Title	
Introduction	Background information
	Thesis statement

	Main idea
	Key details
	Main idea
	Key details
	Main idea
Body paragraphs	Key details
	Main idea
	Key details
	Main idea
	Key details
	Main idea
	Key details

Conclusion	Final statement (summarizes ideas, suggests new directions, reinforces thesis)

Key Elements to Include in a Graphic Organizer
(see Chapter 2, p. 40)

REFLECTIONS

Patterns for Reading and Writing

REFLECTIONS

Patterns for Reading and Writing

Kathleen T. McWhorter

Niagara County Community College

Bedford/St. Martin's

Boston ◆ New York

For Bedford/St. Martin's

Executive Editor: Alexis Walker
Developmental Editors: Randee Falk/Stephanie Butler
Senior Production Editor: Bill Imbornoni
Senior Production Supervisor: Dennis Conroy
Senior Marketing Manager: Christina Shea
Editorial Assistant: Amy Saxon
Copy Editor: Mary Lou Wilshaw-Watts
Indexer: Leoni Z. McVey
Photo Researcher: Julie Tesser
Permissions Manager: Kalina K. Ingham
Art Director: Lucy Krikorian
Text Design: Claire Seng-Niemoeller
Cover Design: Donna Lee Dennison
Cover Photo: Ryan McVay, Glass Brick Abstract. Getty Images.
Composition: Graphic World Inc.
Printing and Binding: RR Donnelley and Sons

President, Bedford/St. Martin's: Denise B. Wydra
Presidents, Macmillan Higher Education: Joan E. Feinberg and Tom Scotty
Editor in Chief: Karen S. Henry
Director of Development: Erica T. Appel
Director of Marketing: Karen R. Soeltz
Production Director: Susan W. Brown
Associate Production Director: Elise S. Kaiser
Managing Editor: Shuli Traub

Manufactured in the United States of America.

1 2 3 4 5 6   16 15 14 13

For information, write: Bedford/St. Martin's, 75 Arlington Street, Boston, MA 02116 (617-399-4000)

ISBN 978-1-4576-3092-7 (high school edition)
ISBN 978-0-312-48688-4

Acknowledgments

Acknowledgments and copyrights are continued at the back of the book on pages 726–29, which constitute an extension of the copyright page.

It is a violation of the law to reproduce these selections by any means whatsoever without the written permission of the copyright holder.

Preface

The goal of *Reflections* is to offer students an integrated approach to reading and writing through scaffolded instruction that guides them through comprehension, analysis, evaluation, and written response — skills that they need to be successful in college.

The title, *Reflections*, emphasizes that reading and writing are mirror images of one another and share the same end result — communication. Readers consider what the writer says and means, and writers are concerned with how to express their ideas clearly and effectively so as to be understood by their readers. Because reading and writing work together and reflect each other, it makes sense that they be taught together. The awareness of connections between reading and writing is important for all college students, perhaps most of all for those who have struggled with reading and writing.

Reflections helps inexperienced readers and writers by applying tools and techniques that I developed in over thirty years of teaching. I have found that students can quickly grasp reading–writing connections if they are provided with clear models, structure, strategies, and processes. That is what the instruction in this book is intended to provide.

Reflections guides students to practice reading and writing skills simultaneously. For example, when students think about a writer's intended audience and purpose, they also learn how to take these factors into account as they write. When they learn to support a thesis with evidence, they also learn to identify and evaluate the evidence other writers offer to support their theses.

The book and its chapters have a unique structure based on a key principle of learning theory — scaffolding. Scaffolding enables students to build on previous learning and uses gradual, small-step learning. Students initially receive extensive direct support and guidance. These cues gradually diminish, and students are able to draw on what they have learned to perform increasingly difficult or complex tasks with less and less guidance.

In this book, reading and writing skills build on one another, and students progress from basic to more complex skills. Chapters in Part 1, "Skills for Success in Reading and Writing," cover all the basic skills. Within each chapter in Part 2, "Readings for Writers," readings and their apparatus increase in difficulty, shifting from an emphasis on understanding to an emphasis on analysis and evaluation. Writing tasks progress from paragraph to essay and move from personal response to more objective interpretation and finally to research.

In each Part 2 chapter, the introductory portions and first essays offer abundant instructional support, including visual aids such as annotations and graphic organizers, to help students develop strategies and build confidence. Later parts of the chapter offer less instructional support, encouraging students to rely on the skills and strategies they have learned to approach reading and writing tasks.

The following features make *Reflections* exceptionally useful for both readers and writers.

Features

INTEGRATION OF READING AND WRITING

While many readers include writing coverage and many composition texts include readings as models, *Reflections* is the first modes reader to truly integrate reading and writing.

- **Part 1 chapters place equal emphasis on the processes of reading and writing,** with a special focus on the connections between them. For example, Chapters 2 and 3 introduce the processes of understanding, analyzing, and evaluating texts both for reading others' work and for revising one's own work.

Table 2.3 Reader's and Writer's Perspectives on Paragraphs		
Paragraph Element	**The Reader's Perspective**	**The Writer's Perspective**
Topic	Identifying the **topic** of each paragraph enables you to build a mental framework for the reading. As you read, your knowledge of the topic increases.	Developing a clear **topic**, for each paragraph is often the key to writing an effective essay.
Main Idea / Topic Sentence	To understand a paragraph, look for a **topic sentence** and the paragraph's **main idea**. Many exams test students' understanding of main ideas.	Writers use a **topic sentence** to state a paragraph's most important point for the reader—that is, its **main idea**.

- **Reading/Writing, special sections** marked with this icon , draw particular attention to areas where reading and writing skills connect.

> Reading|Writing   **Use reading to develop your writing skills.** By studying the writing of others, you can improve your own writing. As you read an article, essay, or textbook assignment, take note of the writer's techniques for presenting information. For example, notice how the writer organizes paragraphs, how she uses language to express ideas, and how she develops ideas throughout the work.

Example of Reading/Writing feature from Chapter 2

- **In Part 2, the rhetorical patterns are taught from the points of view of both readers and writers.** Each chapter starts with a discussion of characteristics of the pattern from both perspectives, followed by a section on reading and writing essays in that pattern.

- **The Readings for Practice, Ideas for Writing section** in each Part 2 chapter includes apparatus that focuses students equally on working with the readings and writing about them or about related topics.

- **The Writing Your Own Essay section** in each Part 2 chapter reactivates the comprehension, analysis, and evaluation skills practiced earlier in the chapter (and in the book), starting with an annotated, color-coded model student essay.

Title: Gilbert identifies process

The Pleasures and Particulars of Philanthropy: How to Publicize Your Fund-Raising Event

Aurora Gilbert

Introduction: Gilbert explains importance of topic

Thesis: Identifies steps in process

One of the most useful and enjoyable skills someone can learn in college is that of organizing and publicizing for a philanthropic event. Putting on such an event certainly requires hard work and dedication, yet the enthusiasm it spreads in your community and support it generates for your charity are invaluable rewards. For the occasion to be successful, it is important to start planning about a month before the event, following a four-step process that includes settling on basic details of the event, gathering the materials for the event, fund-raising, and publicizing the event. In describing these steps, I will discuss an annual all-you-can-eat cupcake event, sponsored by my service group, which raises money for a summer camp for the children of parents affected by cancer.

Writing Your Own Essay sections in each Part 2 chapter start by having students read and work through an annotated student essay.

SCAFFOLDING OF SKILLS

From its general organization through its detailed content, *Reflections* is designed to scaffold students' skill development in reading and writing. Moreover, ample opportunities for active participation and practice — before, during, and after reading — enable students to solidify their acquisition of reading and writing skills.

- **Models in Part 1 chapters help students develop the reading and writing skills they need to work through the assignments in the Part 2 chapters.** In addition to seeing model essays analyzed, students work through model summaries, annotations, analyses, and evaluations.

Revised Draft

A Trend Taken Too Far: The Reality of Real TV

Do you remember life before the reality TV craze? Before reality TV, television viewers seemed interested only in situational comedies and serial dramas. Characters were played by professional actors, and the shows were written by professional writers. Except for a few early reality-type shows, such as *Cops* and *Candid Camera*, this simple formula was what network television offered. Then came

Deleted: One look at a *TV Guide* today shows an overload of reality-based programming, even with the guaranteed failure of most of these shows. Before reality TV there was mostly

---

Abundant models in Part 1 guide students in the fundamentals.

- **The readings in each Part 2 chapter generally progress in difficulty,** so that students' work with shorter, more accessible readings scaffolds their work with longer, more difficult texts. The final selections in each chapter are readings that combine patterns and textbook selections that use the pattern.

- **In Part 2 chapters, each section builds on the previous sections** in a pre-dictable sequence — from an introduction to the rhetorical pattern through a section on writing in the pattern.

- **Questions following reading selections move from understanding through analysis to evaluation;** in addition, as readings become more diffi-cult, the balance of questions shifts. For example, understanding vocabulary in context is especially emphasized in questions following the earlier read-ings in chapters, whereas more analytical and evaluative questions follow later readings.

Understanding the Reading

Analyzing the Reading

Evaluating the Reading

Questions following readings lead students through understanding, analysis, and evaluation.

- **Similarly, the balance of writing prompts shifts across the chapter from paragraph writing to essay writing,** including essays drawing on Internet and other research. Questions are clearly labeled, focusing students on the skills they are practicing.

EMPHASIS ON VISUAL LITERACY AND VISUAL LEARNING

Because students tend to be visual learners, and because they encounter graphics and visuals as they read and may include them in academic papers they write, this book emphasizes visual literacy and appeals to visual learners.

- **Chapters 2 and 3 feature instruction on reading and interpreting graphics.** Students learn strategies for determining what graphics and images are intended to show and for evaluating their effectiveness.

- **Color-coded graphic organizers provide students with a tool both for analyzing readings and for planning and revising their own essays.** Used extensively throughout chapters, these color-coded visual representations of content and structure help students to see at a glance how essays are structured and to work out and assess a structure for their own essays.

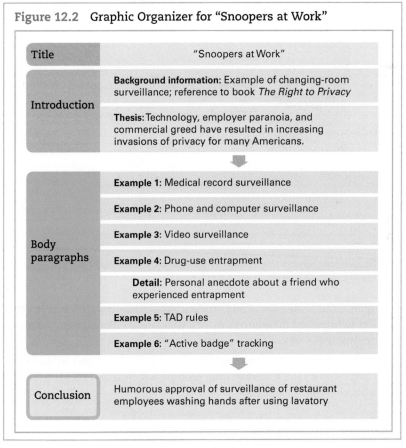

Figure 12.2   Graphic Organizer for "Snoopers at Work"

Title	"Snoopers at Work"
Introduction	**Background information:** Example of changing-room surveillance; reference to book *The Right to Privacy*
	Thesis: Technology, employer paranoia, and commercial greed have resulted in increasing invasions of privacy for many Americans.
Body paragraphs	**Example 1:** Medical record surveillance
	Example 2: Phone and computer surveillance
	Example 3: Video surveillance
	Example 4: Drug-use entrapment
	Detail: Personal anecdote about a friend who experienced entrapment
	Example 5: TAD rules
	Example 6: "Active badge" tracking
Conclusion	Humorous approval of surveillance of restaurant employees washing hands after using lavatory

Each chapter in Part 2 includes one or more graphic organizers showing students how to analyze an essay.

 Understanding the Reading

1. **Structure** To help you see the organization of the reading, complete the graphic organizer below.

Graphic Organizer for "Twitter Goes to College"

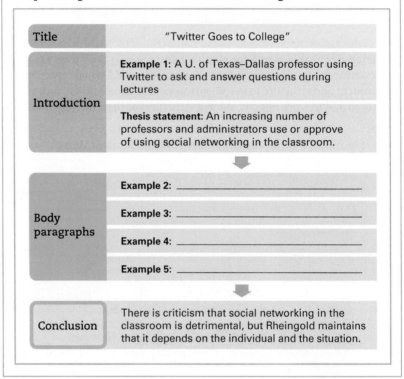

Title	"Twitter Goes to College"
Introduction	**Example 1:** A U. of Texas–Dallas professor using Twitter to ask and answer questions during lectures
	Thesis statement: An increasing number of professors and administrators use or approve of using social networking in the classroom.
Body paragraphs	**Example 2:** _____
	Example 3: _____
	Example 4: _____
	Example 5: _____
Conclusion	There is criticism that social networking in the classroom is detrimental, but Rheingold maintains that it depends on the individual and the situation.

Students are also prompted to use graphic organizers while working with essays they're reading and while revising their own essays.

- **Annotated professional and student essays use consistent color coding to highlight different elements.** This use of color supports students in analyzing the essays.
- **Photographs serve as prompts for writing.** Every chapter in the book opens with a Quick Start writing prompt, which asks students to respond to a photograph.

Chapter 2

Understanding Texts and Images

Quick Start: Study the photograph shown here and discuss its meaning with your classmates. Consider the photograph's content, and ask yourself,

- **Readings frequently include visuals for students to analyze,** reflecting the importance of visuals in college reading and other reading today. In addition, **the design of the readings reflects their appearance in their original context,** whether it be a newspaper, an academic journal, a magazine, or a Web site, to aid students' comprehension, analysis, and evaluation. (See the sample on the next page.)

AskTheInternetTherapist.com

The End of a Relationship: How to Recover from a Broken Heart

Dr. Judith L. Allen

Not all love matches work "forever." Although that is usually the initial hope, dating and practicing relationships are a path of inquiry, looking for a life partner. Even some marriages turn out to be about that search when it comes to light that you may not have known your partner as well as you thought. That once "perfect" pairing turns out to be a match that was perfect for a period of time and now someone has changed their needs and wants to the point that the relationship is no longer fitting into their new life plan.

The term *recovering from a broken heart* usually means that there are still strong feelings and attachments to the person you once loved and whom you depended on. It

Readings are designed to suggest their original place of publication.

AN EMPHASIS ON CRITICAL THINKING

Critical thinking skills are essential for readers and writers, both in college and in the workplace. These skills are emphasized through the following features.

- **Chapter 3 focuses on strategies for interpreting and evaluating text and visuals.** Topics include examining an author's purpose, style, and intended audience; grasping nuances of words; distinguishing between fact and opinion; analyzing tone; looking for omissions; and making inferences. Students learn to read texts critically by identifying bias, evaluating the source, assessing the reliability of supporting information, recognizing assumptions, and judging relevancy and sufficiency of evidence.

Figure 3.1   Sample Advertisement: World Wildlife Fund

Graphics

As discussed in Chapter 2, information-laden graphics can take extra work to understand. Although understanding is always the basis for analysis and evaluation, with graphics it can be especially important to begin with a careful process for understanding.

- **Each chapter in Part 2 offers instruction on analyzing and evaluating the rhetorical pattern taught in the chapter.** These skills are demonstrated by Analysis in Action and Evaluation in Action boxes, examples of student thinking and writing.
- **The apparatus for each reading guides students to think critically about** the focus, content, purpose, and effectiveness of each reading.

AN EMPHASIS ON STUDENT SUCCESS

While reading and writing skills are essential for college success, other skills are needed as well. *Reflections* recognizes that students need to know how to manage their academic life and integrate it with their family, work, and social life.

- **Chapter 1 suggests strategies for setting goals and priorities, managing time, and avoiding procrastination.** Students also learn essential classroom skills such as creating a positive academic image, communicating with instructors, working with classmates, using electronic tools, and taking effective class notes.

Exercise 1.6

Rate your academic image by checking "Always," "Sometimes," or "Never" for each of the following statements.

	Always	*Sometimes*	*Never*
I arrive at classes promptly.	❏	❏	❏
I sit near the front of the room.	❏	❏	❏
I look and act alert and interested in class.	❏	❏	❏
I make eye contact with instructors.	❏	❏	❏
I complete reading assignments before class.	❏	❏	❏
I ask thoughtful questions.	❏	❏	❏
I participate in class discussions.	❏	❏	❏

Quizzes and illustrated examples help students reflect on their academic habits.

- **Many of the readings in Part 2 are related to or promote student success.** In addition, each Part 2 chapter includes a textbook reading, giving students practice in reading and responding to textbooks, using skills such as annotating and highlighting.

ENGAGING AND ACCESSIBLE READINGS

Because students who enjoy what they are reading will approach assignments with interest and enthusiasm, the fifty-eight professional readings and eleven student essays were carefully chosen to engage students and to provide strong rhetorical models.

- **The readings include a mix of reliable, class-tested essays** by well-known writers like Brent Staples, Deborah Tannen, Dave Barry, and Luis Rodriguez, **and contemporary readings on compelling topics,** including reality TV auditions, "green" college campuses, and issue-oriented art.

- **The readings come from a wide range of sources,** including newspapers, popular magazines, Web sites, and textbooks, representing the diverse texts students encounter in both their personal and their academic lives.

 TEXTBOOK

Issue-Oriented and Street Art

Patrick Frank

Today the public accepts most modern art. Exhibitions of work by such former rule-breaking radicals as Henri Matisse, Paul Gauguin, Paul Cézanne, and Claude Monet fill museums with visitors. Nine of the ten most expensive paintings ever sold at auction are modern works (three each by Picasso and van Gogh; one each by Cézanne, Renoir, and Jackson Pollock). The modern-style Vietnam Veterans Memorial is a national shrine. Modern art is no longer controversial.

The impact of this situation is not yet clear. Art of our own time is always the most difficult to evaluate. In general, most artists of the present generation do not appear intent on perfecting form, creating beauty, or fine-tuning their sense of sight. They mostly want to comment on life in all of its aspects. They want to create work that illuminates the relationships between what we see and how we think. Rather than being objects of timeless beauty, most art since the 1980s consists of objects laden with information about the period in which we live. This article will present two movements of the present generation.

Issue-Oriented Art

Many artists in the past twenty years have sought to link their art to current social questions. Issue-oriented artists believe that if they limit their art to **aesthetic** matters, then their work will be only a

aesthetic: concerned with what is beautiful or pleasing in appearance

---

- **Topics help students connect reading with issues relevant to college success and to their lives.** The wide-ranging topics include health, stress management, interpersonal relationships, race relations, consequences of war, virtues and pitfalls of technology, and pros and cons of volunteer work.

- **Readings offer compelling glimpses into various academic disciplines**— for example, general science in Robert Epstein's "How Science Can Help You Fall in Love."

- **Textbook excerpts in each Part 2 chapter give students practice** reading specialized vocabulary, understanding textbook elements, and developing textbook reading skills.

STRATEGIC USE OF RHETORICAL PATTERNS, ALONE AND IN COMBINATION

The rhetorical patterns provide students with a structure and template within which to organize and connect ideas, both when reading and when writing. By learning to think in terms of rhetorical patterns and by seeing how each of these patterns works, students will no longer be overwhelmed by reading or writing assignments, but will be able to approach them analytically.

- Because writers often use more than one pattern in developing an essay, **Chapter 9 focuses on reading and writing essays that combine patterns.**

- **Each Part 2 chapter includes at least one reading that combines patterns,** marked with the icon . This coverage helps students see the day-to-day application of all the patterns.

COMBINING THE PATTERNS

Just Walk On By: A Black Man Ponders His Power to Alter Public Space

Brent Staples

My first victim was a woman—white, well dressed, probably in her early twenties. I came upon her late one evening on a deserted street in Hyde Park, a relatively affluent neighborhood in an otherwise mean, impoverished section of Chicago. As I swung onto the avenue behind her, there seemed to be a discreet, uninflammatory distance between us. Not so. She cast back a worried glance. To her, the youngish black man—a broad six feet two inches with a beard and billowing hair, both hands shoved into the pockets of his bulky military jacket—seemed menacingly close. After a few more quick glimpses, she picked up her pace and was soon running in earnest. Within seconds she disappeared into a cross street.

That was more than a decade ago. I was twenty-two years old, a graduate student newly arrived at the University of Chicago. It was in the echo of that terrified woman's footfalls that I first began to know the unwieldy inheritance I'd come into—the ability to alter public space in ugly ways. It was clear that she thought herself the quarry of a mugger, a rapist, or worse. Suffering a bout of insomnia, however, I was stalking sleep, not defenseless wayfarers. As a softy who is scarcely able to take a knife to a raw chicken—let alone hold one to a person's

---

GRAMMAR AND RESEARCH COVERAGE

Reflections helps students approach writing as a flexible, multifaceted process by offering contextualized support in grammar and research.

- **Practical help with grammar problems that are common in writing** enables students to work on mechanical issues within the context of their own writing. Editing tips in each Part 2 chapter alert students to problems especially likely to arise in writing using a particular rhetorical pattern.

- **A final chapter on finding and using sources** addresses evaluating sources for writing projects, as well as incorporating quotations, avoiding plagiarism, and documenting sources using MLA style.

Support for Instructors and Students

Reflections goes beyond the book. Online and in print, you will find both free and affordable premium resources to help students get even more out of the book and your course. You will also find convenient resources for instructors, such as a downloadable instructor's manual and supplemental exercises. Information on ordering and the ISBNs for packaging these resources with your students' books can be found below, or you may contact your Bedford/St. Martin's sales representative, e-mail sales support (**sales_support@bfwpub .com**), or visit **bedfordstmartins.com/reflections/catalog**). For questions related to content in our textbooks for basic reading and writing courses, please email **developmental@bedfordstmartins.com**.

| 📖 Print | 🖥 Online | 💿 CD-ROM |

Free Instructor Resources

📖 The *Instructor's Edition* of *Reflections* includes all material from the Instructor's Manual bound into the student edition. ISBN 978-1-4576-6723-7

📖 🖥 The *Instructor's Manual,* prepared with assistance from Mark Gallaher, provides new and seasoned instructors alike with the support they need for teaching writing. Unit 1 includes sample syllabi along with chapters on teaching with *Reflections* and helping underprepared students in the first-year writing classroom. Unit 2 includes teaching tips for each chapter in *Reflections*, including brief overviews of each of the readings in the book with sample answers to questions posed in the text. Available in print (ISBN 978-1-4576-3091-0) and online at **bedfordstmartins.com/reflections/catalog**.

💿 *Testing Tool Kit: Writing and Grammar Test Bank* **CD-ROM** allows instructors to create secure, customized tests and quizzes from a pool of nearly two thousand questions covering forty-seven topics. It also includes ten prebuilt diagnostic tests. ISBN 978-0-312-43032-0

📖 *Teaching Developmental Writing: Background Readings,* **Fourth Edition,** is edited by Susan Naomi Bernstein, former co-chair of the Conference on Basic Writing. This professional resource offers essays on topics of interest to basic writing instructors, along with editorial apparatus pointing out practical applications for the classroom. ISBN 978-0-312-60251-2

Teaching Developmental Reading: Historical, Theoretical, and Practical Background Readings, edited by Norman Stahl and Hunter Boylan, offers thirty-seven professional essays by writers such as Martha E. Casazza, Michele L. Simpson, and David C. Caverly, on topics that will engage teachers of basic reading, including strategic learning, the reading/writing connection, and teaching new-to-English learners. ISBN 978-0-312-24774-4

Teaching Study Strategies in Developmental Education: Readings on Theory, Research, and Best Practice, edited by Russ Hodges, Michele Simpson, and Norman Stahl, presents twenty-nine selections that discuss the theory and practice of teaching college students to be efficient and effective learners. Topics include the needs of students in developmental education and learning-assistance programs, current psychological and sociological principles that promote — or hinder — learning, and the role of effective learning strategies and assessment on instruction and student learning. ISBN 978-0-312-66274-5

The Bedford Bibliography for Teachers of Basic Writing, Third Edition, (also available online at **bedfordstmartins.com/basicbib**) has been compiled by members of the Conference on Basic Writing under the general editorship of Gregory R. Glau and Chitralekha Duttagupta. This annotated list of books, articles, and periodicals was created specifically to help teachers of basic writing find valuable resources. ISBN 978-0-312-58154-1

TeachingCentral at **bedfordstmartins.com/teachingcentral** offers the entire list of Bedford/St. Martin's print and online professional resources in one place. You will find landmark reference works, sourcebooks on pedagogical issues, award-winning collections, and practical advice for the classroom — all free for instructors.

Student Resources

FREE AND OPEN

Reflections's companion Web site at **bedfordstmartins.com/reflections** provides students with reading comprehension/skills-building quizzes that guide students in comprehension, analysis, and evaluation; quizzes for each professional essay found in the book; VideoCentral videos of real writers; supplemental exercises from *Exercise Central*; helpful guidelines on avoiding plagiarism and doing research; model essays; advice on writing for the workplace; and links to other useful resources from Bedford/St. Martin's.

⌨ *Exercise Central 3.0* at bedfordstmartins.com/exercisecentral is the largest database of editing exercises on the Internet. This comprehensive resource contains over nine thousand exercises that offer immediate feedback; the program also recommends personalized study plans and provides tutorials for common problems. Best of all, students' work reports to a grade book, allowing instructors to track students' progress quickly and easily.

FREE WITH PRINT TEXT

📖 *The Bedford/St. Martin's ESL Workbook* includes a broad range of exercises covering grammatical issues for multilingual students of varying language skills and backgrounds. Answers are at the back. **Free** when packaged with the print text. Package ISBN 978-1-4576-5710-8

💿 *Exercise Central to Go: Writing and Grammar Practices for Basic Writers* CD-ROM provides hundreds of practice items to help students build their writing and editing skills. No Internet connection is necessary. **Free** when packaged with the print text. Package ISBN 978-1-4576-5714-6

💿 The *Make-a-Paragraph Kit* is a fun, interactive CD-ROM that teaches students about paragraph development. It also contains exercises to help students build their own paragraphs, audiovisual tutorials on four of the most common errors for basic writers, and the content from *Exercise Central to Go: Writing and Grammar Practices for Basic Writers.* **Free** when packaged with the print text. Package ISBN 978-1-4576-5715-3

📖 The *Bedford/St. Martin's Planner* includes everything that students need to plan and use their time effectively, with advice on preparing schedules and to-do lists plus blank schedules and calendars (monthly and weekly). The planner fits easily into a backpack or purse, so students can take it anywhere. **Free** when packaged with the print text. Package ISBN 978-1-4576-5709-2

📖 *Journal Writing: A Beginning* is designed to give students an opportunity to use writing as a way to explore their thoughts and feelings. This writing journal includes a generous supply of inspirational quotations placed throughout the pages, tips for journaling, and suggested journal topics. **Free** when packaged with the print text. Package ISBN 978-1-4576-5713-9

📖 *From Practice to Mastery* (study guide for the Florida Basic Skills Exit Tests) gives students all the resources they need to practice for — and pass — the Florida tests in reading and writing. It includes pre- and post-tests, abundant practices, many examples, and clear instruction in all the skills covered on the exams. **Free** when packaged with the print text. Package ISBN 978-1-4576-5716-0

PREMIUM

🖥 *WritingClass* provides students with a dynamic, interactive online course space preloaded with exercises, diagnostics, video tutorials, writing and commenting tools, and more. *WritingClass* helps students stay focused and lets instructors see how they are progressing. It is available at a significant discount when packaged with the print text. To learn more about *WritingClass*, visit **yourwritingclass.com.** Package ISBN 978-1-4576-5708-5

🖥 *SkillsClass* offers all that *WritingClass* offers, plus guidance and practice in reading and study skills. This interactive online course space comes preloaded with exercises, diagnostics, video tutorials, writing and commenting tools, and more. It is available at a significant discount when packaged with the print text. To learn more about *SkillsClass*, visit **yourskillsclass.com.** Package ISBN 978-1-4576-5718-4

📖 *The Bedford/St. Martin's Textbook Reader,* **Second Edition,** by Ellen Kuhl Repetto, gives students practice in reading college textbooks across the curriculum. This brief collection of chapters from market-leading introductory college textbooks can be packaged inexpensively with *Reflections.* Beginning with a chapter on college success, *The Bedford/St. Martin's Textbook Reader* also includes chapters from current texts on composition, mass communication, history, psychology, and environmental science. Comprehension questions and tips for reading success guide students in reading college-level materials efficiently and effectively. Package ISBN 978-1-4576-5711-5

🖥 *Re:Writing Plus,* **now with VideoCentral,** gathers all of our premium digital content for the writing class into one online collection. This impressive resource includes innovative and interactive help with writing a paragraph; tutorials and practices that show how writing works in students' real-world experience; Video-Central, with over 140 brief videos for the writing classroom; the first-ever peer review game, *Peer Factor; i-cite: visualizing sources;* plus hundreds of models of writing and hundreds of readings. *Re:WritingPlus* can be purchased separately or packaged with *Reflections* at a significant discount. Package ISBN 978-1-4576-5717-7

E-BOOK OPTIONS

The *e-Book for Reflections,* value priced, can be purchased in formats for use with computers, tablets, and e-readers. Visit **bedfordstmartins.com/ebooks** for more information.

ORDERING INFORMATION

To order any ancillary or ancillary package for *Reflections,* contact your local Bedford/St. Martin's sales representative, e-mail **sales_support@bfwpub.com,** or visit our Web site at **bedfordstmartins.com.**

Acknowledgments

A number of instructors and students from across the country have helped me develop *Reflections*. I would like to express my gratitude to the following instructors who provided detailed, valuable comments and suggestions about the manuscript and choice of reading selections: Carolee Ritter (Southeast Community College); Edward Glenn (Miami Dade College); Amy Porter (Kankakee Community College); Kyle Goehner (Community College of Baltimore County); Cindy Beck (Pulaski Technical College); Sharon Cellemme (South Piedmont Community College); Nicole Williams (Community College of Baltimore County); Sharon Hayes (Community College of Baltimore County); Jerri A. Harwell (Salt Lake Community College); Kerry L. Thomas (Rufus King International School — High School Campus); Melissa Lynn Pomerantz (Parkway North High School); Carol Vande Kerkhoff (Millard North High School); David Lawson (Center Grove High School); Michelle Van de Sande (Arapahoe Community College); Maryann Errico (Georgia Perimeter College); Claudia Swicegood (Rowan-Cabarrus Community College); Josie Mills (Arapahoe Community College); Brenda Ashcraft (Virginia Western Community College); Angelina Arellanes-Nunez (El Paso Community College); Sandra Padilla (El Paso Community College); Loren Kleinman (Berkeley College); James Shackle (Owens Community College); Linda Koffman (College of Marin); Regina Barnett (Tidewater Community College); and Courtnay Hornof (Kankakee Community College).

Many people at Bedford/St. Martin's contributed to the creation and development of *Reflections*. Each person with whom I worked demonstrates high standards and expertise in the field of college writing. I thank my development editors, Randee Falk and Stephanie Butler, for their exceptional help planning and composing the book, and Mary Lou Wilshaw-Watts for her careful and judicious copyediting of my final draft. I thank Amy Saxon, Leah Rang, Ryan Larkin, Nick McCarthy, and Emily Wunderlich, who ably oversaw the development of ancillaries, commissioned and synthesized reviews, and performed numerous other essential tasks; Bill Imbornoni, who conscientiously and capably guided the text through the production process; and Christina Shea and Alexis Walker, who provided invaluable advice and guidance on the market and other big-picture issues. I also thank Erica Appel, Karen Henry, Joan Feinberg, Nancy Perry, and Denise Wydra, who have always supported and encouraged my work.

Last, but in no way least, I thank the many students who have inspired me to create a book that directly addresses their needs and learning characteristics. They have shown me how they think and learn, and as a result I have discovered effective teaching strategies that can help all students learn to read and write. My students have made the most significant contribution to this book; they are the reason I enjoy both teaching and writing.

Kathleen McWhorter

Contents

4 Prewriting: How to Find and Focus Ideas   84

5 Developing and Supporting a Thesis   104

14   Comparison and Contrast: Showing Similarities and Differences   383

15 Classification and Division: Explaining Categories and Parts 434

17 Cause and Effect: Using Reasons and Results to Explain   539

What Is Cause and Effect?   540

Reading and Writing Cause-and-Effect Essays   542

Amy Tan, E. coli on the Rocks

"Just when you thought Purell solved all your public hygiene needs, now there's news that the lovely crystalline form of water you get in a restaurant may be dirtier than water from your toilet."

Understanding, Analyzing, and Evaluating Cause-and-Effect Essays   548

Readings for Practice, Ideas for Writing   553

John Clifton, Why Do People Watch Sports on TV?   553

"Win or lose, the sports watcher goes through an emotional journey. Sports becomes an outlet for unspent emotions."

Terry Tempest Williams, The Clan of One-Breasted Women   560

"I cannot prove that my mother, Diane Dixon Tempest, or my grandmothers, Lettie Romney Dixon and Kathryn Blackett Tempest, along with my aunts developed cancer from nuclear fallout in Utah. But I can't prove they didn't."

Thematic Contents

NATURE AND THE ENVIRONMENT

POPULAR CULTURE

RELATIONSHIPS

SCIENCE AND MEDICINE

SPORTS AND HOBBIES

TECHNOLOGY

U.S. AND WORLD CULTURES

THE WAY WE EAT

part

1

Skills for Success in Reading and Writing

Chapter 1

Student Success

Quick Start: The photograph above shows successful students. What does the photo say about academic success? Based on your experiences with education until now, make a list of the skills you think contribute to academic success. What tasks must students perform to be successful? What nonacademic factors, such as job and family responsibilities, play a role in student success? Be specific.

In your response to the Quick Start writing prompt, which skills did you identify as contributing to academic success? You may have mentioned being motivated and organized, knowing how to read and study, or knowing how to write papers and take exams. All of these skills, and many others, contribute to academic success. This chapter presents numerous strategies for success to help you develop the skills you need for a successful academic career.

Strategies for Success

You can start preparing for success even before you enter the classroom. To begin, be sure to use the following strategies.

Focus on Success

You may be concerned about how you will juggle a job, your family life, and school. You also may be wondering whether you have the skills and abilities necessary to get the grades you want. Having doubts and concerns is normal, but it is important to think positively and to focus on success. Here are a few success strategies.

- **Define success.** *Success* means different things to different people, and you need to decide what it means to you. Is a rewarding career your highest priority? Are relationships with family and friends important? Or is your goal to help other people? Figure out how school fits into your definition of *success*.
- **Develop long-term goals that will lead to success.** Once you have defined what success means to you, determine the long-term goals that will get you there. What do you intend to accomplish this term? This year? Next year? Complete Exercise 1.1 (below) to help you define your goals.
- **Take responsibility for achieving your goals.** You are in charge of your own learning and of reaching your goals. Instructors or tutors may help you, but only you can achieve your goals.
- **Visualize success.** Close your eyes and imagine yourself achieving your goals. For example, picture yourself finishing your first year of college with high marks or landing your dream job. Never visualize failure.
- **Develop essential skills that will help you achieve success.** Success is not a matter of luck. It is a matter of learning specific skills—such as strong proficiency in writing, reading, and communication—that will help you achieve your goals.

Exercise 1.1

List where you would like to be and what you would like to be doing at each of the times listed. You may have multiple goals, so list as many as you like.

List what you expect to accomplish in the next two weeks.	1. 2.
List what you expect to accomplish by the end of this term or semester.	1. 2. 3.
List what you will accomplish within the next year.	1. 2. 3.
List what you will have accomplished by graduation.	1. 2. 3.
List what you think you will have accomplished five years after you graduate.	1. 2. 3.

Exercise 1.2

Write a paragraph describing your academic and professional goals. Include the specific steps you need to take to achieve these goals.

Manage Your Time

Examine the two student schedules shown in Figures 1.1 and 1.2. Which student is more likely to meet deadlines? Why? Student 1.2

Figure 1.1 (p. 6) shows a planner with only test dates and assignment deadlines. Figure 1.2 shows a planner detailing how and when the student will meet those deadlines. The student who uses the planner in Figure 1.2 is likely to complete his or her work with less stress and worry.

Managing their time is many students' biggest challenge. Students are required to spend only a certain number of hours per week in class, and for some, organizing unstructured time can be difficult. Others are overwhelmed by integrating their studies into already busy lives. Still others study nonstop, but by never finding free time for relaxation, they set themselves up for burnout.

To avoid these traps and manage your time effectively, you need to establish realistic short-term goals, plan your study time, and avoid procrastination.

Figure 1.1   Planner with Due Dates

	Mon 9/10	Tue 9/11	Wed 9/12	Thu 9/13	Fri 9/14	Sat 9/15	Sun 9/16
GMT-05				Essay 3 due			
9am							
10am							
11am							
12pm							
1pm					1p – 2:40p Anthro quiz		
2pm							
3pm		3p – 4:40p History exam					
4pm							
5pm							
6pm							

Figure 1.2   Planner with Detailed Schedule

	Mon 9/10	Tue 9/11	Wed 9/12	Thu 9/13	Fri 9/14	Sat 9/15	Sun 9/16
GMT-05				Essay 3 due!			
9am	9 – 10:30 outline English Essay 1	9 – 11 draft English Essay 1			9 – 11 review Anthro notes (class notes and notes for Chs. 20-22)	9 – 4p Work	
10am			10 – 12p Revise Essay 1				10 – 11:30 read Bio Ch. 17
11am							
12pm		11:30 – 1p read Anthro Ch. 20					11:30 – 12:30p review Bio lab
1pm				1p – 3p study Anthro Chapters 20-22	1p – 2:40p Anthro quiz		
2pm							2p – 4p read History Ch.15
3pm		3p – 4:40p History exam					
4pm			4p – 6:30p read Anthro Chs. 21-22				
5pm	5p – 6:30p History study group	5p – 8p Work			5p – 8p Work		
6pm							

ESTABLISH REALISTIC SHORT-TERM GOALS

The first step in managing your time is establishing positive and realistic short-term goals. Set a broad, long-term goal—like earning a bachelor's degree in elementary education in four years—before setting short-term goals that you can achieve more quickly. A short-term goal might be to read a textbook chapter by next Monday or to meet with a study partner on Tuesday to review for an upcoming exam. Setting a realistic time frame and sticking to it are critical steps toward accomplishing your short-term goals.

PLAN YOUR STUDY TIME

If you let days "just happen," you're not likely to accomplish much. You need to create a plan, be it tightly structured, loosely structured, or something in between. Try establishing both term and weekly plans, and choose the method that works better for you.

The term plan   Use this approach to establish a study routine for the entire term. Once you have a sense of the work that you need to complete for each of your classes, block out four to six hours per week (outside the classroom) to read and study for each course. The rule of thumb is to work two hours outside of class for every hour you spend in class (more for reading- and writing-intensive courses). Study for each course at the same time each week. The weekly tasks will vary, but you will always have enough time to get everything done. If you have trouble starting assignments, the term plan may be the one for you.

The weekly plan   This alternative approach requires making a schedule each week. Take ten minutes at the beginning of each week to specify what you'll work on for each course, taking into account upcoming assignments. Figure 1.2 (p. 6) is a good example of how to organize a weekly plan.

Regardless of which plan you choose, you should make use of a planner or calendar to record assignments, due dates for papers, and upcoming exams. Purchase a student planner or pocket calendar or use one of the many free calendar and scheduling applications offered for computers, tablets, and smartphones. Make sure to schedule time for reading, completing assignments, and studying; whether you do so daily, weekly, or across the term is up to you. Keep your planner or calendar with you at all times and check it daily. It will help you get and stay organized.

Each time you begin studying, assess what needs to be done and determine the order in which you will complete the required tasks. Tackle the most challenging assignments first, when you are not tired and when your concentration is at its highest level.

AVOID PROCRASTINATION

Procrastination is putting off things that need to be done. For example, you know you should work on an assignment, but you log on to Facebook instead. To avoid procrastination, divide the task into manageable parts that you can complete one at a time. Avoid making excuses. It is easy to say you don't have enough time to get everything done, but often that is not true. You might be able to make more time for your studies by waking up earlier or postponing a get-together with friends. Also avoid escaping into routine tasks such as shopping, cleaning, or washing your car rather than completing the study task.

Exercise 1.3

Use the suggestions above to create a weekly or term plan. Use your plan for the upcoming week and then evaluate how well it worked. Determine whether you got everything done on time. Look for places where you need more or less time. Then, revise your plan and try it for another week.

Organize a Reading, Writing, and Study Area

You don't need a lot of room to create an appropriate space for reading, studying, and writing. Use the following suggestions to organize an efficient work area.

- **Choose a setting that is conducive to reading, writing, and studying.** Your work area should be well lit, comfortable, and equipped with all the tools you need—a clock, a computer, a calculator, pens, pencils, paper, and so on. Make sure your laptop's battery is fully charged. Better yet, choose a spot with plenty of available electrical outlets.
- **Find a quiet area.** If you live somewhere noisy, consider studying in the library or another quiet place. Libraries offer free carrel space where you can work without distractions. Many also provide study rooms for group work or secluded areas with comfortable chairs if you do not need a desk.

  At home, find a place where you won't be disturbed by family or roommates. Your work area need not be a separate room, but it should be a place that won't be disturbed. Otherwise, you may waste time setting up your work, figuring out where you left off, and getting started again.

Develop Concentration Skills

Does either of these situations sound familiar?

"I just read a whole page, and I can't remember anything I read!"

"Every time I start working on this assignment, my mind wanders."

If so, you may need to improve your concentration. If you cannot keep your mind on your work, your classes will be unnecessarily difficult. Try the following concentration tips to help you study smarter, not harder.

- **Work at peak periods of attention.** Determine the time of day or night that you are most efficient and best able to concentrate. Do not try to work when you are tired, hungry, or distracted.

- **Work on difficult assignments first.** Your mind is freshest as you begin to work. Avoid the temptation to put off difficult tasks. Challenging assignments require your fullest attention.

- **Vary your activities.** Do not complete three reading assignments consecutively. Instead, alternate assignments. For example, read a portion of a chapter from your textbook, then work on an essay, then work on math problems, then read another assignment, and so on.

- **Write to keep yourself mentally and physically active.** Highlight and annotate as you read. These processes will keep you mentally alert. (Techniques for highlighting and annotating effectively are found in Chapters 2 and 3.)

- **Avoid electronic distractions.** Turn off the television, your phone, the radio, or anything else that distracts you from your studies.

- **Meet your deadlines.** Before beginning an assignment, estimate how long it will take and work toward completing it by the due date. Many students underestimate the amount of time needed to complete an assignment, so keep track of how long you take to complete a particular task. Then use that information as you schedule time for future assignments.

- **Take a break.** Staring at a textbook or a computer screen for hours at a time can be very draining. Take short breaks every half hour; use the time to get a healthy snack or stretch.

- **Reward yourself.** Use fun activities, such as emailing or sending a text message to a friend, as a reward when you have completed an assignment (or reached an important milestone toward its completion).

Exercise 1.4

Not all students study the same way; they also study differently for different courses. Make a list of the courses you are taking this term and identify a study strategy for each. Compare your strategies with those of other students and write down any new useful strategies that you learn from them.

Manage Stress

The pressures and obligations of school lead many students to feel overwhelmed. Successful students monitor their stress level and take action to lessen it. Take the quiz in Exercise 1.5 to assess your stress level.

Exercise 1.5

Complete the following stress miniquiz. If you answer "Always" or "Sometimes" to more than two or three items, identify at least two ways you can reduce your stress level.

		Always	Sometimes	Never
1.	I worry that I do not have enough time to get everything done.	❏	❏	❏
2.	I regret that I have no time to do fun things each week.	❏	❏	❏
3.	I find myself losing track of details and forgetting due dates, promises, and appointments.	❏	❏	❏
4.	I worry about what I am doing.	❏	❏	❏
5.	I have conflicts or disagreements with friends or family.	❏	❏	❏
6.	I lose patience with small annoyances.	❏	❏	❏
7.	I seem to be late, no matter how hard I try to arrive on time.	❏	❏	❏
8.	I have difficulty sleeping.	❏	❏	❏
9.	My eating habits have changed.	❏	❏	❏
10.	I find myself needing a cigarette, drink, or prescription drug.	❏	❏	❏

Here are some effective ways to reduce stress.

- **Establish your priorities.** Decide what is most important in your life. Let's say you decide school is more important than your part-time job. Once you make this decision, you won't feel conflicted about requesting a work schedule to accommodate your study plan because school is your priority.
- **Learn to say no.** Many people try to do too many things for too many people—family, friends, classmates, coworkers. Allow your priorities to guide your willingness to accept new responsibilities.
- **Focus on the positive.** Do not think, "I'll never be able to finish this assignment on time." Instead ask yourself, "What do I have to do to finish this assignment on time?"
- **Separate work, school, and social worries.** Create mental compartments for your worries. Don't spend time in class thinking about a problem at work. Don't think about a conflict with a friend while attempting to write a paper. Deal with problems at the appropriate time and place.
- **Keep a journal.** Taking a few minutes to write in a journal about your worries and stressors can go a long way toward relieving stress.

Classroom Skills

What you do in the classroom largely determines your academic success. Do all of the following, and success will follow.

Polish Your Academic Image

Your *academic image* is the way you are perceived by your instructors and other students. How you act and respond in class plays a large part in determining this image.

Do ...	Don't ...
Make thoughtful contributions to class discussions.	Read or send text messages during class.
Maintain eye contact with instructors.	Work on homework during class.
Ask questions if information is unclear to you.	Sleep or daydream during class.
Refer to assigned readings in class.	Remain silent during class discussion.
Be courteous to classmates when you speak.	Interrupt others or criticize their contributions.

Don't underestimate the value of communicating daily—through your words and actions—that you are a hardworking student who takes your studies seriously.

Exercise 1.6

Rate your academic image by checking "Always," "Sometimes," or "Never" for each of the following statements.

	Always	Sometimes	Never
I arrive at classes promptly.	❑	❑	❑
I sit near the front of the room.	❑	❑	❑
I look and act alert and interested in class.	❑	❑	❑
I make eye contact with instructors.	❑	❑	❑
I complete reading assignments before class.	❑	❑	❑
I ask thoughtful questions.	❑	❑	❑
I participate in class discussions.	❑	❑	❑
I complete all assignments on time.	❑	❑	❑
I submit neat, complete, well-organized papers.	❑	❑	❑
I refrain from carrying on conversations with or texting other students while the instructor is addressing the class.	❑	❑	❑
I say "hello" when I meet my instructors on campus.	❑	❑	❑

Write a brief statement about how you think others perceive you as a student. Refer to the list of tips about building a positive academic image on page 11. Which tips do you normally follow? Which do you most need to work on?

Demonstrate Academic Integrity

Academic integrity—conducting yourself in an honest and ethical manner—is important in all classrooms. At the simplest level, students with academic integrity do not engage in such obvious forms of dishonesty as copying homework, buying a paper on the Internet, and cheating on exams or helping others do so.

Students with academic integrity also avoid both deliberate and unintentional intellectual dishonesty, which occurs when you **plagiarize, or use others' ideas or language without giving them credit**. An example of **intentional plagiarism** is cutting and pasting information from the Internet into your paper without indicating that it is borrowed. **Unintentional plagiarism** occurs when you use language too similar to that of the original source or forget to place quotation marks around a direct quotation.

Communicate with Your Instructors

Meeting regularly with your instructors will help you understand and meet the course objectives. Take advantage of your instructors' office hours, or speak to them after class. Use the following suggestions to communicate effectively with your instructors.

- **Don't be afraid to approach your instructors.** At first, some of them may seem unapproachable, but most instructors are happy to help you.

- **Learn your instructors' contact information.** Most instructors keep weekly office hours during which they are available to talk with students and answer questions. Some instructors also give out their email addresses and encourage email communication.

- **Prepare for meetings with your instructors.** Write out specific questions in advance. If you need help with a paper, bring along all the work (drafts, outlines, list of research sources) you have done so far.

- **Stay in touch with your instructor.** If you cannot attend class for a valid reason, notify your instructor and explain the situation. Unexcused absences generally lower your grade and suggest that you are not taking your studies seriously. If personal problems interfere with your schoolwork, let your instructors know. They can often refer you to counseling services and may grant you an extension for deadlines missed due to an emergency.

Use Electronic Tools Effectively

Email, texts, and instant messages (IMs) are now widely used for academic purposes at many schools. For example, some colleges allow students to text questions to a reference librarian. Instructors and students can communicate in real time through course management systems. Not all instructors, however, encourage these practices. Use the following guidelines to determine whether electronic communications are appropriate.

- **Text only if invited.** Do not text your instructors unless they have invited you to do so—and then only for appropriate reasons. For example, an instructor may allow you to text the class during an off-campus learning experience.
- **Do not take advantage of access to your instructor.** It would not be appropriate, for instance, to ask your instructor to respond to IMs the night before an exam.
- **Use proper language.** The abbreviations made popular by texting and instant messaging are not appropriate for formal writing. Avoid these abbreviations when writing course assignments or emailing and texting messages to instructors.

Computers are increasingly being used to encourage class participation and collaboration. For example, an instructor might hold "virtual" (online) office hours. Others may schedule a time for an IM chat about an assignment or a reading. Use the following guidelines for participating in online discussions and collaborations.

- **Become familiar with the software or course management system before you attempt to post messages.** If you need assistance, use the software's Help function, try to find print instructions, look for an online demo, or ask classmates or staff at the computer center.
- **Read all previous posts before posting your comments.** Make sure not to repeat something a classmate has already said.
- **Plan ahead.** Think through what you want to post before you post it.
- **Be considerate.** Make it easy for your classmates and instructor to read your postings. Use correct spelling and grammar, and format your comments so they are easy to read. Use boldface and numbered lists as appropriate.
- **Place your comments within a context.** Make it clear whether you are responding to another posting (if so, give the date and poster's name), a reading assignment (give the chapter or page), or a lecture (give the date).

Listen Carefully and Critically

You probably spend far more time listening in class than you do reading, writing, or speaking. Because you spend so much time doing it, you need to listen carefully and critically—grasping what is said and questioning and reacting to what you hear.

BECOMING A CAREFUL LISTENER

Did you know that your brain can process information faster than speakers can speak? As a result, your mind has time to wander while listening. Use the following suggestions to maintain your attention in the classroom.

- **If you are easily distracted, sit in the front of the room.** This helps you focus on the speaker.
- **Take notes.** Writing will help you concentrate.
- **Try to anticipate what the speaker will say next.** This keeps your mind engaged.
- **Sit comfortably but do not sprawl.** A serious posture puts your mind in gear for serious work.
- **Maintain eye contact with the speaker.** You will feel more personally involved and will be less likely to drift off.
- **Avoid sitting with friends.** You will be tempted to talk to them. If you chat with classmates, you risk missing information.

LISTENING CRITICALLY

In many classes, you are expected to understand what the speaker is saying and to respond to it. Here are a few suggestions for developing your critical-listening skills.

- **Maintain an open mind.** It is easy to shut out ideas and opinions that do not conform to your values and beliefs. Avoid evaluating a message until you have more information.
- **Avoid selective listening.** Some listeners hear what they want to hear; they do not remember ideas with which they disagree. Attempt to understand the speaker's viewpoint. Take notes or create an informal outline of the speaker's main points.
- **Avoid oversimplification.** When listening to difficult, emotional, or complex messages, it is tempting to simplify them by eliminating details, reasons, or supporting evidence. Focus on the details in order to comprehend the speaker's message.
- **Focus on the message, not the speaker.** Try not to be distracted by the speaker's clothing, mannerisms, speech patterns, or quirks.

Exercise 1.8

Working with a classmate, identify at least five topics that you would need to listen to critically to avoid the pitfalls listed above.

Ask and Answer Questions

You will learn more from your classes if you actively ask and answer questions. This means not only inquiring when you need information or clarification but also answering questions posed by the instructor to assess and demonstrate your knowledge. Use the following tips to strengthen your questioning and answering skills.

- **Conquer your fear of speaking in class.** Don't worry about what your friends and classmates will think. Speak out. Other students probably have the same questions but may be reluctant to ask.
- **While reading an assignment, jot down questions as they occur to you.** Bring your list to class, and use it when your instructor invites questions.
- **Ask your questions concisely.** Don't ramble.
- **Focus on critical questions.** While it is perfectly acceptable to ask factual questions, instructors particularly appreciate those that center on how the information can be used, how ideas fit together, how things work, and the long-term significance of the information.
- **Think before responding.** When answering questions, compose your response in your head before volunteering to answer.

Exercise 1.9

Working with a classmate, brainstorm a list of questions you could ask about the content presented in this chapter.

Work with Classmates

Many assignments and activities require you to work with other students. Group projects vary depending on the discipline, the course, and the instructor. Some groups may be assembled to discuss problems; others may carry out an activity, such as examining a piece of writing; others may research a topic and present their findings.

UNDERSTANDING THE ASSIGNMENT'S PURPOSE

To benefit most from group projects, be sure you understand the task. Ask yourself, What am I expected to learn from this assignment? You will get more out of an assignment if you focus on its purpose and desired outcomes.

KEEPING GROUPS FUNCTIONING EFFECTIVELY

Some students complain that group projects are time-consuming and unproductive. If you feel this way about a group project, take a leadership role and make it work. Set a good example, and choose to work with serious, energetic classmates.

Assign tasks according to each member's strengths, and establish a firm schedule for completion (with checkpoints along the way). Stay focused on the project during group meetings.

Despite your best efforts and those of other group members, however, not all groups will function effectively. Conflicts may arise; members may complain; a group member may not do his or her share. Because your grade on the project may depend on every other member's work, you must address problems quickly and effectively when they occur. Use the following suggestions to do so.

- If members miss work sessions, offer to remind everyone of the time and place.
- Establish a more detailed timetable if the work is not getting done.
- Offer to take on a greater share of the work if it will help get the assignment done.
- Ask questions that may stimulate unproductive members' ideas and interest.
- Suggest that uncommunicative members share their ideas in written form.
- Encourage the students who are causing the problem to propose solutions.

If you are unable to resolve problems or conflicts, discuss them with your instructor.

Take Effective Notes in Class

To be a successful student, you need to take careful notes and review them at least once a week.

Research has shown that most people retain far more information when they interact with it using more than one sense. For instance, if you only listen to a lecture or discussion, you will probably forget most of it within a couple of weeks, well before the next exam. However, if you take accurate notes and review them regularly, you are more likely to retain the main points and key examples needed. Following are some useful note-taking tips.

- **Read assignments before class.** Read any related textbook material *before* going to class. Familiarity with the topic will make note-taking easier.
- **Don't attempt to record everything.** Record only main ideas and key details. Avoid writing in complete sentences. Use words and phrases instead.
- **Develop a system of abbreviations, signs, and symbols to aid in note-taking.** For example, you might use a star to mark key information.
- **Pay attention to your instructor's cues regarding what is important.** These cues include repetition of key points, changes in voice or speaking rate, listing or numbering of items, and the use of the chalkboard or visuals, such as graphs, photos, and PowerPoint presentations.

- **Don't rewrite your notes.** Your time is valuable; rewriting is time-consuming. You can better use the time reviewing and studying your notes.

- **Leave plenty of blank space in your notes.** Use this space to add examples or fill in information you missed during the lecture or class discussion.

- **When you must miss a class, borrow notes from a classmate who is a good student.**

- **Review and study your notes immediately after the lecture.** While the class is still fresh in your mind, clarify relationships and cement your understanding. If you wait a day or more, your memory of the class will fade. Spending even ten minutes per week reviewing class notes can improve your retention and reduce the stress of "cramming" for tests.

Two of the most popular and efficient methods of taking notes are the two-column method and the modified outline method.

USING THE TWO-COLUMN METHOD

All students can benefit from using the two-column note-taking method illustrated in Figure 1.3. Draw a vertical line from the top of a piece of paper to the bottom. The left-hand column should be about half as wide as the right-hand column.

In the wider, right-hand column, record ideas and facts as your instructor presents them, or as they arise in a discussion group. In the narrower, left-hand column, add your own questions as they arise during the class. When you review your notes later, add summaries of major concepts and sections to the left-hand column. This method allows you to quickly review key information by reading the left-hand column and to study specific information and examples in the right-hand column.

Figure 1.3   Two-Column Method of Note-Taking

Writing Process	Prewriting—taking notes, writing ideas, drawing a cluster diagram, researching, writing questions, noting what you already know, outlining, etc.
	Writing—drafting
(How many drafts does the average writer complete?)	Rewriting—revision = "to see again"
	2 types: global = major overhaul (reconsidering, reorganizing);
	local = rewording, correcting grammar (editing for correctness & style)
NOT linear	Writing is not a linear process. May go back to prewrite after writing, etc.

USING THE MODIFIED OUTLINE METHOD

As Figure 1.4 shows, the modified outline method uses symbols and indentations instead of numbers and letters to separate ideas and suggest relative importance. This sample uses bullets for main ideas and dashes for detailed information within a section. Less important details are simply indented farther. The more detailed the information, the farther to the right you indent your outline entries.

Figure 1.4 Modified Outline Method of Note-Taking

Writing is a process.

- Prewriting
  - —Taking notes
  - —Writing ideas
  - —Drawing a cluster diagram
  - —Researching
  - —Writing questions
  - —Noting what you already know
  - —Outlining
- Writing
  - —First drafts
    - On paper
    - On cards
    - On computer
  - —Later drafts

- Rewriting, or revision (means "to see again")
  - —Global
    - Major revision
    - Reconsidering ideas
    - Reorganizing
  - —Local
    - Rewording for style
    - Rewriting for correct grammar, spelling, punctuation

TAKING NOTES ON YOUR LAPTOP

Some students use their laptop computers to take notes. If you decide to take notes electronically, use the following tips to make your computer work for you.

Do . . .	Don't . . .
Make sure you can plug in your laptop or that you have sufficient battery power.	Allow distractions such as email and instant messages to compete for your attention.
Set up a folder for each course. Create a new file for each day's notes, and include the date in the file name.	Interrupt the class with annoying beeps and buzzes. Turn off the sound.
Save your document frequently so you don't lose anything.	Lose track of your computer. Laptops are easily stolen.
Keep a pen and paper handy to record diagrams, drawings, and other nonverbal material.	

Manage Online Course Work

Online courses are growing in popularity. Although convenient, they require more self-direction and more discipline than traditional classes do. They also require a great deal of online writing, reading, and research. Here are some tips for succeeding in online courses. (You'll read a full student essay comparing online courses to traditional courses in Chapter 2, "Understanding Texts and Images.")

- **Avoid taking online courses in your first college term.** First learn what is expected in college courses by attending traditional classes. When you are familiar with the expectations of a typical college course, you will be better prepared to take an online course.

- **Set aside specific, regular hours to devote to your online course.** Otherwise, it becomes easy to put off class work.

- **Keep up with the work.** Most students who fail online courses do so because they fall hopelessly behind on readings and assignments.

- **Plan to do a lot of reading.** You will read your textbooks, as well as communications from your instructor and other students. Your instructor may also put supplemental (additional) materials online and require you to read them.

- **Maintain your concentration.** Turn off your phone, music, IM, and email while working on your computer.

- **Make sure all your contributions are appropriate and useful.** Comments should be specific and add to the conversation. Avoid posts that simply say "I agree" or "Good job."

These tips and strategies will help you achieve the goals you outlined at the beginning of the chapter. In the rest of Part 1 you will learn how to build on these skills to read and write successfully throughout your academic career.

Chapter 2

Understanding Texts and Images

Quick Start: Study the photograph shown here and discuss its meaning with your classmates. Consider the photograph's content, and ask yourself, What does it portray? Where was it taken? Who are the subjects in the photo and what are they doing? Then write a paragraph explaining what you think is happening in this photograph. Be detailed and specific.

The first step in comprehending the chapter opening photo is to gain a basic understanding of its content. Reading deeply also begins with the process of *understanding*, or comprehending, what the writer *says*. *Active reading* is a process of getting involved with what you read and taking steps to understand, recall, and respond to what you read. It involves thinking about, questioning, reacting to, and evaluating the author's ideas. This chapter will give you the tools to understand what you read and what you see. You will learn what to do before, during, and after reading to strengthen your comprehension and increase your recall. You will learn how to read for meaning and how to extract key information from your reading assignments by conducting an immediate review, writing a summary, and drawing a graphic organizer. You will also learn specific tips for reading professional essays, student essays, textbooks, and visual materials and for reading challenging materials.

In Chapter 3, you will continue to develop your active reading skills by developing *critical reading* skills. You will learn to *analyze* (interpret) and *evaluate* written and visual works. As you improve your ability to read and respond thoroughly and carefully, you'll learn more and do better on exams and quizzes that ask you to apply, connect, and evaluate ideas.

Active Reading Strategies

Active reading is essential for academic success. It is the primary means through which you acquire ideas and gather information. To orient yourself toward reading as a tool for success, keep the following suggestions in mind.

Assume responsibility for reading assignments   Some courses require a heavy reading load. It is tempting to let these assignments go undone, especially when a chapter is long or you feel pressured to complete other work. Use the time-management suggestions in Chapter 1 (pp. 5–8) to organize your workload. Instructors assume that you are keeping up with reading assignments and that you are learning the material. However, most instructors won't tell you *how* to learn. Consequently, you will have to discover how best to learn each subject. Experiment with different methods—taking notes on assignments, preparing study sheets that summarize important information, highlighting (see pp. 33–34), outlining (see pp. 18 and 47), and annotating (see p. 78).

Pay attention to visual aids   Much of what you read will be accompanied by visual aids (for example, drawings, photographs, charts, and graphs). Writers use visual aids to clarify or emphasize ideas, condense information, explain a complicated process, or illustrate a specific viewpoint. Think about the writer's purpose for including them and how they relate to the text that accompanies them. We'll return to this topic later in this chapter and in Chapter 3, "Analyzing and Evaluating Texts and Images."

Adapt your reading skills to different materials   In your studies, you will encounter a wide range of reading materials. In addition to reading textbooks, you may read articles, professionally written essays, student essays, critiques, field reports, and scientific studies. For each type, begin by noticing how the reading is organized and what its purpose might be. Then devise a strategy for identifying what you should learn and remember.

 Reading | Writing   **Use reading to develop your writing skills.** By studying the writing of others, you can improve your own writing. As you read an article, essay, or textbook assignment, take note of the writer's techniques for presenting information. For example, notice how the writer organizes paragraphs, how she uses language to express ideas, and how she develops ideas throughout the work.

Become an active reader   When you attend a baseball game, do you get actively involved? Baseball fans cheer some players and criticize others, evaluate plays and calls, and offer advice and analysis. Like sports fans, active readers get involved with the material they read. They question, think about, and react to ideas. Table 2.1 summarizes the differences between active and passive readers.

Table 2.1   Active versus Passive Readers

Passive Readers	Active Readers
Passive readers begin reading.	Active readers begin by reading the title, evaluating the author, and thinking about what they already know about the subject. Then they decide what they need to know before they begin reading.
Passive readers read the material only because it is assigned.	Active readers read the material while looking for key points and answers to questions.
Passive readers read but do not write.	Active readers highlight or underline, annotate, and write notes as they read.
Passive readers close the book when finished.	Active readers review, analyze, and evaluate what they've read.

To achieve maximum comprehension, you should generally follow a three-step active-reading process.

1. Preview and form prereading questions *before* reading.
2. Read for meaning *during* the reading process.
3. Review the material *after* reading it.

Figure 2.1 shows these steps graphically and in more detail.

Figure 2.1   Strategies for Active Reading

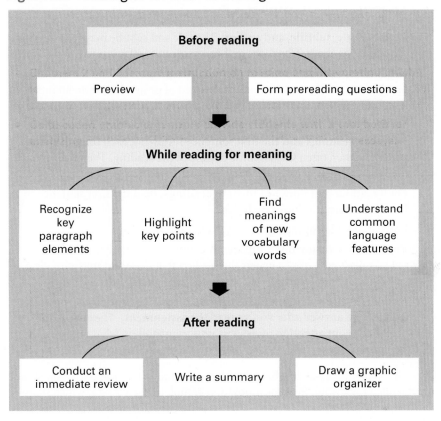

Preview and Form Prereading Questions before Reading

Never start any reading assignment without preparation. Instead, use *previewing* and *prereading questions* to discover what the reading is about and to focus your mind on the topic.

PREVIEW

Previewing is a quick way of familiarizing yourself with a reading's content and organization. Previewing helps you to decide what you need to learn, and it has a number of other benefits as well.

- It helps you get interested in the material.
- It helps you understand the structure of the material and thus focuses your concentration.
- It helps you remember more of what you read.

To preview a reading assignment, use the following guidelines. Remember to read *only* the materials that are listed.

1. **Read the title, subtitle, and author.** The title and subtitle may tell you what the reading is about. Check the author's name to see if it is one you recognize.

2. **Read the introduction and/or the first paragraph.** These sections often provide an overview of the reading. Instead of or in addition to an introduction, some readings include a *headnote* that provides background information about the author or reading.

3. **Read any headings and the first sentence following each one.** Headings, taken together, often form a mini-outline of the reading. The first sentence following a heading often explains the heading.

4. **For a reading that does not include headings, read the first sentence in a few of the paragraphs on each page.**

5. **Look at any photographs, tables, charts, and drawings.**

6. **Read the conclusion or summary.** A conclusion (usually found in the reading's last paragraph) brings the reading to a close and may provide a summary of the piece.

7. *Before* **you begin reading the assignment, read any questions you will be expected to answer** *after* **you've read the assignment.** These questions will help focus your attention on what is important and on what you are expected to know after you have read the assignment.

The following essay has been highlighted to illustrate the parts you should read while previewing. Preview it now and complete Exercise 2.1, which follows.

Comparing Online and Traditional Education

Morgan Lowrie

Morgan Lowrie is a Canadian student studying journalism who lives in Montreal, Quebec. In her autobiography, she says that she writes because she loves learning new things and telling people's stories. She is also an avid reader of everything from "Shakespeare to the backs of cereal boxes."

Prereading Questions

1. **In the context of this article, what does the phrase "traditional education" mean?**

2. **Which type of education, traditional or online, does the author of this article see as the better option?**

In 2008, I completed my bachelor's degree in English literature by taking advantage of my school's distance-education program. I had completed the first two years of study in the conventional, traditional manner: I had attended classes, participated in discussions, and sat for exams. Two years into my four-year degree, I was offered a job which took me away from home, and I was fortunate enough that my school had a significantly large distance-education program that I was able to finish my degree online.

Having experienced both methods of attending school, my preference is   2
for traditional education. Nevertheless, it is worth weighing the benefits and disadvantages of each.

Online Education — Benefits

Without the option of online classes, I would not have been able to both   3
take my dream job and finish my degree. One or the other would have had to have been sacrificed. And therein lies the beauty of online education: It is tremendously flexible.

The traditional classroom is not always particularly accommodating   4
to working adults. Most classes take place in the daytime, and there are not always multiple sections to choose from. Even schools that offer night classes are inconvenient for people who work rotating schedules, such as retail workers. Distance-education course work can usually be accomplished whenever and wherever it suits the student, as long as deadlines are met. Not everybody can afford to take four years out of their lives to attend school, and not everyone has a trust fund set up to pay for their education. Working one's way through school allows a person to graduate without the crippling debt that burdens so many graduating students. Online learning is also an excellent choice for stay-at-home mothers with young children and people with certain disabilities who might need a little more accommodation in order to thrive. Many people who otherwise would not be able to attend college are given the option to do so because of online classes.

Commuting time is also a factor. When I attended traditional classes, I   5
traveled an hour and a half to get to my school. (I was living at home to save money.) Although I managed to do a lot of reading on the two buses and the train that I took, one cannot say that this was a particularly productive or efficient use of time. Even a fifteen or twenty minute drive each way adds up to hours per week spent traveling—time that an online student could put into his or her course work.

Furthermore, as technology improves, so do the conditions for the online   6
student. Most online classes have forums and chat rooms where students can engage in discussions and complete assignments with fellow students. Lectures can be recorded and played back at will by the student. Professors are accessible through email, by phone, and via interactive chats. One geography class I took even included a virtual field trip, thanks to the satellite imagery of Google Earth. Technologies like these ensure that the distance-education student is less isolated than ever before.

Online Learning—Disadvantages

Although the benefits of online learning are numerous, there are also   7
many disadvantages that some students do not consider before enrolling.

The number-one problem that I encountered was that not all classes were   8
offered online. I would have enjoyed my education much more had I been
able to choose the classes that interested me most; instead, I had to take the
classes that were offered online. In the end, I had to change my major and
drop my minor altogether because my school just didn't offer enough courses
for me to complete the major I wanted. This was partially because my school
was a traditional one with an online component, but even fully online schools
tend to have a narrower curriculum and fewer classes to choose from than
their traditional counterparts. For example, it is difficult to take a quality
language course online. It is equally difficult for science classes with a lab
component to be properly taught online. The online student is limited in the
type of degree that can be earned.

Second, because there is less classroom interaction and no time spent in   9
class, the online courses I took placed much more emphasis on writing papers
and exams. Since there were no (or few) marks given for elements such as
participation, group projects, or oral presentations, the courses I took included
very heavy reading loads and several large papers and had a final exam
that was usually worth at least 30% of the final grade. For me, this was not a
problem, since I am a good writer and tend to test extremely well (although I
did have trouble finding quality research materials without access to a good
college library). Students who are not strong in these subjects might have more
difficulty with online classes.

Third, most of the classes that I took still included a final exam. As I was   10
not able to physically make it to the school to write the exam, I had to find a

proctor to supervise me as I wrote. Usually, a proctor has to be a college faculty member or administrator, or a librarian. I was lucky enough to work with someone who met these qualifications and who was happy to assist me, but I have known several people who have expressed surprise at the great difficulty they had finding proctors. Many colleges and libraries charge large fees for this service or else refuse altogether. This can be one of the big hassles of distance education.

Finally, there is the obvious problem: Even with all the technological   11
advances being made, taking a course online is still much less interactive than attending a traditional class. Students who take online classes need to be self-motivated, have good time-management skills, and be able to learn independently. Usually there is far less spoon-feeding of material in distance courses, and there are no lively discussions, anecdotes, or jokes during lectures to make the material more interesting. Perhaps in the future, as online courses become more and more common, some of these hurdles will be overcome. But at the moment, online students need to be prepared to work mostly on their own.

Online or Traditional: Which Is Better?

I will be forever grateful for the existence of online learning, as it gave   12
me the opportunity to take my dream job without having to sacrifice my education. Nevertheless, if personal factors had not intervened, I would have preferred the traditional classroom setting.

Let me put it this way: I think that if a person can attend college   13
traditionally, they should.

When I switched to online education, I missed out on a good chunk   14
of the college experience. To me, the best parts of college were listening to lectures by terrific professors and participating in discussions with other young, intelligent people. Once I became a distance student, I missed out on all of these exchanges of ideas. I missed out on making great friends, on taking some terrific classes, on joining clubs, and on writing for the student newspaper. These are very important parts of a college education, and they are parts that simply cannot be experienced through a computer monitor. I put my education second, behind my job and my personal life. Perhaps, for only a couple of years, I should have put it first.

Online classes can be a godsend for some students, and I think that they   15
provide an incredibly valuable service in opening up the world of college education to some people who otherwise wouldn't be able to earn degrees without great sacrifice. But, take it from someone who has been on both sides of the fence: It isn't the same. It truly isn't.

Exercise 2.1

Based on your preview of the essay "Comparing Online and Traditional Education," answer the following questions either "T" for true or "F" for false. If most of your answers are correct, you will know that previewing helped you gain a sense of the essay's context and organization. (For the answers to this exercise, see p. 52.)

_____ 1. The author believes an online education is the equivalent of a traditional education.

_____ 2. The author is thankful for the opportunities that distance education provided her.

_____ 3. The author has not yet completed her college degree.

_____ 4. The author stopped attending traditional classes so she could accept her dream job.

_____ 5. The author believes that online classes are valuable.

FORM PREREADING QUESTIONS

Before you begin reading, you can improve your _intent to remember_, that is, you can remind yourself that your goal is to remember what you've read. One way to improve retention is to use the reading selection's title and headings to form questions before you begin reading. Then, as you read, answer those questions, thereby strengthening your comprehension and memory of the material. The following guidelines will help you start devising prereading questions.

- **Use the title to devise questions.** Then read to find the answers. Table 2.2 includes a few examples of titles and relevant questions.

- **Use headings to devise questions.** For example, an essay titled "Territoriality" includes two headings, "Types of Territoriality" and "Territorial

Table 2.2   Examples of Titles and Relevant Questions

Title	Question
"Part-time Employment Undermines Students' Commitment to School"	Why does part-time employment undermine commitment to school?
"Human Cloning: Don't 'Just Say No'"	What are good reasons to clone humans?
"Wounds That Can't Be Stitched Up"	What kinds of wounds cannot be repaired?

Encroachment." Each of these headings can easily be turned into a prereading question.

What are the types of territoriality?

What is territorial encroachment and how does it occur?

Not all readings lend themselves to using the title and headings to form prereading questions. For some readings, you may need to dig into the introductory and final paragraphs to form questions. Or you may find the subtitle more useful for forming a question than the title.

Exercise 2.2

Return to the essay "Comparing Online and Traditional Education," and use the title and headings to write three questions you expect the essay to answer.

Read for Meaning

A variety of techniques can help focus your attention and improve your comprehension while you read.

1. Identify the key elements of individual paragraphs.
2. Identify the thesis statement.
3. Highlight key points.
4. Figure out the meanings of unfamiliar words.
5. Understand commonly used language features.

IDENTIFY THE KEY ELEMENTS OF PARAGRAPHS

All readings are composed of paragraphs. A **paragraph** is a group of sentences that explain or develop one idea. Some paragraphs are as short as one sentence; others can go on for pages. As you read, look for the key elements in each paragraph. These include

- the topic,
- the main idea and topic sentence,
- supporting details and transitions.

The topic   The one general subject discussed in the paragraph is its **topic**. Every sentence in the paragraph somehow explains, discusses, or evaluates this topic. Consider paragraph 14 from "Comparing Online and Traditional Education."

> When I switched to online education, I missed out on a good chunk of the college experience. To me, the best parts of college were listening to

lectures by terrific professors and participating in discussions with other young, intelligent people. Once I became a distance student, I missed out on all of these exchanges of ideas. I missed out on making great friends, on taking some terrific classes, on joining clubs, and on writing for the student newspaper. These are very important parts of a college education, and they are parts that simply cannot be experienced through a computer monitor. I put my education second, behind my job and my personal life. Perhaps, for only a couple of years, I should have put it first.

The topic of this paragraph—that is, the *general subject* of the entire paragraph—is the opportunities missed as a result of online education. To find the topic, ask yourself, What is the one thing the writer discusses throughout the entire paragraph?

The main idea and topic sentence   A paragraph's **main idea** is the most important point it is trying to make. The main idea expresses the writer's viewpoint on the topic, and it is often found in a single **topic sentence**. In the paragraph above, the main idea is expressed in the first sentence: "When I switched to online education, I missed out on a good chunk of the college experience." The rest of the paragraph supports the main idea. The topic sentence is often the first sentence in a paragraph, but it can be found at the end of the paragraph or buried in the middle of the paragraph.

The main idea of a paragraph is sometimes not expressed in a single sentence of the paragraph. As an example, look at paragraph 10 of "Comparing Online and Traditional Education." The main idea of this paragraph can be stated as follows: Taking exams for online courses can be inconvenient and expensive. Because main ideas can't always be found in a topic sentence, you should always be able to state the paragraph's main idea in your own words. A correct statement of the main idea takes the entire paragraph into account.

To state the main idea, ask yourself, What is the most important point of this paragraph? If you have difficulty stating the main idea, try the following suggestions.

1. **Determine the topic.** That is, determine the *one general subject* of the paragraph.
2. **Look for the topic sentence.** This will be the most general sentence in the paragraph.
3. **If you cannot find a topic sentence, study the rest of the paragraph.** Formulate a main idea that conveys the paragraph's key point and takes into account all the information provided in the paragraph.

Supporting details and transitions   To fully explain the point they are trying to make, writers provide facts, ideas, and examples. Without these **supporting details**, a paragraph would be undeveloped and unconvincing. The main idea is a *general* statement; the paragraph details provide *specific* support for the main idea. For example, in paragraph 14 from "Comparing Online and Traditional Education," the author provides a number of examples to support her main idea: By switching to online education, she missed (1) hearing lectures by terrific professors, (2) participating in discussions, (3) making friends, (4) taking classes that weren't available in an online format, (5) joining clubs, and (6) writing for the student newspaper.

Supporting details are often signaled by **transitions**, words or phrases that help readers link ideas and follow the author's train of thought. Transitions can signal time sequence (*first, later, next, finally, in the end*); examples (*for instance, to illustrate, for example*); comparison (*like, similarly*); contrast (*on the other hand, in contrast, however, instead*); cause and effect (*because, thus, therefore*); and so on. You will learn more about transitional words and phrases in Chapters 10 to 18.

 Reading|Writing   Understanding the purpose of each paragraph and its parts will allow you to understand the writer's overall message, and it will also help you effectively write your own essays. Table 2.3 (p. 32) summarizes the key paragraph elements from two perspectives: the reader's and the writer's.

IDENTIFY THE CENTRAL THOUGHT OR THESIS STATEMENT

The single main point of a reading (whether an essay, a textbook chapter, or any other source) is called the **central thought** or **thesis statement**. While each paragraph in the reading will have a topic and a main idea, the reading as a whole has only one central idea. It is often found in the first paragraph of the reading, but it may appear anywhere in the selection. It is often, but not always, a single sentence. In "Comparing Online and Traditional Education," the thesis statement appears in the second paragraph: "Having experienced both methods of attending school, my preference is for traditional education. Nevertheless, it is worth weighing the benefits and disadvantages of each."

Note that the thesis statement covers every aspect of the entire reading: the advantages and disadvantages of online education as well as the author's conclusion that a traditional education is preferable.

Exercise 2.3

Answer the questions based on the following excerpt from "Comparing Online and Traditional Education."

> The number-one problem that I encountered was that not all classes were offered online. I would have enjoyed my education much more had I been able to choose the classes that interested me most; instead, I had to take the classes that were offered online. In the end, I had to change my major and drop my minor altogether because my school just didn't

Table 2.3   Reader's and Writer's Perspectives on Paragraphs

Paragraph Element	The Reader's Perspective	The Writer's Perspective
Topic	Identifying the **topic** of each paragraph enables you to build a mental framework for the reading. As you read, your knowledge of the topic increases.	Developing a clear **topic** for each paragraph is often the key to writing an effective essay.
Main Idea / Topic Sentence	To understand a paragraph, look for a **topic sentence** and the paragraph's **main idea**. Many exams test students' understanding of main ideas.	Writers use a **topic sentence** to state a paragraph's most important point for the reader—that is, its **main idea**.
Supporting Details	**Supporting details** clarify, explain, and provide additional details about the main idea. If the main idea is abstract or difficult to understand, supporting details may help you make connections and increase your comprehension.	Use **supporting details** to strengthen your case and to provide specific support for your topic sentence. If you do not provide interesting, relevant supporting details, you will not be able to convince your readers that your ideas or conclusions are valid.
Transitions	**Transitions** are signals to readers; they help you follow the writer's train of thought or hint that a line of thought is about to change.	**Transitions** connect your ideas. They also prevent your essay from sounding choppy or disconnected.

offer enough courses for me to complete the major I wanted. This was partially because my school was a traditional one with an online component, but even fully online schools tend to have a narrower curriculum and fewer classes to choose from than their traditional counterparts. For example, it is difficult to take a quality language course online. It is equally difficult for science classes with a lab component to be properly taught online. The online student is limited in the type of degree that can be earned.

1. What is the topic of the paragraph?
2. Underline the topic sentence.
3. State the main idea in your own words.
4. List at least three supporting details provided by the author.
5. Underline the transitional words or phrases.

HIGHLIGHT KEY POINTS

As you read, you will encounter many new ideas. You will find some ideas more important than others. You will agree with some and disagree with others. Later, as you write about what you have read, you will want to return to the reading's main ideas to refresh your memory.

To locate and remember these ideas easily, it is a good idea to read with a highlighter in hand. If you're using an e-reader, use the note-taking and annotation functions; for anything you read online, keep a blank document open on which you can copy and paste—with quotation marks—any information you want to remember. Highlighting is an active reading strategy that forces you to sort and sift important ideas from less important ideas. In other words, it helps you distinguish main ideas from supporting details at a glance.

Use the following guidelines to make your highlighting as useful as possible.

- **Use a light-colored highlighter (for example, yellow).** Do not use a color that will interfere with your ability to reread the text.

- **Decide what kinds of information to highlight before you begin.** What types of tasks will you be doing as a result of your reading? Will you write a paper, participate in a class discussion, or take an exam? Think about what you need to know and tailor your highlighting to the particular task.

- **Be selective. Do not highlight too much or too little.** If you highlight every idea, none will stand out. Highlighting too much means you are not distinguishing between main ideas and details. Highlighting too little means you are likely missing key information.

- **Read first; then highlight.** First read a paragraph or section; then go back and mark what is important within it. This approach will help you control the tendency to highlight too much.

- **Highlight key elements, words, and phrases.** Mark the thesis statement, the topic sentence in each paragraph, important terms and definitions, and key words and phrases.

In addition to highlighting, many students find it useful to jot down key points in the margins. This process is called *annotating*, and we discuss it in detail in Chapter 3, "Analyzing and Evaluating Texts and Images."

Exercise 2.4

Using the suggestions above, highlight "Comparing Online and Traditional Education." Avoid using a yellow highlighter so your highlighting will be distinct from existing highlighting.

FIGURE OUT THE MEANINGS OF UNFAMILIAR WORDS

If you were to use a dictionary to look up every unfamiliar word you encounter in a reading, you would not have enough time to complete all your assignments. You can often figure out a word's meaning by using one of the following strategies.

- **Look for clues in surrounding text.** You can often figure out a word's meaning from the way it is used in its sentence or in surrounding sentences. Sometimes the author may provide a brief definition or synonym; other times a less obvious context clue reveals meaning.

Brief Definition	Janice *prefaced,* or introduced, her poetry reading with a personal story. [*Prefaced* means "introduced."]
Context Clue	In certain societies young children are always on the *periphery,* and never in the center, of family life. [*Periphery* means "the edges or the fringe," which is far away from the center.]

- **Try pronouncing the word out loud.** Hearing the word will sometimes help you grasp its meaning. By pronouncing the word *magnific,* you may hear part of the word *magnify* and know that it has something to do with enlargement. *Magnific* means "large or imposing in size" and "impressive in appearance."
- **Look at parts of the word.** If you break down the parts of a word, you may be able to figure out its meaning. For example, in the word *nonresponsive* you can see the adjective *responsive,* which means "answering or reacting." *Non* means "not," so you can figure out that *nonresponsive* means "not answering or reacting." You can find a comprehensive list of word parts at **www.learnthat.org/pages/view/roots.html.**
- **Use a dictionary when necessary.** Sometimes you won't be able to continue reading until you understand a particular word. Be sure you have a collegiate dictionary available where you read and study, be it in print or online.

Merriam-Webster (**www.merriam-webster.com**) and Dictionary.com (**dictionary.reference.com**) are two reliable, free dictionary Web sites.

UNDERSTAND COMMONLY USED LANGUAGE FEATURES

As you read the selections in this book, you will encounter interesting and unusual features of language that authors use to express their meaning forcefully and uniquely. Many of these techniques involve **figures of speech**, or language used in nonliteral ways to create a striking impression. Paying attention to these features will expand your vocabulary as well as contribute to your understanding of the reading in which they appear. Table 2.4 (p. 36) summarizes many of these figures of speech.

Review the Material after Reading It

One of the biggest mistakes you can make when you finish reading an assignment is to close the book, periodical, essay collection, or browser window and immediately move on to another, unrelated task. If you do, you will likely forget most of what you read because your brain will not have had time to process and digest the material.

To improve your comprehension and recall, you can use three strategies:

1. Conduct an immediate review.
2. Write a summary.
3. Draw a graphic organizer.

Choose those that fit your purpose for reading and the nature of the material.

CONDUCT AN IMMEDIATE REVIEW

If you spend a few minutes reviewing what you read *immediately after you've finished the reading*, you can dramatically increase the amount of information you remember.

To review material after reading, use the same steps you used to preview the reading (see p. 24). Reviewing does not take much time. Your goal is to touch on each main point once again, not to embark on a long and thorough study. Pay particular attention to the following elements of the reading:

- the headings,
- your highlighting,
- the conclusion.

As you read each heading, look at the prereading questions you composed and see if you can answer them. If you cannot, reread the section until you can. Think of immediate review as a way of solidifying in your mind what you have just learned.

Table 2.4   Figures of Speech and Other Features of Language

Figure of Speech	Explanation	Example
Allusion	A reference to a person, place, thing, or literary work.*	Jackson displayed *Herculean* strength. (Hercules is a Greek hero known for strength and courage.)
Cliché	An overused expression that seldom carries specific meaning.	Don't count your chickens until they are hatched.
Connotative meaning (see also Ch. 3, p. 56)	The feelings and associations that accompany a word.	Both *untidy* and *grubby* mean "messy," but *grubby* suggests something dirty as well.
Doublespeak (see also Ch. 3, p. 57)	Deliberately unclear or evasive language.	The company is *downsizing its staff.* (firing employees)
Euphemism (see also Ch. 3, p. 57)	Words or phrases used in place of others that would be unpleasant, embarrassing, or otherwise objectionable.	The newspaper advertised *previously owned vehicles.* (used cars)
Foreign words and phrases	Words that are taken directly, without translation, from another language, often French or Latin.	The visiting dignitary committed a *faux pas.* (social blunder or mistake)
Hyperbole	A deliberate and obvious exaggeration.	I could eat 40 pounds of that chocolate!
Idiom	Phrase that has a meaning other than what the words literally mean.	My role in the debate was to serve as *devil's advocate.* (take a position for the sake of argument, not necessarily believing in it)

*If you are not familiar with an allusion an author makes, consult a dictionary, encyclopedia, or specialized reference book. Online sources to consult include bartleby.com (**www.bartleby.com**) and britannica.com (**www.brittanica.com**).

Table 2.4   (continued)

Figure of Speech	Explanation	Example
Imagery	Language that creates an impression by appealing to the reader's physical senses, most often sight.	The rich carpet of green grass glinted and rippled in the gentle breeze.
Jargon	Specialized words used in particular academic fields or by special groups and not readily understood by the general public.	Publishing language: trim size and bulk. (trim size = book pages' length and width; bulk = book pages' thickness)
Metaphor	An implied comparison between two things without using the words *like* or *as*.	The woman spoke politely to the gardener, but *icicles were hanging on her every word.* (she spoke in a cold, unfriendly manner)
Personification	Attributing human traits to nonhuman beings or inanimate objects.	As we walked through the jungle, the vines grabbed at our ankles with their wiry fingers.
Restrictive word meaning	The meaning of a commonly used word that is unique to a particular field or discipline.	The word *foul* in baseball has a specific meaning.
Simile	An explicit comparison between two things, typically introduced by the word *like* or *as*.	The surface of the wooden table shone *like a mirror.*

The principle of immediate review applies not only to reading but also to other aspects of learning and studying. Here are some other ways to use immediate review to help you learn.

- **Review your class notes as soon as possible after class.** This review will help cement the ideas in your mind.

- **Review all new course materials at the end of each school day.** This review will help you pull information together and make it more meaningful.

- **Review an essay by identifying its thesis statement (or central thought) and listing at least two or three details that support the thesis.** This will help fix the essay's main ideas and some key details in your memory.

- **Review a textbook chapter as soon as you've completed it.** Conduct this review by rereading each heading and the chapter summary (if one is included). Also look at any learning objectives or goals listed at the start of the chapter. If you can't accomplish any of those objectives, reread the relevant sections until you can. Also review end-of-chapter learning aids such as key terms lists and study or review questions.

WRITE A SUMMARY

As part of your review, it is helpful to write a summary of the reading. A **summary** is a brief statement of the reading's major points with no supporting details. You may not realize it, but you probably compose summaries frequently. For example, when a friend asks, "What was the movie about?" you reply with a summary of the plot but do not include specific scenes or dialogue.

Summarizing is an excellent way of checking your understanding. If you have difficulty writing a summary, you most likely do not fully understand what is important in the reading. A good summary is also an excellent study tool to help you review for exams.

In general, a summary should be less than one-fifth the length of the original (and can be much shorter than that for long readings). Use the following guidelines to write an effective summary.

1. **Complete the entire reading assignment before attempting to write anything.**

2. **Use your highlighting and notes.** Any highlighting or marginal notes you made while reading will help you choose the important points to include in your summary.

3. **Write your summary as you reread the assignment.** Work paragraph by paragraph as you write your summary.

4. **Early in the summary, include a sentence that states the author's thesis (the reading's single most important idea) in your own words.**

5. **To avoid plagiarism, be sure to express the author's ideas and thesis in your own words.** If you want to include the author's words, be sure to use quotation marks.

6. **Include all—and only—the reading's key points.** Your summary should be a factual, brief reporting of the key idea. Do not include your own impressions, reactions, or responses.

7. **Present the ideas in the order in which they appear in the original.** Be sure to use transitional words and phrases as you move from one idea to another.

8. **Read your summary to determine if it contains sufficient information.** Would your summary be understandable and meaningful to someone who had not read the original? If not, revise your summary to include additional information.

The following is an effective summary of "Comparing Online and Traditional Education."

> Morgan Lowrie completed her college degree by taking a mixture of on-campus and online courses. In "Comparing Online and Traditional Education," she outlines the pros and cons of distance-learning courses. Online courses have a flexibility that helps working adults and parents fit their studies into their lives, schedules, and family duties. With online classes, students do not waste precious time commuting. The technologies used in distance education are improving and help students record important information and stay in touch with instructors and classmates. However, distance learning has drawbacks. First, not all courses are offered online, which may limit students to particular majors and classes. Second, online courses require a great deal of reading and writing. Students weak in these areas may find distance-learning challenging. Third, it can be difficult and expensive to find someone to oversee the final exam for an online course. Fourth, online classes require students to work independently. Because they're not on a college campus, online learners miss the classroom experience. So, despite the advantages of online courses, Lowrie would have preferred taking courses on campus, even though distance learning helped her complete her degree. She believes distance-education students miss too many of the opportunities that traditional students have (meeting new people and getting involved in student activities). She recommends campus courses over distance courses whenever possible, even if this choice requires sacrifices. Lowrie concludes that the online college experience is very different from, and not as rewarding as, the campus college experience.

In the summary above, notice that the writer expresses Lowrie's thesis in his own words. The order of ideas parallels the order in Lowrie's essay, but throughout the summary the writer continues to use his own words.

One good way to identify what to include in a summary is to write a **summary note** for most or all paragraphs. Summary notes are marginal annotations that briefly state the key issue presented in each paragraph. You can easily convert these notes into sentences for your summary. For example, a summary note for paragraph 6 of Lowrie's article might read, "technology promotes communication and lecture recording." This note could then be used to create the following sentence in the summary:

"The technologies used in distance education are improving and help students record important information and stay in touch with instructors and classmates."

Exercise 2.5

Read "Talking a Stranger through the Night" (Chapter 10, p. 198) and, using the guidelines on pages 38–39, write a summary of it.

DRAW A GRAPHIC ORGANIZER

A **graphic organizer** is a diagram of the reading's structure and main points. Think of a graphic organizer as a visual means of tracking the author's flow of ideas.

Figure 2.2 shows the format of a graphic organizer. When you draw a graphic organizer, be sure it includes all the key elements shown here. This is a general format that you can adapt to individual readings. An example of a graphic organizer for "Comparing Online and Traditional Education" appears in Figure 2.3. As you work through the organizer in Figure 2.3, reread the essay (pp. 24–27), paragraph by paragraph.

Figure 2.2   Key Elements to Include in a Graphic Organizer

Title	
Introduction	Background information
	Thesis statement
Body paragraphs	Main idea
	Key details
	Main idea
	Key details
	Main idea
	Key details
	Main idea
	Key details
	Main idea
	Key details
	Main idea
	Key details
Conclusion	Final statement (summarizes ideas, suggests new directions, reinforces thesis)

Figure 2.3 Graphic Organizer for "Comparing Online and Traditional Education"

Title	"Comparing Online and Traditional Education"
Introduction	**Background:** Author completed her degree by taking a mixture of traditional and online courses
	Thesis: Having experienced both methods of attending school, the author prefers traditional classes because she believes they have some important advantages over online courses.

Body paragraphs	Benefits of online education	Flexibility
		Helps adults who must work to pay the bills
		Helps parents complete their education
		Helps people with disabilities
		Saves commuting time
		Allows students to use time for studying instead of traveling to and from campus
		Technology allows better communication than in the past
		Online forums and chat rooms
		Lectures can be recorded
		Instructors are available through email, phone calls, interactive chats
	Disadvantages of online education	Not all classes offered online
		Fewer majors and minors offered
		Narrower curriculum
		Fewer classes to choose from
		Heavy emphasis on reading and writing
		No credit for participation, group projects, oral presentations
		Difficult and expensive to find proctor for final exam
		Less interactivity
		Need for self-motivation and good time-management skills
		No lively discussions, anecdotes, jokes

Conclusion	Author believes in the value and opportunity of online education but believes that students are better off attending traditional classes and spending time on campus, which allows for greater social development and a richer college experience.

Strategies for Understanding Texts

In college, at work, and in other areas of your life, you'll have to read many different types of materials, from essays to textbooks to photographs. These materials require different types of attention in order to be understood. Some readings will be more challenging than others, and all students experience difficulty with a reading assignment at one time or another. Perhaps this will happen because you just can't "connect" with the author or because you find the topic uninteresting or the writing style confusing. Regardless of the problem, however, you must complete the assignment. The strategies in this section will help you tackle the types of reading you're most likely to see in school. Table 2.5 highlights particular steps to take when dealing with material you find especially challenging.

Table 2.5   Troubleshooting Guide for Difficult Readings

Problems	Strategies for Solving Them
You cannot concentrate.	1. Take limited breaks. 2. Tackle the assignment at peak periods of attention. 3. Divide the material into sections. Make it your goal to complete one section at a time. 4. Give yourself a reasonable deadline for completing the assignment.
The sentences are long and confusing.	1. Read aloud. 2. Divide each sentence into parts and analyze the function of each part. 3. Express each sentence in your own words.
The ideas are complicated and hard to understand.	1. Reread the material several times. 2. Rephrase or explain each idea in your own words. 3. Create a detailed outline. 4. Study with a classmate; discuss difficult ideas. 5. Look up the meanings of unfamiliar words in a dictionary.
The material seems disorganized or poorly organized.	1. Study the introduction for clues to organization. 2. Pay more attention to headings. 3. Read the summary or conclusion. 4. Try to discover the organization by drawing a graphic organizer (see pp. 40–41) or creating an outline (see pp. 47–48).

Table 2.5   (continued)

Problems	Strategies for Solving Them
The material contains many unfamiliar words.	1. Look for clues to meaning in the surrounding text. 2. Try pronouncing words aloud to see if they remind you of related words. 3. Break words into parts whose meanings you know. 4. Use a dictionary when necessary.
You cannot get interested in the material.	1. Think about something you've experienced that is related to the topic. 2. Work with a classmate, discussing each section as you go.
You cannot relate to the writer's ideas or experiences.	1. Find out some background information about the writer. 2. Imagine yourself having the writer's experiences. How would you react?
The subject is unfamiliar; you lack background information on the subject.	1. Obtain a more basic text or other source that moves more slowly, offers more explanation, and reviews fundamental principles and concepts. 2. For unfamiliar terminology, consult a specialized dictionary within the field of study. 3. Ask your instructor to recommend useful print or online resources and references.

Strategies for Reading Professional Essays

Most of the readings in this book are essays written by professional writers. In general, an **essay** presents information on a specific topic from the writer's point of view. The following are some specific suggestions for reading essays.

Read the headnote   Many essays provide background information about the topic or the author in a *headnote* preceding the essay. (On page 24 you can see the headnote preceding "Comparing Online and Traditional Education.") Headnotes can be valuable sources of information about the author's qualifications. They may also provide a context for the essay and suggestions regarding what to look for in the essay.

Look for meaning in the title and subtitle   In some cases, the title announces the topic and reveals the author's point of view. In others, the meaning or the significance of the title becomes clear only as you read the text. Subtitles, when included, can provide additional clues regarding the topic and author's viewpoint.

Pay close attention to the introduction   An essay's opening paragraph(s) will often announce the topic and provide background information to grab the reader's attention. Some introductory paragraphs define technical or unfamiliar terms; be sure you understand these terms before you attempt to read the entire essay. If the author does not provide sufficient background information, consult other sources to get the information you need.

Look for the thesis statement   Writers often place their thesis statement in the first or second paragraph to let the reader know what lies ahead. But the thesis statement may sometimes appear at the end of the essay instead. Test your understanding of the thesis statement by writing it out in your own words.

Occasionally, a thesis statement will be implied or suggested rather than stated directly. When you cannot find a clear statement of the thesis, ask yourself, What is the one main point the author is making? Your answer is the implied thesis statement.

Look for main ideas (topic sentences), support, and explanation   Highlight main ideas and important supporting details as you read, then review your highlighting as soon as you've completed the reading assignment. Supporting details can fall into any of the following categories: examples, descriptions, facts, statistics, reasons, anecdotes (stories that illustrate a point), personal experiences and observations, and quotations from or references to authorities and experts.

Read the conclusion carefully   An essay's final paragraph or paragraphs often restate the author's thesis and/or offer ideas for further thought or discussion.

Summarize, outline, or draw a graphic organizer of the essay   Reviewing helps cement your understanding of the essay's structure, key points, and supporting details.

Strategies for Reading Student Essays

Some of the essays in Part 2 of this book (Chapters 10–18) were written by college students, not by professional writers. Use the following suggestions when reading student essays.

Read the essay several times   During your first reading, concentrate on the writer's key messages: the thesis statement and topic sentences. Then read the essay again, examining the support and the language used to create a particular impression. Has the writer provided enough support for the thesis? Is the writing clear, concise, and free of grammatical errors?

Read with a pen or marker in hand or be prepared to write notes or use e-reader annotation tools for digital texts   As you discover writing techniques emphasized in the chapter or modeled by your instructor, mark or annotate them.

Focus on the method of organization and its characteristics   Each chapter in Part 2 of this book presents the characteristics of a particular method of essay organization, such as comparison and contrast (Chapter 14) or definition (Chapter 16). Consider how the student essay demonstrates some of or all the characteristics of the specific organizational method.

Look for the specific writing techniques used   Each chapter in Part 2 offers specific techniques and suggestions for writing a particular type of essay. Observe how the student writer makes use of them.

Focus on what is new and different   Ask yourself the following questions as you read: What is the writer doing that you haven't seen before? What catches your attention? What works particularly well? Which writing techniques might be fun to try? Which techniques would be challenging? For example, if a writer begins her essay with a striking statistic, consider whether you could use the same approach to begin one of your essays.

Use student essays to train your critical eye   Although student essays are reasonably good models, they are usually not perfect. Look for ways the essays can be improved. Once you are able to identify ways to improve someone else's essay, you will be better equipped to analyze and improve your own writing.

Use graphic organizers to understand the essay's structure   A graphic organizer is presented for each method of organization discussed in Part 2. Compare the essay to the graphic organizer and notice where the writer conforms to or deviates from it.

Strategies for Reading Textbooks

Textbooks are an essential part of education. These books provide a wealth of accurate information written and vetted by experts in the field. Many of your assigned readings will come from textbooks. (For this reason, one reading in each chapter in Part 2 of this book is taken from a college textbook.)

To get the most from your textbook reading assignments, use the following suggestions.

Understand the role of textbooks   A textbook's primary goal is to convey basic information. Look on textbooks as the base on which to build your learning. Each textbook chapter will present key terms and information that you will explore in more depth in classroom lectures and discussions. In general, textbooks are the most trustworthy of sources because their information is carefully edited and verified. Textbooks also provide summaries of the most important research in the field, combining classic research with the results of important recent studies.

Use textbook features to help you learn   Textbooks provide a wealth of features to help you learn. You can often find a list of the textbook's features in the book's preface. The following are some of the most common textbook features.

> **Learning objectives** These appear at the beginning of the chapter and outline the student's learning goals for the chapter. Upon completing the

chapter, revisit the learning objectives to make sure you can accomplish them. If you can't, go back and reread the relevant sections of the chapter.

Chapter headings Each chapter in a textbook provides a variety of headings to emphasize the chapter's structure and organization. Before reading, conduct a thorough preview of all the headings, formulating prereading questions as you do so.

Marginal definitions Each academic discipline (or subject) has its own special vocabulary. To learn the subject, you must learn many new words and definitions. Key terms frequently appear in **boldface** or *italic* type. You can create flash cards from these key terms to help you study their meanings. Most textbooks also include at the end a **glossary** that lists all the key terms (along with their definitions) in alphabetical order.

Opening vignettes (stories) Many textbook chapters begin with a story that introduces the subject matter in a relevant way. For example, a chapter on social psychology may begin with a story about team sports. Don't skip the introductory vignette; it is an important tool for opening up your mind to the concepts you're about to study.

Minisummaries Some textbooks include a minisummary every few pages to remind readers of key points. Such summaries can be useful because they list the main ideas of the preceding pages in one place. If you have highlighted effectively, your highlights will reflect the content of the minisummaries. Read the minisummary before you move on to the chapter's next section. If you don't understand any of its points, go back and reread the relevant paragraphs.

Visual aids Many of today's textbooks contain numerous visual aids. Text and visual aids are designed to work together, so read the visual aid when the text tells you to. (See "Strategies for Reading Visual Aids," p. 48.)

Boxes Some textbooks include boxes, which have discussions of interesting or relevant topics and key issues in the discipline. For example, a business textbook may include "Ethical Issues" boxes and "Entrepreneurship" boxes because these two issues are widely discussed in business courses.

End-of-chapter material Most textbook chapters end with a summary of key points, a list of key terms, and exercises. These exercises fall in to subject-appropriate categories. For example, a math textbook will have many computations for you to work out, while a sociology textbook might offer critical-thinking questions. Use the end-of-chapter material to help you conduct an immediate review of the chapter. If your instructor has assigned specific exercises, read them *before* you start the chapter. Doing so will give you a sense of what to look for as you read.

Answers or solutions Some, but not all, textbooks include an answer section. Use this section wisely. It is intended to help you check your work after you have completed it. It should not be used as a shortcut.

Index   The final pages of most textbooks contain an **index**, an alphabetical listing of all the key discussions, terms, places, and names in the textbook. Each item comes with a page reference, allowing you to find the discussion quickly and easily.

Tie textbook concepts to your life and experiences   It is much easier to learn new material when you actively think about how the textbook discussions relate to your own life. For example, an economics textbook may talk about prices and how they are set by the forces of supply and demand. How might these concepts help explain why the tickets for a concert you want to see are so expensive?

Study the examples   Many students find examples crucial for gaining an understanding of key terms and concepts. If your textbook or class lecture does not provide an example of an important concept, ask your instructor to provide one.

Get through the "boring" parts   It would be unrealistic for you to find every textbook reading selection interesting or fascinating. Do your best to keep an open mind, and reward yourself (with a healthy snack or something else) to stay motivated to focus on the materials and to finish reading them with a high level of comprehension.

Make use of additional resources   Many textbooks offer companion Web sites featuring chapter quizzes, electronic flash cards, and practice exercises. Use the Web site's resources as part of your review and exam preparation. If you find any materials particularly difficult or frustrating, talk to your instructor or seek help in the tutoring or academic-support center.

Create an outline to help you study   Outlining is an effective way of organizing information and discovering relationships between ideas. To be effective, an outline must show the relative importance of ideas. The easiest way to achieve this goal is to use the following format.

   I.   **First Major Topic**
      A. First major idea
          1.   First important detail
          2.   Second important detail
      B. Second major idea
          1.   First important detail
             a.   Minor detail or example
             b.   Minor detail or example

  II. **Second Major Topic**
      A. First major idea

Notice that the most major ideas and themes are closest to the left margin, while more minor claims and supporting details are found toward the middle of the page. In textbooks, headings often form the basis for an effective outline. For example, here is an effective outline of the beginning of this chapter:

I.   Active Reading Strategies
  A.   Preview and Form Prereading Questions before Reading
    1.   Preview
    2.   Form Prereading Questions

Outlining works not only for textbook readings but also for many other kinds of readings.

Exercise 2.6

Read "Secrets for Surviving College" in Chapter 13, page 369, and prepare an outline of it.

Strategies for Reading Visual Aids

Writers often use **visual aids** to clarify or emphasize ideas, reveal trends, condense information, or illustrate a point of view. For example, an article emphasizing the value of a college education may contain a graph comparing the salaries of people with a college diploma to the salaries of people without a college education. Visual aids can also help readers visualize a place or setting, understand a complicated process, or remember important information.

Visual aids include but are not limited to

- photographs
- cartoons
- advertisements
- illustrations
- drawings
- maps
- charts
- graphs
- tables
- diagrams
- flowcharts

Visual aids are often classified in two categories: (1) **images** and image-based visual aids, such as photographs, cartoons, advertisements, and illustrations; and (2) **graphics**, which generally present or summarize information. Figure 2.4 summarizes the most common types of graphics (pie charts, bar graphs, line graphs, tables, and diagrams and flowcharts).

Writers often include image-based visuals, such as photographs, with their writing to provoke an emotional response or support their thesis. For example, an essay arguing for increased U.S. aid to poor countries may use a photograph of a malnourished child to elicit the reader's sympathy. Because writers use visuals deliberately and creatively to shape their messages, it is important to spend time studying them.

Figure 2.4 Types of Graphics

<table>
<tr><th>Type of Graphic</th><th>Purpose</th><th>Example</th></tr>
<tr><td>Pie (circle) chart
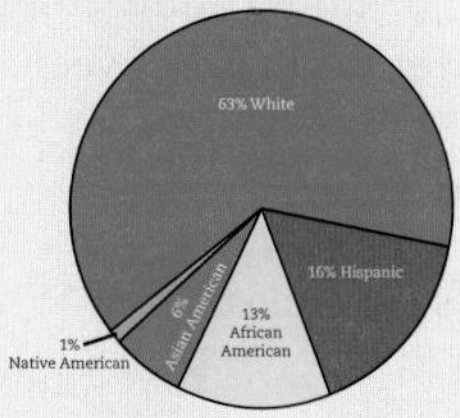
</td><td>To show the relationships among parts of a whole; to show how given parts of a unit are divided or classified</td><td>A chart showing the proportions of different racial and ethnic groups in the U.S. population</td></tr>
<tr><td>Bar graphs
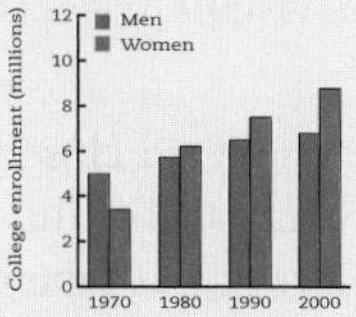
</td><td>To make comparisons between quantities or amounts</td><td>A graph showing college enrollments (in millions) for men and women for selected years between 1970 and 2000</td></tr>
<tr><td>Line graphs
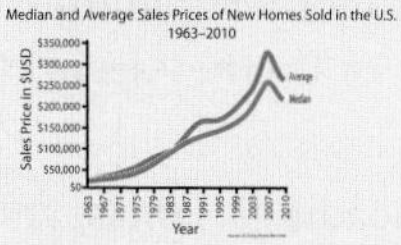
</td><td>To show changes in a variable over time or to compare relationships between two or more variables</td><td>A graph showing the change in average price of new homes sold in the United States from 1963 through 2010</td></tr>
<tr><td>Tables
Table 2-1: Daily Calories
<table>
<tr><th>Age</th><th>Men</th><th>Women</th></tr>
<tr><td>20-25</td><td>1800</td><td>1600</td></tr>
<tr><td>26-35</td><td>2200</td><td>1800</td></tr>
<tr><td>36-50</td><td>2400</td><td>2000</td></tr>
<tr><td>51-75</td><td>2200</td><td>1800</td></tr>
<tr><td>76+</td><td>2000</td><td>1600</td></tr>
</table></td><td>To organize and condense data; to compare and classify information</td><td>A table showing how many calories men and women need daily for various age groups</td></tr>
<tr><td>Diagrams and flowcharts
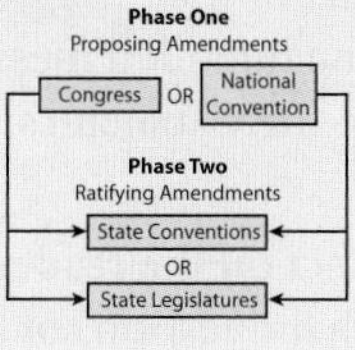
</td><td>To explain processes or procedures or show how things work</td><td>A diagram showing the process by which the U.S. Constitution can be amended</td></tr>
</table>

To achieve a basic comprehension of a visual aid, preview it with your preview of the reading. When reading the text, follow cues in the writing to look at visuals: Many readings will tell you when to look at the visual aid, using a phrase like "As the photograph below illustrates." (Just make sure to finish reading the sentence before jumping to the graphic.) To understand complicated graphics, you may need to go back and forth several times between the text and the visual aid.

As you read the visual aid, consider the following questions.

- **What is your first reaction?** What is the visual aid's general subject? What did you notice first, and how did it affect you?

- **Is the visual aid accompanied by a title, caption, or other explanatory text?** Read any surrounding information and determine how it relates to the visual aid. Do the title and caption fully explain the visual? What is stated and what is left unstated?

- **What exactly does the visual aid show?** Examine the visual aid closely to determine what exactly is being shown. Do any particular parts of the visual aid stand out? Is there an action that is taking place or has taken place? If the image is more informative, what type of information is being presented? Examine the foreground, background, main subject, and details of photographs. How do these elements relate to one another? Do the background and foreground complement each other, or do they seem out of sync? Do any details stand out?

- **How is the visual aid organized?** Read all column headings, labels, and other text used to organize the visual aid. Use the *legend* (a guide to the colors, symbols, terms, and other information in the visual aid) to understand the image's key elements.

- **What is the purpose of the visual aid?** Identify why the writer has included a visual aid and what it contributes to the reading. Has the writer included it to illustrate or emphasize a particular point? Does the visual aid show change over time, present a process or structure, or compare statistics?

- **What does the visual aid mean?** Interpret the meaning of the image, both alone and within the context of the reading. What is the intended message? If words are used within the image, how do they shape the visual aid's overall meaning?

- **What does the visual aid suggest?** The visual aid's effect on the reader is an important part of the reading experience. Consider what questions or issues the image raises or answers.

Two photos are included with "Comparing Online and Traditional Education" (p. 26). These photos help readers visualize the single greatest difference between online and traditional education: the ability to participate in a classroom and learn alongside other students.

Exercise 2.7

Use the text and visual aid provided below to answer the questions that follow.

Environmental racism refers to the likelihood that a racialized minority inhabits a polluted area. As Robert Bullard asserts, "Whether by conscious design or institutional neglect, communities of color in urban ghettos, in rural 'poverty pockets,' or on economically impoverished Native American reservations face some of the worst environmental devastation in the nation." In the United States, Hispanics and blacks are more likely than whites to reside in places where toxic wastes are dumped, polluting industries are located, or environmental legislation is not enforced. Inner-city populations, which in many U.S. cities are disproportionately made up of minorities, occupy older buildings contaminated with asbestos and toxic lead-based paints. As the figure that follows shows, there is an overlap of nonwhite populations and toxic release facilities that is difficult to explain away as simply a random coincidence. Rather, areas such as the city of South Gate, located in Los Angeles County, have seen contaminating industries and activities purposely located in what is today a neighborhood composed of more than 90% Latino residents.

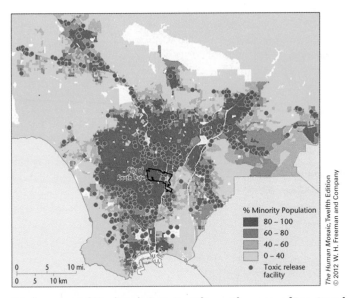

Environmental Racism in Los Angeles.   The map of Los Angeles County's nonwhite population concentrations overlaps closely with the map of toxic release facility locations in Los Angeles County. It is hard to believe that this is simply a coincidence.

1. What two kinds of things mentioned in the text are shown in the map?
2. What is the purpose of the visual aid? Why did the authors choose to include it?
3. Write a one-sentence summary of the visual aid.

Exercise 2.8

For each of the following situations, discuss which type of graphic might be used to advance the writer's purpose and help the reader grasp the material more easily.

1. To show percentage of Americans belonging to each of four major religions in 2012.
2. To show percentages of registered voters who participated in each presidential election from 1988 to 2012 for five age groups.
3. To compare percentages of African Americans, whites, Latinos, and Asian Americans who divorced in each decade from 1970 to 2010.
4. To show the process by which a legal immigrant can become a citizen.
5. To show where divorce in the United States occurs at an average rate, at a below-average rate, and at an above-average rate.

Answers to Exercise 2.1

1. False   2. True   3. False   4. True   5. True

Chapter 3

Analyzing and Evaluating
Texts and Images

Quick Start: The image above shows an example of popular newsstand journalism. Suppose your sociology instructor asked you to examine one or more publications like this one and discuss what they suggest about Americans' values and opinions.

Take a look at the photograph and headline on the front page of the newspaper shown, and then write a list of observations about it. What can you conclude about the article's content, its purpose, and its intended audience? Write a few sentences explaining why the image may have been chosen. How would it be likely to influence readers?

To write about the newspaper's front page, you had to think and react critically; you had to analyze and evaluate. This process is known as **critical thinking**, and it requires skills that go beyond basic comprehension or understanding. Similarly, *critical reading* involves reacting to what you read and evaluating and responding to the author's ideas.

In this chapter you will learn strategies for reading and thinking critically. You will develop strategies for analyzing text and visual aids (including photographs and graphics), as well as strategies for evaluating what you read. All of the critical-reading strategies you'll encounter in this chapter build on the basic comprehension and understanding skills you learned in Chapter 2, "Understanding Texts and Images."

Critical Reading and Thinking

In elementary and high school, you memorized facts and processes to develop a basic foundation of knowledge in reading, writing, science, and mathematics. In college, you are expected to analyze what you learn, develop your own opinions, and conduct your own research. In other words, college instructors expect you to *think critically* and not simply accept something you've read or heard as "the truth." Thinking critically also means not rejecting an idea just because it contradicts what you currently believe or previously learned. In this case, *critical* does not mean "negative." Rather, it means "thoughtful and analytical"—in other words, thinking deeply about the information and ideas you encounter.

Developing your critical-thinking and critical-reading skills has many benefits. Critical thinking will help you

- distinguish good information from incomplete, inaccurate information;
- become a savvy consumer who compares options and avoids scams;
- weigh social issues, examine politicians' campaign platforms and promises, and analyze the political and economic motives of people and businesses;
- recognize trends, analyze causes and effects, and solve problems;
- determine whether research sources and Internet sites are reliable or unreliable.

Analyzing text and images requires you to do the following.

- Examine the author's purpose, style, and intended audience.
- Understand the nuances of words.
- Distinguish fact from opinion.
- Analyze the author's tone.
- Look for purposeful omissions.
- Make reasonable inferences.

We discuss each of these skills in the sections that follow.

Examine the Author's Purpose, Style, and Intended Audience

Writers have many different **purposes** for writing. Sometimes their purpose is to entertain; other times their purpose may be to educate, to advocate for a particular cause, or to elicit a particular emotion from the reader. The writer's purpose determines the words she uses, the details she provides, and the style in which she writes. **Style** is a general term for the characteristics that make a piece of writing unique. For example, one writer's style may be very spare, with short sentences and common words. Another writer's style may be more flowery, with many intense descriptions and complicated words.

The writer's **intended audience** is the group of people the writer expects to read his work. Writers often adjust their style and content to meet the needs of different audiences. For example, a sports writer may write two different essays about the most recent Super Bowl. If his intended audience is composed of devoted football fans, the writer will likely refer to specific plays and highly publicized stories about the personal lives of the players and coaches, assuming that the intended audience already knows about the players. Such an essay might appear in *Sports Illustrated*, a magazine read by devoted sports fans. However, if the intended audience is people who would rather read a book than watch a football game, the writer would likely focus on different aspects of the game. For example, he might talk about why Super Bowl Sunday has become a great American tradition and why football is so important in American culture. He would probably explain football terms, rather than assume the audience knows them. Such an essay might appear in a general-interest newspaper or magazine like *USA Today* or *Newsweek*.

Sometimes a writer's purpose is quite clear. For instance, most textbooks have one specific purpose: to provide information and to educate. But not all writing is so transparent. For example, suppose a writer says, "The recent actions of the British prime minister should be closely examined." You cannot tell from this sentence whether the writer's purpose is to question the prime minister's motives or simply to suggest that the prime minister's actions are worth studying. For this reason, it is important to examine the writer's purpose, style, and intended audience, all of which will help you analyze the author's intentions and messages.

Exercise 3.1

Based on each of the following essay titles, predict the author's purpose and intended audience.

1. Three Simple Ways to Stay Healthy

2. Ten Reasons We Need a New Mayor

3. IRA or 401(k): Which Is the Better Retirement Solution?

Nuances of Words: Denotations, Connotations, Euphemisms, and Doublespeak

Words are powerful, and their power can be used in many ways. Words can inspire, comfort, educate, and calm. But they can also inflame, annoy, and deceive. Professional writers understand that word choices influence readers and listeners, and they choose words that will help them achieve their objectives. Consider the following aspects of word choice.

DENOTATIONS AND CONNOTATIONS

A **denotation** is a word's literal meaning. For example, the denotation of *obese* is "very fat." A **connotation** is the set of additional meanings or associations that a word has taken on. Often, a word's connotation has a much stronger effect on readers or listeners than its denotation does. A politician with a stocky build might be described as "pleasingly plump" (which carries an almost pleasant or jolly connotation), as "quite a bit overweight" (which is an objective-sounding statement), or as "morbidly obese" (which gives readers a negative impression). Always pay attention to the connotations that words carry and consider why the writer has chosen particular words.

Exercise 3.2

For each of the following words, provide one word with a similar denotation but a positive connotation and another word with a similar denotation but a negative connotation.

Example: Group (of people)   Positive: *audience*

Negative: *mob*

1. choosy   **Positive:**

Negative:

2. cheap   **Positive:**

Negative:

3. boss   **Positive:**

Negative:

4. bold   **Positive:**

Negative:

5. walk   **Positive:**

Negative:

EUPHEMISMS AND DOUBLESPEAK

As mentioned in Table 2.4 (p. 36), a **euphemism** is a word or phrase used to avoid an unpleasant, embarrassing, or otherwise objectionable word. For example, a used-car dealer may advertise that it sells "pre-owned fleet vehicles." **Doublespeak** is a type of euphemism that uses deliberately unclear or evasive language. For example, a company may say that it is *moving into international sourcing* when it eliminates jobs in the United States and sends them overseas. Euphemisms and doublespeak seek to sugarcoat an unpleasant reality, and as a critical thinker you should always be alert for them, particularly when reading about politics and business.

Exercise 3.3

1. Much media coverage is devoted to people who come to the United States from other countries without permission from the U.S. government or who stay after their permission to visit has expired. Two terms are often used to refer to these people: *illegal aliens* and *undocumented immigrants*. Discuss which term has a more negative connotation and which seems more neutral. Why does each term carry the connotations it does? Is the more neutral term a euphemism? Why or why not?

2. Brainstorm a list of euphemisms and doublespeak currently in use in business, politics, or the media.

Distinguish Fact from Opinion

Chapter 2, on understanding texts and images, offered strategies for reading two common college assignments: textbooks and essays. Textbooks and essays often differ greatly in terms of their presentation of *facts* and *opinions*.

Textbooks present factual information that has been checked and rechecked, often over many years, and is therefore highly reliable. In addition, when textbook authors write about controversial topics, they usually explain different viewpoints. For example, a marketing textbook that discusses the value of packaging will usually describe the benefits of good packaging (it grabs consumers' attention and makes them more willing to buy the product) as well as the drawbacks (much packaging is expensive, wasteful, and ends up in the trash).

In contrast, essays and other reading materials—newspapers, magazines, advertisements, Web sites, books, and so forth—often present a mixture of fact and opinion without distinguishing between the two. For example, an advertisement may follow some facts about a car's warranty with the opinion that the car maker offers the best warranty coverage.

FACTS

Facts are objective statements of information that can be verified. That is, their truth can be established with valid evidence. Facts are not influenced by personal feelings, interpretations, or prejudices. The following statements are facts.

- Most people who use marijuana do not go on to use more dangerous drugs.
- Texting while driving has caused many accidents.

How do you know a fact when you see it? Facts can be checked in trustworthy sources such as textbooks, encyclopedias, and Web reference sources like refdesk.com. (Note that in academic writing, Wikipedia is *not* considered a trustworthy source for checking facts because its content is not checked by experts and misinformation can and does creep in.)

OPINIONS

Opinions are subjective. That is, they differ by individual. Opinions express attitudes, feelings, or beliefs that cannot be definitely established as either true or false, at least at the present time. They often put forth a particular position or agenda.

Sometimes scholarly journals (which report the results of research and experiments) publish articles that are the authors' opinions based on their own research and that of earlier researchers. Only time and further research will tell if these opinions become facts. The following are opinions.

- It is likely that marijuana use will be legalized in all fifty states by 2020.
- People who text while driving should be fined and have their driver's licenses revoked.
- Because they bring in so much revenue for their schools, college athletes should be paid salaries.

Sometimes opinion statements are signaled by words and phrases such as "In my opinion," "I think," "It seems to me," "It seems," or "Perhaps." However, frequently writers do not use these signal words and phrases to indicate their opinions, so you must read carefully to recognize statements of opinion.

Exercise 3.4

For two of the following topics, write one statement of fact and one statement of opinion. Use the Internet to locate factual information.

1. Voter turnout rates in presidential elections
2. Cell-phone use in classrooms
3. Alternative energy solutions
4. Social media (Facebook)

Analyze the Author's Tone

Have you ever noticed that people can use the same words to mean different things in different situations? The *tone* of the words in each situation can convey a very different meaning. Consider a police officer who pulls you over for speeding and says, "Could you please step out of the car?" His tone would be different from that of an employee at a car wash who says the same words so that he can vacuum your car's interior.

A reading's **tone** refers to the way it sounds to readers, and it is influenced by the writer's approach to her topic and audience. Recognizing a writer's tone will help you analyze and evaluate the message and its effect on you.

Writers reveal tone primarily through word choice and stylistic features, such as sentence patterns and length. For example, a writer can communicate surprise, disapproval, disgust, admiration, gratitude, or amusement. The following are some examples.

- **Disapproval** You really need to discipline your children better.
- **Surprise** I was sitting there, minding my own business, when this stranger came up to me and asked me how old I am!
- **Admiration** I am amazed by your patience, kindness, and generosity.
- **Gratitude** My mother and I were very touched by the beautiful flowers you sent when my father passed away.

Table 3.1 lists some words commonly used to describe tone.

Table 3.1   Words Commonly Used to Describe Tone

angry	disapproving	informative	persuasive
apathetic	earnest	instructive	pessimistic
arrogant	flippant	ironic	playful
assertive	forgiving	irreverent	reverent
bitter	formal	joyful	righteous
caustic	frustrated	loving	sarcastic
cheerful	hateful	malicious	satiric
compassionate	humorous	mocking	serious
condemning	impassioned	nostalgic	sympathetic
condescending	incredulous	objective	vindictive
cynical	indignant	optimistic	worried
detached			

Many writers and speakers feel passionately about their beliefs, and sometimes they have a personal charisma that makes their audience more receptive to their message. Be sure not to get carried away by a writer or speaker's tone or commitment to a cause. As a critical thinker, your job is to analyze words, facts, and tone to determine their effect on you and whether you are being told the complete story. It is also important to watch for subtle or hidden tones within a message. For example, a writer may use an apparently sympathetic tone in describing a political candidate's recent questionable financial deals: "Poor Mayor Jones must not have realized that taking money for political favors is illegal." The apparent sympathy is really sarcasm—the writer's way of criticizing the candidate.

Exercise 3.5

Describe the tone of each of the following statements. Refer to Table 3.1 (p. 59) for specific descriptors if necessary. Which words in the statement are clues to its tone?

1. When you are backpacking, you can reduce the risk of back injury by adjusting your pack so that most of its weight is on your hip belt rather than on your shoulder straps.

2. Do you eat canned tuna? Then you are at least partially responsible for the deaths of thousands of innocent dolphins, who are mercilessly slaughtered by fishermen in their quest for tuna.

3. The penalty for creating and launching a computer virus should include a personal apology to every person who was affected by the virus, and each apology should be typed—without errors!—on a manual typewriter.

4. Piles of solid waste threaten to ruin our environment, pointing to the urgent need for better disposal methods and strategies for lowering the rate of waste generation.

5. All poets seek to convey emotion and the complete range of human feeling, but the only poet who fully accomplished this goal was William Shakespeare.

Exercise 3.6

Consider the following situation: A developer has received permission to bulldoze an entire city block of burned-out tenement buildings and abandoned factories. In their place, the developer plans to build a community of three hundred upscale condominiums for people who work in the city and want to live close to their jobs.

Write three different sentences (or paragraphs) that react to this news. Make the tone of your first sentence outraged. Make the tone of your second sentence joyful. Make the tone of your third sentence nostalgic.

Look for Purposeful Omissions

Writers and speakers sometimes mislead by omission—that is, by what they do *not* say. They may leave out essential background or context, include only details that favor their position, or ignore contradictory evidence. They may also use the passive voice ("damage was done") to avoid taking or assigning responsibility for an action, or use vague nouns and pronouns ("someone did it") to avoid specifying exactly to what or whom they are referring.

Consider an essay written by a woman who has homeschooled her children. As an advocate of homeschooling, she is likely to emphasize her children's educational progress. However, she may not address arguments made by opponents of homeschooling—for example, that homeschooled children sometimes feel lonely or isolated from their peers. She also may refer to homeschooling as "better" for children without specifying exactly what it is better than (her local public school, public schools in general, any kind of school) or in what ways it is better (more personalized attention, fewer distractions, more focus on science or math).

The same writer may also summarize a research study that details the academic excellence of homeschooled children. Other studies, however, have found that homeschooled children do not differ in academic achievement from traditionally educated students. If the writer does not mention these findings, she has chosen to report only evidence that supports her case and to ignore contradictory evidence.

Ask yourself the following questions to be sure you are getting full and complete information.

- Is any important information omitted? What, if anything, am I not being told?
- Has the writer or speaker failed to report any evidence that contradicts his position?
- Has the writer or speaker selectively reported details to further her cause?
- Is there another side to this argument or aspect of this topic that I should consider?
- On the basis of my own experiences, how do I evaluate this material?

To answer these questions, you may need to do some additional reading or research. That is what higher education is all about—learning from as many sources as possible, listening to multiple points of view, and using your critical-thinking skills to formulate your own opinions.

Exercise 3.7

Read the following common scenarios. In each situation, what information is being withheld from you? In other words, what other information do you need to evaluate the situation?

1. You see a TV ad for a fast-food restaurant that shows a huge hamburger topped with pickles, onions, and tomatoes. The announcer says, "For a limited time, get your favorite burger for only ninety-nine cents!"

2. You open your mailbox and find a letter from a credit-card company. The letter invites you to open a charge account with no annual fee and offers you instant credit if you return the attached form in a postage-paid envelope.

3. You get an offer from a DVD club that appears to be a good deal. As part of your introductory package, you can buy five DVDs for only ninety-nine cents, plus shipping and handling.

Make Reasonable Inferences

Some reading materials, such as textbooks and scholarly journals, tend to present information in a straightforward manner. The writers spell everything out clearly so that you don't have to guess at their conclusions.

In other types of reading materials—particularly essays—writers directly state some ideas but hint at, or *imply*, others. You, the reader, must pick up on the clues and determine the writer's unstated messages.

An **inference** is an educated, reasonable guess based on available facts and information, your own experiences, and the content provided in the reading. Inferences are logical connections between what the writer states directly and what he or she implies. Consider the following situation.

> You are walking down a dark city street when you notice someone following you. When you cross the street, so does he. When you turn a corner, so does he. As you run to get to your apartment, the man picks up speed and starts gaining on you.

In this situation, you can reasonably infer that the man is a criminal who is following you and may wish to rob you. It would not be reasonable to infer that the man is a long-lost friend or a lottery agent who wants to tell you that you've won a million dollars.

Making inferences requires active reading and critical thinking. Developing your inference skills requires practice, but here are some suggestions for getting started.

1. **First, understand the author's purpose and the literal meaning.** Before you can make reasonable inferences, you need a clear understanding of the author's purpose and the essay's thesis statement, its main ideas, and the supporting details.

2. **Pay attention to details.** Sometimes a specific detail provides a hint regarding what the writer has left unsaid. When you notice a striking or unusual detail (whether in a description, an image, or a reported conversation), ask yourself, Why is this detail included? For example, read the following passage.

> Susan attends college, works a part-time job, takes care of her two children, and cooks dinner for her husband every night. You'd never know she has MS (multiple sclerosis). She is planning to become an attorney specializing in environmental law, so she's attending a community college now, and plans to transfer to the university.

What is the writer's reason for including the detail about Susan's medical condition? Perhaps she is implying that people who have MS can still maintain normal lives.

3. **Look at the facts.** Consider the complete set of facts provided by the writer. Ask yourself, What is the writer trying to suggest with all of these facts? What conclusion does the complete set of facts support? Suppose a writer presents the following facts.

> It's extremely difficult to get in touch with anyone from Sam's Landscaping Service. Nobody answers the phone or returns messages. Technicians do not show up to conduct lawn maintenance on any specific schedule. The bills sent by Sam's Landscaping Service to customers often include charges for services never performed.

From these sentences, the conclusion is clear: Sam's Landscaping Service is an unreliable, unethical business that you should never hire.

4. **Examine word choice.** A writer's choice of words often conveys his or her feelings toward the subject. Look for words with numerous connotations and ask yourself why the writer chose these words.

5. **Make sure you can support your inference.** Valid inferences are based on fact, context, and personal experiences. Be sure you have ample evidence to back up any inference you make.

Exercise 3.8

Read the following selection, then answer the questions that follow.

> Dissatisfied with your current life? Would you like to become someone else? Maybe someone rich? Maybe someone with no responsibilities? You can. Join a world populated with virtual people and live out your fantasy.
>
> For some, the appeal is strong. Second Life, one of several Internet sites that offer an alternative virtual reality, has exploded in popularity. Of its 8 million "residents," 450,000 spend twenty to forty hours a week in their second life.
>
> —James Henslin, *Sociology: A Down-to-Earth Approach*, 11th Edition

1. What is the purpose of this brief passage?
2. What can you infer from the phrase "live out your fantasy"?
3. Why does the author put the word *residents* in quotation marks?
4. What can you infer from the numbers in the passage?

Strategies for Evaluating What You Read

Once you have understood and analyzed a reading, you will be prepared to take the final step in the critical-thinking process: evaluation. When you evaluate a reading, you form your own opinion and judgment regarding its validity and the strength of its argument. Has the writer presented convincing support for the thesis statement and main ideas?

Understanding, analysis, and evaluation often take place simultaneously. In other words, you may be analyzing and evaluating the reading while you read it. To evaluate what you read, you need to

- identify bias,
- evaluate information sources,
- evaluate the reliability of information,
- examine the relevance and sufficiency of evidence,
- recognize assumptions.

Identify Bias

Bias refers to a writer's prejudice in favor of or against the topic he is writing about. Writers are biased when they present only one side of an argument without considering other viewpoints. For example, an essay biased against amnesty programs for undocumented immigrants will not recognize the benefits of allowing these people to become U.S. citizens. Similarly, an essay biased in favor of such amnesty programs will not recognize the drawbacks of granting privileges to those who have broken the law.

In some reading materials, the author's bias is obvious. In other materials, though, the bias may be hidden or subtle. In these cases, it is up to you to discover the writer's agenda. To determine if a reading selection is biased, ask yourself the following questions.

1. **Is the writer acting as an objective reporter, presenting well-documented facts on all sides of the argument?** If the answer to this question is *yes*, then the author likely is *not* biased.

2. **Does the writer present only one side of the story? Is he providing only positive or only negative information?** If the answer to either of these questions is *yes*, the author likely *is* biased.

3. **Does the writer feel strongly about the issue?** Analyze the writer's tone to determine her attitude toward the subject. The stronger the author's feelings about the subject, the more biased she is likely to be.

4. **Do the words used in the essay generate a strongly positive or strongly negative impression on the reader?** Pay special attention to word

connotations. Writers who repeatedly use words with exclusively positive or exclusively negative connotations tend to be biased.

Exercise 3.9

Review the brief passage about virtual reality and Second Life in Exercise 3.8 (p. 63). Do you detect bias in this selection? If you do, point to specific elements in the passage that show bias. If you do not, explain why you feel the selection is not biased.

Evaluate Information Sources

We live in a world of sensory overload. We are surrounded by news, opinions, advertisements, and other kinds of information everywhere we look (or listen). Developing your comprehension and analytical skills will help you evaluate this avalanche of information. Begin by thinking about various information sources. Ask yourself the following questions about each.

- How factually accurate is it trying to be?
- Is it written by people with valid experiences?
- Has it been reviewed by editors or experts in the field?
- Is it biased in favor of or against a particular person or viewpoint?

TEXTBOOKS

As noted in Chapter 2, "Understanding Texts and Images," textbooks are usually very reliable sources of information. For basic information on any topic, a textbook is often the best place to start.

ESSAYS

Because essays are usually a reflection of the writer's viewpoint, they often have a built-in bias. When reading an essay, identify the writer's purpose and agenda. It is also helpful to know something about the author's background and credentials.

NEWSPAPERS

Newspapers vary in the quality of their reporting. Some newspapers are meticulous about obtaining accurate and complete information and checking facts before publishing a story. Other newspapers are little more than gossip sheets.

Most newspapers have an editorial page or opinion section in which the paper's editors and contributors offer their views on current issues and other topics. These pieces (which are often the equivalent of essays) likely reflect the writers' personal views on controversial questions, so be aware of these biases as you read. Also keep in mind that some newspapers tend to be liberal in their views while others are conservative. These tendencies often show up not just on the editorial page but also in the way news stories are presented.

A newer category of news reporting, *advertorial*, combines a paid advertisement with factual reporting. For example, a local business may pay a newspaper to write a story about the business, describe its services, and present information about the owners. Advertorial content looks just like the content of traditional news stories, so ask yourself, Does the possibility exist that this "article" is actually a paid advertisement? If it seems like it might be an ad, look closely at the layout; often, there's a small heading or footer that states that the content is an advertisement.

BROADCAST NEWS

Television news broadcasts require close scrutiny. Because networks are interested in attracting and keeping viewers, they sometimes focus on events that will boost ratings rather than on more important (but perhaps less immediately interesting) developments. News programs may focus on stories that have high visual appeal at the expense of those with less compelling images. Finally, some networks have a particular political bias or slant, and their news coverage is aimed at furthering their political agenda. Radio news programs and talk shows deserve similar scrutiny, as they, too, may attempt to draw listeners by focusing on "hot" topics, and may have coverage aimed at supporting a particular position.

MAGAZINES

Literally thousands of magazines are published every year. Some are devoted to general interests, such as home improvement, organic food, or American politics. Others report, analyze, and comment on national, state, or local news. Still others focus on specific academic or business topics, such as finance, art, or literature. Although magazines can be excellent sources of information, their content, like that of newspapers and television, is influenced by the perspectives and biases of their editors and writers. Magazines also vary in their attention to careful reporting and fact-checking. Magazines that focus on gossip and celebrities (such as *People* or *Us*) are often less reliable and less detailed than magazines devoted to news coverage (like *Time* or *Newsweek*).

THE INTERNET

Because it is free and easy to access, the Internet is the first place many people go for breaking news and research. However, anyone can create a Web site and post anything on it, regardless of its accuracy. Be particularly cautious when reading blogs (online diaries or columns), which contain personal opinions that are not reviewed by editors. For more information on evaluating Internet sources, see Chapter 19, "Finding and Using Sources."

SCHOLARLY JOURNALS

Scholarly journals report research and developments in a particular academic or professional field. Examples include the *Journal of Psychology* and the *Journal of the American Medical Association.*

Journals tend to be highly trustworthy sources because they are peer-reviewed. In other words, the journals' editors accept only articles that have been evaluated and approved by other authorities in the field. In scientific fields, journal articles must be based on research that follows strict standardized procedures and must make connections to related research on the topic. Articles in scholarly journals often use the specialized vocabulary of the discipline, so you need to read them slowly and carefully. Fortunately, many articles begin with an *abstract*, a one- or two-paragraph summary of the article.

Exercise 3.10

On your own or as part of a class discussion, evaluate the reliability of each of the information sources in the following list. If necessary, do some research to learn more about them. How seriously should you take each source? Which exist solely for entertainment? Which are likely to be biased? Which would be acceptable as references in an academic research paper? Rate the reliability of each on a scale from 1 to 5, with 1 being completely unreliable and 5 being very trustworthy.

1. An opinion column in the *Washington Post* (newspaper)
2. A feature story in the *National Enquirer* (newspaper/magazine)
3. An editorial in the *Wall Street Journal* (newspaper)
4. *Meet the Press* (a TV news program)
5. www.thesmokinggun.com
6. www.census.gov (Web site of the U.S. Census Bureau)
7. www.tmz.com

8. The *Journal of Economic Research*

9. Wikipedia (www.wikipedia.org)

10. A feature article in *InStyle* magazine (a women's fashion magazine)

Evaluate the Reliability of Information

You may have heard the term *spin doctor*. This phrase describes a public relations specialist who puts a positive spin on bad news. Reading and thinking critically require that you understand when information is presented fairly and when it is "spun" for some purpose—to influence public opinion, to sell something, to win votes, and so forth.

In general, the most reliable information is based on solid *evidence*. Just as police look for evidence to discover who committed a crime, you must look for the evidence that supports an assertion made by a writer. If the writer offers little or no evidence, you should question the assertion.

The following types of evidence are often considered relevant and valid.

PERSONAL EXPERIENCE OR EXAMPLES

Personal experience can be powerful evidence. For example, no one understands having cancer like a person who has suffered with the disease and survived. Different people can experience the same event very differently, however; so be careful about generalizing from the experiences of one person. Furthermore, even though several people may report similar experiences, their reports may not be sufficient evidence to support a sweeping generalization.

STATISTICAL AND SURVEY DATA

Academic researchers and professional research organizations routinely collect and distribute statistical (numerical) data. Statistics are often reliable because the people compiling them try to be as objective and accurate as possible. However, be wary of people who use survey data in ways that try to hide the truth rather than reveal it. For example, the Fizzy Soda Company may state, "In a recent taste test, 90% of people preferred our cola to our competitor's cola." Although this statement may be factually true, the test may have been rigged for bias. For instance, suppose the taste test was conducted at the Fizzy Soda Company headquarters? Would the results have been different than if it had been conducted in a neutral location, such as at a mall? In thinking critically about survey data, consider factors such as how many people were surveyed, how they were selected, when the survey was done, and how survey questions were worded.

EYEWITNESS REPORTS

Eyewitness reports are often considered powerful evidence, but studies suggest that eyewitness testimony in criminal cases is often inaccurate. Also, different people can interpret the same situation in different ways. Suppose that a building bursts into flames and two witnesses see a man running out of the building. One person may think, "What a lucky man! He escaped from the burning building." The other person may think, "That man started the fire to burn the building down and collect the insurance money."

EXPERIMENTAL EVIDENCE

The results of scientific experiments and studies are usually considered highly reliable because they are based on the *scientific method*, a specific set of procedures that researchers follow to investigate their theories. However, the conclusions that can be drawn from the results of a single study may be fairly narrow. Moreover, experiments are not always designed or conducted as carefully as they should be. Even when they are, uncontrollable factors can influence the results. For example, two different scientific research studies on the safety of a drug can generate contradictory results.

Although most scientists try to be objective and neutral, you need to consider who is conducting the research and whether the researchers have an interest in its outcome (such as an economic motive or a political agenda) that might influence how they design, conduct, and report their research. In rare cases, researchers have even falsified results and misrepresented data to produce the desired outcome.

Exercise 3.11

Consider each of the following statements and the context in which it is made. What types of information are missing that would help you weigh the evidence and evaluate the claim being made? What further types of evidence would you need to accept or reject the claim?

1. On the label of a bag of cookies: "CONTAINS 45% LESS FAT and 0 grams of TRANS FAT!"

2. In a printed campaign flyer for mayoral candidate Mary Johnson: "My opponent, Joe Smith, has been accused of serious conflicts of interest in the awarding of city contracts during his term as mayor."

3. In large print on the cover of a novel you see at the supermarket checkout: "This novel is a . . . wild and exciting . . . ride through the rough-and-tumble days of the Gold Rush . . . full of . . . adventure and excitement. . . . Memorable."—*New York Times*

Examine the Relevance and Sufficiency of Evidence

In general, the more evidence a writer provides to support a thesis statement, the more convincing her writing is likely to be. Suppose an essay includes the following thesis statement:

> College graduates lead happier lives than those who have only a high-school diploma.

Now suppose the writer includes just one fact to support this statement: "Research shows that most people with college degrees earn substantially more money than people without a college diploma."

Does this one piece of evidence provide enough support for the thesis statement? Most likely, you would argue that it does not. History is full of examples of people who achieved massive success and wealth without a college degree (for example, Steve Jobs of Apple and Bill Gates of Microsoft). In addition, some people who attend technical schools (to learn trades like auto repair, electrical work, or plumbing) earn substantially more than some recent college graduates.

Now consider an essay that supports the thesis statement with the following pieces of evidence.

- College graduates tend to have access to better medical care and therefore live longer.
- College graduates usually have greater job stability and therefore less financial stress in their lives.
- College graduates have lower rates of divorce than people without college degrees.
- College graduates on average earn more money throughout their working lives than those who do not have a college degree.

Each of these points on its own may not be enough to provide sufficient evidence for the thesis statement, but taken together they greatly strengthen the writer's argument.

When evaluating a piece of writing, ask yourself the following questions.

1. **Has the writer provided sufficient data and evidence?** Be careful about accepting the writer's conclusions if he has not given ample evidence.

2. **Has the writer provided relevant information?** It is easy to be distracted by interesting tidbits that are not relevant to the writer's argument or thesis statement. For example, it is interesting that Harvard University's tuition is nearly $37,000 per year, but this fact is not relevant to the thesis statement "College graduates lead happier lives than those who have only a high-school diploma."

When evaluating the relevance of information, check the year of its publication. For example, an article published in 1992 is likely to include outdated information, while an article published in 2012 is much more likely to contain information still relevant today.

Recognize Assumptions

An **assumption** is an idea that a writer believes to be true but does not try to prove. In many cases, assumptions are not directly stated. For example, if someone says to you, "You learned your lesson last time, didn't you?" the unstated assumption is that you made a mistake in the past and the speaker is hoping you won't make the same mistake again. Assumptions can be based on facts, opinions, beliefs, experiences, or any combination of these. They can deal with what is right or wrong, good or bad, or important to the writer specifically or to society in general. For example, if a writer argues that restrictions should be placed on the violence shown in video games rated as acceptable for teenagers, she is assuming that video-game violence is harmful to the teens who play those games.

Often, writers believe that readers will agree with their assumptions because the reader and the writer share a common background or set of values. For example, someone writing an article for a Christian magazine can assume that the reader is familiar with Christian holidays like Easter and Christmas.

As a reader, it is your responsibility to identify the author's assumptions and then decide whether they are realistic and reasonable. Once you've identified the assumptions, you can evaluate whether essays (or other reading materials) based on these assumptions make sense and withstand thorough critical analysis and evaluation.

Here is a tip for identifying assumptions. When you start reading an assignment, you may experience a sense of disagreement or anger that you can't quite describe. As you continue reading, you may become angrier, and you may even stop reading. These reactions are often the result of picking up on the writer's underlying assumptions—and not agreeing with them! Try to determine exactly why the reading is generating these reactions in you, and you'll likely uncover the author's unstated assumptions. Then search the reading for evidence that the writer's assumptions are accurate. If you are unable to find convincing evidence, the reading may be inherently biased and perhaps untrustworthy.

Exercise 3.12

Answer each of the following questions.

1. You read an editorial about aggressive and violent behavior by prisoners in overcrowded prisons. The writer suggests extending prison terms of partici-

pants as the solution to the problem. What is the author assuming about prisoners and their behavior?

2. You read a newspaper article that begins, "Now that you've retired, what will you do with the rest of your life?" What is the writer assuming about the age of her readers?

3. You read a Web article titled "Dieting with a Difference: How to Get Rid of Those Pesky Ten Pounds." What is the author assuming about his readers?

Analyzing and Evaluating Visual Aids

As discussed in Chapter 2, visual aids include images (photographs, cartoons, advertisements, illustrations) and graphics (pie charts, bar graphs, line graphs, tables, diagrams, flowcharts). These powerful tools help writers share information, convey impressions, provoke thought, raise questions, and trigger emotions. As an active and critical reader, you should analyze and evaluate visual aids as carefully as you analyze and evaluate written text. The following are some suggestions for doing so.

Photographs and Other Images

As you critically evaluate images, ask yourself the following questions.

- Are the images typical or representative of the situation or subject? Or do they show exceptions to the rule?
- What is the purpose of the images? In other words, why has the author included them?
- What immediate emotional effects do the images produce?
- Would you feel as strongly about the topic of an essay (or other reading) if the images were not included?
- Do the images achieve their intended purpose?
- What other images might the writer have used to support his or her key points?
- What is the role of the caption, title, or words used in or with the image?

Figure 3.1 is a public service advertisement from the World Wildlife Fund. What do you notice first? Your eye probably goes to the tiger in a lush jungle setting in the small framed snapshot, and you recognize this as a common kind of nature photograph demonstrating the magnificence and beauty of jungle

Figure 3.1   Sample Advertisement: World Wildlife Fund

animals. Then you realize that the photograph is surrounded by a larger one showing a natural habitat destroyed by deforestation. When you then consider the words provided with the images, you realize the ad's purpose: to warn against the human destruction of natural habitats and the animals that live there. This ad makes a dramatic and compelling statement that nature is at risk of being destroyed and is worth protecting. The dual images with their corresponding text deliver a strong and effective message.

Exercise 3.13

Discuss what types of images might be useful to include in each of the following writing tasks.

1. An essay opposing the whaling industry
2. An essay describing problems faced by cyberbullying victims
3. A research paper on teen slang
4. An argumentative essay opposing casino gambling
5. A report about unhealthy fast-food menu items

Graphics

Information-laden graphics can take extra work to understand. Although understanding is always the basis for analysis and evaluation, with graphics it can be especially important to begin with a careful process for understanding.

As discussed in Chapter 2, this process should include reading the reference to the graphic in the main text, to understand the connections between the graphic and the text, and carefully reading all parts of the graphic, in order to understand its purpose and its organization.

To then analyze and evaluate the graphic, use the following process, illustrated with Figure 3.2 (p. 76).

1. **Analyze the data to identify trends or patterns.** Note unexpected changes (such as sudden increases or decreases), surprising statistics, or unexplained variations. For example, in Figure 3.2, you may note that the percentage of students who are at least at the basic level of their grade drops from fourth grade to eighth grade for math while increasing for reading.

2. **Make a brief summary note about any trends or patterns you find.** Writing a summary note will crystallize the idea in your mind, and your note will be useful for review. A summary note of Figure 3.2 might read:

Spending on elementary and secondary public schooling increased considerably from 1980 to 2009. Test scores in 2009 for 4th- and 8th-graders in four states (Missouri, South Dakota, New York, and Maryland) all seem fairly similar to the average scores for the United States, even though two of the states (New York, Maryland) spend much more per pupil than the other two (Missouri, South Dakota).

3. **Critically evaluate the graphic.** Consider questions like these:

- Are the data from a reputable source?
- Is the information current (timely) and accurate?
- How objective (unbiased) is the graphic?
- Are the data presented fairly?
- Is the meaning of the data clear?
- Is anything vague or confusing?
- Is the scale (as shown in the units of measurement) misleading in any way?
- Could the information be presented differently to show a different trend or outcome?

In Figure 3.2, the data come from a source that is considered among the most reputable: the U.S. Bureau of the Census. The data are also current, having been taken from a 2012 publication.

Notice, however, that the graphic might not be objective and unbiased. First, a look at the line graph showing the increase in expenditures over time shows that the numbers along the left do not start at $0 billion but at $90 billion. This misleadingly makes the expenditures at the start of the period visually look less than they were and the increase therefore look greater. Second, the bar graphs at the bottom include bars for ranking state spending along with bars for scores. In these rank-in-spending bars, New York and Maryland look very different from Missouri and South Dakota, which exaggerates the contrast between them, especially in the context of the scores bars, which are quite similar for the four states. The author of the graphic could, instead, have just indicated the rank of each state as a number or could have shown dollar amounts for each state's expenses per pupil. Worse, the author has used data from only four states. There are fifty states, and perhaps some other higher spending states have better results than some other lower spending states. The author has also failed to address the larger context: How much have other expenses increased during this period? Are test scores good measures of learning? Are there factors in addition to learning that might influence test scores? In short, as a critical evaluation of this graphic shows, even data that are reliable can be distorted to "prove" a point.

Figure 3.2   Sample Graphic: U.S. Educational Expenditures, 1980–2009

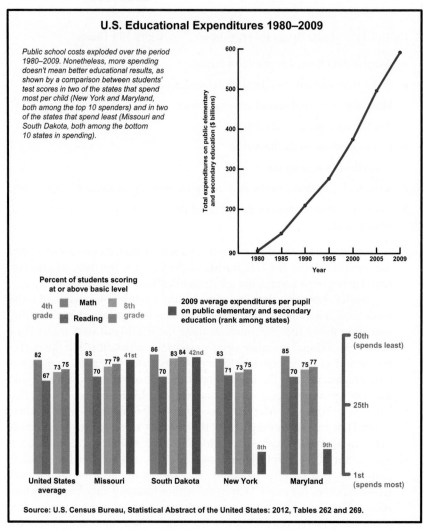

Exercise 3.14

Using the guidelines presented above, study the table and answer the following questions.

Academic Degrees Conferred by Sex

Bachelor's Degree						Master's Degree				
Year	Total	Men	%	Women	%	Total	Men	%	Women	%
1968	632,289	357,682	57	274,607	43	176,749	113,552	64	63,197	36
1978	921,204	487,347	53	433,857	47	311,620	161,212	52	150,408	48
1988	994,829	477,203	48	517,626	52	299,317	145,163	48	154,154	52
1998	1,172,000	523,000	45	649,000	55	406,000	183,000	45	223,000	55
2003	1,312,503	537,079	41	775,424	59	512,645	211,381	41	301,264	59
2007	1,524,092	649,264	43	874,828	57	604,607	238,216	39	366,391	61
2014*	1,582,000	633,000	40	949,000	60	693,000	275,000	40	418,000	60

*Projected

Sources: *Unpublished tabulations, Bureau of Labor Statistics,* Current Population Survey. *2003 and 2014 (projected) data, Tables 27 & 28, "Projections of Education Statistics to 2014," National Center for Education Statistics, U.S. Department of Education; 2007 update. U.S. Department of Education, National Center for Education Statistics (2009). Condition of Education 2009.*

1. How is the table organized?
2. What is the table's purpose?
3. What trends and patterns are evident for bachelor's degrees? For master's degrees? For both degrees? What trends and patterns do you see?
4. Write a brief summary note of the table.
5. Do you consider the source of the data to be reliable?
6. Note that the table reports data in ten-year intervals from 1968 to 1998 and then in five-, four-, and seven-year intervals. Consider possible reasons for this variation. Does an increased frequency of reporting make the changes seem less dramatic?

A Guide to Responding to Texts and Visuals

Active reading (understanding, analyzing, and evaluating) also involves **responding**, or reacting, to the material. When you respond to material, you understand it better.

Responses to a reading can take many formats. Sometimes you'll make informal notes, called *annotations*, while you read. Other times you'll record your reactions in an informal personal journal. Often, your instructor will ask you to write a formal response paper.

Use Annotations

In Chapter 2, "Understanding Texts and Images," you learned how to write an effective summary. Writing a summary is an excellent way to check your understanding of the reading's key points.

In contrast to summaries (which do *not* include your reactions to the reading), **annotations** record your responses to the writer's ideas. When you annotate, you jot down your impressions, reactions, and questions directly in the margins. Later, when you are ready to discuss or write about the reading, your annotations will help you focus on major issues and questions. Here is a list of what you might annotate.

- the thesis statement and other important points
- sections about which you need further information
- sections in which the author reveals his or her reasons for writing
- ideas you agree or disagree with
- inconsistencies
- questions you want to ask your instructor
- particularly meaningful visuals and images

Some students make two sets of annotations: one set during their first reading of the assignment and a second set (in a different color ink) during their second reading. The following is a set of annotations for a portion of the essay "Comparing Online and Traditional Education," in Chapter 2.

Annotation	Text
for me the lectures are OK, but I would really miss the social aspect of college	When I switched to online education, I missed out on a good chunk of the college experience. To me, the best parts of college were listening to lectures by terrific professors and participating in discussions with other young, intelligent people. Once I became a distance student, I missed out on all of these exchanges of ideas. I missed out on making great friends, on taking some

Thesis

I see her point, but I think I would have done the same thing she did. I wouldn't want to turn down my dream job!

Talk to some classmates who took distance-ed courses to get their opinions

terrific classes, on joining clubs, and on writing for the student newspaper. These are very important parts of a college education, and they are parts that simply cannot be experienced through a computer monitor. I put my education second, behind my job and my personal life. Perhaps, for only a couple of years, I should have put it first.

Online classes can be a godsend for some students, and I think that they provide an incredibly valuable service in opening up the world of college education to some people who otherwise wouldn't be able to earn degrees without great sacrifice. But, take it from someone who has been on both sides of the fence: It isn't the same. It truly isn't.

Exercise 3.15

Choose one of the essays in Chapters 10–18 of this book and annotate it.

Keep a Journal

A **journal** is a notebook or computer file in which you record and explore ideas and observations. Experiment with the following two methods of organizing a journal response to a reading assignment.

THE OPEN-PAGE FORMAT

On a blank page, write, outline, draw, or create a diagram to express your reactions to a reading. The open-page format encourages you to let your ideas flow freely. Figure 3.3 (p. 80) shows one student's open-page journal entry for "Comparing Online and Traditional Education." This entry suggests several possible topics to write about—for example, the college experience, the benefits of in-person lectures, and educational options for people with disabilities.

THE TWO-COLUMN FORMAT

Divide several pages of your journal into two columns. If you keep your journal on a computer, you can insert a table with two columns. Label the left column "Quotations" and the right column "Responses." Under "Quotations," jot down five to ten quotations from the text. Choose remarks that seem important—sentences that state an opinion, summarize a viewpoint, offer an important example, and so forth. In the right column, next to each quotation, write your response to the quotation. You might explain it, disagree with or question it, relate it to other information in

Figure 3.3   Sample Open-Page Journal Format

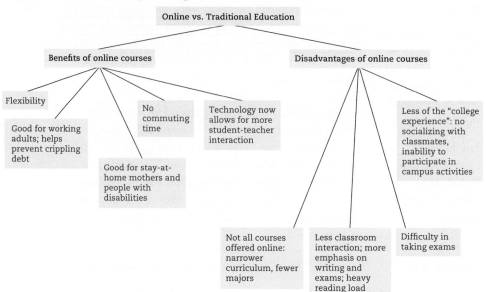

the reading or in another reading, or tie it to your own experiences. The structure of the two-column format forces you to think actively about the reading while you question what you have read and draw connections.

You may find it useful to **paraphrase** the quotation (that is, rewrite it in your own words) before writing your response. Paraphrasing forces you to think about the meaning of the quotation, and ideas for writing may come to mind as a result. To use paraphrasing, add a "Paraphrases" column to your journal between the "Quotations" column and the "Responses" column.

Figure 3.4 follows the two-column format. In this journal entry, the writer has uncovered several possible topics—for example, how the author's experience differs from that of a typical student, as well as the hidden benefits of commuting.

Write in Response to a Reading

When an instructor assigns a reading, some form of response is always expected. You might be expected to participate in a class discussion, summarize the information on an essay exam, or research the topic further and report your findings. Some instructors assign a **response paper**, which requires you to read an essay, analyze it, and write about some aspect of it. In some assignments, your instructor will suggest a particular direction for the paper. Other times, you decide how to respond to the essay.

Figure 3.4   Sample Two-Column Journal Format

Quotations	Responses
"Without the option of online classes, I would not have been able to both take my dream job and finish my degree."	This writer is extremely lucky. How many of us get offered our dream job before we get our degree? Her experience seems like a rare case, not an example of a typical student's experiences.
"Not everybody can afford to take four years out of their lives to attend school, and not everyone has a trust fund set up to pay for their education."	She is so right about this! Many of us have to work to support ourselves, and it can be very stressful to juggle school and work. This is probably a much more common situation than having to take online courses because you've been offered your dream job.
"Although I managed to do a lot of reading on the two buses and the train that I took, one cannot say that this was a particularly productive or efficient use of time."	She has a point, but she also doesn't realize that commuting can be a good experience. It gives you time to yourself, to focus on your studies away from the pressures of family or job. I feel like the only time I have to myself is the time I spend on the bus!

Before beginning any response paper, make sure you understand the assignment. If you are uncertain about your instructor's expectations, ask for clarification. You may also want to check with classmates to find out how they are approaching the assignment. If your instructor does not mention length requirements, ask how long the response paper should be.

In a response paper, you may include a brief summary as part of your introduction, but you should concentrate on analyzing and evaluating what you have read. Do not attempt to discuss all of your reactions, however. Instead, choose one key idea, one question the essay raises, or one issue it explores.

For example, suppose your instructor asks you to read the essay "Advertising: A Form of Institutional Lying," which argues that advertisements deceive consumers by presenting half-truths, distortions, and misinformation, and to write a two-page response paper, but he or she provides no further direction. In writing this response paper, you might take one of the following approaches.

- Discuss how you were once deceived by an advertisement, as a way of confirming the author's main points.

- Evaluate the evidence and examples the author provides to support her claim; determine whether the evidence is relevant and sufficient.

- Discuss the causes or effects of deceptive advertising that the writer has overlooked. (You may need to consult other sources to take this approach.)

- Evaluate the assumptions the author makes about advertising or consumers.

For an assignment like this one or for any response paper, how do you decide which facet of the issue to write about? Begin by reviewing any summary you've written, as well as your annotations and journal entries.

Another way to start ideas flowing for a response paper is to think about how the reading relates to your own experiences. Brainstorming ideas builds a bridge between your ideas and the writer's and suggests ideas to write about.

- **Begin by looking for useful information that you can apply or relate to real-life situations.** Think of familiar situations or examples that illustrate the subject. For example, for "Comparing Online and Traditional Education" you might write a response paper about your experiences with an online course or about your conversation with a friend who has taken a distance-learning course.

- **Think beyond the reading.** Recall other material you have read and events you have experienced that relate to the reading. In thinking about "Comparing Online and Traditional Education," for example, you might recall an article in the student newspaper about the new history, literature, and sociology courses that will be offered online next term.

- **Use the key-word response method for generating ideas.** Choose one or more key words that describe your initial response to the reading, such as *angered, amused, surprised, confused, annoyed, curious,* or *shocked.* For example, fill in the following blank with key words describing your response to "Comparing Online and Traditional Education."

After reading the essay, I felt _____.

The key-word response you just wrote will serve as a point of departure for further thinking. Start by explaining your response, then write down ideas as they come to you, trying to approach the reading from many different perspectives. Here is the result of one student's key-word response to "Comparing Online and Traditional Education."

You have just used *freewriting,* a method of discovering ideas about a topic. Read over what you wrote. Suppose you were asked to write an essay about joy or exuberance. Do you see some starting points and usable ideas in your freewriting? In this chapter, you will learn more about freewriting as well as a number of other methods that will help you find ideas to write about. You will also learn how to focus an essay by considering why you are writing (your purpose), for whom you are writing (your audience), and what perspective you are using to approach your topic (point of view). These steps are all part of the beginning of the process of writing an essay, as illustrated in Figure 4.1 (pp. 86–87).

Choosing and Narrowing a Topic

When you begin an essay assignment, it's a good idea to allow time for choosing a broad topic and then narrowing it to be manageable within the assigned length of your paper. Skipping this step is one of the biggest mistakes you can make in beginning a writing assignment. You can waste a great deal of time working on an essay only to discover that the topic is too large or that you don't have enough to say about it.

Choosing a Topic

In some writing situations, your instructor will assign the topic. In others, your instructor will allow you to write on a topic of your choice. Or you may be given a number of possible topics to choose from. Use the following guidelines when picking your own topic.

1. **Invest time in making your choice.** It may be tempting to grab the first topic that comes to mind, but you will produce a better essay if you work with a topic that interests you and that you know something about.

2. **Focus on questions and ideas rather than on topics.** For example, the question, Do television commercials really sell products? may come to mind more easily than the broad topic of advertising or commercials.

3. **Use your journal as a source of ideas.** If you have not begun keeping a journal, start one now; try writing in it for a few weeks to see if it is helpful. Chapter 3 has tips on using a journal (pp. 79–80).

4. **Discuss possible topics with a friend.** By talking to friends, you may discover worthwhile topics and get feedback on topics you have already thought of.

5. **Consult your course materials for possible ideas.** For instance, many of this chapter's exercises include topics you may want to explore, and each essay in Part 2 includes writing prompts.

See Table 4.1 (p. 88) for a summary of sources of ideas for topics.

Figure 4.1   Overview of the Writing Process

Choosing a topic	Take the time to choose a good topic.
	Use a journal.
	Brainstorm with a friend.
	Consult Table 4.1, "Sources of Ideas for Essay Topics" (p. 88).
Narrowing your topic	Use a branching diagram.
	Ask questions.
Determining your purpose and considering your audience	Decide why you are writing.
	Decide whom you are writing for.
Choosing a point of view	Decide which point of view is most appropriate for your audience.
	Consider which point of view will enable you to present your topic most effectively.
Discovering ideas to write about	Freewrite.
	Map.
	Brainstorm on your own or in a group.
	Ask questions.
	Write assertions.
	Interview a knowledgeable person.
	Use patterns of development.
	Visualize and sketch.
	Research 0your topic.
Developing your thesis statement	Group related ideas together. Evaluate groupings.
	Look for other relationships.
	Do additional prewriting.
	Write your thesis statement.
	Decide where to place your thesis statement.

Figure 4.1   (continued)

Supporting your thesis statement	Supply evidence that is – relevant, – detailed and specific, – representative, – accurate.
	Offer enough evidence and a variety of evidence.
Drafting	Use sources to support your thesis.
	Write effective paragraphs.
	Write a strong introduction, conclusion, and title.
Revising	Analyze your paper's purpose and audience.
	Analyze your thesis, topic sentences, and evidence.
	Analyze your organization.
	Analyze your paragraph development.
	Work with classmates.
Editing and proofreading	See the editing tips in Chapters 10–18.

Essay in Progress 1

Using the suggestions on page 85 and in Table 4.1 (p. 88) for inspiration, record at least three broad topics.

Narrowing a Topic

Once you have chosen a topic, the next step is to narrow it so that it is manageable within the length of the essay your instructor has assigned. For example, a broad topic such as divorce is too large for a two- to four-page paper. However, you might write about one specific cause of divorce or its effects on children.

To narrow a topic, limit it to a specific part or aspect. The following techniques—branching and questioning—will help you do so. Later in the chapter, you

Table 4.1   Sources of Ideas for Essay Topics

Source	What to Look For	Example
Your classes	Listen for issues, controversies, and new ideas that might be worth exploring.	A discussion in your education class leads you to the topic of standardized testing.
Daily activities	Take note of incidents at work and at sporting or social events.	A health inspector's visit at work suggests an essay on restaurant-food safety.
Newspapers and magazines	Flip through recent issues; look for articles that might lead to promising topics.	You find an interesting article on a hip-hop musician and decide to write about her career.
Radio, television, and the Internet	Listen to your favorite radio station for a thought-provoking song, or look for ideas in television programs and commercials or on the Web.	Commercials for diet soda suggest an essay on the diet-food industry.
The world around you	Notice people, objects, and interactions inside your household or outside.	You observe family members reading books and decide to write about the value of leisure time.

will learn idea-generating techniques (pp. 93–101) that may also be used to narrow a broad topic.

USING A BRANCHING DIAGRAM

Start by writing your broad topic at the far left side of your paper or computer screen. Then subdivide the topic into three or more subcategories or aspects. Here is an example for the broad topic of wild-game hunting.

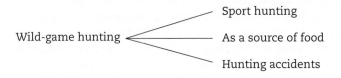

Wild-game hunting
— Sport hunting
— As a source of food
— Hunting accidents

Then choose one subtopic and subdivide it further. Continue narrowing the topic in this way until you feel you have found one that is both interesting and manageable. Keep in mind that once you begin planning, researching, and drafting the essay, you may need to narrow your topic even further. The following example shows additional narrowing of the sport hunting subtopic "effects on environment."

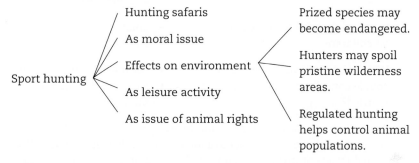

Notice that as the narrowing progresses, the topics change from words and phrases to statements of ideas.

Exercise 4.1

Use branching diagrams to narrow three of the following broad topics to more manageable topics for a two- to four-page essay.

1. Divorce
2. Manned space travel
3. School lunches
4. Air-travel safety measures
5. Campaign-finance rules
6. Alternative-energy sources

Essay in Progress 2

Narrow one of the broad topics you chose in Essay in Progress 1 to a topic manageable for a two- to four-page essay.

ASKING QUESTIONS TO NARROW A BROAD TOPIC

Use questions that begin with *who, what, where, when, why,* and *how* to narrow your topic. This will help you consider specific aspects of the topic. Here is an example of **questioning** for the broad topic of divorce.

Questions	Narrowed Topics
Why does divorce occur?	• Lifestyle differences
	• Infidelity

Questions	Narrowed Topics
How do couples divide their property?	• Division of assets
Who can help couples work through a divorce?	• Role of friends and family • Marital counselor's or attorney's role
What are the effects of divorce on children?	• Emotional • Financial
When might it be advisable for a couple considering divorce to remain married?	• For the sake of their children • Financial benefit of remaining married

As you can see, the questions about divorce produced several workable topics. Ask additional questions to get to a topic that is sufficiently limited. The topic "emotional effects of divorce on children," for example, is still too broad for an essay. Asking questions such as What are the most typical emotional effects on children? and How do divorcing parents prevent emotional problems for their children? would lead to more specific topics.

Exercise 4.2

Use questioning to narrow three of the following subjects to topics that would be manageable within a two- to four-page essay.

1. Senior citizens
2. Mental illness
3. Environmental protection
4. Cyberbullying
5. Television programming

Thinking about Your Purpose, Audience, and Point of View

Once you have decided on a manageable topic, you are ready to determine your purpose and consider your audience.

Determining Your Purpose

A well-written essay should have a specific **purpose** or goal. There are three main purposes for writing—to *express* yourself, to *inform* your reader, and to *persuade* your reader. For example, an essay might express the writer's feelings about an incident of road rage that he or she observed. Another essay may inform readers about the primary causes of road rage. Yet another essay might try to persuade readers that anger management classes are the most effective way of combatting road rage.

As you plan your draft essay, ask yourself two critical questions.

- Why am I writing this essay?
- What do I want this essay to accomplish?

Some essays have more than one purpose. An essay on snowboarding, for example, could be both informative and persuasive: It could explain the benefits of snowboarding and then urge readers to take up the sport because it is good aerobic exercise.

Considering Your Audience

Considering your **audience**—the people who read your essay—is an important part of the writing process. Many aspects of your writing—how you express yourself, your word choice, the details and examples you include, and your attitude toward the topic—all depend on the audience. Your **tone**—how you sound to your audience—is especially important. If you want your audience to feel comfortable with your writing, be sure to write in a manner that appeals to them.

HOW TO CONSIDER YOUR AUDIENCE

As you consider your audience, keep the following points in mind.

- Your readers are not present and cannot observe or participate in what you are writing about.
- Your readers may not know everything that you do about your topic.
- Your readers may not share your opinions and values.
- Your readers may not respond the same way that you do to situations or issues.

The following are questions you can ask when analyzing your audience.

- **What does your audience know or not know about your topic?** If you are proposing a community garden project to city residents who know little about gardening, capture their interest by describing the pleasures and benefits of gardening. Include some basic information.
- **What is the education, background, and experience of your audience?** If you are writing your garden project proposal for an audience of low-income residents, you might emphasize how much money they could save by growing vegetables. For middle-income residents, you might stress instead how relaxing gardening can be.
- **What attitudes, beliefs, opinions, or biases is your audience likely to hold?** If, for example, your audience believes that most development is harmful to the environment, consider emphasizing how the garden will benefit the environment.

- **What tone do your readers expect you to take?** Suppose you are writing to your local city council urging council members to approve the community garden. Your tone should be serious, as community leaders expect to be treated with respect.

WHEN YOUR AUDIENCE IS YOUR INSTRUCTOR

Instructors occasionally direct students to write for a particular audience, such as readers of a certain magazine or newspaper, but you can usually assume that your audience is your instructor. You should not, however, automatically assume that he or she is an expert on your topic. In most cases, it is best to write as if your instructor were unfamiliar with your topic. He or she wants to see if you understand the topic and can write and think clearly about it. For academic papers, then, you should provide enough information to demonstrate your knowledge of the subject. Include background information, definitions of technical terms, and relevant details to make your essay clear and understandable.

Exercise 4.3

1. Write a one-paragraph description of a current television commercial for a particular product. Your audience is another college student.
2. Write a description of the same commercial for one of the following writing situations.
   a. For a business marketing class, analyze the factors that make the advertisement interesting and appealing to consumers. Your audience is your business marketing instructor.
   b. Describe your response to the advertisement in a letter to the company that makes the product. Your audience is the consumer-relations director of the company.
   c. Comment favorably on or complain about the advertisement to a local television station. Your audience is the station director.

Choosing a Point of View

Point of view is the perspective from which you write an essay. There are three points of view possible—*first*, *second*, and *third person*. In choosing a point of view, consider your topic, your purpose, and your audience.

Think of point of view as the "person" you become as you write. For some essays, you may find first-person pronouns (*I, me, mine, we, ours*) effective and appropriate, such as in an essay narrating an event in which you participated. For other types of essays, second-person pronouns (*you, your, yours*) are appropriate, as in an essay explaining how to build a fence: "First, *you* should measure . . .". At times, the word *you* may be understood but not directly stated, as in "First, measure . . .". Many textbooks, including this one, use the second person to address students.

In academic writing, the third-person point of view is prevalent. The third-person point of view is more formal than both the first person and the second person. The writer uses people's names and third-person pronouns (*he, she, they*). Think of the third person as public rather than personal. The writer reports what he or she sees.

Exercise 4.4

Working with a classmate, discuss which point of view (first, second, or third person) would be most appropriate in each of the following writing situations.

1. An essay urging students on your campus to participate in a march against hunger to support a local food drive

2. A description of a car accident on a form that your insurance company requires you to submit in order to collect benefits

3. A paper for an ecology course on the effects of air pollution caused by a local industry

Discovering Ideas to Write About

Many students report that one of the most difficult parts of writing an essay is finding enough to say about a narrowed topic. In the following sections, you will learn a number of useful prewriting strategies for discovering ideas to write about. Experiment with each before deciding which will work for you. The technique you choose for a given essay may depend in part on your topic.

Freewriting

When you use **freewriting**, you write nonstop for a specific period of time, usually five to ten minutes. As you learned in the activity that opens this chapter, freewriting involves writing whatever comes to mind, regardless of its relevance to your topic. If nothing comes to mind, just write the topic, your name, or "I can't think of anything to write." Then let your mind run free: Explore ideas, make associations, jump from one idea to another. The following tips will help you.

- **Be sure to write nonstop.** The act of writing itself often forces thoughts to emerge.
- **Don't be concerned with grammar, punctuation, or spelling.**
- **Write fast!** Try to keep up with your thinking. (Most people can think faster than they can write.)

- **Record ideas as they come to you.** Do this in whatever form they appear—words, phrases, questions, or sentences.
- **If you are freewriting on a computer, darken the screen.** This way, you are not distracted by errors, formatting issues, and the words you have already written.

Next, reread your freewriting, and highlight or underline ideas that seem useful. Look for patterns and connections. Do several ideas together make a point, reflect a sequence, or suggest a larger unifying idea? Here is an excerpt from one student's freewriting on the broad topic of violence in the media.

There seems to be a lot of violence in the media these days, particularly on TV. For example, last night when I watched the news, the cameraman showed people getting shot in the street. What kind of people watch this stuff? I'd rather watch a movie. It really bothered me because people get so turned off by such an ugly, gruesome scene that they won't want to watch the news anymore. Then we'll have a lot of uninformed citizens. There are too many already. Some people do not even know who the vice president of the U.S. is. A negative thing—that is the media has a negative impact on anyone or group who want to do something about violence in the inner city. And they create negative impressions of minority and ethnic groups, too. If the media shows one Latino man committing a crime, viewers falsely assume all Latinos are criminals. It's difficult to think of something positive that can be done when you're surrounded by so much violence. It's all so overwhelming. What we need in the inner city is not more coverage of violence but viable solutions to the violence we have. The media coverage of violent acts only serves to make people think that this violence is a normal state of affairs and nothing can be done about it.

A number of different subtopics surfaced from this student's freewriting.

- The media's graphic portrayal of violence
- The negative effect of media violence on viewers
- The media's portrayal of minority and ethnic groups

Any one of these topics could be narrowed into a manageable topic for an essay.

Exercise 4.5

Set a clock or timer for five minutes and freewrite on one of the following broad topics. Then review and highlight your freewriting, identifying usable ideas with a common theme that might serve as a topic for an essay. With this new potential topic, freewrite for another five minutes to narrow your topic further and develop your ideas.

1. Rap music
2. Blogs
3. How to be self-sufficient
4. Pressures on college students
5. Job interviews

Mapping

Mapping, or **clustering**, is a visual way to discover ideas and relationships. It is also a powerful tool for some writers. Here is how it works.

1. Write your topic in the middle of a blank sheet of paper, and draw a box or circle around it.
2. Think of ideas that are related to or suggested by your topic. As you think of them, write them down in clusters around the topic, connecting them to the topic with lines (see Figure 4.2).
3. Draw arrows and lines or use highlighting to show relationships and connect groups of related ideas.
4. Think of still more ideas, clustering them around the ideas already on your map.

Figure 4.2   Sample Map

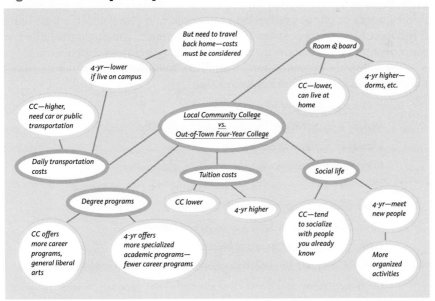

5. If possible, experiment with mapping on a computer, using a graphics program such as the draw function available in Microsoft Word. You can then cut and paste items from your map into an outline or draft of your essay.

The sample map in Figure 4.2 was done by a student working on the topic of the costs of higher education. In this map, the student compared attending a local community college and attending an out-of-town four-year college.

Exercise 4.6

Narrow one of the following topics. Then select one of your narrowed topics, and draw a map of related ideas as they come to mind.

1. Presidential politics
2. Daydreaming
3. Tattoos
4. Cable TV
5. Year-round schooling

Brainstorming

When you do **brainstorming**, you list everything that comes to mind when you think about your topic—impressions, emotions, and reactions, as well as facts. Record words or phrases rather than sentences, and give yourself a time limit: It will force ideas to come faster. If you use a computer, you might use bullets or the indent function to brainstorm to create lists rather than sentences.

The following example shows a student's brainstorming on the narrowed topic of the disadvantages of homeschooling.

Topic: _Disadvantages of Homeschooling_

Parent may not be an expert in each subject

Libraries not easily accessible

Wide range of equipment, resources not available

Child may be confused by parent playing the role of teacher

Child does not learn to interact with other children

Child does not learn to compete against others

Parents may not enforce standards

Parents may not be objective about child's strengths and weaknesses

Child may learn only parent's viewpoint—not exposed to wide range of opinions

Special programs (art, music) may be omitted

Services of school nurse, counselors, reading specialists not available

Three clusters of topics are evident—unavailable services and resources (highlighted in pink), limits of parents (highlighted in violet), and problems of social development (highlighted in tan). Once the student selected a cluster of topics, he did further brainstorming to generate ideas about his narrowed topic.

Brainstorming is somewhat more structured than freewriting because the writer focuses only on the topic at hand instead of writing whatever comes to mind.

Brainstorming can also work well when it is done in groups of two or three classmates. Say your ideas aloud as you record them. You'll find that your classmates' ideas will trigger more of your own.

Exercise 4.7

Choose one of the following subjects and narrow it to a manageable topic for a two- to four-page paper. Then brainstorm, either alone or with one or two classmates, to generate ideas to write about.

1. Value of music
2. National parks
3. Credit-card fraud
4. Texting
5. Web advertising

Questioning

Questioning is another way to discover ideas about a narrowed topic. Working either alone or with a classmate, write down every question you can think of about your topic. As with other prewriting strategies, focus on ideas, not on grammatical correctness. Don't judge or evaluate ideas as you write. It may help to imagine that you are asking an expert on your topic anything that comes to mind.

Here is a partial list of questions one student generated on the narrow topic of the financial problems faced by single parents.

Why do many female single parents earn less than male single parents?

Is there a support group for single parents that offers financial advice and planning?

How do single parents find time to attend college to improve their employability?

Beginning a question with "What if" is a particularly good way to extend your thinking and look at a topic from a fresh perspective. Here are a few challenging *What if* questions about the financial situations of single parents.

What if the government provided national day care or paid for day care?

What if single parents were not allowed to deduct more than one child on their income tax?

What if there were financial support groups for single parents?

Exercise 4.8

Working either alone or with a classmate, choose one of the following topics, narrow it, and write a series of questions to discover ideas about it.

1. The campus newspaper
2. Learning a foreign language
3. Financial-aid regulations
4. Late-night talk radio
5. Government aid to developing countries

Writing Assertions

The technique of **writing assertions** forces you to look at your topic from a number of different perspectives. Begin by writing five to ten statements that take a position on or make an assertion about your topic. Here are a few possible assertions for the topic of the growing popularity of health food.

Supermarkets have increased their marketing of health foods.

Health food is popular because buying it makes people think they are hip.

Health food is popular because it is chemical free.

Health food tricks people into thinking they have a healthy lifestyle.

Review your list of assertions, choose one statement, and try brainstorming, freewriting, or mapping to generate more ideas about it.

Exercise 4.9

Working either alone or with one or two classmates, write assertions about one of the following topics.

1. Advertising directed toward children
2. Buying a used car from a private individual
3. Needed improvements in public education

4. Characteristics of a good teacher

5. Attempts to encourage healthier eating on campus

Using the Patterns of Development

In Part 2 of this book, you will learn nine ways to develop an essay—narration, description, illustration, process analysis, comparison and contrast, classification and division, definition, cause and effect, and argument. These methods are often called **patterns of development**. In addition to providing ways to develop an essay, the patterns of development may be used to generate ideas about a topic. Think of the patterns as doors through which you can gain access to your topic. Just as a building or room looks different depending on which door you enter, so you will see your topic in various ways by approaching it through different patterns of development.

The list of questions in Table 4.2, "Using the Patterns of Development to Explore a Topic" (p. 100), will help you approach your topic through these different "doors." For any given topic, some questions will work better than others. If your topic is voter registration, for example, the questions listed for definition and process analysis would be more helpful than those listed for description.

As you write your answers to the questions, also record any related ideas that come to mind. If you are working on a computer, create a table listing the patterns in one column and your answers to the questions in another. For more information on how to use different patterns of development for a topic, see Chapter 9, "Patterns: An Introduction."

Exercise 4.10

Use a pattern of development to generate ideas on one of the following topics. Refer to Table 4.2 (p. 100) to form questions based on that pattern.

1. Buying only American-made products

2. Effects of email spam

3. Community gardens in urban areas

4. How high-speed trains would change travel

5. Cell-phone usage

Visualizing or Sketching

Especially if you enjoy working with graphics, **visualizing** or actually **sketching** your topic may be an effective way to discover ideas. If you are writing a description of a person, for example, close your eyes and visualize that person in your mind: Imagine what he or she is wearing; study his or her facial expressions and gestures.

Table 4.2   Using the Patterns of Development to Explore a Topic

Pattern of Development	Questions to Ask
Narration (Chapter 10)	What stories or events does this topic remind me of?
Description (Chapter 11)	What does the topic look, smell, taste, feel, or sound like?
Illustration (Chapter 12)	What examples of this topic are particularly helpful in explaining it?
Process Analysis (Chapter 13)	How does this topic work? How does one do this process?
Comparison and Contrast (Chapter 14)	To what is the topic similar? In what ways? Is the topic more or less desirable than those things to which it is similar?
Classification and Division (Chapter 15)	Of what larger group of things is this topic a member? What are its parts? How can the topic be subdivided? Are there certain types or kinds of the topic?
Definition (Chapter 16)	How do I define the term? How does the dictionary define it? What is the history of the term? Does everyone agree on its definition? Why or why not? If not, what points are in dispute?
Cause and Effect (Chapter 17)	What causes the topic? How often does it happen? What might prevent it from happening? What are its effects? What may happen because of it in the short term? What may happen as a result of it over time?
Argument (Chapter 18)	What issues surround this topic?

Exercise 4.11

Visualize one of the following situations. Make notes about or sketch what you "see." Include as many details as possible.

1. A traffic jam
2. A couple obviously in love
3. A class you recently attended
4. The campus snack bar
5. A sporting event

Researching Your Topic

Do some preliminary research on your topic in the library or on the Internet. Reading what others have written about your topic may suggest new approaches, reveal issues or controversies, and help you determine what you do and do not already know about the topic. This method is especially useful for an assigned essay with an unfamiliar topic or for a topic you want to learn more about.

Take notes while reading sources. In addition, be sure to record the publication data you will need to cite each source (author, title, publisher, page numbers, and so on). If you use ideas or information from sources in your essay, you must give credit to the sources of the borrowed material. (For more information on finding and using sources, refer to Chapter 19.)

Exercise 4.12

Do library or Internet research to generate ideas on one of the narrowed topics listed here.

1. A recent local disaster (hurricane, flood)
2. Buying clothing on eBay
3. Preventing terrorism in public buildings
4. Controlling children's access to television programs
5. Reducing the federal deficit

Essay in Progress 3

Keeping your audience and purpose in mind, use one of the prewriting strategies discussed in this chapter to generate details about the topic you narrowed in Essay in Progress 2.

Students Write

In this and the remaining four chapters of Part 1, we follow the work of Christine Lee, a student in a first-year writing course who was assigned to write about a recent trend or fad in popular culture.

Lee decided to use questioning to narrow her topic and freewriting to generate ideas about the topic. Here is an example of her questioning.

Sample Questioning

What are some recent fads or trends?

> *freak dancing*
> *Political blogging*
> *Extreme sports*
> *Tattooing and body piercing*
> *Reality TV*

Lee decided to explore the topic of reality TV further by asking another question.

Why is this trend popular?

Reality TV

> *People are more likely to identify with real people, not actors.*
> *The shows are usually contests, which keep viewers watching until the last episode.*
> *They are unscripted and often unpredictable.*
> *Survivor was popular because money was involved.*

After looking over the answers to her questions, Lee decided to focus on reality TV's evolution and popularity. The following excerpt from her freewriting shows how she started to develop her topic.

Sample freewriting

When *Survivor* was first on TV everyone was watching and talking about it at school and work. It was new and different, and it was interesting to watch how people started to act when a million dollars was at stake. Everybody had a favorite and someone else they loved to hate. After that season it seemed like every network had two or three competition reality shows they were trying out. They get more and more ridiculous and less tasteful with every new show. And now they are coming up with shows based on talent and beauty contests, like *American Idol*. Now I'm getting tired of all of these "real" people as they defend their pettiness by saying, "It's just a game." In the end I'll go back to watching *Modern Family* because it's funny (which *Big Brother* never is) and *Brothers and Sisters* because they talk about serious issues that real people deal with. Maybe we'd all like to think that we wouldn't be as petty and mean as all of these contestants, but with all of these "real" people on TV these days, I can't relate to a single one of them.

As you work through the remaining chapters in Part 1, you will see how Lee develops her tentative thesis statement (Chapter 5), her first draft (Chapter 6), a specific paragraph (Chapter 7), and her final draft (Chapter 8).

Chapter 5

Developing and Supporting a Thesis

"Go ask your search engine."

Quick Start: Study the cartoon above: It humorously depicts a serious situation. Working alone or with one or two classmates, write a statement that expresses the main point of the cartoon. Describe what is happening in the cartoon, and state the idea that the cartoonist is trying to communicate to his audience.

The statement you wrote for the Quick Start prompt is an assertion around which you could build an essay. Such an assertion is called a *thesis statement*. In this chapter, you will learn how to write effective thesis statements and how to support them with evidence. Developing a thesis is an important part of the writing process. In Figure 4.1 (pp. 86–87), you can see it within the context of the process.

What Is a Thesis Statement?

A **thesis statement** (also called *central thought*) is the main point of an essay. It explains what the essay will be about and expresses the writer's position on the subject. It may also give clues about how the essay will develop or how it will be organized. Usually a thesis statement is expressed in a single sentence. When you write, think of the thesis statement as a promise to your reader. The rest of your essay delivers on that promise.

Here is a sample thesis statement.

Playing team sports, especially football and baseball, develops skills and qualities that can make you successful in life because these sports demand communication, teamwork, and responsibility.

In this thesis, the writer identifies the topic—team sports—and states the position that team sports, especially football and baseball, equip players with important skills and qualities. After reading this statement, the reader expects to discover what skills and qualities football and baseball players learn and how these contribute to success in life.

Developing Your Thesis Statement

A thesis statement usually evolves or develops as you explore your topic during pre-writing: Do not expect to be able to sit down and simply write one. As you prewrite, you may discover a new focus or a more interesting way to approach your topic. (For more on prewriting, see Chapter 4.) Expect to write several versions of a thesis statement before you find one that works. For some topics, you may need to do some reading or research to get more information about your topic or tentative thesis. Your thesis may change, too, as you organize supporting evidence and draft and revise your essay. (For more on library and Internet research, see Chapter 19.)

Coming Up with a Working Thesis Statement

To come up with a preliminary or working thesis for your paper, reread your prewriting, and highlight details that have to do with the same subtopic. Write a word or phrase that describes each group of related ideas.

For example, a student working on the topic of intelligence in dogs noticed in her brainstormed list that the details she highlighted could be grouped into two general categories—details about learning and details about instinct. Here is how she arranged her ideas.

Learning
> *follow commands*
>
> *perform new tricks*
>
> *read master's emotions*
>
> *adapt to new owners*
>
> *get housebroken*
>
> *serve as guide dogs for blind people*
>
> *roll up clothing to carry it more easily*
>
> *carry empty water dish to owner*

Instinct
> *females deliver and care for puppies*
>
> *avoid danger and predators*
>
> *seek shelter*
>
> *automatically raise hair on back in response to aggression*

When you've grouped similar details together, the next step is to decide which group or groups of ideas best represent the focus your paper should take. In some instances, one group of details will be enough to develop a working thesis for your paper. At other times, you'll need to use the details in two or three groups. The student working on a thesis for the topic of intelligence in dogs evaluated her groups of details and decided that instinct was unrelated to her topic. Consequently, she decided to write about learning.

If you are not satisfied with how you have grouped or arranged your details, you probably don't have enough details to come up with a good working thesis. If you need more details, prewrite to generate more. Be sure to try a different prewriting strategy than the one you used previously. A new strategy may help you see your narrowed topic from a different perspective. If your second prewriting does not produce better results, consider refocusing or changing your topic.

Essay in Progress 1

If you used a prewriting strategy to generate details about your topic in response to Essay in Progress 3 in Chapter 4 (p. 101), review your prewriting, highlight useful ideas, and identify several sets of related details among those you highlight.

Writing an Effective Thesis Statement

Use the following guidelines to write an effective thesis statement or to evaluate and revise your working thesis.

1. **Make an assertion.** An **assertion**, unlike a fact, takes a position, expresses a viewpoint, or suggests your approach to the topic.

LACKS AN ASSERTION	Hollywood movies, like *127 Hours* and *The King's Speech*, are frequently based on true stories.
REVISED	Hollywood movies, like *127 Hours* and *The King's Speech*, manipulate true stories to cater to the tastes of the audience.

2. **Be specific.** Try to provide as much information as possible about your main point.

TOO GENERAL	I learned a great deal from my experiences as a teenage parent.
REVISED	From my experiences as a teenage parent, I learned to accept responsibility for my own life and for that of my son.

3. **Focus on one central point.** Limit your essay to one major idea.

FOCUSES ON SEVERAL POINTS	This college should improve its tutoring services, sponsor more activities of interest to Latino students, and speed up the registration process for students.
REVISED	To better represent the student population it serves, this college should sponsor more activities of interest to Latino students.

4. **Offer an original perspective on your topic.** If your thesis seems dull or ordinary, it probably needs more work. Search your prewriting for an interesting angle on your topic.

TOO ORDINARY	Many traffic accidents are a result of carelessness.
REVISED	When a driver has an accident, it can change his or her entire approach to driving.

5. **Avoid making an announcement.** Don't use phrases such as "This essay will discuss" or "The subject of my paper is." Instead, state your main point directly.

MAKES AN ANNOUNCEMENT	The point I am trying to make is that people should not be allowed to smoke on campus.
REVISED	The college should prohibit smoking on campus.

6. **Use your thesis to preview the organization of the essay.** Consider mentioning the two or three key concepts on which your essay will focus, in the order in which you will discuss them.

Exercise 5.1

Working in a group of two or three students, discuss what is wrong with each of the following thesis statements. Then revise each thesis to make it more effective.

1. In this paper, I will discuss the causes of asthma, which include exposure to smoke, chemicals, and allergic reactions.
2. Jogging is an enjoyable aerobic sport.
3. The crime rate is decreasing in American cities.
4. Living in an apartment has many advantages.
5. Children's toys can be dangerous, instructional, or creative.

Essay in Progress 2

Keeping your audience in mind, select one or more of the groups of ideas you identified in Essay in Progress 1 and write a working thesis statement based on those ideas.

Placing the Thesis Statement

Your thesis statement can appear anywhere in your essay, but it is usually best to place it in the first paragraph as part of your introduction. When your thesis appears at the beginning of the essay, your readers will know what to pay attention to and what to expect in the rest of the essay. When your thesis is placed later in the essay, you need to build up to the thesis gradually in order to prepare readers for it.

Using an Implied Thesis

In some professional writing, especially in narrative or descriptive essays, the writer may not state the thesis directly. Instead, the thesis may be strongly implied by the details the writer chooses and the way those details are organized. Although professional writers may use an **implied thesis**, academic writers—including professors and students—generally state their thesis. You should always include a clear statement of your thesis for your college papers.

Supporting Your Thesis Statement with Evidence

After you have written a working thesis statement, the next step is to develop evidence that supports your thesis. **Evidence** is any type of information, such as examples, statistics, or expert opinion, that will convince your reader that your thesis is reasonable or correct. This evidence, organized into well-developed paragraphs, makes up the body of your essay. To visualize the basic structure of an essay, look at Figure 6.1 on page 116.

Choosing Types of Evidence

Although there are many types of evidence, it is usually best not to use them all. Analyze your purpose, audience, and thesis to determine which types of evidence will be most effective. If your audience is unfamiliar with your topic, provide definitions, historical background, an explanation of a process, and factual and descriptive details. To persuade, use comparison and contrast, advantages and disadvantages, examples, problems, statistics, and quotations to make your argument. Table 5.1 (pp. 110–11) lists various types of evidence and gives examples of how each type could be used to support a working thesis on acupuncture. Note that many of the types of evidence correspond to the patterns of development discussed in Part 2 of this text.

Exercise 5.2

1. Working in a group of two to three students, discuss and list the types of evidence that could be used to support the following thesis statement for an informative essay.

   The pressure to become financially independent is a challenge for many young adults and often causes them to develop social and emotional problems.

2. For each audience listed here, discuss and record the types of evidence that would offer the best support for the preceding thesis.

   a. Young adults   c. Counselors of young adults
   b. Parents of young adults

Table 5.1   Types of Evidence Used to Support a Thesis

Working Thesis	Acupuncture, a form of alternative medicine, is becoming more widely accepted in the United States.
Types of Evidence	**Example**
Definitions	Explain that in acupuncture, needles are inserted into specific points of the body to control pain or relieve symptoms.
Historical background	Explain that acupuncture is a medical treatment that originated in ancient China.
Explanation of a process	Explain the principles on which acupuncture is based and how scientists think it works.
Factual details	Explain who uses acupuncture, on what parts of the body it is used, and under what circumstances it is applied.
Descriptive details	Explain what acupuncture needles look and feel like.
Narrative story	Relate a personal experience that illustrates the use of acupuncture.
Causes or effects	Discuss one or two theories that explain why acupuncture works. Offer reasons for its increasing popularity.
Classification	Explain types of acupuncture treatments.
Comparison and contrast	Compare acupuncture with other forms of alternative medicine, such as massage and herbal medicines. Explain how acupuncture differs from these other treatments.
Advantages and disadvantages	Describe the pros (nonsurgical, relatively painless) and cons (fear of needles) of acupuncture.
Examples	Describe situations in which acupuncture has been used successfully—for dental procedures, for treating alcoholism, for pain control.

Table 5.1   (continued)

Types of Evidence	Example
Problems	Explain that acupuncture is not always practiced by medical doctors; licensing and oversight of acupuncturists may thus be lax.
Statistics	Indicate how many acupuncturists practice in the United States.
Quotations	Quote medical experts who attest to the effectiveness of acupuncture as well as those who question its value.

Collecting Evidence to Support Your Thesis

Prewriting may help you collect evidence for your thesis. But try a different pre-writing strategy from the one you used to arrive at your working thesis statement. Consider using a strategy from the following list.

1. **Visualize yourself speaking to your audience.** What would you say to convince your audience of your thesis? Jot down ideas as they come to you.

2. **Develop a skeletal outline of major headings with plenty of blank space under each.** Fill in ideas about each heading as they come to you. (For more on outlining, see p. 121 in Chapter 6.)

3. **Draw a graphic organizer of your essay, filling in supporting evidence as you think of it.** (For more on drawing a graphic organizer, see p. 40 in Chapter 2.)

4. **Discuss your thesis statement with a classmate; try to explain why he or she should accept your thesis as valid.**

A worksheet to help you collect evidence and online templates for graphic organizers can be found at bedfordstmartins.com/reflections.

Essay in Progress 3

Using the preceding list of suggestions, generate at least three different types of evidence to support the working thesis statement you wrote in Essay in Progress 2.

Choosing the Best Evidence

In collecting evidence in support of a thesis, you will probably generate more than you need. Consequently, you will need to identify the evidence that best supports your thesis and that suits your purpose and audience. The following guidelines will help you select that evidence.

1. **Make sure the evidence is relevant.** All your evidence must clearly and directly support your thesis. Irrelevant evidence will distract readers and cause them to question the validity of your thesis.

2. **Provide specific evidence.** Avoid general statements that will neither engage your readers nor help you make a convincing case for your thesis. To locate detailed, specific evidence, return to your prewriting or use a different prewriting strategy to generate concrete evidence. You may also need to conduct research to find evidence for your thesis.

3. **Offer a variety of evidence.** Using diverse kinds of evidence increases the likelihood that your evidence will convince your readers. It also shows readers that you are knowledgeable and informed about your topic, thus enhancing your credibility.

4. **Provide a sufficient amount of evidence.** The amount of evidence you need will vary according to your audience and your topic. To discover whether you have provided enough evidence, ask a classmate to read your essay and tell you whether he or she is convinced. If your reader is not convinced, ask him or her what additional evidence is needed.

5. **Provide representative evidence.** Be sure the evidence you supply is typical and usual. Do not choose unusual, rare, or exceptional situations as evidence.

6. **Provide accurate evidence.** Gather your information from reliable sources. Do not guess at statistics or make estimates. If you are not certain of the accuracy of a fact or statistic, verify it through research.

Choosing Evidence for Academic Writing

For most kinds of academic writing, certain types of evidence are preferred over others. In general, your personal experiences and opinions are not considered as useful as more objective evidence, such as facts, statistics, historical background, and research evidence. Suppose you are writing an academic paper on the effects of global warming. Your own observations about climate changes in your city would not be considered adequate or appropriate evidence to support the idea of climatic change as an effect of global warming. Instead, you would need to provide facts, statistics, and research evidence on climatic change in a wide range of geographic areas and demonstrate their relationship to global warming.

Essay in Progress 4

Evaluate the evidence you generated in Essay in Progress 3. Select from it the evidence that you could use to support your thesis in a two- to four-page essay.

Using Sources to Support Your Thesis

For many topics, you will need to research library or Internet sources or interview an expert to collect enough supporting evidence for your thesis. Chapter 19 provides a thorough guide to locating sources in the library and on the Internet and how to cite them in your paper.

Essay in Progress 5

Locate and consult at least two sources to find evidence that supports the working thesis statement you wrote in Essay in Progress 2.

Students Write

In the Students Write section of Chapter 4, you saw how student writer Christine Lee narrowed her topic and generated ideas for her essay on a contemporary trend or fad. You also saw how she decided to focus on reality TV.

After reviewing her responses to questions about her topic and her freewriting, Lee decided that reality TV had become less tasteful and less interesting. She then wrote the following working thesis statement.

> As the trend in competition reality TV wears on, shows are becoming both less interesting and less tasteful.

To generate more details to support her thesis, Lee did more freewriting and brainstorming to help her recall details from shows. The following is an excerpt from what she wrote.

- Early shows: Cops and Candid Camera
- MTV's Real World was first recent reality show to become popular.
- The original Survivor was smart and interesting.
- Big Brother just locked people up together and forced us to watch them bicker.
- The Survivor series continues to be popular, while copycats like Fear Factor get more graphic and unwatchable.
- People will tire of Fear Factor quickly because there is no plot to follow from one episode to the next and watching people eat worms and hold their breath underwater gets boring.

- *Reality TV was popular because it was something different, but now there are dozens of these shows each season and few worth watching.*
- *Shows such as American Idol, America's Got Talent, and America's Next Top Model are a revival of earlier types of TV shows—the talent show and the beauty contest.*
- *Shows like Top Chef and Project Runway focused on special interests.*
- *Celebrity reality shows focusing on real people in weird situations were the next wave.*

Chapter 6

Drafting an Essay

Quick Start: The photograph above shows a college composting program—one example of the many "green initiatives" being tried out at colleges around the country.

Working alone or with two or three classmates, write a sentence that states your opinion on how important (or not) these initiatives are and how likely they are to succeed. Then support this opinion with a list of details (evidence) from the photograph and from your own knowledge of green initiatives, at colleges or elsewhere. Number your best evidence 1, your second-best evidence 2, and so on. Cross out any details that do not support your opinion, or adjust the sentence if the evidence you gathered disagrees with it. Finally, write a paragraph that begins with the sentence you wrote and includes your evidence, in order of importance.

The paragraph you wrote for the Quick Start prompt could be part of an essay on how colleges are making campuses environmentally sustainable. To write an essay you would need to do additional prewriting and research on this topic. Then you would write a thesis statement, develop supporting paragraphs, write an effective introduction and conclusion, and choose a good title. This chapter will guide you through developing an essay in support of a thesis statement, yet another part of the writing process (see Figure 4.1, pp. 86–87).

The Structure of an Essay

Think of an essay as a complete piece of writing, much as a textbook chapter is. For example, a textbook chapter might have the title "Human Rights in Developing Countries," which gives you a clear idea of the chapter's subject. The first few paragraphs would probably introduce and define the concept of human rights. The chapter might then assert that human rights is an important global issue, particularly in developing countries. The rest of the chapter might explain the issue by tracing its history, examining why it is a world issue, and discussing its status in developing countries today. The chapter would conclude with a summary.

Figure 6.1   The Structure of an Essay: Parts and Functions

| Title | May announce your subject |
| | Sparks readers' interest |

Introduction	**Paragraph 1** (or introduction can be two or more paragraphs)
	Identifies your narrowed topic
	Presents your thesis
	Interests your readers
	Provides background

| Body | **Body paragraphs*** |
| | Support and explain your thesis |

Conclusion	**Final paragraph**
	Reemphasizes your thesis (does *not* merely restate it)
	Draws your essay to a close

*There is no set number of paragraphs that an essay should contain. The number depends on your narrowed topic, purpose, and audience.

Similarly, as you see in Figure 6.1, an essay has a title and an introduction. It also makes an assertion (the thesis statement) that is explained and supported throughout the body of the essay. The essay ends with a final statement, its conclusion.

Organizing Your Supporting Details

The body paragraphs of your essay support your thesis. Before you begin writing these paragraphs, decide on the supporting evidence you will use and the order in which you will present it. (For more on developing a thesis and selecting evidence to support it, see Chapter 5.)

Selecting a Method of Organization

The three common ways to organize ideas are most-to-least (or least-to-most) order, chronological order, and spatial order.

MOST-TO-LEAST (OR LEAST-TO-MOST) ORDER

If you choose the **most-to-least** or the **least-to-most** method of organizing an essay, arrange your supporting details from most to least — or least to most — important, familiar, or interesting. You might begin with your most convincing evidence or, alternatively, you might build up to your strongest point. You can visualize these two options in Figure 6.2.

Figure 6.2   Essay Organization: Most-to-Least and Least-to-Most Order

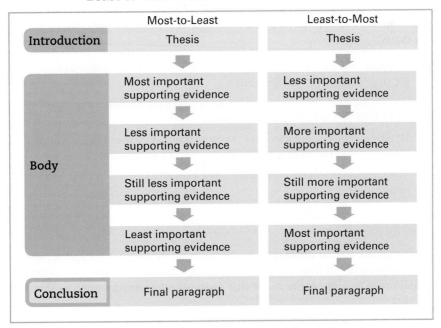

Exercise 6.1

For each of the following narrowed topics, identify several qualities or characteristics that you could use to organize details in most-to-least or least-to-most order.

1. Stores in which you shop
2. Friends
3. Members of a sports team
4. Fast-food restaurants
5. Television shows you watched this week

CHRONOLOGICAL ORDER

When you put your supporting details in the sequence in which they happened, you are using **chronological order**. For this method of organization, begin the body of your essay with the first event, and progress through the others as they occurred or should occur, whether the time increment is in minutes, days, or years. Chronological order is commonly used in narrative essays and in process analyses. You can visualize this order with the help of Figure 6.3.

Exercise 6.2

Working alone or with a classmate, identify at least one thesis statement from those listed below that could be supported by chronological paragraphs. Write a few sentences explaining how you would use chronological order to support this thesis.

1. European mealtimes differ from those of many American visitors, much to the visitors' surprise and discomfort.
2. Despite the many pitfalls that await those who shop at auctions, people can find bargains if they prepare in advance.
3. My first day of kindergarten was the most traumatic experience of my childhood, one that permanently shaped my view of education.
4. Learning how to drive a car increases a teenager's freedom and responsibility.

SPATIAL ORDER

When you use **spatial order**, you organize details about your subject according to its location or position in space. Consider, for example, how you might use spatial order to support the thesis that movie theaters are designed to shut out

Figure 6.3 Essay Organization: Chronological Order

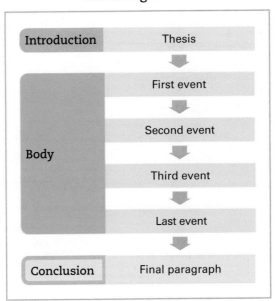

the outside world and create a separate reality within. You could begin by describing the ticket booth, then the lobby, and finally the individual theaters. Similarly, you might describe a basketball court from midcourt to backboard or a person from head to toe. Spatial organization is commonly used in descriptive essays as well as in classification and division essays.

You can best visualize spatial organization by picturing your subject in your mind or by sketching it on paper. "Look" at your subject systematically—from top to bottom, inside to outside, front to back. Cut it into imaginary sections or pieces and describe each one. Figure 6.4 (p. 120) shows two possible options for visualizing an essay that uses spatial order.

Exercise 6.3

Working alone or with a classmate, identify at least one thesis statement listed below that could be supported by means of spatial organization. Write a few sentences explaining how you would use spatial order to support this thesis.

1. Our family's yearly vacation provides us with a much-needed opportunity to renew family ties.

2. My favorite place to escape to is _____ because it _____.

Figure 6.4   Essay Organization: Two Ways to Use Spatial Order

Introduction	Thesis	Thesis
	⬇	⬇
	Far left section	
	⬇	Top part
	Left section	⬇
Body	⬇	Middle part
	Right section	⬇
	⬇	Bottom part
	Far right section	
	⬇	⬇
Conclusion	Final paragraph	Final paragraph

3. The most interesting architectural space on campus is _____.

4. A clear study space can cut down on time-wasting distractions.

Essay in Progress 1

Choose one of the following activities.

1. Using the thesis statement and evidence you gathered for the Essay in Progress activities in Chapter 5, choose a method for organizing your essay. Then explain briefly how you will use that method of organization.

2. Choose one of the following narrowed topics. Then, using the steps in Figure 4.1 (pp. 86–87), prewrite to produce ideas, develop a thesis, and generate evidence to support the thesis. Next, choose a method for organizing your essay and briefly explain how you will use it.

   a. Positive (or negative) experiences with computers

   b. Stricter (or more lenient) regulations for teenage drivers

   c. Factors that account for the popularity of action films

   d. Discipline in public elementary schools

   e. Advantages (or disadvantages) of instant messaging

Preparing an Outline or a Graphic Organizer

After you have written a thesis statement and chosen a method of organization for your essay, take a few minutes to write an outline or draw a graphic organizer of the essay's main points in the order you plan to discuss them. Making an organizational plan is an especially important step when your essay is long or deals with a complex topic.

Outlining or drawing a graphic organizer can help you plan your essay as well as discover new ideas to include. Either method will help you see how ideas fit together and may reveal places where you need to add supporting information.

There are two types of outlines—informal and formal. An **informal outline**, also called a *scratch outline*, uses key words and phrases to list main points and subpoints. An informal outline does not necessarily follow the standard outline format of numbered and lettered headings. Here is an example of one student's informal outline.

Sample Informal Outline

Thesis: Working as a literacy volunteer taught me more about learning and friendship than I ever expected.

Paragraph 1: Learned about the learning process
    Went through staff training program
    Learned about words "in context"

Paragraph 2: Discovered the importance of reading for Marie
    Couldn't take bus, walked to grocery store
    Couldn't buy certain products
    Couldn't write out grocery lists

Paragraph 3: Marie increased her self-confidence
    Made rapid progress
    Began taking bus
    Helped son with reading

Paragraph 4: Developed a permanent friendship
    Saw each other often
    Both single parents
    Helped each other babysit

Conclusion: I benefited more than Marie did.

Formal outlines use Roman numerals (I, II), capital letters (A, B), Arabic numbers (1, 2), and lowercase letters (a, b) to designate levels of importance. There are two categories of formal outline: **Sentence outlines** use complete sentences, and **topic outlines** use only key words and phrases. In a topic or sentence outline, minor entries are indented, as in the sample formal outline below. Each topic or sentence begins with a capital letter. Here is a format showing the beginning of a formal outline.

Format for a Formal Outline

I.   First main topic
 A.   First subtopic of I
 B.   Second subtopic of I
  1.   First detail about I.B
  2.   Second detail about I.B
 C.   Third subtopic of I
  1.   First detail about I.C
   a.   First detail or example about I.C.1
   b.   Second detail or example about I.C.1
  2.   Second detail about I.C

II. Second main topic

Here is a sample outline that a student wrote for an essay for her interpersonal communication class.

Sample Formal Outline

I.   Types of listening
 A.   Participatory
  1.   Involves the listener responding to the speaker
  2.   Has expressive quality
   a.   Maintain eye contact
   b.   Express feelings using facial expressions
 B.   Nonparticipatory
  1.   Involves the listener listening without talking or responding
  2.   Allows speaker to develop his or her thoughts without interruption
 C.   Critical listening
  1.   Involves the listener analyzing and evaluating the message
  2.   Is especially important in college classes
   a.   Listen for instructors' biases
   b.   Evaluate evidence in support of opinions expressed

Remember that all items labeled with the same designation (capital letters, for example) should be at the same level of importance, and each must explain or support the topic or subtopic under which it is placed. Also, all items at the same level should be grammatically parallel.

Not Parallel	I.	Dietary Problems
		A. Consuming too much fat
		B. High refined-sugar consumption

Parallel	I.	Dietary Problems
		A. Consuming too much fat
		B. Consuming too much refined sugar

If your instructor allows, you can use both phrases and sentences within an outline, as long as you do so consistently. You might write all subtopics (designated by capital letters A, B, and so on) as sentences and all supporting details (designated by 1, 2, and so on) as phrases, for instance.

Begin by putting your working thesis statement at the top of a piece of paper or word-processing document. Then list your main points below your thesis. Be sure to leave plenty of space between main points. While you are filling in the details that support one main point, you will often think of details or examples to use in support of a different one. As these details or examples occur to you, jot them down under or next to the appropriate main point of your outline or graphic organizer. (For more about graphic organizers, see Chapter 2, p. 40.)

The graphic organizer shown in Figure 6.5 (p. 124), which was made for the same essay as the informal outline on page 121, follows a chronological method of organization.

Essay in Progress 2

For the topic you chose in Essay in Progress 1, write a brief outline or draw a graphic organizer to show the organizational plan of your essay.

Writing a Draft

Once you have collected your ideas and thought about how to organize them, you are ready to write a first draft. A **draft** is a preliminary or tentative version of your essay. Drafting is a process of putting your ideas into sentence and paragraph form. Drafting is a chance to try out your ideas and see if and how they work together. Expect to write several drafts before you end up with one you are satisfied with. Here are some general suggestions for drafting.

Figure 6.5   Sample Graphic Organizer

Title	"The Value of Volunteering"
Introduction	**Thesis:** Working as a literacy volunteer taught me more about learning and friendship than I ever expected.

Body paragraphs	Learned about the learning process
	Went through staff training program
	Learned about words "in context"
	Discovered the importance of reading for Marie
	Couldn't take bus, walked to grocery store
	Couldn't buy certain products
	Couldn't write out grocery lists
	Marie increased her self-confidence
	Made rapid progress
	Began taking bus
	Helped son with reading
	Developed a permanent friendship
	Saw each other often
	Both single parents
	Helped each other babysit

Conclusion	I benefited more than Marie did.

- **Start by writing or reviewing your thesis statement.** Make sure it is specific and focused. (See Chapter 5 for suggestions on writing a thesis statement.)
- **Work on developing and expressing ideas that explain your thesis.** Use your outline (see pp. 121–22) or your graphic organizer (above) as a guide. Work on ideas that you like best or feel will support your thesis particularly well.
- **Devote one paragraph to each important idea that directly explains your thesis statement.** Refer to Chapter 7 for help with drafting and organizing paragraphs.
- **Think of drafting as a means of experimenting and testing ideas.** Plan on making changes and writing several drafts. As you draft, you may realize

that some ideas do not work. Or you may think of a better way to organize your ideas. Or you may discover new ideas that are better than what you originally started with.

- **Be prepared to change your topic or focus.** Once in a while, you may realize that your topic isn't working or that you should choose a different thesis statement. If your draft isn't working, do not hesitate to start over.
- **Focus on ideas first.** As you draft, first be concerned with expressing your ideas. Once you are satisfied that you have said what you want, then focus on correctness—grammar, spelling, punctuation, and so forth.
- **Allow time between drafts.** You will find that time away from the draft gives you a fresh perspective and allows you to see new ways of working out problems you have identified.
- **Seek help from classmates.** If you think a draft is not working but do not know why, do not hesitate to ask a classmate to read and comment on it (see the section on peer review, Chapter 8, p. 156).

Using Transitions and Repetition to Connect Your Ideas

To show how your ideas are related, be sure to use transitions between sentences and paragraphs as well as repetition of key words and the synonyms and pronouns that refer to them. Use transitions and repetition both within your paragraphs (see Chapter 7, pp. 145–46) and between paragraphs.

Using Transitional Expressions to Connect Ideas

A **transitional expression**—which can be a word, phrase, clause, or sentence—shows the reader how a new sentence or paragraph is connected to the one that precedes it. It may also remind the reader of an idea discussed earlier in the essay.

In the example that follows, the italicized transitional clause connects the two paragraphs by reminding the reader of the main point of the first.

> A compliment is a brief and pleasant way of opening lines of communication and demonstrating goodwill. . . .

> *Although compliments do demonstrate goodwill,* they should be used sparingly; otherwise they may seem contrived. . . .

Especially in lengthy essays (five pages or longer), you may find it helpful to include one or more transitional clauses or sentences that recap what you have said so far and suggest the direction of the essay from that point forward. The following example is from a student essay on the invasion of privacy.

> Thus, the invasion of privacy is not limited to financial and consumer information; invasion of medical and workplace privacy is increasingly common. What can individuals do to protect their privacy in each of these areas?

Thus, at the beginning of the first sentence, signals that the sentence is going to summarize the types of invasion of privacy already discussed in the essay. The second sentence signals that the discussion will shift to the preventive measures that individuals can take.

For a list of commonly used transitions and the connections they suggest, see Table 7.1 on page 147.

Using Repeated Words to Connect Ideas

Repetition of key words or their **synonyms** (words that have similar meanings) from one paragraph to another helps keep your readers focused on the main point of your essay. In the following sentences, the italicized key words focus the readers' attention on the topic of liars and lying.

> There are many types of *liars*, but all put forth *dishonest* or *misleading* information. The occasional *liar* is the most common and *lies* to avoid embarrassing or unpleasant situations.

Writing Your Introduction, Conclusion, and Title

When you write an essay, you don't have to start with the title and introduction and write straight through to the end. Some students prefer to write the body of the essay first and then the introduction and the conclusion. Others prefer to write a tentative introduction as a way of getting started. Some students think of a title before they start writing; others find it easier to add a title when the essay is nearly finished. Regardless of when you write them, the introduction, conclusion, and title are important components of a well-written essay.

Writing a Strong Introduction

Your introduction creates a first, and often lasting, impression. It focuses your readers on your topic and establishes the tone of your essay. Based on your introduction, your readers will form an expectation of what the essay will be about and the approach it will take. Because the introduction is crucial, take the time to get it right.

Two sample introductions to student essays follow. Although they are written on the same topic, notice how each creates an entirely different impression and set of expectations.

Introduction 1

Sexual harassment has received a great deal of attention in recent years. From the highest offices of government to factories in small towns, sexual harassment cases have been tried in court and publicized on national television for all Americans to witness. This focus on sexual harassment has been, in and of itself, a good and necessary thing. However, when a first-grade boy makes national headlines because he kissed a little girl of the same age and is accused of "sexual harassment," the American public needs to take a serious look at the definition of sexual harassment.

Introduction 2

Sexual harassment in the workplace seems to happen with alarming frequency. As a woman who works part-time in a male-dominated office, I have witnessed at least six incidents of sexual harassment aimed at me and my female colleagues on various occasions during the past three months alone. For example, in one incident, a male coworker repeatedly made kissing sounds whenever I passed his desk, even after I explained that his actions made me uncomfortable. A female coworker was invited to dinner several times by her male supervisor; each time she refused. The last time she refused, he made a veiled threat, "You obviously aren't happy working with me. Perhaps a transfer is in order." These incidents were not isolated, did not happen to only one woman, and were initiated by more than one man. My colleagues and I are not the only victims. Sexual harassment is on the rise and will continue to increase unless women speak out against it loudly and to a receptive audience.

In introduction 1, the writer focuses on the definition of sexual harassment. Introduction 2 has an entirely different emphasis—the frequency of incidents of sexual harassment. Each introductory paragraph reveals a different tone as well. Introduction 1 suggests a sense of mild disbelief, whereas introduction 2 suggests anger and outrage. From introduction 1, you expect the writer to examine definitions of sexual harassment and, perhaps, suggest his or her own definition. From introduction 2, you expect the writer to present additional cases of sexual harassment and suggest ways women can speak out against it.

In addition to establishing a focus and tone, your introduction should

- present your thesis statement,
- interest your reader, and
- provide any background information your reader may need.

Introductions are often difficult to write. If you have trouble, write a tentative introductory paragraph and return to it later. Once you have written the body of your essay, you may find it easier to complete the introduction. In fact, as you work out your ideas in the body of the essay, you may think of a better way to introduce them in the opening.

TIPS FOR WRITING A STRONG INTRODUCTION

The following suggestions for writing a strong introduction will help you capture your readers' interest.

1. **Ask a provocative or disturbing question.** Also consider posing a series of short, related questions that will direct your readers' attention to the key points in your essay.

> Should health insurance companies pay for more than one stay in a drug rehabilitation center? Should insurance continue to pay for rehab services when patients consistently put themselves back in danger by using drugs again?

2. **Begin with a story or an anecdote.** Choose one that will appeal to your audience and is relevant to your thesis.

3. **Offer a quotation.** The quotation should illustrate or emphasize your thesis.

4. **Cite a little-known or shocking fact or statistic.**

5. **Move from general to specific.** Begin with the category or general subject area to which your topic belongs, and narrow it to arrive at your thesis.

6. **State a commonly held misconception or a position that you oppose.** Your thesis would then correct the misconception or state your position on the issue.

7. **Describe a hypothetical situation.** This should be a situation the reader can put him- or herself into that relates to your topic.

8. **Begin with a striking example.** Your example should draw readers in with a surprising fact or an interesting anecdote that connects to your topic.

9. **Make a comparison.** Compare your topic with one that is familiar or of special interest to your readers.

MISTAKES TO AVOID

The following advice will help you avoid the most common mistakes students make in writing introductions.

1. **Do not make an announcement.** Avoid opening comments such as "I am writing to explain" or "This essay will discuss."

2. **Keep your introduction short.** An introduction that goes beyond two paragraphs will probably sound long-winded and make your readers impatient.

3. **Avoid statements that may discourage your readers from continuing.** Statements such as "This process may seem complicated, but . . ." may make your readers apprehensive.

4. **Avoid a casual, an overly familiar, or a chatty tone.** Openings such as "Whoa, did it surprise me when" or "You'll never in a million years believe what happened" are not appropriate.

5. **Be sure your topic is clear or explained adequately for your readers.** Do not begin an essay by stating, for example, "I oppose Proposition 413 and urge you to vote against it." Before stating your position on your topic, you need to explain to readers what that legislation is and what it proposes.

Writing an Effective Conclusion

Your essay should not end abruptly with your last supporting paragraph. Instead, it should end with a conclusion—a separate paragraph that reiterates (without directly restating) the importance of your thesis and that brings your essay to a satisfying close.

TIPS FOR WRITING AN EFFECTIVE CONCLUSION

For most essays, your conclusion should summarize your main points and re-affirm your thesis. For many essays, however, you might supplement this information and make your conclusion more memorable and forceful by using one of the following suggestions.

1. **Look ahead.** Take your readers beyond the scope and time frame of your essay.

2. **Remind readers of the relevance of the issue.** Suggest why your thesis is important.

3. **Offer a recommendation or make a call to action.** Urge your readers to take specific steps that follow logically from your thesis.

4. **Discuss broader implications.** Point to larger issues not fully addressed in the essay, but do not introduce a completely new issue.

5. **Conclude with a fact, a quotation, an anecdote, or an example that emphasizes your thesis.** These endings will bring a sense of closure and realism to your essay.

MISTAKES TO AVOID

The following advice will help you avoid common mistakes writers make in their conclusions.

1. **Avoid a direct restatement of your thesis.** An exact repetition of your thesis will make your essay seem dull and mechanical.

2. **Avoid standard phrases.** Don't use phrases such as "To sum up," "In conclusion," or "It can be seen, then." They are routine and tiresome.

3. **Avoid introducing new points in your conclusion.** All major points should have been discussed in the body of your essay.

4. **Avoid apologizing for yourself, your work, or your ideas.** Do not say, for example, "Although I am only twenty-one, it seems to me."

5. **Avoid weakening your stance in the conclusion.** If, for instance, your essay has criticized someone's behavior, do not back down by saying, "After all, she's only human."

Writing a Good Title

The title of your essay should suggest your topic and spark your readers' interest. Depending on the purpose, intended audience, and tone of your essay, your title may be direct and informative, witty, or intriguing. The following suggestions will help you write effective titles.

1. **Write straightforward, descriptive titles for most academic essays.**

   Lotteries: A Game Players Can Little Afford

2. **Ask a question that your essay answers.**

   Who Plays the Lottery?

3. **Use alliteration.** Repeating initial sounds, or *alliteration*, often produces a catchy title.

   Lotteries: Dreaming about Dollars

4. **Consider using a play on words or a catchy or humorous expression.** This technique may work well for less formal essays.

   If You Win, You Lose

5. **Avoid broad, vague titles that sound like labels.** Titles such as "Baseball Fans" or "Gun Control" provide your reader with too little information.

Exercise 6.4

For each of the following essays, suggest a title. Try to use each of the above suggestions at least once.

1. An essay explaining the legal rights of tenants

2. An essay opposing human cloning

3. An essay on causes and effects of road rage

4. An essay comparing fitness routines

5. An essay explaining how to choose a primary-care physician

Essay in Progress 3

Using the outline or graphic organizer you created in Essay in Progress 2, write a first draft of your essay.

Students Write

The first draft of a narrative essay by student writer Christine Lee follows. Lee used her freewriting (see Chapter 4, pp. 102–3) and her working thesis (see Chapter 5, p. 113) as the basis for her draft, adding details after more brainstorming (see Chapter 5, pp. 113–14). Because she was writing a first draft, Lee did not worry about correcting the errors in grammar, punctuation, and mechanics. (You will see her revised draft in Chapter 8.)

First Draft

The Reality of Real TV

Do you remember life before reality TV? One look at a *TV Guide* today   1
shows an overload of reality-based programming, even with the guaranteed failure of most of these shows. Before reality TV there was mostly situational comedies and serial dramas. When *Survivor* caught every viewer's attention, every network in American believed they must also become "real" to keep up its ratings. Shows that followed it were less interesting and less tasteful in the hopes of finding a show as original, inventive, and engaging as the first *Survivor*.

When *Survivor* began in the summer of 2000, there was nothing else   2
like it on TV. *Survivor* had real people in a contest in an exotic location. It had different kinds of players. There was a certain fascination in watching these players struggle week after week for food and shelter but the million dollar prize kept viewers tuning in week after week. Viewers wanted to find out who was going to win and who was getting "voted off the island." The last contestant on the island wins. Players developed a sense of teamwork and camaraderie, as they schemed and plotted. And we as an audience were allowed to watch every minute of it.

Reality shows that followed *Survivor* didn't have the interesting elements   3
that it had. *Big Brother* started as the first of the reality TV spin-offs but audiences didn't have the same things to respond to. It has never been a

success because they took the basic concept of *Survivor* and added nothing new or interesting to it. *Big Brother* locked a bunch of people up together in a house and forced the audience to watch them bicker over nothing. Viewers were forced to watch bored contestants bicker and fight, locked up in a house with nothing else to do. It didn't seem the kind of competition that *Survivor* was, even though there was a cash prize on the line. The cash prize wasn't large enough anyways. We didn't choose favorites because the players weren't up against anything, except fighting off weeks of boredom. *Big Brother* introduced audience participation with the television audience voting off members, which actually only gave the house members less to do and less motive to scheme and plot their allegiances like the castaways on *Survivor*. Voting members off was an arbitrary and meaningless process. But *Big Brother* had the prize component, and it took away the housemates' access to the outside world.

Although nothing seems to capture ratings like the original *Survivor*, networks have continued to use sensational gimmicks to appeal to the audience's basic instincts. Nothing good was carried over from *Survivor*, and the new shows just had extreme situations. *Fear Factor* had contestants commit all sorts of gross and terrifying things like eating worms. Most viewers are disgusted by this.   4

When these gimmicks did not retain viewers, they turned back to two traditional types of reality TV and put modern twists on them: the talent show and the beauty contest. So were born shows like *American Idol*, *America's Got Talent* and *America's Next Top Model*. Again, there was no built in drama like in *Survivor* so they tried to create drama with the colorful judges and supportive fans. At first, the shows were exciting with the singing and the beauty, but after a while, audiences lost interest. Even showing the long lines that contestants had to wait in, and footage of those who did not make the cut did not help to keep viewers hooked on these types of reality shows. Viewers could only stomach so much loud singing and mascara.   5

The next round of shows had to do with special interests like cooking and shows like *Hell's Kitchen* and *Top Chef*. There were also dance shows like *So You Think You Can Dance* and *Dancing with the Stars*. *The Biggest Loser* was a weight loss competition. *Project Runway* was a fashion designer competition. *The Apprentice* was about business and *Shear Genius* was about hair stylists. These shows appealed to only small numbers of people and had manufactured and contrived situations for the contestants to act in.   6

Recently reality shows are about everyday lives or celebrities. *The Real World* was the first kind, following young adults as they drank and slept around. *The Simple Life* was a celebrity show with Paris Hilton and Nicole Richie. Soon it seemed every celebrity had a reality show—Ozzy Osbourne, Paula   7

Abdul, Tori Spelling, Bret Michaels, and more. The next wave of shows was people in weird situations like *Jon & Kate Plus Eight*. These programs showed people at their worst. Networks had to try hard to find new and different scenarios to show since these shows are getting more tasteless.

Since *Survivor*, reality shows have gone from terror and violence to talent and beauty to special interest shows and last to shows following real people. It's the viewers who decide what is popular. Reality shows continue to be popular even though they're getting more tasteless and contrived-looking. I hope viewers get tired of all these cheap gimmicks and call for more entertaining programming.

8

Analyzing the Writer's Technique

1. Evaluate Lee's title and introduction. Which tip for writing a strong conclusion did Lee use?

2. Evaluate Lee's thesis statement. Is it clear? How could it be improved?

3. Does Lee provide adequate details for her essay? If not, what additional information might she include?

4. How does Lee organize her ideas? Is her organization clear and effective?

5. Evaluate her supporting paragraphs. Which paragraphs need more detail? Identify where Lee uses transitional expressions and repetition.

6. Evaluate the conclusion. How does it draw the essay to a close?

Chapter 7

Writing Effective Paragraphs

Quick Start: Study the photograph above. At what kind of event does it seem to have been taken? Write a sentence that states the main point of the photograph. Then write several more sentences explaining what is happening in the photograph. Describe what details in the photo enabled you to identify the event.

In much the same way as a photograph does, a paragraph makes an overall impression, or main point, and includes details that support this main point. In a paragraph, the topic sentence states the main idea and the remainder of the sentences provide the details that support it. The topic sentence is often the first sentence in a paragraph; however, it may instead follow a transition sentence or may come at the end of the paragraph.

The Structure of a Paragraph

A paragraph is a group of connected sentences that develop an idea about a topic. Each paragraph in your essay should support your thesis and contribute to the overall meaning and effectiveness of your essay. A well-developed paragraph contains

- a well-focused topic sentence;
- unified, specific supporting details (definitions, examples, explanations, or other evidence);
- transitions and repetition that show how the ideas are related.

Here is a sample paragraph with its parts labeled.

Topic sentence

Audiences gather with varying degrees of willingness to hear a speaker. Some are anxious to hear the speaker, and may even have paid a substantial admission price. The "lecture circuit,"

Details and transitions

for example, is a most lucrative aspect of public life. But whereas some audiences are willing to pay to hear a speaker, others don't seem to care one way or the other. Other audiences need to be persuaded to listen (or at least to sit in the audience). Still other audiences gather because they have to. For example, negotiations on a union contract may require members to attend meetings where officers give speeches.

—DeVito, *The Essential Elements of Public Speaking*

In addition to the well-focused topic sentence, specific supporting details, and helpful transitions, notice how the writer repeats the words *audience(s)* and *speaker*, along with the synonyms *lecture* and *speeches*, to help tie the paragraph to the idea in the topic sentence.

For a paragraph to develop a single idea, it needs to have unity. A unified paragraph stays focused on one idea, without switching or wandering from topic

Figure 7.1   The Structure of a Paragraph

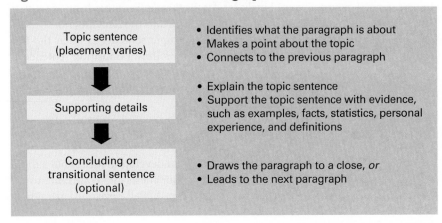

to topic. A paragraph also should be of a reasonable length, neither too short nor too long. Short paragraphs look skimpy and are often underdeveloped; long paragraphs are difficult for readers to follow.

To visualize the structure of a well-developed paragraph, see Figure 7.1 above.

Writing a Topic Sentence

A topic sentence is to a paragraph what a thesis statement is to an essay. Just as a thesis announces the main point of an essay, a topic sentence states the main point of a paragraph. In addition, each paragraph's topic sentence must support the thesis of the essay. A topic sentence has several specific functions.

A Topic Sentence Should Focus the Paragraph

A topic sentence should make clear what the paragraph is about (its topic) and express a view or make a point about the topic.

The topic sentence should tell readers what the paragraph is about in specific and detailed language. Avoid vague or general statements. Compare these examples of unfocused and focused topic sentences.

UNFOCUSED   Some members of minority groups do not approve of affirmative action.

FOCUSED   Some members of minority groups disapprove of affirmative action because it implies that they are not capable of obtaining employment based on their own accomplishments.

If you have trouble focusing your topic sentences, review the guidelines for writing an effective thesis statement—many of which also apply to writing effective topic sentences—in Chapter 5 (pp. 107–8).

A Topic Sentence May Preview the Organization of the Paragraph

A topic sentence may suggest the order in which details are discussed in the paragraph, thereby helping readers know what to expect.

first detail

Teaching employees how to handle conflicts through anger management

second detail

and mediation is essential in high-stress jobs.

Readers can expect anger management to be discussed first, followed by a discussion of mediation.

Exercise 7.1

Revise each topic sentence to make it focused and specific. At least two of your revised topic sentences should also preview the organization of the paragraph.

1. In society today, there is always a new fad or fashion in clothing.
2. People watch television talk shows because they find them irresistible.
3. Body piercing is a popular trend.
4. Procrastinating can have a negative effect on your success in college.
5. In our state, the lottery is a big issue.

A Topic Sentence Should Support Your Thesis

Each topic sentence must in some way explain the thesis or show why the thesis is believable or correct. This sample thesis, for example, could be supported by the topic sentences that follow it.

THESIS   Adoption files should not be made available to adult children who are seeking their biological parents.

Topic Sentences

Research has shown that not all biological parents want to meet with the sons or daughters they gave up many years before.

Adult adoptees who try to contact their biological parents often meet resistance and even hostility, which can cause them to feel hurt and rejected.

Both topic sentences support the thesis because they offer valid reasons for keeping adoption files closed.

Exercise 7.2

For each of the following thesis statements, identify the topic sentence in the list below that does not support it.

1. To make a marriage work, a couple must build trust, communication, and understanding.
   a. Knowing why a spouse behaves as he or she does can improve a relationship.
   b. People get married for reasons other than love.
   c. The ability to talk about feelings, problems, likes, and dislikes should grow as a marriage develops.
   d. Marital partners must rely on each other to make sensible decisions that benefit both of them.
2. Internet sales are capturing a larger market share relative to in-store sales.
   a. Internet retailers that target a specific audience tend to be most successful.
   b. The convenience of ordering any time of day or night accounts, in part, for increased Internet sales.
   c. Many customers use Paypal for online purchases.
   d. Web sites that locate and compare prices for a specified item make comparison shopping easier on the Internet than in retail stores.

A Topic Sentence Should Be Strategically Placed

Where you place the topic sentence will determine the order and structure of the rest of the paragraph. The topic sentence also may have different effects, depending on its placement.

TOPIC SENTENCE FIRST

The most common, and often the best, position for a topic sentence is at the beginning of the paragraph. A paragraph that opens with the topic sentence should follow a logical sequence: You state your main point, and then you explain it. The topic sentence tells readers what to expect in the rest of the paragraph, making it clear and easy for them to follow.

Topic sentence	Advertising is first and foremost based on the principle of visibility—the customer must notice the product. Manufacturers often package products in glitzy, even garish, containers to grab the consumer's
Explanatory details	attention. For example, one candy company always packages its candy in reflective wrappers. When the hurried and hungry consumer glances at the candy counter, the reflective wrappers are easy to spot. It is only natural for the impatient customer to grab the candy and go.

TOPIC SENTENCE EARLY IN THE PARAGRAPH

When one or two sentences at the beginning of a paragraph are needed to smooth the transition from one paragraph to the next, the topic sentence may follow these transitional sentences.

Transitional sentence	However, visibility is not the only principle in advertising; it is simply the first. A second and perhaps more subtle principle is identity: The manufacturer attempts to lure the consumer into
Topic sentence	buying a product by linking it to a concept with which the consumer can identify. For instance, Boundaries perfume is advertised on television as the choice of "independent" women. Since independent women are admired in our culture, women identify with the concept and therefore are attracted to the perfume. Once the consumer identifies with the product, a sale is more likely to occur.

TOPIC SENTENCE LAST

The topic sentence can also appear last in a paragraph. With this strategy, you first present the supporting details and then end the paragraph with the topic sentence, which usually states the conclusion that can be drawn from the details. Common in argumentative writing, this arrangement allows you to present convincing evidence before stating your point about the issue.

Evidence

The saying "Guns don't kill people; people kill people" always makes me even more certain of my own position on gun control. That statement is deceptive in the same way that the statement "Heroin doesn't kill people; people kill themselves" is deceptive. Naturally, people need to pull the trigger of a gun to make the gun kill other people, just as it is necessary for a person to ingest heroin for it to kill him or her. However, these facts do not excuse us from the responsibility of keeping guns (or heroin) out of people's hands as much as possible. People cannot shoot people unless they have a gun. This fact alone should persuade the government to institute stiff gun-control laws.

Topic sentence

Essay in Progress 1

Return to your first draft for Essay in Progress 3 in Chapter 6 (p. 131) and evaluate each of your topic sentences for content and placement. Revise as needed to make each more effective.

Including Supporting Details

In addition to including well-focused topic sentences, effective paragraphs are unified and well developed and provide concrete details that work together to support the main point.

Effective Paragraphs Have Unity

In a unified paragraph, all of the sentences directly support the topic sentence. Including details that are not relevant to the topic sentence makes your paragraph unclear and distracts your reader from the point you are making. To identify irrelevant details, evaluate each sentence by asking the following questions.

1. Does this sentence directly explain the topic sentence? What new information does it add?

2. Would any essential information be lost if this sentence were deleted? (If not, delete it.)

3. Is this information distracting or unimportant? (If so, delete it.)

The following sample paragraph lacks unity. Sentences that don't relate to the ways the media promote violence should be deleted.

Paragraph Lacking Unity

Topic sentence

(1) Much of the violence we see in the world today may be caused by the emphasis on violence in the media. (2) More often than not, the front page of the local newspaper contains stories involving violence. (3) In fact, one recent issue of my local newspaper contained seven references to violent acts.

Not related to topic (4) There is also violence in public school systems. (5) Television reporters frequently hasten to crime and accident scenes and film every grim, violent detail.

Not related to topic (6) The other day, there was a drive-by shooting downtown. (7) If the media were a little more careful about the ways in which they glamorize violence, there might be less violence in the world today and children would be less influenced by it.

Exercise 7.3

Working alone or in a group of two or three students, read each paragraph and identify the sentences that do not support the topic sentence. In each paragraph, the topic sentence is underlined.

1. (a) Today many options and services for the elderly are available that did not exist years ago. (b) My grandmother is eighty-five years old now. (c) Adult care for the elderly is now provided in many parts of the country. (d) Similar to day care, adult care provides places where the elderly can go for meals and social activities. (e) Retirement homes for the elderly, where they can live fairly independently with minimal supervision, are another option. (f) My grandfather is also among the elderly at eighty-two. (g) Even many nursing homes have changed so that residents are afforded some level of privacy and independence while their needs are being met.

2. (a) Just as history repeats itself, fashions have a tendency to do the same. (b) In the late 1960s, for example, women wore miniskirts that came several inches above the knee; some forty years later, the fashion magazines are featuring this same type of dress, and many teenagers are wearing them. (c) The miniskirt has always been flattering on slender women. (d) I wonder if the fashion industry deliberately recycles fashions. (e) Men wore their hair long in the hippie period of the late 1960s and 1970s. (f) Today, some men are again letting their hair grow. (g) Beards, considered "in" during the 1970s, have once again made an appearance.

Effective Paragraphs Are Well Developed

A unified paragraph provides adequate and convincing evidence to explain the topic sentence. Include enough supporting details to demonstrate that your topic sentence is accurate and believable. Evidence can include explanations, examples, or other kinds of information that help the reader understand and believe the assertion in the topic sentence. The following example shows an underdeveloped paragraph that is revised into a well-developed paragraph.

Underdeveloped Paragraph

Email and instant messaging (IM) are important technological advances, but they have hidden limitations, even dangers. It is too easy to avoid talking to people face-to-face. Using email can be addictive, too. Plus, they encourage ordinary people to ignore others while typing on a keyboard.

Developed Paragraph

Email and instant messaging (IM) are important technological advances, but they have hidden limitations, even dangers. While email and instant messaging allow fast and efficient communication and exchange of information, they provide a different quality of human interaction. It is too easy to avoid talking to people. It is easier to click on a chat list and check to see if someone wants to meet for dinner than it would be to look up her number and actually talk to her. Online you can post a "be right back" message, avoiding an intrusion into your life. In fact, using these services can become addictive. For example, some students on campus are obsessed with checking their email several times throughout the day. They spend their free time talking to email acquaintances across the country, while ignoring interesting people right in the same room. Because computer interaction is not face-to-face, email and instant messenger addicts are shortchanging themselves of real human contact. There is something to be said for responding not only to a person's words but to his or her expressions, gestures, and tone of voice.

These two versions of the paragraph differ in the degree to which the ideas are developed. The first paragraph has skeletal ideas that support the topic sentence, but those ideas are not explained. For example, the first paragraph does not explain why email and instant messaging are important or provide any evidence of how or why email can be addictive. Notice that the second paragraph explains how email and instant messaging allow for fast and efficient communication and gives further information about the addictive qualities of email. The second paragraph also explains the qualities of face-to-face interaction that are absent from online communication.

To discover if your paragraphs are well developed, begin by considering your audience. Have you given them enough information to make your ideas understandable and believable? Try reading your essay aloud, or ask a friend to do so. Listen for places where you jump quickly from one idea to another without explaining the first idea. To find supporting evidence for a topic sentence, use a prewriting strategy from Chapter 4. Also, the same types of evidence used to support a thesis (Table 5.1, p. 110–11) can be used to develop a paragraph. You may need to do some research to find this evidence.

Exercise 7.4

Use Table 5.1 (p. 110–11) to suggest the type or types of evidence that might be used to develop a paragraph based on each of the following topic sentences.

1. Many people have fallen prey to fad diets, risking their health and jeopardizing their mental well-being.

2. One can distinguish experienced soccer players from rookies by obvious signs.

3. To begin a jogging routine, take a relaxed but deliberate approach.

4. The interlibrary loan system is a fast and convenient method for obtaining print materials from libraries affiliated with the campus library.

5. Southwest Florida's rapid population growth poses a serious threat to its freshwater supply.

Exercise 7.5

Create a well-developed paragraph by adding details to the following paragraph.

Although it is convenient, online shopping is a different experience from shopping in an actual store. You don't get the same opportunity to see and feel objects. Also, you can miss out on other important information. There is much that you miss. If you enjoy shopping, turn off your computer and support your local merchants.

Effective Paragraphs Provide Specific Supporting Details

The evidence you provide to support your topic sentences should be concrete and specific. Specific details interest your readers and make your meaning clear and forceful. Compare the following two examples.

Vague

Many people are confused about the difference between a psychologist and a psychiatrist. Both have a license, but a psychiatrist has more education than a psychologist. Also, a psychiatrist can prescribe medication.

The example above contains general statements that do not completely explain the topic sentence.

Concrete and Specific

Many people are confused about the difference between psychiatrists and psychologists. Both are licensed by the state to practice psychotherapy. However, a psychiatrist has earned a degree from medical school and can also practice medicine. Additionally, a psychiatrist can prescribe psychotropic medications. A psychologist, on the other hand, usually has earned a Ph.D. but has not attended medical school and therefore cannot prescribe medication of any type.

Concrete details make clear the distinction between the two terms in the example above.

To make your paragraphs concrete and specific, use the following guidelines.

1. **Focus on *who*, *what*, *when*, *where*, *how*, and *why* questions.** Ask yourself these questions about your supporting details, and use the answers to expand and revise your paragraph.
2. **Name names.** Include the names of people, places, brands, and objects.
3. **Use action verbs.** Select strong verbs that will help your readers visualize the action.
4. **Use descriptive language that appeals to the senses (smell, touch, taste, hearing, sight).** When you use words that appeal to the senses, they enable your readers to feel as if they are observing or participating in the experience you are describing.
5. **Use adjectives and adverbs.** Including carefully chosen adjectives and adverbs in your description of a person, a place, or an experience can make your writing more concrete.

Exercise 7.6

Working alone or in a group of two or three students, revise and expand each sentence in the following paragraph to make it concrete and specific. Feel free to add new information and new sentences.

I saw a great concert the other night in Dallas. Two groups were performing. The music was great, and there was a large crowd. In fact, the crowd was so enthusiastic that the second group performed one hour longer than scheduled.

DETAILS ARE ARRANGED LOGICALLY

The details in a paragraph should follow a logical order to make them easier to follow. You might arrange the details from most-to-least (or least-to-most) important, in chronological order, or in spatial order. Refer to Chapter 6, pages 117–20, for more information on each of these arrangements.

Essay in Progress 2

Evaluate the supporting details you used in each paragraph of your draft for Essay in Progress 1 (p. 140). Revise to make each paragraph unified, well developed, and logically organized. Make sure you have provided concrete, specific details.

Using Transitions and Repetition

All the details in a paragraph must fit together and function as a connected unit of information. When a paragraph has **coherence**, its ideas flow smoothly, allowing readers to follow its progression with ease. Using one of the methods of organization discussed earlier in this chapter can help you show the connections among details and ideas. Two other useful devices for linking details are transitions between sentences and repetition of key terms.

As mentioned in Chapter 6, **transitions** are words, phrases, or clauses that lead your reader from one idea to another. Think of transitional expressions as guideposts, or signals, of what is coming next in a paragraph. Some commonly used transitions are shown in Table 7.1 (on p. 147). They are grouped according to the type of connections they show.

In the two examples that follow, notice that the first paragraph is disjointed and choppy because it lacks transitions, whereas the revised version is easier to follow.

Without Transitions

Most films are structured much like a short story. The film begins with an opening scene that captures the audience's attention. The writers build up tension, preparing for the climax of the story. They complicate the situation by revealing other elements of the plot, perhaps by introducing a surprise or additional characters. They introduce a problem. It will be solved either for the betterment or to the detriment of the characters and the situation. A resolution brings the film to a close.

With Transitions

Most films are structured much like a short story. The film begins with an opening scene that captures the audience's attention. Gradually, the writers build up tension, preparing for the climax of the story. Soon after the first scene, they complicate the situation by revealing other elements of the plot, perhaps by introducing a surprise or additional characters. Next, they introduce a problem. Eventually, the problem will be solved either for the betterment or to the detriment of the characters and the situation. Finally, a resolution brings the film to a close.

Notice that the **repetition** of key terms, or pronouns that stand in for the key terms, also lends coherence to the paragraph. For example, *they* (which stands in for *writers*) appears twice, and the word *film* appears three times.

Essay in Progress 3

Evaluate your use of transitions and repetition within each paragraph of your draft for Essay in Progress 2 (p. 145). Add transitions and repetition where needed to make the relationship among your ideas clearer and your paragraph more coherent.

Students Write

Chapters 4 to 6 show student writer Christine Lee's progress planning and drafting an essay on reality television. Below is one of her first-draft paragraphs (also included in Chapter 6 as part of her first-draft essay, pp. 131–33) and her revised, strengthened paragraph.

First-Draft Paragraph

Reality shows that followed *Survivor* didn't have the interesting elements that it had. *Big Brother* started as the first of the reality TV spin-offs, but audiences didn't have the same things to respond to. It has never been a success because they took the basic concept of *Survivor* and added nothing new or interesting to it. *Big Brother* locked up a bunch of people in a house and forced the audience to watch them bicker over nothing. Viewers were forced to watch bored contestants bicker and fight, locked up in a house with nothing else to do. It didn't seem the kind of competition that *Survivor* was, even though there was a cash prize on the line. The cash prize wasn't large enough anyways. We didn't choose favorites because the players weren't up against anything, except fighting off weeks of boredom. *Big Brother* introduced audience participation with the television audience voting off members, which gave the house members less to do and less motive to scheme and plot their allegiances like the castaways on *Survivor*. Voting members off was an arbitrary and meaningless process. But *Big Brother* had the prize component, and it took away the housemates' access to the outside world.

Table 7. 1   Commonly Used Transitional Expressions

Type of Connection	Transitions
Logical Connections	
Items in a series	then, first, second, next, another, furthermore, finally, as well as
Illustration	for instance, for example, namely, that is
Result or cause	consequently, therefore, so, hence, thus, then, as a result
Restatement	in other words, that is, in simpler terms
Summary or conclusion	finally, in conclusion, to sum up, all in all, evidently, actually
Similarity/agreement	similarly, likewise, in the same way
Difference/opposition	but, however, on the contrary, nevertheless, neither, nor, on the one/other hand, still, yet
Spatial Connections	
Direction	inside/outside, along, above/below, up/down, across, to the right/left, in front of/behind
Nearness	next to, near, nearby, facing, adjacent to
Distance	beyond, in the distance, away, over there
Time Connections	
Frequency	often, frequently, now and then, gradually, week by week, occasionally, daily, rarely
Duration	during, briefly, hour by hour
At a particular time	at two o'clock, on April 27, in 2010, last Thanksgiving, three days ago
Beginning	before then, at the beginning, at first
Middle	meanwhile, simultaneously, next, then, at that time
End	finally, at last, eventually, later, at the end, subsequently, afterward

Revised Paragraph

Reality TV shows that followed *Survivor* had none of the interesting elements that it had. *Big Brother* was the first spin-off reality TV show to try to repeat the success of *Survivor*, but it did not offer the drama that *Survivor* did. In *Big Brother*, contestants were locked in a house without any outside contact for weeks. As in *Survivor*, there was a cash prize on the line, but in *Big Brother* there were not any competitions or struggles. Contestants were expelled by a viewer phone poll, so the poll gave them no motive to scheme and plot allegiances the way *Survivor* contestants did. In fact, the contestants had little to do except bicker and fight. Viewers lost interest in players who were not up against any challenge except weeks of boredom. In the end, *Big Brother* was simply not interesting.

Analyzing the Writer's Technique

1. How did Lee strengthen her topic sentence?
2. What irrelevant details did she delete?
3. What transitions did she add to provide coherence?
4. What words are repeated that contribute to coherence?
5. What further revisions do you recommend?

Chapter 8

Revising Content and Organization

Quick Start: Looking at the photograph above from left to right, list everything that is happening in the picture.

Then examine your list, looking for ways to make it more understandable to someone who has not seen the photo. Write a few sentences summarizing what you think is going on in the photo. Add details and rearrange them in your original list to describe the photo more fully. After you make these changes, will it be easier for a reader who has not seen the photo to understand what is happening in it?

Exchange papers with a classmate and examine how your classmate organized ideas. Look for parts that you find confusing and that need more detail. Write down your comments for your classmate. Finally, using your own comments and those of your classmate, make changes to improve your own description of the photograph.

When you changed your list in the Quick Start exercise, did you include more details from the photo? Leave some unimportant details out? Change the content of any details? Whatever changes you made improved the content of your writing. In other words, you *revised* the description of the photo.

Revising an essay works in much the same way. **Revision** is a process of making changes to improve both what your essay says and how it is said. This chapter offers several approaches to revising an essay. It lists some general suggestions, describes how to use a graphic organizer for revision, offers specific questions to guide your revision, and discusses the implications of learning style for the revision process. As noted in Figure 4.1 (pp. 86–87), revision is an essential part of the writing process.

Why Revise?

A thorough, thoughtful revision can change a C paper to an A paper! Revising can make a significant difference in how well your paper achieves your purpose and how effectively it expresses your ideas to your intended audience. Although revision takes time and hard work, it pays off and produces results.

Most professional writers revise frequently and thoroughly, as do successful student writers. Revision is a process of looking again at your *ideas* to make them clearer and easier to understand. It is not merely a process of correcting grammatical errors. It may mean adding, eliminating, or reorganizing key elements within the essay. It may even mean revising your thesis statement and refocusing the entire essay.

The amount of revision you need to do depends, in part, on how you approach the task of writing. Some writers spend more time planning; others spend more time revising. A well-planned draft usually requires less revision than one that was spontaneously written. However, any first draft will require at least some revision.

Useful Techniques for Revision

The following techniques will help you get the most benefit from the time you spend revising your essays.

- **Allow time between drafting and revising.** Once you have finished writing, set your draft aside for a while, overnight if possible. When you return to your draft, you will be able to approach it from a fresh perspective.

- **Read your draft aloud.** Hearing what you have written will help you discover main points that are unclear or that lack adequate support. You will notice confusing paragraphs, awkward wording, and vague or overused expressions.

- **Ask a friend to read your draft aloud to you.** When your reader hesitates, slows down, misreads, or sounds confused, it may signal that your message is not as clear as it should be. Keep a copy of your draft in front of you as you listen, and mark places where your reader falters or seems baffled.

- **Seek the opinions of classmates.** Ask a classmate to read and comment on your paper. This process, called **peer review**, is discussed in detail later in this chapter (see p. 156).
- **Look for consistent problem areas.** After writing and revising several essays, you may discover consistent problem areas, such as a lack of concrete details.
- **Use a typed and printed copy.** Because computer-generated, typed copy seems less personal, you will be able to analyze and evaluate it more impartially. You will also be able to see a full page at a time on a printed copy, instead of only a paragraph at a time on a computer screen. Finally, on a printed copy you can write marginal annotations, circle troublesome words or sentences, and draw arrows to connect details.

One of the best ways to reexamine your essay is to draw a graphic organizer—a visual display—of your thesis statement and supporting paragraphs. A graphic organizer allows you to see how your thesis and topic sentences relate to one another. It also can help you evaluate both the content and the organization of your essay.

As you draw your graphic organizer, record next to it issues you find in the essay, such as an example that does not support a topic sentence, as shown in Figure 8.3 (p. 165).

Another option, instead of drawing a graphic organizer, is to write an outline of your draft. (For more information on outlining, see Chapter 6, pages 121–23.)

Key Questions for Revision

The six key questions listed below will help you make changes when you revise. Use the questions to identify broad areas of weakness in your essay.

- **Does your essay clearly convey a purpose and address the appropriate audience?**
- **Does your essay state a thesis?**
- **Do you have enough reasons and evidence to support your thesis?**
- **Do the ideas in your essay fit together?**
- **Is each paragraph well developed?**
- **Does your essay have a strong introduction and conclusion?**

After reading your draft or after discussing it with a classmate, answer each of these six questions to pinpoint areas that need improvement. Then refer to the flowcharts in the following sections. In addition to the revision suggestions and flowcharts in this chapter, the chapters in Part 2, "Readings for Writers," provide revision flowcharts tailored to the specific assignments in each pattern of development.

Analyzing Your Purpose and Audience

First drafts are often unfocused and lack a clear purpose. For instance, one section of an essay on divorce may inform readers of its causes, and another section may argue that it harms children. A first draft may contain sections that appeal to different audiences. For instance, one section of an essay on counseling teenagers about drug abuse might seem to be written for parents; other sections might be more appropriate for teenagers. (For more information about purpose and audience, see Chapter 4, pp. 90–92.)

To find out if your paper has a clear focus, write a sentence stating what your paper is supposed to accomplish. If you cannot write such a sentence, your essay probably lacks a clear purpose. To find a purpose, do some additional thinking or brainstorming, listing as many possible purposes as you can think of.

To find out if your essay is directed to a specific audience, write a sentence or two describing your intended readers. Describe their knowledge, beliefs, and experience with your topic. If you are unable to do so, try to zero in on a particular audience and revise your essay with it in mind.

Essay in Progress 1

Evaluate the purpose and audience of the draft essay you wrote for Essay in Progress 3 in Chapter 7 (p. 146) or of any essay that you have written. Make notes on your graphic organizer or annotate your outline.

Analyzing Your Thesis, Topic Sentences, and Evidence

Once your paper is focused on a specific purpose and audience, your next step is to evaluate your thesis statement and your support for that thesis. Use Figure 8.1 to examine your thesis statement, topic sentences, and evidence.

Essay in Progress 2

Using Figure 8.1, evaluate the thesis statement, topic sentences, and evidence in your Essay in Progress 3 from Chapter 7 (p. 146). Make notes on your graphic organizer or annotate your outline.

Analyzing Your Organization

Your readers will not be able to follow your ideas if your essay does not hold together as a unified piece of writing. To be sure that it does, examine your essay's organization. The graphic organizer or outline of your draft that you

Figure 8.1   Flowchart for Evaluating Your Thesis Statement, Topic Sentences, and Evidence

QUESTIONS	REVISION STRATEGIES
1. Thesis Does your essay have a thesis statement that identifies your topic and states your position or suggests your slant on the topic?	• Reread your essay and determine the one main point it is mostly concerned with. • Write a thesis statement that expresses that main point. • Revise your paper to focus on that main point. • Delete parts of the essay that do not support your thesis statement.
2. Background information Have you given your readers all the background information they need to understand your thesis?	• Answer *who, what, when, where, why,* and *how* questions to discover more background information.
3. Evidence Have you presented enough convincing evidence to support your thesis? Would *you* accept the thesis?	• Use prewriting strategies or do additional research to discover more supporting evidence. • Add the most convincing evidence to your essay.
4. Topic sentences Does each topic sentence logically connect to and support the thesis?	• Rewrite the topic sentences so that they clearly support the thesis. • If necessary, broaden your thesis to include all your supporting points.
5. Evidence Is your evidence specific and detailed? Does it answer *Who? What? When? Where? Why? How?*	• Name names, give dates, specify places. • Use action verbs and descriptive language. • Answer *who, what, when, where, why,* and *how* questions to discover more detailed evidence.

Between questions the arrows read "No" (pointing right to the Revision Strategies) and "Yes" (pointing down to the next question).

completed will help you analyze the draft's organization and discover any flaws.

To determine if the organization of your draft is clear and effective, you can also ask a classmate to read your draft and explain to you how your essay is organized. If your classmate cannot describe your essay's organization, it probably needs further work. Use one of the methods in Chapter 6 (pp. 117–20) or one of the patterns of development described in Part 2 to reorganize your ideas.

Analyzing Your Introduction, Conclusion, and Title

Once you are satisfied with the draft's organization, analyze your introduction, conclusion, and title. Use the following questions as guides.

1. **Does your introduction interest your reader and provide needed background information?** If your essay jumps into the topic without preparing readers for it, your introduction needs to be revised. Ask the five *W*s and an *H* question—*who*, *what*, *when*, *where*, *why*, and *how* — to determine the background information that you need.

2. **Does your conclusion draw your essay to a satisfactory close and reinforce your thesis statement?** Imagine explaining the significance of your essay to a friend. Use this explanation to rewrite your conclusion.

3. **Does your title accurately reflect the content of your essay?** To improve your title, write a few words that "label" your essay. Also, reread your thesis statement, looking for a few key words that can serve as part of your title.

You should also use the suggestions in Chapter 6 to help you revise your introduction (p. 128), conclusion (p. 129), and title (p. 130).

Essay in Progress 3

Evaluate the organization of your essay in progress. Make notes on your draft copy.

Analyzing Your Paragraph Development

Each paragraph in your essay must fully develop a single idea that supports your thesis. (Note: Narrative essays are an exception to this rule. As you will see in Chapter 10, in a narrative essay, each paragraph focuses on a separate part of the action.)

In a typical first draft, paragraphs are often weak or loosely structured. They may contain irrelevant information or lack a clearly focused topic sentence. Study each paragraph separately in conjunction with your thesis statement. You may need to delete or combine some paragraphs, rework or reorganize others, or move paragraphs to a more appropriate part of the essay. If you need to supply additional information to support your thesis, you may need to add paragraphs to the draft. Use Figure 8.2 to help you analyze and revise your paragraphs and refer to Chapter 7, "Writing Effective Paragraphs," for more on paragraph development.

Essay in Progress 4

Using Figure 8.2, examine each paragraph of your essay in progress. Make notes on the draft copy of your essay.

Figure 8.2   Flowchart for Evaluating Your Paragraphs

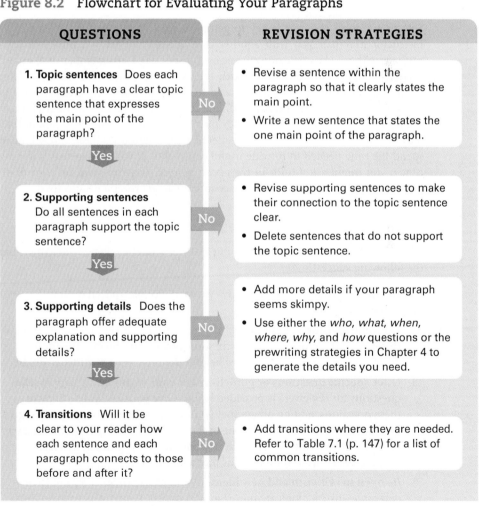

Working with Classmates to Revise Your Essay

In your writing classes and in other academic disciplines, you may be expected to participate in **peer review**, a process in which two or more students read and comment on each other's papers. Students might work together in class, outside of class, via email, or online. Working with classmates is an excellent way to get ideas for improving your essays. You'll also have the opportunity to discover how other students view and approach the writing process. The following suggestions will help both the writer and the reviewer get the most out of peer review.

How to Find a Good Reviewer

Selecting a good reviewer is key to getting good suggestions for revision. Your instructor may pair you with another class member or let you find your own reviewer, either a classmate or someone outside of class. Class members make good reviewers, since they are familiar with the assignment and with what you have learned so far in the course. If you need to find someone outside of class, try to choose a person who has already taken the course and done well. Close friends are not necessarily the best reviewers; they may be reluctant to offer criticism, or they may be too critical. Instead, choose someone who is serious, skillful, and willing to spend the time needed to provide useful comments. If your college has a writing center, you might ask a tutor in the center to read and comment on your draft. Consider using more than one reviewer so you can get several perspectives.

Suggestions for the Writer

To get the greatest benefit from having another student review your paper, use the following suggestions.

1. **Be sure to provide readable copy.** A typed, double-spaced draft is preferred.

2. **Do some revision yourself first.** If your essay is not very far along, think it through a little more, and try to fix some obvious problems. The more developed your draft is, the more helpful the reviewer's comments will be.

3. **Offer specific questions or guidelines for your reviewer.** A sample set of questions for reviewers is provided below. Give your reviewer a copy of these questions, adding others that you need answered. You might also give your reviewer questions from one of the revision flowcharts in this chapter or, if you have written an essay in response to an assignment in a later chapter, the revision flowchart for that assignment.

4. **Be open to criticism and new ideas.** As much as possible, try not to be defensive; instead, look at your essay objectively, seeing it as your reviewer sees it.

5. **Don't feel obligated to accept all the advice you are given.** A reviewer might suggest a change that will not work well in your paper or wrongly identify something as an error. If you are uncertain about a suggestion, discuss it with your instructor.

QUESTIONS FOR REVIEWERS

1. What is the purpose of the paper?
2. Who is the intended audience?
3. Is the introduction fully developed?
4. What is the main point or thesis? Is it easy to identify?
5. Does the essay offer evidence to support each important point? Where is more evidence needed? (Be sure to indicate specific paragraphs.)
6. Is each paragraph clear and well organized?
7. Are transitions used to connect ideas within and between paragraphs?
8. Is the organization easy to follow? Where might it be improved, and how?
9. Does the conclusion draw the essay to a satisfying close?
10. What do you like about the draft?
11. What are its weaknesses, and how could they be eliminated? Underline or highlight sentences that are unclear or confusing.

Suggestions for the Reviewer

Be honest but tactful. Criticism is never easy to accept, so keep your reader's feelings in mind. The following tips will help you provide useful comments.

1. **Read the draft through completely before making any judgments or comments.** You will need to read it at least twice to evaluate it.
2. **Concentrate on content; pay attention to what the paper says.** Focus on the main points and how clearly they are expressed and organized. If you notice a misspelling or a grammatical error, you can circle it, but correcting errors is not your primary task.
3. **Offer some positive comments.** It will help the writer to know what is good as well as what needs improvement.
4. **Be specific.** For instance, instead of saying that more examples are needed, tell the writer which ideas in which paragraphs are unclear without examples, and suggest what kind of example would be most useful in each case.
5. **Use the "Questions for Reviewers" above as well as any additional questions that the writer provides to guide your review.** If the essay was written in response to an assignment in one of the chapters in Part 2, you might use the revision flowchart in that chapter.

6. **Write notes and comments directly on the draft.** At the end, write a note that summarizes your overall reaction, pointing out both strengths and weaknesses.

7. **If you are reviewing a draft on a computer, type your comments in brackets following the appropriate passage, or highlight them in some other way.** The writer can easily delete your comments after reading them. Some word-processing programs have features for adding comments.

8. **Do not rewrite paragraphs or sections of the paper.** Instead, suggest how the writer might revise them.

Essay in Progress 5

Give your essay in progress to a classmate to read and review. Ask your reviewer to respond to the "Questions for Reviewers" (p. 157). Revise your essay using your revision outline, your responses to the evaluation flowcharts in Figures 8.1 and 8.2 (pp. 153 and 155), and your reviewer's suggestions.

Using Your Instructor's Comments

Another resource to use in revising your essays is the commentary your instructor provides. These comments can be used not only to submit a revised version of a particular essay but also to improve your writing throughout the course.

Revising an Essay Using Your Instructor's Comments

Your instructor may want to review a draft of your essay and suggest revisions you can make for the final version. Some instructors allow students to revise and resubmit a paper and then give the students an average of the two grades. Either way, your instructor's comments can provide a road map for you to begin your revision. Carefully review the comments on your essays, looking for problems that recur so that you can focus on these elements in your future writing.

Different instructors may use different terminology when they mark up writing assignments, but most like to point out several common problems. The marks on your essay will often address spelling and grammar errors and problems with organization and clarity or development of ideas.

Exercise 8.1

If your instructor has returned a marked-up first draft to you, read the comments carefully. Then draw a line down the middle of a blank piece of paper. On the left, write the instructor's comments; on the right, jot down ways you might revise the essay in response to each. Put a check mark next to any problems that recur throughout your essay; these are areas you will want to pay particular attention to in your future writing.

Using Your Instructor's Comments to Improve Future Essays

When you receive a graded essay back from an instructor, it is tempting to note the grade and then file away the essay. To improve your writing, however, take time to study each comment. Use the following suggestions.

- **Reread your essay more than once.** Read it once to note grammatical corrections, and then read it again to study comments about organization or content. Processing numerous comments on a wide range of topics takes more than one reading.

- **For grammar errors, make sure you understand the error.** Check a grammar handbook or ask a classmate; if the error is still unclear, check with your instructor. Make note of your errors in an error log. When you proofread your next essay, look carefully for those errors.

- **If you did not get a high grade, try to determine why.** Was the essay weak in content, organization, or development?

- **Using the evaluation flowcharts in Figures 8.1 (p. 153) and 8.2 (p. 155), highlight or mark weaknesses that your instructor identified.** When writing your next essay, refer back to these flowcharts. Pay special attention to these areas as you evaluate your next paper.

- **If any of your instructor's comments are unclear, first ask a classmate if he or she understands them.** If not, then ask your instructor, who will be pleased that you are taking time to study the comments.

Editing and Proofreading

Some of the comments you've received from instructors and your classmates will refer not to larger issues like ideas, evidence, and organization, which call for thoughtful revision, but to more local issues like style, mechanical and grammatical correctness, and word choice. Reviewing your work for such local issues is generally referred to as *editing;* giving your revised and edited work a final read-through for any remaining problems, such as transposed letters or missing punctuation, is generally referred to as *proofreading.*

The following sections draw your attention to some key things to keep in mind when you edit and proofread your papers. In Part 2 you will find further advice specific to different types (modes or patterns) of writing. The editing and proofreading advice we provide here is necessarily brief. Your instructor may provide other references and resources, like a grammar handbook, or you may refer to **www.bedfordstmartins.com/reflections** for further help.

Improving Your Sentences

To make your sentences stronger and more interesting, use the following questions.

1. **Are your sentences concise?** Look for places where you can use fewer words, avoid saying the same thing twice, or cut unnecessary phrases or clauses.

    ▶ ~~It is my opinion that~~ *f*ast-food restaurants should post nutritional information for each menu item.

2. **Are your sentences varied?** Use short sentences only rarely and only for emphasis or clarity; otherwise, your writing will sound choppy. Use sentences that combine different types of phrases and clauses to show relationships between your ideas.

    ▶ Leon asked a question/ *, and the* ~~The~~ entire class was surprised. OR

    ▶ *When* Leon asked a question/ *, the* ~~The~~ entire class was surprised.

3. **Do your sentences have strong, active verbs?** Consider replacing *to be* verbs (*is, was, were,* etc.) with verbs that are descriptive and help your readers visualize what you're trying to communicate.

    ▶ The puppy *whimpered and quivered during the storm* ~~was afraid of thunder~~.

4. **Are your sentences parallel in structure?** The parts of a sentence that serve a similar purpose should be expressed with words that have the same grammatical form.

    ▶ The children were rowdy and *noisy* ~~making a great deal of noise~~.

Improving Your Word Choice

Each word in your essay has the power either to contribute to or take away from your meaning. Use the following questions to evaluate and improve your choice of words.

1. **Is the tone appropriate, not too formal or too casual?** You should write as naturally as possible, but not the same way you'd talk to friends. Try for the kind of language you'd use in speaking to an instructor who's on the strict side. Avoid slang or any language you wouldn't use in speaking with this instructor.

2. **Do your words convey the connotations—feelings or attitudes—you intend?** As a test, try setting your writing aside for a bit; then, reread it, aloud if you can, and pay attention to how it sounds or how it makes you feel. If possible, give it to a couple of friends or classmates to read and ask them for their impressions.

3. **Have you used as many specific words as possible and avoided vaguer, more general words?** Try to make your language come to life.

   > ▸ The ~~red flowers grew~~ in our yard.
   >   *crimson petunias bloomed*

4. **Have you avoided clichés and trite expressions?** A *cliché*—a phrase that is overused—is like rock-hard bread: People will eat it if they're hungry enough, but they won't enjoy it. Try invented descriptions if you can manage it; otherwise, stick to plain language.

   > ▸ ~~I felt as sick as a dog~~.
   >   *My stomach was a bowl of curdled milk*

Avoiding Common Errors

Seven common errors are listed below. Be on the lookout for these errors as you revise and edit your essays.

1. **Sentence fragments** *Fragments* lack a subject, a verb, or both, and do not express a complete thought. For example, "A serious threat to society" is a fragment because it lacks a verb. Correct fragments in either of these ways.

   1. By combining them with a nearby sentence

      > ▸ Jenny speaks Spanish fluently/ ~~And~~ reads French well.
      >   *and*

   2. By rewriting them to include the missing subject and/or verb

      > ▸ Jenny speaks Spanish fluently. ~~And~~ reads French well.
      >   *She also*

2. **Run-on sentences and comma splices** *Independent clauses* are word groups with a subject and verb that can stand on their own as sentences. A *run-on sentence* contains two or more independent clauses run together without a punctuation mark or connecting word. The following sentence is a run-on: "Facial expressions are revealing they also are an important communication tool." A *comma splice* occurs when two or more independent clauses are joined only with a comma. The following sentence is a comma splice: "Facial expressions are revealing, they also are an important communication tool." (Note that some people call both run-ons and

comma splices *fused sentences*.) Both run-ons and comma splices can be corrected in any of the following ways.

1. By separating the independent clauses into separate sentences

    ►   Facial expressions are revealing ~~they~~ *. They* also are an important communication tool.

2. Through the use of a semicolon

    ►   Facial expressions are revealing *;* they also are an important communication tool.

3. Through use of a comma and coordinating conjunction (usually *and*, *but*, or *so*)

    ►   Facial expressions are revealing *, and* they also are an important communication tool.

3. **Errors in subject-verb agreement** Subjects and verbs must agree in person and number. For *person*, the forms *I* and *we* are first person; *you* is second person; and *he*, *she*, *it*, and *they* are third person. Subjects that are nouns (*Luis*, *restaurants*) are also third person. *Number* refers to whether subjects and verbs are singular or plural. Find the subject and verb of a sentence and correct any verb that does not agree with the subject.

    ►   The number of farmworkers ~~have~~ *has* remained constant in recent years.

4. **Unclear pronoun reference** A *pronoun*—a word that replaces a noun— should refer clearly to its *antecedent*, the noun or pronoun it substitutes for. Find and fix any unclear pronoun references or vague uses of words such as *they*, *it*, and *you*.

    ►   The hip-hop station battled the alternative rock station for the highest ratings. Eventually, ~~it~~ *the alternative rock station* won.

    ►   On the Internet, ~~they~~ *a Web page* claimed that an asteroid would collide with the earth.

5. **Errors in pronoun-antecedent agreement** A pronoun must agree with its antecedent in person, number, and *gender* (male, female, or the neuter *it/its*). Change any pronouns that do not agree with their antecedents.

his
▶   A father should pay ~~their~~ dues.

6. **Misplaced and dangling modifiers** A *modifier* is a word or group of words used to describe other words in a sentence. Make sure modifiers are placed close to the words they describe. A *misplaced modifier* is in the wrong place in the sentence. Fix it by moving it next to the word it describes.

angrily
▶   The police officer scolded the pedestrians for jaywalking ~~angrily~~.

A *dangling modifier* does not modify anything in the sentence. (In the sentence below, for example, the television didn't do any realizing.) Fix a dangling modifier by rewriting the sentence so the modifier does modify something.

we left   *on*
▶   Without realizing it, the television ~~played~~ all night.

7. **Confusing shifts** Avoid *shifts*, or unexpected changes that may confuse readers, for example, shifts in *verb tense*. (For more on shifts, see pages 230, 330, and 382.) To avoid a shift in verb tense, keep tense the same, unless meaning requires you to change tense.

forgot
▶   He took [**past tense**] the package with him and then he ~~forgets~~

[past tense]
~~[present tense]~~.

Proofreading Your Essay

To proofread, or make a final check for errors, print out a clean double-spaced copy of your essay. Do not attempt to work with a previously marked-up copy on a computer screen. Use the following suggestions to produce an error-free essay.

1. **Read your essay several times.** Each time focus on *one* error type—spelling, punctuation, grammar, and so on.
2. **Read your essay backward.** Reading from the last sentence to the first will help you concentrate on spotting errors.
3. **Use the spell-check and grammar-check functions cautiously.** These functions can help you spot many errors, but they will miss certain kinds of errors and are not a reliable substitute for careful proofreading.
4. **Read your essay aloud.** Reading aloud slowly will help you catch problems such as missing words, errors in verb tense, and errors in singular and plural forms of nouns.
5. **Ask a classmate to proofread your paper.** Another reader may spot errors you have overlooked.

Students Write

After writing her first draft, which appears in Chapter 6 (pp. 131–33), student writer Christine Lee used the guidelines and revision flowcharts in this chapter to help her decide what to revise. For example, she decided that she needed to add more details about what happened on the TV show *Survivor*. She also decided that she should de-emphasize the uninteresting details of the examples of some other reality TV shows.

Lee asked a classmate named Sam to review her essay. A portion of Sam's comments is shown below.

Reviewer's Comments

The trend that you have chosen to write about is well-known and interesting. Beginning your introduction with a question piques the reader's interest, and your thesis is clear: Reality TV shows are becoming less interesting and tasteful. You mention why people enjoyed *Survivor* and why they didn't enjoy the other shows. You should also emphasize why television viewers watched *Survivor*. Once that point is clear, many of your ideas might fit better.

I think some specific details about the reality TV shows you mention would help readers who are not familiar with the shows. It would also help prove your point: These shows are getting worse. The title and conclusion could better help make this point too. The title doesn't indicate what the reality of reality TV is, and the conclusion could look ahead to what you think the fate of reality TV will be.

Using her own analysis and her classmate's suggestions, Lee created a graphic organizer (Figure 8.3) to help her decide how to revise her draft, using the format for an illustration essay provided in Chapter 12 (p. 286).

After creating the graphic organizer, Lee revised her first draft. A portion of her revised draft, with her revisions indicated using the Track Changes (in Microsoft Word) function, follows.

Revised Draft

A Trend Taken Too Far: The Reality of Real TV

Deleted: One look at a *TV Guide* today shows an overload of reality-based programming, even with the guaranteed failure of most of these shows. Before reality TV there was mostly

Do you remember life before the reality TV craze? Before reality TV, television viewers seemed interested only in situational comedies and serial dramas. Characters were played by professional actors, and the shows were written by professional writers. Except for a few early reality-type shows, such as *Cops* and *Candid Camera*, this simple formula was what network television offered. Then came

Figure 8.3   Graphic Organizer for Christine Lee's Revision Plans

Introduction		
	TV Guide reveals an overload of reality TV shows.	**Detail to delete:** Mention of *TV Guide*
	Before *Survivor* there were mostly sitcoms and dramas.	**Detail to add:** Mention earlier reality-type shows (*Cops, Candid Camera*).
	Survivor caused networks to become real.	
	Thesis: Shows that followed *Survivor* were less interesting and less tasteful.	**Information to add:** Shows that followed had less drama and relied on gimmicks.

Body paragraphs			
	Paragraph 2	When *Survivor* began, there was nothing like it.	
		Exotic location	**Details to add:**
		Different kinds of real people played	• Audience response • Popularity of "getting voted off the island" phrase
		Competition for million-dollar prize	• Appeal of the drama involved
		Development of player camaraderie and sense of teamwork	
	Paragraph 3	*Big Brother* didn't offer audiences the same things to respond to.	
		People bickered over nothing.	**Unnecessary details:** • "Nothing new added"
		The audience did not choose favorites.	• "Took away access to outside world"
		Participants weren't up against anything.	**Details to add:** • Not as much drama as *Survivor* had
		The audience voted off members, which led to members doing less and scheming less.	
	Paragraph 4	Networks have continued to use gimmicks to appeal to the audiences' instincts.	
		Shows revolving around flirtation and sex	**Unnecessary details:** • Shows revolving around extreme situations • *Fear Factor* demonstrated this.
		Pushing limits of good taste	**Details to add:** • Explain what contestants had to do. • Viewers not interested and stopped watching

Continued >

Figure 8.3 (continued)

Body paragraphs	Paragraph 5	Two types of reality TV became popular.	
		Talent shows	**Details to add:** • Colorful judges • Supportive fans • Audiences lost interest. • Long lines for contestants to wait in and too much mascara
		Beauty contests	
		There was no built-in drama.	
	Paragraph 6	The next shows were about special interests.	
		Cooking (*Hell's Kitchen* and *Top Chef*)	**Details to add:** • Weight-loss shows • Fashion shows • Business shows • Hairstyling shows
		Dancing (*So You Think You Can Dance*)	
	Paragraph 7	Recent shows are about everyday lives or celebrities.	
		Every celebrity seemed to get a show.	**Details to add:** • Stars of *The Simple Life* and what they did • Jessica Simpson's show
		Everyday people in weird situations got shows.	

Conclusion	Reality shows have evolved.	
	The viewer decides what's popular.	**Details to add:** • Previous shows were copycat spin-offs. • *Jersey Shore* is a new show that shows people at their worst.
	Networks have to try to find new scenarios.	**Unnecessary detail:** • "I hope"

MTV's *The Real World* in 1992. The high ratings that this cable show garnered made network executives take notice of the genre. Eventually *Survivor* debuted in the summer of 2000. When *Survivor* caught the attention of even more viewers, television networks changed their programming.

Deleted: every viewer's

It seemed that networks acted as though they had to become "real" to compete with *Survivor* and maintain viewer interest. The problem with this copycat strategy, though, was that the original *Survivor* offered more interesting elements to its audience than any reality TV show modeled after it. *Survivor* was engaging and dramatic, but the shows that followed it were less interesting and less tasteful, lacking drama and relying on gimmicks.

> **Deleted:** every network in America believed they must also

> **Deleted:** keep up its ratings

> **Deleted:** Shows

> **Deleted:** in the hopes of finding a show as original, inventive, and engaging as the first *Survivor*.

Before Lee submitted her final draft, she read her essay several more times, editing it for sentence structure and word choice. She also proofread it once to catch errors in grammar and punctuation as well as typographical errors. The final version of Lee's essay follows.

Final Draft

Title: A play on words catches the reader's attention.

A Trend Taken Too Far: The Reality of Real TV

Christine Lee

Do you remember life before reality TV? Before reality TV, television viewers seemed interested only in the fictional lives of characters in situational comedies and serial dramas. Characters were played by professional actors, and the shows were written by professional writers. Except for a few early reality-type shows such as *Cops* and *Candid Camera*, this simple formula was what network television offered. Then came MTV's *The Real World* in 1992. The high ratings that this cable show garnered made network executives take notice of the genre. Eventually *Survivor* debuted in the summer of 2000. When *Survivor* caught the attention of even more viewers and dominated television ratings, television networks changed their programming. It seemed that networks acted as though they had to become "real" to compete with *Survivor* and maintain viewer interest. The problem with this copycat strategy, though, was that the original *Survivor* offered more interesting elements to its audience than any reality TV show modeled after it. *Survivor* was engaging and dramatic, but the shows that followed it

Background information on shows leading up to reality TV

The **thesis statement** is focused and detailed.

1

were less interesting and less tasteful, lacking drama and relying on gimmicks.

The **topic sentence** supports part of the thesis: *"Survivor was engaging and dramatic."*

Survivor captured the interest of a wide viewing audience because it was fresh and entertaining. The show introduced real participants in a contest where they competed against each other in an exotic location. The participants on *Survivor* were ethnically and socially diverse and represented a variety of ages including young, middle-aged, and older adults. The location was fascinating; a South Pacific island was more interesting than any house full of people on a sitcom. However, the most unique feature of *Survivor* was to make the participants compete for a million-dollar prize. Contestants were divided into two camps that had to compete to win everyday supplies, like food and shelter. At the end of each episode, players voted, and one of them was kicked off the show and lost his or her chance for the million dollars. The last contestant on the island won. To win the game, contestants created alliances and manipulated other contestants. All of these unique elements drew television viewers back each week.

Details offer reasons that support the topic sentence.

The **topic sentence** continues to support the thesis by explaining engaging aspects of *Survivor*.

The television audience responded favorably to the dramatic elements of *Survivor*. The competition gave viewers something to speculate about as the show progressed. Viewers' allegiance to one team over another or one player over another developed from episode to episode. Viewers were fascinated watching these players struggle in primitive situations, compete in tasks of strength and skill, and decide on how to cast their votes. The phrase "getting voted off the island" became a recognizable saying across America. Although players displayed positive human traits like teamwork, compassion, and camaraderie, they also schemed and plotted to win the allegiance of their fellow players. This situation made *Survivor* dramatic, and the viewers were attracted to the drama. Reality TV shows that followed *Survivor* had none of its interesting elements.

Specific details about dramatic elements support the topic sentence.

The **topic sentence** supports the thesis that later shows were "less interesting."

Big Brother was the first spin-off reality TV show to try to repeat the success of *Survivor*, but it did not offer the drama that *Survivor* did. In *Big Brother*, contestants were locked in a house without any outside contact for weeks. As in *Survivor*, there was a cash prize on the

2

3

4

Concrete details
about *Big Brother*
contestants

line, but in *Big Brother* there were not any competitions
or struggles. Contestants were expelled by a viewer
phone poll, but the poll gave them no motive to scheme
and plot allegiances the way the *Survivor* contestants
did. In fact, the contestants had little to do except
bicker and fight. Viewers were not interested in players
who were not up against any challenge except weeks
of boredom. In the end, *Big Brother* was simply not
interesting.

The topic sentence
supports thesis that
later shows relied on
gimmicks

The next wave of reality TV shows tried to use   5
graphic displays of terror and violence to attract viewers.
Fear Factor, the most successful of these shows, has its
contestants commit all manner of gross and terrifying
acts, like eating worms or being immersed in a container
of live rats. Some viewers may be interested in watching
how far the contestants will go, but the majority
of viewers regard these acts with disgust. Viewers
might tune in once or twice but, disgusted, will not be
interested in the long run.

The topic sentence
identifies other new
gimmicks.

When this gimmick did not retain viewers, two   6
traditional types of reality TV were revived with modern
twists added—the talent show and the beauty contest.
So shows like *American Idol*, *America's Got Talent*, and
America's Next Top Model were born. Again, there was
no built-in drama as in *Survivor*, so the shows tried
to create drama using colorful judges and supportive

Details about talent
shows and beauty
contests

fans. At first, these twists provided enough spectacle
to engage viewers, but after a while, audiences lost
interest. Even footage showing the long lines that
contestants had to wait in and the despair of those who
did not make the cut did not keep viewers hooked on
these types of reality shows. Viewers could only tolerate
so much loud singing and mascara.

The topic sentence
identifies a new
focus on special
interests.

The next incarnation of reality shows focused on   7
special interests such as cooking, with shows like *Top
Chef* and *Hell's Kitchen*, or dance, with shows such as
Dancing with the Stars and *So You Think You Can Dance*.
The net was spread wider with *The Biggest Loser*, a
weight-loss competition; *Project Runway*, where fashion

Details about special-
interest shows

designers are pitted against each other; *The Apprentice*,
a business competition; and *Shear Genius*, which offered
competition among hairstylists. The problems with

these shows were that they each appealed to only a very small segment of the population and offered manufactured and increasingly contrived situations for the contestants to act within.

The topic sentence identifies the latest focus of reality shows.

More recently, reality-show programming has turned increasingly to examining the everyday lives of groups of people and showcasing celebrities. *The Real World* was an early example of the first category, simply following the lives of a group of young adults as they drank and slept around. *The Simple Life* was one of the earliest celebrity reality shows, following Paris Hilton and sidekick Nicole Richie in ridiculously contrived situations. Soon it seemed every B-list celebrity had a reality show—Jessica Simpson, Ozzy Osbourne, Paula Abdul, Tori Spelling, Bret Michaels, and more. The next wave of shows featured ordinary people in interesting, strange, or controversial situations, such as *Jon & Kate Plus 8*, *Dog the Bounty Hunter*, *The Real Housewives*, *The Little Couple*, *Cake Boss*, *Choppers*, and more. These programs often showed people at their worst, as seen with a recent hit, *The Jersey Shore*, in which a cast of unknowns became famous for carousing and becoming caricatures of themselves. Networks have had to stretch to find new and different scenarios to offer to viewers as these shows have become increasingly tasteless.

Details about shows focused on ordinary people and celebrities

Examples continue to support thesis of "less tasteful."

The conclusion returns to the thesis and calls for more entertaining programming.

In the decade following the advent of *Survivor*, reality shows have evolved from copycat spin-offs to programs featuring terror and violence, talent and beauty contests, special-interest competitions, and finally to shows following real people's lives. In the end, the viewers determine what gets shown on television. Reality shows continue to be popular, despite becoming steadily more contrived and tasteless. One can hope that viewers will tire of all of these cheap gimmicks and call for more entertaining programming. If there were fewer reality shows, viewers could then return to more entertaining situational comedies and serial dramas or perhaps to another form of engaging program that may evolve.

Analyzing the Writer's Technique

1. Identify the major revisions that Lee made from the earlier draft in Chapter 6 (pp. 131–33). How did she carry out the plan indicated in her graphic organizer?

2. Choose one major revision that Lee made, and explain why you think it improved her essay.

3. Evaluate Lee's introduction and conclusion. In what ways are they more effective than the introduction and conclusion in her first draft (pp. 131–33)? What additional improvements could she make?

4. Choose one paragraph, and compare the details provided in it with those in the corresponding paragraph of the first draft (pp. 131–33). Which added details are particularly effective, and why?

Readings
for Writers

Chapter 9

Patterns: An Introduction

Quick Start: Carefully examine the photographs on this page, noting any details that would help someone who cannot see the images to understand the differences and similarities between the two types of dancing. How would you define each type of dancing? How would you describe each style? How is each performed? In what ways are they the same and different? Consider also the dancers. How would you describe them? How are they similar or different? Working on your own or with a partner, brainstorm answers to these questions.

An Overview of Patterns

The different ways in which you analyzed the photos for the Quick Start prompt demonstrate different ways—or patterns—of understanding one topic. You will recall that **essays** present information on a topic from the writer's point of view. Effective essays have a *specific* topic and provide adequate support for the thesis statement.

Beyond presenting a specific viewpoint, writers often have different reasons, or *purposes*, for writing. Once a topic is chosen, the writer selects a particular aspect of that topic to explore. Consider the very general topic *winter*. On which aspect(s) of winter might the writer choose to focus in his essay? How might he focus on that aspect?

- He can tell a story about a memorable ski vacation he took with friends. **(narration)**

- He can describe winter in a particular location. For example, a person writing about winter in New York would write a very different essay than a person writing about winter in Hawaii. **(description)**

- He can outline survival techniques for living in a brutal winter climate, such as Siberia or Alaska. **(illustration)**

- He can focus on a main characteristic of winter—snow—and explain exactly how it forms and falls to earth. **(process analysis)**

- He can examine the similarities and differences between an extremely cold winter and an extremely hot summer. **(comparison and contrast)**

- He can explore how different cultures experience winter. For example, the Saami people of northern Europe have words to describe many different kinds of snow. **(classification and division)**

- He can define and analyze the word *winter*. For instance, the scientific definition of winter refers not to a season but to Earth's position relative to the sun. **(definition)**

- He can discuss how winter affects people. Cold weather causes some people to spend more time indoors, while others spend more time outdoors taking part in winter sports. **(cause and effect)**

- He can make the case that winters are becoming less severe across the world as a result of global climate change. **(argumentation)**

Reading|Writing   An essay using any of these approaches to the general topic of *winter* will have a specific thesis statement and follow a specific pattern. Writing **patterns** are systems of developing and organizing information, and they are extremely helpful for both readers and writers. They help writers present their ideas in a logical, useful manner, giving them a specific writing plan to follow. They also help readers follow the writer's key points. Essays organized around writing patterns are easy to read and remember because their purpose and organization are clear and specific.

Chapters 10 to 18 are devoted to specific patterns. Each chapter presents guidelines for effectively reading and writing in each pattern and includes professionally written essays that use the pattern.

The following table summarizes the most common patterns and their purposes. You will find that essay examinations in many college courses ask you to answer questions with a pattern-based essay.

Table 9.1   Writing Patterns and Purposes with Examples

Writing Pattern	Purpose	Sample Thesis Statement	Sample Essay Exam Question
Narration (Chapter 10)	Relates a series of real or imaginary events in an organized sequence	The ski trip I took with three college friends taught me a great deal about friendship and loyalty.	Provide a brief biography of Harriet Tubman's life.
Description (Chapter 11)	Presents information in a way that appeals to one or more of the five senses (sight, smell, touch, taste, or hearing)	Summer in New Jersey can be summarized in three words: hot, humid, and unbearable.	Describe the climate of sub-Saharan Africa.
Illustration (Chapter 12)	Uses specific information (examples) to reveal the essential characteristics of a topic or to reinforce the thesis	Minnesotans, who live through extremely cold winters, have developed many coping mechanisms for getting through the coldest months of the year.	List three benefits and three drawbacks to social media like Facebook and Twitter, using examples to explain each.

Continued >

Table 9.1   (continued)

Writing Pattern	Purpose	Sample Thesis Statement	Sample Essay Exam Question
Process Analysis (Chapter 13)	Explains in a step-by-step fashion how something works, is done, or is made	Snow occurs when water crystallizes into ice in the atmosphere and then falls to earth.	Explain how to administer the flu shot.
Comparison and Contrast (Chapter 14)	Looks at the differences and similarities between two or more ideas, things, or phenomena	Winters in the Northern Hemisphere are often brutal and unpleasant; in the Southern Hemisphere, however, winter means warm, pleasant conditions and even a trip to the beach.	Explore the similarities and differences between the works of Nathaniel Hawthorne and of Mark Twain.
Classification and Division (Chapter 15)	Explains the categories or groups into which a given subject can be divided	The Saami of northern Europe have many words for snow. These include *soalvi* (slushy snow), *luotkku* (loose snow), and *skáva* (a very thin layer of frozen snow).	List and explain the cultural characteristics of the seven key regions within the United States (the Northeast, the Southwest, etc.).
Definition (Chapter 16)	Provides, in detail, the meaning of a specific word, phrase, or term	Winter begins on the winter solstice, which occurs when Earth's axial tilt is farthest away from the sun.	What is the pathetic fallacy? How does Mary Shelley use the pathetic fallacy in *Frankenstein*?
Cause and Effect (Chapter 17)	Analyzes why an event or phenomenon happens (*causes*) and what happens as a result of the event or phenomenon (*effects*)	In general, winter makes humans more likely to stay indoors, put on weight, and go to sleep earlier.	Describe three causes of the American Civil War.

Table 9.1   (continued)

Writing Pattern	Purpose	Sample Thesis Statement	Sample Essay Exam Question
Argument (Chapter 18)	Presents logical, reliable evidence to support a claim	As global warming continues, we can expect to see shorter, warmer winters but, strangely enough, much more snow.	Should teachers be required to assign at least two hours of homework each night? Why or why not?

Combining Patterns

Many writers find that combining different patterns helps them achieve their purpose. A writer who is *arguing* that the U.S. school year should be extended from ten to twelve months may want to *compare* the U.S. school system to that of countries in Europe and Asia.

Here is an example of a paragraph that combines different writing patterns.

Definition	A nor'easter is a hurricane-like storm that travels along the East Coast of the United States and Canada, starting in the waters of the Southeast (usually off the coast of Florida, Georgia, or the Carolinas) and traveling in a northeastern direction along the coast. Nor'easters
Cause/Effect	are known for their extreme destructiveness. They often cause heavy winds, blizzard conditions, severe flooding,
Illustration	and beach erosion. A particularly devastating nor'easter hit the United States in October 2011, when more than thirty inches of snow fell on parts of the
Cause/Effect	East Coast. The storm disrupted power for about three million people, and winds gusted as high as seventy miles per hour in Massachusetts. In New Jersey, the trees hadn't lost their leaves yet, which allowed wet, heavy snow to collect on them. As a result, heavy branches came crashing down all over the state, causing millions of dollars in damage.

Because writers combine patterns so often, each chapter on individual patterns (Chapters 10 to 18) includes an essay that uses more than one pattern. In your own writing, you should feel free to combine patterns to suit your purpose.

Writing an Essay That Combines Patterns

Chapters 10 through 18 explore in detail how to use each single pattern. To write an essay that combines patterns, use the following suggestions for each stage of the writing process.

PLANNING AN ESSAY THAT COMBINES PATTERNS

Choose a topic   When prewriting, use your knowledge of the various patterns to think about your topic in unique, creative, and diverse ways.

Determine which patterns to use   You would not use all the patterns in a single essay, but two or more could be combined effectively to support a thesis statement about, for example, eating organically. The list of questions in "Using the Patterns of Development to Explore a Topic" (Table 4.2, p. 100) can help you consider how your essay may combine different patterns.

Select only those patterns that contribute to the essay by supporting the thesis statement. Using too many patterns can overwhelm the reader and make the essay difficult to follow.

Develop your thesis   After deciding how to approach your topic, develop an effective thesis statement. The thesis statement should reveal your primary method of development. It may also suggest other patterns you will use in the essay, but the primary method should be clear to readers. Following is an example of a good thesis statement that combines patterns.

> Student services are divided into two main programs, Health and Counseling Services and Disability Services, each providing valuable services and support to students and prospective students.

This thesis statement makes it clear that classification is the predominant pattern. It also suggests that cause and effect will be used to explain how these services help students.

Generate evidence to support your thesis   Understanding the patterns of development can help you generate relevant supporting evidence. For example, while including narrative elements may pique readers' interest, an illustration essay should rely on examples to explain its main topic.

DRAFTING AN ESSAY THAT COMBINES PATTERNS

Determine the essay's organization   The way you organize your essay will be determined by the primary pattern and any other patterns you plan to use. In choosing a pattern, consider the nature of your topic and the needs and characteristics of your audience. See the coverage in Chapters 10 to 18.

Use transitions between different patterns   Transition words and phrases signal that you are moving from one pattern to another, enabling the reader to follow your train of thought easily. Specific transitional words and phrases for each pattern are discussed in Chapters 10 to 18.

Make sure your introduction and conclusion emphasize the primary pattern
The introduction should provide necessary background, provide the thesis statement, and suggest the primary pattern. The conclusion should draw the essay to a satisfying close while restating the main ideas, suggesting a new direction, or making a call to action—again, framed in language that echoes the primary pattern.

ANALYZING AND REVISING AN ESSAY THAT COMBINES PATTERNS

Set your essay aside for a day or two   Doing so will allow you to revisit it with a fresh, critical eye. As you reread it, pay particular attention to whether your primary pattern is evident and well-developed. Secondary patterns should all be used to explain or support the primary pattern.

EDITING AND PROOFREADING AN ESSAY THAT COMBINES PATTERNS

Use the "Editing and Proofreading Your Essay" sections in Chapters 10 to 18
These will help you identify common errors in each of the writing patterns.

For general editing suggestions, use tools from Chapter 8   In addition to consulting the revision flowcharts in Chapters 10 to 18 to analyze the primary pattern used in your essay, use the tools from Chapter 8, "Revising Content and Organization."

Chapter 10

Narration: Recounting Events

Quick Start: Take a look at the photograph above, and imagine the events that might have caused the two people in it to gather these balloons. Was it a dare? Are they celebrating something? If so, what? Why would they take the balloons to this setting? Working by yourself or with a classmate, construct a series of events that might have led up to this situation. Then write a summary of the events you imagined.

What Is Narration?

A **narrative** relates a series of events, real or imaginary, in an organized sequence. It is a story but *a story that makes a point*. It presents actions and details that build toward a climax, the point at which the conflict of the narrative is resolved. Most narratives use dialogue to present selected portions of conversations that move the story along. You probably exchange family stories, tell jokes, read biographies or novels, and watch television sitcoms or dramas—all of which are examples of the narrative form. Narratives are an important part of the writing you will do in college and in your career. For instance, a sociology instructor may ask students to describe a situation in which they were in conflict with an authority figure. Salespeople are often required by their employers to submit travel reports that describe the people they meet, meetings they attend, and clients they gain when on business trips.

Narration does the following:

1. It makes a point.
2. It conveys action and detail.
3. It presents a conflict and creates tension.
4. It sequences events.
5. It uses vivid details that advance the story and the main point.
6. It uses dialogue.
7. It is told from a particular point of view.

Narratives do all this to provide human interest, spark curiosity, and draw in readers.

1. Narratives Make a Point

A narrative makes a point or supports a thesis by telling readers about an event or a series of events. The point may be to describe the significance of the events, make an observation, or present new information. Often the writer will state the point directly, using an explicit thesis statement, but at other times he or she may leave the main point unstated, using an implied thesis.

The following excerpt is from a brief narrative, written by a student, based on a photo of a homeless person sleeping on a street bench. After imagining the series of events that might have brought the woman to homelessness, the student wrote this concluding paragraph, which makes an explicit point about the homeless.

> Karen is a kind, older woman in an unfortunate circumstance who wants nothing more than to live in a house or an apartment instead of on the street.

Purpose: Explain
misunderstandings
about the homeless.

Unfortunately, thousands of Americans, through no fault of their own, share her hopeless plight. Too often, passersby shun them and their need for a helping hand. They either look away, repulsed by the conditions in which the homeless live, or gaze at them with disapproving looks and walk away, wrongly assuming that such people live this way out of choice rather than necessity.

2. Narratives Convey Action and Detail

A narrative presents a detailed account of an event or a series of events. In other words, it is like a camera lens that zooms in and makes readers feel like they can see the details and experience the action. Writers of narratives can involve readers in several ways: through **dialogue**, with *physical description*, and by *recounting action*. This paragraph from Barbara Ehrenreich's book *Nickel and Dimed: On (Not) Getting by in America* describes her time as a low-wage worker at Wal-Mart.

Detail 1: physical
description
Detail 2: dialogue

Detail 3: recounting
action

Still, for the first half of my shift, I am the very picture of good-natured helpfulness. Amazingly, I get praised by Isabelle, the thin little seventyish lady who seems to be Ellie's adjutant: I am doing "wonderfully," she tells me, and — even better — am "great to work with." But then, somewhere around 6:00 or 7:00, when the desire to sit down becomes a serious craving, a Dr. Jekyll/Mr. Hyde transformation sets in. I cannot ignore the fact that it's the customers' sloppiness and idle whims that make me bend and crouch and run.

3. Narratives Present a Conflict and Create Tension

An effective narrative presents a **conflict**—such as a struggle, question, or problem—and works toward its **resolution**. The conflict can be between participants or between a participant and some external force, such as a law, a value, a moral, or an act of nature. **Tension** is the suspense created as the story unfolds and as the reader wonders how the conflict will be resolved. The point just before the conflict is resolved is called the **climax**.

For example, a writer might begin a narrative essay by saying he had planned a relaxing afternoon before describing the following harrowing events.

Surprising scene creates tension	The relaxing day took a strange turn. While driving to the beach I stopped at a traffic signal and saw the driver in front of me slump over the steering wheel as his car rolled forward.
Conflict	As a trained EMT and first responder, I suspected the driver was having a heart attack.
Tension builds	I put my car in park, leapt out, ran, and forced myself into the car, guided it to the curb, and put it
Climax	in park. Then I administered CPR and revived the driver.
Resolution follows the climax	My anticipated day at the beach was replaced by saving a life and preventing possible injury to others.

4. Narratives Sequence Events

The events in a narrative must be arranged in an order that is easy for readers to follow. Often, but not always, a narrative presents events in chronological order. At other times, writers may use the techniques of flashback and foreshadowing to make their point. A **flashback** returns the reader to events that took place in the past. **Foreshadowing** hints at events that will happen in the future. Both techniques are used frequently in drama, fiction, and film. A movie, for instance, might start with a pitcher on a baseball field at the end of an important game, flash back to the events that made this game so crucial, and then return to the game. A television show might begin with a wedding reception that foreshadows problems the bride and groom will have in the future. When used sparingly, these techniques can build interest and add variety to a narrative, especially a lengthy chronological account.

5. Narratives Use Vivid Details That Advance the Story and the Main Point

Narratives include specific types of details about the scene, key actions, key participants, and the writer's feelings, which help make the story clear and compelling.

The Scene Should Have Relevant Sensory Details   Narration essays include enough detail about the place where the experience occurred to allow readers to feel as if they are there. Details that appeal to the senses work best. A successful essay will focus on important details that direct readers' attention to the main points of the narrative and avoid irrelevant details that distract from the main point.

Key Actions Should Create Tension, Build It to a Climax, and Resolve It   A successful narration essay provides the details about the conflict and answers the following questions.

Why did the experience or incident occur?

What events led up to it?

How was it resolved?

What were its short- and long-term outcomes?

What is its significance now?

When reading a narration essay, make note of the author's answer to each of these questions to help you focus on the conflict discussed. When writing your own narration essay, be sure that you've addressed these questions in order to effectively convey the conflict.

Narration Essays Include Details Only about the Appearance and Actions of the Main Characters   People who were present but not part of the incident or experience need not be described in detail or even included in the narration.

6. Narratives Use Dialogue

Just as people reveal much about themselves by what they say and how they say it, dialogue can reveal a great deal about the characters in a narrative. In fact, dialogue is often used to dramatize the action, emphasize the conflict, and reveal the personalities or motives of the key participants in a narrative. Keep in mind that dialogue should resemble everyday speech; it should sound natural, not forced or formal. Consider these examples.

TOO FORMAL	Eva said to her grandfather, "I enjoy talking with you. The stories you tell of your early life in Mexico are very interesting. I wish I could visit there with you."
NATURAL	Eva said to her grandfather, "Your stories about Mexico when you were a kid are great. I'd love to go there with you."

Reading | Writing   When reading a narration essay, ask yourself what each line of dialogue reveals about the person saying it. When writing a narration essay, include key dialogue that is interesting, revealing, and related to the main point of the story. To make sure the dialogue sounds natural, read the lines aloud or ask a friend to do so.

7. Narratives Are Told from a Particular Point of View

Many narratives use the first-person **point of view**, in which the key participant speaks directly to the reader ("*I* first realized the problem when . . ."). Other narratives use the third-person point of view, in which an unknown storyteller describes what happens to the key participants ("The problem began when *Saul. . .*").

Both the first and third person offer distinct advantages. The first person allows the narrator to assume a personal tone and to speak directly to the audience, easily expressing his or her attitudes, feelings, interpretation, and commentary. When you narrate an event that occurred in your own life, the first person is probably your best choice.

The third-person point of view gives the narrator more distance from the action and generally provides a more objective perspective than the first-person point of view. It also allows the narrator to reveal insights about a character's actions or personality, as can be seen in the following third-person narrative taken from the Hispanic folktale "La Llorona" ("The Crying Woman").

<table>
<tr><td>Reveals character's
personality</td><td>People said Maria was certainly the prettiest girl in New Mexico. She might even be the most beautiful girl in the world. But because Maria was so beautiful, she thought she was better than everyone else.</td></tr>
<tr><td>Objective view of
Maria's life</td><td>Maria came from a hard-working family, and they had one of the finest homes in Santa Fe. They provided her with pretty clothes to wear. But she was never satisfied. She thought she deserved far better things.</td></tr>
</table>

—Joe Hayes, *The Day It Snowed Tortillas*

Reading and Writing Narration Essays

In this section you will learn about the structure of a narration essay, read a sample essay, and practice using the guidelines for understanding, analyzing, and evaluating narration essays. This will help you skillfully read and write essays that use narration.

How Is a Narration Essay Structured?

The structure of a narration essay follows the familiar structure of a short story, novel, or movie.

1. The **introduction** of a narration essay includes important background information and introduces the sequence of events. It may include the **thesis statement**.

Figure 10.1 Graphic Organizer for a Narration Essay

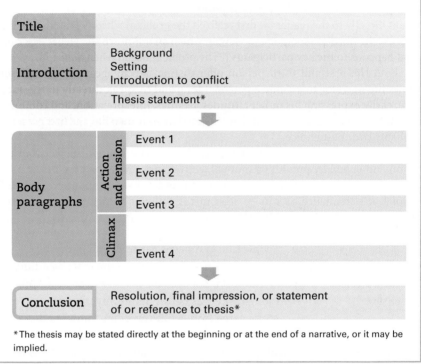

Title

Introduction
Background
Setting
Introduction to conflict

Thesis statement*

Body paragraphs

Action and tension

Event 1

Event 2

Event 3

Climax

Event 4

Conclusion
Resolution, final impression, or statement
of or reference to thesis*

*The thesis may be stated directly at the beginning or at the end of a narrative, or it may be implied.

2. The **body paragraphs** of a narration essay tell the story using action and tension that build to a climax.

3. The **conclusion** to a narration essay ends the story in a satisfying manner.

Figure 10.1 represents these major components visually.

1. THE INTRODUCTION PROVIDES BACKGROUND INFORMATION

The introduction to a narrative essay should

- catch the reader's attention,
- provide useful background information,
- set up the sequence of events, and
- contain the thesis, if the writer chooses to include it there.

In an essay that uses narration, the thesis states the purpose of the story being told (see "Narratives Make a Point," p. 183, for more information). Here are a few sample thesis statements.

> The silver serving platter, originally owned by my great-grandmother, became our most prized family heirloom after a robbery terrorized our family.
>
> (The body of the essay would tell the story of the robbery.)

Many events that seem coincidental often have simple explanations; however, sometimes these incidents have no simple explanation.

(The body of the essay would describe an event that proves this point.)

In a narrative the thesis does not necessarily need to appear in the introduction.

 Reading|Writing   When reading a narration essay, start by previewing the text to get an overview of its content and organization. When writing a narration essay, be sure that your thesis statement clearly states the purpose of the story you will tell. Make sure that you draw readers in and signal your organization.

2. THE BODY PARAGRAPHS TELL THE STORY

The body paragraphs of a narration essay tell a story that makes the point stated in the thesis (or implied if there is no direct thesis). These paragraphs use action, description, and dialogue to create conflict and build tension that lead to the climax of the story (see "What Is Narration?" p. 183).

Organization is important to the effectiveness of a narration essay. The events may all occur in chronological order from beginning to end, which makes the actions clear. Some narratives create drama or tension by presenting some events as flashbacks or by foreshadowing.

 Reading|Writing   When reading a narration essay, it is easy to become immersed in the story and to overlook its importance or significance. Therefore, it's a good idea to read the story several times. First, familiarize yourself with the events and action, noting who did what, when, where, and how. Then reread the narrative, this time concentrating on its meaning. When writing a narration essay, devote a separate paragraph to each major action or distinct part of the story. Use transitional words and phrases—such as *during, after,* and *finally*—to connect events and guide readers along.

3. THE CONCLUSION ENDS THE STORY AND CONNECTS TO THE THESIS

The final paragraph of a narrative should finish the story and reinforce the thesis. A summary is usually unnecessary and may detract from the effectiveness of the narrative. An effective conclusion to a narration essay will do one or more of the following things.

Make a final observation about the experience or incident   For an essay on part-time jobs in fast-food restaurants, a writer might conclude by writing, "Overall, I learned a lot more about getting along with people than I did about how to prepare fast food."

Ask a probing question   For an essay on adventure travel, a writer might conclude, "Although the visit to Nepal was enlightening for me, do the native people really want or need us there?"

Suggest a new but related direction of thought   For an essay on racial profiling, a writer might conclude by suggesting that sensitivity training for the police may have changed the outcome of the situation.

Reveal a surprising piece of information   For an essay that uses narration to explain the effects of serious phobias, a writer might conclude by stating that less serious phobias also exist—such as arachibutyrobphobia, which is the fear of peanut butter sticking to the roof of one's mouth.

Refer back to the beginning   For an essay about home burglary, the writer might return to the beginning of the story, when family members still felt safe and unviolated.

Restate the thesis or broaden its scope   When restating, be sure to use different words. To broaden the scope of a thesis statement, extend its applicability beyond the immediate situation. For an essay using narration to relate an incident of workplace gender inequality, the writer might refer back to the thesis, either stated or implied, and then comment that the gender inequality illustrated by these events is far too common in numerous other workplace environments as well.

A Model Narration Essay

Title

Right Place, Wrong Face

Alton Fitzgerald White

Alton Fitzgerald White majored in musical theater at Cincinnati's College Conservatory of Music. He made his Broadway debut with Miss Saigon *in 1991 and has since appeared in five other musicals, including* The Lion King *and* Ragtime. *The following essay, which was first published in the* Nation *in 1999, recounts an ordeal he suffered in New York City.*

Introduction
Background
information:
description of White's
upbringing
Thesis: An incident
changes his
perspective on the
police.

As the youngest of five girls and two boys growing up in Cincinnati, I was raised to believe that if I worked hard, was a good person, and always told the truth, the world would be my oyster. I was raised to be a gentleman and learned that these qualities would bring me respect.

   While one has to earn respect, consideration is something owed to every human being. On Friday, June 16, 1999, when I was wrongfully arrested at my Harlem apartment building, my perception of everything I had learned as a young man was forever changed—not only because I wasn't given even a second to use the manners my parents taught me, but mostly because the police, whom I'd always naively thought were supposed to serve and protect me, were actually hunting me.

Body paragraphs: the story

I had planned a pleasant day. The night before was a payday, plus I had received a standing ovation after portraying the starring role of Coalhouse Walker Jr. in the Broadway musical *Ragtime*[1]. It is a role that requires not only talent but also an honest emotional investment of the morals and lessons I learned as a child.

Comparison between what happens to him and what the character he plays experiences

Coalhouse Walker Jr. is a victim (an often misused word, but in this case true) of overt racism. His story is every black man's nightmare. He is hardworking, successful, talented, charismatic, friendly, and polite. Perfect prey for someone with authority and not even a fraction of those qualities. On that Friday afternoon, I became a real-life Coalhouse Walker. Nothing could have prepared me for it. Not even stories told to me by other black men who had suffered similar injustices.

Sets the scene for action to begin

Friday for me usually means a trip to the bank, errands, the gym, dinner, and then off to the theater. On this particular day, I decided to break my pattern of getting up and running right out of the house. Instead, I took my time, slowed my pace, and splurged by making strawberry pancakes. Before I knew it, it was 2:45; my bank closes at 3:30, leaving me less than 45 minutes to get to midtown Manhattan on the train. I was pressed for time but

State of mind prior to action is established

in a relaxed, blessed state of mind. When I walked through the lobby of my building, I noticed two light-skinned Hispanic men I'd never seen before. Not thinking much of it, I continued on to the vestibule, which is separated from the lobby by a locked door.

Action begins

As I approached the exit, I saw people in uniforms rushing toward the door. I sped up to open it for them. I thought they might be paramedics, since many of the building's occupants are elderly. It wasn't until I had opened the door and greeted them that I recognized that they were police officers. Within seconds, I was told to "hold it"; they had received a call about young Hispanics with guns. I was told to get against the wall.

5

[1] The character Coalhouse Walker Jr. is a black New Yorker in the early twentieth century who snaps under the strain of racist treatments.

I was searched, stripped of my backpack, put on my knees, handcuffed, and told to be quiet when I tried to ask questions.

With me were three other innocent black men who had been on their way to their U-Haul. They were moving into the apartment beneath mine, and I had just bragged to them about how safe the building was. One of these gentlemen got off his knees, still handcuffed, and unlocked the door for the officers to get into the lobby where the two strangers were standing. Instead of thanking or even acknowledging us, they led us out the door past our neighbors, who were all but begging the police in our defense.

Tension builds

The four of us were put into cars with the two strangers and taken to the precinct station at 165th and Amsterdam. The police automatically linked us, with no questions and no regard for our character or our lives. No consideration was given to where we were going or why. Suppose an ailing relative was waiting upstairs, while I ran out for her medication? Or young children, who'd been told that Daddy was running to the corner store for milk and would be right back? My new neighbors weren't even allowed to lock their apartment or check on the U-Haul.

Tension continues

After we were lined up in the station, the younger of the two Hispanic men was identified as an experienced criminal, and drug residue was found in a pocket of the other. I now

Realizes how naive he was

realize how naive I was to think that the police would then uncuff me, apologize for their mistake, and let me go. Instead, they continued to search my backpack, questioned me, and put me in jail with the criminals.

The rest of the nearly five-hour ordeal was like a horrible dream. I was handcuffed, strip-searched, taken in and out for questioning. The officers told me that they knew exactly who I was, knew I was in *Ragtime*, and that in fact they already had the men they wanted.

Expresses outrage

How then could they keep me there, or have brought me there in the first place? I was told it was standard procedure. As if the average law-abiding citizen knows what that is and can dispute it. From what I now know, "standard procedure" is something that every citizen, black and white, needs to learn, and fast.

I felt completely powerless. Why, do you think? Here I was, young, pleasant, and successful, in good physical shape, dressed in clean athletic attire. I was carrying a backpack

10

containing a substantial paycheck and a deposit slip, on my way to the bank. Yet after hours and hours I was sitting at a desk with two officers who not only couldn't tell me why I was there but seemed determined to find something on me, to the point of making me miss my performance.

Identifies himself as victim of racial profiling

It was because I am a black man!

White analyzes the experience

I sat in that cell crying silent tears of disappointment and injustice with the realization of how many innocent black men are convicted for no reason. When I was handcuffed, my first instinct had been to pull away out of pure insult and violation as a human being. Thank God I was calm enough to do what they said. When I was thrown in jail with the criminals and strip-searched, I somehow knew to put my pride aside, be quiet, and do exactly what I was told, hating it but coming to terms with the fact that in this situation I was a victim. They had guns!

Climax

Before I was finally let go, exhausted, humiliated, embarrassed, and still in shock, I was led to a room and given a pseudo-apology. I was told that I was at the wrong place at the wrong time. My reply? "I was where I live."   15

Conclusion: reference to thesis statement

Everything I learned growing up in Cincinnati has been shattered. Life will never be the same.

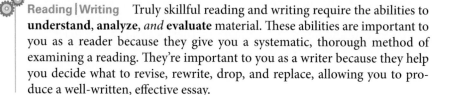

Understanding, Analyzing, and Evaluating Narration Essays

In reading and writing narration essays, your goal is to get beyond mere competence: That is, you want to be able to do more than merely understand the content of the essays you're reading or convey just your basic ideas to the audience you're writing for.

Reading | Writing   Truly skillful reading and writing require the abilities to **understand, analyze,** *and* **evaluate** material. These abilities are important to you as a reader because they give you a systematic, thorough method of examining a reading. They're important to you as a writer because they help you decide what to revise, rewrite, drop, and replace, allowing you to produce a well-written, effective essay.

◼ Understanding a Narration Essay

Preview the essay first to get a basic overview of what is happening. Then read it slowly and carefully to familiarize yourself with the specific events and actions, finding out who did what, when, where, and how. When reading a narrative essay the first time, it is easy to get lost in the story and overlook its importance. So be sure to reread it, concentrating on its meaning and message. As you read and reread, use the skills you learned in Chapter 2, "Understanding Texts and Images," and look for the answers to the following questions.

- **What is the writer's thesis?** If the thesis is implied, try to state it in your own words.
- **What is the role of each participant in the story?** Determine who is important in the story and how the important participants interact and relate to one another.
- **What does the dialogue reveal about the characters?** Also consider how the dialogue contributes to the essay's main point.
- **What actions occur within the narrative?** Pay attention to what the participants are doing and where, when, and how they are doing it.
- **What is the conflict?** Consider its causes or how it was brought about. Observe how the writer builds the conflict.
- **What is the climax?** Determine how, why, and where the conflict is resolved.
- **What is the sequence of events?** Especially for lengthy or complex narratives or for those involving flashback or foreshadowing among events, it is helpful to draw a graphic organizer. Refer to Figure 10.1, the graphic organizer for narrative essays on page 188, before starting to draw your own diagram.

Understanding in Action

Look at the following graphic organizer for "Right Place, Wrong Face," reread the essay, and write a summary of it. (For advice about writing summaries, see pp. 38–39.) As an example, below is one student's summary of paragraphs 6–8 of "Right Face, Wrong Place."

> He was leaving his building when police officers rushed in. They ordered him against the wall and took his backpack and handcuffed him. Three other innocent black men were also held, along with the real suspects, two light-skinned Hispanic men. They were put in police cars and taken to headquarters. There was no chance to let anyone know what was happening.

Figure 10.2   Graphic Organizer for "Right Place, Wrong Face"

Title	"Right Place, Wrong Face"
Introduction	**Background:** Youngest of seven; raised to be a gentleman **Setting:** June 1999, Harlem Narrator plays Coalhouse Walker Jr., an African American who experiences the injustice of racism, in *Ragtime*.
	Thesis: Narrator's wrongful arrest changes his perception of everything he learned while growing up.

⬇

Body paragraphs	Action and tension	1. Narrator is on his way to cash his paycheck.
		2. He notices strange men in his building's lobby.
		3. He opens door for police officers.
		4. Narrator and neighbors (African Americans) are arrested; suspects police seek are Hispanic.
		5. Narrator is jailed, searched, repeatedly questioned.
	Climax	Narrator is finally released; "I was told that I was at the wrong place at the wrong time. My reply? 'I was where I live.'"

⬇

Conclusion	"Everything I learned growing up in Cincinnati has been shattered."

Figure 10.2 is a visual representation of Alton Fitzgerald White's "Right Place, Wrong Face."

📊 *Analyzing a Narration Essay*

Analyzing a narrative involves examining how and why the story was told and determining the point that is being made through the story. Use the following questions to guide your analysis of narrative essays.

- **What is the author's purpose?** Determine the writer's point or message.
- **Does the point of the story follow logically and clearly from the events in the story?** The story should lead up to and demonstrate the point the writer is attempting to make.

- **How does the writer create tension?** Determine what factors created the tension that leads up to the climax. Does the author give you clues about what is about to happen?
- **How objective is the writer?** Narratives are often personal accounts and, therefore, influenced by the writer's perceptions, attitudes, values, and beliefs. It is possible that different writers may describe the same event differently. If you suspect a writer is one-sided, or biased, seek further information from other sources.

Analysis in Action

Using the preceding questions as a guide, make notes on the rest of White's narration. The following example shows one student's notes analyzing paragraph 14 of the essay.

Connects his experience to other black men's	I sat in that cell crying silent tears of disappointment and injustice with the realization of how many innocent black men are convicted for no reason. When I was handcuffed, my first instinct had been to pull away out of pure insult and violation as a human being. Thank God I was calm
Ties in with lessons from childhood	enough to do what they said. When I was thrown in jail with the criminals and strip-searched, I somehow knew to put my pride aside, be quiet, and do exactly what I was
Would police see this differently?	told, hating it but coming to terms with the fact that in this situation I was the victim. They had guns!

Evaluating a Narration Essay

Evaluating a narration essay involves judging how effectively the writer told the story and determining how well the story makes its intended point or message. Unless you have reason to believe otherwise, assume that the writer is honest about the events presented. You should also assume, however, that the writer chose details selectively to put forth his or her message. Use the following questions to guide your evaluation of narrative essays.

- **Is the story realistic, believable, and well explained?** Consider whether the writer clearly and effectively told the story, maintained your interest, and led you to understand the point of the story.
- **Is the conflict resolution believable and well explained?** Determine if there is adequate detail to enable you to understand how and why events happened.

- **Does the writer leave anything unspoken or unreported?** The writer should report all relevant conversations and actions. Pay attention to what is reported, but also consider what might be left unsaid.

- **Does the writer reveal his feelings about the incident or events?** Writers often reveal their feelings through their tone, which is established through word choice and other language features (see "Analyze the Author's Tone," p. 59).

Evaluation in Action

Use the evaluating a narration essay questions, your own summary, and your annotation of the essay to write an evaluation of White's narration. The following example is by the same student whose notes appear in the Analysis in Action exercise (p. 196). That student used those notes to write an evaluation of paragraph 14 as it relates to White's thesis.

In this paragraph White successfully supports and expands on his thesis. He shows how the manners his parents taught him helped him do what the police officers told him to do. He didn't resist them, which would definitely have made the situation worse. He also strengthens his point about how naive he had been to think that the police were there to protect him. Instead he was their victim. He links his experience to the experiences of other black men who have actually been convicted because of police injustice. It is clear why White's youthful hopes were shattered that day.

Readings for Practice, Ideas for Writing

Talking a Stranger through the Night

Sherry Amatenstein is an author, a journalist, and a noted relationship expert. She offers advice in an online column and through such books as *The Complete Marriage Counselor: Relationship-Saving Advice from America's Top 50+ Couples Therapists* (2011). The article that follows, which was first published in *Newsweek*, describes her experience volunteering at Help Line, New York City's oldest crisis and suicide hotline.

Reading Tip

As you read, notice how Amatenstein thrusts you immediately into the situation and creates suspense about the crisis. Pay attention to the way her use of dialogue reveals both the caller's and the author's states of mind.

Previewing the Reading

Preview the reading (see pp. 23–24 for guidelines), and then answer the following questions.

1. What experience does the author describe in this reading?
2. What benefit does the author derive from working a hotline?

SHERRY AMATENSTEIN

Talking a Stranger through the Night

The call came sixty minutes into my third shift as a volunteer at the crisis hotline. As the child of Holocaust[1] survivors, I grew up wanting to ease other people's pain. But it wasn't until after September 11 that I contacted Help Line, the nonprofit telephone service headquartered in New York. The instructor of the nine-week training course taught us how to handle a variety of callers, from depressed seniors to

"repeats" (those who checked in numerous times a day).

We spent two sessions on suicide calls, but I prayed I wouldn't get one until I felt comfortable on the line. Drummed over and over into the thirty trainees' heads was that our role wasn't to give advice. Rather, we were to act as empathetic[2] sounding boards and encourage callers to figure out how to take action.

My idealism[3] about the hotline's value faded that first night, as in quick succession I heard from men who wanted to masturbate while I listened, repeats who told me again and again about their horrific childhoods, know-nothing shrinks

---

[1] **Holocaust** Persecution of Jews and other minorities by the Nazis from 1933 to 1945.

[2] **empathetic** Understanding of others' emotions and feelings.
[3] **idealism** The act or practice of envisioning things in the best possible form.

and luckless lives, and three separate callers who railed about the low intellect of everyone living in Queens (my borough!). Sprinkled into the mix were people who turned abusive when I refused to tell them how to solve their problems.

I tried to remain sympathetic. If I, who had it together (an exciting career, great friends and family) found New York isolating, I could imagine how frightening it was for people so untethered they needed a hotline for company. That rationale didn't help. After only ten hours, I no longer cringed each time the phone rang, terrified it signified a problem I wasn't equipped to handle. Instead I wondered what fresh torture this caller had up his unstable sleeve.

5   Then Sandy's (not her real name) quavering voice nipped into my ear: "I want to kill myself." I snapped to attention, remembering my training. Did she have an imminent plan to do herself in? Luckily, no. Sandy knew a man who'd attempted suicide via pills, threw them up, and lived. She was afraid of botching a similar attempt. Since she was handicapped, she couldn't even walk to her window to jump out.

Sandy's life was certainly Help Line material. Her parents had disowned her forty years before. She'd worked as a secretary until a bone-crushing fall put her out of commission. Years later she was working again and had a boyfriend who stuck with her even after a cab struck Sandy and put her back on the disabled list. They became engaged, and then, soap-opera like, tragedy struck again. Sandy's boyfriend was diagnosed with cancer and passed away last year. Now she was in constant pain, confined to a dark apartment, her only companion a nurse's aide. "There's nothing left," she cried. "Give me a reason to live."

Her plea drove home the wisdom of the "no advice" dictum. How could I summon the words to give someone else's

life meaning? The best I could do was to help Sandy fan the spark that had led her to reach out. I tossed life-affirming statements at her like paint on a canvas, hoping some would stick. I ended with "Sandy, I won't whitewash[4] your problems. You've had more than your share of sorrow. But surely there are some things that have given you pleasure."

She thought hard and remembered an interest in books on spirituality. The downside followed immediately. Sandy's limited eyesight made it difficult for her to read. She rasped, "My throat hurts from crying, but I'm afraid if I get off the phone I'll want to kill myself again."

I said, "I'm here as long as you need me."

10   We spoke another two hours. She recalled long-ago incidents—most depressing, a few semi-joyful. There were some things she still enjoyed: peanuts, "Oprah," the smell of autumn. I again broached the topic of spirituality. My supervisor, whom I'd long ago motioned to listen in on another phone, handed me a prayer book. I read, and Sandy listened. After "amen," she said, "I think I'll be all right for the night."

Naturally, she couldn't promise to feel better tomorrow. For all of us, life is one day, sometimes even one minute, at a time. She asked, "When are you on again?"

I said, "My schedule is irregular, but we're all here for you, anytime you want. Thanks so much for calling."

As I hung up, I realized the call had meant as much to me as to Sandy, if not more. Despite having people in my life, lately I'd felt achingly lonely. I hadn't called a hotline, but I'd manned one, and this night had been my best in a long time. Instead of having dinner at an overpriced restaurant or watching HBO, I'd connected with another troubled soul in New York City.

[4] **whitewash** Hide the truth.

Understanding the Reading

1. **Background** What motivated Amatenstein to volunteer for the crisis hotline?
2. **Detail** Why was Amatenstein initially disappointed by her experiences speaking with callers on the hotline?
3. **Action** How did Amatenstein respond when she first answered Sandy's call?
4. **Detail** What did Amatenstein find out about Sandy as she spoke to her?
5. **Detail** What important lesson that she learned during her training did Amatenstein recall during her conversation with Sandy?
6. **Action** How did Amatenstein help Sandy?
7. **Main point** What did Amatenstein learn about herself because of her experience?
8. **Vocabulary** Using context clues (see p. 34) and consulting a dictionary if necessary, briefly define these words: *horrific* (para. 3), *rationale* (4), *signified* (4), *imminent* (5), *botching* (5), and *dictum* (7).
9. **Vocabulary** "Fan the spark" (para. 7) is an idiom. Explain its meaning as Amatenstein uses it.
10. **Structure and sequence** To help you see the organization of "Talking a Stranger through the Night," complete the graphic organizer on page 201.

Analyzing the Reading

1. **Conflict** What is the central conflict presented in Amatenstein's narrative? (Hint: *Conflict* can refer to any kind of struggle, not just one involving opposition.)
2. **Tension and suspense** What is the primary source of tension and suspense in "Talking a Stranger through the Night"? What kept you reading?
3. **Climax** When and how is the tension resolved, providing the narrative with its climax?

Evaluating the Reading

1. **Character** Evaluate the kinds of detail Amatenstein provides about Sandy— for example, that Sandy enjoyed "peanuts, 'Oprah,' the smell of autumn" (para. 10). Does she make you care about Sandy?
2. **Main point** How do you respond to Amatenstein's implied thesis in her concluding paragraph? Should she have been more specific?

Discussing the Reading

1. Amatenstein gives advice on relationships in her professional life. However, at Help Line she is told not to offer advice to callers. Why might a crisis hotline differ from other resources for people seeking help?

Graphic Organizer for "Talking a Stranger through the Night"

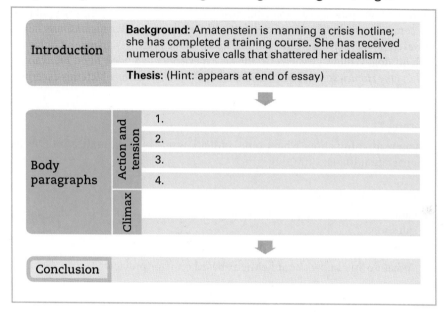

Introduction

Background: Amatenstein is manning a crisis hotline; she has completed a training course. She has received numerous abusive calls that shattered her idealism.

Thesis: (Hint: appears at end of essay)

Body paragraphs

Action and tension

1.
2.
3.
4.

Climax

Conclusion

2. In a group discussion or in your journal, explore the various reasons someone might call a crisis hotline. What qualities would you expect a volunteer answering the phone lines to possess?

3. Discuss some of the reasons people choose to volunteer. Are they generally the same as Amatenstein's reasons?

Writing about the Reading

1. **Paragraph** Write a paragraph narrating a situation in which talking to someone helped you solve a problem or provided you with a fresh perspective. Brainstorm some of the conversations you had with the other person. Pick out the most important advice or information that helped you solve your problem and include it in the draft of your paragraph.

2. **Paragraph** Write a paragraph about a situation you had approached idealistically only to find the reality to be less than what you had expected. As you plan your paragraph, be sure to include enough detail to contrast your idealism with the reality of the situation.

3. **Essay** Write a narrative essay about a time when, like Amatenstein, you helped another person and found that the experience benefited you as well. Start by brainstorming a list of such experiences. Select the best example and organize a sequence of events relating to it. Be sure to include a thesis statement about some results of helping others.

The Lady in Red

Richard LeMieux was a successful businessman who operated his own publishing company and lived a life of comfort and even luxury. After his business failed, however, he was evicted from his home and became homeless, living out of his car with his dog, Willow. LeMieux details his experiences in a book titled *Breakfast at Sally's: One Homeless Man's Inspirational Journey* (2009), from which this excerpt is taken.

Reading Tip

As you read, think about what point LeMieux wants to make and about how he uses narration to make it.

Previewing the Reading

Preview the reading (see pp. 23–24 for guidelines), and then answer the following questions.

1. What action does LeMieux describe in the reading?
2. What do you know about LeMieux based on your preview?

RICHARD LEMIEUX

The Lady in Red

It went back to last Thanksgiving Day, 2002. That was the day I learned to beg.

I was up in Poulsbo. I had used the last of my change to buy Willow a hamburger at the McDonald's drive-thru. My gas tank was almost empty, and my stomach was growling. Desperate for money just to keep moving and get something to eat, I began to consider the only option I seemed to have left: begging.

My whole life I had been a people person. As a sportswriter for the *Springfield Sun*, I had seen Woody Hayes motivate players at Ohio State and Sparky Anderson put the spark into Pete Rose. As a sales rep, I had sold hundreds of thousands of dollars of advertising, convincing people they needed to invest in the product I was publishing. I wore the right suits and ties and kept my cordovans shined and did the corporate dance for twenty years. But this, this *begging*, was far more difficult.

I had given to others on the street. They had all types of stories: "I need to buy a bus ticket to Spokane so I can go visit my dying mother." "I lost my wallet this morning, and I need five dollars for gas." I had always given, knowing all along that their tales were suspect. So I decided to just straight-up ask for money. No made-up stories. No sick grandmas waiting for my arrival. No lost wallets.

I started at the store I had shopped 5 at for many years—Central Market. It was a glitzy, upscale place with its own Starbucks, $120 bottles of wine, fresh crab, line-caught salmon, and oysters

Rockefeller to go. It was a little bit of Palm Springs dropped into Poulsbo. The parking lot was full of high-priced cars: two Cadillac Escalades, three Lincoln Navigators, and a bright yellow Hummer. I had spent at least $200 a week there ($800 a month, $9,600 a year, $192,000 in twenty years), so I rationalized that I could beg there for *one* day—Thanksgiving Day at that.

I was wrong.

After watching forty people walk by, I finally asked a lady for help. "Ma'am, I'm down on my luck. Could you help me with a couple of dollars?" I blurted out.

"Sorry," she said. "All I have is a credit card," and she moved on.

A man in a red Porsche pulled in. I watched him get out of his car, lock the doors from his key-chain remote, and head for the store. "Sir, I hate to bother you. This is the first time I have ever done this, and I'm not very good at it. But I am down on my luck and need help. Could you—"

10 "Get a Goddamned job, you bum!" he interrupted and kept walking.

Stung, I wanted to run to the van and leave, but I knew I couldn't go far; I barely had enough gas to leave the parking lot.

I spent the next twenty minutes trying to recover from the verbal blast I had received and could not approach anyone else. But the exclamation point had not yet been slapped in place on my failure at begging. The young manager of the store, maybe twenty-five years old, came out to do the honors. "Sir, sir," he called out to me as he approached. "We have a . . ." He halted mid-sentence. "Don't I know you?" he asked instead.

"Probably," I replied. "I've been shopping here for twenty years."

"I thought I'd seen you in the store," he said. "Well," he sighed heavily, "a man complained about you begging in front of the store. You're going to have to move on."

I could tell he didn't want to hear 15 about the $192,000 I had spent in his store. He just wanted to hear what I was going to spend today. So I said, "Okay." He didn't offer me a sandwich, a loaf of bread, a soy latte, or even a plain old cup of coffee.

I had no choice. I had to keep trying. I decided to go across the street to Albertsons. As I walked back to the van, tears filled my eyes. I remembered Thanksgivings of the past. By now, I would be pouring wine for our family and friends, rushing to the door to welcome guests, and taking their coats to be hung in the hall closet. My home would be filled with the smells of turkey and sage dressing. At least twenty people would be there. Children would be jumping on the sofa and racing up and down the hallways and stairs. The football game between the Cowboys and the Packers would be blaring in the background. There would be a buzz. A younger, friskier Willow would stay close to the kitchen, hoping for the first bites of the bird from the oven.

But that was yesterday. Today, I drove across the highway to the "down-market" store, nestled in the strip mall between the drugstore and the card shop. I stepped out of the van to try my luck again. It was getting late, and the shoppers were rushing to get home to their festivities. I had little time to succeed.

I saw an old friend of mine pull into the parking lot and get out of her car. She headed for the grocery store. I turned my back to her and hid behind

Continued >

a pillar. I waited for her to enter the store, and then I approached a man as he walked toward the entrance. "Sir, I'm down on my luck. Could you help me with a little money for food?" I asked.

He walked away muttering, "Jesus Christ, now we've got worthless beggars on the streets of *Poulsbo*."

20   I closed my eyes for a moment against the failure and fatigue, and then I felt a tap on my shoulder. "Sir," a lady was saying. As I opened my eyes and turned around, a lady in a red hat and an old red coat with a big brooch of an angel pinned to her lapel was standing there. She was digging through her purse as she talked.

"I overheard your conversation with that man. I hope you don't mind. I—well, I can help you a little bit," she said, holding out some rolled-up bills. Her presence and the offered gift surprised me. I stood there a moment, looking into her eyes. "Here," she said, reaching her hand out again. "Take it."

I reached out my hand and took the money from her. "Thank you so much," I said softly. "This is very kind of you."

"Thank you. I know what . . ." she began, and then her sentence was interrupted by a cough. She clutched her purse to her chest with one hand and did her best to cover her mouth with the other. She stiffened and then bent her head toward the pavement as the cough from deep in her chest consumed her. She moved her hand from her mouth to her bosom and just held it there. When the cough subsided, she took a deep breath. She looked up at me with watery eyes. "I've had this darned hacking cough for a month or more now," she said after she recovered. "I can't seem to shake this cold. It's going to be the death of me," she added with a smile. "I'm going back to the doctor after the holiday."

"I hope you get better soon," I said.

The lady then moved her purse from 25 her chest and opened it again. "Wait," she said, looking inside her bag and then reaching in. "I might have some change in here too." She dug to the bottom of her purse. She took out a handful of change and handed it to me. I put my hands together and held them out, and she poured the coins into them. "I hope this helps you," she said, gently placing her hand on mine. "Remember me. I'll see you in heaven. Happy Thanksgiving!" She turned and walked away.

I watched her disappear into her car before I counted the money she had given me. It was sixty-four dollars and fifty cents. I was stunned! I walked back to the van, counted the money again, and then counted my blessings.

I sat there in the drizzle, contemplating what had just happened. A sporadic churchgoer my entire life, I had spent recent months asking God to send his angels to me. But no angels came. Maybe *I* had to go looking for *them*.

With the glimmer of faith I still had left on that Thanksgiving Day, I said a prayer, thanking God for the visit from the Lady in Red.

And now, in the church parking lot, it was time to sleep. I closed the doors of my mind, one by one, and snuggled with Willow.

Understanding the Reading

1. **Detail** Why did LeMieux avoid telling hard-luck stories to those he asked for money?

2. **Background** Describe LeMieux's lifestyle prior to being homeless.

3. **Reasons** Why is Lemieux uncomfortable with begging and why does he resort to it?

4. **Vocabulary** Using context clues (see p. 34), briefly define these words: *glitzy* (para. 5), *rationalized* (5), *verbal blast* (12), *fatigue* (20), and *subsided* (23).

5. **Main point** What main point does LeMieux want to convey to his readers through his narrative? (Hint: look at paragraph 27.)

Analyzing the Reading

1. **Tension** What actions create tension in the narrative?

2. **Climax** What is the climax of the narrative?

3. **Flashback** Where in the narrative does LeMieux use the technique of flashback? (Hint: Look for places where LeMieux recalls his life before he became homeless.) Why is flashback useful here? Why does he include it?

4. **Vocabulary** What is the *corporate dance* that LeMieux refers to in paragraph 3?

5. **Dialogue** What does the dialogue reveal about LeMieux and about those he asked for money?

6. **Structure and sequence** How does LeMieux use a series of dialogues and a couple of changes in specific settings to structure his narrative?

Evaluating the Reading

1. **Evidence** LeMieux relies on personal experience to make his point in this narrative. Do you think he provides sufficient personal evidence and details to support his ideas?

2. **Inference** Why does the Lady in Red give LeMieux money? What clues does LeMieux provide in the narrative? Does he provide sufficient information?

3. **Details** Why did LeMieux include details about previous Thanksgiving dinners in his home? How do these details affect the impact of his story?

4. **Point of view** Imagine the narrative were told by an observer unknown to LeMieux or by one of the people from who he begged for money. How would this change in point of view affect the narrative and possibly its message?

5. **Descriptive detail** What details are particularly vivid and descriptive? Choose several and explain what each contributes to the narrative.

Discussing the Reading

1. What are some of the reasons people become homeless? What are some of the unique challenges faced by homeless people? Should society be doing more to help them?

2. Why does LeMieux explain his background as a salesperson? How are the skills of a salesperson relevant to begging and why are they not enough?

3. Why is it significant that the events described in the narrative occur on Thanksgiving Day?

Writing about the Reading

1. **Paragraph** LeMieux was in dire need of help when the Lady in Red offered assistance. Write a narrative paragraph describing a situation when you needed help and someone came to your aid.

2. **Essay** The Lady in Red performs a charitable act by giving LeMieux money. Write a narrative essay describing a particular charitable act you or someone you know has performed. Be sure to explain how tension is built and describe the climax in detail.

3. **Essay** LeMieux suggests that one has to work and take action to help oneself out of difficult situations, rather than wait for help to arrive. Write a narrative essay describing a situation in which direct action helped you or someone you know solve a problem or overcome negative circumstances.

Singing for the Cameras: Reality TV = Community Exposure?

Janel Healy earned a B.A. in communication from the University of Southern California, where she also performed in an a cappella group. She now lives, writes, and sings at Twin Oaks, a commune in rural Virginia. This essay documents her attempt to leverage her living situation into a show business opportunity whereby she could educate the public about intentional communities. Healy's piece first appeared in the summer 2011 issue of *Communities Magazine*, a periodical that promotes the communal lifestyle.

Reading Tip

As you read, pay attention to Healy's organization. Consider the effect this organization has on her ability to build suspense.

Previewing the Reading

Preview the reading (see pp. 23–24 for guidelines), and then answer the following questions.

1. What event in her life does the author relate in this narration?
2. What is unusual about the author's lifestyle?

JANEL HEALY

Singing for the Cameras: Reality TV = Community Exposure?

Just days before moving to the Twin Oaks Community in Louisa, Virginia, I auditioned for a musical reality TV show. My brief foray into the world of reality TV actually began on a trip to East Wind, Twin Oaks' sister egalitarian community in Missouri. A bunch of folks were sitting around a campfire one night when someone asked me to serenade the group, and I obliged. When I'd finished, the person said to me, "Janel, have you ever thought about auditioning for [popular show that aims to find the next singing superstar]? Because you have heart, and that's what they're looking for!" "I don't know," I replied tentatively. "They're looking for someone with a story . . ." The person laughed. "Look around you!" With a sweep of her arm, she motioned toward the group, the fire, and the dark mountains around us. "Look where you are. I'd say you have a story to tell!" That night, a thought was planted in my mind: *If I auditioned for the show and actually got airtime, I could expose the idea of intentional community[1] to 30 million viewers . . .*

[1] **intentional community** A group of people who share a common goal or cause choosing to live together.

Continued >

So, on August 19th, after eleven hours of waiting outside a San Francisco stadium with 10,000 fellow hopefuls, I finally found myself standing before the two producers' assistants who would decide my fate. "Hi," I said. "My name is Janel, and I live on a commune." I then sang my song, and waited for a reaction. The two assistants just stared at me. Finally, the man asked, "You really live on a commune?" I nodded enthusiastically. "For the past six months, I've been visiting intentional communities throughout the country, and now I'm about to move to one." "How did you find out about these communities in the first place?" "I typed in 'commune' on Google!" After a few more hilarious questions (e.g., "How do you listen to music on these communes? Are there radios?!"), the assistants motioned me forward. "You're in," the woman said to me with a wink.

I was escorted to a room where the handfuls of other people deemed worthy were signing paperwork. As I begrudgingly signed a slew of forms giving the show permission to publicly ridicule and/ or invent fictitious information about me, another minion of the producers approached me. "So. What's the most interesting thing about you?" I knew he was looking for filming material, and I was ready. "I live on a commune," I answered confidently. His eyes widened. "Do you think they would let us film there?" "Well, I'll bet at least one of the intentional communities I've spent time at this year would be up for that," I said, trying to sound casual despite the excited pounding of my heart.

Two days later, I was standing in front of the show's producers. They asked me a slew of questions about communes, and before I had even sung for ten seconds, I got a "yes." Thrilled that my angle was working, I then walked into

PHOTO COURTESY OF JANEL HEALY

the executive producer callback—lights, cameras, and microphones following my every movement—and again explained that I live on an intentional community. After fielding questions about slaughtering animals by hand and installing wind turbines (neither of which I know anything about, but hey, I tried), I sang my heart out. But the executive producers dismissively told me that my voice "wasn't special enough." "Sorry, it's a 'no.'"

Perhaps they thought I needed a more "folk-y" sound to go with my "hippie" persona.[2] Or perhaps they thought I was the kind of person who, upon being rejected, would deliver a dramatic show of emotion for the camera. But I didn't feel sadness at their response. In fact, I felt relieved that I would now get to enjoy my Twin Oaks experience with no strings attached. I

[2] **persona** A perceived personal image.

cheerfully said, "OK, thanks!" and walked out of the room. When I burst into the waiting room, a camera crew descended upon me. "How do you feel right now?" A man behind a camera asked me. I knew he was hoping I would dissolve into a fit of tears, or start swearing profusely. But I shrugged. "I know I'm going to do incredible things with my life," I said with a smile, "but not this, I guess!" I began to gather up my things, but the crew was still glued to my side. Finally, as I was walking out the door, the cameraman called out to me. "Won't you flash a peace sign for the camera?"

I did, knowing that a sound bite about "the girl that lives on a commune" might therefore appear on prime time TV a few months later. I was eager to clue more Americans in on the fact that there are alternative ways to live one's life in this country. But I also knew that if it didn't happen, it would be all right—I'd find some other way to spread the good news.

Understanding the Reading

1. **Action** What happened while the author was visiting the East Wind community in Missouri? Why did this experience lead her to audition for the musical reality show?

2. **Action** How did the various producers' assistants and producers who conducted her first three auditions respond to Healy's story, her "angle" as she puts it (para. 4)?

3. **Narrative action** Why did Healy respond to her eventual rejection as she did? When asked to "flash a peace sign for the camera" as she was leaving, why was she happy to oblige?

4. **Main point** What central idea does Healy communicate in her essay?

5. **Vocabulary** Throughout, Healy uses the terms *intentional community* and *commune* to describe her living situation. How do these terms differ in connotation? Why might she have told the producers she lives on a "commune" rather than in an "intentional community"?

Analyzing the Reading

1. **Audience** Healy first published this essay in a journal aimed at people with an interest in living communally. What elements can you identify in the essay that suggest this fairly specific audience?

2. **Narrative suspense** How does Healy create suspense in telling her story, particularly in paragraphs 2–4? What techniques does she use to keep readers interested?

3. **Tone** What is Healy's attitude toward the people who interview her and the process of auditioning for the show? Look particularly at her language in paragraphs 2 and 3.

4. **Climax and conclusion** Where does the climax of the narration occur? What is the purpose of the somewhat lengthy conclusion that follows?

5. **Visualizing the reading** Using this chart or a similar one, record several examples of each of the characteristics of narrative essays used by Healy.

Narrative Characteristics	Examples
Makes a point or thesis	
Uses dialogue	
Includes sensory details	
Recounts action	
Builds tension	
Presents a sequence of events	

Evaluating the Reading

1. **Purpose and audience** As suggested in the first Analyzing the Reading question, Healy was writing with a specific audience in mind. Do you think she succeeds in interesting a general audience in reading about her experience and thinking about her central point? Why, or why not?

2. **Character** How effective is Healy's presentation of the people she writes about here? Given her purpose, do you think she should have provided more detail about the woman at East Wind or about the staff at the audition?

3. **Dialogue** Why do you think Healy uses so much dialogue in the essay? Does the dialogue she writes seem to echo the way people really speak?

4. **Strategy** Healy chooses not to name the reality competition she auditioned for, referring to it only as a "popular show that aims to find the next singing superstar." Why might she have done this? Do you think she should have named the specific show?

5. **Tone** How do you think Healy herself comes across in the essay? Do you find her sympathetic, or would you use another word to describe her?

6. **Visuals** The photograph that accompanies this piece was provided by Healy. Why do you think she chose to include this particular photo? How does it contribute to your overall impression of her (see your answer to question 5 in this section)? (Hint: Think about the focus of the photo and how it connects to Healy's reasons for trying out for the show.)

Discussing the Reading

1. Why do you think people might choose to live together on a commune? Does communal living seem like a legitimate alternative lifestyle? Or do you consider it odd, as the people who interview Healy obviously do?

2. How do you feel about the kinds of reality talent shows like the one Healy auditioned for? Do you think, as Healy does, that part of their function is to "publicly ridicule and/or invent fictitious information" about contestants and to get contestants to break down on camera? Do these shows generally reward talent?

3. Healy is described as singing with "heart." What does this mean? How do you recognize such singing when you hear it? Give examples of performers that you think sing with heart.

Writing about the Reading

1. **Essay** Auditions such as the one Healy describes have a lot in common with the process of applying and interviewing for a job. Write an essay about such a job-hunting experience you've had. (Hint: In narrating your experience, characterize the people doing the interviewing, and try to create some suspense—as Healy does—about whether or not you made the cut.)

2. **Essay** Healy writes about pursuing a dream. In an essay, narrate your own pursuit of a dream, your own story of wanting something badly and how you went about trying to achieve it, even if there were setbacks along the way. It doesn't have to be something you've fulfilled already, as long as you can trace a sequence of events from the source of your dream to the present and speculate about the future. (Hint: Don't forget to include interactions you've had with other people while in pursuit of this dream.)

3. **Essay** Healy has clearly chosen to live a life out of the mainstream. Have you ever chosen to rebel against what was expected of you, to go your own way in spite of what others thought, whether they were your peers, your family, or mainstream society as a whole? Share your experience in a narrative essay that explores the development of your decision to pursue a course others didn't expect for you and how you put your decision into practice. (Hint: In planning your narrative, be sure to think about how to present conflict, both with others and within yourself.)

COMBINING THE PATTERNS

It's a Mad, Mad Marathon

Leslie Jamison, a Ph.D. candidate at Yale University, has been published in *Best New American Voices 2008, A Public Space,* and *Black Warrior Review.* Her debut novel, *The Gin Closet,* appeared in 2010. This piece followed in a 2011 issue of the *Believer.*

Reading Tip

Jamison employs aspects of other patterns of organization in addition to narration in this essay. As you read, note which other pattern(s) she uses. For an overview of the patterns, refer to Chapter 9, "Patterns: An Introduction."

Previewing the Reading

Preview the reading (see pp. 23–24 for guidelines) to get a sense of what the "mad, mad marathon" involves. What seems to be the author's involvement in the race?

LESLIE JAMISON

It's a Mad, Mad Marathon

On the western edge of Frozen Head State Park, just before dawn, a man in a rust brown trench coat blows a giant conch shell. Runners stir in their tents. They fill their water pouches. They tape blisters. They eat thousand-calorie breakfasts. Some pray. Others ready fanny packs. The man in the trench coat sits in an ergonomic lawn chair beside a famous yellow gate, holding a cigarette. He calls the two-minute warning.

The runners gather in front of him, stretching. They are about to travel more than a hundred miles through the wilderness—if they are strong and lucky enough to make it that far, which they probably aren't. They wait anxiously. We, the watchers, wait anxiously.

At 7:12, the man in the trench coat rises from his lawn chair and lights his cigarette. Once the tip glows red, the race known as the Barkley Marathons has begun.

The first race was a prison break. On June 10, 1977, James Earl Ray, the man who shot Martin Luther King Jr., escaped from a federal penitentiary and fled across the briar-bearded hills of northern Tennessee. Fifty-four hours later he was found. He'd gone about eight miles. Some hear this and wonder how he squandered his escape. One man heard this and thought: I need to see that terrain!

5   Over twenty years later, that man, the man in the trench coat—self-dubbed Lazarus Lake (known as Laz)—has turned this terrain into the stage for a legendary ritual: the Barkley Marathons, held yearly (traditionally on Lazarus Friday or April Fools' Day) outside Wartburg, Tennessee. Laz used to run the race himself, but never managed to finish it. Only eight men have ever finished. The event is considered extreme even by those who specialize in extremity.

What makes it so bad? No trail, for one thing. A cumulative elevation gain nearly twice the height of Everest. Saw briars that turn a man's legs to raw meat. Hills with names like Rat Jaw, Little Hell, Big Hell, Coffin Springs.

The race consists of five loops on a course that's been listed at twenty miles but is more like twenty-six. Standard metrics are irrelevant, the laws of physics replaced by Laz's personal whims. Guys who could finish a hundred miles in twenty hours might not finish a single loop here. If you finish three, you've completed what's known as the Fun Run. If you do not finish, Laz plays taps to commemorate your quitting.

There are no published entry requirements. It helps to know someone. Admissions are decided by Laz's discretion, and his application includes questions like "What is your favorite parasite?" Only thirty-five entries are admitted. This year, one of them is my brother. Julian is a "virgin," one of fifteen newbies who will do their damndest to finish a loop.

The day before the race, runners start arriving at camp. Their license plates say 100 RUNNR, ULT MAN, CRZY RUN. They bring camouflage tents and orange hunting vests and skeptical girl-friends and acclimated wives.

10   I help sort Julian's supplies in the back of the car. He earned his Ph.D. at age twenty-five and, in his nonsuperhero incarnation as a development economist, is working on a microfinance project in Liberia. Here, he needs a compass. He needs pain pills and NoDoz and electrolyte pills and a blister "kit" (a needle and Band-Aids). He needs tape for when his toenails fall off. He needs batteries. Running out of batteries is the *must-avoid-at-all-costs worst possible thing that could happen*. Julian's coup de grâce[1] is a pair of duct-tape pants designed to fend off saw briars.

Traditionally, the epicenter of camp is a chicken fire. This year it's manned by someone named Doc Joe. We arrive as he's spearing the first thighs from the grill.

At this particular potluck, small talk rarely stays banal for long. I fall into conversation with a bearded veteran. Our conversation starts predictably. He asks where I'm from. I say Los Angeles. He says he loves Venice Beach. I say I love Venice Beach, too. Then he says, "Next fall I'm running from Venice Beach to Virginia Beach to celebrate my retirement."

> **The desire seems to be to devise an unrunnable race, to sustain the immortal horizon of an unbeatable challenge.**

I learn that there are a couple of major contenders to complete a hundred: Blake and A.T. They are two of the "alumni" (former finishers) who are running this year. Finishing twice would make history.

Blake Wood is a nuclear engineer at Los Alamos with a doctorate from Berkeley and an incredible Barkley

[1] **coup de grâce** Fatal blow.

Continued >

record: six for six Fun Run comple-
tions, one finish, another near finish
blocked only by a flooded creek. In
person, he's a friendly middle-aged dad
with a salt-and-pepper mustache.

15   Andrew Thompson is a youngish
guy from New Hampshire famous for
a near finish in 2005, when he was
strong heading into his fifth loop but
literally lost his mind out there. He
completely forgot about the race.

There's J. B., Jonathan Basham,
A.T.'s best support crew for years, at
Barkley for his own race this time
around. I mainly hear him mentioned
in the context of his relationship to
A.T., who calls him Jonboy.

There are some strong virgins in the
pack, including Charlie Engle, an
accomplished ultra-runner (he's "done"
the Sahara). Like many ultra-runners,
he's a former addict. He's been sober
for nearly twenty years, and many
describe his recovery as the switch from
one addiction to another—drugs for
adrenaline, trading that extreme for
this one.

Watching Laz from across the
campfire, I can't help thinking of *Heart
of Darkness*.[2] Like Kurtz, Laz is bald
and charismatic, leader of a minor
empire, trafficker in human pain. He's
a cross between the Colonel and your
grandpa. There's an Inner Station
splendor to his orchestration of this
hormone extravaganza, testosterone
spread like fertilizer across miles of
barren wilderness. He speaks to "his
runners" with comfort and fondness.
Most have been running "for him"
(their phrase) for years. Everyone pays
a $1.60 entry fee.

All through the potluck, runners
pore over their instructions, five single-
spaced pages with details like "the coal
pond beavers have been very active this
year, be careful not to fall on one of
the sharpened stumps they have left."
The instructions tend to cite land-
marks like "the ridge" or "the rock"
that seem less than useful. And then
there's the issue of the night.

The runners are out on their loops   20
anywhere from eight to thirty-two
hours. Between loops, if they're continuing, they stop at camp for a few
moments of food and rest. Dropping,
unless you drop at the single point
accessible by trail, involves a three-to-
four-hour commute back into camp.
Which means that the act of *ceasing to
compete* in the Barkley race is comparable to running a marathon.

Ten books are placed at various
points along the course, and runners are
responsible for ripping out pages that
match their race number. Laz is playful
in his book choices: *The Most Dangerous Game, Death by Misadventure, A
Time to Die*—even *Heart of Darkness*.[3]

The talk this year is about Laz's latest addition to the course: a quarter-
mile cement tunnel that runs under the
old penitentiary, where, rumor has it,
the snakes are the size of arms. Whose
arms? I wonder. Most of the guys here
are pretty wiry.

Laz gives himself the freedom to
start the race whenever he wants. He
offers only two guarantees: that it will
begin between midnight and noon, and
that he will blow the conch shell an
hour beforehand.

At the start gate, Julian is wearing
a light silver jacket and his duct-tape

---

[2] *Heart of Darkness* A well-known adventure
story by Joseph Conrad featuring the narrator's journey up the Congo River, reaching
the Inner Station and encountering the
mysterious Kurtz.

[3] Books and stories that pertain to competition and adventure.

chaps. He looks like a robot. He disappears uphill in a flurry of camera flashes.

After the runners take off, Doc Joe and I start grilling waffles. Laz strolls over with his glowing cigarette, its gray cap of untapped ash quaking. I introduce myself. He introduces himself. He asks us if we think anyone has noticed that he's not actually smoking. "I can't this year," he explains, "because of my leg." He has just had surgery on an artery and his circulation isn't good.

I tell him the cigarette looks great as an accessory. Doc Joe tells him that he's safe up to a couple packs. Doc Joe, by the way, really is a doctor.

I ask Laz how he chooses the time. "One time I started at three," he says, as if in answer. "That was fun."

"Last year you started at noon, right? I heard the runners got a little restless."

"Sure did." He shakes his head, smiling at the memory. "Folks were just standing around getting antsy."

As we speak, he mentions sections of the course—Danger Dave's Climbing Wall, Raw Dog Falls, Pussy Ridge. Laz's greatest desire seems to be to devise an unrunnable race, to sustain the immortal horizon of an unbeatable challenge. After the first year, when no one came close to finishing, Laz wrote an article headlined: THE "TRAIL" WINS THE BARKLEY MARATHONS.

Two public trails intersect the course, although Laz generally discourages meeting runners. "Even just the sight of other human beings is a kind of aid," he explains. "We want them to feel the full weight of their aloneness."

Whenever I see Laz around camp, he says, "You think Julian is having fun out there?" I finally say, "I fucking hope not!" and he smiles.

But I can't help thinking his question dissolves precisely the kind of loneliness he seems so interested in producing: The idea that when you are alone out there, someone back at camp *is thinking of you alone out there*, is, of course, just another kind of connection.

When Julian comes in from his first loop, it's almost dark. He's been out for twelve hours and is in good spirits. He's got ten page 61s, including one from an account of teenage alcoholism called *The Late Great Me*. The duct tape has been ripped from his pants. "You took it off?" I ask.

"Nope," he says. "Course took it off."

He eats hummus sandwiches and Girl Scout cookies and gulps a butter pecan Ensure. He takes another bib number, for his second round of pages, and Laz and I send him into the woods. His rain jacket glows silver in the darkness.

Julian has completed five hundred-mile races so far. He explained to me that he wants to achieve a completely insular system of accountability, one that doesn't depend on external feedback. He wants to run a hundred miles when no one knows he's running, so that the desire to impress people, or the shame of quitting, won't constitute his sources of motivation.

It starts to rain. I make a nest in the back of my car and try to sleep. I'm awoken every once in a while by the mournful call of taps.

Julian arrives back in camp around eight in the morning. He was out for another twelve hours but reached only two books. There were a couple hours lost, another couple spent lying down, in the rain, waiting for first light. He is proud of himself for going out, even though he didn't think he'd get far, and I am proud of him, too.

We join the others under the rain tent. People are speculating about

Continued >

whether anyone will even finish the Fun Run. There are only six runners left. If anyone can finish the full hundred, everyone agrees, it will be Blake.

The wife of one of the runners has packed a plastic bag of clothes and is planning to meet him at Lookout Tower. If he decides to drop, she'll hand him his dry clothes and escort him down the three-mile trail back into camp. If he decides to continue, she'll wish him luck as he prepares for another uphill climb — soaked in rainwater and pride, unable to take the dry clothes because accepting aid would get him disqualified.

The crowd stirs. There's a runner coming up the paved hill. Coming from this direction is a bad sign — it means he's dropping rather than finishing. People guess it's J. B. or Carl, but after a moment Laz gasps.

"It's Blake," he says.

45   Blake is soaked and shivering. "I'm close to hypothermia," he says. "I couldn't do it." He says that climbing Rat Jaw was like scrambling up a playground slide in roller skates.

Laz hands over the bugle. It's as if he can't bear to play taps for Blake himself. He's clearly disappointed, but there's a note of glee in his voice when he says: "You never know what'll happen around here."

How does the race turn out? Turns out J. B. pulls off a surprising victory. In my attention to flashier runners, I'd somehow managed to forget about J. B. Good old Jonboy. This is what Barkley specializes in, right? It swallows the story you imagined and hands you another one.

Why do people do this, anyway? Whenever I pose the question, runners reply ironically: I'm a masochist; I need somewhere to put my craziness; type A

from birth. Nobody has to answer this question seriously, because they are already answering it seriously — with their bodies and their willpower and their pain. Maybe this is why so many ultra-runners are former addicts: They want to redeem the bodies they once punished, master the physical selves whose cravings they once served.

The persistence of "why" is the point: the elusive horizon of an unanswerable question, the conceptual equivalent of an unrunnable race.

One of the most compelling inqui- 50 ries into *why* lies in a tale of temporary madness: A.T.'s account of his fifth loop back in 2004. He describes wandering without any clear sense of how he'd gotten to the trail or what he was meant to be doing there: "The Barkley would be forgotten for minutes on end although the premise lingered. I *had* to get to the Garden Spot, for . . . *why*?" His amnesia captures the endeavor in its starkest terms. But his account offers flashes of wonder: "I stood in a shin-deep puddle for about an hour — squishing the mud in and out of my shoes. . . . I sat and poured gallon after gallon of fresh water into my shoes."

By the end of A.T.'s account, the facet of Barkley deemed most brutally taxing, that sinister and sacred "self-sufficiency," has become an inexplicable miracle: "When it cooled off, I had a long-sleeve shirt. When I got hungry, I had food. When it got dark, I had a light. I thought: *Wow, isn't it strange that I have all this perfect stuff, just when I need it?*"

This is evidence of a grace beyond the self that has, of course, come *from* the self — the same self that loaded the fanny pack hours before, whose role has been obscured by bone-weary delusion, turned *other* by the sheer fact of the body losing its own mind.

Understanding the Reading

1. **Character** Identify the personalities and the motives of the participants in the marathon. Consider what Jamison tells readers about them (for example, in paragraphs 3–5, 9–10, 13–18, and 38), as well as what she reveals through dialogue. Why is Jamison herself in attendance, and what do you learn about her?

2. **Action** Summarize what happens over the course of this narrative and the conflicts the participants face. Keep in mind that, because of the nature of the race, different things happen to different individuals at different times. Where does the climax occur?

3. **Thesis** What main point is the author making in relating this story? Where does she state this point most directly?

4. **Vocabulary** Jamison's brother told her that "he wants to achieve a completely insular system of accountability, one that doesn't depend on external feedback" (para. 38). What does he mean, and how does this relate to his participation in extreme racing?

Analyzing the Reading

1. **Audience** How can you tell that Jamison's intended audience was not primarily extreme racers but a more general group of readers? Point to some specific details she provides to support your answer.

2. **Purpose** What overall impression do you think Jamison hoped to leave readers with? What did she want to communicate about the marathon's participants?

3. **Sequence of events** Why do you think Jamison chose to move back and forth in time as she does in the essay? Was it necessary for her to do so, or could she have told the story strictly in chronological sequence?

4. **Technique** Look again at paragraphs 16 and 47. Why are these two isolated paragraphs crucial to Jamison's narrative?

Evaluating the Reading

1. **Story** How well does Jamison relate the incidents in her narrative? Do you feel that you have a clear understanding of the race and its implications, or do you have questions you wish Jamison had answered?

2. **Point of view** If this story were being written for a newspaper, the reporter would not use the first person or share personal thoughts, feelings, and observations, as Jamison does. How would a straightforward retelling of the external events of the race alter the effectiveness of the story?

3. **Character** Does Jamison make the people she describes come to life for you? Why, or why not?

4. **Setting** Throughout the essay, Jamison describes the physical location of the race. Point to some of her descriptions that you find particularly effective and explain what makes them so.

Discussing the Reading

1. Reread the essay's final paragraph. Discuss how this paragraph can be interpreted.

2. Ultimately, Jamison doesn't have a simple answer to her question, "Why do people do this, anyway?" (para. 48). How would you answer this question?

3. Lazarus Lake, or Laz, seems quite a character, as presented by Jamison. Discuss your responses to this man who so obviously enjoys stage-managing the grueling Barkley Marathons.

Writing about the Reading

1. **Essay** Write a personal narrative about an experience that seriously tested your strength and resolve. The challenge could have been a physical one, as described in "It's a Mad, Mad Marathon," but it could also have been one that involved the courage to stand up for something, such as your personal beliefs or someone you cared about. Make sure your essay communicates a central point about why the experience had special meaning for you.

2. **Essay** In "It's a Mad, Mad Marathon," the underdog wins the race. Brainstorm a list of occasions when you came from behind to succeed beyond your expectations, whether in a contest of some kind or in another aspect of your life. If you can't come up with any underdog experiences of your own, you might consider those experiences of friends or family members. Write an essay narrating one of those experiences.

3. **Combining patterns** In "It's a Mad, Mad Marathon," description of the setting and characters is crucial to supporting the action of the narrative. Write a personal narrative that also communicates the physical environment and, if appropriate, the appearance and personalities of other people involved. Use description along with narration to create a compelling story for readers. (If you have written another personal narration already, you might ask your instructor if you may revise it with an eye toward fleshing out the descriptive elements.)

📖 **TEXTBOOK**

History of the Future

Ben Beekman is a writer, Web and multimedia designer, consultant, and technology educator. **George Beekman** is also a writer, teacher, consultant, and multimedia developer. "History of the Future" is an excerpt from their textbook *Digital Planet: Tomorrow's Technology and You.*

Reading Tip

As you read this excerpt, highlight and annotate the reading using the guidelines for active reading discussed in Chapter 2, "Understanding Texts and Images." Consider what information you would need to remember for a class discussion or an in-class exam on the material.

Previewing the Reading

Preview the reading (see pp. 23–24 for guidelines), and write a sentence summarizing what you expect its main point will be.

History of the Future
Ben Beekman and George Beekman

*First we shape our tools, thereafter **they shape us**.*   — *Marshall McLuhan*

Today's technology raises fascinating and difficult questions. But these questions pale in comparison to the ones we'll have to deal with as the technology evolves in the coming years. Imagine . . .

> *You wake up to the sound of your radio playing songs and news stories that match your personal interest profile. The newscaster is talking about the hacker uprising that has crippled China's **infrastructure**, but you have other things on your mind.*
>
> *Today's the day of your big trip. You're looking forward to spending time in the same room with Tony, your Italian lab partner. Over the past few months you've become close friends, working and chatting by videophone, conquering virtual reality games together, and creating truly terrible music in those late-night long-distance jam sessions. Still, there's no substitute for being in the same space, especially after Tony's accident. Tony says that the chip implant and the prosthetic hand will make him almost as good as new, but you know he can use some moral support while he recovers.*

infrastructure: fundamental facilities and systems that service a country

The "Meteor" subway line of the Paris Metro is completely automated. The trains have no drivers.

On the way to the airport, your electric car's computer pipes up, "Ben's Bagels ahead on the right is running a special on cinnamon bagels. Nobody is at the drive-up window, so you can pick up a bagel and still make your flight."

5   "I thought I told you already: I don't like cinnamon bagels," you grumble.

Noting your annoyance, the car responds, "Sorry. I knew you didn't like cinnamon buns. No more cinnamon bagel ads or notifications, either." You wonder if the computer's spam and ad filter needs fixing, or you just forgot to tell it about your bagel preferences. Before you can ask, the computer announces that the next freeway entrance is blocked because of an accident. It suggests another entrance and talks you through the traffic to that entrance.

Once you get on the freeway, you join the "auto train" in the fast lane. Your car, now controlled by a network computer, races along at exactly the same speed as the car that's a few feet in front of it. You take this opportunity to ask your phone, "Which bus do I take to get from Rome airport to Tony's place?" The phone responds, "Bus 64. Watch out for pickpockets." You shiver when you remember what happened the last time you lost your wallet; it took months to undo the damage from that identity thief.

At the airport, you step out of the car near the shuttle station, remove your suitcase, and tell the car to park itself in the long-term lot. It says "Goodbye" and glides away.

On the shuttle you use your phone to try to learn a few Italian phrases. You say "Translate Italian" then "I would like to convert dollars into Euros." The phone responds, "Vorrei convertire i dollari in Euro," into your *tiny wireless earpiece. You know the phone can translate for you on the fly, but you'd like to be able to say a few things without its help.*

10   *At the security station, you insert your passport into the slot, put your hand on the scanner, and put your face into a shielded enclosure. After the system confirms your identity by taking your handprint and scanning your retinas, it issues a boarding pass, baggage claim slip, and routing tag. Under the watchful eye of the security guard, you attach the routing tag to your bag and place it on the conveyer belt leading to the baggage handling area. You notice that a nearby passenger is being vigorously questioned, and you hope that she's not the victim of yet another security system error.*

You realize you forgot to pack your jet lag medication. You enter the airport gift shop and insert your medical ID card under the pharmacy scanner. A dispenser issues a vial of pills that should work well with your genetic structure. You also download a best-selling book into your phone for the trip. As you leave the store, a sensor detects your two purchases. Your phone tells you that $33.97 has just been deducted from your account and asks if you want to know the remaining balance. You don't answer; you're trying to remember the last time you bought something from a human cashier.

The Kurzweil KNFB Mobile Reader makes it possible for a blind person to read signs, menus, and money.

This isn't far-fetched fantasy. Early versions of most of the devices in this story already exist. And exponential growth in computing power . . . makes it likely that you'll see similar technology in your everyday life in just a few years.

For better and for worse, we will be coexisting with information technology until death do us part. As with any relationship, a little understanding can go a long way.

Understanding the Reading

1. **Textbook reading** As part of the first chapter in a computer-science textbook, what does "History of the Future" communicate to readers? What do you learn from it?

2. **Language** Choose five words or phrases in the reading that refer to concepts related to the subject of digital technology. Briefly define each, using context clues or a dictionary.

3. **Meaning** How does the opening quotation by Marshall McLuhan support the point of the excerpt?

Analyzing the Reading

1. **Strategy** Why is this textbook excerpt structured as narrative? What is the goal of this narrative?

2. **Looking ahead** What does this excerpt from the opening chapter suggest about what you might expect from later chapters in the textbook?

3. **Similarities and differences** Compare this reading to other narrative essays in this chapter. What are some striking differences?

Evaluating the Reading

1. **Detail** What are some details in the narrative that you find particularly strong and helpful in communicating the main message of the excerpt?

2. **Language** The authors write in paragraph 12 that this is no "far-fetched fantasy" and that what they imagine will result from "exponential growth in computing power." How do you respond to the language they use here?

3. **Technique** This narrative is developed using the second person, "you." Evaluate this technique. Do you see yourself in the story, as the authors apparently intended you to?

Discussing the Reading

1. What differences and similarities do you see between this "factual" narrative of the future and science fiction?

2. The narrative suggests both positive and negative aspects of technology. Point to several examples of each. Do the positives outweigh the negatives in your mind?

3. Which predictions made in the reading do you find most surprising or intriguing? Do you find any disturbing?

Writing about the Reading

1. **Response paper** Write a narrative of your own in response to this reading. That is, imagine yourself at some point in the future going through your daily life using the technology you predict will be available then—no matter how far-fetched. See "Write in Response to a Reading," on pages 80–83 in Chapter 3, for guidelines.

2. **Summary for class** Assume you are preparing for a class discussion about this essay. Write a summary in which you answer the following question: What will be involved in the future for people "coexisting with information technology"?

3. **Essay** In an essay, react to the statement by Marshall McLuhan that opens the reading: "First we shape our tools, thereafter **they shape us**." How are you, and people generally, "shaped" by currently available technology?

Writing Your Own Narration Essay

Now that you have learned about the major characteristics, structure, and purposes of a narration essay, you know everything necessary to write your own narrative. In this section you will read a student's narration essay and get advice on finding ideas, drafting your essay, and revising and editing it. You may want to use the essay prompts in "Readings for Practice, Ideas for Writing" (p. 198) or choose your own topic.

A Student Model Narration Essay

Mina Raine, an education major, wrote this essay for an assignment given by her first-year writing instructor. She had to describe a situation in which her involvement made a difference or affected others. As you read the essay, notice how Raine's narrative creates conflict and tension and builds to a climax and resolution. Highlight the sections where you think the tension is particularly intense.

Title

Taking Back Control

Mina Raine

Introduction: Raine gives background about her relationship with Beth.

My friend Beth is soft spoken but strong in faith and character. She is one of those rare people who can light up a room with her smile or make you feel at ease just by simply being near you. We met freshman year at a gathering of mutual friends in the largest dorm on campus. Since then, we've spent our time together among a close-knit circle of friends. Beth has always seemed, to me, so mature and composed and so in control of herself and her life, so giving, so caring, so nurturing in all her relationships, which is why I was deeply concerned and very much surprised when I began to notice a drastic change in her.

Thesis statement: Raine gives a rationale for her concern.

Transitions help sequence events.
Action: begins with specific detail

First I noticed that Beth was making a habit out of eating her dinner from a small cereal bowl instead of a plate. I didn't think much of that, at first. Maybe the dining hall had temporarily run out of plates and a bowl was all she could find. Or maybe it was just one of those funny little habits we all find ourselves adopting, eventually. (Later I would learn that the small bowl is a way to monitor and control the amount of food she eats; you can only fit so much food into the shallow dish.)

Tension begins to build.

A few weeks later, my friends and I noticed a dramatic change in Beth's appearance—sunken, tired eyes void of their usual sparkle, a smile that seemed forced, and the clothes that once hugged her lovely curves in a subtle and conservative way now hanging off her fragile frame. This coupled with her strange cereal bowl habit was finally enough to make us realize something was definitely wrong. Of course, we weren't sure yet if Beth really was struggling with an eating disorder, but it was certainly evident that she was not herself, and from her somewhat depressed and rather distracted demeanor, she seemed to be seriously struggling with something.

Then, on one particular evening in the dining hall, my friends and I overheard Beth discussing her new workout regimen with her boyfriend, Steve. She had recently started fitting in evening running sessions between all of her studies and extracurricular activities. Steve had been running on the treadmill daily and carefully monitoring what he ate in an effort to lose the "freshman fifteen" (or twenty) he had gained. Unfortunately, it seemed his new efforts to live a healthy lifestyle had rubbed off on Beth, in an unhealthy way. My friend, who had been at a perfect weight and had been eating properly, was now eating less and exercising more. It was a sure recipe for disaster. I heard Steve talking to Beth about how many miles they had run that evening and how many more they would run the next day. He had her on the same workout schedule he was on, but she wasn't the one who was overweight. As I sat there listening to him influence her in this way, I felt myself getting angry. I didn't know for sure what was wrong with Beth at that point (though I had a pretty good idea), but it was obvious something was wrong. How could he not see

Tension increases.

that? The dark circles under Beth's eyes showed her obvious lack of sleep, and her low energy and lack of focus showed that her body wasn't getting the nutrition it needed.

After listening to the unsettling conversation between Beth and Steve about their strict workout routine, my friends and I began discussing the matter among ourselves and deciding on the best way to address the issue with Beth. I spent a few days wondering how best to approach her or if I even should. What if I upset her and she stopped talking to me? What if we were wrong and Beth was fine? Or worse, what if we were right and she pulled away from us? Then, Beth solved this dilemma for me: *She* came to *me*.

Dialogue leads to a climax.

Three weeks after my friend's struggle with food and weight became glaringly obvious, she knocked on my door. "I need to talk to you," she said, "and I think you already know what it's about."

5

I felt unprepared for this moment. Beth responded in a calm, serious tone to my anxious silence: "First, I feel I owe you an apology for making you worry about me. You're a good friend and I'm sorry." Here she broke down, and it was my turn to try to be stoic.

"It's OK. It's nothing you have to apologize for. But are you OK?"

Climax

"Not really," Beth answered in an unsteady voice. "I have an eating disorder."

Conclusion: Raine returns to the idea in her thesis statement — her knowledge of Beth as someone in control of her life.

What do you say to that? You know it happens, but you never think it will be you or someone close to you who will be plagued by a nagging, evil voice in the back of her head telling her she's had enough to eat today (even though she's still very hungry) or that despite the fact that she is a size 5 she really shouldn't enjoy a piece of cake for dessert. "Is it bulimia?" I asked Beth. She had regained her composure now, and spoke matter-of-factly.

"No, I don't make myself sick. It's not really anorexia either because I do eat. I just don't eat much. It's more of a control thing. When I eat my meals out of a cereal bowl, I can control the portion size, keep it small, and I'm aware of exactly how much I am eating."

"When did this start?" I asked, expecting her to say only a few weeks, maybe a few months ago.

"I've struggled with it most of my life, but I had it mostly under control until around a year ago."

A year! She had been fighting this ugly thing for a year, and we, I, had only just noticed in the past few weeks? How could that be? Beth later told me that her now ex-boyfriend had made a trivial but insensitive comment about her weight around a year ago. That was what had triggered the disorder to resurface. I was furious with myself and at a loss for words. All I could do was hug her, tell her that I have absolute faith in her and her ability to fight this thing, this disgusting thing that has taken over her body and her life, and cry into the comfort of my hands when she was finally too far down the hall to hear me.

When I checked in with Beth a couple days after her disconcerting but unsurprising revelation, she broke down and gave me an intimate glimpse into the complicated and disturbing battle being fought within her head. She seemed so defeated but aware of this feeling of defeat, which only made her angry at herself. I did my best to console her with the reassuring fact that her awareness of the problem and the need to make some serious changes in her life was already a giant step toward her recovery. I also told her that while I would always be there for her, to support and encourage her, I'm not qualified to truly help her deal with her disorder.

"I know," she said, a few silent tears sliding down her pale cheeks, "I've made an appointment with the counseling office on campus."

"I'm so proud of you," I responded as I embraced her.

"I'm hoping you'll come with me, at least for the first visit."

"Of course," I answered. "You're strong and smart. You will beat this. You'll get better. And I'm always here if you need to talk or just need a hug. Just please promise me you'll stop working out until you get back to more normal eating habits. That means no more cereal bowls. Unless, of course, you're eating cereal."

Beth laughed a little at this last comment, which is what I had been hoping for. Even if only for a moment, the Beth I knew shone through in that brief smile and soft chuckle. I knew then that though she'll probably have to work on it every day, Beth will regain control of her body and her life.

15

Responding to Raine's Essay

1. Evaluate the strength of Raine's thesis. How clear and specific is it?
2. What ideas in the essay, if any, do you think should be discussed more fully? Where did you feel more details were needed? Which details — if any — are unnecessary?
3. How does Raine establish conflict and create tension?
4. Where does Raine use foreshadowing? How effective is it?
5. Evaluate the title, introduction, and conclusion of the essay.

Finding Ideas for Your Narration Essay

One way to find ideas to write about is to look for topics *as you read* material in this book, in other classes, or in your spare time. Pay particular attention as you read to the issue, struggle, or dilemma at hand. Try to discover what broader issue the essay is concerned with. For example, a narrative about a worker's conflict with a supervisor is also concerned with the larger issue of authority. Once you've identified the larger issue, you can begin to develop ideas about it by relating it to your own experience.

Choosing an Event or Incident for Your Narration Essay

As you think about an experience or incident to write about, be sure that it is memorable and vivid enough that you can recall the details. After all, you don't want to discover, when your draft is nearly completed, that you cannot remember important details about the experience. Make sure you're comfortable writing about the incident. At this stage, you should also decide whether to tell your story in the first or the third person.

Gathering Details about the Experience or Incident

This step involves recollecting as many details about the experience or incident as possible and recording them on paper or in a computer file. Reenact the story, sketching each scene in your mind. Identify key actions, describe the main participants, and express your feelings. Here are a few ways to gather details.

- **Replay the experience or incident in your mind.** Jot down exactly what you see, hear, smell, taste, and feel—colors, dialogue, sounds, odors, flavors, and sensations. Also note how these details make you feel.
- **Write the following headings on a piece of paper, or type them on your computer screen:** *Scene, Key Actions, Key Participants, Key Dialogue,* **and** *My Feelings.* List your ideas under each heading systematically.
- **Describe the incident or experience to a friend.** Have your friend ask questions as you retell the story. Jot down the details that the retelling and questioning help you recall.
- **Describe the incident or experience aloud while recording it.** Then listen to the recording and make notes.
- **Consider different aspects of the incident or experience by asking** *who, what, when, where, how,* **and** *why* **questions.** Record your answers.

Developing and Supporting a Thesis

Once you have enough details, it is time to focus your thesis—the main point of your narrative. You probably have a working thesis in mind. Now is the time to improve it.

A thesis statement may be placed at the beginning of a narrative essay. It may also be placed at the end of a narrative, or it may be implied. Once you have a thesis, you may need to do some additional prewriting to develop supporting details.

Drafting Your Narration Essay

When you are satisfied with your thesis and your support for it, you are ready to organize your ideas and write the first draft. Decide whether you will put all events in chronological order or whether you will use flashbacks or foreshadowing for dramatic effect. As you write, refer to the graphic organizer in Figure 10.1 (p. 188) to remind yourself of the structure and elements of a narration essay. Use the following guidelines to help keep the narrative on track.

1. **The introduction should contain an attention-getting opening, provide any necessary background information, and introduce the conflict.** The introduction should also contain your thesis if you have decided to place it at the beginning of the essay.

2. **The narrative should build tension as it leads up to the final resolution.** Each major action should have its own paragraph. Use transitional words and phrases to help readers understand the sequence of events.

3. **The conclusion should end the essay in a satisfying manner.** Resist providing a summary at the end of the narrative, as it may detract from the impact of the story. Instead, try ending in one of the ways described in "How Is a Narration Essay Structured?" (p. 187).

Revising Your Narration Essay

If possible, set your draft aside for a day or two before rereading and revising it. As you reread, don't worry about errors in spelling, grammar, and mechanics; focus instead on improving the overall effectiveness of the narrative. Will it interest readers and make them want to know what happens next? Does it make your point clearly? To discover weaknesses in your draft, use the revision flowchart in Figure 10.3.

Editing and Proofreading Your Essay

The last step is to check your revised narrative essay for errors in grammar, spelling, punctuation, and mechanics. In addition, be sure to look for the types of errors that you tend to make in any writing assignments, whether for this class or another situation. For narrative essays, pay particular attention to the following kinds of sentence problems.

1. **Be certain that your sentences vary in structure.** A string of sentences that are similar in length and structure is tedious to read.

   ▶   We went to the Ding Darling National Wildlife Preserve located on Sanibel Island, Florida. It was ~~e~~*E*stablished in 1945 as the Sanibel Refuge/ *it was renamed* ~~Its name was changed~~ in 1967 to honor the man who helped found it.

2. **Be sure to punctuate dialogue correctly.** Use commas to separate the quotation from the phrase that introduces it, unless the quotation is

Figure 10.3 Revising a Narration Essay

QUESTIONS		REVISION STRATEGIES
1. Main point Is the main point clear?	No	• Make your thesis more explicit.
Yes		
2. Conflict Does the narrative present a clear conflict related to the main point?	No	• Add events specific to the conflict. • Rework your thesis to make it better relate to the conflict.
Yes		
3. Key scenes, people, and action Do they clearly relate to the main point and conflict?	No	• Delete unnecessary scenes, people, or actions.
Yes		
4. Descriptions Is each key scene, person, or action vividly described?	No	• Brainstorm vivid details. • Consider adding dialogue.
Yes		
5. Major events Is the sequence of events clear? Is it clear when you use foreshadowing or flashbacking?	No	• Add missing events. • Consider rearranging the events. • Use transitions to clarify the sequence of events.
Yes		
6. Topic sentences Is each paragraph focused on a separate part of the action?	No	• Be sure each paragraph has a topic sentence and supporting details. (See Chapter 7.) • Combine paragraphs about closely related events and split those that cover more than one event.
Yes		
7. Dialogue Is it realistic when you say it aloud? Does it directly relate to the conflict?	No	• Record yourself telling someone what you want your dialogue to express. Use that recording to revise your dialogue and make it more natural. • Eliminate dialogue that does not add to the story.
Yes		
8. Point of view Do you use a consistent point of view and verb tense?	No	• Reconsider your point of view. • If the tense changes for no reason, revise for consistency.
Yes		
9. Introduction and conclusion Do they address the main point? Does the conclusion resolve the conflict?	No	• Revise your introduction and conclusion. (See pp. 126–30.)

integrated into the sentence. If the sentence ends with a quotation, the period stays inside the quotation marks.

As the wildlife refuge guide noted, "American crocodiles are an endangered species and must be protected."

The wildlife refuge guide noted that "American crocodiles are an endangered species and must be protected."

3. **Use strong active verbs to make the narrative lively and interesting.**

| WEAK | The puppy was afraid of the fireworks. |
| STRONG | The puppy whimpered and quivered as the fireworks exploded. |

Use verbs in the **active voice** (the subject performs the action). Avoid verbs in the **passive voice** (the subject is acted upon).

| PASSIVE | It was claimed by the cyclist that the motorist failed to yield the right of way. |
| ACTIVE | The cyclist claimed that the motorist failed to yield the right of way. |

4. **Use consistent verb tense.** Most narratives are told in the past tense ("Yolanda *discovered* the glass in the front door was shattered."). Fast-paced, short narratives, however, are sometimes related in the present tense ("Yolanda *discovers* the glass."). Whichever tense you choose, be sure to use it consistently. Avoid switching between past and present tenses unless the context of the narrative clearly requires it.

| INCONSISTENT TENSE | Marissa raced down the street and hugs her brother. |
| CONSISTENT TENSE | Marissa races down the street and hugs her brother. |

Chapter 11

Description: Portraying People, Places, and Things

Quick Start: Suppose you are moving to a large city and need to sell your car because the apartment you just rented does not include parking. You place the following advertisement in the local newspaper:

6-year-old VW bug. $4500 or best offer. Call 555-2298.

Although the ad runs for two weeks, you get only a few calls and no offers. Then a friend advises you to write a more appealing description of your unique vehicle that will make people want to contact you. Rewrite the advertisement, describing the car shown in the photograph in a way that will convince prospective buyers to call you.

What Is Description?

The ad you wrote in response to the Quick Start prompt uses description. Description presents information in a way that appeals to one or more of the five senses, usually with the purpose of creating a specific impression or feeling. Descriptive writing makes your ideas vivid so that the audience can almost see, hear, smell, taste, or touch what you are writing about. People use description every day. For example, in a conversation with a friend you might describe a pair of new shoes you recently bought, a flavor of ice cream you tasted last night, or a concert you attended last weekend. You will use description in many situations in college and on the job. For instance, you may be asked to describe the odor and appearance of a substance made by combining two chemicals in a chemistry lab report for college. As a nurse at a local burn treatment center, you might be responsible for recording on each patient's chart the overall appearance of and changes in second- and third-degree burns.

Description does the following:

1. It uses sensory details.
2. It uses active verbs and varied sentences.
3. It creates a dominant impression.
4. It uses connotative language effectively.
5. It uses comparisons.
6. It assumes a vantage point.
7. It is often combined with other patterns.

Successful descriptions offer readers more than a list of sensory details or a catalog of characteristics. In a good description, the details work together to create a single dominant impression. Writers often use comparison to help readers understand the experience.

1. Description Uses Sensory Details

Sensory details appeal to one or more of the five senses and can help readers experience the object, sensation, event, or person described in an essay.

Sight   When you describe what something looks like, you help the reader create a mental picture of it. In the following excerpt, Loren Eiseley uses visual detail to describe what he found in a field.

One day as I cut across the field which at that time extended on one side of our suburban shopping center,

Size: "giant"
Shape: "funnel"

I found a giant slug feeding from a funnel of pink ice cream in an abandoned Dixie cup. I could see his eyes

Color: "pink" and "dark"	telescope and protrude in a kind of dim, uncertain ecstasy as his dark body bunched and elongated in the
Action: "bunched and elongated"	curve of the cup.

—Loren Eiseley, "The Brown Wasps"

The description enables the reader to imagine the slug eating the ice cream in a way that a bare statement of the facts—"On my way to the mall, I saw a slug in a paper cup"—could never do. Notice also how he includes specific details ("suburban shopping center," "Dixie cup") to help readers visualize the scene.

Sound   Sound can also be a powerful descriptive tool. Can you "hear" the engines in the following description?

Active verbs: "throbbed and fluttered," "purred," "whined"	They were one-cylinder and two-cylinder engines, and some were make-and-break and some were jump-spark, but they all made a sleepy sound across the lake. The one-lungers throbbed and fluttered, and the twin-
Descriptive adjectives: "sleepy," "petulant," "irritable," "still"	cylinder ones purred and purred, and that was a quiet sound too. But now the campers all had outboards. In the daytime, in the hot mornings, these motors made
Comparison: "whined about one's ears like mosquitoes"	a petulant, irritable sound; at night, in the still evening when the afterglow lit the water, they whined about one's ears like mosquitoes.

—E. B. White, "Once More to the Lake"

Writers of description also use *onomatopoeia*—that is, words that approximate the sounds they describe. The words *hiss, whine, spurt,* and *sizzle* are examples.

Smell   Smells are sometimes difficult to describe, partly because there are not as many adjectives for smells as there are for sights and sounds. However, smell can be an effective descriptive device, as shown here.

> Driving through farm country at summer sunset provides a cavalcade of smells: manure, cut grass, honeysuckle, spearmint, wheat chaff, scallions, chicory, tar from the macadam road.
>
> —Diane Ackerman, *A Natural History of the Senses*

Notice how Ackerman lists nouns that evoke distinct odors and leaves it to the reader to imagine how they smell.

Taste   Words that evoke the sense of taste can make descriptions very lively, as in Rowen Jacobsen's description of eating a raw oyster from *A Geography of Oysters*:

After the initial sensation of salt, you will sense the body of the oyster. For this, you will have to chew. Some squeamish eaters don't like to chew their oysters. I'm sorry, but chewing is where all the toothsome pleasure of the oyster comes out — the snappy way it resists your teeth for just a moment before breaking, like a fresh fig. Chewing also begins to release an oyster's sweetness.

Touch   Descriptions of texture, temperature, and weight enable a reader not only to visualize but almost to tactilely experience an object or a scene. In the excerpt that follows, Annie Dillard uses tactile descriptions to accurately describe the experience of holding a Polyphemus moth cocoon.

Weight	We passed the cocoon around; it was heavy. As we held it in our hands, the creature within warmed and squirmed. We were delighted, and wrapped it tighter in our fists. The pupa began to jerk violently, in heart-stopping knocks. Who's there? I can still feel those
Texture	thumps, urgent through a muffling of spun silk and leaf, urgent through the swaddling of many years, against the curve of my palm. We kept passing it around. When
Temperature	it came to me again it was hot as a bun; it jumped half out of my hand. The teacher intervened. She put it, still heaving and banging, in the ubiquitous Mason Jar.

—Annie Dillard, *Pilgrim at Tinker Creek*

2. Description Uses Active Verbs and Varied Sentences

Sensory details are often best presented by using active, vivid verbs in sentences with varied structure. In fact, active verbs are often more effective than adverbs in creating striking and lasting impressions, as the following example demonstrates.

ORIGINAL   The team captain *proudly* accepted the award.

REVISED   The team captain *marched* to the podium, *grasped* the trophy, and *gestured* toward his teammates.

To maximize the effective expression of sensory details, writers must be sure to use different types of sentences and to vary sentence lengths. It is also important to avoid wordy or repetitive sentences, especially those with strings of mediocre adjectives or adverbs (*pretty, really, very*), which detract from the vivid impression you want to create.

3. Description Creates a Dominant Impression

An effective description leaves the reader with a **dominant impression**—an overall attitude, mood, or feeling about the subject. The impression may be awe, inspiration, anger, or distaste, for example. The dominant impression is the **implied thesis** of a descriptive essay; it suggests the author's main point about the subject.

A descriptive essay about an old storage box in the writer's parents' attic might emphasize, or give a "slant" to, *memories of childhood*. Given this slant, the writer can describe the box in several different ways, each of which would convey a different dominant impression.

> A box filled with treasures from my childhood brought back memories of long, sunny afternoons playing in our backyard.
>
> (The essay goes on to describe those afternoons.)

> Opening the box was like lifting the lid of a time machine, revealing toys and games from another era.
>
> (The essay describes the games that the speaker no longer plays.)

> When I opened the box I was eight years old again, fighting over my favorite doll with my twin sister, Erica.
>
> (The essay focuses on describing a sibling relationship.)

Because each example provides a different impression of the contents of the storage box, each would require a different type of support—that is, only selected objects from within the box would be relevant to each impression. Also, it is significant that in all of these examples the dominant impression is stated directly rather than implied. Many times, writers rely on descriptive language to imply a dominant impression.

4. Description Uses Connotative Language Effectively

As noted in Chapter 3, most words have two levels of meaning: **denotative** and **connotative**. The denotation of a word is its precise dictionary meaning (for instance, the denotation of *flag* is "a piece of cloth used as a national emblem"). Usually, however, feelings and attitudes are also associated with a word; these are the word's connotations. (A common connotation of *flag* is patriotism—love and respect for one's country.) As you write, be careful about the connotations of the words you choose. Select words that strengthen the dominant impression you are creating.

5. Description Uses Comparisons

When describing a person or an object, writers can help their audience by comparing it to something familiar. Several types of comparison are used in descriptive writing: similes, metaphors, personification, and analogies.

In a **simile** the comparison is direct and is introduced by the word *like* or *as*. For example, in the essay "Twelve Moments in the Life of the Artist," David Sedaris uses this simile in describing a theater space: "My parents attended the premiere, sitting cross-legged on one of the padded mats spread like islands across the filthy concrete floor."

A **metaphor** is an indirect comparison, describing one thing as if it were another. Instead of the simile shown above, Sedaris could have used a metaphor to describe the theater space: "The mats were islands in a filthy concrete sea."

Personification is a figure of speech in which an object is given human qualities or characteristics. "The television screen stared back at me" is an example. An **analogy** is an extended comparison in which one subject is used to explain the other. Often, a more familiar subject is used to explain one that is less familiar. For example, you might explain how the human eye works by comparing it to a camera, emphasizing the similarities. Both have a lens, both project an image, the pupil of the eye contracts or expands to adjust the amount of light as does the shutter of a camera, and so forth. Like similes and metaphors, analogies add interest to writing while making your ideas more accessible to the reader.

6. Description Assumes a Vantage Point

A **vantage point** is the point or position from which one writes a description. With a *fixed vantage point*, you describe what you see from a particular position. With a *moving vantage point*, you describe your subject from a number of different positions. In this way, the vantage point is similar to a movie camera: A fixed vantage point is like a stationary camera trained on a subject from one direction, whereas a moving vantage point is like a handheld camera that moves around the subject, capturing it from many directions.

7. Description Is Often Integrated with Other Patterns

Sometimes a description alone fulfills the purpose of an essay. In most cases, however, description is used in other types of essays. For instance, in a narrative essay, description helps readers experience events, reconstruct scenes, and visualize action. Similarly, description can explain the causes or effects of a phenomenon, compare or contrast animal species, and provide examples that illustrate defensive behavior in children. Writers use description to keep their readers interested in the material. Description, then, is essential to many types of academic and business writing.

Reading and Writing Description Essays

In this section you will learn about the structure of a description essay, read a sample essay, and practice using the guidelines for understanding, analyzing, and evaluating description essays. This will help you skillfully read and write essays that use description.

How Is a Description Essay Structured?

The structure of a description essay will depend somewhat on the subject, but all description essays have a structure that includes a dominant impression, supporting details, and a conclusion.

1. The **introduction** provides the background and setting, and the **thesis** states or suggests the dominant impression.
2. The **body paragraphs** provide supporting details and comparisons, which can be organized in several different ways.
3. The **conclusion** references the dominant impression and brings the essay to a close.

Figure 11.1 represents these major components visually.

Figure 11.1 Graphic Organizer for a Description Essay

Title	
Introduction	Background Setting
	Dominant impression (stated or suggested in thesis)
Body paragraphs	Supporting details
	Supporting details
	Supporting details
Conclusion	Reference to the dominant impression Draws essay to a close

1. THE INTRODUCTION PROVIDES THE BACKGROUND
   AND SETTING, AND THE THESIS STATES OR SUGGESTS
   THE DOMINANT IMPRESSION

In a descriptive essay, the introduction provides a context for the description and presents the thesis statement, which states or suggests the dominant impression. Any relevant background information necessary for understanding the description should be included here; the setting is likely to be part of this background. The introduction establishes the dominant impression that will also hold the rest of the essay together. This impression may be stated directly in the thesis or it may be implied. Either way, the dominant impression creates a mood or feeling about the subject, which all the other details in the essay will explain or support. The dominant impression should appeal to the writer's audience, offer an unusual perspective, and provide new insights into the subject.

 Reading|Writing   When reading a description essay, ask yourself, How does the author want me to feel about the subject? The answer will be the dominant impression the writer wants to convey. When writing a description essay, you should carefully consider what dominant impression of your subject you would like to convey.

2. THE BODY PARAGRAPHS PROVIDE SUPPORTING DETAILS
   AND COMPARISONS, WHICH CAN BE ORGANIZED IN SEVERAL
   DIFFERENT WAYS

The body of a descriptive essay expands on the dominant impression established in the introduction, through supporting details and comparisons. Effective descriptions, like other kinds of writing, must follow a clear method of organization in order to be easy to read. Three common methods of organization used in descriptive writing are spatial order, chronological order, and most-to-least or least-to-most order.

- **Spatial order** systematically describes a subject from top to bottom, inside to outside, or near to far away. Essays start from a central focal point and then describe the objects that surround it. For example, a description of a college campus might start with a building at the center of the campus, then describe the buildings next to it, and conclude by describing something on the outskirts.

- **Chronological order** works well for describing events or changes that occur in objects or places over a given period. For example, chronological order would be appropriate to describe the changes in a puppy's behavior as it grows.

- **Most-to-least** or **least-to-most order** (see p. 117) might be used to describe the different smells in a flower garden or the sounds of an orchestra tuning up.

Description essays can also be arranged according to the five senses. For example, an essay describing a chocolate-chip cookie could give details about how it looks, smells, tastes, sounds (its crunch), and feels.

No matter which organization the essay follows, the details included in the body paragraphs should follow these guidelines.

1. **Include only relevant details.** The sensory details should enhance the reader's understanding of the event, person, or scene being described.

2. **Keep the description focused.** Select enough details to make your essential points and dominant impression clear. Readers may become impatient if you include too many details.

3. **Make sure the description fits the essay's tone and point of view.** A personal description, for example, is not appropriate in an essay explaining a technical process.

Reading|Writing   When reading the body of a description essay, highlight particularly striking details and images that you may want to refer to again or that may help you assess the essay's effectiveness. When writing the body of a description essay, select striking sensory details that make your point effectively; leave out details that tell the reader little or nothing. Consider providing a few metaphors or similes to make your essay understandable and vivid, but only do so if the comparison comes naturally. A contrived metaphor or simile will only lessen the impact of your essay.

3.   THE CONCLUSION REFERENCES THE DOMINANT IMPRESSION AND BRINGS THE ESSAY TO A CLOSE

The conclusion draws the description to a close and makes a final reference to the dominant impression. It may offer a final detail or make a closing statement.

Reading|Writing   When reading the conclusion of a description essay, ask yourself if the writer brings the essay to a satisfying close. Is it consistent with the dominant impression? When writing a conclusion to a description essay, be sure to ask yourself, Have I provided vivid details that are consistent with the dominant impression? What final statement will make this impression stick in my reader's mind?

A Model Description Essay

Title

Eating Chilli Peppers

Jeremy MacClancy

Jeremy MacClancy is an anthropologist who studies the everyday choices people make and how those choices vary from culture to culture. As a professor of social anthropology at Oxford Brookes University in England, MacClancy has written on a variety of topics, but he has a particular interest in food. The following essay comes from MacClancy's book *Consuming Culture: Why You Eat What You Eat* (1993).

***

Introduction: creates interest through questions that are answered in essay

Body paragraphs: sensory details and comparison: vivid simile

Sensory details: taste, touch, feel

Sensory details and comparison: another vivid simile

Comparison to drug use

How come over half of the world's population have made a powerful chemical irritant the center of their gastronomic lives? How can so many millions stomach chillies?

Biting into a tabasco pepper is like aiming a flame-thrower at your parted lips. There might be little reaction at first, but then the burn starts to grow. A few seconds later the chilli mush in your mouth reaches critical mass and your palate prepares for liftoff. The message spreads. The sweat glands open, your eyes stream, your nose runs, your stomach warms up, your heart accelerates, and your lungs breathe faster: All this is normal. But bite off more than your body can take, and you will be left coughing, sneezing, and spitting. Tears stripe your cheeks, and your mouth belches fire like a dragon celebrating its return to life. Eater, beware!

As a general stimulant, chilli is similar to amphetamines—only quicker, cheaper, nonaddictive, and beneficial to boot. Employees at the tabasco plant in Louisiana rarely complain of coughs, hay fever, or sinusitis. (Recent evidence, however, suggests that too many chillies can bring on stomach cancer.) Over the centuries, people have used hot peppers as a folk medicine to treat sore throats or inflamed gums, to relieve respiratory distress, and to ease gastritis induced by alcoholism. For aching muscles and tendons, a chilli plaster is more effective than one of mustard, with the added advantage that it does not blister the skin. But people do not eat tabasco, jalapeño, or cayenne peppers because of their pharmacological side effects. They eat them for the taste—different varieties have different flavors—and for the fire they give off. In other words, they go for the burn.

Eating chillies makes for exciting times: the thrill of anticipation, the extremity of the flames, and then the slow descent back to normality. This is a benign form of masochism, like going to a horror movie, riding a roller coaster, or stepping into a cold bath after a sauna. The body flashes danger signals, but the brain knows the threat is not too great. Aficionados, self-absorbed in their burning passion, know exactly how to pace their whole chilli eating so that the flames are maintained at a steady maximum. Wrenched out of normal routines by the continuing assault on their mouths, they concentrate on the sensation and ignore almost everything else. They play with fire and just ride the burn, like experienced surfers cresting along a wave. For them, without hot peppers, food would lose its zest and their days would seem too dull. A cheap, legal thrill, chilli is the spice of their life.

In the rural areas of Mexico, men can turn their chilli habit into a contest of strength by seeing who can stomach the most hot peppers in a set time. This gastronomic test, however, is not used as a way to prove one's machismo, for women can play the game as well. In this context, chillies are a nonsexist form of acquired love for those with strong hearts and fiery passions—a steady source of hot sauce for their lives.

The enjoyable sensations of a running nose, crying eyes, and dragon-like mouth belching flames are clearly not for the timorous.

More tabasco, anyone?

Sensory details: taste, feel

Describes use of chillies in Mexico

Conclusion: Author ends as he began, with a question.

5

Understanding, Analyzing, and Evaluating Description Essays

In reading and writing description essays, your goal is to get beyond mere competence: That is, you want to be able to do more than merely understand the content of the essays you're reading or convey just your basic ideas to the audience you're writing for.

Reading|Writing   Truly skillful reading and writing require the abilities to **understand, analyze,** *and* **evaluate** material. These abilities are important to you as a reader because they give you a systematic, thorough method of examining a reading. They're important to you as a writer because they help you decide what to revise, rewrite, drop, and replace, allowing you to produce a well-written, effective essay.

Understanding a Description Essay

To understand a descriptive essay, focus on the dominant impression and the details, both factual and sensory, that support it. You may find it helpful to read the essay more than once. Read it the first time to get a general sense of what is going on. Then reread it, paying attention to the details and the language used. Use the reading skills you learned in Chapter 2 and answer the following questions.

- **What is the subject and what aspect of the subject does the essay focus on?** Almost any subject has many aspects or facets. Determine with what trait, characteristic, or part the essay is concerned.

- **What is the essay's dominant impression?** If it is not directly stated, ask yourself how the author wants you to feel about the subject. Your answer is the dominant impression.

- **How does each paragraph contribute to the dominant impression?** Figure out what new information each paragraph adds.

- **What sensory details are particularly important?** Highlight particularly striking details and images that you may want to refer to again or that may be helpful in analyzing the essay.

- **What is the author's vantage point?** The vantage point (see p. 236) will help you understand how the author is looking at the subject.

- **How is the essay organized?** Draw a graphic organizer that shows the structure of the essay. Figure 11.2 provides a graphic organizer of Jeremy MacClancy's "Eating Chilli Peppers." Refer back to the graphic organizer for description essays on page 237 before starting your own diagram.

Understanding in Action

Following is one student's brief summary of paragraph 3 of Jeremy MacClancy's "Eating Chilli Peppers." In a paragraph, summarize the dominant impression created in the essay, quoting specific words that contribute to this impression.

> Chillies are a "stimulant" more "beneficial" than any drug. They are also a "folk medicine" used to treat many ailments. But that's not really why people eat them. People eat chillies for the "fire" and the "burn" they enjoy in their taste.

Figure 11.2 Graphic Organizer for "Eating Chilli Peppers"

Title	"Eating Chilli Peppers"
Introduction	Many people like eating chilli peppers despite the possible pain caused by doing so.
	Dominant impression: Chilli acts as stimulant, thrilling the senses

Body paragraphs	Sensory details and comparisons
	Eating chillies is "like going to a horror movie, riding a roller coaster."
	Eating chillies can become a contest of strength.
	"Biting into a tabasco pepper is like aiming a flame-thrower at your parted lips" "...your mouth belches fire..."

Conclusion	Eating chilli peppers can be painful, exciting, and in some cases, beneficial to one's health.

Analyzing a Description Essay

Analyzing a descriptive essay involves examining how the writer describes the subject and how he or she shapes your response to it. The words and details a writer chooses can make a subject sound pleasant or unpleasant, attractive or repellant, and so forth. Consider the difference between a stranger described as having an "impish, childlike grin" versus one with "cold, vacant eyes." Use the following questions to analyze descriptive essays.

- **Is the essay intended to be objective, subjective, or both?** An **objective** essay is written to inform—to present information or communicate ideas without bias or emotion. A **subjective** essay, often written in the first person (*I, me, mine*), is intended to create an emotional response. An objective essay describes only what the writer observes or experiences, while a subjective essay includes both observations and the writer's feelings about them. For subjective essays, be sure to ask yourself what attitude the writer is trying to convey.

- **What impression of the subject did the writer create?** Authors choose sensory details carefully and intentionally, usually to make a point. Added together, what feelings, impressions, or responses do the sensory details leave you with? What do they point to, suggest, or imply?

The sensory details writers choose often reveal their feelings and attitudes toward the subject. Descriptive words, and their connotative meanings (see p. 235), are used intentionally to create a particular emotional response. As you read, get in the habit of highlighting descriptive words with strong connotative meanings.

- **What types of language did the writer use to create his or her impression?** To which senses do the sensory images appeal? Examine the figures of speech (similes and metaphors) and analogies that are used. What do they add to the dominant impression?

- **Why did the writer choose a particular vantage point?** Consider what else you might have learned had a different vantage point been used. What does the chosen vantage point emphasize that another would not?

Analysis in Action

Following is an example of a student's analysis of how the language in one paragraph creates an appealing impression of the topic. Based on your reading of "Eating Chilli Peppers," answer one of the questions above.

> In paragraph 4, MacClancy uses language that describes chillis as a positive experience, at least for people who enjoy them. They make "for exciting times" and create "the thrill of anticipation." The experience is like the fun of seeing a horror movie or riding a roller coaster. For fans they add "zest" and are the "spice of their life." Without chillies everything would be "dull." MacClancy's use of words and phrases that convey excitement and thrills makes the description of the experience of peppers seem like a positive one.

Evaluating a Description Essay

Evaluating a descriptive essay involves judging how effective the writer's description of the subject is, as well as determining how fair and accurate it is. As you evaluate the essay, ask yourself the following questions.

- **Is the dominant impression fair and accurate?** Determine whether the writer presents a biased or unbiased impression of the subject. If biased, determine whether the writer openly reveals the bias or whether it is subtle or hidden.

- **What details might the writer have chosen to omit?** As you read, ask yourself, What hasn't the author told me? or What else would I like to know about the subject? Authors may omit details because they are not relevant, but they may also omit details that disprove the dominant impression they are trying to convey. To be sure you are getting a complete picture of the subject, do some research, consulting several other sources of information. Then pull together what you have learned and form your own impression.

- **If comparisons or analogies were made, do they work?** That is, are they representative, logical, and effective?

- **Is the writer trying to be convincing or persuasive?** If so, consider whether this intent is up-front and obvious, subtle, or hidden.

- **If photographs, graphics, or other visuals are included, why are they used?** Are they used effectively? Are they intended to sway or persuade you to take a particular viewpoint toward the subject?

Evaluation in Action

The following evaluation of the appeal of language in paragraph 4 of Jeremy MacClancy's "Eating Chilli Peppers" is by the student who wrote the earlier summary and analysis. Using your Analysis in Action response, write a paragraph evaluating the aspect of the essay you focused on.

> While a lot of the language in paragraph 4 might be meant to create an appealing impression of eating chillies, I'm not convinced. The "extremity of the flames" doesn't appeal to me, and I don't like horror movies or roller coasters. The last thing I want is an "assault" on my mouth when I'm eating that makes me "ignore almost everything else." I don't want to "play with fire," and I don't need a "cheap" thrill like chillies. The description is effective but doesn't appeal to me!

Readings for Practice, Ideas for Writing

The Discus Thrower

Richard Selzer is a former surgeon who has written several books and articles presenting frank descriptions of life as a physician knows it. His works include *Mortal Lessons* (1977), *Raising the Dead* (1994), and most recently, *Diary* (2011). This essay first appeared in *Harper's* magazine in 1977.

Reading Tip

As you read, notice Selzer's use of detail. These sensory elements create a vivid picture of his patient. Also pay attention to his use of dialogue: It is important for what is *not* said as much as for what *is* said.

Previewing the Reading

Preview the reading (see pp. 23–24 for guidelines), and then answer the following questions.

1. What word does Selzer use to describe his observations of his patients?
2. Who is the subject of this essay?

The Discus Thrower

Richard Selzer

I spy on my patients. Ought not a doctor to observe his patients by any means and from any stance, that he might the more fully assemble evidence? So I stand in the doorways of hospital rooms and gaze. Oh, it is not all that furtive an act. Those in bed need only look up to discover me. But they never do.

From the doorway of Room 542 the man in the bed seems deeply tanned. Blue eyes and close-cropped white hair give him the appearance of vigor and good health. But I know that his skin is not brown from the sun. It is rusted, rather, in the last stage of containing the vile repose within. And the blue eyes are frosted, looking inward like the windows of a snowbound cottage. This man is blind. This man is also legless—the right leg missing from midthigh down, the left from just below the knee. It gives him the look of a bonsai, roots and branches pruned into the dwarfed facsimile of a great tree.

Propped on pillows, he cups his right thigh in both hands. Now and then he shakes his head as though acknowledging the intensity of his suffering. In all of this he makes no sound. Is he mute as well as blind?

The room in which he dwells is empty of all possessions—no get-well cards, small, private caches of food, day-old flowers, slippers, all the usual kickshaws[1] of the sickroom. There is only the bed, a chair, a nightstand, and

[1] **kickshaw:** Trinkets.

a tray on wheels that can be swung across his lap for meals.

5   "What time is it?" he asks.

"Three o'clock."

"Morning or afternoon?"

"Afternoon."

He is silent. There is nothing else he wants to know.

10   "How are you?" I say.

"Who is it?" he asks.

"It's the doctor: How do you feel?"

He does not answer right away.

"Feel?" he says.

15   "I hope you feel better," I say.

I press the button at the side of the bed.

"Down you go," I say.

"Yes, down," he says.

He falls back upon the bed awkwardly. His stumps, unweighted by legs and feet, rise in the air, presenting themselves. I unwrap the bandages from the stumps, and begin to cut away the black scabs and the dead, glazed fat with scissors and forceps. A shard of white bone comes loose. I pick it away. I wash the wounds with disinfectant and redress the stumps. All this while, he does not speak. What is he thinking behind those lids that do not blink? Is he remembering a time when he was whole? Does he dream of feet? Of when his body was not a rotting log?

20   He lies solid and inert. In spite of everything, he remains impressive, as though he were a sailor standing athwart a slanting deck.

"Anything more I can do for you?" I ask.

For a long moment he is silent.

"Yes," he says at last and without the least irony. "You can bring me a pair of shoes."

In the corridor, the head nurse is waiting for me.

25   "We have to do something about him," she says. "Every morning he orders scrambled eggs for breakfast, and, instead of eating them, he picks up the plate and throws it against the wall."

"Throws his plate?"

"Nasty. That's what he is. No wonder his family doesn't come to visit. They probably can't stand him any more than we can."

She is waiting for me to do something.

"Well?"

"We'll see," I say.   30

The next morning I am waiting in the corridor when the kitchen delivers his breakfast. I watch the aide place the tray on the stand and swing it across his lap. She presses the button to raise the head of the bed. Then she leaves.

In time the man reaches to find the rim of the tray, then on to find the dome of the covered dish. He lifts off the cover and places it on the stand. He fingers across the plate until he probes the eggs. He lifts the plate in both hands, sets it on the palm of his right hand, centers it, balances it. He hefts it up and down slightly, getting the feel of it. Abruptly, he draws back his right arm as far as he can.

There is the crack of the plate breaking against the wall at the foot of his bed and the small wet sound of the scrambled eggs dropping to the floor.

And then he laughs. It is a sound you have never heard. It is something new under the sun. It could cure cancer.

Out in the corridor, the eyes of the   35
head nurse narrow.

"Laughed, did he?"

She writes something down on her clipboard.

A second aide arrives, brings a second breakfast tray, puts it on the nightstand, out of his reach. She looks over at me shaking her head and making her mouth go. I see that we are to be accomplices.

"I've got to feed you," she says to the man.

"Oh, no you don't," the man says.   40

Continued >

"Oh, yes I do," the aide says, "after the way you just did. Nurse says so."

"Get me my shoes," the man says.

"Here's oatmeal," the aide says. "Open." And she touches the spoon to his lower lip.

"I ordered scrambled eggs," says the man.

45   "That's right," the aide says.

I step forward.

"Is there anything I can do?" I say.

"Who are you?" the man asks.

In the evening I go once more to that ward to make my rounds. The head nurse reports to me that Room 542 is deceased. She has discovered this quite by accident, she says. No, there had been no sound. Nothing. It's a blessing, she says.

I go into his room, a spy looking for   50 secrets. He is still there in his bed. His face is relaxed, grave, dignified. After a while, I turn to leave. My gaze sweeps the wall at the foot of the bed, and I see the place where it has been repeatedly washed, where the wall looks very clean and very white.

Understanding the Reading

1. **Background** According to Selzer, what is wrong with the patient? What don't we know about his medical condition?

2. **Details** In paragraph 25, we learn that the head nurse is upset. What is upsetting her, and how does the doctor react to the nurse's complaints?

3. **Dominant impression** The author does not include a stated thesis. Instead, Selzer uses description to build a single dominant impression. Identify his dominant impression. What might this tell you about his purpose for writing about this patient?

4. **Subject** What emotion does the patient exhibit as he throws his food? Why might he feel this way?

5. **Actions** How does the doctor find out that the patient has died? What is the head nurse's reaction to the patient's death? How does Selzer react to his death?

6. **Vocabulary** Explain the meaning of each of the following words as it is used in the reading: *furtive* (para. 1), *shard* (19), *inert* (20), *athwart* (20), and *hefts* (32). Refer to your dictionary as needed.

7. **Organization** To analyze the descriptive elements used in Selzer's essay, complete the graphic organizer that follows.

Analyzing the Reading

1. **Sensory details** Highlight several sections in which sensory details are particularly effective. What makes these details most successful?

Title	"The Discus Thrower"
Introduction	**Background and setting:** Doctor spies on his patients
	Dominant impression

⬇

Body paragraphs: sensory details and comparisons, organized chronologically	1.
	2.
	3.

⬇

| Conclusion | |

2. **Vantage point** This story is told from the vantage point of the doctor. Is this point of view effective? What does it achieve? What do you learn, and what information remains untold?

3. **Conclusion** What does the doctor notice about the patient and his room after the death? How do these details contrast with earlier descriptions of the patient and his room?

4. **Language** What are the connotative meanings of the word *spy* as used in paragraphs 1 and 50?

Evaluating the Reading

1. **Tone** How would you characterize Selzer's overall tone in "The Discus Thrower"?

2. **Dialogue** How does the author's use of dialogue contribute to the tone of the essay? How does it contribute to your overall impression of the essay's subject?

3. **Meaning** How does Selzer's tone affect your reading of the situation described in the essay? How does it make you feel about doctors and nurses? How does it make you feel about the patient?

4. **Figurative language** Evaluate the use of figurative language in this essay. Consider the statements that liken the patient to a cottage (para. 2), a bonsai tree (2), a log (19), and a sailor (20). What do you learn about the patient from each?

Discussing the Reading

1. Suggest how the doctor might have approached the patient differently or offered more help and support.

2. Why does the doctor refer to himself as a spy? Are there certain things about a patient that a doctor should not know or ask about?

3. The discus thrower dies quietly and alone. In class or in your journal, write about a time when you were alone and wished you had a friend or family member nearby.

Writing about the Reading

1. **Paragraph** Selzer focuses on one particular patient in "The Discus Thrower"; but other than the man's medical condition, we know little about him. Using descriptive details, write a paragraph that describes briefly who this man might be and why he is alone at the hospital.

2. **Paragraph** The patient Selzer describes is, at least in his last stages of life, a pretty unpleasant man, as the head nurse suggests in paragraph 27. Write a paragraph describing a person you know whose personality and actions you find objectionable, even "nasty" — someone you would avoid if you could. (Hint: Begin by explaining your relationship to this person, and then detail specific aspects of his or her personality and behavior that you find distasteful.) Unlike Selzer, you might make your subject the object of some humor.

3. **Essay** Brainstorm a list of reactions and/or feelings you or someone you know experienced when undergoing a medical procedure of some kind. What dominant impression do they suggest? Develop and support this dominant impression by writing an essay that describes the medical treatment and experience.

The Hawk

Brian Doyle is a prolific writer and editor of *Portland Magazine* at the University of Portland. He has published five essay collections, three compilations of short prose, two nonfiction books, and a novel. The list of his accolades is comparably long and includes a 2008 Award in Literature from the American Academy of Arts and Letters.

Reading Tip

As you read, think about why the writer is so interested in the man he identifies only as the "Hawk." Why does he think readers should want to learn about the Hawk?

Previewing the Reading

Preview the reading using the guidelines on pages 23–24, and then answer the following questions.

1. Why is football important in this essay?
2. Based on your preview, what do you know about Hawk?

The Hawk

Brian Doyle

Recently a man in my town took up residence on the town football field, in a tent in the northwestern corner. He had been a terrific football player in high school, and then in college, and then in the nether reaches of the pros, and then he had entered into business ventures, but these had not gone well, and he had married and had children, but that had not gone so well either, and finally he returned to the football field, because that was where things had gone well, and he needed to get balanced again, so, with all due respect to people who thought he was a nut, he thought he would stay there a while. He had already spoken with the cops, and it was a mark of the general decency of our town that he was told he could stay a while as long as he didn't interfere with use of the field, which of course he would never think of doing.

He had been nicknamed the Hawk when he was a player, for his habit of lurking around on defense and then making a stunning strike, and he still speaks the way he played, quietly but then amazingly, and when we talked recently he said some quietly amazing things, which I think you should hear.

"A reporter came by the other day, and she wanted to write about the failure of the American dream, and the collapse of the social contract, and I know she was just trying to do her job, but I kept telling her things that didn't fit her story, like that people come by and leave me sandwiches, and the kids who play lacrosse at night set up a screen so my tent wouldn't get peppered by stray shots, and the cops drift by at night to make sure no one's giving me grief. Everyone understands

Continued >

someone getting nailed and trying to get back up again. I just lost my balance. People are good to me. I keep the field clean. Lost cell phones I hang in a plastic bag by the gate. I walk the perimeter a lot. I saw coyote pups the other day. I don't have anything smart to say. Things just are what they are. Someone leaves coffee for me every morning by the gate. The other day a lady came by with twin infants and she let me hold one while we talked about football.

That baby weighed about half of nothing. You couldn't believe a human being could be so tiny, and there were two of him. That reporter kept asking me what I had learned, what would I say to her readers if there was one thing to say, and I told her what could possibly be better than standing on a football field holding a brand-new human being the size of a coffee cup, you know what I mean? Everything else is sort of a footnote."

Understanding the Reading

1. **Dominant impression** What dominant impression does this description create of its subject? How does it primarily do so?

2. **Introduction** What does the first paragraph tell you about the Hawk and his relationship to the town where he and Doyle live?

3. **Meaning** How did the subject of the essay get the name *the Hawk*? How does Doyle use this information to help describe the man in his present situation?

4. **Descriptive detail** What do you learn about the Hawk from the long quotation that makes up paragraph 3? Note specific details that contribute to your sense of the kind of person he is.

5. **Vocabulary** Define the following words as they are used in the essay, consulting a dictionary if necessary: *nether reaches* (para. 1), *ventures* (1), *decency* (1), and *perimeter* (3).

6. **Language** The Hawk says that the reporter who interviewed him wanted to write about "the collapse of the social contract" (para. 3). What does this mean, and why does the Hawk feel he can't give her an answer?

Analyzing the Reading

1. **Intention** Is this description mainly subjective or objective? How can you tell?

2. **Descriptive detail** Highlight some of the adjectives Doyle uses in paragraphs 1–2 in describing the Hawk. What do these contribute to the dominant impression?

3. **Presentation** Why do you suppose Doyle refers to his subject only as the Hawk, a nickname he received as a high-school football player?

4. **Language** Doyle writes that some might think of the Hawk as a "nut" but that, in fact, he just "needed to get balanced" (and he later echoes the Hawk saying that he "lost" his "balance"). What do you see as the difference between these two characterizations of the subject?

5. **Vantage point** What is Doyle's vantage point in relation to his subject? Where does he seem to be for the major part of this description?

6. **Support** Doyle writes in paragraph 1 of the "general decency" of his town. How does he back up his assertion?

7. **Conclusion** Why does Doyle end the Hawk's story as he does, particularly with the final two sentences?

Evaluating the Reading

1. **Dominant impression** Do you find Doyle's description of the Hawk generally biased or unbiased? Do you think he tries to hide any biases?

2. **Descriptive details** The Hawk is living as a homeless man on a football field. What details do you suppose Doyle has chosen to omit about him? Would the inclusion of such details change the dominant impression in any way?

3. **Intention** What is Doyle trying to persuade readers of in this essay? Do you think he succeeds?

4. **Personal response** In three words, summarize how you respond to the Hawk as he is described here. (For example, fill in the following blanks: "I think that the Hawk is _____, _____, and _____.") Are all your descriptive words similar, or do they reveal some conflict in your attitude? What in the essay makes you feel as you do?

Discussing the Reading

1. The Hawk is clearly a person who achieved success as an athlete in high school and college but couldn't live up to that early success later in life. How common do you think that scenario is? Do the "stars" in high school continue to be stars afterward, or are they often outshone by students who initially appeared to have much lower "success" profiles?

2. Doyle writes that the Hawk "needed to get balanced again" (para. 1). Does the Hawk's choice of taking up residence on the football field where he played as a teenager strike you as a good way of doing this?

3. The Hawk says that what he had to say didn't fit the story that the reporter who came to interview him had in mind. Do you think that the news media often have preconceived "stories" that reporters then find evidence to support? How trustworthy, in general, do you find commercial news, whether printed, televised, or online?

Writing about the Reading

1. **Paragraph** Like Doyle, describe a person you know whom some might think a "nut" but you feel more sympathetically about. (Hint: Before drafting, make a list of the person's characteristics that might seem odd and another list of

the characteristics that you find sympathetic; of course, there may be some overlap. Use these lists to provide the basis for your paragraph.)

2. **Essay** Write an extended story, like the Hawk's in paragraph 3, in which you describe yourself or someone you know well in terms of how you or him or her react to the world and how the world reacts to you or him or her. Write freely and conversationally as you draft, but then go back to edit for clarity and to make sure you create a dominant impression. Consider adding an introduction and a conclusion to clarify and give context to your dominant impression.

3. **Essay** Doyle describes the "general decency" of his community. Write an essay in which you describe a community to which you belong, focusing on its general embodiment of decency or anything else that basically characterizes it. Be sure to include details of how the people in the community demonstrate your central characterization of it.

The Secret Latina

Veronica Chambers is a fiction writer, journalist, and former editor at the *New York Times Magazine.* In the acclaimed memoir *Mama's Girl* (1996), she examines her complex relationship with her mother. The following essay, which originally appeared in *Essence* magazine, also explores her family heritage.

Reading Tip

As you read, think about the relationship between the writer and her mother. How does the writer feel about her mother, and how does her mother feel about the writer?

Previewing the Reading

Preview the reading (see pp. 23–24 for guidelines), and then write a sentence summarizing what you have learned about the meaning of the title.

The Secret Latina

Veronica Chambers

She's a platanos-frying, malta Dukesa-drinking, salsa-dancing Mamacita—my dark-skinned Panamanian mother. She came to this country when she was twenty-one, her sense of culture intact, her Spanish flawless. Even today, more than twenty years since she left her home country to become an American citizen, my mother still considers herself Panamanian and checks "Hispanic" on census forms.

As a Black woman in America, my Latin identity is murkier than my mother's, despite the fact that I, too, was born in Panama, and call that country "home." My father's parents came from Costa Rica and Jamaica, my mother's from Martinique. I left Panama when I was two years old. My family lived in England for three years then came to the States when I was five. Having dark skin and growing up in Brooklyn in the 1970s meant I was Black, period. You could meet me and not know I was of Latin heritage. Without a Spanish last name or

my mother's fluent Spanish at my disposal, I often felt isolated from the Latin community. And frankly, Latinos were not quick to claim me. Latinos can be as racist as anybody else, favoring blue-eyed, blond *rubias* over *negritas* like me.

I found it almost impossible to explain to my elementary-school friends why my mother would speak Spanish at home. They would ask if I was Puerto Rican and look bewildered when I told them I was not. To them, Panama was a kind of nowhere. There weren't enough Panamanians in Brooklyn to be a force. Everybody knew where Jamaicans were from because of famous singers like Bob Marley. Panamanians had Ruben Blades, but most of my friends thought he was Puerto Rican, too.

In my neighborhood, where the smell of somebody's grandmother's cooking could transform a New York corner into Santo Domingo, Kingston, or Port-au-Prince, a Panamanian was a

Continued >

sort of fish with feathers—assumed to be a Jamaican who spoke Spanish. The analogy was not without historical basis: A century ago, Panama's Black community was largely drawn to the country from all over the Caribbean as cheap labor to build the Panama Canal.

5 My father didn't mind that we considered ourselves Black rather than Latino. He named my brother Malcolm X, and if my mother hadn't put her foot down, I would have been called Angela Davis Chambers. It's not that my mother didn't admire Angela Davis, but you have only to hear how *Veronica Victoria* flows off her Spanish lips to know that she was homesick for Panama and for those names that sang like *timbales*[1] on carnival day. So between my father and my mother was a Black-Latin divide. Because of my father, we read and discussed books about Black history and civil rights. Because of my mother, we ate Panamanian food, listened to salsa, and heard Spanish at home.

Still it wasn't until my parents divorced when I was ten that my mother tried to teach Malcolm and me Spanish. She was a terrible language teacher. She had no sense of how to explain structure, and her answer to every question was "That's just the way it is." A few short weeks after our Spanish lessons began, my mother gave up and we were all relieved. But I remained intent on learning my mother's language. When she spoke Spanish, her words were a fast current, a stream of language that was colorful, passionate, fiery. I wanted to speak Spanish because I wanted to swim in the river of her words, her history, my history, too.

As school I dove into the language, matching what little I knew from home

with all that I learned. One day, when I was in the ninth grade, I finally felt confident enough to start speaking Spanish with my mother. I soon realized that by speaking Spanish with her, I was forging an important bond. When I'd spoken only English, I was the daughter, the little girl. But when I began speaking Spanish, I became something more—a *hermanita*, a sisterfriend, a Panamanian homegirl who could hang with the rest of them. Eventually this bond would lead me home.

Two years ago, at age twenty-seven, I decided it was finally time. I couldn't wait any longer to see Panama, the place my mother and my aunts had told me stories about. I enlisted my cousin Digna as a traveling companion and we made arrangements to stay with my godparents, whom I had never met. We planned our trip for the last week in February—carnival time.

Panama, in Central America, is a narrow sliver of a country: You can swim in the Caribbean Sea in the morning and backstroke across the Pacific in the afternoon. As our plane touched down, bringing me home for the first time since I was two, I felt curiously comfortable and secure. In the days that followed, there was none of the culture shock that I'd expected—I had my mother and aunts to thank for that. My godmother, Olga, reminded me of them. The first thing she did was book appointments for Digna and me to get our eyebrows plucked and our nails and feet done with Panamanian-style manicures and pedicures. "It's carnival," Aunt Olga said, "and you girls have to look your best." We just laughed.

10 In Panama, I went from being a lone Black girl with a curious Latin heritage to being part of the *Latinegro*

---

[1] **timbales** Drums played with the hands.

tribe or the *Afro-Antillianos*, as we were officially called. I was thrilled to learn there was actually a society for people like me. Everyone was Black, everyone spoke Spanish, and everyone danced the way they danced at fiesta time back in Brooklyn, stopping only to chow down on a smorgasbord of souse,[2] rice with black-eyed peas, beef patties, *empanadas*,[3] and codfish fritters. The carnival itself was an all-night bacchanal[4] with elaborate floats, brilliantly colored costumes, and live musicians. In the midst of all this, my godmother took my cousin and me to a photo studio to have our pictures taken in *polleras*, the traditional dress. After spending an hour on makeup and hair and donning a rented costume, I looked like Scarlett in *Gone with the Wind*.

[2] **souse** Pig parts preserved in brine.
[3] **empanadas** Small pies with meat or other fillings.
[4] **bacchanal** Celebration.

Back in New York, I gave the photo to my mother. She almost cried. She says she was so moved to see me in a *pollera* because it was "such a patriotic thing to do." Her appreciation made me ridiculously happy; ever since I was a little girl, I'd wanted to be like my mother. In one of my most vivid memories, I am seven or eight and my parents are having a party. Salsa music is blaring and my mother is dancing and laughing. She sees me standing off in a corner, so she pulls me into the circle of grown-ups and tries to teach me how to dance to the music. Her hips are electric. She puts her hands on my sides and says, "Move these," and I start shaking my hip bones as if my life depends on it.

Now I am a grown woman, with hips to spare. I can salsa. My Spanish isn't shabby. You may look at me and not know that I am Panamanian, that I am an immigrant, that I am both Black and Latin. But I am my mother's daughter, a secret Latina, and that's enough for me.

Understanding the Reading

1. **Subject** This description focuses both on Chambers herself and on her mother. How does the connection between the two of them help make this "double description" work?

2. **Dominant impression** What main impression does Chambers create of herself and of her mother? What do the final two paragraphs contribute to this dominant impression?

3. **Descriptive details** Annotate the essay to highlight the specific details that help you "see" Chambers and her mother. What words does Chambers use to describe herself and her mother?

4. **Meaning** What is the point of paragraphs 3–4? What do they contribute to Chambers's underlying point about herself?

5. **Meaning** Why was it important for Chambers to make the trip to Panama she writes about in paragraphs 8–10?

6. **Organization** To understand the organization of "The Secret Latina," complete the following graphic organizer.

Title	"The Secret Latina"
Introduction	Opening description of the writer's mother today

⬇

Paragraph 2
Paragraphs 3–4
Paragraph 5
Paragraphs 6–7
Paragraphs 8–10

⬇

Conclusion

📊 Analyzing the Reading

1. **Attitude** This is obviously a subjective description. What attitude is the writer trying to convey about herself and her mother?

2. **Introduction** Why does the opening paragraph focus only on Chambers's mother? And the why does Chambers shift her focus to herself in paragraph 2?

3. **Language** In paragraph 3, Chambers writes that in her neighborhood Panamanians were viewed as "fish with feathers." What is her point, and why does she go on to put this analogy in historical context?

4. **Development** What do paragraphs 6–7 contribute to your understanding of Chambers's relationship with her mother? How is this point echoed in the final paragraph?

📊 Evaluating the Reading

1. **Descriptive details** How well do you think Chambers describes her mother? What details do you find most effective? Are there any aspects of her mother about which you would like to learn more?

2. **Language and audience** Throughout the essay Chambers sprinkles in Spanish vocabulary, which she doesn't always define for a non-Spanish-reading audience: for example, *rubias* (para. 2), *timbales* (5), and *souse* (10). Do you think this is appropriate for the general audience of a publication like *Essence*?

3. **Presentation** How do you respond to Chambers's presentation of herself in the essay? Point to specific details that contribute to your response.

4. **Opening and conclusion** How well do you think the concluding paragraph provides a connection to the opening paragraph? That is, do the opening and conclusion serve to give the essay a sense of cohesion?

Discussing the Reading

1. Why does Chambers make such a point of the fact that her friends in elementary school didn't understand who she was culturally? Do you think this should be an issue in personal relationships?

2. Chambers says that it was important for her to learn Spanish, her mother's native language. In what other ways do children as they grow up attempt to connect with their parents?

3. While we generally think about prejudice as occurring across racial and ethnic divides, Chambers writes about prejudice *within* the Latino community regarding skin color. Within your own community, are some "types" valued more highly while other "types" receive prejudicial treatment? Why might this be the case?

Writing about the Reading

1. **Essay** Like Chambers, write an essay of "double description," focusing on both yourself and a significant person in your life whom you mirror in some way: a parent, a sibling, a partner, or a close friend. (Hint: As you plan your essay, use Chambers's organization as a model: how she opens by describing her mother, ends by describing herself to echo that opening description, and uses her body paragraphs to develop the connections between herself and her mother.)

2. **Essay** Chambers could have written an extended descriptive essay just about her experiences during carnival time in Panama (paras. 8–10). Brainstorm a list of holiday celebrations and festivals you have participated in. Then choose one as the basis for a descriptive essay, being sure that you can re-create it for readers using as many details of the senses — sight, smell, hearing, touch, taste — as possible.

3. **Essay** In paragraph 4, Chambers writes about the memories created by "the smell of somebody's grandmother's cooking." Write an essay describing a vivid childhood memory of your own that can be called up by something that occurs in the present. It might be positive, as Chambers's example is, or might focus on a different kind of memory — one that is unpleasant or even frightening. Be sure to develop your essay by explaining what evokes the memory and using sensory details to communicate the memory vividly.

COMBINING THE PATTERNS

A Step in the Right Direction

The *Economist*, a renowned British weekly magazine, publishes news and opinion pieces on politics, business, and world affairs. It is printed in six countries and distributed worldwide. In order to emphasize its "collective voice" and the collaborative nature of the writing and editorial process, authors' names do not appear with articles in the magazine.

Reading Tip

This reading is quite technical and contains detailed information on the mechanics and biology of artificial limbs. Use the footnotes for help with unfamiliar terms. You may need to reread some sections several times to fully understand them. As you read, highlight and list some of the implications of Hugh Herr's technological developments — both for disabled people and for people who are able to walk normally.

Previewing the Reading

Preview the reading (see pp. 23–24 for guidelines), and then briefly summarize how the title predicts what this description is primarily about.

A Step in the Right Direction

The Economist

Hugh Herr lost his lower legs as a teenager. He has since gone on to become a leading light in the development of artificial limbs.

"Fifty years from now I want people to be running to work," says Hugh Herr, director of the biomechatronics group at the Massachusetts Institute of Technology (MIT). Far from being some kind of motivational guru, Dr. Herr hopes to achieve this using technology. His goal is to augment people's limbs with what he calls a "mobility platform," akin to a pair of magic trousers, that allows people to move quickly with minimal effort—like riding a bicycle, but without the bicycle. "They won't need parking lots," says Dr. Herr. "People can run straight into their offices, remove their mobility platform, as if they were undressing, and then hang it right on their coat rack."

It sounds implausible. Roboticists have struggled for decades to understand bipedal locomotion,[1] and even today's most sophisticated robots require huge amounts of energy and computer power to walk on two legs. But Dr. Herr's credentials are sound. He is a leading authority on the biomechanics[2] of legs, and in the past

---

[1] **bipedal locomotion** Two-footed movement.
[2] **biomechanics** Study of the mechanical nature of body processes, such as muscle movement.

Hugh Herr wearing artificial limbs he has developed.

decade he has made several advances in the development of artificial legs and assistive walking devices, or "orthoses," enabling amputees to walk with a more natural gait than was previously possible.

As well as enhancing the lives of disabled people, Dr. Herr's work on exoskeletons[3]—the precursors of his planned mobility platforms—could make life easier for able-bodied people, too. By contrast with the bulky, cumbersome exoskeletons featured in science-fiction movies like *Aliens* and *Avatar*, or those being developed for military use, Dr. Herr's devices are smaller and lighter, and will require much less power. This will, he hopes, allow people to walk and run greater distances, or carry heavier loads, than they would otherwise be able to.

[3] **exoskeletons** Protective outer covering of a body.

Dr. Herr's interest in the biomechanics of walking stems from his own personal experience. He is a double amputee, having lost both his legs below the knee after a climbing accident in 1982, at the age of seventeen. At the time he was regarded as one of the best climbers in America. But after ascending a 200-meter wall of ice on Mount Washington, in New Hampshire, Dr. Herr and his climbing partner Jeff Batzer found themselves caught in a blizzard. Blinded by the snow, they became lost in the wilderness as they struggled to find their way to safety. By the time they were rescued, more than three days later, they were both suffering from severe hypothermia and frostbite. "We were in pretty bad shape," Dr. Herr recalls. He had both his legs amputated below the knee and Mr. Batzer lost a leg, the toes from his remaining foot, and all the fingers from his right hand.

Continued >

5   "Climbing was my life's passion," says Dr. Herr. Angry with the mistakes he'd made on Mount Washington, he was determined to rebuild his life and prove to himself that he could climb responsibly once again. Within just a few months he was out climbing once again, wearing a pair of temporary legs made of plaster that could, he was warned, easily fracture. "I think my family saw it as great therapy," says Dr. Herr. "They were probably more frightened that I would become frustrated and depressed if I hadn't been able to climb again." He is certain if he hadn't got back on the rock he would be a very different person today. Driven on by the desire to create better legs for himself he has spent the past three decades turning his loss into a personal gain that has also benefited many others.

Climb Every Mountain

He began by customizing his new artificial limbs so that they were optimized for climbing. "I realized I didn't need a rock climbing shoe—I could just bond climbing rubber right to the artificial foot," he says. Convinced that artificial limbs could be improved further, he started to make his own. "I studied tool-and-die at school so I knew my way around tools," says Dr. Herr. His efforts resulted in a dedicated pair of limbs that could be adjusted for different types of climbing, and could even have their length extended or reduced to match the demands of the wall. As a result he was soon climbing at an even higher standard than before the accident, and certainly better than the vast majority of able-bodied people.

Having created better legs for moving vertically, he turned his attention to ordinary, horizontal locomotion. He studied physics at university, on the basis that it would provide a good foundation for designing prostheses. His first focus was to make artificial limbs more comfortable to wear. By his senior year he had been granted his first patent, for a socket interface that used a series of bladders[4] to compensate for the wide variation in the shapes of different people's residual limbs. Over the next few years, as he studied for a master's degree in mechanical engineering at MIT and a Ph.D. in biophysics at Harvard before returning to MIT as a postdoctoral fellow, Dr. Herr worked on a novel knee-joint mechanism.

This work, which was eventually commercialized as the Rheo Knee, used a magnetorheological (MR) fluid—a fluid whose viscosity can be controlled by applying a magnetic field—to act as a variable damper, and thus create a more natural knee swing. Traditionally, artificial knee joints use hydraulic damping, which presents more angular resistance to fast rotational motion than to slow motion. A joint with a computer-controlled "smart" MR fluid, by contrast, can present a more even resistance, allowing for a more natural gait and enabling a prosthetic[5] leg to adapt the knee swing as the wearer's gait changes. The joint can also be more easily tuned to meet a particular user's needs.

Having improved upon existing artificial knees, Dr. Herr decided that designing radically better prostheses and orthoses required a return to first principles, and a greater understanding of how human limbs work. "It's surprising to most people that we, the human race, do not yet understand biological walking," he says. It turns out to be complex and often counterintuitive. "In many respects walking should be an inefficient process, but because of the way the human body is designed, it is quite the opposite," says Dr. Herr.

[4] **bladders** Air-filled sacs.
[5] **prosthetic** Artificial substitute or replacement.

Although effort is required to bend a joint or flex a muscle, the body is able to recycle much of the energy expended through spring-like tendons and elegantly arranged muscles. There is a constant shuffling, as potential energy is transformed into kinetic or elastic energy, and then back again. "That's why, when you walk, it's so economical and uses so little energy," he says.

10   With most prosthetic devices, including the Rheo Knee, much of the energy put into them by the body is lost, rather than being recovered. With this in mind Dr. Herr went on to develop, in 2003, the first powered ankle-foot orthosis—a device designed to fit around the ankle joint of someone with walking difficulties, such as a stroke patient. It provides active correction, ensuring that the foot flexes in the right way, and is used to teach a patient how to walk again. Then in 2007 Dr. Herr took this a step further by incorporating assistive power into an artificial leg, or prosthesis. The result, the PowerFoot One, will be launched this year by Dr. Herr's spin-out company, iWalk, and will be the first powered artificial leg on the market.

The PowerFoot One uses motors, springs, sensors, and an elaborate control system to emulate[6] the energy-transfer mechanisms of the foot and ankle at each stage of a stride. It adapts to different terrain angles and different gaits, can tell whether the user is going up or down stairs, and increases both speed and stability. It will even hang naturally when the user crosses his legs. "Some of our patients actually start to cry when they use it," says Dr. Herr. The powered mechanism, which will require daily recharging, creates a natural gait and ensures that no "metabolic[7] cost" is imposed on the wearer, he says.

An Unfair Leg Up?

The question of metabolic cost was highlighted by the case of Oscar Pistorius,[8] the South African double-amputee sprinter who runs using blade-like prosthetics made of carbon fiber. In 2007 he was banned from trying to qualify for the 400-meter race at the 2008 Beijing Olympics by the International Association of Athletics Federations. The IAAF argued that his prosthetics gave him an unfair advantage by enabling him to run at a much lower metabolic cost—in other words, with much less effort—than an able-bodied person. Dr. Herr was brought in by Mr. Pistorius's legal team to argue against this claim. With less than a month to prepare a defense, Dr. Herr and his colleagues Rodger Kram and Peter Wyand carried out tests to demonstrate that Mr. Pistorius's prosthetics, which are not powered, do not enable him to run with less effort. As a result the decision to ban Mr. Pistorius was overturned. (In the event, he did not qualify for the South African team and did not compete in Beijing.)

The science is still very immature when it comes to assessing whether prosthetics provide an advantage, says Dr. Herr, though the evidence so far suggests that they do not. "We want to get the science done," he says, "because the next time Oscar or anyone else wants to compete against people with intact limbs, there will be certain people in the world who will claim augmentation[9]— so we need to be prepared for that." He would like to produce prosthetics that can emulate biological limbs so precisely that they ensure that the likes of Mr. Pistorius are neither advantaged nor disadvantaged.

[6] **emulate** Imitate.
[7] **metabolic** Referring to chemical processes by which cells produce energy.

[8] Pistorius competed in the 2012 Olympics in London, reaching the semifinals.
[9] **augmentation** Added help or assistance.

Continued >

Although Mr. Pistorius's unpowered prosthetics do not provide any metabolic advantage, there is no reason why powered prosthetics, or exoskeletons worn by able-bodied people, cannot do so. Indeed, with his latest work on exoskeletons, Dr. Herr is moving in this direction. His latest powered exoskeleton, which in effect helps carry the wearer, has already been shown to reduce the metabolic effort involved in hopping by 30% (the tests for running have not yet been completed). And it does not require much energy to work: In its current form the exoskeleton has just two small clutches which only draw a quarter of a watt of power each. "That's negligible," says Dr. Herr. He plans to add regenerative capabilities to the exoskeleton, so that it will require little or no power when moving on level ground.

15   This sort of device is primarily aimed at improving distance rather than speed, says Dr. Herr. Wearing it enables you to walk or run with less effort, so it will improve your marathon time (because you will not get tired so quickly over long distances) but will not enable you to sprint any faster than your existing top speed. "Think of it as a bicycle for your legs," he says. "A bicycle profoundly augments human locomotion in terms of human metabolic rate and speed, and yet it requires zero energy itself."

Dr. Herr plans to add regenerative capabilities to his prosthetic devices, such as the PowerFoot One. After all, one advantage of having artificial limbs is that you can upgrade them. And for Dr. Herr, there will always be room for improvement in the speed, stability, and energy efficiency of his legs. "When I'm eighty I want the artificial part of my body to be completely superior to the biological part," he says. It is a distant goal, but he has already taken several steps in the right direction.

Understanding the Reading

1. **Subject** Summarize in a sentence or two exactly what is being described in this essay. Why does the writer think this subject would be of interest to readers?

2. **Meaning** What special qualifications allow Hugh Herr to pursue advancements in helping people walk? Why is he so passionate about what he does?

3. **Meaning** What two main points are made about the act of walking in paragraph 9? How do these relate to Herr's goals?

4. **Language** The writer quotes Herr's dream of creating a human "mobility platform" (para. 1). After reading the essay, how would you define this term?

5. **Vocabulary** Define the following words as they are used in the essay, consulting a dictionary if necessary: *biomechatronics* (para. 1), *guru* (1), *augment* (1), *implausible* (2), *bipedal* (2), *locomotion* (2), *cumbersome* (3), *hypothermia* (4), *prostheses* (7), *viscosity* (8), *hydraulic* (8), *counterintuitive* (9), *tendons* (9), *terrain* (11), and *regenerative* (14).

Analyzing the Reading

1. **Purpose and audience** What is the writer's purpose? How does the writer seem to define the audience for the essay, and what makes you think so?

2. **Descriptive details and dominant impression** Point to specific details in the essay that contribute to the dominant impression that the writer wishes to make. Then briefly summarize this dominant impression.

3. **Presentation and vantage point** The writer obviously wants readers to view Herr quite positively. What information provided about him is intended to help achieve this goal?

4. **Combining patterns** Where in the essay does the writer use process analysis to further the description? Where is cause and effect used?

5. **Language** Highlight some examples of technical or scientific vocabulary used in the essay. Why is such language appropriate for this particular subject?

Evaluating the Reading

1. **Dominant impression** Does the writer persuade you, as Herr believes, that his prostheses can have many positive benefits now and in the future?

2. **Analogy** In paragraph 1 and again in paragraph 15, one of Herr's prosthetic devices is compared to a bicycle. How well does this analogy help you understand the nature of the device?

3. **Development** Paragraphs 12–13 are something of an aside, not directly related to Herr's own devices. Rather, they focus on Herr being brought in as a consultant in a case involving a controversy over the use of other prosthetics by athletes. How appropriate do you find this sidetrack?

4. **Language and presentation** Point out any sections of this reading that you found difficult to understand. What questions might you ask the writer or what suggestions might you make that would help clarify these sections?

Discussing the Reading

1. How appealing do you find the description in paragraph 1 of people running to work fifty years from now? Would you be interested in a device that would help you do this with little effort?

2. What's your response to the idea of allowing athletes with disabilities to use prosthetic devices to compete with able-bodied athletes? Do you believe such devices would provide an unfair advantage in the sense that they would allow athletes with disabilities to expend less energy?

3. Currently, Herr's devices are aimed at amputees and people with walking difficulties. Do you think he's right to expand his research into creating devices to augment the performance of able-bodied people? Is this a good use of his time?

Writing about the Reading

1. **Essay** Herr imagines a device in the future that will allow people to run long distances with little physical effort. Brainstorm a list of devices to make people's lives easier that you can imagine being developed over the next half century or so. Don't limit yourself to those that might augment physical performance; think also about devices that would improve performing household chores; make traveling easier; enhance entertainment, work, and learning; or whatever else comes to mind. Then choose one as the subject for a descriptive essay. (Hint: Once you make your choice, you'll need to sketch out your device's physical properties and how it will make users' lives easier.)

2. **Researched essay** Visit the Web site for Herr's business, iWalk.com, and research his prosthetic products, such as the Rheo Knee and the PowerFoot One, on other sites to find photographs of these products and information about how people use them. Then write an essay describing one or more of these products in detail for an audience who has never heard of them.

3. **Combined patterns** In paragraphs 4–5, the writer describes and narrates a devastating ordeal Herr underwent — a climbing accident that resulted in the amputation of his legs — and then goes on to explain a causal effect of this ordeal — Herr's determination to find a way to climb again. Think about a difficult incident you've faced in your life. Then write an essay using narration and description to communicate to readers what happened to you and cause-and-effect analysis to show how it affected you — perhaps in a life-changing way, perhaps more subtly.

📖 TEXTBOOK

Costumes

Louis Giannetti is an emeritus professor of film studies and English at Case Western Reserve University. His books on the cinema include *Flashback: A Brief History of Film* and *Masters of the American Cinema* (2010). The selection here comes from *Understanding Movies* (2010), his introductory textbook on the language of film.

Reading Tip

As you read, think about how the caption below the still of Marilyn Monroe from *The Seven Year Itch* relates to the rest of the text discussion and whether you find the two discussions equally informative.

Previewing the Reading

Preview the reading (see pp. 23–24 for guidelines), and list three things you think it will cover in more detail.

Costumes

Louis Giannetti

In the most sensitive films and plays, costumes and makeup aren't merely frills added to enhance an illusion, but aspects of character and theme. Costumes can reveal class, self-image, even psychological states. Depending on their cut, texture, and bulk, ceratin costumes can suggest agitation, **fastidiousness**, delicacy, dignity, and so on. A costume, then, is a medium, especially in the cinema, where a close-up of a fabric can suggest information that's independent even of the wearer.

> **fastidiousness:** excessively particular about details, hard to please

Color symbolism is used by Zeffirelli in *Romeo and Juliet*. Juliet's family, the Capulets, are characterized as aggressive **parvenues**: Their colors are appropriately "hot" reds, yellow, and oranges. Romeo's family, on the other hand, is older and perhaps more established, but in obvious decline. They are costumed in blues, deep greens, and purples. These two color schemes are echoed in the liveries of the servants of each house, which helps the audience identify the combatants in the brawling scenes. The color of the costumes can also be used to suggest change and transition. Our first view of Juliet, for example, shows her in a vibrant red dress. Afer she marries Romeo, her colors are in the cool blue spectrum. Line as well as color can be used to suggest psychological qualities. Verticals, for example, tend to emphasize stateliness and dignity (Lady Montague); horizontal lines tend to emphasize earthiness and comicality (Juliet's nurse).

> **parvenue:** someone who has risen economically or socially but lacks the appropriate social skills for his or her new position

Publicity photo of Marilyn Monroe in *The Seven Year Itch* **(U.S.A., 1955),**
directed by Billy Wilder.   Variations of this image have become **iconographic** in
popular culture, replicated millions of times, and recognized by virtually everyone
on the planet. Why did this image in particular capture the imagination of so many
people? Perhaps it was the costume. (1) The *period* of the garment is 1955, but so
classic in its lines that variations of the dress can still be found in stores. (2) The
class of the dress is middle to upper middle: It's an elegant, well-made party
dress. (3) The *sex* is feminine in the extreme, emphasizing such erotic details as a
plunging neckline and bare arms and back. (4) The *age* level would be suitable to
any mature woman (from the late teens to the mid-forties) in good physical shape.
(5) The *silhouette* is form-fitting from the waist up, emphasizing Marilyn's famous
breasts. The accordion-pleated flare skirt ordinarily would obscure her shape below
the waist, but the updraft from the subway below swooshes the skirt toward her
face. Her gesture of holding the skirt down near the crotch suggests a childish
innocence and spontaneity. (6) The *fabric* is lightweight, suitable for a summer
evening, probably a silk/cotton blend. (7) The *accessories* include only the circular
earrings (hard to see in this photo) and the high-heeled strap sandals. The shoes
are sexy and delicate, but not very practical. They make her look pampered and
vulnerable and easy to catch. (8) The dress's *color* is white—pure, clean,
untouched by the city's dirt. (9) There is quite a bit of *body exposure*—the arms,
shoulders, back, cleavage, and—at least here—much of the upper thighs. (10) The
function of the dress is recreational, not work-related. It's meant to attract
attention. It's a dress to have fun in. (11) Marilyn's *body attitude* is childish
exuberance—she's not in the least ashamed or embarrassed by her body and
wears the outfit with confidence. (12) The general *image* suggests innocence,
femininity, spontaneity, and a riveting sexual allure. *(Twentieth Century Fox)*

iconographic:
something that
has become a
symbol of the art
form

Perhaps the most famous costume in film history is Charlie Chaplin's tramp outfit. The costume is an indication of both class and character, conveying the complex mixture of vanity and dash that makes Charlie so appealing. The moustache, derby hat, and cane all suggest the fastidious dandy. The cane is used to give the impression of self-importance as Charlie swaggers confidently before a hostile world. But the baggy trousers several sizes too large, the oversized shoes, the too-tight coat—all these suggest Charlie's insignificance and poverty. Chaplin's view of humanity is symbolized by that costume: vain, absurd, and—finally—poignantly vulnerable.

In most cases, especially period films, costumes are designed for the performers who will be wearing them. The costumer must always be conscious of the actor's body type—whether he or she is thin, overweight, tall, short, and so on—to compensate for any deficiency. If a performer is famous for a given trait—Dietrich's legs, Marilyn's bosom, Matthew McConaughey's chest—the costumer will often design the actor's clothes to highlight these attractions. Even in period films, the costumer has a wide array of styles to choose from, and his or her choice will often be determined by what the actor looks best in within the **parameters** defined by the **milieu** of the story.

During the Hollywood studio era, powerful stars often insisted on costumes and makeup that heightened their natural endowments, regardless of period accuracy. This was a practice that was encouraged by the studio bosses, who wanted their stars to look as glamourous as possible by suggesting a "contemporary look." The results are usually jarring and **incongruous**. Even prestigious directors like John Ford gave in to this tradition of vanity. In Ford's otherwise superb western, *My Darling Clementine* (1946), which is set in a rough frontier community, actress Linda Darnell wore glamourous star makeup and a 1940s-style hairdo, even though the character she was playing was a cheap Mexican "saloon girl"—a coy period euphemism for a prostitute. She looks as though she just stepped out of a hoity-toity beauty salon after receiving the deluxe treatment. She's groomed to within an inch of her life.

In realistic contemporary stories, costumes are often bought off the rack rather than individually designed. This is especially true in stories dealing with ordinary people, people who buy their clothes in department stores. When the characters are lower class or poor, costumers often purchase used clothing. For example, in *On The Waterfront*, which deals with dockworkers and other working-class characters, the costumes are frayed and torn. Costumer Anna Hill Johnstone bought them in used clothing stores in the neighborhood adjoining the waterfront area.

Costumes, then, represent another language system in movies, a symbolic form of communication that can be as complex and revealing as the other language systems filmmakers use. A systematic analysis of a costume includes a consideration of the following characteristics:

parameters: boundaries, guidelines

milieu: setting

incongruous: out of place, not fitting together, inconsistent

Continued >

1. **Period** What era does the costume fall into? Is it an accurate reconstruction? If not, why?
2. **Class** What is the apparent income level of the person wearing the costume?
3. **Sex** Does a woman's costume emphasize her femininity or is it neutral or masculine? Does a man's costume emphasize his virility or is it fussy or effeminate?
4. **Age** Is the costume appropriate to the character's age or is it deliberately too youthful, dowdy, or old-fashioned?
5. **Silhouette** Is the costume form-fitting or loose and baggy?
6. **Fabric** Is the material coarse, sturdy, and plain or sheer and delicate?
7. **Accessories** Does the costume include jewelry, hats, canes, and other accessories? What kind of shoes?
8. **Color** What are the symbolic implications of the colors? Are they "hot" or "cool"? Subdued or bright? Solids or patterns?

Understanding the Reading

1. **Textbook reading** Highlight each of the reading's seven main paragraphs as if you were preparing for an objective exam on the material. Compare your highlighting with that of a classmate.
2. **Language** Reread the long photo caption analyzing Marilyn Monroe's costume in *The Seven Year Itch*. What is the meaning of the italicized words, and why are they italicized?
3. **Thinking visually** Why does the author reproduce this particular photo of Marilyn Monroe in costume? What does this costume represent?

Analyzing the Reading

1. **Predicting exam questions** To prepare for an essay exam, it can be helpful to predict possible questions your instructor might ask. Write an essay question that might be asked about this reading.
2. **Considering examples** In addition to Marilyn Monroe's costume in *The Seven Year Itch*, what other specific examples does the author describe? What do these examples contribute to the discussion?
3. **Viewpoint** What is the author's basic view of costumes in film? Where is the viewpoint stated directly?

Evaluating the Reading

1. **Language** Choose five words in the caption analyzing Marilyn Monroe's costume that would be important to learn when reading or writing about costume design. Write a definition of each, using your own words.

2. **Technique** How does the topic of paragraph 5 differ from what is covered in the rest of the reading? Is this information necessary?

3. **Strategy** How effective is this reading in terms of its use of description? What do you see as its strengths and weaknesses, if any?

Discussing the Reading

1. The author includes examples describing costumes from films student readers may not be familiar with, such as Zeffirelli's *Romeo and Juliet* and *On the Waterfront*. Is this a problem in terms of understanding the points being made?

2. The author suggests that the image of Marilyn Monroe from *The Seven Year Itch* might be so well known around the world because of the costume. Are you convinced? Can you offer other reasons for why it is famous?

3. In general, how closely do you pay attention to what characters are wearing in films? Has this reading changed how you will look at costumes in movies? Why, or why not?

Writing about the Reading

1. **Essay exam question** Write a brief essay answering the question you posed for Analyzing the Reading.

2. **Applying the reading** Watch the video of a film that you regard highly. Take notes about the costumes, and write an essay that both describes and analyzes some of them in terms of what they communicate symbolically about the characters. (Take into consideration the eight characteristics that conclude the reading.)

3. **Thinking on your own** In paragraph 1, the author writes that costumes can reveal "class, self-image, even psychological states" as well as traits such as "agitation, fastidiousness, delicacy, dignity, and so on." Using these images as a guideline, write an essay in which you describe and analyze what people in real life may reveal about themselves by how they dress.

Writing Your Own Description Essay

Now that you have learned about the major characteristics, structure, and purposes of a description essay, you know everything necessary to write your own. In this section you will read a student's description essay and get advice on finding ideas, drafting your essay, and revising and editing it. You may want to use the essay prompts in "Readings for Practice, Ideas for Writing" (p. 246) or choose your own topic.

A Student Model Description Essay

Ted Sawchuck, a journalism student at the University of Maryland at College Park, wrote this essay in response to an assignment in one of his classes. He was asked to describe a workplace situation that he had experienced. As you read, study the annotations and pay particular attention to Sawchuck's use of sensory language that helps you see and feel what he experienced.

Title: foreshadows dominant impression

Heatstroke with a Side of Burn Cream

Ted Sawchuck

Introduction

Builds toward dominant impression by describing restaurant kitchen

I sprinkle the last layer of cheese on top of my nachos—no time to watch the cheddar melt—and turn sideways, nearly falling face-first on grimy, spongy rubber mats. Catching my fall and the plate, I whip a towel from my belt with my free hand, open the scalding-hot oven door, and slide in the chips to toast before slapping a palm on top of the now-light-brown quesadilla on the rack below and pulling it out onto a clean part of the towel for a 180 degree turn to the counter behind. A pizza cutter makes three smooth cuts; the quesadilla is plated with three small cups (guac, salsa, sour cream) and handed to the window. I slap the bell, bellow "Jamie! Nachos!", and spin back to my station too fast to see a gorgeous grad student scoop up the plate and scoot it out to her table.

Dominant impression: identifies topic of description
Vivid, active verbs help readers visualize setting

Welcome to a restaurant kitchen during lunch or dinner rush, the time when the restaurant is packed with hungry people and the kitchen is maniacally cranking away at their orders. I'm thrashing appetizers, trying to keep up with college students' demands for fried goodies, nachos, and quesadillas. My friend A is working the grill, cooking fifteen burgers and a couple of chicken breasts for sandwiches, and M, a mutual friend, is buzzing around prepping plates, flirting with waitresses, and handling salads and desserts, both of which require time away from the main preparation line.

Sensory details: comparison adds humor and realism to visual details.

The kitchen space I spend eight hours a day in is about the size of my one-room apartment, which is slightly larger than your average prison cell. Three people, and more on horribly busy days, work in that space, crammed in with four fryers, a massive grill, a griddle, an oven, a microwave, two refrigeration units with prep counters, bins of tortilla chips, a burning-hot steam table bigger than the grill, and vast tubs of bacon. If I put both arms out and rotated, I'd severely injure at least two people.

Sensory details: describe heat in kitchen and efforts to deal with it

The most common problem for nonchefs is dealing with the heat. On one side of my work station are four fryers full of 350-degree oil. On the other, there is the steam table, so named because it boils water to keep things warm—especially deadly for forearms. Burns aren't the worst of it. You'll lose some skin, but you won't die. Overheating or dehydration can kill. When it's over 110 degrees in your workplace, fluid consumption is essential. I start gushing sweat the second I clock in and don't stop until about half an hour after clocking out. Even though we have huge buzzing exhaust fans to suck the greasy smoke away from our lungs and a warehouse-sized room fan to keep it at a low triple digits, I drink enough water to fill the steam table twice during busy times. My bandana frequently restrains ice cubes as well as rapidly tangling hair.

Sensory details: describe sounds in kitchen

The fans add to the noise, as do the chattering servers, the head chef yelling out orders, other cooks yelling out updates, and the music. Some kitchens run on music, others don't. I like to blare NPR when it is just me and A working, but on nights with a full staff, the rap music that gives rap music a bad name is trotted out—you know the kind I mean—the mainstream, with prechoreographed dances, predictable couplets about the joys of 'caine and loose women, and frequently more bleeped words than heard. The volume at which such music is played means I have to scream everything and never hear orders. It's like playing tennis with a ball that randomly disappears.

Sensory details: describe physical dangers of job

There are uncountable ways to damage yourself in a restaurant kitchen. If you didn't touch anything—just stood there—you'd still be at risk for smoke inhalation, steam burns, knife cuts from other people, spills, splatters, and being bowled over—because no one stands still in a professional kitchen. Even walking in a kitchen is dangerous. The only time the kitchen floor

5

Sentences vary in length and structure.

at the to-remain-nameless restaurant at which I cook is clean is immediately after washing, a process that results in innumerable gallons of grody gray water and the inadvertent freeing of at least one mouse from his glue trap. Moving in that kitchen is a constant struggle. Because the floor is slippery red tile, we put down thick rubber mats, which make standing for eight hours much easier on the knees. Unfortunately, these mats are coated, nay permeated, with everything we've ever spilled on them. Moving is like trying to skate across a frying pan with butter strapped to your feet. Sometimes you'll need to use a skating-like sliding motion to get through without falling face-first in the awfulness. Falling is worse, because if you grab to catch something your options are a fryer (bad), the grill (worse), or your head chef (worst of all).

Comparison: comparisons used to convey essence of restaurant kitchen work

Working in a restaurant during rush makes journalism on deadline look like elementary basket-weaving. While reporters are expected to get everything right in every story, they're only writing at most three stories a day. At one point during the worst dinner rush I can remember, I was cooking five nachos, eight quesadillas, four sampler plates, and three orders of wings at the same time. I had to get every component of those dishes right, from the plate they were served on to the garnish, serving size, cooking temperature, and appearance—and I needed to have done it fifteen minutes ago because the customers have been waiting. They don't care that we're so stacked up there's no more room in the oven for the nachos and quesadillas that are stacking up. Did I mention sampler plates have four items each, all with different cooking times and prep methods?

Organization: after several paragraphs presenting concrete, physical details, shift to more abstract issues of mental complexity and time pressure

Working in a restaurant kitchen is like speaking a foreign language. Once you stop thinking about it and just do it, you can keep up, sometimes. Other times, the pressure builds up. Maybe half the restaurant fills up in five minutes, or it's game night in a college town. Maybe the servers screwed up and gave you all their tables' orders at once instead of as they came in. Either way, you've got to shift into the next gear. Sometimes it means throwing on ten orders of wings in fryers only meant to hold eight, then garnishing a stack of plates for the main-course guys so they can focus on getting twenty burgers of different doneness levels cooked properly. For the appetizer guy, it usually means never being allowed to make a mistake, because any delay in appetizer futzes the flow of the meal. The main course is being cooked at the same time, so if my stuff comes

Vivid words: connotations of *futzes* support dominant impression better than a more formal word, such as *disrupts,* would

in late, then the properly cooked main course will either be overdone or arrive cold because no one wants the main course five minutes after receiving an appetizer.

Explains term used in restaurant work that most readers will not know

When you're late in the restaurant world, it's called being in the weeds. The origin of the name is unclear, but friends of mine note that you hide bodies where weeds grow because it's a sign of low foot traffic. Being in the weeds is not as bad as rendition to Egypt, but everyone, servers and management included, can see you're behind. In addition to getting chewed out by the head chef (who would rather yell at you than help you), you lose any chance you had with that subtle, kittenish server. Not holding your own on the line means much less fun after work. When you're in the weeds (or "weeded"), you can ask for help or suck it up. Asking for help is frowned upon; your only route is taking a breath and pulling yourself out. I spend a lot of time in the weeds, unsurprising for a kid whose only chef-like experience was making breakfast on Sundays at home and the occasional grilled cheese sandwich.

Conclusion:
makes direct appeal to readers

Like print journalism and the armed forces, professional cooking requires a very specific skill set. If you've got it, get a good knife and get to practicing. If not, be a little nicer next time the entree doesn't come exactly when you expect it.

10

Responding to Sawchuck's Essay

1. Sawchuck notes that falling behind on the job results in less fun after work. Have you found that job performance can affect off-the-job relationships with coworkers? If so, how does this effect manifest itself?

2. Do you think Sawchuck is satisfied with his job despite the adverse working conditions? Discuss to what degree working conditions affect job performance and satisfaction.

3. Is it possible to be "in the weeds" academically? Write a journal entry exploring either reasons for being in the weeds or ways to get yourself out of the weeds.

4. Sawchuck describes the time pressures he experiences. Write an essay describing the time pressures you experience in either an academic or a workplace setting.

Finding Ideas for Your Description Essay

Since you may be asked to write a response to a descriptive essay, keep an eye out for ideas as you read. Try to think of parallel situations that evoked similar images for and feelings in you. For example, for an essay describing the peace and serenity the author experienced while sitting beside a remote lake in a forest, try to think of situations in which you felt peace and serenity or how you felt when you visited a national park or wilderness area. Perhaps you had negative feelings, such as anxiety about being in a remote spot. Negative feelings are as worthy of exploration as positive feelings are.

Choosing a Subject for Your Description Essay

Your first step is to choose a subject. Make sure it is one you are familiar with or one you can readily observe. Also be aware that you may need to observe the object, activity, or person several times as you work through your essay.

Because almost any subject will encompass many more details than you could possibly include, you'll need to emphasize a particular slant or angle. If your subject is a person, you might focus on a character trait such as compulsiveness or sense of humor. To describe an object, you might emphasize its usefulness, value, or beauty.

Collecting Details That Describe Your Subject

Once you've decided on a slant or an angle, you're ready to collect and record additional sensory details. The following suggestions will help you generate details. Also refer to Table 11.1 on page 278 to stimulate your thinking.

1. **Brainstorm about your subject.** Record any sensory details that support the slant or angle you have chosen.
2. **Describe the subject to a friend, concentrating on your particular slant.** You may discover that details come more easily during conversation. Make notes on what you say and on your friend's response.
3. **Draw a quick sketch of the subject, and label the parts.** You may recall additional details as you draw.
4. **List the sensory details.** Divide a piece of paper or a computer file into five horizontal sections. Label the sections *sight, hearing, taste, touch*, and *smell*. Work through each section in turn, systematically recording what the subject looks like, sounds like, and so forth.

Finding Comparisons and Choosing a Vantage Point

Look over your list of details. Try to think of appropriate comparisons—similes, metaphors, analogies, personification—for as many details as possible. Jot down your comparisons in the margin next to the relevant details in your list. Don't expect to find a comparison for each detail. Instead, your goal is to discover one or two strong comparisons that will be most effective.

Next, consider whether to use a fixed or a moving vantage point. Think about the aspect of your subject you are emphasizing and how it can best be communicated. Ask yourself the following questions.

- What vantage point(s) will give the reader the most useful information?
- From which vantage point(s) can I provide the most revealing or striking details?

Creating a Dominant Impression

As noted earlier, think of the dominant impression as the thesis that conveys your main point and holds the rest of the essay together. It also creates a mood or feeling about the subject, which all other details in the essay explain or support.

The dominant impression you decide on should be the one about which you feel most confident. It should also appeal to your audience, offer an unusual perspective, and provide new insights on the subject. Finally, keep in mind that you may need to do additional prewriting to gather support for your dominant impression. This step is similar to collecting evidence for a thesis, except the "evidence" for a descriptive essay consists of sensory details. Therefore, before drafting your essay, check to see if you have enough sensory details to support your dominant impression.

Drafting Your Description Essay

Once you are satisfied with your dominant impression and sensory details, you can choose the method of organization that will best support the dominant impression (see p. 238). As you draft the essay, remember that all details must support the dominant impression. For example, if you are describing the way apes in a zoo imitate one another and humans, only details about how the apes mimic people and other apes should be included. Other, unrelated details, such as the condition of the apes' environment and types of animals nearby, do not belong in the essay. Be careful as well about the *number* of details you include. Too many details will tire your readers, but an insufficient number will leave them unconvinced of your main point. Select striking sensory details that make your point effectively; leave out details that tell the reader little or nothing. For example, instead of selecting five or six ordinary details to describe a concert, choose one revealing detail such as the following.

> As the band performed the final song, the lights dimmed and every single member of the audience of twelve hundred people silently held a lighted candle before his or her face.

Try also to include one or two telling metaphors or similes. If you cannot think of any, however, don't stretch to construct them. Effective comparisons

Table 11.1   Characteristics to Consider in Developing Sensory Details

Sight	Color
	Pattern
	Shape
	Size
Sound	Volume (loud or soft)
	Pitch
	Quality
Taste	Pleasant or unpleasant
	Salty, sweet, sour, or bitter
Touch	Texture
	Weight
	Temperature
Smell	Agreeable or disagreeable
	Strength

usually come to mind as you examine your subject. Contrived comparisons will only lessen the impact of your essay.

As you write, remember that the sensory language you use should enable readers to re-create the person, object, or scene in their minds. Keep the following three guidelines in mind.

1. **Create images that appeal to the five senses.** Your descriptions should appeal to one or more of the senses. See pages 232–34 for examples of ways to engage each of the five senses.

2. **Avoid vague, general descriptions.** Use specific, not vague, language to describe your subject.

   VAGUE   The pizza was cheaply prepared.

   CONCRETE   The supposedly "large" pizza was miniature, with a nearly imperceptible layer of sauce, a light dusting of cheese, a few paper-thin slices of pepperoni, and one or two stray mushroom slices.

3. **Use figures of speech and analogies effectively.** Figures of speech (similes, metaphors, analogies, and personification) create memorable images that enliven your writing and capture the readers' attention.

- **Choose fresh, surprising images.** Avoid overused clichés such as "cold as ice" and "it's a hop, skip, and a jump away."
- **Make sure the similarity between the two items being compared is apparent.** If you write "*Peter* looked like an *unpeeled tangerine*," your reader will not be able to guess what characteristics Peter shares with the tangerine. "Peter's *skin* was as dimpled as a *tangerine peel*" gives the reader a clearer idea of what Peter looks like.
- **Don't mix or combine figures of speech.** Such expressions, called **mixed metaphors**, are confusing and often unintentionally humorous. For example, what follows mixes images of a hawk and a wolf: "The fighter jet was a hawk soaring into the clouds, growling as it sought its prey."

Revising Your Description Essay

If possible, set aside your draft for a day or two before rereading and revising. As you reread, focus on overall effectiveness, not on grammar and mechanics. Use the revision flowchart in Figure 11.3 (p. 280) to discover the strengths and weaknesses of your descriptive essay.

Editing and Proofreading Your Essay

The last step is to check your revised essay for errors in grammar, spelling, punctuation, and mechanics. In addition, be sure to look for the types of errors you tend to make in writing assignments, whether for this class or another situation. For descriptive writing, pay particular attention to the punctuation of adjectives. Keep the following rules in mind.

1. **Use a comma between adjectives only where needed.**

    ▶ Singh was a confident, skilled pianist.

    The order of adjectives can usually be scrambled (*skilled, confident pianist* or *confident, skilled pianist*). To be sure a comma is needed, try reversing the two adjectives. If the phrase sounds correct when the adjectives are reversed, a comma is needed. However, if changing the adjective order makes the sentence nonsensical, then those adjectives are cumulative. Cumulative adjectives act together to modify the noun and should not be separated by commas.

    ▶ We ate at an excellent Chinese restaurant.

    You would not write *Chinese excellent restaurant*.

2. **Use a hyphen to connect two words that work together as an adjective before a noun.** Using hyphens properly can avoid misunderstanding, for

Figure 11.3 Revising a Description Essay

QUESTIONS	REVISION STRATEGIES
1. Dominant impression Does your essay express the dominant impression you wish to convey? — No →	• Reread your essay. Make a list of the different impressions it conveys. • Choose one impression that you have the most to say about, and develop additional details that support it.
Yes ↓	
2. Sensory details Does each detail support your dominant impression? — No →	• Eliminate irrelevant sensory details.
Yes ↓	
3. Vivid language Is there enough vivid language to help your reader visualize the topic? Are the connotations of your language appropriate? — No →	• Brainstorm additional sensory details. • Replace passive verbs with active ones. • Vary your sentences. • Replace words with inappropriate connotations with ones that better support your dominant impression.
Yes ↓	
4. Comparisons Is each simile, metaphor, and analogy fresh and effective? — No →	• Look for and eliminate clichés. • Brainstorm new comparisons.
Yes ↓	
5. Organization Are the details arranged in a clear way? — No →	• Experiment with several arrangements of details to see which works best. • Add transitions to connect your ideas.
Yes ↓	
6. Topic sentence Does the topic sentence make clear what the paragraph is describing? — No →	• Revise so that each paragraph has a clear topic sentence and supporting details that relate to it.
Yes ↓	
7. Introduction and conclusion Is each effective? — No →	• Revise your introduction and conclusion so that they meet the guidelines given in Chapter 6.

example, between *green and brown toads* and *green-and-brown toads*. Here are a few examples.

- ▶   *well-used* book

- ▶   *perfect-fitting* shoes

- ▶   *foil-wrapped* pizza

3. **Avoid misplaced modifiers.** Modifiers are words or phrases that describe, change, qualify, or limit the meaning of another word or phrase in a sentence. Be sure your modifiers give readers a clear picture of the details you want to convey.

- ▶   *In the Caribbean, w*
    We visited a tremendously powerful telescope searching distant stars
    for signs of life *in the Caribbean.*

- ▶   *I sent him .*
    Hoping to get a message to John, an urgent fax ~~was sent~~.

- ▶   *carefully*
    The FBI monitors Web sites coming from known terrorist groups .
    ~~carefully.~~

Chapter 12

Illustration:
Explaining with Examples

Quick Start: In a social problems class, the instructor shows the photograph on this page and makes the following statement: "Environmental pollution is a growing global problem." She asks the class to think of situations similar to the one shown here that confirm this view. With a small group of classmates, brainstorm a list of examples of environmental pollution that you have observed or read about.

What Is Illustration?

Illustration is a technique that uses one or more examples to make a point. For instance, you might argue that two movies have similar plots and give examples of *how* they're similar. Or, if you are making a point that holidays no longer have the same meaning as they used to, you could give several examples of their increasing commercialization. (Note that the last two sentences *illustrate* the definition of *illustration* provided in the first sentence!) Examples make ideas concrete, often connecting them to situations within the reader's experience. Most textbooks are filled with examples for this very reason, and writers in academic and work situations commonly use illustration, as well.

Illustration does the following:

1. It brings ideas to life.
2. It helps clarify unfamiliar or difficult topics, concepts, or terms.
3. It helps readers and writers connect.

Knowing how writers (and other communicators) use illustration will help you understand, analyze, and evaluate it when you read and help you use it in your own writing.

1. Illustration Brings Ideas to Life

Many ideas are only meaningful and clear when they are fully explained. Providing examples is a simple, effective way to make a concept clear in a lively, interesting manner. For instance, if someone says that a child's behavior is *atrocious*, examples can illustrate the degree of the child's misbehavior (such as, "he pulled the cat's tail, broke two plates, and drew on my wall with permanent markers"). Examples bring ideas to life by enabling readers and listeners to understand and visualize real and concrete situations.

In the following example from the book *Adventures in the Screen Trade*, William Goldman presents a **generalization** (a statement offered as a general truth) and supports it with specific examples that make it concrete, specific, and understandable.

Example 1: *Raiders of the Lost Ark*

Not one person in the entire motion picture field knows for a certainty what's going to work. . . . *Raiders [of the Lost Ark]* is the number-four film in history as this is being written. I don't remember any movie that had such power going in. It was more or less the brainchild of George Lucas and was directed by Steven Spielberg, the two unquestioned wunderkinder of show business (*Star Wars, Jaws,* etc.). Probably you all knew that. But did you know that *Raiders of the Lost Ark* was offered

> to every single studio in town—*and they all turned it down?*
>
> All except Paramount.
>
> ... [W]hy did all the other studios say no? Because nobody knows anything. And why did Universal, the mightiest studio of all, pass on *Star Wars*...? Because nobody, *nobody*—not now, not ever—knows the least thing about what is or isn't going to work at the box office.
>
> —William Goldman, *Adventures in the Screen Trade*, pp. 39–41

Example 2: *Star Wars*

2. Illustration Explains Unfamiliar Topics and Difficult Concepts or Terms

One of the best ways to explain something unfamiliar or difficult to understand is to give an example that demonstrates how the idea works.

Unfamiliar topics   When the audience has little or no knowledge of a topic, examples can help them understand it. Note how examples are used to explain how occasional reinforcement works in the following excerpt from a textbook chapter on consumer learning.

> Marketers have found that product quality must be consistently high and provide customer satisfaction with each use for desired consumer behavior to continue. However, they have also discovered that some nonproduct rewards do not have to be offered each time the transaction takes place; even an occasional reward provides reinforcement and encourages consumer patronage. For example, airlines may occasionally upgrade a passenger at the gate, or a clothing discounter may from time to time announce a one-hour sale over the store sound system. The promise of possibly receiving a reward provides positive reinforcement and encourages patronage.
>
> —Schiffman and Kanuk, *Consumer Behavior*, p. 223

Example 1: Airlines

Example 2: Clothing discounter

Difficult concepts or terms   Complicated or abstract concepts can be difficult for readers to grasp, even when they're defined; illustration can help. For instance, note how the following passage from a communications textbook begins by defining the term *channels* as "simply the vehicles or mechanisms that transmit messages from senders to receivers." The definition alone offers little help. To clarify the concept, the authors go on to list examples that will help readers make the abstract idea of channels concrete.

> Channels are simply the vehicles or mechanisms that transmit messages from senders to receivers. . . . Consider, for example, the possible channels used for written communication (memos, letters), electronic communication (radio, television), and computer-transmitted communication (email, Internet).
>
> —Dan O'Hair et al., *Competent Communication*

Examples: written, electronic, computer-assisted

The term might not be difficult but might be abstract and open to different interpretations.

In other situations, writers clarify what they mean by a term. Suppose you were to use *unfair* to describe an employer's treatment of employees; readers might have different ideas of fairness. Providing examples of the working conditions or treatment of workers that you consider unfair would give readers enough information so they could understand your point and either agree or disagree.

3. Illustration Helps Readers and Writers Connect

Illustration is also useful for enabling readers and writers to share experiences. For instance, a writer who has traveled extensively in the Middle East could share his or her experiences with readers, who then learn and benefit from the writer's travels.

In this paragraph, the example allows the writer to make a connection to readers' own lives by giving examples of smells that are familiar to them.

> Smell communication, or olfactory communication, is extremely important in a wide variety of situations and is now big business. For example, there's some evidence (though not very conclusive evidence) that the smell of lemon contributes to a perception of health, the smells of lavender and eucalyptus increase alertness, and the smell of rose oil reduces blood pressure. Research also finds that smells can influence your body's chemistry, which in turn influences your emotional state. For example, the smell of chocolate results in the reduction of theta brain waves, which produces a sense of relaxation and a reduced level of attention.
>
> —DeVito, *Human Communication*, p. 152

Examples 1–3: Smells of lemon, lavender and eucalyptus, and rose oil

Example 4: Smell of chocolate

Reading and Writing Illustration Essays

In this section you will learn about the structure of an illustration essay, read a sample essay, and practice using the guidelines for understanding, analyzing, and evaluating illustration essays. This will help you skillfully read and write essays that use illustration.

How Is an Illustration Essay Structured?

The structure of an illustration essay is straightforward.

1. The **introduction** presents the topic. It also contains background information and usually includes the **thesis statement**.
2. The **body paragraphs** give one or more examples that support the thesis. A clear organization and the use of transitions make it easy to identify the examples.
3. The **conclusion** presents a final statement.

Figure 12.1 represents these major structural components visually.

Figure 12.1   Graphic Organizer for an Illustration Essay

Title	
Introduction	Background information
	Thesis statement*

Body paragraphs		or	One extended example with details
	Example 1		
	Detail		
	Detail		
	Detail		
	Example 2		
	Detail		
	Detail		
	Detail		
	Example 3		
	Detail		
	Detail		
	Detail		

Conclusion	Final statement

*In some essays the thesis statement may be implied or appear in a different position.

1. THE INTRODUCTION PRESENTS THE TOPIC

The introduction of an illustration essay should

- present the topic,
- state the thesis, and
- suggest why the topic is worth reading about.

Background information should include relevant material to help orient readers to the topic. For instance, an essay on misconceptions about the welfare system might provide background information on eligibility, distribution of benefits, and so forth.

As you learned in Chapter 5 (p. 105), the heart of every essay is its thesis—the point or main idea that a writer wants to persuade his or her audience to accept. In essays that use illustration, the thesis is often a **generalization**—a broad statement about a subject—that the writer attempts to make specific and concrete through the use of examples. Here are a few sample thesis statements.

> Teenagers use various forms of self-expression, including clothing, body art, and hairstyles, to establish their identity.
>
> (The body of the essay would give examples of each form.)

> Facebook, an online social network, has changed how college students communicate, both positively and negatively.
>
> (The body of the essay would give examples of how communication has changed for better and for worse.)

> Effective decision making in the workplace requires two essential skills: planning and assessment.
>
> (The body of the essay would give examples of situations in which each skill is used.)

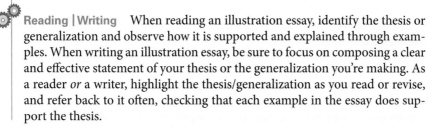

Reading | Writing   When reading an illustration essay, identify the thesis or generalization and observe how it is supported and explained through examples. When writing an illustration essay, be sure to focus on composing a clear and effective statement of your thesis or the generalization you're making. As a reader *or* a writer, highlight the thesis/generalization as you read or revise, and refer back to it often, checking that each example in the essay does support the thesis.

2. THE BODY CONTAINS SUPPORTING EXAMPLES IDENTIFIABLE THROUGH A CLEAR ORGANIZATION AND TRANSITIONS

To maintain readers' interest and to cover topics thoroughly, writers must select their examples carefully when they use illustration, and they must be sure to provide a sufficient number of examples to make their points understandable and believable. Examples in illustration essays should be relevant, representative, detailed and complete, and striking. They should also be appropriate in length and number and appropriate for the audience the essay addresses.

Examples should be relevant   Examples should clearly demonstrate the point or idea the essay illustrates. For instance, a thesis that states that publicly funded and operated preschool programs should be expanded should be supported with examples of public programs, not private ones.

Examples should be representative   Typical cases, not specialized or unusual ones, best support an essay's main point. In many essays, several of these examples are necessary. In an essay arguing that preschool programs advance children's prereading skills, one example of an all-day, year-round preschool would not be characteristic of preschool programs in general.

Examples should be detailed and complete   In order for readers to understand the connection between the generalization and the examples, the examples must be thoroughly explained. Illustration essays that report statistics should do so objectively and provide enough information so that readers can evaluate the reliability of the data.

EXAMPLE LACKING DETAIL	Most students in preschool programs have better language skills than children who don't attend such programs.
DETAILED EXAMPLE	According to an independent evaluator, 73% of children who attended the Head Start program in Clearwater had better language skills after one year of attendance than did children who did not attend the program.

Examples should be striking   Include examples that capture readers' attention and make a vivid impression.

GENERIC EXAMPLE	old car
VIVID EXAMPLE	a '96 Chevy with exhaust belching, rust flaking

Examples should be appropriate in length and number   The appropriate number of examples depends on how complex the generalization—or thesis—is. For a focused thesis statement, a single, extended example may be sufficient.

> In New York, a wealthy city, pollution can be severe in poor neighborhoods. Consider the South Bronx.

An extended discussion of conditions in the South Bronx would clearly explain and support the thesis. Consider, on the other hand, the more complex thesis statement that follows.

Poor neighborhoods across America bear a disproportionate environmental burden because they lack political, social, and economic power to fight back.

Here, multiple examples of neighborhoods victimized for social, political, and economic reasons would probably be necessary to persuade the audience that the thesis is reasonable.

Either method can be effective, as long as the material included serves to adequately support the author's thesis.

Examples should be appropriate to the purpose and audience   Audience and purpose are key factors in deciding what types of examples to include. Suppose you want to persuade readers that the Food and Drug Administration should approve a new cancer drug. If your audience is composed of physicians, the most effective examples would include clinical studies and technical explanations of how the drug works and what the potential side effects are. But if your audience is the general public, it would be better to include personal anecdotes about lives being saved because of the drug's effectiveness.

 Reading | Writing   When reading an illustration essay, be sure to understand how the example or examples support the thesis. Also analyze and evaluate the examples using the criteria explained in "Understanding, Analyzing, and Evaluating Illustration Essays," (p. 293). When writing an illustration essay, be sure to select examples that best support your thesis. As you review your examples, don't hesitate to revise or entirely change your thesis.

Effective essays use a clear method of organization. Often, illustration essays employ one of the organization methods discussed in Chapter 6: most-to-least, least-to-most, chronological, or spatial order. For instance, in an essay explaining how teenagers today typically dress, the examples might be arranged spatially, starting with footwear (such as flip-flops) and moving upward to facial piercings and hairstyles.

In some instances, illustration essays may use a secondary pattern of development, such as classification and division or comparison and contrast. To support the thesis below you could use examples like the ones following it, which are arranged into different classes, or categories, of prepared foods (home-cooked dishes, restaurants' "signature" dishes, and "global" dishes).

Thesis: Many of the acts that today are called "piracy" with regard to movies and music are traditional practices when it comes to food.

Example 1: The green bean casserole recipe was distributed by Campbell's Soup Company and quickly spread from personal recipe card to personal recipe card without giving credit.

Example 2: A restaurant's signature dishes, no matter how distinctive, cannot be copyrighted or patented and are picked up by other restaurants.

Example 3: Some foods, like pizza, have become so popular that they have crossed all national boundaries to become a kind of global cuisine.

Reading | Writing   When reading an illustration essay, be sure to examine how the essay is organized and use the organization to guide you through the reading. Watch for transitions that signal the next example, and note how the organization guides you through the generalization that is being illustrated. When writing an illustration essay, use a diagram to help you plan and organize your examples.

Effective illustration essays use clear **transitions** to guide the reader from example to example or from one aspect of the extended example to the next. Transitional words and phrases particularly useful for illustration essays include the following:

for example	for instance	to illustrate
another example	in another situation	such as

3.   THE CONCLUSION REINFORCES THE THESIS

The conclusion usually returns to or references the generalization and makes a final statement that draws the essay to a close.

Reading | Writing   As a reader, pay attention to whether the writer has logically connected the examples and whether the examples lead to the stated conclusion. As a writer, be sure to give your reader a sense of unity and closure, perhaps by referring back to one or more examples. Be sure to refer to your generalization by restating it, suggesting further directions to pursue, or by expanding on it.

A Model Illustration Essay

Title

Snoopers at Work

Bill Bryson

Bill Bryson (b. 1951) grew up in the United States and then lived in England from 1977 to the mid-1990s, where he wrote for newspapers and then branched out to write about travel. The essays in *I'm a Stranger Here*

Myself (1999), one of Bryson's nonfiction works about traveling in the United States, began as a column in a British newspaper, the *Mail on Sunday.* In the following piece from that collection, Bryson discusses the invasion of workers' privacy by their employers.

Introduction

Now here is something to bear in mind should you ever find yourself using a changing room in a department store or other retail establishment. It is perfectly legal—indeed, it is evidently routine—for the store to spy on you while you are trying on their clothes.

Background information: example of changing-room surveillance; reference to book *The Right to Privacy*

I know this because I have just been reading a book by Ellen Alderman and Caroline Kennedy called *The Right to Privacy*, which is full of alarming tales of ways that businesses and employers can—and enthusiastically do—intrude into what would normally be considered private affairs.

The business of changing-cubicle spying came to light in 1983 when a customer trying on clothes in a department store in Michigan discovered that a store employee had climbed a stepladder and was watching him through a metal vent. (Is this tacky or what?) The customer was sufficiently outraged that he sued the store for invasion of privacy. He lost. A state court held that it was reasonable for retailers to defend against shoplifting by engaging in such surveillance.

Thesis: Technology, employer paranoia, and commercial greed have resulted in increasing invasions of privacy for many Americans.

He shouldn't have been surprised. Nearly everyone is being spied on in some way in America these days. A combination of technological advances, employer paranoia, and commercial avarice means that many millions of Americans are having their lives delved into in ways that would have been impossible, not to say unthinkable, a dozen years ago. . . .

Body paragraphs: examples of privacy violation

Many companies are taking advantage of technological possibilities to make their businesses more ruthlessly productive. In Maryland, according to *Time* magazine, a bank searched through the medical records of its borrowers—apparently quite legally—to find out which of them had life-threatening illnesses and used this information to cancel their loans. Other companies have focused not on customers but on their own employees—for instance, to

Example 1: medical-record surveillance

check what prescription drugs the employees are taking. One large, well-known company teamed up with a pharmaceutical firm to comb through the health records of employees to

5

see who might benefit from a dose of antidepressants. The idea was that the company would get more serene workers; the drug company would get more customers.

According to the American Management Association, two-thirds of companies in the United States spy on their employees

Example 2: methods of spying

in some way. Thirty-five percent track phone calls, and 10 percent actually tape phone conversations to review at leisure later. About a quarter of companies surveyed admitted to going through their employees' computer files and reading their email.

Still other companies are secretly watching their employees at work. A secretary at a college in Massachusetts discovered that

Example 3: video surveillance

a hidden video camera was filming her office twenty-four hours a day. Goodness knows what the school authorities were hoping to find. What they got were images of the woman changing out of her work clothes and into a track suit each night in order to jog home from work. She is suing and will probably get a pot of money. But elsewhere courts have upheld companies' rights to spy on their workers.

Example 4: drug-use entrapment

There is a particular paranoia about drugs. I have a friend who got a job with a large manufacturing company in Iowa a year or so ago. Across the street from the company was a tavern that was the company after-hours hangout. One night my friend was having a beer after work with his colleagues when he was approached by a fellow employee who asked if he knew where she could get some marijuana. He said he didn't use the stuff

Detail: personal anecdote

himself, but to get rid of her — for she was very persistent — he gave her the phone number of an acquaintance who sometimes sold it.

The next day he was fired. The woman, it turned out, was a company spy employed solely to weed out drug use in the company. He hadn't supplied her with marijuana, you understand, hadn't encouraged her to use marijuana, and had stressed that he didn't use marijuana himself. Nonetheless, he was fired for encouraging and abetting the use of an illegal substance.

Already, 91 percent of large companies — I find this almost

Example 5: TAD rules

unbelievable — now test some of their workers for drugs. Scores of companies have introduced what are called TAD rules — TAD

10

being short for "tobacco, alcohol, and drugs"—which prohibit employees from using any of these substances at any time, including at home. There are companies, if you can believe it, that forbid their employees to drink or smoke at any time—even one beer, even on a Saturday night—and enforce the rules by making their workers give urine samples.

Example 6: "active badge" tracking

But it gets even more sinister than that. Two leading electronics companies working together have invented something called an "active badge," which tracks the movements of any worker compelled to wear one. The badge sends out an infrared signal every fifteen seconds. This signal is received by a central computer, which is thus able to keep a record of where every employee is and has been, whom they have associated with, how many times they have been to the toilet or water cooler—in short, to log every single action of their working day. If that isn't ominous, I don't know what is.

Conclusion: humorous approval of surveillance of restaurant employees washing hands after using lavatory

However, there is one development, I am pleased to report, that makes all of this worthwhile. A company in New Jersey has patented a device for determining whether restaurant employees have washed their hands after using the lavatory. Now *that* I can go for.

Understanding, Analyzing, and Evaluating Illustration Essays

In reading and writing illustration essays, your goal is to get beyond mere competence: That is, you want to be able to do more than merely understand the content of the essays you're reading or convey just your basic ideas to the audience you're writing for.

Reading | Writing   Truly skillful reading and writing require the abilities to **understand**, **analyze**, *and* **evaluate** material. These abilities are important to you as a reader because they give you a systematic, thorough method of examining a reading. They're important to you as a writer because they help you decide what to revise, rewrite, drop, and replace, allowing you to produce a well-written, effective essay.

📊 Understanding an Illustration Essay

To understand an illustration essay—that is, to understand the point it's making—focus on the thesis and the examples used to support it. Use the reading skills you learned in Chapter 2 as well as the following questions to assist you.

- **What is the essay's thesis?** Read the essay to identify the thesis or generalization.
- **What examples does the author use to illustrate the thesis?** As you read, take note of each example offered to support that generalization. Highlight the examples as you read. If the author uses one extended example, be sure to identify all aspects of that example.
- **How is the essay organized?** Draw a diagram that shows the structure of the essay and the sequence of ideas. Figure 12.2 provides a diagram of the structure of Bryson's essay. Refer back to the model graphic organizer for illustration essays on page 286 before starting your own.

Understanding in Action

Use the completed graphic organizer in Figure 12.2 to write a brief summary of Bryson's essay.

📊 Analyzing an Illustration Essay

Analyzing an illustration essay involves investigating more precisely *how* an essay works, not just the message it conveys. Whether you're reading someone else's essay or your own, analysis requires you to look closely at the examples and study their relationship to the thesis (or generalization). You may need to reread the essay, perhaps several times, considering each example by itself first and then in conjunction with the other examples. Here are key questions to ask.

- **How does each example illustrate the thesis?** As you read, note in the margin the aspect of the thesis that each example illustrates.
- **What kinds of examples did the author choose? Why? How do the examples suit the intended audience and the author's purpose?** Study the examples to discover how they appeal to the intended audience. Consider whether different examples might produce different results.
- **What is the emotional impact of the examples, if any?** If an example stirs your emotions or seems to evoke a response, ask how and why the

writer chose this example. What was he or she attempting to accomplish?

- **What is the author's tone? How does the tone contribute to the essay's intended effect?** How does the author present the examples? Does he or she treat them seriously and suggest their value?

- **What type of evidence other than examples, if any, does the author offer in support of the thesis? What effect does this evidence have on the reader?** In many situations, using facts, details, statistics, and expert opinion may also be effective ways to support a thesis.

Figure 12.2   Graphic Organizer for "Snoopers at Work"

Title	"Snoopers at Work"
Introduction	**Background information:** Example of changing-room surveillance; reference to book *The Right to Privacy*
	Thesis: Technology, employer paranoia, and commercial greed have resulted in increasing invasions of privacy for many Americans.
Body paragraphs	**Example 1:** Medical record surveillance
	Example 2: Phone and computer surveillance
	Example 3: Video surveillance
	Example 4: Drug-use entrapment
	Detail: Personal anecdote about a friend who experienced entrapment
	Example 5: TAD rules
	Example 6: "Active badge" tracking
Conclusion	Humorous approval of surveillance of restaurant employees washing hands after using lavatory

Analysis in Action

Reread Bill Bryson's essay (pp. 290–93) and use the Analyzing an Illustration Essay questions outlined above to make notes on the piece.
  A sample of one student's analysis annotations is included below.

Stat supports claim.	Already, 91 percent of large companies—I find this almost unbelievable—now test some of their workers for drugs.
Example would appeal to general audience—everyone works!	Scores of companies have introduced what are called TAD rules—TAD being short for "tobacco, alcohol, and drugs"—which prohibit employees from using any of these substances at any time, including at home. There are companies, if you can believe it, that forbid their
Author sounds upset here.	employees to drink or smoke at any time—even one beer, even on a Saturday night—and enforce the rules by making their workers give urine samples.

📊 Evaluating an Illustration Essay

Evaluate how well the examples support the thesis using the following questions.

- **Is each example accurate and clearly presented?** That is, are the examples believable and documented, if necessary? Are all relevant aspects of the example well explained?

- **Are the examples representative or exceptional?** That is, are the examples the author uses to support his or her thesis typical or are they rare or unusual? If they are *not* typical, does this affect the persuasiveness of the essay?

- **Are all the examples relevant?** Do they relate specifically to the thesis?

- **Is there a sufficient number of examples to fully explain the generalization?** Are more examples needed to demonstrate that the generalization applies to a wide variety of situations?

- **Can you think of any examples that have been omitted that would contradict the author's thesis and that he or she should have taken into account?** Be sure the writer offers fair and objective examples, not those that show only one side of an issue or point of view.

Evaluation in Action

Use Figure 12.2 (p. 295), the Evaluating an Illustration Essay questions on p. 296, and your notes analyzing Bill Bryson's "Snoopers at Work" (pp. 290–93) to write an evaluation of the whole piece.

The student whose notes were shown in Analysis in Action used them to write the following evaluation of that same paragraph.

> This paragraph is relevant to Bryson's thesis that employers invade employees' privacy. It shows that companies force employees to behave in certain ways even when they're not at work. He uses a statistic to make the example seem common, which is persuasive. However, he doesn't say how many companies forbid alcohol and smoking on the weekend. His examples appeal to his audience. As newspaper readers, they are likely to be employed and would probably not like the idea of their employer spying on them.

Readings for Practice, Ideas for Writing

Thinking Purple and Living Green

Celestina Phillips has contributed to several Fort Worth publications, including *Fort Worth, Texas: The City's Magazine, Parker County Today*, and *Downtown Fort Worth, Inc.* "Thinking Purple and Living Green" was first published in the *Fort Worth Business Press* in 2008.

Reading Tip

As you read, identify the thesis statement and notice whether each example directly supports it. Also notice whether Phillips provides adequate details about each example.

Previewing the Reading

Preview the reading (see pp. 23–24 for guidelines), and then answer the following questions.

1. What is the subject of the essay?
2. What college is discussed throughout?
3. Who is involved in the effort described in the essay?

CELESTINA PHILLIPS

Thinking Purple and Living Green

While many of us are just now learning to incorporate such terms as *carbon footprint*[1] and *eco-friendly* into our vocabulary, the lingo is a matter of business as usual at Texas Christian University. Students, faculty, and staff members have been participating in campus-wide sustainability[2] initiatives long before the notion of "going green" became fashionable.

[1] **carbon footprint** Measure of the carbon dioxide produced by a person, an organization, or a location at a given time.
[2] **sustainability** Capability of being continued with minimal long-term effect on the environment.

The university is leading the way in implementing environmentally conscious programming that allows the campus community to make real differences in its everyday lives. From purple bikes to biodegradable potato-fiber spoons, TCU thinks purple (the school's signature color) and lives green. TCU has been named the North Texas Clean Air Coalition Gold award winner for Employer of the Year, more than 500 employees.

"I've never seen so much enthusiasm," says Tim Barth, chair of psychology at TCU and North Richland Hills City Council member. "So much of it comes from the students. That age group, in particular, gets really excited about having the opportunity to put their stamp on the world and be a part of this great change."

"It also provides a lot of energy for the faculty and staff," Barth adds. "They get excited because the students are excited. More than anything, you see a real awareness of these issues, much more than we've seen in the past."

5   TCU students and staff have the opportunity to participate in many earth-friendly programs that can impact the environment in a positive manner. For example, the school's successful Purple Bike Program allows both students and staff members to use custom purple-painted cruiser-style bicycles to get to and from campus at no fee, reducing the number of cars on campus. The program is such a hit that there is often a waiting list for bikes.

The Purple Bike Program was founded by Keith Whitworth, a professor of sociology who champions a curriculum covering social justice and environmental stewardship[3] across the global economy. Students recently worked to harvest solar energy at the TCU–Stanford football game. The class in sustainability is now a requirement for sociology, criminal justice, and anthropology majors.

The university also provides metro-area public-transportation passes for all students, faculty, and staff, free of charge. Earlier this year, TCU handed out reusable shopping bags with the slogan, "Live Purple, Bleed Green." The concept was so well received that the university developed the idea of "Think Purple, Live Green" as a theme for the present semester. Faculty members and students work together to create programs and events that address global issues and inspire action.

"Even though this theme is for one semester, these initiatives are going to

[3] **stewardship** Taking responsibility for the care of something owned by someone else or by a group.

continue for some period of time," Barth says.

One teamwork contest in progress encourages individual commitments to a green way of life. TCU also is competing in an intercollegiate program called Recyclemania, in which students and staff rally to achieve high recycling rates and to produce the least amount of trash.

"Right now, it's cool to be environ- 10 mentally conscious," Barth says. "I think we are riding the tide of that and giving these opportunities to the students in particular."

One of the more unusual green initiatives is TCU's new "SpudWare"— cutlery made from 80% potato starch and 20% soy oil that biodegrades in 180 days. "Ecotainers" also are used, which are compostable chlorine-free cups that have an inner lining made of corn instead of petroleum. Additionally, many TCU offices and processes are now paperless, including financial services, human resources, and the registration process. The university also offers green book clubs, film programs, speaker forums, and easy-to-use carbon-footprint measurement tools.

Regarding campus buildings and construction, a new student union facility provides the first opportunity for TCU to have a building certified under LEED (Leadership in Energy and Environmental Design), Barth says.

"The union is in reach of those criteria and is close to it," Barth said. "In the future, LEED certification is going to be an important part of new building construction on campus."

As TCU continues to evoke a new sense of sustainability on campus, the university is looking to expand its efforts throughout the city. The new

Continued >

Center for Applied Psychology will play a key role in performing behavioral research that one day could lead Fort Worth to a greener way of life.

15   "We will become involved in determining people's attitude toward environmentally friendly lifestyles, assessing what it is they are willing to change," Barth says. "We would try to come up with programs that are evidence-based on our research, and apply them toward this issue that is so important to the region. That is what the Center for Applied Psychology is all about . . . trying some things here with our students, but then bringing it out into the community to see if it could be effective in real life."

A new "sustainability coordinator" also is on the horizon[4] for the school.

According to Barth, this individual would focus on carbon offsets, a field that studies the fragile act of balancing negative and positive practices that affect carbon emissions.

"We would ideally get to a point where we are carbon-neutral,[5] which is a very difficult thing to do," Barth explains. "The idea is for everything we do that's bad, we do something that offsets it. In the end, we are neutral in emitting carbon into the environment. While it's a great goal, if you ever achieve it, I don't know."

But unknowns won't stop TCU in pursuing environmental sustainability even further, as proven with the many initiatives the campus is already implementing.

[4] **on the horizon** In the future.

[5] **carbon-neutral** Having a net zero carbon footprint.

📊 Understanding the Reading

1. **Topic** What is the main topic of the selection?

2. **Main idea** What is the main idea the author is trying to convey about the topic?

3. **Detail** Why are TCU students interested in the living-green program (refer to para. 3)?

4. **Detail** How does course content at TCU reflect the emphasis on living green (para. 6)?

5. **Detail** What products and services does TCU offer to help students live green (paras. 5–8)?

6. **Detail** What policies and procedures has TCU implemented to encourage green living (paras. 9–13)?

7. **Detail** How has TCU expanded its living-green efforts into the community (paras. 14–16)?

8. **Detail** What is TCU's long-term goal (para. 17)?

9. **Vocabulary** Using context clues (see Chapter 2, p. 34), write a brief definition of each of the following words as it is used in the reading, checking a dictionary if necessary: *incorporate* (para. 1), *implementing* (2), *impact* (5), *champions* (6), and *fragile* (16).

10. **Vocabulary** Suppose you are reading this article for an environmental studies class. Circle the specialized vocabulary (see Chapter 2, p. 37) that would be important to learn.

11. **Summary** Write a summary of the reading that would be useful to help you recall the article's main points.

Analyzing the Reading

1. **Critical thinking** Based on the examples the author uses to illustrate the thesis, who is the intended audience of the piece?

2. **Evidence** How does each example support the author's thesis?

3. **Tone** Describe the tone of the piece. How does it help or hinder the author's thesis?

Evaluating the Reading

1. **Evidence** Are all the author's examples relevant to her claim that TCU is a leader in green living on universities?

Discussing the Reading

1. With your classmates, discuss whether or not you think the TCU living-green initiatives would work at your school. Give your reasons.

2. Do you think there is strong peer pressure at TCU to live green? If so, how might it create problems for some students?

3. TCU has a large campus and a significant presence in its community. Do you think initiatives such as riding purple bikes would work at other colleges, regardless of campus location and the colleges' importance within their communities?

Writing about the Reading

1. **Paragraph** Brainstorm a list of your college's efforts to go green. Consider ways this list is similar to and different from TCU's efforts. Then write a paragraph comparing your college's efforts to live green with those of TCU. Your topic sentence might begin, "Compared to TCU, the living-green efforts at (name of your school) are . . . ." Draft your paragraph using the strongest examples of your college's green initiatives to support this topic sentence.

2. **Paragraph** TCU is making an effort to go paperless, as are many other organizations and businesses. Write a paragraph explaining whether you could go paperless. Your draft should include examples of why doing so would be convenient or inconvenient.

3. **Essay** Devise a "recyclemania" program for your school, and write an essay describing the details of your plan. Begin by brainstorming possible plans and their details. Choose the plan that seems most workable. Write a clear thesis statement, such as "[Name of your program] is a campus-wide recycling plan designed to build student interest and commitment through competition." Then draft your essay, being sure to include examples of how your plan would work.

Twitter Goes to College

Zach Miners is a former reporter for *U.S. News and World Report* and currently writes for Elsevier, a publishing company specializing in health and science. The following illustration essay, which was published in *U.S. News and World Report* in 2009, shows how social networking is used as a teaching tool in colleges around the country.

Reading Tip

As you read this essay, think about ways social media—like Facebook and Twitter — have changed the way you interact with people.

Previewing the Reading

Preview the reading (see pp. 23–24 for guidelines), and then answer the following questions.

1. What do you already discover about how Twitter is being used in the college classroom other than for communicating with friends?
2. What types of examples does the author supply?

Twitter Goes to College

Zach Miners

At the University of Texas–Dallas, history professor Monica Rankin needed a better way to get students involved in the classroom. The ninety-person lecture hall was too big for back-and-forth conversation. So, with help from students in the school's emerging media program, she had her students set up accounts on Twitter—a micro-blogging service—and then use the technology to post messages and ask questions that were displayed on a projector screen during class. Rankin says that although the technology has its limitations, the experiment encouraged students to participate when they otherwise might not have.

Though Twitter might not be quite as popular among students as Facebook or MySpace, a growing cadre[1] of professors and administrators are embracing it and using it to introduce their classes to a different kind of communication and networking—one that doesn't involve "poking" friends or posting your results from quizzes and polls.

At Champlain College in Vermont, Elaine Young, a professor of marketing and online business, went from using Twitter—which lets people send 140-character messages, or "tweets," out for anyone to see—as a tool to help teach in the classroom to seeing it as something that business and marketing students can call on to build networks and make connections

[1] **cadre** Group.

Continued >

in the professional world. Compared to other social networking sites, "Twitter is more about creating connections with others who may not be your real friends," she says.

In the moment. The biggest challenge, Young says, is getting students who are convinced that they will never need the technology to give Twitter a try. But many of her students are jumping in and have taken on business projects with local companies and made recommendations on whether the firms should use services like Twitter, blogs, or email newsletters. When the Internet-based marketing class ended in May, the students continued to post tweets, Young says.

5   Young even had several of her students tweeting from their cell phones during the school's 2009 commencement. The result was a play-by-play of quips on the ceremony, right down to one student complaining that her "sash is falling off." And because all the tweets were uniformly tagged and updated, other members of the audience—as well as those watching online and on the local public-access TV channel—stumbled upon the Twitter feed and posted their own tweets. "It's all right in the moment," says Young.

Another educator who's leveraging[2] that instant-access information is David Parry, a professor of emerging media at the University of Texas–Dallas. Parry uses Twitter to enhance his classes and as a means of keeping students engaged in course content beyond the classroom walls. He has them create Twitter profiles and "follow," or track, his updates along with those of friends and others outside the unversity. Many of his students go one step further and use the site to alert their classmates to world events or issues that are relevant to the course.

"One thing that has changed about higher education is the idea that people come and sit in a dorm and, after class, they share ideas," says Parry. "A lot of that is gone now, because students work two jobs, they don't live in dorms. . . . But Twitter is making up for it, in a way."

Parry's students helped Rankin use Twitter in her classroom. And a former student of Parry's, who now works for the UT Southwestern Medical Center, made history when she helped provide the first Twitter log of a kidney transplant. Family members were able to view timely updates of the six-hour procedure as they were posted. (The Twitter account is "ChildrensTheOne.")

Howard Rheingold, who teaches at the University of California–Berkeley and Stanford University, was an early adopter of Twitter and often turns to it for teaching advice. He explains to his digital journalism students how to use the site to establish a network of sources and, using tweets, how to entice those sources to follow them in return. In his social-media course, he has his students employ Twitter for what he describes as "student-to-teacher-to-student ambient[3] office hours."

10   Bringing sites like Twitter into an academic environment is a teaching style that has seen a fair share of criticism. Some say that restricting users to 140-character blurbs ruins students' writing skills and destroys their attention spans.

Rheingold says that how useful Twitter is depends on the individual person. "If you want to share information in small bites with a group of people who share your interest," he says, "that's what it's for."

---

[2] **leveraging** Using power to get things done.

[3] **ambient** In the surrounding area.

Understanding the Reading

1. **Structure** To help you see the organization of the reading, complete the graphic organizer below.

2. **Detail** Why and how did Rankin use Twitter?

3. **Detail** How does Twitter differ from other social networks?

4. **Detail** How did reluctant students respond to Twitter when Young encouraged them to use it?

5. **Detail** How does Parry use Twitter?

6. **Detail** How can Twitter help students prepare for careers?

7. **Detail** Why do some people object to using Twitter in the classroom?

8. **Vocabulary** Using context clues (see Chapter 2, p. 34), write a brief definition of each of the following words and phrases as they are used in the reading, checking a dictionary if necessary: *quips* (para. 5), *emerging* (6), *entice* (9), *blurbs* (10), and *attention spans* (10).

9. **Vocabulary** Identify at least five words and phrases that reveal Miners's positive, enthusiastic attitude toward social networking.

Graphic Organizer for "Twitter Goes to College"

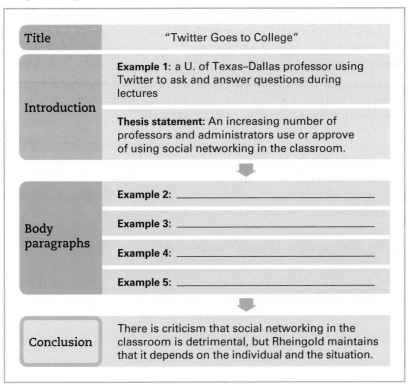

Title	"Twitter Goes to College"
Introduction	**Example 1:** a U. of Texas–Dallas professor using Twitter to ask and answer questions during lectures
	Thesis statement: An increasing number of professors and administrators use or approve of using social networking in the classroom.
Body paragraphs	**Example 2:** _____
	Example 3: _____
	Example 4: _____
	Example 5: _____
Conclusion	There is criticism that social networking in the classroom is detrimental, but Rheingold maintains that it depends on the individual and the situation.

10. **Vocabulary** What does the phrase "student-to-teacher-to-student ambient office hours" mean?

11. **Paraphrase** Write a paraphrase of paragraphs 1 and 2. Refer to page 80 for help with writing paraphrases.

Analyzing the Reading

1. **Evidence** For each example in the reading, decide what aspect of classroom use of Twitter it illustrates.

2. **Audience** Who is Miners's intended audience? Which examples are particularly appealing to this audience?

3. **Tone** Describe the tone of this reading. How does this tone help put forth the author's thesis?

4. **Evidence** In addition to the examples offered, what other types of evidence could have been used to support the thesis?

Evaluating the Reading

1. **Evidence** Examine the author's examples. How does each one support the thesis? Are all of them relevant? If not, which ones do not help the author's argument? What arguments would you use instead?

2. **Evidence** Consider whether each example is representative or exceptional. Are any of the examples unusual or atypical? How does this affect the persuasiveness of the article? What examples would you include if you were to rewrite the piece?

3. **Inferences** The author states that Twitter helps replace traditional dorm life. Based on the article, what has led to changes in the way students interact? How has Twitter maintained or altered student life?

Discussing the Reading

1. Discuss how you use Twitter or explain why you don't use it. Do you agree that Twitter is better used for creating connections than for keeping in touch with friends?

2. Do you think that Twitter or other social media can make up for a lack of face-to-face interaction in college dorms or other social settings? What is gained with electronic interaction? What is lost?

3. Do you share the concern that Twitter may ruin students' writing skills and narrow their attention spans? Explain your reasons.

Writing about the Reading

1. **Paragraph** Use examples to support the following topic sentence: Extensive use of Twitter will (or will not) have a detrimental effect on a user's writing skills and attention span. (Hint: Brainstorm examples that support both options. Thinking about one will help you come up with ideas for the other.) Refer to pages 287–90 for help in choosing effective examples.

2. **Essay** The reading mentions a live Twitter feed describing a kidney transplant. Write an essay about possible innovations using Twitter or another electronic social medium in educational or training situations. (Hint: Brainstorm a list of situations, either academic or workplace, in which immediate, step-by-step feedback is useful and important.)

3. **Essay** Young encouraged her students to use Twitter from their cell phones during graduation. Write an essay agreeing or disagreeing with the appropriateness of participants' moment-by-moment, real-time commentary on social situations or public events. (Hint: Brainstorm a list of other situations or events for which such participant commentary would be appropriate or inappropriate.)

Hey Mom, Dad, May I Have My Room Back?

Cristina Rouvalis's essays and articles have appeared in such magazines as *Inc.*, *AARP Bulletin*, *Pittsburgh Quarterly*, *Carnegie Mellon Today*, and *Carnegie Magazine*. She has also been a staff writer for the *Pittsburgh Post-Gazette*, where the following piece appeared in August 2008.

Reading Tip

As you read the selection, look for and highlight the examples Rouvalis uses to support her thesis.

Previewing the Reading

Preview the reading (see pp. 23–24 for guidelines), and then answer the following questions.

1. What trend among college graduates does this reading address?
2. Why is this trend necessary or popular?

CRISTINA ROUVALIS

Hey Mom, Dad, May I Have My Room Back?

Bobby Franklin Jr., confident and energetic, seemed on a trajectory to an independent life — going to college, moving into an off-campus apartment, and jumping into the banking industry just weeks after his last final exam. Only, the Clarion University graduate circled back home like a boomerang[1]. Inside his parents' elegant five-bedroom house in Plum, he has settled into a roomy bedroom, with its own staircase leading outside. His return home has raised nary an eyebrow with his peers. After all, he said, most of his friends have moved home, too. "Everyone is doing it. No one says, 'Why are you still at

[1] **boomerang** A wooden object thrown so as to return to the thrower.

home?'" said the twenty-four-year-old. "I never get that. It is more like, 'Stay at home as long as you can and save.'"

Some parents who pondered the loneliness of empty-nest syndrome are facing a surprising new question. When will their young adult children leave home — and this time for good? The sight of a college graduate moving into his or her childhood bedroom, filled with dusty high school trophies and curling rock-star posters, is no longer an oddity. A sour economy, big college loans, and sky-high city rents have made some new graduates defer their plans to strike out on their own.

Boomerangers, as they are called, are everywhere you look. Some 14.5 million children age eighteen to twenty-four lived at home in 2007, up from 6.4 million in 1960, according to U.S. Census figures. To be sure, much of the increase simply reflects overall population growth — as the actual percentage of men living at home is up only slightly, from 52% in 1960 to 55% in

Laptop in hand, Bobby Franklin moves about his room at his parent's home in Plum. A recent graduate of Clarion, Mr. Franklin says his dream job would be in pharmaceutical sales.

JOHN HEILER/POST-GAZETTE

2007. The bigger change has occurred with women. Nearly half in this age range were living at home in 2007, up from 35% nearly a half century ago—a shift attributed in part to the delay in marriage.

Other reports suggest the number of boomerangers is even higher—and has grown as a tough economy has made it harder for debt-laden college grads to find jobs. Some 77% of college graduates who responded to an unscientific readers' survey by the online entry job site CollegeGrad.com said they were living with mom and dad in 2008, up from 67% in a 2006 survey. "We see a larger percentage of Gen-Yers or Millennials, or whatever tag we want to use, have a closer relationship to their parents and feel more comfortable relying on parental support," said Heidi Hanisko, director of

client services for CollegeGrad.com. "There is less of a stigma than there was five or ten years ago. We see that as a good thing that college grads are willing to go to their parents for support, but we encourage students to stand on their own. It seems the reliance can be too much and spill over on their ability to do the job."

Others also wonder if this generation is coasting and letting their parents do too much. But Jeffrey Jensen Arnett, author of *Emerging Adulthood: The Winding Road from the Late Teens through the Twenties*, is tired of hearing all the judgments against the Boomerang generation. Most of them move home for a year or two while they go through a transition and a period of self-discovery—waiting for graduate school, looking for a fulfilling career option, paying down a huge loan, or

5

Continued >

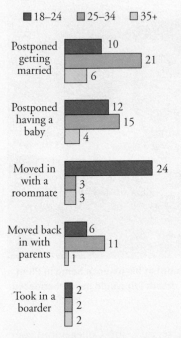

Life Interrupted: Percent of each group who say they did the following because of the recession...

■ 18–24   ▨ 25–34   ☐ 35+

Postponed getting married: 10, 21, 6

Postponed having a baby: 12, 15, 4

Moved in with a roommate: 24, 3, 3

Moved back in with parents: 6, 11, 1

Took in a boarder: 2, 2, 2

Note: "Don't know/Refused" responses not shown.
Pew Research Center

saving enough so they can afford big-city rent. "People jump to the conclusion that they are lazy and irresponsible and pampered and self-indulgent," said Dr. Arnett, a research professor at Clark University in Worcester, Massachusetts. "It is not true. Think about the ones you know. Are they lazy? Do they stand around in their underwear watching TV? No. They are out working their bottoms off trying to make money in these crummy jobs available to them in their twenties."

"Grandma's Boy"

Mike Masilunas's old childhood bedroom—the one with photos of him fly-fishing and Jerome Bettis playing football—was converted into an office inside his family's Peters house. So when Mr. Masilunas, a graduate of Penn State Erie, moved home in May of 2007, he had to share a room with his older brother. In the musical bedrooms of his household, Mr. Masilunas later took over his younger sister's bedroom when she headed off to college. "We joke about the movie *Grandma's Boy*, hanging out all the time, sleeping on the coach," said Mr. Masilunas, referring to the comedy about the guy who gets evicted from his apartment and moves in with his grandmother.

The twenty-three-year-old financial consultant said it made sense to live at home because it is close to his office. Plus, there is the matter of $40,000 in student loans. "I can put $600 toward school loans instead of rent," he said. "Rather than living for right now, I am thinking about a house and retirement. I can put up with this for a few years." Most of his friends understand because they are at home too. Sometimes he catches flak. "You gotta get out of there," one friend told him recently. "The ones who give me flak are the ones spending money like idiots," he said. "They are also the same ones who complain about not having money."

And there are trade-offs to his rent-free existence. He gets along well with his parents and pitches in with chores, but it is an adjustment to go from total freedom to being under his mother's watch. "A mother will always be a mother. They only want the best for you. They are always nagging you. I kind of zone it out. 'Do this. Do that.' The first month it was like, 'Let's pull back the reins a little bit.'" Plus there is the culture shock of going from a college campus to a quiet residential neighborhood—something

Brenna O'Shea experienced after graduating from West Virginia University and heading back to her parents' home in Mt. Lebanon.

Even though the twenty-one-year-old Ms. O'Shea has plenty of company—most of her friends from elementary school have done the same thing—she misses the energy of the campus. Her first night back in Mt. Lebanon, she caught herself yelling a little on the street. "I had to check myself." "It can be a hard adjustment both ways," Dr. Arnett said. "If children regret coming home, it is not because of the stigma. They like their parents and their parents like them. But they want to make their own decisions without parental commentary. Parents aren't that crazy about it either. They like not knowing. If they don't have any idea what time their kids come home or who they are with, ignorance is bliss."

In the Franklin home, Jan and 10 Bobby Franklin, parents of Bobby Jr., can't help but worry about their son when he is out. Even so, they like having him around, especially since he follows the house rules of picking up after himself. Mrs. Franklin knows another mother who put her thirty-year-old son's mattress on the porch, a not-so-subtle hint to fly on his own. "I could never do that to my son—as long as he is not causing any problems." Still mother and son have a standing joke about his boomerang back home.

"When are you going to move out?" she asks Bobby Jr.

Bobby, who plans to leave in a year or two, quips back, "I am not going anywhere until I am at least thirty."

Understanding the Reading

1. **Detail** What difficulties do boomerangers experience when they move back home?

2. **Detail** How do parents respond to their children moving back in?

3. **Visuals** Summarize the data that is included in the graph that accompanies the essay.

Analyzing the Reading

1. **Audience** What audience is Rouvalis addressing? How do her examples address this audience?

2. **Evidence** What other types of supporting evidence, in addition to examples, does Rouvalis use?

3. **Tone** What is the author's attitude toward boomerangers?

4. **Visual evidence** Analyze the effectiveness of Rouvalis's examples by completing the following chart. For each example, indicate what information it adds to the author's thesis.

Example	What It Contributes
Franklin (paras. 1, 10–11)	
Masilunas (paras. 6–8)	
O'Shea (paras. 8–9)	

5. **Visuals** Look carefully at the photograph that accompanies the essay. How is the subject presented in the photo? What does it suggest about the author's tone? How is it similar to or different from the tone of the essay itself?

Evaluating the Reading

1. **Purpose** Express Rouvalis's thesis in your own words. Is it directly stated in the essay? If not, should it be?

2. **Evidence** The essay opens with an example that illustrates the topic and then returns to it in the final paragraph. Why is this an effective technique?

3. **Evidence** Does Rouvalis provide enough examples to support her thesis? Are these examples fair and representative of the situation that college graduates face?

4. **Evidence** Rouvalis includes statistics from the U.S. Census and from an "online entry job site." How trustworthy do you consider each of these sources to be?

5. **Evidence** What information, if any, is not presented that would help you understand the situation more completely?

6. **Visuals** Rouvalis's article is about recent college graduates, and the people she interviews all fit the eighteen-to-twenty-four age category in the graph on page 310. But the graph suggests that people age twenty-five to thirty-four have been about twice as likely as the younger group to move back in with their parents because of the recession. Those in the younger group are more likely to live with roommates. What might be the reasons for these patterns?

Discussing the Reading

1. What would be the most compelling reason for you or someone you know to live with parents after college?

2. With your classmates, discuss what adult children and parents could do to make living together easier.

3. Brainstorm options, other than moving back home, for adult children who cannot afford to live on their own.

4. Given current economic conditions, do you expect the numbers of boomerangers to increase or decrease in the next year? Justify your answer.

Writing about the Reading

1. **Essay** Mike Masilunas explains that he's willing to put up with some of the problems of living with his parents in order to get the benefits of the situation. Describe a decision you made to put up with the problems associated with something (other than living with your parents) in order to experience the benefits. Use the benefits as examples to support your thesis.

2. **Essay** Family members of different generations have often been forced or chosen to live together; elderly parents moving in with their adult children (and often with their grandchildren as well) is an example of one such arrangement. Write an essay discussing either the problems or the benefits of multigenerational households, other than those containing boomerangers. Give examples from your own experience or observations to support your thesis.

3. **Essay** Write an essay describing and giving examples of the long-term effects on boomerangers of moving back in with their parents. How will their lives be affected? (Hint: You might consider how delaying marriage and childbearing will affect them and how their feelings of independence and self-worth will be affected.)

COMBINING THE PATTERNS

Just Walk On By: A Black Man Ponders His Power to Alter Public Space

Brent Staples (b. 1951) is a journalist who has written numerous articles, essays, and editorials as well as a memoir, *Parallel Time: Growing Up in Black and White* (1994). Staples holds a Ph.D. in psychology and is currently a member of the editorial board at the *New York Times.* This essay was first published in *Harper's* magazine in 1986.

Reading Tip

As you read the selection, highlight or underline the author's thesis and the examples he uses to support it.

Previewing the Reading

Preview the reading (see pp. 23–24 for guidelines) to discover what the public space referred to in the title is and how the author has the power to "alter" it.

Just Walk On By: A Black Man Ponders His Power to Alter Public Space

Brent Staples

My first victim was a woman — white, well dressed, probably in her early twenties. I came upon her late one evening on a deserted street in Hyde Park, a relatively affluent neighborhood in an otherwise mean, impoverished section of Chicago. As I swung onto the avenue behind her, there seemed to be a discreet, uninflammatory distance between us. Not so. She cast back a worried glance. To her, the youngish black man — a broad six feet two inches with a beard and billowing hair, both hands shoved into the pockets of his bulky military jacket — seemed menacingly close. After a few more quick glimpses, she picked up her pace and was soon running in earnest. Within seconds she disappeared into a cross street.

That was more than a decade ago. I was twenty-two years old, a graduate student newly arrived at the University of Chicago. It was in the echo of that terrified woman's footfalls that I first began to know the unwieldy inheritance I'd come into — the ability to alter public space in ugly ways. It was clear that she thought herself the quarry of a mugger, a rapist, or worse. Suffering a bout of insomnia, however, I was stalking sleep, not defenseless wayfarers. As a softy who is scarcely able to take a knife to a raw chicken — let alone hold one to a person's throat—I was surprised, embarrassed, and dismayed all at once. Her flight made me feel like an accomplice in tyranny. It also made it clear that I was indistinguishable from the muggers who occasionally seeped into the area from the surrounding ghetto. That first encounter, and those that followed, signified that a vast, unnerving gulf lay between nighttime pedestrians—particularly women—and me. And I soon gathered that being perceived as dangerous is a hazard in itself. I only needed to turn a corner into a dicey situation, or crowd some frightened, armed person in a foyer somewhere, or make an errant move after being pulled over by a policeman. Where fear and weapons meet—and they often do in urban America—there is always the possibility of death.

In that first year, my first away from my hometown, I was to become thoroughly familiar with the language of fear. At dark, shadowy intersections, I could cross in front of a car stopped at a traffic light and elicit the *thunk, thunk, thunk, thunk* of the driver—black, white, male, or female—hammering down the door locks. On less traveled streets after dark, I grew accustomed to but never comfortable with people crossing to the other side of the street rather than pass me. Then there were the standard unpleasantries with policemen, doormen, bouncers, cabdrivers, and others whose business it is to screen out troublesome individuals *before* there is any nastiness.

I moved to New York nearly two years ago and I have remained an avid night walker. In central Manhattan, the near-constant crowd cover minimizes tense one-on-one street encounters. Elsewhere—in SoHo, for example, where sidewalks are narrow and tightly spaced buildings shut out the sky—things can get very taut indeed.

After dark, on the warrenlike streets 5 of Brooklyn where I live, I often see women who fear the worst from me. They seem to have set their faces on neutral, and with their purse straps strung across their chests bandolier-style, they forge ahead as though bracing themselves against being tackled. I understand, of course, that the danger they perceive is not a hallucination. Women are particularly vulnerable to street violence, and young black males are drastically overrepresented among the perpetrators of that violence. Yet these truths are no solace against the kind of alienation that comes of being ever the suspect, a fearsome entity with whom pedestrians avoid making eye contact.

It is not altogether clear to me how I reached the ripe old age of twenty-two without being conscious of the lethality nighttime pedestrians attributed to me. Perhaps it was because in Chester, Pennsylvania, the small, angry industrial town where I came of age in the 1960s, I was scarcely noticeable against a backdrop of gang warfare, street knifings, and murders. I grew up one of the good boys, had perhaps a half-dozen fistfights. In retrospect, my shyness of combat has clear sources.

As a boy, I saw countless tough guys locked away; I have since buried several, too. They were babies, really—a teenage cousin, a brother of twenty-two, a childhood friend in his mid-twenties—all gone down in episodes of bravado[1] played out in the streets. I came to doubt the virtues of intimidation early on. I chose, perhaps unconsciously, to remain a shadow—timid, but a survivor.

The fearsomeness mistakenly attributed to me in public places often

---

[1] **bravado** Display of courage and self-confidence.

Continued >

has a perilous flavor. The most frightening of these confusions occurred in the late 1970s and early 1980s, when I worked as a journalist in Chicago. One day, rushing into the office of a magazine I was writing for with a deadline story in hand, I was mistaken for a burglar. The office manager called security and, with an ad hoc posse,[2] pursued me through the labyrinthine[3] halls, nearly to my editor's door. I had no way of proving who I was. I could only move briskly toward the company of someone who knew me.

Another time I was on assignment for a local paper and killing time before an interview. I entered a jewelry store on the city's affluent Near North Side. The proprietor excused herself and returned with an enormous red Doberman pinscher straining at the end of a leash. She stood, the dog extended toward me, silent to my questions, her eyes bulging nearly out of her head. I took a cursory look around, nodded, and bade her good night.

10   Relatively speaking, however, I never fared as badly as another black male journalist. He went to nearby Waukegan, Illinois, a couple of summers ago to work on a story about a murderer who was born there. Mistaking the reporter for the killer, police officers hauled him from his car at gunpoint and but for his press credentials would probably have tried to book him. Such episodes are not uncommon. Black men trade tales like this all the time.

Over the years, I learned to smother the rage I felt at so often being taken for a criminal. Not to do so would surely have led to madness. I now take precautions to make myself less threatening. I move about with care, particularly late in the evening. I give a wide berth to nervous people on subway platforms during the wee hours, particularly when I have exchanged business clothes for jeans. If I happen to be entering a building behind some people who appear skittish, I may walk by, letting them clear the lobby before I return, so as not to seem to be following them. I have been calm and extremely congenial on those rare occasions when I've been pulled over by the police.

And on late-evening constitutionals[4] I employ what has proved to be an excellent tension-reducing measure: I whistle melodies from Beethoven and Vivaldi and the more popular classical composers. Even steely New Yorkers hunching toward nighttime destinations seem to relax, and occasionally they even join in the tune. Virtually everybody seems to sense that a mugger wouldn't be warbling bright sunny selections from Vivaldi's *Four Seasons*. It is my equivalent of the cowbell that hikers wear when they know they are in bear country.

[2] **ad hoc posse** Group formed for a special purpose.
[3] **labyrinthine** Intricate, mazelike.

[4] **constitutionals** Regular walks, often for health benefits.

📊 Understanding the Reading

1. **Detail** Explain how Staples alters public space and why it happens.

2. **Detail** Staples considers himself a "survivor" (para. 7). To what does he attribute his survival?

3. **Language** What is the connotative meaning of the word *victim* (para. 1)?

4. **Language** Explain the analogy of cowbells and hikers used in the last sentence of the essay.

5. **Language** Beginning with the word *victim* in paragraph 1, Staples uses a number of terms that relate to hunting or pursuit. Find several other words or phrases that carry this connotation. How do they shape the reader's attitude toward Staples's subject?

6. **Thinking visually** Draw a diagram outlining the structure of the reading. Compare yours to that of a classmate and discuss the similarities and differences.

Analyzing the Reading

1. **Evidence** Does Staples provide enough examples to adequately support his thesis? Explain your answer.

2. **Language** Staples uses descriptive language to make his examples engaging and striking. Find several places where he does so. In each place, how does the descriptive language contribute to the effectiveness of the example?

3. **Audience** Define Staples's intended audience. Are the examples that Staples provides appealing to and appropriate for this audience? (Hint: *Harper's* magazine is a general-interest periodical that explores issues of national concern, including politics, society, the environment, and culture.)

4. **Structure** Staples opens and closes his essay with examples. Are these effective ways to begin and end? What other ways might be equally or more effective?

5. **Evidence** Staples's essay is based on personal experiences. What other types of evidence could he have used to support his thesis?

Evaluating the Reading

1. **Inference** What advice might Staples offer to others at risk of racial profiling?

2. **Voice** If the incidents in this essay were reported by an uninvolved third-person narrator rather than told by Staples in the first person, how would the essay's impact change?

3. **Evidence** What additional details might have made the essay even more realistic, convincing, or compelling?

4. **Themes** This essay was written several decades ago. Evaluate how closely it reflects current reality with regard to the issues Staples raises. To what extent, if at all, have public perceptions of black men and their effect on public space changed since Staples wrote this piece?

5. **Tone** How do Staples's tone and attitude change as the essay progresses? What could account for this change?

Discussing the Reading

1. Staples's "unwieldy inheritance" gives him the power to alter public space. Discuss some other ways that people can alter public space, and how they use that power.

2. Why do you think whistling tunes by Beethoven or Vivaldi makes Staples's presence less threatening? Analyze his choice of music in relation to his purpose and audience. According to your analysis, what other strategies might work to make him less intimidating?

3. Why does Staples mention his upbringing on his mean streets of Chester, Pennsylvania? How does his experience growing up in a tough neighborhood affect his perspective on the issues he raises in this essay? Discuss this with your classmates.

Writing about the Reading

1. **Essay** Staples describes himself as a "survivor" (para. 7) of the streets he grew up on. In a sense, everyone is a survivor of certain decisions or circumstances that, if they had played out differently, might have resulted in misfortune or, at least, a different direction in life. Using illustration write an essay that explains a situation in which you were a survivor.

2. **Combining patterns** Rewrite Staples's essay from his "first victim['s]" point of view, using illustrative techniques. Include a thesis that makes a generalization, and provide supporting examples. (Tip: You might begin with a thesis statement such as "An experience that I had on a December night in Chicago made me realize the extent to which I engage in racial stereotyping.") You might include the woman's background, past experiences, and emotional state. Discuss how encountering Staples on the street affects her and whether she changes her behavior as a result of the experience.

3. **Using Internet research** Visit the part of the American Civil Liberties Union Web site that deals with racial profiling (www.aclu.org/racialjustice /racial-profiling) or another site of your choice that also deals with the topic. Using what you learn from the Web site, along with your own knowledge and experience, write an essay that takes a position or makes a recommendation on racial profiling. Be sure to include examples to support your thesis.

TEXTBOOK

Issue-Oriented and Street Art

Patrick Frank is adjunct professor of visual and public art at California State University, Monterey Bay. He is the author of *ARTFORMS: An Introduction to the Visual Arts,* the textbook from which this reading was taken. His recent scholarly work is devoted to Latin American graphic artists.

Reading Tip

As you read this textbook excerpt, look for language that is particular or unique to the field of visual arts.

Previewing the Reading

Preview the reading (see pp. 23–24 for guidelines), and write a list of three things you expect to learn from it.

Issue-Oriented and Street Art

Patrick Frank

Today the public accepts most modern art. Exhibitions of work by such former rule-breaking radicals as Henri Matisse, Paul Gauguin, Paul Cézanne, and Claude Monet fill museums with visitors. Nine of the ten most expensive paintings ever sold at auction are modern works (three each by Picasso and van Gogh; one each by Cézanne, Renoir, and Jackson Pollock). The modern-style Vietnam Veterans Memorial is a national shrine. Modern art is no longer controversial.

The impact of this situation is not yet clear. Art of our own time is always the most difficult to evaluate. In general, most artists of the present generation do not appear intent on perfecting form, creating beauty, or fine-tuning their sense of sight. They mostly want to comment on life in all of its aspects. They want to create work that illuminates the relationships between what we see and how we think. Rather than being objects of timeless beauty, most art since the 1980s consists of objects laden with information about the period in which we live. This article will present two movements of the present generation.

Issue-Oriented Art

Many artists in the past twenty years have sought to link their art to current social questions. Issue-oriented artists believe that if they limit their art to **aesthetic** matters, then their work will be only a distraction from pressing problems. Furthermore, they recognize that what

aesthetic: concerned with what is beautiful or pleasing in appearance

Continued >

Barbara Kruger. *Untitled (I Shop Therefore I Am)*. 1987. Photographic silkscreen/vinyl. 111″ × 113″. Courtesy Mary Boone Gallery, New York.

we see influences how we think, and they do not want to miss an opportunity to influence both.

Photographer Richard Misrach presents new kinds of landscape in new ways. His photograph *Submerged Lamppost, Salton Sea* captures the silent yet ironic beauty of a small town in California that was flooded by a misguided irrigation system. In other works he has documented in chilling detail the bloated carcasses of animals killed on military proving grounds in Nevada. His brand of nature photography is the opposite of the common calendars that include soothing views of pristine landscapes. He wants us to know that such scenes are fast disappearing.

Barbara Kruger was trained as a magazine designer, and this profession shows in her piece *Untitled (I Shop Therefore I Am)*. She invented the slogan, which sounds as though it came from advertising. The position of the hand, too, looks like it came from an ad for aspirin or sleeping medication. Do our products define us? Are we what we shop for? Often we buy a product because of what it will say about us and not for the thing itself. These are some of the messages present in this simple yet fascinating work. Perhaps its ultimate irony is that the artist had it **silkscreened** onto a shopping bag.   5

silkscreened: printed using a special stencil process

Artists who create works about racism and class bias show how common practices of museum display contribute to such problems. In 1992, the Maryland Historical Society invited African American artist Fred Wilson to rearrange the exhibits on one floor to create an **installation** called *Mining the Museum*. He spent a year preparing for the show, rummaging through the Society's holdings and documentary records; the results were surprising. He found no portraits, for example, of noted African American Marylanders Benjamin Banneker (who laid out the boundaries of the District of Columbia), Frederick Douglass (noted abolitionist and journalist), or Harriet Tubman (founder of the Underground Railroad). He found instead busts of Henry Clay, Andrew Jackson, and Napoleon Bonaparte, none of whom ever lived in Maryland. He exhibited those three busts next to three empty pedestals to symbolize the missing African Americans. He set out a display of colonial Maryland silverware and tea utensils, and included a pair of slave shackles. This lesser-known form of metalwork was perhaps equally vital to the functioning of nineteenth-century Maryland. He dusted off the Society's collection of wooden cigar-store Indians and stood them, backs to the viewers, facing

installation: a work of art made up of multiple components, often in different media, and exhibited in an arrangement specified by the artist

photographs of real Native Americans who lived in Maryland. In an accompanying exhibition brochure he wrote that a museum should be a place that can make you think. When *Mining the Museum* went on display, attendance records soared.

The Swiss-born Thomas Hirschhorn took up the issue of the Iraq war, but only indirectly, in the context of today's media-saturated society. His 2006 installation *Superficial Engagement* filled the entire gallery space with a *dizzying* array of objects that resembled a parade float on drugs, or a cross between an insane asylum and a grocery store. Photos of mangled war dead competed for space with coffins, nail-studded mannequins, blaring headlines, and reproductions of abstract artworks. The nailed bodies refer to traditional African magic sculptures, and the abstract art was mostly copied from the Austrian mystic Emma Kunz in what the artist called "friendly piracy." The headlines shout the aimless alarmism of cable news channels: "Decision Time Approaches," "Broken Borders," "An Assault on Hypocrisy," "The Real Crisis." The artist used only cheap materials (cardboard, plastic, plywood, package tape) in an effort to avoid art-world pretense and make it more accessible. He said of his brash style, "Art is a tool, a tool to encounter the world, to confront the reality and the time I am living in." The shrill volume of this exhibition only paralleled the strident intensity of today's news, where a disaster might follow a fashion show. At the opening reception, the artist provided hammers and screwdrivers, and the crowd joined in attaching nails and screws, thus finishing the piece.

Street Art

In the late 1990s, many galleries in various cities began to exhibit work by artists who had previously made illegal graffiti. Many of these "street artists" were based in the culture of skateboards and Punk music, and they used materials bought at the hardware store rather than the art supply house. Their creations were only rarely related to gang-oriented graffiti, which usually marks out territories of influence. Nor were they autobiographical or personal. Rather, the street artists made much broader statements about themselves and the world in a language that was widely understandable. The ancestors of the movement in the 1980s were Keith Haring and Jean-Michel Basquiat, both of whom worked illegally for years before exhibiting in galleries. By the turn of the twenty-first century, Street Art was a recognized movement, and most of its main practitioners work both indoors and out.

The career of Shepard Fairey is exemplary. He studied at the Rhode Island School of Design, but was never satisfied in the art world, which seemed to him closed-off and elitist. He began working outdoors, and quickly acquired notoriety for posting dozens of signs and stickers with the single word "Obey" below the ominous-looking face of wrestler Andre the Giant. His vocabulary soon expanded to

Continued >

include advertising symbols, propaganda posters, and currency, even as the scale of his work increased to billboard size.

His 2006 work *Revolution Girl* is an antiwar mural created on a   10 legal wall for a three-month show in West Hollywood. The dominant motif is a huge female Communist soldier from the Vietnam War that the artist borrowed from Chinese propaganda, but her rifle has a flower protruding; her weapon has become an elaborate vase. Other motifs from Chinese propaganda decorate the center right, repurposed for a peace campaign. In the lower corner, posters of a female face with flowery hair symbolize nurturing. The message of the mural is antiwar, but the artist made the statement positive rather than negative, expressing the hope that we can convert our weapons into flower holders. His friend and fellow street artist Blake Marquis provided the vivid leafy patterns at the left. . . .

Some of today's most skillful street art is created by Swoon, a woman who uses the pseudonym to avoid prosecution. She carves large linoleum blocks and makes life-sized relief prints from them, usually portraits of everyday people. She prints them on large sheets of cheap (usually recycled) newsprint and pastes them on urban walls, beginning on the Lower East Side of Manhattan but now in cities on every continent. Her *Untitled* installation at Deitch Projects was a recent indoor work. Against objections that her work is mostly illegal, she replies that her creations are far easier to look at than advertising, that they lack any persuasive agenda, and that they glorify common people. Moreover, the newsprint that she uses decays over time so that her work is impermanent. Although she works mostly outdoors, she sometimes

Banksey, *Graffiti Removal Hotline, Pentonville Road.* 2006. Steve Cotton/artofthestate .co.uk. *Source:* Frank, Patrick L., *Prebles' Artforms (Book Alone)*, 9th Edition, © N/A. Reprinted by permission of Pearson Education, Inc., Upper Saddle River, NJ.

shows in galleries because, she admits, "I have to make a living," but she charges far less for her work than most other artists of wide repute.

Probably the most famous street artist is Banksy (who also uses a pseudonym). He placed his own art in the collections of several major museums in 2005 by merely entering the galleries and sticking his pieces to the wall. His street graffiti is generally witty, as we see in his *Graffiti Removal Hotline, Pentonville Road*. There is no such thing as a graffiti removal hotline; the artist stenciled the words and then created the youth who seems to paint out the phone number. Banksy is currently one of the most popular artists in England, and many of his outdoor works have been preserved. When a prominent work of his was recently defaced by another graffiti artist, protests ensued and the defacer was arrested for vandalism! Thus street artists often blur the line between legal and illegal.

Understanding the Reading

1. **Textbook reading** Highlight the reading, identifying important information you would need to learn for an art-history exam based, in part, on it.

2. **Language** What terminology specific to the art field is used in this reading? Select five words (other than those noted in the margin) that are important in an art-history course. Write the meaning of each.

3. **Thinking visually** Select one of the photographs included in the reading, and discuss how it is used as an example to support Frank's thesis about issue-oriented or street art. What does the photograph add to the reading? Why was it included?

Analyzing the Reading

1. **Organizing information** Other than highlighting, what strategies might you use to organize information from this essay about the artists and their works so as to better learn and recall it for an exam? Use one of these strategies to create a study guide for this piece.

2. **Predicting exam questions** A useful way to prepare for an essay exam is to predict possible questions your instructor might ask and then to practice answering them. Compose several essay-exam questions that would likely appear on an exam covering "Issue-Oriented and Street Art."

3. **Similarities and differences** In what ways is this textbook excerpt similar to and different from other illustration essays included in this chapter?

4. **Expert opinion** The opinion of experts is known as "informed" opinion. Patrick Frank, the author of this textbook reading, is an expert in the field of art, and an example of his informed opinion is that the "shrill volume of [Hirschhorn's] exhibition only paralleled the strident intensity of today's news, where a disaster might follow a fashion show" (para. 7). While considered

trustworthy, different experts may present differing opinions on an issue. Identify several other statements of informed opinion in the reading. For each, discuss what further evidence may be helpful in analyzing the opinion.

📊 Evaluating the Reading

1. **Language** Identify at least five words or phrases that contribute to the effectiveness of the essay. Select words or phrases that are particularly descriptive, revealing, insightful, or striking.

2. **Visuals** How important and useful are the visuals included in this chapter? Choose one and explain what it illustrates.

3. **Evidence** Write a paragraph evaluating the effectiveness of illustration as it is used in this reading. Consider each of the characteristics of illustration explained on pages 283–85, and discuss whether the characteristic is evident in the reading and, if so, what it contributes or what problems you see with it.

Discussing the Reading

1. Do you agree with Frank's interpretation of Kruger's *Untitled (I Shop Therefore I Am)*? Do you think that the products we purchase define us? Are there exceptions to this generalization?

2. In what circumstances can you envision art being "only a distraction from pressing problems" (para. 3)?

3. What is the author's attitude toward modern artists in contrast to classic art masters?

4. What similarities and differences do you observe between issue-oriented art and street art? How does the notion of "impermanent art" fit with your definition of art?

Writing about the Reading

1. **Essay exam question** Choose one of the questions you predicted in Analyzing the Reading question 2 (p. 323) and write an essay answering it.

2. **Response paper** In art classes you are often asked to understand, analyze, evaluate, and respond to a particular work. Choose one of the pieces of art included in this excerpt and write a response to it. Explain what it accomplishes and how it affects you or what feelings or ideas it draws out.

3. **Using Internet research** Explore the Web site for street art exhibitions at the Tate Modern in London (www.tate.org.uk/modern/exhibitions/streetart/) or locate other sites that focus on such art. View some examples of street art and form a thesis about the value, function, or purpose of this art form. Write an essay explaining your thesis and supporting it with examples drawn from the art you viewed.

Writing Your Own Illustration Essay

Now that you have learned about the major characteristics, structure, and purposes of an illustration essay, you know everything necessary to write your own. In this section you will read a student's illustration essay and get advice on finding ideas, drafting your essay, and revising and editing it. You may want to use the essay prompts in "Readings for Practice, Ideas for Writing" (p. 298) or choose your own topic.

A Student Model Illustration Essay

Assigned to write an essay describing a cultural event for a writing course, Dusty Henry decided to focus on Black Friday, the intense shopping event that occurs the day after Thanksgiving. Henry used his personal experience with the day to write this illustration essay. As you read, pay attention to how he uses his examples to illustrate a generalization about Black Friday.

Title: Henry indicates topic and suggests focus of essay.

Black and Blue Friday: Fear of Shopping

Dusty Henry

Introduction

Background information: Henry explains Black Friday.

Thesis: Henry presents main idea he will illustrate.

Example 1: Wal-Mart

Detail: Wal-Mart shoppers' behavior invokes fear in the author.

Before the turkey and stuffing can even settle in America's collective digestive systems, people are heading out the door to snag the best deals they can for Christmas shopping. It is the phenomenon known as Black Friday: a bizarre twenty-four hours when primal instincts and territorial mentalities are released to ensure the purchase of cheap DVD players or big-screen televisions. It occurs on the day after Thanksgiving, although some stores open their doors late Thanksgiving night. Stores tout ridiculously low prices and deals available only for one day or even a few hours. The best deals go fast, so many shoppers will wait at the doors hours before stores open. This year, I went to Wal-Mart, Best Buy, and Macy's to observe how extreme bargain hunting has the power to turn normal people into frightening warriors.

At the Wal-Mart I visited, customers were allowed in on Thanksgiving evening, but the items would not be available for the sale price till midnight. At 10 p.m., when we got there, the aisles were already swarming with fierce competitors. Throughout the store, black garbage bags covered electronics, like television sets, that could not be removed from their kiosks until the sale started at midnight. Walking through the crowd, I got skeptical and hungry stares from fellow shoppers clinging to these kiosks. I knew to not bother these people because they were not going to let anyone interfere with their purchases no matter what they would need to do. For fear of what might happen when these people were allowed to make their purchases, I decided to leave before midnight.

Example 2: Best Buy

At Best Buy, die-hard shoppers were also scrambling for entertainment deals. When I arrived, a bedraggled employee was handing out video games by the handful. He would call out the names and as soon as a popular title was announced the crowd turned from an audience into a mosh pit; people clawed, pushed, and screamed just to get their copy of *Kinect Sports* or *Modern Warfare 3* for a discount.

Detail: Shoppers scramble for video-game deals.

Example 3: Macy's

Macy's customers faced a similar physical fight that could have become dangerous. Wrestling for clothes, elbowing for decorative furniture, and diving for jewelry sale items were all normal on Black Friday. Some people even brought their families and children with them. On any other day, bringing a child to a department store would seem normal, even expected. The hordes of aggressive bargain hunters penned into a tense building on Black Friday make this decision a bit questionable. I had been standing in the store just long enough that Thanksgiving dinner began to seem like a distant memory.

Detail: Shoppers' behavior makes author question the safety of Black Friday.

Conclusion: Henry sums up concern for personal safety among Black Friday shoppers.

Maybe Black Friday is just a way to universally kick off the Christmas spirit of consumerism. Though I did find it fascinating to observe people's whacky antics while holiday shopping, I would have felt concerned for my safety if I had stayed any longer than I did. Hearing stories of black eyes and deaths at these events is enough for me to not wish to experience the chaos again. In the end, a $5 DVD wouldn't be worth the hospital bill that followed or the momentary loss of self amidst the savings.

Responding to Henry's Essay

1. Does Henry provide enough information in his opening to clearly introduce the subject of Black Friday?

2. How does Henry's thesis statement predict the essay's organization?

3. How well do Henry's descriptions of the shoppers in the three stores show that they are "frightening," as he suggests in this thesis?

4. Why might Henry have ended paragraph 4 as he does?

5. What specific details in the conclusion reemphasize the key points of the essay?

Finding Ideas for Your Illustration Essay

When you are asked to write an illustration essay, keep an eye out for ideas to write about as you read. While reading "Snoopers at Work," for instance, you might have thought about your own experience with surveillance. What surveillance issues concern you? What type of surveillance is acceptable? Is the British-style crime-prevention surveillance good or bad? What's your stance on antiterrorism-related wiretapping in America? How do you feel about parental surveillance of children, especially their Internet use? When does that surveillance violate children's privacy and when is it for their own good? Each of these examples could lead you to a thesis and ideas for writing.

Choosing a Subject for Your Illustration Essay

Your first step is to choose a subject and then narrow it to a topic so it becomes manageable—so it can be supported by one or more examples. Use the characteristics of an illustration essay described in "What Is Illustration?" (pp. 283–85) to help guide you in finding a topic that is specific, yet expansive enough, that you can make a generalization and support it with detailed, relevant evidence.

Gathering Examples for Your Illustration Essay

Once you are satisfied with your subject, you'll need to generate examples that illustrate it. As you do so, begin to think about the generalization that will become your thesis. As you work, you may think of situations that illustrate a different or more interesting thesis than the one you first had in mind. Take advantage of such developments, which will make your thesis and essay better.

Here are a few techniques you can use to generate examples.

- **Brainstorm examples that relate to your subject.** Jot down all instances or situations you can think of that are relevant to your subject and that illustrate your tentative thesis.

- **Visualize situations that illustrate your subject.** Close your eyes and imagine situations, images, stories, or scenes that relate to your subject.

- **Use your memory.** Systematically review your life—year by year, place by place, or job by job—to recall situations that illustrate the topic.

- **Talk to someone else.** Discuss your tentative thesis with a classmate. Try to match or better each other's examples.

- **Research your topic.** At the library or on the Internet, search to discover examples outside your own experience.

Developing and Supporting Your Thesis

The next step is to develop a working thesis about the narrowed topic by making a generalization about it. The thesis in an illustration essay expresses the idea that all your examples will support. In "Snoopers at Work," Bryson makes such a generalization when he says, "A combination of technological advances, employer paranoia, and commercial avarice means that many millions of Americans are having their lives delved into in ways that would have been impossible, not to say unthinkable, a dozen years ago" (para. 4). All his examples support this thesis. For more examples of illustration essay thesis statements, see "The Introduction Presents the Topic" on page 287.

Drafting Your Illustration Essay

As you draft your essay, refer to the graphic organizer in Figure 12.1 (p. 286) to remind yourself of the elements of an illustration essay. Use the suggestions that follow it to write effective drafts.

1. **Begin with a clear introduction.** In most illustration essays, the thesis is stated in the first paragraph. Besides stating the generalization the essay will illustrate, your introduction should also spark readers' interest and include background information about the topic.

2. **Remember that each paragraph should express one key idea; the example(s) or details in that paragraph should illustrate that key idea.** Develop the body paragraphs so that each one presents a single example or a group of closely related examples or closely related details about the extended example.

3. **Use the topic sentence in each paragraph to make clear the particular point that each example or set of examples or details makes.**

4. **Provide sufficient detail about each example.** Explain each one with vivid descriptive language. Your goal is to make readers feel as if they are experiencing or observing the situation themselves.

5. **Use transitions to move readers from one idea to another.** Without transitions, your essay will seem choppy and disconnected. Use transitions such as *for example* and *in particular* to keep readers on track when you move to a new example or detail.

6. **End with an effective conclusion.** Your essay should conclude with a final statement that pulls your ideas together and reminds readers of your thesis. In less formal writing situations, you may end with a final example—as Bryson does in "Snoopers at Work"—as long as it effectively concludes the essay and reminds readers of the thesis.

Revising Your Illustration Essay

If possible, set aside your draft for a day or two before rereading and revising it. As you reread and review, concentrate on organization, level of detail, and overall effectiveness—not on grammar or mechanics. Use the flowchart in Figure 12.3 to discover the strengths and weaknesses of your illustration essay.

Figure 12.3   Revising an Illustration Essay

QUESTIONS	REVISION STRATEGIES
1. Thesis statement Does your thesis clearly indicate the generalization that your examples support? No	• Revise your thesis so that the generalization fits your examples.

Yes

| **2. Audience** Will your examples appeal to your audience? After eliminating those that do not, do you have enough left? No | • Brainstorm examples that will appeal to your audience, and add them to your essay. |

Yes

| **3. Purpose** Do all of your examples fulfill your purpose? After eliminating those that do not, do you have enough left? No | • Brainstorm examples that are more appropriate to your purpose, and add them to your essay. |

Yes

| **4. Examples** Is each one relevant, representative, detailed, and striking? Are they varied? No | • Eliminate irrelevant, unrepresentative, or dull examples.
• Brainstorm or conduct research to discover better examples.
• Add details to vague examples.
• Omit misleading examples.
• Consider adding other kinds of examples. |

Yes

| **5. Topic sentences** Does each paragraph have a topic sentence that clearly states the point that the paragraph develops? No | • Add a topic sentence or revise the existing one to clearly indicate the paragraph's point.
• Reorganize examples according to the idea they demonstrate. |

Yes

| **6. Organization** Is your organization clear and effective? Do you use transitional phrases to make it clear? No | • Add or revise transitions to make your organization clear.
• Consider using a different organization strategy from Chapter 6. |

Yes

| **7. Introduction and conclusion** Is each effective? No | • Revise each so that they meet the guidelines on pages 287–290. |

Editing and Proofreading Your Essay

The last step is to check your revised essay for errors in grammar, spelling, punctuation, and mechanics. In addition, look for the types of errors you commonly make in writing assignments, whether for this class or any other situation. For illustration essays, pay particular attention to the following common errors.

1. **Be consistent in your use of first, second, or third person.** Be sure to use first person (*I, me*), second person (*you*), or third person (*he, she, it, him, her*) consistently throughout your essay. Do not shift from one person to another unless you have a reason for doing so.

   ▶ I visited my daughter's first-grade classroom during parents'

   week last month. Each parent was invited to read a story to the

   class, and ~~you~~ *we* were encouraged to ask the children questions

   afterward.

2. **Use full sentences.** Although professional writers such as Bill Bryson occasionally use fragments, student writers should avoid them; each sentence should have both a subject and a verb.

   ▶ Technology is becoming part of teenagers' daily lives. ~~For example, high~~ *High*

   school students who carry pagers~~, for example.~~ *are an example.*

3. **Be consistent in your use of tense.** This can be especially tricky when using an extended example. For instance, when citing an event from the past as an example, always use the past tense to describe it.

   ▶ Special events are an important part of children's lives. For example,

   parent visitation day at school ~~is~~ *was* an event my daughter talked about

   for an entire week. Children are also excited by . . .

Chapter 13

Process Analysis: Explaining How Something Works or Is Done

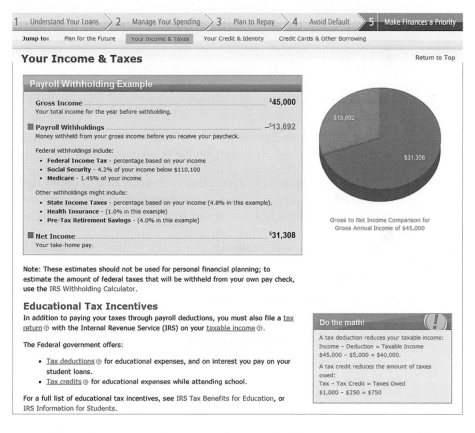

Quick Start: This screen shot is from a Web site (**www.studentloans.gov**) that offers college students help managing their finances. As you know, the process of earning, saving, budgeting, and spending money involves important skills and has serious consequences. Write a paragraph describing your own process in deciding how to spend and/or save money. Include the steps you follow when budgeting each week or month.

What Is Process Analysis?

The paragraph you wrote for the Quick Start prompt followed a pattern of development called **process analysis**. A process analysis explains in step-by-step fashion how something works, is done, or is made. Process analyses provide people with practical information (such as directions for assembling something) or inform people about things that affect them (such as an explanation of how a medication works). Regardless of the purpose, the information in a process analysis must be accurate, clear, and easy to follow.

Process analysis is a common type of writing in college. For example, a student writing a chemistry lab report will summarize the procedure she followed in preparing a solution or conducting an experiment. This type of organization helps on the job, too. An engineer at a water-treatment plant might write an explanation for his supervisors about how the city's drinking water is tested and treated for contamination.

There are two basic types of process analysis essays.

- A **how-to essay** explains how something works or is done for readers *who want or need to perform the process.*

- A **how-it-works essay** explains how something works or is done for readers *who want to understand the process but not actually perform it.*

At times, you may read or write essays that contain elements of both types of process analysis. In writing about how a car alarm system works, for example, you might include explicit instructions on how to activate and deactivate the system.

Process analysis does the following.

1. It defines technical terms.
2. It provides background information.
3. It describes necessary equipment.
4. It provides an appropriate level of detail.
5. It anticipates trouble spots and offers solutions.

1. Process Analysis Defines Technical Terms

In most cases, a writer will assume her audience is not familiar with technical terms associated with the process she is describing. In a process essay, it is necessary to define specialized terms. In describing how cardiopulmonary resuscitation (CPR) works, for instance, an essay would need to include meanings of such terms as *airway*, *sternum*, and *cardiac compression*.

2. Process Analysis Provides Background Information

In some process analysis essays, readers may need background information to fully understand the process. For example, in an explanation of how CPR works, general readers might need to know how the heart functions before they can understand how pressing down on a person's breastbone propels blood into the arteries.

3. Process Analysis Describes Necessary Equipment

When special equipment is needed to perform or understand the process, the writer must describe the equipment. If necessary, he should also mention where to obtain it. In an essay about how to make chili for a large group, for example, the student writer made sure to describe the specific materials necessary for cooking in bulk.

Special size pot for the particular task	To start off, you'll need a huge pot with a lid. Mine's a 32-quart monstrosity you could boil a cow's head in. (Don't ask how I know.) Cooking the chili in several smaller pots results in different kinds of chili—great, but not what we're looking for here. Beg, borrow,
Additional equipment needed	or rent a good large pot and lid for this one. Also essential are a knife, a cutting board, a cool drink (never cook without refreshment), and something for
Specific types of equipment that work best for the task	stirring the chili. A wooden spoon works great, as does a silicone spatula. Just don't use anything that'll melt in bubbling chili.

4. Process Analysis Provides an Appropriate Level of Detail

A process analysis essay should provide just enough detail—not too much, not too little. It should not overwhelm readers with too many technical details. For example, an essay about how to perform CPR would be highly technical if written by and for physicians, but it would be less technical if written for paramedics and even less so if written for restaurant staff who wanted to be prepared in case of emergencies. No matter the circumstance, the analysis must include enough detail to show readers how to perform the steps of the CPR process.

Keep in mind that essays explaining technical or scientific processes benefit from sensory details and figures of speech that make the writing lively and interesting. Descriptive details help readers digest technical details.

5. Process Analysis Anticipates Trouble Spots and Offers Solutions

Process analysis essays, especially how-to essays, must anticipate potential trouble spots or areas of confusion for readers and offer advice on how to avoid or resolve them. A how-to essay should also alert readers to difficult, complicated, or critical steps. In the following paragraph, the author anticipates problems readers might have doing sit-ups.

Precaution 1: neck stress

Precaution 2: hitting head

Advice: use mat

> Begin [the sit-up] by lying on your back with your arms crossed on your chest. Your knees should be bent at approximately 90-degree angles, with your feet flat on the floor. The complete sit-up is performed by bringing your chest up to touch your knees and returning to the original lying position. . . . Two precautions should be mentioned. First, avoid undue stress on your neck during the "up" phase of the exercise. That is, let your abdominal muscles do the work; do not whip your neck during the sit-up movement. Second, avoid hitting the back of your head on the floor during the "down" phase of the sit-up. Performance of the [exercise] on a padded mat is helpful.
>
> —Scott K. Powers and Stephen L. Dodd, *Total Fitness and Wellness*, 3rd ed.

Reading and Writing Process Analysis Essays

In this section you will learn about the structure of a process analysis essay, read a sample essay, and practice using the guidelines for understanding, analyzing, and evaluating process analysis essays. This will help you skillfully read and write essays that use process analysis.

How Is a Process Analysis Essay Structured?

A process analysis essay is structured so that the reader will understand or be able to perform the process after reading the essay.

1. The **introduction** identifies the process and usually includes an explicit **thesis statement**.
2. **Body paragraphs** are organized chronologically to present a clear, step-by-step description of the process.
3. A **conclusion** draws the essay to a close and refers back to the thesis.

Figure 13.1 represents these major structural components visually.

Figure 13.1   Graphic Organizer for a Process Analysis Essay

Title	
Introduction	Background information
	Thesis statement*

⬇

Body paragraphs: steps in the process	Step 1**
	Substep 1
	Substep 2
	Step 2
	Step 3
	Step 4

⬇

Conclusion	Draws essay to a close and refers back to the thesis

* In some essays, the thesis statement may be implied or may appear in a different position.
** In some essays, substeps may be included.

1.   THE INTRODUCTION IDENTIFIES THE PROCESS

The introduction to a process analysis essay usually contains a clear thesis that identifies the process to be discussed and suggests the writer's attitude or approach toward it. The thesis statement also tells why the process is important or useful. Thesis statements for how-to process analyses suggest the usefulness or importance of the process. In a how-it-works essay, the writer either reveals why the information is worth knowing or makes an assertion about the nature of the process itself.

> **How-To Thesis:** Switching to a low-carbohydrate diet can improve weight control dramatically.
>
> (The body of the essay will inform readers of the steps to take to change their diets.)
>
> **How-It-Works Thesis:** Although understanding the grieving process will not lessen the grief that you experience after the death of a loved one, knowing that your experiences are normal does provide some comfort.
>
> (The body of the essay will explain the intricacies of the grieving process.)

 Reading | Writing   When reading a process essay, identify the process being explained and look for clues in the thesis statement about the value of the process. This will help you determine the most important information as you read. When writing a process essay, be sure to make it clear to your readers why they should care about and want to read the essay. Point out the value, importance, or usefulness of becoming familiar with the process.

2.   THE BODY PARAGRAPHS EXPLAIN EACH STEP IN THE PROCESS

The steps or events in a process analysis are usually organized in chronological order—that is, the order in which the steps are completed. Think of process analysis as being organized by the clock or calendar. A process essay presents what happens first in time, then what happens next in time, and so forth. In the following example, literary critic and legal scholar Stanley Fish humorously describes the process of buying a cup of coffee in a modern-day coffee shop in the order the actions happen.

Step 1: Wait in line.   It turns out to be hard [to get coffee]. First you have to get in line, and you may have one or two people in front of you who are ordering a drink with more parts than an internal combustion engine, something about "double shot," "skinny," "breve," "grande," "au lait," and a lot of other words that never pass my lips. If you are patient

Steps 2–3: Order and   and stay in line (no bathroom breaks), you get to put in wait for coffee.   your order, but then you have to find a place to stand while you wait for it. There is no such place. So you shift your body, first here and then there, trying not to get in the way of those you can't help get in the way of.

Step 4: Receive   Finally, the coffee arrives.
coffee.   —Stanley Fish, "Getting Coffee Is Hard to Do," *New York Times*

On occasion, the steps of a process may not have to occur in any particular order. For example, in an essay on how to resolve a dispute between two coworkers, the order may depend on the nature of the dispute. In this type of situation, a logical progression of recommended actions should be used, such as starting with informal or simple steps and progressing to more formal or complex ones.

 Reading | Writing   When reading a process essay, use transitional words and phrases as guides or markers. For complicated processes, stop after each step and mentally review what the process involves thus far and consider what the new step contributes to the process. When writing a process essay, be sure to make it easy for your readers to identify and follow the steps. For complicated or lengthy processes, consider grouping the steps into stages, such as before, during, and after or setting up, carrying out, and following up. Use transitional words and phrases to guide your reader from step to step.

3.   THE CONCLUSION SUMMARIZES THE VALUE OF THE PROCESS

Especially in how-it-works essays, simply ending with the final step in the process may sound incomplete to readers. Therefore, a successful process analysis will emphasize the value or importance of the process, describe particular situations in which it is useful, or offer a final amusing or emphatic comment or anecdote. The following conclusion to a process analysis essay describing why leaves change color in the fall gives that process much more meaning.

Concisely step

At last the leaves leave. But first they turn color and thrill us for weeks on end. Then they crunch and crackle underfoot. They shush, as children drag their small feet through leaves heaped along the curb. Dark, slimy mats of leaves cling to one's heels after the rain. . . . Sometimes one finds in fossil stones the imprint of a leaf, long since disintegrated, whose outlines remind us how detailed, vibrant, and alive are the things of this earth that perish.

Process provides a valuable reminder about life

—Diane Ackerman, *A Natural History of the Senses*

 Reading | Writing   When reading process essays, use the conclusion to gauge your understanding of the process. Mentally review the entire process, making sure you understand why or how each step is done. Doing so will help you remember it and be able to carry it out or discuss it with others. When writing process essays, use your conclusion to set the importance or usefulness of the process firmly in your reader's mind. You might conclude with an interesting example that describes a situation in which knowing the process was helpful or essential. Another option is to condense the steps into a summary statement that will help your readers understand the information.

A Model Process Analysis Essay

Title

Gabby Giffords: Portrait of a Brain Being Rebuilt

William Saletan

William Saletan covers science, technology, and politics for the online magazine *Slate*. He is also the author of *Bearing Right: How Conservatives Won the Abortion War* (2004). The following article first appeared in *Slate* in November 2011.

Introduction

Background information: summarizes the shooting that injured Giffords

Thesis: As the video shows, a damaged brain repairs itself.

On January 8, Gabrielle Giffords was shot through the head at point-blank range. Two weeks later, as she lay mute and glassy-eyed in a hospital bed, her husband, Mark Kelly, began to video-record her recovery. The result, excerpted last night on ABC's 20/20, is one of the greatest home movies ever made: a day-by-day portrait of a crippled brain repairing itself.

Background information: how the brain works

The brain has powers unlike any machine. It organizes the world. It organizes itself. When it's damaged—even when it's transected by a skull-shattering bullet—it can regain not just knowledge, but the ability to learn. If it can't use old circuits, it invents new ones. Where there's a will, the brain finds a way.

Gabrielle Giffords (P. K. Weis/Giffords Campaign via Getty Images)

Body paragraphs: steps in the process

Giffords was shot through her left hemisphere. The bullet took out chunks of her cortex that processed speech and language comprehension. In the opening scenes, captured in late January, she lies motionless, her skull cracked across its dome like an egg. Her eyes are glazed. Her face is blank.

Step 1: physical tasks to get an unresponsive brain working and learning

Kelly and a team of therapists get to work. Their work is to make Giffords work, because that's how the brain learns: by doing. Kelly pats her arm, clasps her hand, tells her to give him a high five. A therapist manipulates Giffords's forearm, tapping it to a tune. The attendants constantly challenge, prod, and encourage her. "You look great," Kelly tells her, though she looks awful. "You just got a little work to do."

Kelly puts Giffords's shoes on a chair. "Here are your tennis shoes," he tells her. "You're going out for a jog today. How does that sound?" He instructs her to hold up his wedding ring on her finger, then take it off. "Can you do that, Sweetie?" he asks. "There you go." He gets her to make a thumbs-up gesture. Two weeks later, the therapists are pushing her to walk. They assist her useless right leg so she can exercise her left and regain her sense of balance.

Step 2: thinking tasks

There are thinking tasks, too. They show her a magazine article. They lay pictures on a table. They make her select cards from a hand. They get her to draw. Sometimes, like a child, she learns by observing her teachers. They show her how to sigh and pucker. "Watch me," says a therapist. "Watch me," Giffords repeats. Now and then she closes her eyes in fatigue or frustration. It's hard work.

5

Having lost some parts of her brain, Giffords has to enlist others. At first, unable to rotate her eyes, she learns to identify and remove Kelly's ring using her sense of touch. Her therapists feed her phrases—"Zip up your . . . ," "You tell time with a . . ."— so that she can reabsorb, through context, words that were blown away. But the chief teaching tool is music, which persists in mental regions safely clear of the devastated language centers. Through melody, she recovers lyrics and eventually spoken words.

Step 3: word tasks using songs and cues

"I love . . ." a therapist sings to Giffords. "You," the patient mouths back. At five weeks, Giffords is chanting along: "Let it shine, let it shine, let it shine." A friend playing a piano keyboard leads her: "It's great to see you looking . . ." Giffords finishes the sentence: "swell." Later, she grins from ear to ear, singing with amusement, "Girls just want to have fun."

Step 4: emotional stimulation

Since emotion and cognition are interwoven, emotional stimulation is crucial to Giffords's recovery. "Can you smile, Sweetie?" Kelly asks. When she doesn't respond, he teases her: "That's not a smile!" At this, the left side of her mouth curls up. "That's better!" he laughs.

Step 5: finally, communicating with speech and gesture

At four weeks, Giffords speaks her first word. She learns to sigh. She gestures while talking. She reaches out in a fluid motion to gently touch her therapist. She cries but can't find the word for what she feels: sadness. The therapist assures her that life will be better and gives her a hug. Then the therapist accidentally knocks a water bottle off the table. Giffords begins to laugh.   10

At seven weeks, Giffords crinkles her nose to say no. She squints wryly at Kelly. She pokes fun at herself. "Goofball Giffords," she says.

Finally, at ten months, Giffords sits down for an ABC interview. Her voice is strong, her eyes full of life. She reaches over to fix Diane Sawyer's hair. Giffords's vocabulary is much improved. She says moving her right arm is "difficult," despite "two hours of therapy" every day. She looks at a picture and pronounces it "beautiful." Thinking back to the people who died at the scene of her shooting, she finds the word she couldn't summon earlier: "sad." She gropes for simple terms to express her feelings: "Better. Stronger. Hard." And for her husband: "Brave."

Conclusion

The interview shows how extensively Giffords has recovered. "Awful," she snorts when Kelly jokes that she likes football. "Stinks!" she adds. But the most remarkable thing caught on camera is her struggle to regain what's still missing. When Sawyer asks Giffords whether she really thinks she can return to Congress, Giffords, at a loss for words, shapes her hand into a gesture that conveys what she wants to say. Giffords's face is tight with concentration and effort, her eyes locked on her hand. She seems to be speaking in sign language, but not to Sawyer or anyone else. The brain, through the hand, is rewiring itself.

Giffords's healing process connected to new research about the mind

What you see in Giffords is what researchers are learning about the mind. Right now, at the annual meeting of the Society of Neuroscience, thirty thousand humans are swarming around the Washington, D.C., convention center, exchanging the latest discoveries about neurons, receptors, and circuits. What they're finding everywhere is plasticity. The brain isn't built once. It rebuilds itself, day after day, editing a network of one hundred trillion synapses that absorb, represent, and manage experience. It makes us who we are. And, when necessary, it remakes us. Just ask Gabby Giffords.

Understanding, Analyzing, and Evaluating Process Analysis Essays

In reading and writing process analysis essays, your goal is to get beyond mere competence: That is, you want to be able to do more than merely understand the content of the essays you're reading or convey just your basic ideas to the audience you're writing for.

 Reading | Writing   Truly skillful reading and writing require the abilities to **understand**, **analyze**, *and* **evaluate** material. These abilities are important to you as a reader because they give you a systematic, thorough method of examining a reading. They're important to you as a writer because they help you decide what to revise, rewrite, drop, and replace, allowing you to produce a well-written, effective essay.

Understanding a Process Analysis Essay

Begin by previewing the essay to find out what process is being explained and to get an overall sense of how complicated or complex it may be. Then consider how much, if anything, you already know about the process. These tasks will help you determine how to read the essay and what to look for. Read complicated essays about unfamiliar topics slowly—and perhaps several times—highlighting each step. You may be able to read an essay that is about a familiar topic and offers general advice much faster, with less or no rereading. As you read and reread, use the skills you learned in Chapter 2 and look for the answers to the following questions.

- **What process is being explained and what is the author's thesis?** The writer's view of why the topic is important or useful may suggest what parts of the process to pay most attention to.

- **Is it a "how-to" or "how-it-works" essay?** Your answer will determine what types of information are important to remember. For how-to essays, you need exact, detailed comprehension because you will be performing the process. For how-it-works essays, you need to understand the logic of the process, mechanical and technical aspects of executing it, and how steps relate to one another.

- **Can steps be grouped into larger categories?** For complicated or lengthy processes, categorize the steps and label those groupings in the margin.

- **Are there cautions or warnings about difficult or troublesome steps?** You might highlight these in a different color.

- **Can you visualize the process?** For a how-to essay, imagine yourself carrying out the process. For a complex how-it-works essay, draw the object and label working parts. These techniques will cement the steps of the process in your memory and improve your recall.

- **Can you summarize the process?** To test whether you understand the process, try to summarize it without looking back at the essay. If you cannot, this means you have not learned the process fully and that review would be helpful.

Figure 13.2 (p. 342) is a visual representation of William Saletan's "Gabby Giffords: Portrait of a Brain Being Rebuilt."

Understanding in Action

Following is one student's understanding of the main idea of William Saletan's process analysis. Write a summary of the stages described in the process. Use the graphic organizer on page 342 to help structure your summary.

A seriously damaged brain can actually repair itself over time. It can take in lost information. It can even learn how to learn again. The recordings of Gabby Giffords's recovery show how this process works.

Analyzing a Process Analysis Essay

Analyzing a process analysis essay involves assessing how clearly and accurately the writer presented the process. Use the following questions to guide your analysis of process essays.

- **Does the writer explain why the process is important and useful?** Determine whether the reasons are sound, practical, and logical.
- **Are the steps clear, sequential, and distinct?** Steps should be explicit, should be sequentially or logically arranged, and should not overlap.
- **Does the writer provide sufficient background information?** Assess whether the writer adequately explains unfamiliar terminology, unusual equipment, and complicated techniques.
- **Is the level of detail appropriate for the intended audience?** Writers should neither assume knowledge that readers lack nor tire them by explaining things they already know.

Figure 13.2   Graphic Organizer for "Gabby Giffords: Portrait of a Brain Being Rebuilt"

Title	"Gabby Giffords: Portrait of a Brain Being Rebuilt"
Introduction	Gabby Giffords suffered a serious brain injury from a gunshot wound in early 2011, and later that year *20/20* aired her husband's video of her recovery process.
	Thesis: The video of Giffords's recovery demonstrates the steps a damaged brain goes through as it repairs itself.
Body paragraphs: steps in the process	**Step 1:** Physical tasks to get an unresponsive brain working and learning
	Step 2: Thinking tasks
	Step 3: Word tasks using songs and cues
	Step 4: Emotional stimulation
	Step 5: Finally, communicating with speech and gesture
Conclusion	The *20/20* interview shows Giffords's progress and how far she still has to go. The video and interview also show what researchers are learning about the human brain: It is constantly remaking itself.

Analysis in Action

Following is an analysis of how Saletan presents the first stage of the process in his essay (paras. 4–5) written by the student who wrote the summary in Understanding in Action. Write your own analysis of how Saletan presents the subsequent stages.

> The first stage of the process is getting Giffords to work, to do things physically. To make this stage clear, Saletan describes some of the specific tasks she's asked to do by her husband and therapists, like take off her wedding ring, give a high five, and exercise her good leg. The author describes the process using these familiar actions. This helps the audience, who are not doctors, understand.

📊 Evaluating a Process Analysis Essay

Although most process analysis essays are straightforward and informative, you should still consider the author's motives for writing, the author's qualifications to write about the topic, and the quality, accuracy, and completeness of the information presented. Use the following questions to guide your evaluation of process analysis essays.

- **What are the writer's motives?** As you read, ask yourself, Why does the writer want me to understand or carry out this process? A writer may have a particular motive for explaining a process. For example, a writer opposed to the death penalty may use graphic details about the process of execution to shock readers and persuade them to actively oppose the death penalty. Sometimes a writer may have a hidden agenda, even in an article on a noncontroversial topic. For example, an essay titled "How to Lose Ten Pounds" written by the owner of a weight-loss clinic may be attempting to sell clinic services.

- **Is the writer knowledgeable and experienced?** Always consider whether the writer has sufficient knowledge, training, education, or experience to write about the topic. This question is particularly important for how-to essays in which you will learn how to perform the task. Following the advice of someone unqualified could be a waste of time or even dangerous. Check the author's credentials and determine if he or she is an expert in the field. Also consider whether the writer supports his or her assertions by referring to outside sources or mentioning or quoting other experts in the field.

- **Is the information complete and sufficiently detailed?** Authors writing for a particular audience make assumptions about what readers do and do not know. If they wrongly assume them to be more knowledgeable than they are, readers may not be able to understand or carry out the process. For example, in explaining how to prepare for an interview, a writer may advise readers to research a company beforehand, assuming they know what information to look for and how to find it. But if readers are unfamiliar with this research process, they will be unable to complete the step.

Evaluation in Action

Based on his analysis (p. 343), our student writer composed the following evaluation of the presentation of the first stage of Saletan's process analysis. Write your own evaluation of the presentation of the rest of the process.

> The first stage of the process is presented very clearly in paragraphs 4–5. The author provides many details about what the medical workers and her husband did to get Gabby's brain working again. He seems to be proud of Gabby and her husband. Words like *challenge*, *prod*, *encourage*, and *pushing* emphasize how much she and others did to help her recovery.

Readings for Practice, Ideas for Writing

The End of a Relationship:
How to Recover from a Broken Heart

Judith L. Allen, Ph.D., is a licensed marriage and family therapist. She specializes in relationship and communication issues for adults and children. In addition to private practice, she offers online counseling at AskTheInternetTherapist.com, where this article first appeared.

Reading Tip

As you read, think about the kind of connection the author creates between herself and her potential audience, as well as how she establishes that connection.

Previewing the Reading

Preview the reading (see pp. 23–24 for guidelines), and then answer the following questions.

1. What process is described in this essay?
2. What are the main steps in the process?

AskTheInternetTherapist.com

The End of a Relationship: How to Recover from a Broken Heart

Dr. Judith L. Allen

Not all love matches work "forever." Although that is usually the initial hope, dating and practicing relationships are a path of inquiry, looking for a life partner. Even some marriages turn out to be about that search when it comes to light that you may not have known your partner as well as you thought. That once "perfect" pairing turns out to be a match that was perfect for a period of time and now someone has changed their needs and wants to the point that the relationship is no longer fitting into their new life plan.

The term *recovering from a broken heart* usually means that there are still strong feelings and attachments to the person you once loved and whom you depended on. It

Continued >

AskTheInternetTherapist.com

also may tend to imply that the breakup was not the outcome you desired, leaving you feeling some form of powerlessness. There is probably some underlying message that somehow you've failed or that you may not have been good enough in some way.

Those who have faced an ending to an important relationship with someone they loved, and perhaps still love very much, can certainly relate to an aftermath of sadness, grief, disorientation, self-doubt, and often a temporary feeling of depression and despair.

It takes time for your heart to mend, which usually involves a time of thinking through and reliving all the shared experiences. It takes time to reevaluate your choices from beginning to end, to look for clues that may not have been apparent at the time. This can mean weeks or months and even years for some, of feeling waves of emotion as your mind revisits experiences that keep getting triggered by your daily activities.

One of the most difficult parts of breaking up is getting through the initial shock, sadness, and loss. Even those who feel that it was their choice to end the relationship go through a period of feeling lost and confused without their former partner. After all, life has changed drastically and quickly!

5

It's important not to misinterpret the pain you're feeling as a sign that you did something wrong when the relationship came to an end. Most people tend to feel that they are in more pain than the other person. It's a natural part of the healing process to feel this and it means that you are now focused on yourself and what you need, instead of thinking in terms of the other person's needs. Allow yourself time to engage in recognition of your pain and your loss.

You may have read rule-of-thumb statements similar to one that goes "It takes as much time to heal as the time involved in the relationship." In my experience this has not been a fact for most people. The deepness and dependence on the relationship is often rooted in unfulfilled needs from childhood. What seems like a brief relationship may take a year to heal, where a long-term relationship may end and be processed in a relatively short time. There are no real rules for how much time it takes, but it's a good idea to seek help if the time seems extensive and protracted, beyond what would seem a normal time to each person, or if there seems to be no progress in the healing.

If you want to see how that progress is going for you, watch for these steps and work on getting through each one completely.

Step One: Adjusting from Being Part of a Couple to Being on Your Own

This may be the hardest step. When you care for another person, over time, you blend your energies in the form of hopes, dreams, plans, and expectations with that person. When the relationship ends, you go through a process of individuation, pulling back and reclaiming yourself and your evolved identity. This can feel for a time like part of you is actually missing. Even if you want someone out of your life, the ending of

AskTheInternetTherapist.com

the pattern of familiarity leaves a feeling that you are not whole for a time. Your mind is searching to rebuild the feeling of independence you once knew, while incorporating the development which has taken place during the time you were involved in the relationship.

Because of the newness, the strangeness, and the confusion of your mind during this 10 time, you may experience a period of tearfulness, hopelessness, and not feeling joy. You may not feel like socializing or eating, and you may experience physical symptoms such as an aching in the pit of your stomach. You may feel loneliness even in the presence of close friends. It's interesting to note that these symptoms are similar to those reported from people recovering from drug, food, and alcohol addiction in the earliest stages. It's normal during this step to feel sorry for yourself as you review many painful memories. People experience strong longings to return to the situation that has ended, to prevent or stop the emotional and mental processing of this first step. It's a longing for the familiar and the ensuing confusion that drives people at this time to want it to be over.

Allow yourself to feel sorry for your loss. This means allowing tears, feelings of loss, and wanting to be alone for a time. If you ignore these feelings or try to distract yourself, they will only remain for a longer period. Cry about it, write about it, talk about it with a therapist or close friend who will listen without judging.

After an initial period of grieving and mourning your loss, make a commitment to begin to get back to rebuilding other connections which you may have neglected while you were part of a couple and through your grieving period. Begin to make plans with old friends, sign up for a class to make new friends, plan a gathering at your home or have one at the home of a friend. Only schedule part of your time with others, and use some constructive alone time to continue the review of the past relationship. Your mind needs to find answers to your questions. You may need to do research to gain the understanding you need, and/or talk to a professional to do some soul searching. You'll want to know if you lost something positive in your life, or something that was negative and needed changing even before the actual breakup.

Based on what you will learn about the past experience, you can begin to build a listing of what you want in your future. That evaluation can help move your mind from the past to the future, where hope exists. The only part of life you can control is what you think and do today, and what you make plans for in your future.

Practice healthy avoidance. Avoid seeing or interacting with your former partner, avoid excess in the use of alcohol, food, and medications. You may think you are reducing emotional pain, but you are actually setting up to continue it for a longer time. Calling him/her to relieve the pain is simply continuing the connection where your recovery will be destined to start over and over again.

Continued >

AskTheInternetTherapist.com

Don't avoid feelings. Don't avoid what can really help, such as exercise (at the gym or   15 maybe dancing), communication with friends, and reading.

Step Two: Starting to Smile Again!

When you find yourself free of thinking about your past relationship for a few hours at a time, you are starting to move from the hardest first step. You are now at a place that you can quantitatively[1] measure your progress. Make a notation of each event, thought, or experience that makes you smile. Those can begin the new foundation you are building for yourself. You were there before, you are getting there again, almost as a reward for facing the hard work you have done up to this step.

You may even have periods where you are able to think of the past relationship in terms of being needed in your life for that specific period of time. You may find that you are becoming more philosophical and enlightened about the meaning of the past relationship. Look for new meaning each time your mind goes back to cover more details.

There is a phenomenon that most people find disconcerting for many months. You may feel that you're doing better, you're beginning to smile, and you may even have started feeling good enough to date again. Then, out of nowhere, you are hit with a flood of emotions! You think to yourself, "I thought I was doing better than this, what's wrong with me?" Know that it is part of the process that can be looked at with a metaphor of the ocean and the waves coming in and out. Recovering from a relationship comes in waves that cover you, but as time goes on, the waves become more infrequent and have less power. Eventually, the tide will go out and not return, but during recovery from a breakup, understand that you have little control over the pattern and frequency. Don't lose sight of your path to find things and people who make you feel like smiling again.

Step Three: Getting Back to Being Yourself

Life is now returning to some semblance of normalcy. You'll find that you're able to concentrate, get excited by prospects of the future, and you no longer feel as if you are in transition. You have returned to a place where you have your identity back, and you may be ready to date and get involved in a new relationship. You may have another path, such as working on your career for the time being. You'll find that your mind has found many answers to your questions that arose during the period of grief and that you have come to a settled place of feeling like you know what was wrong with the past relationship. Hopefully, you can find it comfortable to say with honesty—Nice person, bad match. Additionally you may honestly see why it was perfect for a

---

[1] **quantitatively** Keep track numerically.

AskTheInternetTherapist.com

time, but destined to be only for that specific period of your life. Your needs are changing all the time. Still, watch out for the occasional wave of memories.

Step Four: Maturity about How Relationships Work (and Don't Work)

When you get to this point, you're well on your way in your development of complete 20 healing. You may have even talked about or seen your former partner, and the stinging pain was gone. You are involved and connected with friends and maybe in a new relationship. As time has gone on, you've reevaluated what is important in your life and changed your list somewhat of what you want in a partner. It may have gotten longer or even shorter based on your previous experiences. You know now that you can and did recover and that if it ever happens in your future, you can depend on the strength you demonstrated to get you through the process again. No, of course you don't want it to happen again, but you also don't want to waste any time getting out of a relationship which is fundamentally over. Each relationship is giving you more information as the desired picture of your life comes into clear focus. Remind yourself that you survived before and you can do it whenever it is needed in the future.

Understanding the Reading

1. **Thesis** What is the author's thesis, and where does she state it?

2. **Audience** Throughout the essay Allen writes to "you." What specific audience does she have in mind?

3. **Purpose** Is this a how-to essay or a how-it-works essay? How does Allen hope readers will benefit from her essay? Where does she state this idea specifically?

4. **Meaning** How long does Allen say this process should take?

5. **Meaning** What does Allen say is the hardest step in the process? What advice does she give for getting through this stage?

6. **Meaning** What progress does Allen say people make in the second stage of the process? What setbacks do they encounter?

7. **Meaning** What is the goal of this process?

8. **Vocabulary** Using context clues (p. 34), write a brief definition of each of the following words as it is used in the reading, checking a dictionary if necessary: *disorientation* (para. 3), *protracted* (7), *individuation* (9), *ensuing* (10), *disconcerting* (18), *semblance* (19), and *fundamentally* (20).

9. **Organization** To help understand the organization of the essay, complete the graphic organizer that follows.

Title	"The End of a Relationship: How to Recover from a Broken Heart"
Introduction	Description of "brokenhearted" person
	Thesis: It takes time for the heart to heal.
Body paragraphs: steps in process	**Step 1:**
	Step 2:
	Step 3:
	Step 4 (and Conclusion):

Analyzing the Reading

1. **Background information** Allen doesn't begin to focus on the process she describes until paragraph 9. What is the point of her eight introductory paragraphs?

2. **Level of detail** Allen describes the first step in great detail (paras. 9–15), the second step more briefly (16–18), and the final two steps in only a single paragraph each. What do you think accounts for this difference in level of detail?

3. **Technique** Allen points to a potential trouble spot in paragraph 18. How does she help guide readers through this?

4. **Purpose and audience** If you have not recently experienced an emotional breakup, do you still find Allen's analysis and advice pertinent? Why, or why not?

5. **Conclusion** Why does Allen refer to the "future" twice in her final paragraph?

Evaluating the Reading

1. **Author expertise** Consider Allen's background. Does she seem knowledgeable and experienced? Why, or why not? (Hint: Use the headnote that precedes the essay, as well as her own words, to better understand her background.)

2. **Level of detail** As noted in question 2 of Analyzing the Reading, Allen describes the second step somewhat briefly (16–18), and the final two steps in only a single paragraph each. Is this evidence sufficient?

3. **Figurative language** How well does the "metaphor of the ocean" in paragraph 18 help you understand the point Allen is making here?

Discussing the Reading

1. In her opening Allen writes that "dating and practicing relationships are a path of inquiry." What can people learn from relationships that don't ultimately succeed?

2. Allen likens what one experiences after a romantic breakup to the early stages of recovering from an addiction (para. 10). Why might these feelings be so similar?

3. In her final paragraph, Allen refers to the list people have of what they want in a life partner. Do you think most people have such a list, and does it evolve over time, as Allen suggests?

Writing about the Reading

1. **Paragraph** Summarize the four steps of Allen's process analysis in your own words. Start with a topic sentence and perhaps some further information to introduce the process. (Hint: Use transitional words, such as *first*, to replace *Step* headings in the essay.)

2. **Paragraph** Brainstorm a list of changes you would like to make in your life. Then choose one that seems challenging but doable. Write a paragraph in which you describe the process you would follow to accomplish that change. Make sure you start with a topic sentence explaining your goal before describing the steps.

3. **Essay** Imagine you have a friend who has just gone through a painful breakup. Write an essay describing for that friend the steps to take in mending his or her broken heart. (Hint: Draw on the advice Allen offers, tailoring it to your friend, but also include information from your own experience and observations.)

Dater's Remorse

Cindy Chupack served as an executive producer and, frequently, a writer for the HBO show *Sex and the City*. Before working in television, she contributed a personal essay to *New York Woman* magazine that attracted the attention of an industry writer who encouraged her to create sitcom scripts. The selection here appears in a collection of Chupack's writings titled *The Between Boyfriends Book* (2003).

Reading Tip

As you read, notice the way Chupack builds her humorous analogy between shopping and dating, from her opening description of her telephone-company "suitors" to her concluding warning of *Caveat emptor*—"Let the buyer beware."

Previewing the Reading

Preview the reading (see pp. 23–24 for guidelines), and then answer the following questions.

1. What clues do you have about the meaning of the title?

2. What type of information does the author present about dating?

Dater's Remorse

CINDY CHUPACK

I never imagined this would happen, but three men are fighting over me. They call me repeatedly. They ply me with gifts. They beg me for a commitment. Yes, they're just AT&T, MCI, and Sprint salesmen interested in being my long-distance carrier, but what I'm relishing—aside from the attention—is the sense that I am in complete control.

In fact, just the other day my ex (phone carrier, that is) called to find out what went wrong. Had I been unhappy? What would it take to win me back? Turns out all it took was two thousand frequent flier miles. I switched, just like that. I didn't worry about how my current carrier would feel, or how it might affect my Friends and Family. Now if only I could use that kind of healthy judgment when it comes to my love life.

The unfortunate truth is that while most of us are savvy shoppers, we're not sufficiently selective when looking for relationships, and that's why we often suffer from dater's remorse. Perhaps we should try to apply conventional consumer wisdom to men as well as merchandise. How satisfying love might be if we always remembered to:

Go with a classic, not a trend. We all know it's unwise to spend a week's salary on vinyl hip-huggers. But when it comes to men, even the most conservative among us occasionally invests in the human equivalent of a fashion fad. The furthest I ever strayed from a classic was during college. I wrote a paper about the Guardian Angels, those street toughs who unofficially patrol inner-city neighborhoods, and being a very thorough student, I ended up dating one. He wore a red beret and entertained me by demonstrating martial arts moves in my dorm room. I remember telling my concerned roommate how he was *sooo* much more interesting than those boring MBA[1] types everybody else was dating. Of course, what initially seemed like a fun impulse buy turned out to require more of an emotional investment than I was willing to make. It took me two months to break up with him— two months of getting persistent late-night calls, angry letters, and unannounced visits to my dorm room door, which I envisioned him kicking down someday. The good thing about MBAs: They're familiar with the expression "Cut your losses."

Beware of the phrase "Some assembly required." Anyone who has tried to ₅ follow translated-from-Swedish directions for putting together a swivel chair understands that when you've got to assemble something yourself, the money you save isn't worth the time you spend. The same goes for men. Many women think that even though a guy is not exactly "together," we can easily straighten him out. The fact is that fixer-uppers are more likely to stay forever flawed, no matter what we do. My friend Jenny fell for a forty-one-year-old bachelor, despite the fact that he spent their first few dates detailing his dysfunctional family and boasting that he went to the same shrink as the Menendez brothers.[2] "Six weeks later, when he announced he couldn't handle a relationship, it shouldn't have surprised me," says Jenny, who now looks for men requiring a little less duct tape.

Make sure your purchase goes with the other things you own. I once fell in love with a very expensive purple velvet couch, and I seriously considered buying it, even though it would mean getting my cat declawed, and I had signed an agreement when I adopted her that I would never do that. But the couch . . . the couch . . . I visited it a few more times, but I didn't buy, and not just out of sympathy for my cat. I realized that if I owned that couch, I'd have to replace all my comfy old stuff with new furniture equal in quality and style to the purple couch. Men can be like that, too. You're drawn to them because they're attractively different, but being with them may mean changing your entire life. For example, while dating a long-distance bicyclist, my friend Janet found herself suddenly following his training regimen: bowing out of social events just as the fun began, rising at an hour at which she normally went to bed, and replacing fine dining with intensive carbo-loading. And the only bike she ever rode was the stationary one at the gym.

Check with previous owners. Once beyond age twenty-five, most men would have to be classified as secondhand, and we all know how risky it is to buy used merchandise. Therefore, it's up to you to do some basic consumer research. Find out how many previous owners your selection has had. If he's such a steal, why is he still on the lot? Is it because his exterior is a bit unsightly, or because he's fundamentally a lemon? (Before becoming too critical, bear in mind that *you* are still on the lot.)

---

[1] **MBA** Master of Business Administration, an advanced business degree.
[2] **Menendez brothers** Two brothers who were convicted in 1996 of killing their parents.

Continued >

Caveat emptor.[3] Following these guidelines won't guarantee a great relationship, but it will help you cut down on the number of times you feel dater's remorse. Obviously looking for a husband is a bit more complicated than choosing a major appliance, but since there are no lifetime guarantees or lemon laws for men, it pays to be a savvy shopper.

[3] *Caveat emptor* Latin phrase meaning "Let the buyer beware."

Understanding the Reading

1. **Thesis** Identify Chupack's thesis. How does the author's relationship with long-distance phone companies relate to the topic of dating?

2. **Steps in the process** According to Chupack, what can happen when you date someone who is "the human equivalent of a fashion fad" (para. 4)?

3. **Process warnings** Explain the connection Chupack makes between dating and assembling furniture. Why does the author advise women to stay away from "fixer-uppers" (para. 5)?

4. **Vocabulary** Explain the various ways the word *lot* is used in paragraph 7.

5. **Vocabulary** Explain the meaning of each of the following words as it is used in the reading: *relishing* (para. 1), *conventional* (3), *classic* (4), *envisioned* (4), *dysfunctional* (5), and *regimen* (6). Refer to your dictionary as needed.

6. **Visualizing the reading** Chupack explains the process of avoiding dater's remorse by comparing it to shopping. Match each step to the corresponding aspect of the analogy in this chart. The first one has been done for you.

Step	Shopping Analogy	Dating Advice
1	"Go with a classic, not a trend." (para. 4)	Avoid men who are radically different from the types you usually date.
2	"Beware of the phrase 'Some assembly required.'" (para. 5)	
3	"Make sure your purchase goes with the other things you own." (para. 6)	
4	"Check with previous owners." (para. 7)	
5	"*Caveat emptor.*" (para. 8)	

Analyzing the Reading

1. **Audience** What assumption does the author make about her readers as revealed in the final paragraph?

2. **Thesis** Chupack's thesis involves dating as well as shopping. How does she use the idea of shopping to create a process for dating?

3. **Organization** What type of organization does Chupack use to order the steps in her process analysis essay? If the essay is not organized chronologically, does the author use any sort of logical progression, such as starting with simple steps and progressing to more complex ones?

4. **Language** What is the connotative meaning of *secondhand* and *used merchandise* in paragraph 7?

Evaluating the Reading

1. **Analogy** An **analogy** is a comparison in which an author illustrates one point, thing, or situation by likening it to another. How does Chupack develop her analogy? Analyze each part. Do all the aspects of the analogy make sense? How closely are the two concepts related? Do the two ideas have enough in common? For what purpose is the analogy used? Explain.

2. **Meaning** Are there ways in which shopping and dating differ? If yes, how? Does the author address these? Why, or why not?

3. **Detail** Highlight the details Chupack includes as part of her process. How specific are her steps? Is the essay detailed enough to be of practical use?

Discussing the Reading

1. Discuss some experiences you or a friend have had with dating. How difficult is it to find someone with whom you are compatible?

2. Write a journal entry about a successful relationship that you have now or had in the past or that you have observed in those close to you. What made this relationship work out so well?

Writing about the Reading

1. **Paragraph** Chupack warns readers about men who are "fixer-uppers" (para. 5). Think of a person from your own experience for whom there was "some assembly required." In a paragraph, list the steps that this person would need to follow to repair flaws in his or her personality or lifestyle.

2. **Essay** Write a process analysis essay offering your own advice on dating or marriage. Present suggestions for maintaining a workable and satisfying relationship. Include potential trouble spots and advice on how to avoid or resolve them. Title your essay "How to Make a Relationship Work."

3. **Internet research** Conduct online research about "speed dating." In a how-it-works essay, explain what speed dating is and outline the steps one must follow to participate in this activity. Include background information about the process and interesting and relevant details to keep readers informed and interested. In your essay, address your own feelings about speed dating. What are its advantages and disadvantages over traditional ways of meeting people?

Inside the Engine

Tom and his brother, **Ray Magliozzi**, better known to their listening audience as Click and Clack, the Tappet Brothers, are the award-winning hosts of *Car Talk* on National Public Radio. This call-in show has a devoted following because of the brothers' use of humor as they offer automobile repair advice. The selection here was taken from *Car Talk*, a book published in 1991 featuring some of the best advice from the brothers' radio show.

Reading Tip

As you read, notice how effectively the authors explain complex terms and technology in order to make their how-it-works essay easy to understand.

Previewing the Reading

Preview the reading (see pp. 23–24 for guidelines), and then answer the following questions.

1. What is the purpose of the reading?

2. Do you predict that this reading will be technical and specialized or practical and readable?

Inside the Engine

TOM AND RAY MAGLIOZZI

A customer of ours had an old Thunderbird that he used to drive back and forth to New York to see a girlfriend every other weekend. And every time he made the trip he'd be in the shop the following Monday needing to get something fixed because the car was such a hopeless piece of trash. One Monday he failed to show up and Tom said, "Gee, that's kind of unusual." I said jokingly, "Maybe he blew the car up."

Well, what happened was that he was on the Merritt Parkway in Connecticut when he noticed that he had to keep the gas pedal all the way to the floor just to go 30 m.p.h., with this big V-8 engine,[1] and he figured something was awry.

So he pulled into one of those filling stations where they sell gasoline and chocolate-chip cookies and milk. And he asked the attendant to look at the engine and, of course, the guy said, "I can't help you. All I know is cookies and milk." But the guy agreed to look anyway since our friend was really desperate. His girlfriend was waiting for him and he needed to know if he was going to make it.

---

[1] **V-8 engine** Powerful engine so called because of its eight cylinders arranged in two rows situated at right angles to each other.

Anyway, the guy threw open the hood and jumped back in terror. The engine was glowing red. Somewhere along the line, probably around Hartford, he must have lost all of his motor oil. The engine kept getting hotter and hotter, but like a lot of other things in the car that didn't work, neither did his oil pressure warning light. As a result, the engine got so heated up that it fused itself together. All the pistons melted, and the cylinder heads deformed, and the pistons fused to the cylinder walls, and the bearings welded themselves to the crankshaft—oh, it was a terrible sight! When he tried to restart the engine, he just heard a *click, click, click* since the whole thing was seized up tighter than a drum.

That's what can happen in a case of extreme engine neglect. Most of us wouldn't do that, or at least wouldn't do it knowingly. Our friend didn't do it knowingly either, but he learned a valuable lesson. He learned that his girlfriend wouldn't come and get him if his car broke down. Even if he offered her cookies and milk.

The oil is critical to keeping things running since it not only acts as a lubri- 5 cant, but it also helps to keep the engine cool. What happens is that the oil pump sucks the oil out of what's called the sump (or the crankcase or the oil pan), and it pushes that oil, under pressure, up to all of the parts that need lubrication.

The way the oil works is that it acts as a cushion. The molecules of oil actually separate the moving metal parts from one another so that they don't directly touch; the crankshaft *journals,* or the hard parts of the crankshaft, never touch the soft connecting-rod *bearings* because there's a film of oil between them, forced in there under pressure. From the pump.

It's pretty high pressure too. When the engine is running at highway speed, the oil, at 50 or 60 pounds or more per square inch (or about 4 bars, if you're of the metric persuasion—but let's leave religion out of this), is coursing through the veins of the engine and keeping all these parts at safe, albeit microscopic, distances from each other.

But if there's a lot of dirt in the oil, the dirt particles get embedded in these metal surfaces and gradually the dirt acts as an abrasive and wears away these metal surfaces. And pretty soon the engine is junk.

It's also important that the motor oil be present in sufficient quantity. In nontechnical terms, that means there's got to be enough of it in there. If you have too little oil in your engine, there's not going to be enough of it to go around, and it will get very hot, because four quarts will be doing the work of five, and so forth. When that happens, the oil gets overheated and begins to burn up at a greater than normal rate. Pretty soon, instead of having four quarts, you have three and a half quarts, then three quarts doing the work of five. And then, next thing you know, you're down to two quarts and your engine is glowing red, just like that guy driving to New York, and it's chocolate-chip cookie time.

Continued >

In order to avoid this, some cars have gauges and some have warning lights; 10
some people call them "idiot lights." Actually, we prefer to reverse it and call them
"idiot gauges." I think gauges are bad. When you drive a car—maybe I'm weird
about this—I think it's a good idea to look at the road most of the time. And you
can't look at the road if you're busy looking at a bunch of gauges. It's the same
objection we have to these stupid radios today that have so damn many buttons
and slides and digital scanners and so forth that you need a copilot to change stations. Remember when you just turned a knob?

Not that gauges are bad in and of themselves. I think if you have your choice,
what you want is idiot lights—or what we call "genius lights"—and gauges too. It's
nice to have a gauge that you can kind of keep an eye on for an overview of what's
going on. For example, if you know that your engine typically runs at 215 degrees
and on this particular day, which is not abnormally hot, it's running at 220 or 225,
you might suspect that something is wrong and get it looked at before your radia-
tor boils over.

On the other hand, if that gauge was the only thing you had to rely on and
you didn't have a light to alert you when something was going wrong, then you'd
look at the thing all the time, especially if your engine had melted on you once. In
that case, why don't you take the bus? Because you're not going to be a very good
driver, spending most of your time looking at the gauges.

Incidentally, if that oil warning light ever comes on, shut the engine off! We
don't mean that you should shut it off in rush-hour traffic when you're in the
passing lane. Use all necessary caution and get the thing over to the breakdown
lane. But don't think you can limp to the next exit, because you can't. Spend the
money to get towed and you may save the engine.

It's a little-known fact that the oil light does *not* signify whether or not you
have oil in the engine. The oil warning light is really monitoring the oil *pressure*.
Of course, if you have no oil, you'll have no oil pressure, so the light will be on.
But it's also possible to have plenty of oil and an oil pump that's not working for
one reason or another. In this event, a new pump would fix the problem, but if
you were to drive the car (saying, "It must be a bad light, I just checked the oil!")
you'd melt the motor.

So if the oil warning light comes on, even if you just had an oil change and 15
the oil is right up to the full mark on the dipstick and is nice and clean—don't
drive the car!

Here's another piece of useful info. When you turn the key to the "on" position, all the little warning lights *should light up*: the temperature light, the oil
light, whatever other lights you may have. Because that is the *test mode* for these
lights. If those lights *don't* light up when you turn the key to the "on" position
(just before you turn it all the way to start the car), does that mean you're out of

oil? No. It means that something is wrong with the warning light itself. If the light doesn't work then, it's not going to work at all. Like when you need it, for example.

One more thing about oil: Overfilling is just as bad as underfilling. Can you really have too much of a good thing? you ask. Yes. If you're half a quart or even a quart overfilled, it's not a big deal, and I wouldn't be afraid to drive the car under those circumstances. But if you're a quart and a half or two quarts or more over-filled, you could have so much oil in the crankcase that the spinning crankshaft is going to hit the oil and turn it into suds. It's impossible for the pump to pump suds, so you'll ruin the motor. It's kind of like a front-loading washing machine that goes berserk and spills suds all over the floor when you put too much deter-gent in. That's what happens to your motor oil when you overfill it.

With all this talk about things that can go wrong, let's not forget that modern engines are pretty incredible. People always say, "You know, the cars of yesteryear were wonderful. They built cars rough and tough and durable in those days."

Horsefeathers.[2]

The cars of yesteryear were nicer to look at because they were very individu-alistic. They were all different, and some were even beautiful. In fact, when I was a kid, you could tell the year, make, and model of a car from a hundred paces just by looking at the taillights or the grille. 20

Nowadays, they all look the same. They're like jellybeans on wheels. You can't tell one from the other. But the truth is, they've never made engines as good as they make them today. Think of the abuse they take! None of the cars of yester-year was capable of going 60 or 70 miles per hour all day long and taking it for 100,000 miles.

Engines of today—and by today I mean from the late '60s on up—are far superior. What makes them superior is not only the design and the metallurgy, but the lubricants. The oil they had thirty years ago was lousy compared to what we have today. There are magic additives and detergents and long-chain polymers and what-have-you that make them able to hold dirt in suspension and to neu-tralize acids and to lubricate better than oils of the old days.

There aren't too many things that will go wrong, because the engines are made so well and the tolerances are closer. And aside from doing stupid things like running out of oil or failing to heed the warning lights or overfilling the thing, you shouldn't worry.

But there's one word of caution about cars that have timing belts: Lots of cars these days are made with overhead camshafts. The camshaft, which opens the valves, is turned by a gear and gets its power from the crankshaft. Many cars today use a notched rubber *timing belt* to connect the two shafts instead of a chain because it's cheaper and easy to change. And here's the caveat: *If you don't change*

[2] **horsefeathers** Nonsense.

Continued >

it and the belt breaks, it can mean swift ruin to the engine. The pistons can hit the valves and you'll have bent valves and possibly broken pistons.

So you can do many hundreds of dollars' worth of damage by failing to heed the manufacturer's warning about changing the timing belt in a timely manner. No pun intended. For most cars, the timing belt replacement is somewhere between $100 and $200. It's not a big deal. 25

I might add that there are many cars that have rubber timing belts that will *not* cause damage to the engine when they break. But even if you have one of those cars, make sure that you get the belt changed, at the very least, when the manufacturer suggests it. If there's no specific recommendation and you have a car with a rubber belt, we would recommend that you change it at 60,000 miles. Because even if you don't do damage to the motor when the belt breaks, you're still going to be stuck somewhere, maybe somewhere unpleasant. Maybe even Cleveland! So you want to make sure that you don't fall into that situation.

Many engines that have rubber timing belts also use the belt to drive the water pump. On these, don't forget to change the water pump when you change the timing belt, because the leading cause of premature belt failure is that the water pump seizes. So if you have a timing belt that drives the water pump, get the water pump out of there at the same time. You don't want to put a belt in and then have the water pump go a month later, because it'll break the new belt and wreck the engine.

The best way to protect all the other pieces that you can't get to without spending a lot of money is through frequent oil changes. The manufacturers recommend oil changes somewhere between seven and ten thousand miles, depending upon the car. We've always recommended that you change your oil at 3,000 miles. We realize for some people that's a bit of an inconvenience, but look at it as cheap insurance. And change the filter every time too.

And last but not least, I want to repeat this because it's important: Make sure your warning lights work. The oil pressure and engine temperature warning lights are your engine's lifeline. Check them every day. You should make it as routine as checking to see if your zipper's up. You guys should do it at the same time.

What you do is, you get into the car, check to see that your zipper's up, and then turn the key on and check to see if your oil pressure and temperature warning lights come on. 30

I don't know what women do.

Understanding the Reading

1. **Thesis** Identify the thesis statement. Does it state why the process is important or useful to readers?

2. **Detail** Why did their customer's car break down? What lesson relating to this story do the authors teach?

3. **Detail** Why is oil so important to a car? What does a car's oil warning light mean when it goes on?
4. **Detail** What problem do the authors associate with gauges?
5. **Detail** What do the authors say is the best way to protect your car?
6. **Visualizing the reading** "Inside the Engine" includes practical advice for keeping your car operating properly. Use the following chart to summarize the how-to advice offered in each of these paragraphs. The first one has been done for you.

Paragraph	How-to Advice
13	Shut the engine off if the oil warning light comes on.
16	
17	
24	
26	
27	
28	

Analyzing the Reading

1. **Audience** Analyze the level of detail in the selection. Is it appropriate for the intended audience, or do the authors include unnecessary technical details? Explain your answer.
2. **Process** What techniques do the authors use to make the process of taking care of one's car interesting and understandable? What level of knowledge and mechanical savvy do the authors assume their readers possess?
3. **Cautions** What potential trouble spots or areas of confusion do the authors identify? Are their suggested solutions easy to understand? Why, or why not?
4. **Techniques** What techniques do the authors use to make technical terms understandable to readers who lack mechanical knowledge?

Evaluating the Reading

1. **Authors' reliability** Are the authors of "Inside the Engine" qualified to give professional car advice? Why, or why not? (Hint: Review any background information included or conduct a quick online search about the authors to help determine whether their expertise includes this area.)

2. **Authors' reliability** Do the authors offer advice about anything outside their realm of expertise? If so, what is it, and do you trust it?

3. **Language** The oil is described as "coursing through the veins of the engine" (para. 7). How does this use of metaphor enhance the process being described?

4. **Language** Evaluate the similes "like a front-loading washing machine" (para. 17) and "like jellybeans on wheels" (para. 21). How effective are they in helping you understand the term or concept being described?

Discussing the Reading

1. Discuss why good car repair advice is hard to find.

2. Have you ever listened to *Car Talk* on National Public Radio? If so, how would you describe the program to someone who has never heard the show? Based on your description, would you say that this essay is typical of how the Magliozzi brothers approach automotive issues on their show?

3. Discuss the authors' attitude toward the increasing complexity of technology. Do you agree with their assessment? Why, or why not?

Writing about the Reading

1. **Essay** Write a how-it-works process analysis essay explaining how a machine that you use every day works. For example, you could explain how the elevator in your building works or how a microwave oven operates. Depending on your level of knowledge about the machine, it may be necessary to do a bit of research. Be sure to include a thesis and an explanation of the steps in the process, using relevant and apppropriate details. Personalize your essay by describing how the item influences your daily life.

2. **Essay** Brainstorm a list of people whom you have gone to for advice. Choose one and write a process analysis essay about seeking advice from this person. For example, you may have sought the help of a guidance counselor when applying to colleges. Describe the process you undertook in identifying whom to approach for help, how you arranged a meeting, any preparation that you did before the meeting, and the type of advice given. Be sure to include a conclusion that explains the process and how the advice ultimately affected you.

3. **Internet research** Visit the *Car Talk* Web site at **www.cartalk.com** or another Web site devoted to car operation, repair, or maintenance. Explore the site and then choose a process that is explained there—for example, how to set your side-view mirrors so that there is no blind spot. In your own words, write a process analysis essay that explains the steps to a group of new drivers. Be sure to define technical terms, and use sensory details and figures of speech to keep your writing lively and interesting.

COMBINING THE PATTERNS

The Warrior's Brain

Andrew Bast has reported for the *New York Times*, the *Village Voice*, and *Newsweek*, where this article first appeared (in November 2010). He currently serves as Web editor of foreign affairs for the Council on Foreign Relations.

Reading Tip

As you read, use one color of highlighting to indicate those sections of the essay that focus on process analysis and another color to identify those that focus on explaining cause-and-effect relationships.

Previewing the Reading

Preview the reading (see pp. 23–24 for guidelines) to get an idea of the specific person the essay focuses on and how he was affected by his wartime experiences.

The Warrior's Brain

Andrew Bast

The worst was the day Brooke Brown came home to find her husband with a shotgun in his mouth. But there had been many bad days since Lance Corporal David Brown had returned from Iraq. Days when he would shake uncontrollably in crowded places, when a family visit to a restaurant would send him on a frantic search for the nearest exit. He couldn't concentrate; he couldn't do his job. After a second deployment, the Marine Corps placed him on leave, then discharged him. Brooke quit her job to care for him and their three children. The bills piled up.

It sounds like another troubling case of post-traumatic stress disorder, or PTSD, the up-to-the-moment diagnosis for the anxiety and depression that has afflicted returning veterans at least since the Napoleonic wars. (In the times of French conquest, it was called nostalgia.) But Brown's case is more complicated. He also suffered a succession of mild seizures that culminated in a devastating grand mal episode[1] that sent him to the hospital covered in his own blood, vomit, and excrement. He had vision problems and excruciating headaches, dating back almost two years to his first deployment, when a mortar attack on his post in Fallujah knocked him to the ground.

Brown, now twenty-three, didn't sustain visible injuries in the attack, but clearly the man who returned from war was not the same as the proud, can-do soldier whom Brooke had kissed and sent off to battle. "Our middle son clings to David; he knows something is wrong," says Brooke, twenty-two. "Our four-year-old doesn't know what caused it, but he knows Daddy's sick and he needs help."

[1] **grand mal episode** A seizure involving convulsions and loss of conciousness.

Continued >

But what kind of help does Brown need? His case perplexed civilian doctors—one of whom suggested the painkiller tramadol for his headaches, which instantly made the seizures worse—as well as the Department of Veterans Affairs. The headaches and seizures suggest the aftereffects of an undiagnosed concussion—or, in the current jargon, mild traumatic brain injury (TBI). But his other symptoms point to PTSD. Or perhaps it's both—and if so, are they reinforcing one another in a vicious cycle? Several federally funded research projects now aim to answer the question of exactly how PTSD might aggravate the long-term effects of brain injuries. Dr. Murray Stein, a psychiatry professor at the University of California, San Diego, who's leading a consortium[2] of scientists at ten clinical trial sites around the country, says that while his team is "agnostic"[3]

> **Doctors suspect the high stress of combat interferes with recovery.**

about what they'll find, "you have to figure they are linked in most people." Brooke is unqualified: She believes the emotional weight of David's best friend's deployment last year with the Second Battalion, Eighth Marines, as part of President Obama's surge in Afghanistan caused one of his worst seizures.

5   If that's the case, Brown may be in the vanguard[4] of a wave of badly wounded warriors for which the military and veterans' medical systems are woefully unprepared. A common estimate inside the military is that 20% of veterans in combat theaters return with some degree of PTSD, although—largely because of the stigma within the military ranks—less than half of those actually seek treatment. Some 2.1 million service members have been deployed to Iraq and Afghanistan, implying more than 400,000 potential cases. While the Pentagon claims to count battlefield concussions with precision, the official figure of 144,453 since 2000 might understate the real number by as much as 40%, according to a study done at the Army's Fort Carson in Colorado. Nobody can accurately estimate how many veterans might be walking around with both.

The interrelationship between PTSD and TBI is still mostly unexplored. The same event may give rise to both, and the symptoms overlap and shade into one another. "You may have been injured, may have lost a buddy during an attack," says Colonel John Bradley, head of psychiatry at Walter Reed Army Medical Center. "Traumatic brain injury has both a physical and psychological component, and so does PTSD." After a concussion, one is almost certain to have headaches, but headaches are also common among people with a mental-health disorder. Concussions cause trouble sleeping—and so can PTSD. Difficulty concentrating is common to both. "It's very difficult to determine if it's a psychological problem or the results of an organic brain injury," says Terry Schell, a behavioral scientist at the RAND Corporation.

One problem is that military medicine is coming late to the science of TBI, which until very recently was mostly studied in the context of car crashes and football injuries. The definition of a concussion is injury to the brain caused by a blow to the head, typically resulting in headache,

---

[2] **consortium** A group of individuals or institutions with a shared purpose.
[3] **agnostic** Holding none of differing opinions on an area of study.
[4] **vanguard** At the forefront.

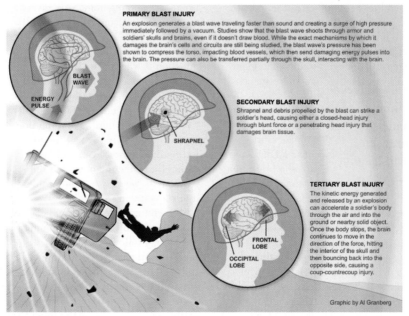

PRIMARY BLAST INJURY
An explosion generates a blast wave traveling faster than sound and creating a surge of high pressure immediately followed by a vacuum. Studies show that the blast wave shoots through armor and soldiers' skulls and brains, even if it doesn't draw blood. While the exact mechanisms by which it damages the brain's cells and circuits are still being studied, the blast wave's pressure has been shown to compress the torso, impacting blood vessels, which then send damaging energy pulses into the brain. The pressure can also be transferred partially through the skull, interacting with the brain.

BLAST WAVE

ENERGY PULSE

SECONDARY BLAST INJURY
Shrapnel and debris propelled by the blast can strike a soldier's head, causing either a closed-head injury through blunt force or a penetrating head injury that damages brain tissue.

SHRAPNEL

TERTIARY BLAST INJURY
The kinetic energy generated and released by an explosion can accelerate a soldier's body through the air and into the ground or nearby solid object. Once the body stops, the brain continues to move in the direction of the force, hitting the interior of the skull and then bouncing back into the opposite side, causing a coup-countrecoup injury.

FRONTAL LOBE

OCCIPITAL LOBE

Graphic by Al Granberg

Hurt Inside the Head

memory loss, and general confusion. In most civilian cases, the prescription is rest, and the brain heals in as little as a week.

But on the battlefield, concussions are more vexing. According to the Department of Veterans Affairs, symptoms such as vision, memory, and speech problems; dizziness; depression; and anxiety last far longer in men and women returning from combat. Doctors suspect the high-stress environment of combat interferes with recovery. So does the desert heat of Iraq, "which can make the effects of a concussion worse," says David Hovda, director of the UCLA Brain Injury Research Center. There is no specific test for concussion, although the military is funding research seeking biomarkers[5]

[5] **biomarker** An indicator of a particular biological condition or process.

that could give an accurate diagnosis in the field. Currently, if an injured fighter reports symptoms that match the concussion watch list, he or she is pulled from action for twenty-four hours of observation. In seemingly mild cases, that may be the only treatment. The standard, says Brooke, has been "if you ain't bleeding, you ain't hurt."

At the same time, though, civilian researchers are learning more about the effects of sustained head trauma, in athletes in particular. Repeated concussions give rise to a condition called chronic traumatic encephalopathy, which may appear ten to fifteen years later and is linked to Parkinson's disease, dementia, and a devastating neurological condition resembling Lou Gehrig's disease. Depression and suicidal thoughts also seem associated with this condition, as well as with PTSD. A Pentagon report in August put

Continued >

the military suicide rate at one death every thirty-six hours.

10   What researchers have discovered so far is not reassuring. Animal models suggest that a head trauma can make one more susceptible to PTSD.

> **Animal models suggest a head trauma can make one more susceptible to PTSD.**

"Minor traumatic brain injury does not necessarily cause PTSD, but it puts the brain in a biochemical and metabolic state that enhances the chances of acquiring post-traumatic stress disorder," says UCLA's Hovda, who serves on a civilian task force studying the problem for the military. On the agenda for the next meeting, in December, is the question of special treatment for patients with both PTSD and TBI. Hovda also played a key role in the development of the National Intrepid Center of Excellence, a military medical facility in Bethesda, Maryland, devoted to the care of returning vets who suffer from PTSD and/or head trauma. "When they get to Bethesda, or get home, a lot of times individuals will be suffering from symptoms related to these multiple concussions," he says. "They don't understand that it's related to a brain injury, and they become very depressed and confused."

There's another unsettling aspect to Brown's case, of course: that PTSD and TBI may not be the only culprits in his condition. Headaches present for a large number of illnesses. And depression, anxiety, and trouble sleeping? Those are often the result of living with an unexplainable illness. In reality, the troops are coming home with myriad medical issues, some new, like TBI; some, like PTSD, as old as war itself; and some a hybrid of the two. The question is whether we have the tools and treatments to figure out which is which. At the moment, those tools are few, and they're not terribly useful. "What has been hard is that [on brain injuries] people really feel we are letting them down," General Peter Chiarelli, vice chief of staff of the Army, told *Newsweek*. "The problem is that we just don't know."

Brown finally found some peace of mind thanks to Lieutenant Colonel Tim Maxwell, a fellow Marine, who was pierced in the skull with shrapnel in Iraq and later lost his leg to mortar fire. Maxwell has established a quiet network of wounded warriors and maintains a Web site on the topic, SemperMax.com. Earlier this year he heard of Brown's struggle and helped him reenlist in the Marines and be admitted to the TBI ward at the National Naval Medical Center in Bethesda. After being treated there for four weeks in August, Brown is back at Camp Lejeune awaiting a medical discharge. "I spend most of my time over at the wounded-warrior tent doing rehab," he says. He's taking Topamax, a drug usually prescribed to epileptics to stave off seizures, and it seems to be effective, despite the side effects. "He's lost his speech for thirty minutes a couple of times," Brooke says, but he hasn't had any more grand mal seizures. His wife is fighting for him at every turn. "I'm going to stand by my man," she said this August. She stiffened her spine. "He stood for me over in Iraq. The least I can do is stand by him now."

Understanding the Reading

1. **Thesis** Bast suggests his thesis in paragraphs 4 and 5. How would you summarize this thesis?

2. **Meaning** Why does Bast say it is so difficult to make an accurate diagnosis for former soldiers with symptoms like David Brown's? What evidence does he offer?

3. **Meaning** In paragraph 8, Bast writes that battlefield concussions are "more vexing" than civilian concussions. Why is this so?

4. **Vocabulary** Using context clues (p. 34), write a brief definition of each of the following words as it is used in the reading, checking a dictionary if necessary: *stigma* (5), *biochemical* (10), *metabolic* (10), and *myriad* (11).

Analyzing the Reading

1. **Purpose and audience** "The Warrior's Brain" was originally published in *Newsweek*. What does this tell you about Bast's purpose and audience?

2. **Combining patterns** Where in the essay does Bast use process analysis? Where does he detail a relationship between cause and effect?

3. **Fact versus opinion** Paragraph 10 opens with what might be considered Bast's opinion. How does he go about suggesting that the statement is a fact?

4. **Tone** Bast poses questions twice, in paragraph 4 and again in paragraph 11. What is the purpose of these questions in an essentially factual report?

5. **Introduction and conclusion** How are the opening and concluding paragraphs linked? What is the effect of this linkage?

Evaluating the Reading

1. **Technique** Bast opens with a highly dramatic image. How do you respond to his opening sentence?

2. **Evidence** In paragraph 5, Bast provides statistical evidence of the incidence of PTSD and TBI among combat veterans. How convincing do you find his sources for these statistics?

3. **Assumptions** One of Bast's central points is that the "interrelationship between PTSD and TBI is still mostly unexplored" (para. 6). What is his underlying assumption in the essay? Do you agree with this assumption?

4. **Quotation** Bast includes quotation and paraphrase throughout the essay, both from Brown and his wife and from various medical and military experts. How effective do you find his use of quotation and paraphrase?

5. **Visuals** How effectively does the diagram "Hurt Inside the Head" explain the process of traumatic brain injury? How could it be improved? Does anything need clarification or explanation?

6. **Visuals** What is the purpose of the diagram that accompanies the reading?

Discussing the Reading

1. Why do you think the relationship between PTSD and TBI has been studied so little? Base your response on both what Bast suggests and your own conclusions.

2. Bast writes in paragraph 5 that PTSD is greatly underreported by returning veterans "largely because of the stigma within the military ranks" and in paragraph 8 that concussions among military personnel often aren't treated because of the standard "'if you ain't bleeding, you ain't hurt.'" How do you respond to these observations?

3. Write a brief response to this essay, starting with "After reading the essay, I felt _____." Share your response with classmates, and discuss similarities and differences among the responses.

Writing about the Reading

1. **Essay** Both Bast and William Saletan in "Gabby Giffords: Portrait of a Brain Being Rebuilt" (p. 337) write about a process of gradual recovery. Think of a time when you underwent a process of personal recovery, whether from an illness, an accident, an emotional blow, or even an addiction. In an essay, chart the process of your recovery. (Hint: Before drafting, be sure to outline the specific stages you can define in terms of the recovery process.) You might relate the process from your own perspective using the first person or use the second person *you* to suggest how readers could experience such a recovery themselves.

2. **Essay** Rewrite the process of David Brown's ongoing recovery from either his perspective or that of his wife, Brooke. (Hint: To start, you'll need to reread Bast's essay carefully to determine a chronology, beginning with Brown's initial deployment and injury and ending with his time at Camp Lejeune awaiting discharge.)

3. **Combining patterns** Process analysis often involves cause-and-effect analysis when steps in the process directly result in subsequent steps and, of course, in the ultimate outcome or goal. Write an essay analyzing a process familiar to you in which you emphasize this cause-and-effect aspect.

◫ TEXTBOOK

Secrets for Surviving College

Saundra K. Ciccarelli is a professor of psychology at Gulf Coast State College, where she has taught for more than thirty years. **J. Noland White** is an associate professor of psychology at Georgia College, Georgia's Public Liberal Arts University. The following selection from the introduction to their textbook *Psychology* reflects their scholarly interest in the effectiveness of incorporating technology in and out of the college classroom to facilitate student learning.

Reading Tip

As you read, highlight each of the stages in the process the authors recommend, and briefly summarize the whole process when you've finished reading. Then evaluate which steps are likely to be most helpful to you.

Previewing the Reading

Preview the reading (see pp. 23–24 for guidelines), and then list the five main stages recommended for reading textbooks.

Secrets for Surviving College
Saundra K. Ciccarelli and J. Noland White

Reading Textbooks: Textbooks Are Not Meatloaf

There are two common mistakes that people make in regard to reading a textbook. The first mistake is simple: Many people don't bother to read the textbook before going to the lecture that will cover that material. Trying to get anything out of a lecture without reading the material first is like trying to find a new, unfamiliar place without using a map or any kind of directions. It's easy to get lost. This is especially true because of the assumption that most instructors make when planning their lectures: They assume that the students have already read the assignment. The instructors then use the lecture to go into detail on the information the students supposedly got from the reading. If the students haven't done the reading, the instructor's lecture isn't going to make a whole lot of sense.

The second mistake that most people make when reading textbook material is to try to read it the same way they would read a novel: They start at the first page and read continuously. With a novel, it's easy to do this because the plot is usually interesting and people want to know what happens next, so they keep reading. It isn't necessary to remember every little detail—all they need to remember are the main plot points. One could say that a novel is like meatloaf—some meaty

Continued >

parts with lots of filler. Meatloaf can be eaten quickly, without even chewing for very long.

With a textbook, the material may be interesting but not in the same way that a novel is interesting. A textbook is a big, thick steak—all meat, no filler. Just as a steak has to be chewed to be enjoyed and to be useful to the body, textbook material has to be "chewed" with the mind. You have to read slowly, paying attention to every morsel of meaning.

So how do you do that? Probably one of the best-known reading methods is called SQ3R, first used by F. P. Robinson in a book called *Effective Study* (1970). The first letters S-Q-R-R-R stand for:

SURVEY

Look at the chapter you've been assigned to read.

- Take a look at the outline at the beginning of the chapter or whatever opening questions, learning objectives, or other material the author has chosen to let you, the reader, know what the chapter is about.
- Flip through the chapter and read the headings of each section, and look at the tables, figures, graphs, and cartoons to get an idea about the kinds of things that you will be learning.
- Finally, quickly read through the chapter summary if there is one.

It might sound like it takes too much time to do this, but you should just be skimming at this point—a couple of minutes is all it should take. Why do this at all? Surveying the chapter, or "previewing" it, as some experts call it, helps you form a framework in your head around which you can organize the information in the chapter when you read it in detail. . . . [O]rganization is . . . one of the main ways to improve your memory for information. Think of it this way: As mentioned earlier, if you are going to drive to a new place, it's helpful to have a road map to give you an idea of what's up ahead. Surveying the chapter is giving yourself a "road map" for the material in the chapter.

QUESTION

After previewing the chapter, read the heading for the first section. *Just* the first section! Try to think of a question based on this heading that the section should answer as you read. For example, in Chapter One [of *Psychology*] there's a section titled "Pavlov, Watson, and the Dawn of Behaviorism." You could ask yourself, "What did Pavlov and Watson do for psychology?" or "What is behaviorism?" Some textbooks even include questions at the start of many sections. In this text, there is a list of learning objectives for the key concepts in the chapter in the form of questions that can be used with the SQ3R method. There are also student questions that can serve the same purpose. These questions, which are based on

5

Table 1   Study Tips for Different Learning Styles

Visual/Verbal	Use different colors of highlighter for different sections of information in text or notes. Use flash cards of main points or key terms. Write out key information in whole sentences or phrases in your own words. When looking at diagrams, write out a description. Use "sticky" notes to remind yourself of key terms and information, and put them in the notebook or text or on a mirror that you use frequently. Visualize spellings of words or facts to be remembered. Rewrite things from memory. Study alone in a quiet place.
Visual / Nonverbal	Make flash cards with pictures or diagrams to aid recall of key concepts. Make charts and diagrams and sum up information in tables. Use different highlighter colors for different information but highlight symbols and diagrams as well as key terms and ideas. Visualize charts, diagrams, and figures. Redraw things from memory. Study alone in a quiet place.
Auditory	Join or form a study group or find a study partner so that you can discuss concepts and ideas. Talk out loud while studying or into a tape recorder that you can play back later. Make speeches. Tape the lectures (with permission). Take notes on the lecture sparingly, using the tape to fill in parts that you might have missed. Read notes or text material into a tape recorder or get study materials on tape and play back while driving or doing other chores. When learning something new, state the information in your own words out loud or to a study partner.
Tactile / Kinesthetic	Sit near the front of the classroom and take notes by jotting down key terms and making pictures or charts to help you remember what you are hearing. When you study, read information out loud while walking back and forth. Study with a friend. While exercising, listen to tapes that you have made containing important information. Write out key concepts on a large board or poster. Make flash cards, using different colors and diagrams, and lay them out on a large surface. Practice putting them in order. Make a three-dimensional model. Spend extra time in the lab. Go to outside areas such as a museum or historical site to gain information. Trace letters and words to remember key facts. Use musical rhythms as memory aids, putting information to a rhyme or a tune.

Continued >

the authors' years of hearing and answering similar questions from students in the classroom, will be in gray type in the margin, often with the picture of a typical student who is asking the question. Now when you read the section, you aren't *just* reading—you're reading to *find an answer*. That makes the material much easier to remember later on.

READ

Now read the section, looking for the answer to your question. As you read, take notes by making an outline of the main points and terms in the section. This is another area where people make a big mistake. They assume that using a highlighter to mark words and phrases is as good as writing notes. One of the author's former students is conducting research on the difference between highlighting and note-taking, and her preliminary findings are clear: Students who write their own notes during the reading of a text or while listening to a lecture scored significantly higher on their exam grades than students who merely used a highlighter on the text (Boyd & Peeler, 2004). Highlighting requires no real mental effort (no "chewing," in other words), but writing the words down yourself requires you to read the words in depth and understand them. . . .

RECITE

It may sound silly, but reciting *out loud* what you can remember from the section you've just read is another good way to process the information more deeply and completely. How many times have you thought you understood something, only to find that when you tried to tell it to someone, you didn't understand it at all? Recitation forces you to put the information in your own words, just as writing it down in the form of notes does. Writing it down accesses your visual memory; saying it out loud gives you an auditory memory for the same information. If you have ever learned something well by teaching it to someone else, you already know the value of recitation. If you feel self-conscious about talking to yourself, talk into a tape recorder—it makes a great way to review while traveling in the car.

Now repeat the Question, Read, and Recite instructions for each 10 section, taking a few minutes' break after every two or three sections. Why take a break? There's a process that has to take place in your brain when you are trying to form a permanent memory for information, and that process takes a little bit of time. When you take a break every ten to twenty minutes, you are giving your brain time to do this process. Doing this avoids a common problem in reading texts in which you find yourself reading the same sentence over and over again because your brain is too overloaded with trying to remember what you just read to continue reading.

RECALL/REVIEW

Finally, you've finished reading the entire chapter. If you've used the guidelines listed previously, you'll only have to read the chapter in this depth once instead of having to read it over and over throughout the semester and just before exams. Once you've read the chapter, take a few minutes to try to remember as much of what you learned while reading it as you can. A good way to do this is to take any practice quizzes that might be available, either in your text or in a student workbook that goes with the text. Many publishers have Web sites for their textbooks that have practice quizzes available online. If there are no quizzes, read the chapter summary in detail, making sure that you understand everything in it. If there's anything that's confusing, go back to that section in the chapter and read again until you understand it.

Reading textbooks in this way means that you only have to read them once. When it comes time for the final exam, all you will have to do is carefully review your notes to be ready for the exam—you won't have to read the entire textbook all over again. What a time-saver!

Understanding the Reading

1. **Textbook reading** Write a summary of the five stages described in the reading, using a sentence or two for each.

2. **Language** According to the author, why are novels like "meatloaf" while textbooks are like "steak." How is "eating" the two different?

3. **Purpose** What is the purpose of each of the five stages in this process? Why is each important?

4. **Process** This reading process obviously requires a good deal of time. According to the author, how is it ultimately a time-saver?

5. **Organizing information** Create a chart, table, or map of this process that you can refer to as you read textbooks for other courses.

Analyzing the Reading

1. **Study questions** Make a list of five questions that could be used as a practice quiz for this reading during the final stage of "Recall/Review" (para. 11).

2. **Applying the reading** Follow the advice in paragraph 9 ("Recite"). Reread one section of the essay, and then try "reciting *out loud* what you can remember" from that section. How might doing so help you remember the information?

3. **Visuals** Why did the authors include Table 1? Explain its purpose and how it relates to other advice offered in the reading.

Evaluating the Reading

1. **Strategy** How useful do you find the process as presented here? Do you think each stage is explained in enough detail to answer most students' questions?

2. **Writer's voice** How do you respond to the way the authors write to you, the reader? How is the authors' approach different from that employed in textbooks in other subject areas?

3. **Argument** This textbook excerpt is essentially an argument for a particular method of study. Do you find it convincing? Explain your answer.

4. **Visuals** How useful is Table 1 to you? What additional information do you need to use the table to help you study?

Discussing the Reading

1. Do you agree that in most cases instructors expect students to have read the textbook assignment before class? Do college instructors generally adhere to what's covered in the text?

2. In your experience so far, how different are college textbooks from textbooks you studied while in high school? Do they seem to require a different reading process?

3. What is the best advice you take away from this reading? What might you actually apply to your own study habits?

Writing about the Reading

1. **Response paper** Write a letter to the authors of this reading, first explaining problems you experience with textbook reading and then detailing whether the advice they offer addresses your concerns.

2. **Essay** You do not study each subject the same way; you study differently for a math course than for a literature class, for example. This selection offers general advice for all textbook reading. The SQ3R method could be adapted by adding or deleting steps to suit specific disciplines. Choose a discipline and write an essay explaining how you would adapt the SQ3R method to suit it.

3. **Internet research** The SQ3R method of reading detailed in this selection has been interpreted and explained in various ways. First read several different articles about SQ3R online, using "SQ3R" as a search term. Then write an essay analyzing how the process described in these articles relates to the selection reproduced here.

Writing Your Own Process Analysis Essay

Now that you have learned about the major characteristics, structure, and purposes of a process analysis essay, you know everything necessary to write your own process analysis essay. In this section you will read a student's process analysis essay and get advice on finding ideas, drafting your essay, and revising and editing it. You may want to use the essay prompts in "Readings for Practice, Ideas for Writing" (p. 345) or choose your own topic.

A Student Model Process Analysis Essay

Aurora Gilbert wrote the following essay in response to an assignment that asked her to explain a process that she had mastered. As you read the essay, consider whether the steps described in the essay clearly explain the process of planning a fund-raising event.

Title: Gilbert identifies process

The Pleasures and Particulars of Philanthropy: How to Publicize Your Fund-Raising Event

Aurora Gilbert

Introduction: Gilbert explains importance of topic

Thesis: identifies steps in process

One of the most useful and enjoyable skills someone can learn in college is that of organizing and publicizing for a philanthropic event. Putting on such an event certainly requires hard work and dedication, yet the enthusiasm it spreads in your community and support it generates for your charity are invaluable rewards. For the occasion to be successful, it is important to start planning about a month before the event, following a four-step process that includes settling on basic details of the event, gathering the materials for the event, fund-raising, and publicizing the event. In describing these steps, I will discuss an annual all-you-can-eat cupcake event, sponsored by my service group, which raises money for a summer camp for the children of parents affected by cancer.

Body paragraphs

Step 1: Name the event, pick a date, and communicate these to group members. Topic sentence previews step discussed

The first step in putting on an event is taking care of the basic details: the name and the date. Choose a name that is simple yet appealing and informative. Make sure it is catchy and at the same time refers to the main attraction of the event. We chose the name Eat Your Heart Out because it utilizes a simple, well-known phrase to indicate that our event centers around both food ("eat") and charity ("heart"). At the same time that you name the event, finalize the date, location, and time, and notify all members of your group of these details. For instance, in early September, an email announced to my service group that Eat Your Heart Out was to be held on October 10th at Artopolis Espresso from 8 to 11 p.m.

Transitions help readers keep track of process.
Step 2: Gather materials.

Next, begin gathering the materials, which include T-shirts and raffle prizes, that you will need to publicize and run the event. Do this about three and a half weeks before the event; in this time, your committee must design and order publicity T-shirts and ask members to start collecting raffle prizes for the event. Like the event name, T-shirts must be simple yet informative. Design your T-shirts in a style that reflects the tone of your event and make sure to include the names of your organization and event, as well as the event's logo.

Specific details about T-shirts

Our shirts, for example, were emblazoned with a silver heart and the phrase "Eat Your Heart Out" in white and blue script on the front; the back read "Philanthropy 2011" in white script. The sleek black of the shirts implied professionalism while the aesthetically pleasing detail promised entertainment and satisfaction.

Step 3: Solicit raffle donations for fund-raising efforts.

If your event will include a raffle, you should begin gathering prizes at the same time that you design your T-shirts. By selling raffle tickets for fun prizes, many organizations entice people to attend a charity event and donate. At this time, you must require all members of your organization to begin soliciting businesses

Detailed advice for complex stage in process

to donate these prizes. Among these donations, try to receive a particularly exciting one that gives people an incentive to buy raffle tickets; for Eat Your Heart Out, we received an iPad that we advertised constantly in the weeks leading up to our event. Create and distribute a flyer that outlines the details and purpose of the event that members can give to businesses. This flyer should display the logo and name of your event, the date, location, and time, raffle ticket prices, a paragraph about planned activities, and a description of your featured charity. Make sure to play up the importance of the charity in order to ensure that the businesses know they are donating to a good cause.

Step 4: Publicize event in three substeps.
Substep 1: initial publicity
Effective example illustrates this stage

Publicizing your event in several stages is key to having a well-attended, successful event. Two weeks before the event, your group should begin publicizing the event and selling tickets. One great way to reach students on a college campus and maximize attendance is to create a Facebook event and start selling tickets to prospective attendees. Use your event name as the title of the Facebook page and upload an image of your logo. Include the same information that you provided to businesses. Invite all organization members to "attend" the Facebook event and

5

encourage them to invite all their Facebook friends to attend as well. At the same time, create tickets with the event name, date, location, and charity printed on them and distribute them among group members. Require each member to sell a certain number of tickets (for Eat Your Heart Out, it was three), and ask them to generate enthusiasm for the event in the weeks leading up to it.

Substep 2: Distribute flyers and display banners.

Everything starts to come together one week before the event; your group must post its flyer around campus, create and display a banner advertising the event, collect raffle prizes from the businesses donating them, and have members sign up for time slots to staff the event. The publicity flyers must be simpler than the raffle flyers and more aesthetically pleasing; make sure all the necessary information is included and presented in a way that will excite and motivate people to attend your event. The flyer for Eat

Detailed examples

Your Heart Out consisted of our logo and the information from the tickets in a creative font arranged neatly on the page. We enticed potential attendees by emphasizing the cupcakes, raffle prizes, and charitable aspect of the event, using a larger font size for "All you can eat cupcakes for only $5!!!" "Raffle GRAND PRIZE: iPad," and "All proceeds go to the Camp Kesem Chapter at Columbia University."

Reminder of other important, simultaneous tasks

Each group member should be assigned a dorm or building in which to post flyers within one day of his or her assignment. Your group should also create a banner to display in a public place on campus; like the other publicity material, this banner should be informative, easy to read, and pleasing to the eye. All raffle prizes donated by businesses should be collected by this time, and a spreadsheet should be sent out to the group by email that allows members to sign up for time slots during which they will staff the event. It is important to require each member to sign up for at least one slot to ensure that the work is distributed evenly.

Substep 3: final push

In the four days before the event comes the last extreme publicity push. Four days before the event, all group members must wear their event shirts on campus and change their Facebook profile pictures to the event's logo; this will remind the campus of your upcoming event and inspire enthusiasm and anticipation in your prospective attendees. Remind your members to keep selling tickets and inviting all their friends to the event in the following days.

Step 5: Hold fundraiser (the result is a successful event).

The last step is to hold your event. On the day of the event, members should wear their shirts again and post Facebook statuses linking viewers to the event. Have your group meet early to set up equipment and decorations, make sure each member is present for his or her time slot, have fun, and watch all your careful planning pay off with a great event.

Conclusion: emphasizes importance of process

While planning a fund-raising event can be time-consuming and stressful, using these steps will make it both successful and rewarding. There is little that surpasses the joy and satisfaction one can gain from arranging an event that not only provides entertainment for those involved but also generates support and funds for a worthy cause.

Responding to Gilbert's Essay

1. Do you think the essay's introduction helps engage readers in wanting to learn about the fund-raising process? Why, or why not?

2. From the start the writer uses as an example of the process a fund-raising event her own campus organization sponsored. Do you find this an effective strategy throughout the essay?

3. Do the steps of the process as the writer presents them follow clearly from the thesis?

4. Do you find the level of detail adequate? Could you follow the instructions here to create a successful fund-raising event?

5. How well do you think the two final paragraphs conclude this process analysis?

Finding Ideas for Your Process Analysis Essay

Look for ideas to write about *as you read*. Record your ideas and impressions as marginal annotations. Think about why you want or need to understand the process. Consider situations in which you can apply the information. Consider also how other processes are the same and/or different from the one in the essay. If metaphors or analogies come to mind, such as the similarity of a dream catcher to a spider's web, make a note of them. Finally, evaluate the usefulness and completeness of the information provided.

Choosing a Process for Your Essay

The first step is to select a process to write about. Be sure to keep the following tips in mind.

- For a how-to essay, choose a process that you can visualize or actually perform as you write. Keep the object or equipment nearby for easy reference. In explaining how to scuba dive, for example, it may be helpful to have your scuba equipment in front of you.

- For a how-it-works essay, choose a topic about which you have background knowledge or for which you can find adequate information. Unless you are experienced in woodworking, for example, do not try to explain how certain stains produce different effects on various kinds of wood.

- Choose a topic that is useful and of interest to readers. For example, unless you can find a way to make an essay about how to do the laundry interesting, do not write about it.

Developing and Supporting Your Thesis

Once you have chosen a process to write about, the next step is to develop a working thesis. As noted earlier, the thesis of a process analysis essay tells readers *why* the process is important, beneficial, or relevant to them (see p. 335). In a how-to essay on jogging, for instance, your thesis might be "Jogging, an excellent aerobic activity, provides both exercise and a chance for solitary reflection." Note how the benefits of the activity are clearly stated in the thesis statement.

Considering your particular audience is especially important in developing a thesis for a process analysis because what may be of interest or importance to one audience may be of little interest to another audience.

Listing the Steps and Gathering Details

Once you are satisfied with your working thesis statement, it is time to list the steps in the process and to gather appropriate and interesting details. You will probably need to do additional prewriting at this point to generate ideas and details that help explain the process. Use the following suggestions.

1. **List the steps in the process as they occur to you, keeping these questions in mind.**
   - What separate actions are involved?
   - What steps are obvious to me but may not be obvious to someone unfamiliar with the process?
   - What steps, if omitted, will lead to problems or failure?
2. **Record the process aloud, and then take notes as you play back the recording.**
3. **Discuss the process with classmates to see what kinds of details they need to know about it.**
4. **Generate details for the steps you are describing by doing additional prewriting or conducting research online or in the library.** Make sure you have sufficient detail about unfamiliar terms, equipment, and trouble spots. If you are explaining how to hike in the Grand Canyon, for example, you might include details about carrying sufficient water and dressing in layers.

Drafting Your Process Analysis Essay

Once you have an effective thesis and enough details to explain the steps in the process, it is time to organize your ideas and draft the essay. For a process that involves fewer than ten steps, you can usually arrange the steps in chronological order, devoting one paragraph to each. However, for a process with ten or more steps, divide the steps into three or four major groups.

After organizing the steps, you are ready to write a first draft. Use the following guidelines.

1. **Write an effective introduction.** The introduction usually presents the thesis statement and includes necessary background information. It should also capture the readers' interest and focus their attention on the process. For some essays, you may want to explain that the process you are describing is related to other processes and ideas (for example, the process of jogging is related to running). For a lengthy or complex process, consider including an overview of the steps or providing a brief introductory list.

2. **Include reasons for the steps.** Unless the reason is obvious, explain why each step or group of steps is important and necessary. In explaining why a step is important, consider including a brief anecdote as an example.

3. **Consider using graphics.** For a process involving many complex steps, consider using a drawing or diagram to help readers visualize each step. Remember, however, that a graphic is no substitute for a clearly written explanation.

4. **Consider adding headings.** Headings divide the body of a lengthy or complicated process analysis into manageable segments. They also call attention to the main topics and signal readers that a change in topic is about to occur.

5. **Use transitions.** To avoid writing a process analysis that sounds monotonous, use transitions such as *before*, *next*, and *finally*.

6. **Use an appropriate tone.** Your tone should be appropriate for your audience and purpose. In some situations a direct, matter-of-fact tone is appropriate; at other times an emotional or humorous tone may be suitable.

7. **Write a satisfying conclusion.** Make sure you remind readers of the importance of the process or explain situations in which it would be useful.

Review "How Is a Process Analysis Essay Structured?" (pp. 334–35) for the characteristics of each part of a process analysis essay.

Revising Your Process Analysis Essay

If possible, wait at least a day before rereading and revising your draft. As you reread, concentrate on the organization and your ideas, not on grammar or mechanics. Use the flowchart in Figure 13.3 to guide your analysis.

Figure 13.3 Revising a Process Analysis Essay

QUESTIONS	REVISION STRATEGIES

1. Thesis Is the importance of the process clear? *No* →

- Consider why readers want or need to know this process and its importance. Incorporate the answer into your thesis statement.

 Yes

2. Organization Are the steps of the process in chronological, or another logical, order? Is the order clear? *No* →

- Use your graphic organizer or outline to determine if any steps are out of order.
- Visualize or perform the process to discover the best order in which to do it.
- Rearrange the steps into the right order.
- Add transitions if necessary.

 Yes

3. Background information Is it sufficient? Have you provided an overview of the process, if needed? *No* →

- Give an example of a situation in which the process might be used.
- Explain that related processes and ideas depend on the process.

 Yes

4. Unfamiliar or technical terms Is each term clearly defined? *No* →

- Ask a classmate to read your draft and identify any missing or unclear definitions.
- Add or revise definitions as needed.

 Yes

5. Equipment Have you described all necessary equipment? Will it all be familiar to readers? *No* →

- Mention equipment you have overlooked.
- Describe potentially unfamiliar equipment.

 Yes

6. Key details Have you included an appropriate level of detail for your readers? *No* →

- Add or delete background information, definitions of technical terms, or other details.

 Yes

7. Potential difficulties For a how-to essay, have you anticipated all likely trouble spots? Are these sections clear and reassuring? *No* →

- Add more detail about critical steps.
- Add warnings about confusing or difficult steps.
- Offer advice on what to do if things go wrong.

 Yes

8. Introduction and conclusion Is each effective? *No* →

- Revise your introduction and conclusion so that they meet the guidelines given in Chapter 6, pages 126–30.

Editing and Proofreading Your Essay

The last step is to check your revised essay for errors in grammar, spelling, punctuation, and mechanics. In addition, be sure to look for errors that you tend to make in any writing assignments, whether for this class or another situation. As you edit and proofread your process analysis essay, watch out for two grammatical errors in particular: comma splices and shifts in verb mood.

1. **Avoid comma splices.** A comma splice occurs when two independent clauses are joined only by a comma. To correct comma splices, do the following.

   Add a coordinating conjunction (*and, but, for, nor, or, so,* or *yet*) after the comma.

   ▶ The first step in flower arranging is to choose an attractive container, *but* the container should not be the focal point of the arrangement.
   ^

   Change the comma to a semicolon.

   ▶ Following signs is one way to navigate a busy airport, looking for a map is another.
   ; ^

   Divide the sentence into two sentences.

   ▶ To place a long-distance call using a credit card, first dial 0 and the ten-digit number, next punch in your credit card number and PIN.
   . Next ^

   Subordinate one clause to the other.

   ▶ *After you have placed* Place the pill on the cat's tongue, hold its mouth closed, rubbing its chin ^ until it swallows the pill.

2. **Avoid shifts in verb mood.** A verb can have three *moods*: the indicative mood (used for ordinary statements and to ask questions), the imperative mood (used for orders, advice, and directions), and the subjunctive mood (used for statements contrary to fact or for wishes and recommendations). When writing a process analysis, avoid switching between the indicative and imperative moods.

   ▶ The firefighters told the third-grade class about procedures to follow if a fire occurred in their school. They emphasized that children should leave the building quickly. Also, *children should* move at least 100 feet away ^ from the building.

Chapter 14

Comparison and Contrast: Showing Similarities and Differences

Quick Start: Study this photograph of a young man who enjoys watching a basketball game on TV. Think about how watching a sport on TV is similar to and different from actually playing the sport. Make two lists — one of the similarities and one of the differences. Base your lists on basketball or on some other sport. You can include details about the degree of physical activity, nature of interaction with others, setting, emotions, and so on. Then write a paragraph comparing the experiences of playing a sport and watching it on television.

What Is Comparison and Contrast?

As you discovered in writing your paragraph in response to the Quick Start prompt, using **comparison and contrast** involves looking at both similarities and differences. For example, when you compare and contrast two used cars, you might consider how they are similar in terms of size, body type, and gas mileage and how they are different in terms of price, color, and engine size. There are many occasions to use comparison and contrast in writing in college and on the job. For instance, for a course in criminal justice, an instructor might ask students to compare organized crime in three countries: Italy, Japan, and Russia. On the job, a computer technician for a pharmaceutical firm may have to compare and contrast several notebook computers and recommend one the company should purchase.

There are two basic types of comparison-and-contrast essays.

- A **subject-by-subject essay** describes the key points or characteristics of one subject before moving on to those of the other subject.
- A **point-by-point essay** moves back and forth between two subjects, comparing or contrasting them on the basis of several key points.

When writers use comparison and contrast, they consider subjects with characteristics in common, examining similarities, differences, or both. Whether used as the primary pattern of development or alongside another pattern, comparison and contrast can help writers achieve their purpose and make a clear point about their subjects.

Comparison and contrast does the following.

1. It has a clear purpose.
2. It considers subjects that can be compared.
3. It fairly examines similarities, differences, or both.
4. It makes a point.
5. It considers a sufficient number of significant characteristics and details.

1. Comparison and Contrast Has a Clear Purpose

A comparison-and-contrast essay usually has one of three purposes: *to express ideas, to inform,* or *to persuade.* In an essay about playing virtual and actual sports, the purpose could be to express your ideas about the subject based on your experiences with Wii or Kinect and actual sports. Alternatively, the purpose could be to inform readers who are going to play either form of the sport, explaining what they can expect in each case. Finally, the purpose could be to persuade readers that playing the Wii or Kinect form of a sport is convenient, accessible, and entertaining.

2. Comparison and Contrast Considers Subjects That Can Be Compared

You have probably heard the familiar expression "You can't compare apples and oranges." Although it is overused, the cliché makes a useful point about comparisons: You cannot compare two things that have nothing in common. Of course, we *can* compare apples and oranges because they are both fruits—so we can compare them on characteristics such as nutritional value. When making a comparison, then, a writer needs to choose subjects that have some *basis of comparison*—that is, one or more characteristics on which they can reasonably be compared.

3. Comparison and Contrast Fairly Examines Similarities, Differences, or Both

Depending on their purpose, writers using comparison and contrast may focus on similarities, differences, or both. In an essay intended to *persuade* readers that performers Beyoncé Knowles and Jennifer Lopez have much in common in terms of talent and cultural influence, the writer would focus on similarities—hit records, millions of fans, and parts in movies. However, an essay intended to *inform* readers about the singers would probably cover both similarities and differences, discussing the singers' different childhoods or singing styles.

An essay focusing on similarities often mentions a few differences, usually in the introduction, to let readers know that the writer is aware of the differences. Conversely, an essay that focuses on differences might mention a few similarities.

Whether you focus on similarities, differences, or both in an essay, you should strive to treat your subjects fairly. Relevant information should not be purposely omitted to show one subject in a more favorable light. In an essay about Knowles and Lopez, for instance, you should not leave out information about Lopez's charity work in an effort to make Knowles appear to be the nicer person.

4. Comparison and Contrast Makes a Point

Regardless of the purpose of a comparison-and-contrast essay, its main point should spark readers' interest and therefore must be more than a mechanical listing of similarities or differences. This main point can serve as the thesis, or the thesis can be implied by the writer's choice of details. In the following excerpt, an Indian-born novelist compares herself to her sister in order to describe their differing views of changes to immigration policy in the United States.

Purpose: Describe sisters' differing opinions on immigration by contrasting their situations.

This is a tale of two sisters from Calcutta, Mira and Bharati, who have lived in the United States for some thirty-five years, but who find themselves on different sides in the current debate over the status of immigrants. I am an American citizen and she is not. I am moved that thousands of long-term residents are finally taking the oath of citizenship. She is not.

—Bharati Mukherjee, "Two Ways to Belong in America," *New York Times*

5. Comparison and Contrast Considers a Sufficient Number of Significant Characteristics and Details

A comparison-and-contrast essay considers various points or characteristics through which to discuss both subjects. These **points of comparison** should be significant as well as relevant to the essay's purpose and thesis. Although the number of points of comparison can vary by topic, usually at least three or four significant points are needed to support a thesis. Each point should be fully described or explained so readers can fully grasp the thesis.

A writer may use sensory details, dialogue, examples, expert testimony, and other kinds of detail in a comparison-and-contrast essay. Consider the following paragraph in which humorist David Sedaris compares his childhood to that of his partner, Hugh.

Four points of comparison: location, pets, their activities, and their mothers' activities

Certain events are parallel, but compared with Hugh's, my childhood was unspeakably dull. When I was seven years old, my family moved to North Carolina. When he was seven years old, Hugh's family moved to the Congo. We had a collie and a house cat. They had a monkey and two horses named Charlie Brown and Satan. I threw stones at stop signs. Hugh threw stones at crocodiles. The verbs are the same, but he definitely wins the prize when it comes to nouns and objects. An eventful day for my mother might have involved a trip to the dry cleaner or a conversation with the potato-chip deliveryman. Asked one ordinary Congo afternoon what she'd done with her day, Hugh's mother answered that she and a fellow member of the Ladies' Club had visited a leper colony on the outskirts of Kinshasa. No reason was given for the expedition, though chances are she was staking it out for a future field trip.

—David Sedaris, *Me Talk Pretty One Day*

Reading and Writing Comparison-and-Contrast Essays

In this section you will learn about the structure of a comparison-and-contrast essay, read a sample essay, and practice using the guidelines for understanding, analyzing, and evaluating such essays. This will help you skillfully read and write essays that use comparison and contrast.

How Is a Comparison-and-Contrast Essay Structured?

A comparison-and-contrast essay is structured to help the reader follow and understand the points of comparison.

1. The **introduction** introduces the subjects that will be compared, contrasted, or both and usually includes a **thesis statement**.
2. The **body paragraphs** make the comparison or contrast, either point by point or subject by subject, depending on the organization.
3. The **conclusion** reinforces the thesis and summarizes the main points.

Figures 14.1 (p. 388) and 14.2 (p. 389) represent these major components visually.

1. THE INTRODUCTION ESTABLISHES THE COMPARISON OR CONTRAST

The introduction should identify the subjects being compared or contrasted and present the thesis statement. It should also provide any background information readers may need to understand the comparison. A piece comparing the sports football, which is familiar to Americans, and rugby, which is unfamiliar to many Americans, should include a brief overview of what rugby is. A comparison-and-contrast essay's introduction should spark readers' interest and draw them in to the essay; one way to do this is to suggest why the comparison and/or contrast is useful or important.

Most comparison-and-contrast essays include an explicit thesis statement in the introduction. The thesis has three functions.

1. It identifies the *subjects* being compared or contrasted.
2. It suggests whether the focus is on *similarities, differences,* or *both.*
3. It states the *main point* of the comparison and contrast.

Here are some examples of thesis statements that make clear the main point of the comparison or contrast.

Although different in purpose, weddings and funerals each draw families together and confirm family values.

(The essay would go on to compare the effects of weddings and funerals.)

The two cities Niagara Falls, Ontario, and Niagara Falls, New York, demonstrate two different approaches to appreciating nature and preserving the environment.

(The essay would go on to contrast the two cities' environmental preservation methods.)

Figure 14.1   Graphic Organizer for a Subject-by-Subject Comparison-and-Contrast Essay

Title	
Introduction	Background information
	Subjects: A comparison/contrast of Houses A and B
	Thesis statement

Body paragraphs: subject by subject	Subject A (House A)
	Point 1 applied to Subject A (Layout of House A)
	Point 2 applied to Subject A (Size of House A)
	Point 3 applied to Subject A (Building materials used in House A)
	Point 4 applied to Subject A (Landscaping around House A)
	Subject B (House B)
	Point 1 applied to Subject B (Layout of House B)
	Point 2 applied to Subject B (Size of House B)
	Point 3 applied to Subject B (Building materials used in House B)
	Point 4 applied to Subject B (Landscaping around House B)

Conclusion	Reinforces thesis
	Summarizes main points

 Reading | Writing   When reading a comparison-and-contrast essay, study the introduction to get a sense of what the writer knows about the subjects and determine how detailed or complex the essay will be. Also determine how much you already know about the subjects. This information will help you determine how slowly and carefully you should read the essay and what strategies (such as highlighting, annotating, or summarizing) may be most useful for understanding and recalling the information. When writing a comparison-and-contrast essay, be sure your introduction speaks directly to your audience, indicating why the comparison and contrast is relevant to them. Explain the benefits or advantages of knowing how your subjects are similar or different.

Figure 14.2   Graphic Organizer for a Point-by-Point Comparison-and-Contrast Essay

Title	
Introduction	Background information
	Subjects: A comparison/contrast of Houses A and B
	Thesis statement

⬇

	Point 1 (Layout)
	Subject A (House A)
	Subject B (House B)
	Point 2 (Size)
	Subject A (House A)
Body paragraphs: point by point	Subject B (House B)
	Point 3 (Building materials)
	Subject A (House A)
	Subject B (House B)
	Point 4 (Landscaping)
	Subject A (House A)
	Subject B (House B)

⬇

Conclusion	Reinforces thesis
	Summarizes main points

2. THE SUBJECTS ARE COMPARED OR CONTRASTED IN THE BODY PARAGRAPHS

Comparison-and-contrast essays are organized in one of two ways: subject by subject or point by point. In a subject-by-subject essay, the first paragraph or set of paragraphs will discuss all the points of comparison or contrast of one subject. The next paragraph or set of paragraphs will introduce the same points of comparison or contrast for the second subject. The body paragraphs of a point-by-point essay are arranged by each point of comparison or contrast: Both subjects are discussed in each paragraph.

For example, a writer who is going to compare two houses (A and B) by layout, size, building material, and landscaping has two options for organizing the essay: subject by subject or point by point.

Subject-by-subject organization In a *subject-by-subject organization*, the writer would first discuss all points about House A — its layout, size, building materials, and landscaping. Then the writer would do the same for House B. This pattern is shown in the graphic organizer in Figure 14.1 (p. 388).

Point-by-point organization In a *point-by-point organization*, the writer would first discuss the layout of the houses, then their sizes, then their building materials, and finally their landscaping. The writer would go back and forth between the two houses, noting similarities and differences on each point of comparison. This pattern is shown in the graphic organizer in Figure 14.2 (p. 389).

Each organization is appropriate for certain topics and purposes.

1. The subject-by-subject method tends to emphasize the larger picture, whereas the point-by-point method emphasizes details and specifics.

2. The point-by-point method often works better for lengthy essays if you want to keep both subjects current in your reader's mind.

3. The point-by-point method is often preferable for complicated or technical subjects. For example, if you compare two computer systems, it would be easier to explain the functions of a memory card once and then describe the memory cards in each of the two systems.

A successful comparison-and-contrast essay will use the organization that best suits its subject and length.

Reading | Writing When reading a comparison-and-contrast essay, identify the method of organization as soon as possible. It may be suggested in the introduction, but it will definitely be evident as you begin reading the body paragraphs. Knowing the chosen method will help you begin to construct a mental outline as you read, slotting in details as you encounter them. When writing a comparison-and-contrast essay, carefully define your purpose for writing, since it will determine, in part, which method of organization you choose. Consider your audience: Which method are they likely to respond to better and find easier to follow?

3.   THE CONCLUSION SUMS UP THE COMPARISON OR CONTRAST

The conclusion should draw the essay to a satisfying close. You might offer a final comment on your comparison or contrast, as well as sum up and remind your readers of your thesis.

Reading | Writing When reading a comparison-and-contrast essay, use the conclusion to help you pull together the entire essay to understand points of similarity and difference. Also, for an essay discussing both similarities and differences, consider whether the subjects are mostly similar or mostly different. Finally, consider whether the author achieved his or her purpose: Did he or she convince you of the relevance and importance of comparing or contrasting the subjects? When writing a comparison-and-contrast essay, you might refer back to the introduction by mentioning again the usefulness or value of the comparison or contrast. For lengthy or complicated comparisons, you might want to summarize the main points as well.

A Model Comparison-and-Contrast Essay

Title

Unstoppable Double-Fudge Chocolate Mudslide Explosion

John Scalzi

John Scalzi is the best-selling author of *The Last Colony* (**2009**), *Fuzzy Nation* (**2012**), and other science-fiction novels. He has also received a Hugo Award for *Your Hate Mail Will Be Graded* (**2010**), a collection of essays from his blog *Whatever*. As a nonfiction writer, he treats topics from personal finance to film to chocolate, as evidenced here.

Introduction

Chocolate is God's way of reminding men how inadequate they are. I am vividly confronted with this fact every time my wife and I go out to a restaurant. When it gets to dessert, my wife usually orders the most chocolate-saturated dessert possible. It's the one called "Unstoppable Double-Fudge Chocolate Mudslide Explosion" or some such thing. I always wonder why anyone would want to eat anything that promises a catastrophic natural disaster in your mouth.

Background information: humorous story about his wife sets up thesis

The dark brown monstrosity arrives at the table, and my wife takes the first bite. Before the fork is even removed from her mouth, a small moan escapes her lips. Her eyes, previously perfectly aligned, first cross slightly then glaze completely, pupils dilating in pure chocolate pleasure before the eyelids clamp down in ecstasy. The hand not holding the fork clenches into a fist and starts pounding the table. The silverware rattles.

After about six minutes of this, she finally manages to swallow the bite, realign her eyes, and take the next shuttle back from whatever transcendental plane she's been visiting. Slowly, her sphere of consciousness expands to include me, her husband, her life-long mate, her presumed partner in all things ecstatic.

Subject A: men & chocolate;

Subject B: women & chocolate

Thesis

Body paragraphs (point by point)

Point 1: response to question

A: trivial

B: essential

Point 2: chocolate and sex

B: better than sex

A (implied): sex is better

Point 3: importance (elaborates Point 1)

A: fine, a little bonus

B (implied): essential

Conclusion

implies that understanding the difference in attitude is important because it helps the author make his wife happy

"Hey, this is pretty good," she'll say. "You want some?"

No, I don't. I want nothing to do with an object that does to   5
my wife in one bite what I've worked for an entire relationship to achieve. It wouldn't do any good, anyway. Men just don't have the same relationship with chocolate that women do. It's not even close. I wandered around the office today and asked men— "Chocolate. Your thoughts?"—and the result was always the same. First, a confused look as to why they're being asked about something so trivial, and then some lame, obvious statement like "Uh . . . it's brown?"

Ask women the same question, and you get responses like "The ONLY food group," "ESSENTIAL to life as we know it," and the ultimate casual swipe at every member of the Y-chromosome brigade, "better than sex." Ouch. Some women will try to make up for the last one by quickly adding that chocolate is supposed to be an aphrodisiac.

Uh-huh. Chocolate certainly increases desire; problem is the desire is usually for more chocolate. The best a guy can do is buy a box of chocolates and hope he'll be considered somewhere between the cherry truffle and the strawberry nougat.

Don't get me wrong. Guys like chocolate just fine; it's just not essential to life as we know it. Respiration is essential to life as we know it; chocolate is simply one of those nice little bonuses you get. We won't usually pass it up if it's offered, but I don't know too many guys who would get substantially worked up if it were to suddenly disappear from the face of the earth (ironic in a way, as back in the days of the Aztecs, only men were allowed to have the stuff). When I eat a chocolate dessert, I enjoy it, yes. My worldview doesn't narrow to include only the plate that it's on.

Maybe we're missing something. On the other hand, we don't have to pick up our silverware from the floor after we're done with our tiramisu. Life is about trade-offs like that. All I know is that come Valentine's Day, chocolate will be among the things I offer my wife. I can't truly appreciate it, but I can truly appreciate what it does for her. Which is close enough.

Understanding, Analyzing, and Evaluating Comparison-and-Contrast Essays

In reading and writing comparison-and-contrast essays, your goal is to get beyond mere competence: That is, you want to be able to do more than merely understand the content of the essays you're reading or convey just your basic ideas to the audience you're writing for.

> **Reading | Writing**   Truly skillful reading and writing require the abilities to **understand**, **analyze**, *and* **evaluate** material. These abilities are important to you as a reader because they give you a systematic, thorough method of examining a reading. They're important to you as a writer because they help you decide what to revise, rewrite, drop, and replace, allowing you to produce a well-written, persuasive essay.

Understanding a Comparison-and-Contrast Essay

Reading a comparison-and-contrast essay is somewhat different from reading other kinds of essays. First, the essay addresses two (or more) subjects instead of just one. Second, the subjects are being compared, contrasted, or both, so you must follow the writer's points of comparison between them. These differences make comparison-and-contrast essays more difficult to read, so plan on rereading them several times.

Begin by previewing the essay to determine the subjects being considered and whether the writer is concerned with similarities, differences, or both. Also consider your familiarity with the subjects, as this will determine, in part, how difficult the essay will be to read. Then, as you read, use the skills you learned in Chapter 2 and look for the answers to the following questions.

- **What is the author's purpose?** Determine whether the essay is written to express ideas, inform, or persuade. Depending on the purpose, you will be looking for different things as you read. If the purpose is to express ideas, you will be looking for the author's attitudes, opinions, and beliefs. If the purpose is to inform, you will be looking for factual statements and their support. If the purpose is to persuade, you will be looking for reasons and evidence.

- **What method of organization is used?** Determine this as soon as possible, since your mind-set and focus will differ for each. Both methods can present the same information, but what you expect to come next depends on whether you are reading a point-by-point or subject-by-subject essay.

- **What is the basis of comparison?** Identifying this will help you focus your attention and identify the most important supporting details.

Figure 14.3   Graphic Organizer for "Unstoppable Double-Fudge Chocolate Mudslide Explosion"

Title	"Unstoppable Double-Fudge Chocolate Mudslide Explosion"
Introduction	**Opening story:** Story of the wife's over-the-top reaction to tasting the chocolate dessert and the author's incomprehension
	Subjects: Men's and women's relationship with chocolate (= Subject A and Subject B)
	Thesis: Men and women have very different relationships with chocolate.

Body paragraphs: subject by subject	Point 1: Answer to question: "Chocolate. Your thoughts?"
	Subject A: Trivial—it's brown
	Subject B: Essential to life; better than sex
	Point 2: Chocolate vs. sex
	Subject B: Chocolate is better
	Subject A (implied): Sex is better
	Point 3: Importance
	Subject A: Chocolate is a bonus
	Subject B (implied): Essential

Conclusion	Elaborates further on men's view of chocolate and explains that understanding that his wife feels differently helps him make her happy

- **What are the points of comparison?** The points of comparison are the most important key ideas of the essay. Be sure to highlight each as you identify it. The points of comparison are usually directly tied to the writer's purpose, so be sure to connect the two. For example, if a writer's purpose is to express ideas about two popular films, the points of comparison are likely to be subjective—expressing the writer's preferences. If, however, the purpose is to inform, then more objective, factual points of comparison are likely to be made.

Figure 14.3 is a visual representation of John Scalzi's "Unstoppable Double-Fudge Chocolate Mudslide Explosion."

Understanding in Action

Following is one student's summary of John Scalzi's introduction for "Unstoppable Double-Fudge Chocolate Mudslide Explosion." In a paragraph, summarize the author's thesis, the body of the comparison, and the conclusion. Use the Understanding Comparison-and-Contrast Essays guidelines and Figure 14.3 (pp. 393–94) to make sure you include all the important points.

> The author begins by describing himself and his wife out to dinner when she orders, as always, a very chocolaty dessert. After one bite she reacts, as Scalzi puts it, "in ecstasy." Her reaction reminds him of "how inadequate" men are because chocolate does for his wife "in one bite what I've worked for an entire relationship to achieve."

Analyzing a Comparison-and-Contrast Essay

Analyzing a comparison-and-contrast essay involves assessing how effectively and clearly the writer explains similarities and/or differences between two or more subjects. Use the following questions to guide your analysis of comparison-and-contrast essays.

- **Does the thesis statement identify whether the writer intends to express ideas, inform, or persuade?** A good writer should help his or her readers form a mind-set and know what to expect. If the writer does not have a clear purpose in mind or does not express it clearly, you might notice a mixed basis of comparison or overlapping points of comparison.

- **Is the basis of comparison clear and does it fulfill the writer's purpose?** If the writer's purpose is to inform readers about two football sports figures' athletic skills, he or she should not, for example, discuss the players' off-field behavior.

- **Do the points of comparison cover some of the major similarities and differences?** For many subjects it would be impossible to cover all similarities or differences, but at least some of the major ones should be covered. In comparing two musical groups, it would be important to identify the type of music each plays, for instance.

- **Are the points of comparison relevant to the thesis statement?** Writers should choose points that are common and typical and that support the thesis statement. For example, in an essay about two medical specialties, contrasting them according to the ethnicities of their practitioners would not be pertinent, whereas comparing types of training and uses of surgery would pertain.

Analysis in Action

The student who wrote the summary in Understanding in Action made notes as she read and turned them into the following analysis of the introduction to John Scalzi's "Unstoppable Double-Fudge Chocolate Mudslide Explosion." Choose a two- or three-paragraph section of the essay. Use the questions on page 395 to analyze the section you choose. Write marginal notes recording your thoughts.

Expressing an idea	Chocolate is God's way of reminding men how inadequate they are. I am vividly confronted with this fact every time
Implies thesis: He and his wife have different reactions to chocolate.	my wife and I go out to a restaurant. When it gets to dessert, my wife usually orders the most chocolate-saturated dessert possible. It's the one called "Unstoppable Double-Fudge Chocolate Mudslide Explosion" or some such thing. I always wonder why anyone would want to eat anything that promises a catastrophic natural disaster in your mouth.
Humor used to support thesis	The dark brown monstrosity arrives at the table, and my wife takes the first bite. Before the fork is even removed from her mouth, a small moan escapes her lips.

Evaluating a Comparison-and-Contrast Essay

Comparison-and-contrast essays written to inform can be direct and straightforward. However, when the purpose is to express ideas or to persuade, closer evaluation is needed. Use the following questions to guide your evaluation of comparison-and-contrast essays.

- **Does the writer treat each subject fairly and provide balanced coverage of all subjects?** Determine whether the writer gives equal and objective coverage to each subject. If one of the subjects seems to be favored or given special consideration (or if one subject seems not to be treated fairly, fully, or adequately), the writer might be biased—that is, introducing his or her own values and attitudes into the comparison.

- **How does the organization affect meaning?** The two methods of development provide different emphases. Point-by-point organization provides a steady back-and-forth between subjects, keeping the reader's attention focused on both subjects simultaneously. Subject-by-subject organization tends to allow in-depth consideration of each subject separately. To present one subject more positively than another, a writer may choose to discuss the favored subject and all its characteristics first, thereby shaping the reader's impression in a positive way before the reader encounters the second subject. Or a writer may present the less-favored subject first, bringing out its faults, and then move to the more-favored second subject, pointing out its merits and leaving the reader with a final positive impression of the second subject.

- **What points of comparison are omitted?** Be sure to ask yourself what other points of comparison could have been made that were not made. For example, in an essay comparing landlines and cell phones, it would be odd if the convenience and accessibility factors were not discussed.

Evaluation in Action

The student writer who was featured understanding and analyzing John Scalzi's essay wrote the following evaluation of its introduction after reviewing her notes analyzing the piece. Use the questions above to help you write your evaluation of the rest of the essay.

> The author's opening story is funny and works so well because it is really exaggerated. The name of the dessert combines a lot of different chocolate desserts into something that would never appear on a menu. He calls it a "dark brown monstrosity," as if it looks like something you wouldn't want to go near. His wife's sexy reaction to the first bite lasts "about six minutes." The author's whole style makes me enjoy what he has to say.

Readings for Practice, Ideas for Writing

New York vs. Chicago Pizza

Sarah Spigelman is a writer, editor, and foodie based in New York City. She chronicles her cooking and eating adventures in the blog *Fritos and Foie Gras*. She also contributes to msnbc.com, where the following article first appeared.

Reading Tip

As you read, think about the quotations the author includes and how these contribute to her comparison and contrast.

Previewing the Reading

Preview the reading (see pp. 23–24 for guidelines), and then answer the following questions.

1. What two things are compared in the essay?
2. What is one major difference between the two?

---

msnbc.com

New York vs. Chicago Pizza: Supreme Court Justice Makes Ruling

Sarah Spigelman

One thing can be said about Supreme Court justices—they have strong opinions and they stand by them.

msnbc.com

Even about pizza. In January, Justice Antonin Scalia praised New York pizza as "infinitely better" than Chicago pizza, and on Tuesday he reinforced that fact, stating that although he likes Chicago style deep-dish pizza, "It should not be called 'pizza.' It should be called 'a tomato pie.' Real pizza is Neapolitan [from Naples, Italy]. It is thin. It is chewy and crispy, OK?"

There are those who agree with him, those who disagree, and those who fall somewhere in the middle.

In Justice Scalia's corner, you have people who think pizza should have a thin crust that, according to Serious Eats, is "at once crisp and chewy . . . best with only one or two toppings applied (so crust remains crisp)." The tomato sauce is applied underneath the cheese and toppings. Fans of this style of pizza include Anthony Bourdain, who, as a proud New Yorker, says "I think even our ordinary, 'utility' pizza is better than anybody else's." NYC pizza is so popular, it is even favored by First Lady Michelle Obama, who proclaimed her pizza lunch at famous pizzeria Grimaldi's "better than Chicago pizza." Now THAT'S some serious love! New York's most famous classic pizzerias include the aforementioned Grimaldi's, John's of Bleecker Street, and Lombardi's.

Those who love Chicago pizza shouldn't get their feathers ruffled, though — there   5
are plenty in that camp. Chicago pizza lovers enjoy a crust that has been, according to Serious Eats, "cooked in a deep pan, with a deep, thick, buttery crust, and a chunky tomato sauce. Lots of cheese, lots of (and/or copious amounts of) toppings." Some restaurants assemble the pizza like it is made in NYC (but on a thicker crust and with more toppings), while some put the cheese and toppings on the bottom of the crust, topping off the whole thing with tomato sauce and a sprinkling of Parmesan.

This is the case at the Original Gino's East, of which Ace of Cakes star Duff Goldman is a devotee: "Gino's has the giant disk of sausage that they put inside the pizza. It's genius. Every bite has the same amount of sausage. You don't get one bite with more sausage and one bite without any." He loves it so much that he named it the best pizza he ever ate. *Travel + Leisure* magazine readers evidently agree with him, because in 2011 they rated Chicago as the best pizza city in America in the mag's America's Favorite Cities Poll. New York didn't even come in until number three on that poll, which just goes to prove that not everyone goes for the two pizza heavyweight cities.

Celebrity chef and restaurateur David Burke loves pizza from his home state of New Jersey, citing Fort Lee's Baggio's for its "different kind of sauce — it's more caramelized, and has more flavor." When "The Price is Right" wrapped production, host Drew Carey flew out forty-five pizzas from Antonio's in Parma, Ohio, to celebrate with the cast and crew. And of course, New Haven, Connecticut's Sally's and Pepe's are still waging an ages-old battle.

Continued >

msnbc.com

Where do you stand on the pizza issue? Thin, foldable, and crunchy from New York? Fork-and-knife, cheesy, buttery Chicago deep dish? Or something else altogether? The only wrong opinion is not having one! New York vs. Chicago (or Ohio!)—who wins the pizza showdown?

Understanding the Reading

1. **Thesis** What is Spigelman's thesis, and where does she state it most directly?

2. **Basis of comparison** What characteristics do New York and Chicago pizzas share that allow a comparison between them to be made?

3. **Contrasts** According to their fans, what are the strengths of New York and Chicago pizzas?

Strengths of New York Pizza	Strengths of Chicago Pizza
1.	1.
2.	2.
3.	3.

4. **Language** Using context clues (p. 34), write a brief definition of each of the following words as it is used in the reading, checking a dictionary if necessary: *infinitely* (para. 2), *utility* (4), *proclaimed* (4), *copious* (5), and *waging* (7).

5. **Development** What other regional pizzas are cited in the essay? What point is Spigelman making by mentioning them?

Analyzing the Reading

1. **Purpose** Is Spigelman's purpose mainly to inform or to persuade? Why do you think as you do?

2. **Organization** Is the organization of the comparison subject by subject or point by point?

3. **Sources** List the sources Spigelman quotes or paraphrases in the essay. Why might she have included all these sources?

4. **Visuals** How do the visuals that accompany the piece support the comparison that Spigelman is making?

5. **Conclusion** Spigelman's last paragraph includes five questions. What is the purpose of the questions?

Evaluating the Reading

1. **Introduction** Why do you suppose Spigelman begins by quoting a Supreme Court justice's views on pizza? Is this an effective opening strategy?

2. **Level of detail** Spigelman provides considerably more descriptive details about Chicago pizza than about New York pizza. How do you respond to the difference in level of development?

3. **Audience** Does Spigelman's naming of specific pizzerias contribute positively to the essay, given that most readers may not be familiar with them?

4. **Tone** In her last paragraph, Spigelman includes the sentence, "The only wrong opinion is not having one!" Given her intended audience and purpose, is the exclamation point appropriate?

Discussing the Reading

1. Why do you think people have such strong opinions about pizza? Is there such a thing as the country's "best" pizza?

2. Clearly, part of the difference in pizza preference described here is based on a rivalry between New Yorkers and Chicagoans. How serious do you feel such regional rivalries are?

3. What, in your opinion, are the characteristics of a superior pizza pie?

Writing about the Reading

1. **Paragraph** Write a paragraph comparing and contrasting two versions of a dish you know well, whether homemade or produced in a restaurant. (Hint: You can remain neutral, as Spigelman does, or you can express your personal preferences between the two versions.)

2. **Paragraph** Brainstorm a list of casual dining restaurants, such as pizzerias or fast-food chains. Then choose two specific establishments to compare and contrast in a paragraph. (Hint: Make sure that the two have enough commonalities to provide a basis of comparison but also enough differences to develop in the paragraph.)

3. **Essay** In an essay describe how your personal tastes—perhaps in terms of food, clothing, music, movies, hobbies, political views, or other things—are similar to and different from those of someone with whom you are close. (Hint: Before drafting, think about whether a subject-by-subject or point-by-point organization will be more effective.)

We've Got the Dirt on Guy Brains

Dave Barry began his professional writing career covering local events for a Pennsylvania newspaper. In 1983 he began writing a humor column for the *Miami Herald* that appeared in more than five hundred newspapers; Barry stopped writing the column in 2004. Barry has written thirty books; plays guitar in the Rock Bottom Remainders, a rock band made up of well-known writers such as Stephen King and Amy Tan; and received a Pulitzer Prize for Commentary in 1988. "We've Got the Dirt on Guy Brains" originally appeared in November 2003.

Reading Tip

As you read, pay attention to the comparisons Barry draws and the "evidence" he uses to back up his humorous points. In addition, notice how he presents and refutes "opposing viewpoints" (supposedly from irate readers of a previous column).

Previewing the Reading

1. What two subjects are being contrasted?
2. Do you predict this essay will be factual or subjective?

We've Got the Dirt on Guy Brains

Dave Barry

I like to think that I am a modest person. (I also like to think that I look like Brad Pitt naked, but that is not the issue here.)

There comes a time, however, when a person must toot his own personal horn, and for me, that time is now. A new book has confirmed a theory that I first proposed in 1987, in a column explaining why men are physically unqualified to do housework. The problem, I argued, is that men — because of a tragic genetic flaw — cannot see dirt until there is enough of it to support agriculture. This puts men at a huge disadvantage against women, who can detect a single dirt molecule twenty feet away.

This is why a man and a woman can both be looking at the same bathroom commode, and the man — hindered by Male Genetic Dirt Blindness (MGDB) — will perceive the commode surface as being clean enough for heart surgery or even meat slicing; whereas the woman can't even *see* the commode, only a teeming, commode-shaped swarm of bacteria. A woman can spend two hours cleaning a toothbrush holder and still not be totally satisfied; whereas if you ask a man to clean the entire New York City subway system, he'll go down there with a bottle of Windex and a single paper towel, then emerge twenty-five minutes later, weary but satisfied with a job well done.

When I wrote about Male Genetic Dirt Blindness, many irate readers complained that I was engaging in sexist stereotyping, as well as making lame excuses for the fact that men are lazy pigs. All of these irate readers belonged to a gender that I will not identify here, other than to say: Guess what, ladies? There is now scientific proof that I was right.

5   This proof appears in a new book titled *What Could He Be Thinking? How a Man's Mind Really Works*. I have not personally read this book, because, as a journalist, I am too busy writing about it. But according to an article by Reuters,[1] the book states that a man's brain "takes in less sensory detail than a woman's, so he doesn't see or even feel the dust and household mess in the same way." Got that? We can't see or feel the mess! We're like: "What snow tires in the dining room? Oh, *those* snow tires in the dining room."

And this is only one of the differences between men's and women's brains. Another difference involves a brain part called the "cingulate gyrus," which is the sector where emotions are located. The Reuters article does not describe the cingulate gyrus, but presumably in women it is a structure the size of a mature cantaloupe, containing a vast quantity of complex, endlessly recalibrated emotional data involving hundreds, perhaps thousands, of human relationships; whereas in men it is basically a cashew filled with NFL highlights.

In any event, it turns out that women's brains secrete more of the chemicals "oxytocin" and "serotonin," which, according to biologists, cause humans to feel they have an inadequate supply of shoes. No, seriously, these chemicals cause humans to want to bond with other humans, which is why women like to share their feelings. Some women (and here I am referring to my wife) can share as many as three days' worth of feelings about an event that took eight seconds to actually happen. We men, on the other hand, are reluctant to share our feelings, in large part because we often don't have any. Really. Ask any guy: A lot of the time, when we look like we're thinking, we just have this low-level humming sound in our brains. That's why, in male-female conversations, the male part often consists entirely of him going "hmmmm." This frustrates the woman, who wants to know what he's really thinking. In fact, what he's thinking is, literally, "hmmmm."

So anyway, according to the Reuters article, when a man, instead of sharing feelings with his mate, chooses to lie on the sofa, holding the remote control and monitoring 750 television programs simultaneously by changing the channel every one-half second (pausing slightly longer for programs that feature touchdowns, fighting, shooting, car crashes, or bosoms) his mate should *not* come to the mistaken conclusion that he is an insensitive jerk. In fact, he is responding to scientific biological brain chemicals that require him to behave this way for scientific reasons, as detailed in the scientific book *What Could He Be Thinking? How a Man's Mind Really Works*, which I frankly cannot recommend highly enough.

In conclusion, no *way* was that pass interference.

[1] **Reuters** International news and financial information service providing reports and stories to the media.

Understanding the Reading

1. **Author** How does the author describe himself?

2. **Thesis** What is Barry's thesis? What characteristics about men and women does he emphasize to support this idea?

3. **Sources** What information does Barry give from the book he mentions? What other sources does he cite in his essay?

4. **Examples** Give two examples of the types of situations in which Barry feels men and women differ in their thinking.

5. **Description** Barry describes the "cingulate gyrus" as a "cantaloupe" and a "cashew" (para. 6). Explain the effectiveness of these images in the context of the essay.

6. **Vocabulary** Explain the meaning of each of the following words as it is used in the reading: *modest* (para. 1), *teeming* (3), *irate* (4), *recalibrated* (6), and *secrete* (7). Refer to your dictionary as needed.

7. **Organization** Complete the graphic organizer to better understand the structure of the piece.

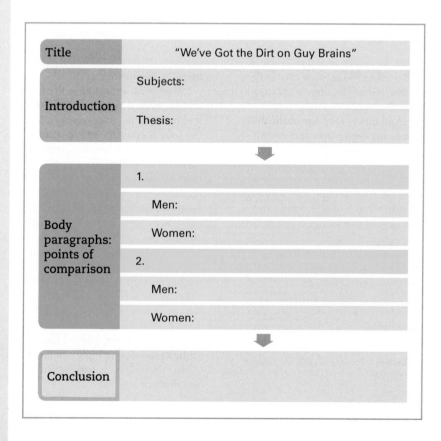

Title	"We've Got the Dirt on Guy Brains"	
Introduction	Subjects:	
	Thesis:	

⬇

Body paragraphs: points of comparison	1.	
	Men:	
	Women:	
	2.	
	Men:	
	Women:	

⬇

Conclusion	

Analyzing the Reading

1. **Basis of comparison** Consider Barry's purpose in writing. What basis of comparison does he use to convey his message? Does he cover the major similarities and differences sufficiently?

2. **Examples** Does Barry give enough examples to compare and contrast each characteristic? Are his details relevant and interesting? Explain.

3. **Language** Explain the allusion to Brad Pitt in paragraph 1.

Evaluating the Reading

1. **Humor** When encountering humor in an essay, readers must evaluate the purpose and appropriateness of the statements that are intended to be funny. Writers use humor in different ways: to entertain, to lighten the tone of an otherwise serious essay, or to expose the negative side of an issue through *sarcasm*—bitter or dark humor. Why do you think Barry uses humor in this essay? How does the use of humor relate to the subject matter? How would the essay be different if it had been written without humor? Would it be as effective? Explain.

2. **Humor** Do you think this essay is funny? Why, or why not? Support your answer.

3. **Organization** Does Barry organize his essay point by point or subject by subject? Would the essay be equally effective if the other method were used? Why, or why not?

Discussing the Reading

1. Discuss your reaction to Barry's essay. Do you agree with his assessment of male and female thinking patterns?

2. Barry uses humor to discuss the perennial "battle of the sexes." How does humor help or hinder discussions about sensitive issues?

3. In class, explain your personal living style. Are you a "neat freak," a slob, or something in between? Has this ever caused a problem with your roommate or siblings? Explain.

Writing about the Reading

1. **Paragraph** Write a paragraph comparing two people you know in terms of their attitudes toward "dirt." Begin by choosing your subjects. Then use one of the brainstorming techniques you've learned to consider their similarities and differences. As you construct your paragraph, remember to use the topic sentence to establish the comparison or contrast in their attitudes.

2. **Essay** Barry claims that men are unqualified to do housework. What other activities do you think either men or women seem less qualified than the

opposite sex to do? Write an essay describing one such activity, comparing and contrasting men's and women's ability to perform it.

3. **Internet research** Visit the online site for the humorous newsmagazine the *Onion* (**www.theonion.com**) or another site that spoofs current events and find a story based on a real current event. Then use cnn.com or another online news source to find the nonsatirical version of the story. Write an essay describing the differences and similarities between the two accounts. Be sure to give background information on the story and to explain how the humorous version gives insight into or makes a political comment on the issue reported on.

Sex, Lies, and Conversation

Deborah Tannen holds a Ph.D. in linguistics and is currently a professor at Georgetown University. Tannen has written several books about communication and language, including *I Only Say This Because I Love You* (2001), in which she examines communication between family members. The following essay first appeared in the *Washington Post* in 1990.

Reading Tip

Notice how the author begins with a personal example, immediately catching the reader's interest. Pay attention also to her use of supporting evidence.

Previewing the Reading

1. What is Tannen comparing and contrasting in this essay?
2. Identify at least one point of comparison.
3. Why does Tannen think understanding is important?

DEBORAH TANNEN

Sex, Lies, and Conversation

I was addressing a small gathering in a suburban Virginia living room—a women's group that had invited men to join them. Throughout the evening, one man had been particularly talkative, frequently offering ideas and anecdotes, while his wife sat silently beside him on the couch. Toward the end of the evening, I commented that women frequently complain that their husbands don't talk to them. This man quickly concurred. He gestured toward his wife and said, "She's the talker in our family." The room burst into laughter; the man looked puzzled and hurt. "It's true," he explained. "When I come home from work I have nothing to say. If she didn't keep the conversa-tion going, we'd spend the whole evening in silence."

This episode crystallizes the irony that although American men tend to talk more than women in public situations, they often talk less at home. And this pattern is wreaking havoc with marriage.

The pattern was observed by political scientist Andrew Hacker in the late '70s. Sociologist Catherine Kohler Riessman reports in her new book *Divorce Talk* that most of the women she interviewed—but only a few of the men—gave lack of communication as the reason for their divorces. Given the current divorce rate of nearly 50%, that amounts to millions of cases in the United States every year—a vir-tual epidemic of failed conversation.

In my own research, complaints from women about their husbands most often focused not on tangible inequities such as having given up the chance for a career to accompany a husband to his,

Continued >

or doing far more than their share of daily life-support work like cleaning, cooking, social arrangements, and errands. Instead, they focused on communication: "He doesn't listen to me." "He doesn't talk to me." I found, as Hacker observed years before, that most wives want their husbands to be, first and foremost, conversational partners, but few husbands share this expectation of their wives.

5   In short, the image that best represents the current crisis is the stereotypical cartoon scene of a man sitting at the breakfast table with a newspaper held up in front of his face, while a woman glares at the back of it, wanting to talk.

Linguistic Battle of the Sexes

How can women and men have such different impressions of communication in marriage? Why the widespread imbalance in their interests and expectations?

In the April issue of *American Psychologist*, Stanford University's Eleanor Maccoby reports the results of her own and others' research showing that children's development is most influenced by the social structure of peer interactions. Boys and girls tend to play with children of their own gender, and their sex-separate groups have different organizational structures and interactive norms.[1]

I believe these systematic differences in childhood socialization make talk between women and men like cross-cultural communication, heir to all the attraction and pitfalls of that enticing but difficult enterprise. My research on men's and women's conversations uncovered patterns similar to those described for children's groups.

[1] **norms** Behavior that is typical of a group or culture.

For women, as for girls, intimacy is the fabric of relationships, and talk is the thread from which it is woven. Little girls create and maintain friendships by exchanging secrets; similarly, women regard conversation as the cornerstone of friendship. So a woman expects her husband to be a new and improved version of a best friend. What is important is not the individual subjects that are discussed but the sense of closeness, of a life shared, that emerges when people tell their thoughts, feelings, and impressions.

Bonds between boys can be as intense 10 as girls', but they are based less on talking, more on doing things together. Since they don't assume talk is the cement that binds a relationship, men don't know what kind of talk women want, and they don't miss it when it isn't there.

Boys' groups are larger, more inclusive, and more hierarchical, so boys must struggle to avoid the subordinate position in the group. This may play a role in women's complaints that men don't listen to them. Some men really don't like to listen, because being the listener makes them feel one-down, like a child listening to adults or an employee to a boss.

But often when women tell men, "You aren't listening," and the men protest, "I am," the men are right. The impression of not listening results from misalignments in the mechanics of conversation. The misalignment begins as soon as a man and a woman take physical positions. This became clear when I studied videotapes made by psychologist Bruce Dorval of children and adults talking to their same-sex best friends. I found that at every age, the girls and women faced each other directly, their eyes anchored on each other's faces. At every age, the boys and men sat at angles to each other and looked elsewhere in the room, periodically glancing at each other. They were obviously attuned to each other, often mirroring each other's movements. But the tendency of men to face away can give women the impression they aren't listening even when they are. A young woman in college was frustrated: Whenever she told her boyfriend she wanted to talk to him, he would lie down on the floor, close his eyes, and put his arm over his face. This signaled to her, "He's taking a nap." But he insisted he was listening extra hard. Normally, he looks around the room, so he is easily distracted. Lying down and covering his eyes helped him concentrate on what she was saying.

Analogous to the physical alignment that women and men take in conversation is their topical alignment. The girls in my study tended to talk at length about one topic, but the boys tended to jump from topic to topic. The second-grade girls exchanged stories about people they knew. The second-grade boys teased, told jokes, noticed things in the room, and talked about finding games to play. The sixth-grade girls talked about problems with a mutual friend. The sixth-grade boys talked about fifty-five different topics, none of which extended over more than a few turns.

Listening to Body Language

Switching topics is another habit that gives women the impression men aren't listening, especially if they switch to a topic about themselves. But the evidence of the tenth-grade boys in my study indicates otherwise. The tenth-grade boys sprawled across their chairs with bodies parallel and eyes straight ahead, rarely looking at each other. They looked as if they were riding in a car, staring out the windshield. But they were talking about their feelings. One boy was upset because a girl had told him he had a drinking problem, and the other was feeling alienated from all his friends.

Now, when a girl told a friend about 15 a problem, the friend responded by asking probing questions and expressing agreement and understanding. But the boys dismissed each other's problems. Todd assured Richard that his drinking was "no big problem" because "sometimes you're funny when you're off your butt." And when Todd said he felt left out, Richard responded, "Why should you? You know more people than me."

Women perceive such responses as belittling and unsupportive. But the boys seemed satisfied with them. Whereas women reassure each other by implying, "You shouldn't feel bad because I've had similar experiences," men do so by implying, "You shouldn't feel bad because your problems aren't so bad."

There are even simpler reasons for women's impression that men don't listen. Linguist Lynette Hirschman found that women make more listener-noise, such as "mhm," "uhuh," and "yeah," to show "I'm with you." Men, she found, more often give silent attention. Women who expect a stream of listener-noise interpret silent attention as no attention at all.

Women's conversational habits are as frustrating to men as men's are to women. Men who expect silent attention interpret a stream of listener-noise as overreaction or impatience. Also, when women talk to each other in a close, comfortable setting, they often overlap, finish each other's sentences, and anticipate what the other is about to say. This practice, which I call

Continued >

"participatory listenership," is often perceived by men as interruption, intrusion, and lack of attention.

A parallel difference caused a man to complain about his wife, "She just wants to talk about her own point of view. If I show her another view, she gets mad at me." When most women talk to each other, they assume a conversationalist's job is to express agreement and support. But many men see their conversational duty as pointing out the other side of an argument. This is heard as disloyalty by women, and refusal to offer the requisite support. It is not that women don't want to see other points of view, but that they prefer them phrased as suggestions and inquiries rather than as direct challenges.

20   In his book *Fighting for Life*, Walter Ong points out that men use "agonistic" or warlike, oppositional formats to do almost anything; thus discussion becomes debate, and conversation a competitive sport. In contrast, women see conversation as a ritual means of establishing rapport. If Jane tells a problem and June says she has a similar one, they walk away feeling closer to each other. But this attempt at establishing rapport can backfire when used with men. Men take too literally women's ritual "troubles talk," just as women mistake men's ritual challenges for real attack.

The Sounds of Silence

These differences begin to clarify why women and men have such different expectations about communication in marriage. For women, talk creates intimacy. Marriage is an orgy of closeness: You can tell your feelings and thoughts, and still be loved. Their greatest fear is being pushed away. But men live in a hierarchical world, where talk maintains independence and status. They are on guard to protect themselves from being put down and pushed around.

This explains the paradox of the talkative man who said of his silent wife, "She's the talker." In the public setting of a guest lecture, he felt challenged to show his intelligence and display his understanding of the lecture. But at home, where he has nothing to prove and no one to defend against, he is free to remain silent. For his wife, being home means she is free from the worry that something she says might offend someone, or spark disagreement, or appear to be showing off; at home she is free to talk.

The communication problems that endanger marriage can't be fixed by mechanical engineering. They require a new conceptual framework about the role of talk in human relationships. Many of the psychological explanations that have become second nature may not be helpful, because they tend to blame either women (for not being assertive enough) or men (for not being in touch with their feelings). A sociolinguistic approach by which male–female conversation is seen as cross-cultural communication allows us to understand the problem and forge solutions without blaming either party.

Once the problem is understood, improvement comes naturally, as it did to the young woman and her boyfriend who seemed to go to sleep when she wanted to talk. Previously, she had accused him of not listening, and he had refused to change his behavior, since that would be admitting fault. But then she learned about and explained to him the differences in women's and men's habitual ways of aligning themselves in conversation. The next time she told him she wanted to talk, he began, as usual, by lying down and covering his eyes. When the familiar negative reaction bubbled up, she reassured herself that he really was listening. But then he sat up and looked at her. Thrilled, she asked why. He said, "You like me to look at you when we talk, so I'll try to do it." Once he saw their differences as cross-cultural rather than right and wrong, he independently altered his behavior.

25   Women who feel abandoned and deprived when their husbands won't listen to or report daily news may be happy to discover their husbands trying to adapt once they understand the place of small talk in women's relationships. But if their husbands don't adapt, the women may still be comforted that for men, this is not a failure of intimacy. Accepting the difference, the wives may look to their friends or family for that kind of talk. And husbands who can't provide it shouldn't feel their wives have made unreasonable demands. Some couples will still decide to divorce, but at least their decisions will be based on realistic expectations.

In these times of resurgent ethnic conflicts, the world desperately needs cross-cultural understanding. Like charity, successful cross-cultural communication should begin at home.

Understanding the Reading

1. **Thesis** What is Tannen's thesis about gender communication?

2. **Introduction** What does the opening anecdote about the man at a women's group illustrate?

3. **Contrasts** What differences in communication are observable between young girls and boys?

4. **Contrasts** In what ways does body language differ between men and women? How do these differences affect communication between the sexes?

5. **Organization** What method of organization does Tannen use?

Analyzing the Reading

1. **Thesis** Is Tannen's thesis effectively placed? Why, or why not?

2. **Points of comparison** Identify the points of comparison that Tannen uses to support her thesis. Does she focus on similarities, differences, or both? Does she treat her subjects fairly? Explain.

3. **Evidence** In explaining the communication differences between men and women, Tannen explores the causes of these differences. How does this information strengthen the essay?

4. **Language** What sort of image does the phrase "wreaking havoc" (para. 2) bring to mind?

5. **Visualizing evidence** Tannen includes different types of evidence to support
    her thesis. Analyze the purpose of the supporting evidence by completing the
    following chart. The first entry has been done for you.

Evidence	Purpose
Reference to political scientist Andrew Hacker (para. 3)	Gives legitimacy to the thesis and demonstrates that the thesis is not a new idea
Sociologist Catherine Kohler Riessman's observations from her book *Divorce Talk* (para. 3)	
The author's own research (para. 4)	
American Psychologist article by Stanford University's Eleanor Maccoby (para. 7)	
Psychologist Bruce Dorval's videotapes (para. 12)	
The author's own research (paras. 13–16)	
Linguist Lynette Hirschman's research (para. 17)	
Reference to *Fighting for Life* by Walter Ong (para. 20)	

Evaluating the Reading

1. **Organization** Why do you think Tannen chose the organization she used?
    Would the essay be as effective with a different organizational plan? Explain.

2. **Language** Tannen, a linguist, uses some linguistic jargon even though she is
    writing for the general public. Highlight these terms and evaluate their effec-
    tiveness. Are they a benefit or a detriment to your understanding of the essay?

3. **Original sources** Sometimes when authors are reporting on research for a
    general audience, they do not provide full citations for the work—that is, the
    original sources — they mention. Review the chart of sources included in
    question 5 under Analyzing the Reading (above). Next to each source, indi-
    cate whether full (i.e., author, title, date, publisher), incomplete (e.g., author
    and title but no date or publisher), or no source information has been given.

Then, jot down your ideas on how to find the original sources mentioned in the essay. For example, you might use your library catalog to locate Catherine Kohler Riessman's book *Divorce Talk*.

4. **Evidence** Use Tannen's essay as a basis for observing how men and women communicate around you. Observe the men and women with whom you attend class, participate in extracurricular activities, live, or work. Make a chart or list of your observations in relation to Tannen's descriptions. For each of Tannen's points of comparison, decide whether you agree or disagree with her findings based on this exercise and on your own knowledge and experience.

5. **Purpose** At the end of the piece, Tannen provides a reason for why we should work toward better communication between men and women. Evaluate her reasoning. Does it follow logically from the rest of her essay? Does her evidence (the comparisons and contrasts she offers) relate to her conclusion? Defend your answer using specific examples from the essay.

Discussing the Reading

1. Discuss the importance of clear communication in a relationship you have experienced.

2. Discuss how Tannen's findings are similar to or different from those of Dave Barry as expressed in "We've Got the Dirt on Guy Brains" (p. 402).

3. In class or in your journal, describe an incident from your own experience that confirms or contradicts Tannen's findings.

Writing about the Reading

1. **Essay** Tannen provides many points of comparison to support her thesis. Choose one of them and expand it into a comparison-and-contrast essay of your own. Develop the point of comparison by using information from your own experiences. For example, you could show how differences in body language do indeed reflect a common communication pattern.

2. **Essay** Tannen's essay addresses differences in communication between men and women. Consider how communication is similar or different between two other groups—parents and teenagers, employers and employees, or twenty-year-olds and forty-year-olds, for example. Then write an essay that defines each group and compares or contrasts their differences or similarities. Include descriptive details and narration to help readers "see" your subjects. Conclude with possible reasons for the differences you observed.

3. **Internet research** Using a search engine, look for articles on communication between men and women. For example, the *Purdue News* includes a short article on this subject at http://news.uns.purdue.edu/UNS/html4ever /2004/040217.MacGeorge.sexroles.html. After choosing an article, write an essay that compares and contrasts it with Tannen's report. Are their findings similar or different? If they disagree, why might their findings differ?

COMBINING THE PATTERNS

Why Chinese Mothers Are Superior

Amy Chua is a professor at Yale Law School whose expertise includes international business transactions and globalization. Her personal account of extreme parenting, *Battle Hymn of the Tiger Mother*, propelled her onto *Time* magazine's 2011 list of the "100 Most Influential People in the World." The following excerpt comes from *Battle Hymn*.

Reading Tip

This essay is relatively long. As you read, look specifically for the point at which the author begins to focus most directly on comparing and contrasting her two subjects.

Previewing the Reading

Preview the reading (see pp. 23–24 for guidelines) to learn what two specific subjects the author is comparing.

Why Chinese Mothers Are Superior

AMY CHUA

A lot of people wonder how Chinese parents raise such stereotypically successful kids. They wonder what these parents do to produce so many math whizzes and music prodigies, what it's like inside the family, and whether they could do it too. Well, I can tell them, because I've done it. Here are some things my daughters, Sophia and Louisa, were never allowed to do:

- attend a sleepover
- have a playdate
- be in a school play
- complain about not being in a school play
- watch TV or play computer games
- choose their own extracurricular activities
- get any grade less than an A
- not be the No. 1 student in every subject except gym and drama
- play any instrument other than piano or violin
- not play piano or violin

I'm using the term "Chinese mother" loosely. I know some Korean, Indian, Jamaican, Irish, and Ghanaian parents who qualify too. Conversely, I know some

Amy Chua with her daughters, Louisa and Sophia, at their home in New Haven, Connecticut.

mothers of Chinese heritage, almost always born in the West, who are not Chinese mothers, by choice or otherwise. I'm also using the term "Western parents" loosely. Western parents come in all varieties.

All the same, even when Western parents think they're being strict, they usually don't come close to being Chinese mothers. For example, my Western friends who consider themselves strict make their children practice their instruments for thirty minutes every day. An hour at most. For a Chinese mother, the first hour is the easy part. It's hours two and three that get tough.

Despite our squeamishness about cultural stereotypes, there are tons of studies out there showing marked and quantifiable differences between Chinese and Westerners when it comes to parenting. In one study of fifty Western American mothers and forty-eight Chinese immigrant mothers, almost 70% of the Western mothers said either that "stressing academic success is not good for children" or that "parents need to foster the idea that learning is fun." By contrast, roughly 0% of Chinese mothers felt the same way. Instead, the vast majority of the Chinese mothers said that they believe their children can be "the best" students, that "academic achievement reflects successful parenting," and that if children did not excel at school then there was "a problem" and parents "were not doing their job." Other studies indicate that compared to Western parents, Chinese parents spend approximately ten times as long every day drilling academic activities with their children. By contrast, Western kids are more likely to participate in sports teams.

What Chinese parents understand is that nothing is fun until you're good at it. To get good at anything you have to work, and children on their own never want to work, which is why it is crucial to override their preferences. This often

Continued >

requires fortitude on the part of the parents because the child will resist; things are always hardest at the beginning, which is where Western parents tend to give up. But if done properly, the Chinese strategy produces a virtuous circle. Tenacious practice, practice, practice is crucial for excellence; rote repetition is underrated in America. Once a child starts to excel at something—whether it's math, piano, pitching, or ballet—he or she gets praise, admiration, and satisfaction. This builds confidence and makes the once not-fun activity fun. This in turn makes it easier for the parent to get the child to work even more.

Chinese parents can get away with things that Western parents can't. Once 5 when I was young—maybe more than once—when I was extremely disrespectful to my mother, my father angrily called me "garbage" in our native Hokkien dialect. It worked really well. I felt terrible and deeply ashamed of what I had done. But it didn't damage my self-esteem or anything like that. I knew exactly how highly he thought of me. I didn't actually think I was worthless or feel like a piece of garbage.

As an adult, I once did the same thing to Sophia, calling her garbage in English when she acted extremely disrespectfully toward me. When I mentioned that I had done this at a dinner party, I was immediately ostracized. One guest named Marcy got so upset she broke down in tears and had to leave early. My friend Susan, the host, tried to rehabilitate me with the remaining guests.

The fact is that Chinese parents can do things that would seem unimaginable— even legally actionable—to Westerners. Chinese mothers can say to their daughters, "Hey fatty—lose some weight." By contrast, Western parents have to tiptoe around the issue, talking in terms of "health" and never ever mentioning the f-word, and their kids still end up in therapy for eating disorders and negative self-image. (I also once heard a Western father toast his adult daughter by calling her "beautiful and incredibly competent." She later told me that made her feel like garbage.)

Chinese parents can order their kids to get straight As. Western parents can only ask their kids to try their best. Chinese parents can say, "You're lazy. All your classmates are getting ahead of you." By contrast, Western parents have to struggle with their own conflicted feelings about achievement, and try to persuade themselves that they're not disappointed about how their kids turned out.

I've thought long and hard about how Chinese parents can get away with what they do. I think there are three big differences between the Chinese and Western parental mind-sets.

First, I've noticed that Western parents are extremely anxious about their chil- 10 dren's self-esteem. They worry about how their children will feel if they fail at something, and they constantly try to reassure their children about how good they are notwithstanding a mediocre performance on a test or at a recital. In other words, Western parents are concerned about their children's psyches. Chinese parents aren't. They assume strength, not fragility, and as a result they behave very differently.

For example, if a child comes home with an A-minus on a test, a Western parent will most likely praise the child. The Chinese mother will gasp in horror and ask what went wrong. If the child comes home with a B on the test, some Western parents will still praise the child. Other Western parents will sit their child down and express disapproval, but they will be careful not to make their child feel inadequate or insecure, and they will not call their child "stupid," "worthless," or "a disgrace." Privately, the Western parents may worry that their child does not test well or have aptitude in the subject or that there is something wrong with the curriculum and possibly the whole school. If the child's grades do not improve, they may eventually schedule a meeting with the school principal to challenge the way the subject is being taught or call into question the teacher's credentials.

If a Chinese child gets a B—which would never happen—there would first be a screaming, hair-tearing explosion. The devastated Chinese mother would then get dozens, maybe hundreds of practice tests and work through them with her child for as long as it takes to get the grade up to an A.

Chinese parents demand perfect grades because they believe that their child can get them. If their child doesn't get them, the Chinese parent assumes it's because the child didn't work hard enough. That's why the solution to substandard performance is always to excoriate, punish, and shame the child. The Chinese parent believes that their child will be strong enough to take the shaming and to improve from it. (And when Chinese kids do excel, there is plenty of ego-inflating parental praise lavished in the privacy of the home.)

Second, Chinese parents believe that their kids owe them everything. The reason for this is a little unclear, but it's probably a combination of Confucian filial piety and the fact that the parents have sacrificed and done so much for their children. (And it's true that Chinese mothers get in the trenches, putting in long grueling hours personally tutoring, training, interrogating, and spying on their kids.) Anyway, the understanding is that Chinese children must spend their lives repaying their parents by obeying them and making them proud.

By contrast, I don't think most Westerners have the same view of children 15 being permanently indebted to their parents. My husband, Jed, actually has the opposite view. "Children don't choose their parents," he once said to me. "They don't even choose to be born. It's parents who foist life on their kids, so it's the parents' responsibility to provide for them. Kids don't owe their parents anything. Their duty will be to their own kids." This strikes me as a terrible deal for the Western parent.

Third, Chinese parents believe that they know what is best for their children and therefore override all their children's own desires and preferences. That's why Chinese daughters can't have boyfriends in high school and why Chinese kids can't go to sleepaway camp. It's also why no Chinese kid would ever dare say to their mother, "I got a part in the school play! I'm Villager Number Six. I'll have to stay after school for rehearsal everyday from 3:00 to 7:00, and I'll also need a ride on weekends." God help any Chinese kid who tried that one.

Continued >

Don't get me wrong. It's not that Chinese parents don't care about their children. Just the opposite. They would give up anything for their children. It's just an entirely different parenting model.

Here's a story in favor of coercion, Chinese-style. Lulu was about seven, still playing two instruments, and working on a piano piece called "The Little White Donkey" by the French composer Jacques Ibert. The piece is really cute—you can just imagine a little donkey ambling along a country road with its master—but it's also incredibly difficult for young players because the two hands have to keep schizophrenically different rhythms.

Lulu couldn't do it. We worked on it nonstop for a week, drilling each of her hands separately, over and over. But whenever we tried putting the hands together, one always morphed into the other, and everything fell apart. Finally, the day before her lesson, Lulu announced in exasperation that she was giving up and stomped off.

"Get back to the piano now," I ordered.   20

"You can't make me."

"Oh yes, I can."

Back at the piano, Lulu made me pay. She punched, thrashed, and kicked. She grabbed the music score and tore it to shreds. I taped the score back together and encased it in a plastic shield so that it could never be destroyed again. Then I hauled Lulu's dollhouse to the car and told her I'd donate it to the Salvation Army piece by piece if she didn't have "The Little White Donkey" perfect by the next day. When Lulu said, "I thought you were going to the Salvation Army, why are you still here?" I threatened her with no lunch, no dinner, no Christmas or Hanukkah presents, no birthday parties for two, three, four years. When she still kept playing it wrong, I told her she was purposely working herself into a frenzy because she was secretly afraid she couldn't do it. I told her to stop being lazy, cowardly, self-indulgent, and pathetic.

Jed took me aside. He told me to stop insulting Lulu—which I wasn't even doing, I was just motivating her—and that he didn't think threatening Lulu was helpful. Also, he said, maybe Lulu really just couldn't do the technique—perhaps she didn't have the coordination yet—had I considered that possibility?

"You just don't believe in her," I accused.   25

"That's ridiculous," Jed said scornfully. "Of course I do."

"Sophia could play the piece when she was this age."

"But Lulu and Sophia are different people," Jed pointed out.

"Oh no, not this," I said, rolling my eyes. "Everyone is special in their own special way." I mimicked sarcastically. "Even losers are special in their own special way. Well don't worry, you don't have to lift a finger. I'm willing to put in as long as it takes, and I'm happy to be the one hated. And you can be the one they adore because you make them pancakes and take them to Yankees games."

I rolled up my sleeves and went back to Lulu. I used every weapon and tactic   30 I could think of. We worked right through dinner into the night, and I wouldn't let Lulu get up, not for water, not even to go to the bathroom. The house became a war zone, and I lost my voice yelling, but still there seemed to be only negative progress, and even I began to have doubts.

Then, out of the blue, Lulu did it. Her hands suddenly came together—her right and left hands each doing their own imperturbable thing—just like that.

Lulu realized it at the same time I did. I held my breath. She tried it tentatively again. Then she played it more confidently and faster, and still the rhythm held. A moment later, she was beaming.

"Mommy, look—it's easy!" After that, she wanted to play the piece over and over and wouldn't leave the piano. That night, she came to sleep in my bed, and we snuggled and hugged, cracking each other up. When she performed "The Little White Donkey" at a recital a few weeks later, parents came up to me and said, "What a perfect piece for Lulu—it's so spunky and so *her*."

Even Jed gave me credit for that one. Western parents worry a lot about their children's self-esteem. But as a parent, one of the worst things you can do for your child's self-esteem is to let them give up. On the flip side, there's nothing better for building confidence than learning you can do something you thought you couldn't.

There are all these new books out there portraying Asian mothers as scheming, callous, overdriven people indifferent to their kids' true interests. For their part, many Chinese secretly believe that they care more about their children and are willing to sacrifice much more for them than Westerners, who seem perfectly content to let their children turn out badly. I think it's a misunderstanding on both sides. All decent parents want to do what's best for their children. The Chinese just have a totally different idea of how to do that. 35

Western parents try to respect their children's individuality, encouraging them to pursue their true passions, supporting their choices, and providing positive reinforcement and a nurturing environment. By contrast, the Chinese believe that the best way to protect their children is by preparing them for the future, letting them see what they're capable of, and arming them with skills, work habits, and inner confidence that no one can ever take away.

Understanding the Reading

1. **Thesis** What is Chua's thesis, and where does she state it most directly?

2. **Meaning** What is Chua's point in paragraph 4? How does she go on to illustrate this point at length later in the essay?

3. **Meaning** Summarize paragraphs 5–7. What does the brief anecdote about the Western father and daughter at the end of paragraph 7 contribute to Chua's meaning?

4. **Points of comparison** What three main points of distinction does Chua make between Chinese and Western parents?

5. **Argument** Without quite saying so directly, Chua is arguing a point as she contrasts Chinese and Western parents. What is this argument, and where in the essay does she suggest it clearly?

6. **Language** In paragraph 10, what does Chua mean when she writes that Western parents are concerned for their children's "psyches"? Why do Chinese parents not worry that sometimes they may have to "excoriate" their children (13)?

7. **Language** In paragraph 35, Chua writes that Asian mothers have been portrayed as "scheming, callous, overdriven people indifferent to their kids' true interests." Do you think this describes Chua?

8. **Organization** Create a graphic organizer of the reading (see pp. 388–89). Is the organization subject by subject or point by point?

Analyzing the Reading

1. **Audience** Would you say Chua is writing primarily for Western readers or readers of Asian heritage? What makes you think so?

2. **Technique** Chua opens with a list of things she doesn't allow her daughters to do. What effect does she expect this list to have on readers?

3. **Evidence** Early in the essay, Chua offers statistical data from several different sources. What role do these statistics serve?

4. **Structure** What is the purpose of paragraph 9?

5. **Structure** Why do you suppose Chua relates in such detail the story of her struggle with her daughter over learning the piano piece (paras. 18–33)?

6. **Visual** How does the photograph of Chua and her daughters contribute to the thesis of this essay?

Evaluating the Reading

1. **Opening** Evaluate Chua's four opening paragraphs. How do they create interest in her topic?

2. **Bias** How fairly do you think Chua represents Western parents? Do your own biases contribute to your response?

3. **Strategy** Why do you think Chua gives voice to her non-Asian husband in paragraph 15 and when she tells about her struggle with Lulu (paras. 25–29)? Do you think she presents his views adequately?

4. **Technique** How well do you think Chua narrates the story of her struggle with Lulu (paras. 18–33)? Do the action and dialogue seem believable to you?

5. **Argument** How well do you think Chua makes her case for her Chinese parenting philosophy and methods? Are you convinced that they work as she claims?

Discussing the Reading

1. Chua writes in paragraph 4 that "practice, practice, practice is crucial for excellence; rote repetition is underrated in America." How do you respond to this statement?

2. Chua has no qualms about parents referring to their children as "garbage," "fatty," "lazy," "cowardly," "self-indulgent," even "pathetic." Can she really believe this and still consider herself a loving parent?

3. In not allowing her daughters to participate in extracurricular activities of their own choosing, is Chua limiting her daughters' lives? Or do parents know best?

4. Chua writes of telling her husband that she's "'happy to be the one hated'" and to allow him to be the parent their daughters "'adore'" (para 29). What does this suggest to you about Chua as a person?

Writing about the Reading

1. **Essay** Write an essay comparing and contrasting the parenting styles of two parents—or sets of parents—that you know. You might choose your own parents and a friend's parents, yourself as a parent and your parents when you were a child, or perhaps a mother and a father with different parenting styles. While planning, be sure to focus on types of parental differences, as Chua does in paragraphs 9–17.

2. **Essay** Just as parents have different approaches to child rearing, teachers have different approaches to educating. Think of two teachers you've had whose ways of dealing with students and presenting material differ, at least in some respects. Then write an essay comparing and contrasting the two styles. Like Chua, you might cast your essay as a comparison not so much of individuals but of the more general types each represents. (Another possibility might be to focus on two different coaching styles.)

3. **Combined patterns** Using either of the previous two suggestions, write an essay in which you both compare and contrast your subjects and make the argument that one style is preferable to the other.

📖 TEXTBOOK

Dealing with Cultural Differences

Carole Wade holds a Ph.D. in cognitive psychology from Stanford University. She and **Carol Tavris**, a writer and public lecturer on psychology, have co-authored four books. Among their collaborations is *Invitation to Psychology*, from which the following selection is taken.

Reading Tip

As you read, consider what the authors mean by *critical thinking*, a term they use several times in the selection, and why they think critical-thinking skills are important.

Previewing the Reading

Preview the reading (see pp. 23–24 for guidelines), and then list three questions you expect it to answer.

Dealing with Cultural Differences
Carole Wade and Carol Tavris

A French salesman worked for a company that was bought by Americans. When the new American manager ordered him to step up his sales within the next three months, the employee quit in a huff, taking his customers with him. Why? In France, it takes years to develop customers; in family-owned businesses, relationships with customers may span generations. The American manager wanted instant results, as Americans often do, but the French salesman knew this was impossible and quit. The American view was, "He wasn't up to the job; he's lazy and disloyal, so he stole my customers." The French view was, "There is no point in explaining anything to a person who is so stupid as to think you can acquire loyal customers in three months."

Both men were committing the fundamental attribution error: assuming that the other person's behavior was due to personality rather than the situation, in this case a situation governed by cultural rules. Many corporations now realize that such rules are not trivial and that success in a global economy depends on understanding them. But you don't have to go to another country to encounter cultural differences; they are right here at home.

If you find yourself getting angry over something a person from another culture is doing or not doing, use the skills of critical thinking to find out whether your expectations and perceptions of that person's behavior are appropriate. Take the time to examine your assumptions and biases, consider other explanations of the other person's actions, and avoid emotional reasoning. For example, people who shake hands as a gesture of friendship and courtesy are likely to feel insulted if a person from a non-hand-shaking culture refuses to do the same, unless they have asked themselves the question, "Does everyone have the custom of shaking hands the way I do?"

Similarly, people from Middle Eastern and Latin American cultures are used to bargaining for what they buy; Americans and northern Europeans are used to having a fixed price. People who do not know how to bargain, therefore, are likely to find bargaining an exercise in frustration because they will not know whether they got taken or got a great deal. In contrast, people from bargaining cultures will feel just as exasperated if a seller offers a flat price. "Where's the fun in this?" they'll say. "The whole human transaction of shopping is gone!"

Learning another culture's rule or custom is hard enough, but it 5 is much more difficult to comprehend cultural differences that are deeply embedded in its language. For instance, in Iran, the social principle of *taarof* describes the practice of deliberate insincerity, such as giving false praise and making promises you have no intention of keeping. Iranians know that they are supposed to tell you what you want to hear to avoid conflict or to offer hope for a compromise. To Iranians, these practices are a part of good manners; they are not offended by them. But Americans and members of other English-speaking cultures are used to "straight talking," to saying directly and succinctly what they want. Therefore they find *taarof* hard to learn, let alone to practice. As an Iranian social scientist told the *New York Times* (August 6, 2006), "Speech has a different function than it does in the West"—in the West, "yes" generally means yes; in Iran, "yes" can mean yes, but it often means maybe or no. "This creates a rich, poetic linguistic culture," he said. "It creates a multidimensional culture where people are adept at picking up on nuances. On the other hand, it makes for bad political discourse. In political discourse people don't know what to trust."

You can see why critical thinking can help people avoid the tendency to stereotype and to see cultural differences in communication solely in hostile, negative ways. "Why are the Iranians lying to me?" an American might ask. The answer is that they are not "lying" in Iranian terms; they are speaking in a way that is completely natural for them, according to their cultural rules for communication.

To learn the unspoken rules of a culture, you must look, listen, and observe. What is the pace of life like? Do people regard brash individuality and loud speech as admirable or embarrassing? When customers enter a shop, do they greet and chat with the shopkeeper or ignore the person as they browse? Are people expected to be direct in their speech or evasive? Sociocultural research enhances critical

Continued >

thinking by teaching us to appreciate the many cultural rules that govern people's behavior, values, attitudes, and ways of doing business. Before you write off someone from a culture different from your own as being rude, foolish, stubborn, or devious, consider other interpretations of that person's behavior—just as you would want that person to consider other, more forgiving, interpretations of yours.

Understanding the Reading

1. **Textbook reading** This reading is from a featured section called "Taking Psychology with You" at the end of a psychology textbook chapter titled "Behavior in Social and Cultural Context." What does this suggest about the purpose of this section in terms of the rest of the chapter?

2. **Summary** In a sentence or two, summarize the main idea of the reading. What underlying argument is being made?

3. **Language** In paragraph 2, the authors define the term *attribution error*. Where else in the reading are terms used and then defined? Highlight them.

Analyzing the Reading

1. **Similarities and differences** In what way does the use of comparison and contrast in this reading differ from that in other essays in this chapter? How does the subject of the reading account for this difference?

2. **Technique** What is the point of the opening example? How does it function in making the larger point of the reading?

3. **Conclusion** The final paragraph includes a series of questions. What do they contribute to the conclusion?

4. **Language** The final sentence suggests that readers should not assume that the behavior of someone from another culture is "rude, foolish, stubborn, or devious." How do these adjectives relate to the rest of the selection?

Evaluating the Reading

1. **Value of information** Do you feel that this selection taught you something useful? Explain your answer.

2. **Examples** The authors present four examples of specific cultural behavior in paragraphs 1, 3, 4, and 5. Do you think these examples are sufficient to communicate the point being made?

3. **Technique** In paragraphs 1, 3, 4, and 6, the authors create imaginary quotations of people they suppose are experiencing cultural miscommunication. How realistic do you find these?

Discussing the Reading

1. The authors' underlying assumption is that "success in a global economy" (para. 2) requires understanding differences among cultures. How do you respond to this idea?

2. The authors write in paragraph 7 that learning "the unspoken rules of a culture" requires one to "look, listen, and observe." What would you add to this advice?

3. Paragraph 5 suggests that, unlike Iranians, English speakers are "straight talking" and don't practice "deliberate insincerity." In your experience, is this the case? Further, is political discourse in the United States, therefore, basically trustworthy?

Writing about the Reading

1. **Response paper** Write an essay responding to the examples of cultural difference described in paragraphs 1, 3, 4, and 5. Which behavior in each case does your background lead you to view more favorably, and why do you feel as you do?

2. **Applying the reading** Based on the information in the selection, as well as on your own experience, write an essay providing advice about potential cultural misunderstandings about someone you know well.

3. **Using the strategy** This selection considers "the tendency to stereotype" (para. 6). Write an essay comparing and contrasting a widely held cultural stereotype with the reality as you know it. Potential subjects include ethnic stereotypes, regional stereotypes, and stereotypes based on people's activities and interests.

Writing Your Own
Comparison-and-Contrast Essay

Now that you have learned about the major characteristics, structure, and purposes of a comparison-and-contrast essay, you know everything necessary to write your own. In this section you will read a student's comparison-and-contrast essay and get advice on finding ideas, drafting your essay, and revising and editing it. You may want to use the essay prompts in "Readings for Practice, Ideas for Writing" (p. 398) or choose your own topic.

A Student Model Comparison-and-Contrast Essay

Heather Gianakos was a first-year student when she wrote the following comparison-and-contrast essay for her composition course. Although she had always enjoyed the two styles of cooking she chose to discuss, she needed to do some research in the library and on the Internet to learn more about their history. As you read the essay, observe how Gianakos integrates information from sources into her essay.

Border Bites

Heather Gianakos

Introduction indicates essay examines similarities and differences but focuses on differences.

Thesis

Subject A: Southwestern food

Subject B: Mexican food

Chili peppers, tortillas, tacos: All these foods belong to the styles of cooking known as Mexican, Tex-Mex, and southwestern. These internationally popular styles often overlap; sometimes it can be hard to tell which style a particular dish belongs to. Two particular traditions of cooking, however, play an especially important role in the kitchens of Mexico and the American Southwest—native-derived Mexican cooking ("Mexican"), and Anglo-influenced southwestern cooking, particularly from Texas ("southwestern"). The different traditions and geographic locations of the inhabitants of Mexico and of the Anglo American settlers in the Southwest have resulted in subtle, flavorful differences between the foods featured in Mexican and southwestern cuisine.

Body paragraphs: point by point

Point 1: the physical conditions in which the two styles developed

A: difficult conditions

Many of the traditions of southwestern cooking grew out of difficult situations—cowboys and ranchers cooking over open fires, for example. Chili, which can contain beans, beef, tomatoes, corn, and many other ingredients, was a good dish to cook over a campfire because everything could be combined in one pot. Dry foods, such as beef jerky, were a convenient way to solve food storage problems and could be easily tucked into saddlebags. In

B: fresh foods available

Notice the use of transitions and sources

Mexico, by contrast, fresh fruits and vegetables such as avocados and tomatoes were widely available and did not need to be dried or stored. They could be made into spicy salsa and guacamole. Mexicans living in coastal areas could also enjoy fish and lobster dishes (Jamison and Jamison 5).

Point 2: the use of corn and wheat

Corn has been a staple in the American Southwest and Mexico since the time of the Aztecs, who made tortillas (flat, unleavened bread, originally made from stone-ground corn and water) similar to the ones served in Mexico today (Jamison and Jamison 5). Southwesterners, often of European descent, adopted the tortilla but often prepared it with wheat flour, which was easily available to them. Wheat-flour tortillas can now be found in both Mexican and southwestern cooking, but corn is usually the primary grain in dishes with precolonial origins. Tamales (whose name derives from a word in Nahuatl, the Aztec group of languages) are a delicious example: A hunk of cornmeal dough, sometimes combined with ground meat, is wrapped in corn husks and steamed. In southwestern cooking, corn is often used for leavened corn bread, which is made with corn flour rather than cornmeal and can be flavored with jalapeños or back bacon.

A and B: in tortillas
B: corn especially important; example: tamales
A: corn bread

Point 3: the use of chicken
A: fried
B: stewed or baked

Meat of various kinds is often the centerpiece of both Mexican and southwestern tables. However, although chicken, beef, and pork are staples in both traditions, they are often prepared quite differently. Fried chicken rolled in flour and dunked into sizzling oil or fat is a popular dish throughout the American Southwest. In traditional Mexican cooking, however, chicken is often cooked more slowly, in stews or baked dishes, with a variety of seasonings, including ancho chiles, garlic, and onions.

Point 4: the use of beef
A: grilled
B: fajita or taco

Ever since cattle farming began in Texas with the early Spanish missions, beef has been eaten both north and south of the border. In southwestern cooking, steak—flank, rib eye, or sirloin—grilled quickly and served rare is often a chef's crowning glory. In Mexican cooking, beef may be combined with vegetables and spices and rolled into a fajita or served ground in a taco. For a Mexican food purist, in fact, the only true fajita is made from skirt steak, although Mexican food as it is served in the United States often features chicken fajitas.

Point 5: the use of pork
A: BBQ

In Texas and the Southwest United States, barbecued pork ribs are often prepared in barbecue cook-offs, similar to chili-cooking competitions. Such competitions have strict rules for the preparation and presentation of the food and for sanitation

B: originated BBQ; chorizo

(Central Texas). However, while the BBQ is seen as a southwestern specialty, barbecue ribs as they are served in southwestern-themed restaurants today actually come from a Hispanic and Southwest Mexican tradition dating from the days before refrigeration: Since pork fat, unlike beef fat, has a tendency to become rancid, pork ribs were often marinated in vinegar and spices and then hung to dry. Later the ribs were basted with the same sauce and grilled (Campa 278). The resulting dish has become a favorite both north and south of the border, although in Mexican cooking, where beef is somewhat less important than in southwestern cooking, pork is equally popular in many other forms, such as chorizo sausage.

Conclusion: Gianakos returns to the idea of overlap mentioned in the introduction and makes clear her purpose—to inform readers about the differences between the two cuisines.

    Cooks in San Antonio or Albuquerque would probably tell you that the food they cook is as much Mexican as it is southwestern. Regional cuisines in such areas of the Southwest as New Mexico, Southern California, and Arizona feature elements of both traditions; chimichangas—deep-fried burritos—actually originated in Arizona (Jamison and Jamison 11). Food lovers who sample regional specialties, however, will note—and savor—the contrast between the spicy, fried or grilled, beef-heavy style of southwestern food and the richly seasoned, corn- and tomato-heavy style of Mexican food.

Works Cited

Campa, Arthur L. *Hispanic Culture in the Southwest*. Norman: U of Oklahoma P, 1979. Print.

Central Texas Barbecue Association. "CTBA Rules." *Central Texas Barbecue Association*. CTBA, 16 Aug. 2004. Web. 6 May 2005.

Jamison, Cheryl Alters, and Bill Jamison. *The Border Cookbook*. Boston: Harvard Common, 1995. Print.

Responding to Gianakos's Essay

1. What is Gianakos's purpose in writing the essay? How effectively does she present and support her thesis?

2. What method of organization does Gianakos use?

3. Consider Gianakos's points of comparison. How effective is she in presenting details to support each point? What types of examples and sensory details describe each characteristic?

4. How does Gianakos's use of sources contribute to the essay?

Finding Ideas for Your Comparison-and-Contrast Essay

To write a comparison-and-contrast essay, consider the following strategies.

- If you read an essay that interested you, try comparing its subjects by using a different basis of comparison. If, for example, an essay compares or contrasts athletes in two sports on the basis of salary, you could compare them according to the training required.

- If an essay that interested you emphasized differences between its subjects, consider writing about their similarities, or vice versa. For example, in response to an essay on the differences between two late-night television hosts, you might write about their similarities.

- If a reading has a point of comparison that you would like to develop in more depth, you might do research to discover further information or interview an expert on the topic.

Choosing a Basis of Comparison and a Purpose

The first step is to choose specific subjects to write about. You may want to compare subjects that are concrete (such as two public figures) or abstract (such as teaching styles or views on an issue). Be sure, in any case, to choose subjects with which you have some firsthand experience or that you can learn about through research. Also choose subjects that interest you. It will be more fun writing about them, and your enthusiasm will enliven your essay.

After selecting your subjects, you need to establish a basis of comparison and a purpose for writing. To compare or contrast two well-known football players—a quarterback and a linebacker—you could compare them on the basis of the positions they play, describing the skills and training needed for each position. Your purpose in this instance would be to *inform* readers about the two positions. Alternatively, you could base the comparison on their performances on the field; in this case, your purpose might be to *persuade* readers to accept your evaluation of both players and your opinion on who is the better athlete. Other bases of comparison might be the players' media images, contributions to their respective teams, or service to the community.

Once you have a basis of comparison and a purpose, try to state them clearly in a few sentences. Refer to these sentences throughout the process of writing your essay to keep on track.

Discovering Similarities and Differences and Generating Details

The next step is to discover how your two subjects are similar and how they are different. You can approach this task in a number of ways.

1. **Create a two-column list of similarities and differences.** Jot down ideas in the appropriate column.

2. **Ask a classmate to help you brainstorm aloud by mentioning only similarities; then counter each similarity with a difference.** Take notes as you brainstorm, or record your session.

3. **If your subjects are concrete, try visualizing them.** Take notes on what you "see," or draw a sketch of the subjects.

4. **Create a scenario in which your subjects interact.** For example, if your topic is automobiles of the 1920s and 2004, imagine taking your great-grandfather, who owned a Model T Ford, for a drive in a 2004 luxury car. How would he react? What would he say?

5. **Do research on your two subjects at the library or on the Internet.**

Keep in mind that your readers will need plenty of details to grasp the similarities and differences between the subjects. Vivid descriptions, interesting examples, and appropriate facts will make your subjects seem real.

To maintain an even balance between the two subjects, do some brainstorming, freewriting, or library or Internet research to gather roughly the same amount of detail for each. This guideline is especially important if your purpose is to demonstrate that Subject A is preferable to or better than Subject B. Readers will become suspicious if you provide plenty of detail about Subject A and only sketchy information about Subject B.

Developing and Supporting Your Thesis

The thesis statement for a comparison-and-contrast essay needs to fulfill the three criteria noted earlier: It identifies the subjects; suggests whether you will focus on similarities, differences, or both; and states your main point. In addition, the thesis should tell why your comparison and contrast of the two subjects is important or useful. Look at the following sample thesis statements.

WEAK   The books by Robert Parker and Sue Grafton are similar.

REVISED   The novels of Robert Parker and Sue Grafton are popular because readers are fascinated by the intrigues of witty, independent private detectives.

The first thesis is weak because it presents the two subjects in isolation, without placing the comparison within a context or giving readers a reason to care about it. The second thesis provides a basis for comparison and indicates why the similarity is worth reading about. As you develop your thesis, consider what large idea or worthwhile point the comparison demonstrates.

Selecting Points of Comparison

With your thesis in mind, review your notes and try to identify the points or characteristics by which you can best compare your subjects. For example, if your thesis involves evaluating the performance of two football players, you would probably select various facts and details about their training, the plays they make, and their records. Think of points of comparison as the main similarities or differences that support your thesis. Make sure to have enough points of comparison to support the thesis and enough details to develop those points. If necessary, do additional brainstorming.

Drafting Your Comparison-and-Contrast Essay

Before you begin writing, decide whether you will use a point-by-point or a subject-by-subject organization. To select a method of organization, consider the complexity of your subjects and the length of your essay. You may also need to experiment with the two approaches to see which one works better. It is a good idea to make an outline or draw a graphic organizer at this stage. To experiment with different methods of organization, create a new computer file for each possibility and try each one out.

Here are a few other points to consider when deciding what method of organization to use.

- The subject-by-subject method tends to emphasize the larger picture, whereas the point-by-point method emphasizes details and specifics.
- The point-by-point method often works better for lengthy essays because it keeps both subjects current in the reader's mind.
- The point-by-point method is usually preferable for complicated or technical subjects.

After choosing a method of organization, your next step is to write a first draft. Use the following guidelines.

1. **Write an effective introduction.** The introduction should spark readers' interest, present your subjects, state your thesis, and include any background information readers may need.

2. **For a point-by-point essay, work back and forth between the two subjects, mentioning the subjects in the same order.**

3. **For a point-by-point essay, arrange the points of comparison carefully.** Start with the clearest, simplest points and then move on to more complex ones.

4. **For a subject-by-subject essay, cover the same points for both subjects.** Address the points of comparison for each subject in the same order for both halves of your essay.

5. **Use transitions to alert readers to the organization of the essay and to shifts between subjects or to a new point of comparison.** To move between subjects, use transitional words and phrases such as *similarly, in contrast, on the one hand . . . on the other hand,* and *not only . . . but also.*

Figure 14.4 Revising a Comparison-and-Contrast Essay

QUESTIONS	REVISION STRATEGIES

1. Thesis Does it identify the subjects being compared and state your main point? Does it or do nearby sentences express a clear purpose?

No →
- Brainstorm a list of reasons for making the comparison. Make the most promising reason your purpose.

Yes ↓

2. Basis of comparison Is it clear? Does it relate to your thesis?

No →
- Brainstorm a clear or new basis of comparison with a friend or classmate.

Yes ↓

3. Points of comparison Have you included all significant points of comparison and fairly examined them? Does each support your thesis?

No →
- Delete any insignificant similarities or differences or ones that do not support your thesis.
- Add any significant points of comparison from your prewriting that you have not already included.
- Conduct research or talk to a classmate to find new points of comparison.

Yes ↓

4. Topic sentences Does each paragraph have a clear topic sentence? For a point-by-point comparison, is each paragraph focused on a single point or shared characteristic?

No →
- Consider splitting paragraphs that focus on more than one point or characteristic and combining paragraphs that focus on the same one.

Yes ↓

5. Details Are there enough details to make your comparisons vivid and interesting? Is there roughly the same amount of detail for each subject?

No →
- Add or delete details as necessary.
- Review your prewriting to see if you overlooked any significant details.
- Conduct research to come up with additional details.

Yes ↓

6. Organization Did you use either point-by-point or subject-by-subject organization consistently? Is your organization clear to your reader?

No →
- Study your graphic organizer or outline to find inconsistencies or gaps.
- Reorganize your essay using one method of organization consistently.
- Add transitions if necessary.

Yes ↓

7. Introduction and conclusion Does the introduction provide a context for your comparison? Is the conclusion satisfying and relevant to the comparison?

No →
- Revise your introduction and conclusion to meet the guidelines in Chapter 6.
- Consider proposing an action or a way of thinking that is appropriate in light of the comparison.

6. **Write a satisfying conclusion.** The conclusion should offer a final comment on the comparison and contrast, reminding readers of your thesis. For a lengthy or complex essay, it is a good idea to summarize the main points as well.

Revising Your Comparison-and-Contrast Essay

If possible, set your draft aside for a day or two before rereading and revising it. As you reread, concentrate on your ideas and not on grammar or mechanics. Use the flowchart in Figure 14.4 to guide your analysis of the draft's strengths and weaknesses.

Editing and Proofreading Your Essay

The last step is to check your revised essay for errors in grammar, spelling, punctuation, and mechanics. In addition, be sure to look for errors that you tend to make in any writing assignment, whether for this class or another situation. As you edit and proofread your comparison-and-contrast essay, watch out for the types of errors discussed below.

1. **Look at adjectives and adverbs and their degrees of comparison—***positive* **(the form that describes without comparing),** *comparative,* **and** *superlative.* Make sure to change the form of adjectives and adverbs when comparing two items (comparative) and three or more items (superlative). The following examples show how adjectives and adverbs change forms.

	Adjectives	Adverbs
POSITIVE	sharp	early
COMPARATIVE	sharper	earlier
SUPERLATIVE	sharpest	earliest

 ▶ Both *The Village* and *The Sixth Sense* were suspenseful movies, but
   I liked *The Sixth Sense* ~~best~~. [*better*]

 ▶ George, Casey, and Bob all play basketball badly, but Bob's game is
   ~~worse~~. [*the worst*]

2. **Use correlative conjunctions properly.** Make sure that items linked by correlative conjunctions (conjunctions used in pairs, such as *either . . . or, neither . . . nor, not only . . . but also*) are in the same grammatical form.

 ▶ The Grand Canyon is not only a spectacular tourist attraction but also
   ~~scientists consider it~~ a useful geological record/ [*for scientists.*]

Chapter 15

Classification and Division: Explaining Categories and Parts

Quick Start: Study this photograph of a grocery store. Notice how similar items on the shelves are grouped together. Think of a favorite store that you frequent, and write a paragraph describing for someone who has never been there how the different categories of merchandise are arranged. Be sure to clearly identify all the categories.

What Are Classification and Division?

The paragraph you wrote in response to the Quick Start prompt uses **classification**, a method of development that is based on putting items into categories or groups. You use classification every day to organize things and ideas. Your dresser drawers and kitchen cabinets are probably organized by categories—with socks and sweatshirts in different drawers and pots and glasses in different cabinets. Classification, then, is a process of sorting people, things, or ideas into groups or categories to make them more understandable. For example, your college classifies course offerings by schools, divisions, and departments. Imagine how difficult it would be to find courses in a catalog if it were arranged alphabetically instead of by categories.

Division is similar to classification, but instead of involving items grouped into categories, division involves *one* item being broken down into parts. Thus, for example, the humanities department at your college may be divided into English, modern languages, and philosophy; the modern language courses might be further divided into Spanish, French, Chinese, and Russian. Division is related to process analysis (see Chapter 13) in that both involve breaking a thing down into smaller parts.

A classification or division essay explains a topic by describing its categories or parts. For example, a classification essay might explore types (categories) of advertising: direct mail, radio, television, newspaper, online, and so forth. A division essay might describe the parts of an art museum: exhibit areas, museum store, visitor-services desk, and the like. You will find many occasions to use these patterns of development in the writing you do in college and the workplace. For instance, for a course in anatomy and physiology, students might be asked to review the structure and parts of the human ear by identifying the function of each part. In the work world, a facilities planner might conduct a feasibility study of several new sites by sorting them into categories such as within state, out of state, and out of country.

A successful classification or division essay does the following:

1. It groups or divides ideas according to one principle.
2. It develops a principle meaningful to the audience.
3. It uses categories (if classification) or parts (if division) that are exclusive and comprehensive.
4. It fully explains each category or part.

1. Classification and Division Group or Divide Ideas According to One Principle

To sort items into groups for a classification essay, a writer must decide how to categorize them. For example, birds could be classified in terms of size, habitat, or diet, while microwave ovens could be classified by price, size, or manufacturer.

For a division essay, the writer must decide into what parts to divide the topic. The writer of an article surveying the field of psychology could divide the topic of psychology into periods in the development of psychology or into subfields in psychology today.

To develop an effective set of categories or parts, a writer must choose *one principle of classification or division* and use it consistently throughout the essay or within a particular section of the essay. For instance, a college president might classify professors by experience or teaching style, but he or she would not mix categories by classifying some professors by experience and others by teaching style. The president could, however, classify all professors by experience in the first part of a report and then by teaching style in another part.

Once a writer chooses an appropriate principle of classification or division, the next step is to identify a manageable number of categories or parts. An essay classifying birds according to diet, for example, might address five or six types of diet, not twenty.

2. The Principle of Classification or Division Is Meaningful to the Audience

Because several different bases—or principles—can be used to categorize any particular group, the writer's purpose will determine the principle of classification that is chosen. To develop a meaningful classification, therefore, writers must focus on their readers and purpose for writing. When the purpose is to inform, essays should focus on a principle of classification that will be of interest to its readers. If, for instance, a writer wishes to inform parents about the types of day-care centers in the local area, he or she could classify the centers according to the services they offer because readers would be looking for that information.

Division essays, too, are guided by purpose and audience. For example, a writer who divides the day in a kindergarten into time spent on active play, imaginative play, and formal learning might be writing to persuade readers that the kindergarten program is well balanced. His or her audience might be parents considering the program.

3. Categories of a Classification or Parts of a Division Are Exclusive and Comprehensive

Categories or parts should not overlap. In other words, a particular item or person should fit into no more than one category. A familiar example is age: The age categories *25 to 30* and *30 to 35* are not mutually exclusive because someone who is thirty years old would fit into both. The second category should be changed to *31 to 35*. In an essay about the nutritional value of pizza, you could divide the topic into carbohydrates, proteins, and fats, but you would not add a separate category for saturated fat because that is already contained in the fats category.

Categories or parts should also be comprehensive. In a division essay, all the major parts of an item should be included. In a classification essay, the categories must be able to include all the items related to the topic. For example, an essay classifying fast-food restaurants according to type of food served would have to include a category for pizza parlors, as many fast-food establishments belong to this category.

4. A Classification or Division Essay Fully Explains Each Category or Part

A classification or division essay should contain adequate detail so that each category or part can be well understood. In the following excerpt from a student essay on types of sales, the writer describes one source of consumer purchases—vending machines. Notice how the student begins with some background and an explanation of how vending machines work before talking about the advantages of this type of sales. She concludes with details about the types of products one can buy from a vending machine.

Background information	While automatic vending machines have been around since the turn of the century, the accessibility and low overhead associated with them continue to make them a popular sales option. To make a purchase, the consumer simply inserts cash and the machine dispenses the product. This makes vending machines
Advantage 1: Cost effective	cost effective because they do not require sales staff or a high-maintenance selling floor. They are also accessible
Advantage 2: Convenient	twenty-four hours a day and can be placed in convenient locations, such as hotels, malls, and office buildings. A
Advantage 3: Variety of goods available	wide assortment of goods can now be purchased through vending machines: from steaming hot coffee to calorie-packed snacks, everyday items like stamps and subway tokens, and even travel insurance at airports.

Descriptive details such as these enable readers to "see" the writer's categories or parts.

Reading and Writing Classification and Division Essays

In this section you will learn about the structure of classification and division essays, read a sample essay, and practice using the guidelines for understanding, analyzing, and evaluating classification and division essays. This will help you skillfully read and write essays that use classification and division.

How Is a Classification or Division Essay Structured?

Knowing how to structure a classification or division essay will help you write it more effectively and will also help you understand, analyze, and evaluate such essays when you read. The structure of a classification or division essay is straightforward.

1. The **introduction** identifies the subject to be classified or divided and presents the **thesis statement**.
2. The **body paragraphs** explain and describe each category or part.
3. The **conclusion** reinforces the thesis and offers a new insight or perspective.

Figure 15.1 represents these major components visually.

The following sections explain the different parts of the classification and the division essay in more detail.

1.   THE INTRODUCTION EXPLAINS THE CLASSIFICATION OR DIVISION

The introduction, which usually includes the thesis statement, provides background information and may explain or justify the principle of classification or division used. It might also suggest why the classification or division is significant or worth knowing. The thesis statement in a classification or division essay identifies the topic and may reveal the principle used to classify or divide it. The categories or parts may also be briefly identified. In most cases, the writer also suggests why the classification or division is relevant or important. Here are a few examples of thesis statements.

CLASSIFICATION ESSAY   Most people consider videos a form of entertainment; however, videos can also serve educational, commercial, and political functions.

(The essay goes on to classify the subject, the functions of videos, into three types in addition to entertainment.)

DIVISION ESSAY   The Grand Canyon is divided into two distinct geographical areas, the North Rim and the South Rim; each offers different views, facilities, and climatic conditions.

(The essay goes on to discuss the differences between the two parts of the Grand Canyon.)

 Reading | Writing   When reading a classification or division introduction, identify the subject and examine how it is classified or divided. Then assess how familiar you are with the subject and decide how carefully you need to read the essay, what you need to look for and remember, and what strategies to use to read it effectively. When writing a classification or division essay introduction, draw your readers in by explaining why the classification or division is important. You might describe a situation in which familiarity with the classification or division was useful, for instance.

Figure 15.1 Graphic Organizer for a Classification or Division Essay

Title	
Introduction	Topic announcement
	Background information
	Thesis statement
Body paragraphs: categories or parts	Category 1 or Part 1
	Characteristic
	Characteristic
	Characteristic
	Category 2 or Part 2
	Characteristic
	Characteristic
	Characteristic
	Category 3 or Part 3
	Characteristic
	Characteristic
	Characteristic
	Category 4 or Part 4
	Characteristic
	Characteristic
	Characteristic
Conclusion	Reinforces thesis
	Offers new insight or perspective

2. THE BODY PARAGRAPHS EXPLAIN AND DESCRIBE THE CATEGORIES OR PARTS

The body paragraphs each deal with a category or part. These categories or parts result from the principle of classification or division, which should be meaningful to the audience and appropriate to the subject and should make possible an essay with a worthwhile point. An essay discussing highway drivers might classify them by driving habit; its point might be that there are many annoying or unsafe drivers on the road.

Reading | Writing   When reading the body of a classification or division essay, pay attention to the author's organization, noting when he or she moves from category to category or part to part. Creating an outline or a graphic organizer can help you track the organization. Highlight categories and parts and the features of each, using one color to identify categories and parts and another to identify features of each. Also mark important definitions and useful examples for future reference. If you find a category or part confusing, make a marginal annotation and then, later, reread, research, or check with a classmate. When writing the body of a classification or division essay, focus on developing and explaining each category or part, offering roughly the same amount of detail and description for each. To help your reader follow your classification or division, use transitional words and phrases to signal when you are moving on to a new category or part.

3.   THE CONCLUSION REINFORCES THE THESIS AND MAY OFFER NEW INSIGHT

The conclusion should do more than just repeat categories or parts. It should bring the essay to a satisfying close, reemphasizing the thesis or offering a new insight or perspective on the topic.

 Reading | Writing   When reading the conclusion of a classification or division essay, take a moment to summarize the categories or parts presented and their importance. If you find that you can't recall the major points, reread the essay and review your outline or graphic organizer to better understand the topic. When writing a conclusion for a classification or division essay, reread your essay. Then ask yourself, Will my readers care about the topic? Make sure your conclusion addresses this question by reasserting the thesis or shedding new light on the topic.

A Model Classification Essay

Title

Online Dating—Five Things to Avoid

Joshua Fruhlinger

As editor in chief of *TapOnline*, Joshua Fruhlinger helped create the first twenty-four-hour online reality show. He later joined AOL and served as editorial director of *Engadget*, a Web magazine covering electronics and technology. This article appeared in 2007 on Switched, a Web site devoted to the intersection of the digital world and popular culture that is now part of the technology section of the *Huffington Post*.

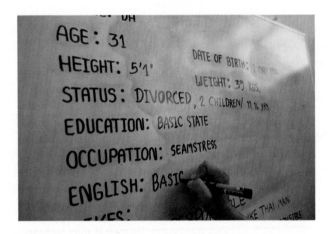

Introduction

Everyone's doing it—over 40% of U.S. singles are finding matches online. That's more than 40 million single Americans cruising the Internet looking for love (based on census results that say there are over 100 million single Americans).

So the Internet *must* be a great place to find true love, right? Not so fast. While online dating can be a great way to find someone new, dating *sites* are littered with scam artists, cheaters, and straight-up liars.

Thesis: Avoid these five types of online daters to spare yourself heartbreak.

Now, this doesn't mean you should avoid online dating altogether—just don't believe everything you see out there. In order to help sort out the winners from the losers, we've compiled a list of the top five types of online daters you should definitely avoid, along with some tips to help you save some heartache. Be careful out there, and good luck!

1. Liars

Category 1: Liars
don't tell the truth
about themselves.

In a recent survey, it was found that most online profiles contain some sort of lie, whether it's the person's age or—in some cases—relationship status. White lies—adding an inch to height or dropping a couple pounds—are the most common and not a big deal to most people.

Consider these facts according to the April 2007 issue of *Proceedings of Computer/Human Interaction*:

Characteristic 1:
Height, weight, and
age are among the
smaller lies told by
online daters.

- About 52.6% of men lie about their height, as do 39% of women.
- Slightly more women lie about their weight (64.1%) than men (60.5%).
- When it comes to age, 24.3% of men lie compared with 13.1% of women.

Characteristic 2:
Misrepresentation of
age or relationship
status can cause
serious problems for
the person who falls
for them.

When it comes to misrepresentations of age or relationship status, be careful or you could get seriously burned. In one recent case, a woman met a man on a popular dating site with whom she immediately hit it off. She even put her life on hold to go with him to Dubai when he was transferred for work. Eleven months into the relationship, she came across an email—from his son! What's more, the email said something about "Mom" saying hi. In one fell swoop, our poor girl found out the man she met online was not only a father—he was married! She moved back to the United States and has given up on online dating since.

How to Avoid Them:

Ask questions. Though it may be listed on someone's profile, someone's age is fair game in the questions department, so feel free to ask your potential date how old (or young!) they are. You may find that thirty-five suddenly becomes forty-two. While you don't want to ask too many questions and scare the person away, it's perfectly fair to verify the big things: age, weight, height, and—most of all—whether or not that person is, in fact, single. Half the time, people lie on their profiles to get people interested—nine times out of ten, someone will level with you about their stats once you show some real interest, since they know they might have a chance of meeting you in person.

2. Photo Fakes

Dating-site traffic analyses show that profiles with pictures are clicked on twice as much as those without. Having a good picture of yourself can be the difference between getting seen and getting

Category 2: Photo fakes post unusually good-looking photos.

lost. However, some people take the notion of "looking good" a little too far. They post misleading pictures that can trap you into thinking you're meeting your dreamboat only to find a shipwreck waiting for you. Let's face it, not everyone looks as good as George Clooney or Angelina Jolie.

Joan, a woman from New Jersey, had thought she met Mr. Right. He was charming and—according to the picture on his profile—quite handsome. She looked forward to seeing his auburn hair and deep eyes when it turned out that Mr. Right had gone gray. He also hadn't

Characteristic 1: They post old photos.

seen a gym in years. Turns out that his profile picture was over five years old. While there's nothing wrong with gray hair or a couple extra pounds, people who misrepresent their looks aren't being honest.

Characteristic 2: They post only one, especially flattering photo.
Characteristic 3: They post photos only taken at flattering angles.

How to Avoid Them:

Look for profiles with more than one picture. People who choose   10
only flattering angles could be hiding something. Ask for a recent picture, and if the person refuses, you could be looking at that person's high school yearbook photo. And if someone looks as good as George Clooney or Angelina Jolie, you need to double-check that it's for real.

Category 3: Fixer-uppers are still healing from previous relationships.
Characteristic 1: They are likely to be critical of potential partners.
Characteristic 2: They list what they don't want in a partner, not what they do want.

3. Fixer-Uppers

Most marriages end in divorce—that's just a fact of life. But many people on the rebound make their profiles about what they *don't* want. The truth is, these people are on the rebound and are likely to still be living with the wounds of their last relationship. You may be in for some serious scrutiny, criticism, and baggage handling, so beware. Imagine, for example, what any of Sir Paul McCartney's new lovers must think as he talks about his past relationships!

Consider these recent profile headlines:

- Cheaters Need Not Apply
- Tired of Meeting Women in Bars
- No Manipulative B*tches, please!
- Please Don't Be a Liar
- Felons, Potheads, and Jerks Need Not Apply

What we have here are jilted lovers. Run. Run away. While it's a good idea to learn from your past relationships, no one wants to date a bitter, angry person. By telling people what you don't want, you're scaring off potential mates.

On the other side, if you're reading profiles, avoid these singles as they are either recently out of relationships or still getting over something pretty big. They're not ready, and you don't want to be their fixer-upper.

How to Avoid Them:

To steer clear of the fixer-upper at all costs, watch out for the aforementioned profile headlines. While you may hate the same things these rebounders do, you still shouldn't pursue a relationship with them. Having something in common can be great, but those things should be positive, not negative. As the old saying goes, You must love yourself before you love another.

Category 4: Membership fishers are trying to lure you to another dating site. **Characteristic 1:** The person's profile is on another site; that site requires you to join. **Characteristic 2:** The person does not exist.

4. Membership Fishers

You finally got a response to your profile, and she's hot! You're all set to respond to the beauty queen, but there's one problem: Her profile happens to be over at some other site.   15

Of course, before you can send her a note on her profile, you're asked by the new dating site she's listed with to sign up. Before you know it, you're a member of a new dating site, and it has your credit card info, and, it turns out, your new love doesn't exist.

Dating sites make their money on membership dues, and with thousands of them competing for daters, they're in a vicious fight to get you to sign up. Some wily sites have taken to trolling single people from other sites, making them think that a new lovely wants to meet them . . . at a new site that requires signing up.

How to Avoid Them:

Make sure anyone you hear from is already signed up with the online dating site you're signed up with. If someone responds to your profile, it means they already have a profile at the site you are using. Don't fall for the "meet me over here" tactic. If they really like you, they'll come talk to you where you are.

5. Cheaters

How is it possible that this new, wonderful person is still single? In fact, he or she may not be. While there are some great singles out there waiting to steal your heart away, some of them are not, in fact, single. Surprise, surprise, it turns out that some people use dating sites as a way to get a little something on the side when they're out of town.

Category 5: Cheaters are already in relationships.

Consider this story about Jill, a twenty-seven-year-old Washington, D.C., marketing executive, who met the "man of her dreams" online: 20

Characteristic 1: He or she might live in a different city than you.

Characteristic 2: He or she may cancel many dates at the last minute.

Characteristic 3: He or she might call you only when on the move or only from a cell phone.

"Since he lived in a different city—Roanoke, Virginia—it was easy for him to sneak around." She told iVillage, "Although he made excuse after excuse about why he continually had to cancel a date at the last minute—one time claiming he'd been in a car accident—I got suspicious only after I knew everything." There had been numerous red flags. For instance, he only called from his cell phone while driving in his car. It turns out that Joe (not his real name) was talking to several women online. According to his wife, Jill was the only one he'd met and kissed.

Note: This essay does not include an explicit conclusion, but ends with some general advice.

How to Avoid Them:

Look out for people who can only talk to you during the day, will only talk online or via text message, or who mysteriously disappear at night and on weekends. Other warning signs include out-of-town lovers who happen to be in town a lot. And be especially cautious of people who live thousands of miles away, since you have no real way of verifying what's actually going on with them day-to-day. There's a good chance you could be on the back burner. Also, look out for people who list their status as "separated"—they could be separated in mind, only.

Understanding, Analyzing, and Evaluating Classification and Division Essays

In reading and writing classification and division essays, your goal is to get beyond mere competence: That is, you want to be able to do more than merely understand the content of the essays you're reading or convey just your basic ideas to the audience you're writing for.

 Reading | Writing   Truly skillful reading and writing require the abilities to understand, analyze, *and* evaluate material. These abilities are important to you as a reader because they give you a systematic, thorough method of examining a reading. They're important to you as a writer because they help you decide what to revise, rewrite, drop, and replace, allowing you to produce a well-written, persuasive essay.

Understanding a Classification or Division Essay

Preview the essay before reading to identify the subject being classified or divided and, if possible, to identify the categories or parts. Then read to become familiar

Understanding in Action

Following is one student's summary of the essay's introduction and the first category it describes. Using this as a model, write a summary of the whole essay.

> While online-dating sites can be a good way to meet possible matches, there is also a lot to beware of. The first thing to look out for is people who lie in their profile. Some lies may be minor, like age or height. Others can be major, like marital status. To protect yourself, ask questions. Make sure in particular that the person is actually single.

with specifics about each category or part. As you read and reread, use the skills you learned in Chapter 2 and look for answers to the following questions.

- **What is the writer's thesis?** State it in your own words. Why is the classification or division important? When might you use this or need to explain it to someone else?

- **What is the principle of classification?** If the author does not explicitly state the principle, try explaining it in your own words. Identifying the principle is the key to understanding the entire essay.

- **What are the categories or parts?** Mark or highlight each as you encounter it. Creating a graphic organizer can help you identify the categories or parts. Figure 15.2 shows a graphic organizer for "Online Dating—Five Things to Avoid."

Analyzing a Classification or Division Essay

Analyzing a classification or division essay involves examining how and why the classification or division was made. Use the following questions to guide your analysis.

- **Is each category or part clearly named or titled?** The author should make it easy for the reader to identify each and to move from one category or part to another.

- **Is each category or part distinct from the others?** The author should make clear how each differs, using details, descriptions, examples, comparisons or contrasts, or personal experiences.

- **Is each category or part explained clearly and understandably?** Each description should be clear, with any terms defined, and should not require background knowledge the reader does not have.

Figure 15.2   Graphic Organizer for "Online Dating—Five Things to Avoid"

Title	"Online Dating—Five Things to Avoid"
Introduction	**Topic:** Online-dating site profiles
	Background: A large percent of singles today are looking for matches online. Online-dating sites can be helpful, but there are also potential problems to consider.
	Thesis: Here are five types of online daters to avoid.
Body paragraphs: categories or parts	**Category 1:** Liars
	May lie about little or major things about themselves in their profiles.
	Can be avoided by asking questions.
	Category 2: Photo fakes
	Post photos that are misleadingly good.
	Can be avoided by asking for recent photos and multiple photos.
	Category 3: Fixer-uppers
	Make negative comments and are really just on the rebound.
	Can be avoided by looking for positive things in common.
	Category 4: Membership fishers
	The person's on another site, which tries to get you to spend money to sign up.
	Can be avoided by staying with people on the site you're signed up with.
	Category 5: Cheaters
	Pretend to be single and may often be unavailable.
	Can be avoided by watching for people who aren't available on nights or weekends.

Evaluating a Classification or Division Essay

Evaluating a classification or division essay involves judging how accurately and effectively the author has classified or divided the subject. Use the following questions to guide your evaluation of such essays.

- **Is the classification or division comprehensive and complete?** Determine whether all essential categories or all essential parts are included. It would be misleading, for example, for a writer to classify unemployed workers into

Analysis in Action

The student who wrote the summary for Understanding in Action wrote the following analysis of the author's purpose in "Online Dating—Five Things to Avoid." Using it as a starting point, write a brief analysis of the essay's intended audience and how the author tries to connect with them.

> The author of "Online Dating—Five Things to Avoid" wants to help readers recognize that you have to be careful when you're reading profiles on dating sites. To do so, he lists five types of postings that could be iffy. For each type he also offers tips to avoid being burned.

only two groups—those who have been laid off or downsized and those who lack skills—because many people are out of work for other reasons. Such a classification fails to consider, for example, those who are unable to work due to illness or those who have recently completed college and have not yet found a job.

- **Does each category or part have fair and equal coverage?** Each category or part should be given roughly the same amount of coverage and use the same level of detail. To provide many details for some categories and just a few for others suggests bias. For example, if a writer classifying how high school students spend their time goes into great detail about leisure activities and offers little detail on part-time jobs or volunteer work, the writer may create a false impression that students care only about having fun and make few meaningful contributions to society.

Evaluation in Action

The student who wrote the summary and analysis of "Online Dating—Five Things to Avoid" wrote this brief evaluation of the essay's strengths and weaknesses. Read it and then write your own evaluation of the essay.

> I think the best thing about the essay is that it doesn't just classify the iffy types of postings to dating sites. It goes further and offers specific advice about what to do to avoid being fooled by them. This is helpful information. The only negative I see is that the first and last categories overlap a little bit.

Readings for Practice, Ideas for Writing

Types of Women in Romantic Comedies Who Are Not Real

Mindy Kaling is an Emmy-nominated writer, actress, and producer and is well known for her role on NBC's sitcom *The Office*. This excerpt from her book *Is Everyone Hanging Out Without Me? (And Other Concerns)* (2011) classifies the types of female characters that appear in Hollywood films.

Reading Tip

As you read, identify the author's attitude toward the characters she classifies. Summarize her attitude in a word or two.

Previewing the Reading

Preview the reading (see pp. 23–24 for guidelines), and then perform the following task: name several types of female characters in romantic comedies that Kaling defines.

Types of Women in Romantic Comedies Who Are Not Real

=== MINDY KALING ===

When I was a kid, Christmas vacation meant renting VHS copies of romantic comedies from Blockbuster and watching them with my parents at home. *Sleepless in Seattle* was big, and so was *When Harry Met Sally*. I laughed along with everyone else at the scene where Meg Ryan fakes an orgasm at the restaurant without even knowing what an orgasm was. In my mind, she was just being kind of loud and silly at a diner, and that was hilarious enough for me.

I love romantic comedies. I feel almost sheepish writing that, because the genre has been so degraded in the past twenty years or so that admitting you like these movies is essentially an admission of mild stupidity. But that has not stopped me from watching them.

I enjoy watching people fall in love on-screen so much that I can suspend my disbelief for the contrived situations that only happen in the heightened world of romantic comedies. I have come to enjoy the moment when the normal lead guy, say, slips and falls right on top of the hideously expensive wedding cake. I actually feel robbed when the female lead's dress *doesn't* get torn open at

Continued >

a baseball game while the JumboTron is on her. I simply regard romantic comedies as a subgenre of sci-fi, in which the world created therein has different rules than my regular human world. Then I just lap it up. There is no difference between Ripley from *Alien* and any Katherine Heigl character. They're all participating in the same level of made-up awesomeness, and I enjoy every second of it.

So it makes sense that in this world there are many specimens of women who I do not think exist in real life, like Vulcans or UFO people or whatever. They are:

The Klutz

When a beautiful actress is in a movie, executives wrack their brains to find some   5
kind of flaw in her that still allows her to be palatable. She can't be overweight or not perfect-looking, because who would want to see that? A not 100-percent-perfect-looking-in-every-way female? You might as well film a dead squid decaying on a beach somewhere for two hours.

So they make her a Klutz.

The 100-percent-perfect-looking female is perfect in every way, except that she constantly falls down. She bonks her head on things. She trips and falls and spills soup on her affable date. (Josh Lucas. Is that his name? I know it's two first names. Josh George? Brad Mike? Fred Tom? Yes, it's Fred Tom.) Our Klutz clangs into stop signs while riding a bike, and knocks over giant displays of expensive fine china. Despite being five foot nine and weighing 110 pounds, she is basically like a drunk buffalo who has never been a part of human society. But Fred Tom loves her anyway.

The Ethereal Weirdo

The smart and funny writer Nathan Rabin coined the term *Manic Pixie Dream Girl* to describe a version of this archetype[1] after seeing Kirsten Dunst in the movie *Elizabethtown*. This girl can't be pinned down and may or may not show up when you make concrete plans. She wears gauzy blouses and braids. She decides to dance in the rain and weeps uncontrollably if she sees a sign for a missing dog or cat. She spins a globe, places her finger on a random spot, and decides to move there. This ethereal[2] weirdo abounds in movies, but nowhere else. If she were from real life, people would think she was a homeless woman and would cross the street to avoid her, but she is essential to the male fantasy that even if a guy is boring, he deserves a woman who will find him fascinating and pull him out of himself by forcing him to go skinny-dipping in a stranger's pool.

[1] **archetype** Typical example or model.
[2] **ethereal** Extremely delicate or refined, heavenly.

The Woman Who Is Obsessed with Her Career
and Is No Fun at All

I, Mindy Kaling, basically have two full-time jobs. I regularly work sixteen hours a day. But like most of the other people I know who are similarly busy, I think I'm a pleasant, pretty normal person. I am slightly offended by the way busy working women my age are presented in film. I'm not, like, always barking orders into my hands-free phone device and telling people constantly, "I have no time for this!" I didn't completely forget how to be nice or feminine because I have a career. Also, since when does having a job necessitate women having their hair pulled back in a severe, tight bun? Often this uptight woman has to "re-learn" how to seduce a man because her estrogen leaked out of her from leading so many board meetings, and she has to do all sorts of crazy, unnecessary crap, like eat a hot dog in a libidinous[3] way or something. Having a challenging job in movies means the compassionate, warm, or sexy side of your brain has fallen out.

The Forty-Two-Year-Old Mother
of the Thirty-Year-Old Male Lead

I am so accustomed to the young mom phenomenon, that when I saw the poster   10 for *The Proposal* I wondered for a second if the proposal in the movie was Ryan Reynolds suggesting he send his mother, Sandra Bullock, to an old-age home.

However, given the popularity of teen moms right now, this could actually be the wave of the future.

The Sassy Best Friend

You know that really horny and hilarious best friend who is always asking about your relationship and has nothing really going on in her own life? She always wants to meet you in coffee shops or wants to go to Bloomingdale's to sample perfumes? She runs a chic dildo store in the West Village? Nope? Okay, that's this person.

The Skinny Woman Who Is Beautiful
and Toned but Also Gluttonous and Disgusting

Again, I am more than willing to suspend my disbelief during a romantic comedy for good set decoration alone. One pristine kitchen from a Nancy Meyers movie like in *It's Complicated* is worth five Diane Keatons being caught half-clad in a topiary[4] or whatever situation her character has found herself in.

But sometimes even my suspended disbelief isn't enough. I am speaking of the gorgeous and skinny heroine who is also a disgusting pig when it comes to

---

[3] **libidinous** Full of sexual lust; lewd.
[4] **topiary** Tree or bush trimmed in a decorative shape.

Continued >

food. And everyone in the movie—her parents, her friends, her boss—are all complicit in this huge lie. They are constantly telling her to stop eating and being such a glutton. And this actress, this poor skinny actress who so clearly lost weight to play the likeable lead, has to say things like "Shut up you guys! I love cheesecake! If I want to eat an entire cheesecake, I will!" If you look closely, you can see this woman's ribs through the dress she's wearing—that's how skinny she is, this cheesecake-loving cow.

You wonder, as you sit and watch this movie, what the characters would do if they were confronted by an actual average American woman. They would all kill themselves, which would actually be kind of an interesting movie. 15

The Woman Who Works in an Art Gallery

How many freakin' art galleries are out there? Are people constantly buying visual art or something? This posh-smart-classy job is a favorite in movies. It's in the same realm as kindergarten teacher in terms of accessibility: Guys don't really get it, but the trappings of it are likeable and nonthreatening.

> ART GALLERY WOMAN: Dust off the Rothko.[5] We have an important buyer coming into town and this is a really big deal for my career. I have no time for this!

This is one of the rare clichés that actually has a male counterpart. Whenever you meet a handsome, charming, successful man in a romantic comedy, the heroine's friend always says the same thing. "He's really successful—he's an . . .
(say it with me)
. . . architect!"
There are like nine people in the entire world who are architects, and one of them is my dad. None of them look like Patrick Dempsey.[6]

---

[5] **Rothko** A twentieth-century American painter.
[6] **Patrick Dempsey** Well-known American actor.

Understanding the Reading

1. **Thesis** What is Kaling's thesis, and where does she state it most directly?

2. **Principle of classification** What is Kaling's main principle of classification? That is, on what basis does she compare the members of each category?

3. **Categories** Briefly summarize each of Kaling's categories using your own words. How does her final category explanation differ somewhat from those preceding it?

4. **Supporting details** What types of supporting details does Kaling offer to explain each category?

5. **Vocabulary** Using context clues (p. 34), write a brief definition of each of the following words as it is used in the reading, consulting a dictionary if necessary: *sheepish* (para. 2), *degraded* (2), *contrived* (3), *heightened* (3), *palatable* (5), *archetype* (8), *complicit* (14), *posh* (16).

Analyzing the Reading

1. **Introduction** What do the first four paragraphs contribute to introducing Kaling's topic?

2. **Audience** How would you define Kaling's intended audience? In your answer, highlight several references she makes that she expects readers to be familiar with.

3. **Purpose** What is Kaling's purpose? Is this essay basically informative, or does it have another purpose?

4. **Language** In paragraph 4, how does Kaling's reference to "Vulcans" and "UFO people" relate to her thesis?

5. **Technique** Why does Kaling begin paragraphs 11 and 16 with a series of questions? What do these questions and those used throughout the piece contribute to her thesis?

Evaluating the Reading

1. **Audience** Based on your response to Analyzing the Reading question 2, how well do you think Kaling appeals to her intended audience?

2. **Voice** Do you agree with Kaling's claim in paragraph 2 that saying one likes romantic comedies is "an admission of mild stupidity"? Why might she say this about herself?

3. **Language** In paragraph 3, Kaling uses the phrase "suspend my disbelief" and calls romantic comedies a "subgenre of sci-fi" in which "the world created therein has different rules than my regular human world." How well do you think she carries through with this idea? Is there consistency in the language she uses? How effective is this idea?

4. **Categories** Based on your movie-watching experience, which of Kaling's types of romantic-comedy characters make most sense to you? Do any not correspond with the female characters you've seen in such comedies?

Discussing the Reading

1. Kaling does not provide a traditional conclusion to this essay. How do you think she should conclude it? Which ideas—either stated or implied—are most important and the ones that readers should be reminded of at the end?

2. Kaling briefly mentions the male characters that appear in romantic comedies. What do you think her attitude is toward these characters? Is it similar

to or different from her attitude toward female characters? What might this say about how men and women are presented in movies?

3. What is your attitude toward romantic comedies? Do you agree with Kaling that they have nothing to do with the "regular human world"?

Writing about the Reading

1. **Paragraph** In a paragraph summarize "Types of Women in Romantic Comedies Who Are Not Real." Write a brief introduction, and then in just a sentence or two describe each of Kaling's seven categories. (Hint: Note that Kaling's formal classification begins with para. 5.)

2. **Paragraph** In a paragraph classify three types of male characters in romantic comedies. (Hint: Kaling, for example, mentions the "boring" guy [para. 8], the male lead son [10], and the "architect" [19] and also refers specifically to the actors Ryan Reynolds [10] and Patrick Dempsey [20]. Use these to help you develop categories based on your own movie viewing.)

3. **Essay** Kaling likens romantic comedies to science-fiction films and refers specifically to Vulcans and UFO people (para. 4). Write a classification essay about science-fiction films. You might focus on different types of films, various sorts of characters, even kinds of plot devices. (Hint: Start by brainstorming a list of films, characters, and so forth in the science-fiction genre. Then separate appropriate individual examples according to a clear basis of classification.)

Friends, Good Friends—Such Good Friends

Judith Viorst has written poetry, nonfiction, a novel, and eighteen children's books, including *Alexander and the Terrible, Horrible, No Good, Very Bad Day* (1972). She graduated from the Washington Psychoanalytic Institute, and her work has often addressed psychological aspects of human behavior. Viorst was a contributing editor for over twenty-five years at *Redbook*, where this essay first appeared in 1977.

Reading Tip

As you read, notice how many concrete examples Viorst includes, both from her own experience and from the experiences of others, to help make each of her categories clear.

Previewing the Reading

Preview the reading using the guidelines on pages 23–24. Then answer the following questions.

1. Is this a classification or a division essay?
2. Identify several types of friends that the author discusses.

Friends, Good Friends—Such Good Friends

Judith Viorst

Women are friends, I once would have said, when they totally love and support and trust each other, and bare to each other the secrets of their souls, and run—no questions asked—to help each other, and tell harsh truths to each other (no, you can't wear that dress unless you lose ten pounds first) when harsh truths must be told.

Women are friends, I once would have said, when they share the same affection for Ingmar Bergman, plus train rides, cats, warm rain, charades, Camus, and hate with equal ardor Newark and Brussels sprouts and Lawrence Welk and camping.

In other words, I once would have said that a friend is a friend all the way, but now I believe that's a narrow point of view. For the friendships I have and the friendships I see are conducted at many levels of intensity, serve many different functions, meet different needs, and range from those as all-the-way as the friendship of the soul sisters mentioned above to that of the most nonchalant and casual playmates.

Consider these varieties of friendship:

1. Convenience friends. These are women with whom, if our paths weren't crossing all the time, we'd have no particular reason to be friends: a

5

Continued >

next-door neighbor, a woman in our car pool, the mother of one of our children's closest friends, or maybe some mommy with whom we serve juice and cookies each week at the Glenwood Co-op Nursery.

Convenience friends are convenient indeed. They'll lend us their cups and silverware for a party. They'll drive our kids to soccer when we're sick. They'll take us to pick up our car when we need a lift to the garage. They'll even take our cats when we go on vacation. As we will for them.

But we don't, with convenience friends, ever come too close or tell too much; we maintain our public face and emotional distance. "Which means," says Elaine, "that I'll talk about being overweight but not about being depressed. Which means I'll admit being mad but not blind with rage. Which means that I might say that we're pinched this month but never that I'm worried sick over money."

But which doesn't mean that there isn't sufficient value to be found in these friendships of mutual aid, in convenience friends.

2. Special-interest friends. These friendships aren't intimate, and they needn't involve kids or silverware or cats. Their value lies in some interest jointly shared. And so we may have an office friend or a yoga friend or a tennis friend or a friend from the Women's Democratic Club.

10 "I've got one woman friend," says Joyce, "who likes, as I do, to take psychology courses. Which makes it nice for me—and nice for her. It's fun to go with someone you know and it's fun to discuss what you've learned, driving back from the classes." And for the most part, she says, that's all they discuss.

"I'd say that what we're doing is *doing* together, not being together," Suzanne says of her Tuesday-doubles friends. "It's mainly a tennis relationship, but we play together well. And I guess we all need to have a couple of playmates."

I agree.

My playmate is a shopping friend, a woman of marvelous taste, a woman who knows exactly *where* to buy *what*, and furthermore is a woman who always knows beyond a doubt what one ought to be buying. I don't have the time to keep up with what's new in eyeshadow, hemlines, and shoes and whether the smock look is in or finished already. But since (oh, shame!) I care a lot about eyeshadow, hemlines, and shoes, and since I don't *want* to wear smocks if the smock look is finished, I'm very glad to have a shopping friend.

3. Historical friends. We all have a friend who knew us when . . . maybe way back in Miss Meltzer's second grade, when our family lived in that three-room flat in Brooklyn, when our dad was out of work for seven months, when our brother Allie got in that fight where they had to call the police, when our sister married the endodontist from Yonkers, and when, the morning after we lost our virginity, she was the first, the only, friend we told.

The years have gone by and we've 15 gone separate ways and we've little in common now, but we're still an intimate part of each other's past. And so whenever we go to Detroit we always go to visit this friend of our girlhood. Who knows how we talked before our voice got un-Brooklyned. Who knows what we ate before we learned about artichokes. And who, by her presence, puts us in touch with an earlier part of ourself, a part of ourself it's important never to lose.

"What this friend means to me and what I mean to her," says Grace, "is having a sister without sibling rivalry. We know the texture of each other's lives. She remembers my grandmother's cabbage soup. I remember the way her uncle played the piano. There's simply no other friend who remembers those things."

4. Crossroads friends. Like historical friends, our crossroads friends are important for *what was*—for the friendship we shared at a crucial, now past, time of life. A time, perhaps, when we roomed in college together; or worked as eager young singles in the Big City together; or went together, as my friend Elizabeth and I did, through pregnancy, birth, and that scary first year of new motherhood.

Crossroads friends forge powerful links, links strong enough to endure with not much more contact than once-a-year letters at Christmas. And out of respect for those crossroad years, for those dramas and dreams we once shared, we will always be friends.

5. Cross-generational friends. Historical friends and crossroads friends seem to maintain a special kind of intimacy—dormant but always ready to be revived—and though we may rarely meet, whenever we do connect, it's personal and intense. Another kind of intimacy exists in the friendships that form across generations in what one woman calls her daughter-mother and her mother-daughter relationships.

20   Evelyn's friend is her mother's age—"but I share so much more than I ever could with my mother"—a woman she talks to of music, of books, and of life. "What I get from her is the benefit of her experience. What she gets—and enjoys—from me is a youthful perspective. It's a pleasure for both of us."

I have in my own life a precious friend, a woman of sixty-five who has lived very hard, who is wise, who listens well; who has been where I am and can help me understand it; and

who represents not only an ultimate ideal mother to me but also the person I'd like to be when I grow up.

In our daughter role we tend to do more than our share of self-revelation; in our mother role we tend to receive what's revealed. It's another kind of pleasure—playing wise mother to a questing younger person. It's another very lovely kind of friendship.

6. Part-of-a-couple friends. Some of the women we call our friends we never see alone—we see them as part of a couple at couples' parties. And though we share interests in many things and respect each other's views, we aren't moved to deepen the relationship. Whatever the reason, a lack of time or—and this is more likely—a lack of chemistry, our friendship remains in the context of a group. But the fact that our feeling on seeing each other is always, "I'm *so* glad she's here" and the fact that we spend half the evening talking together says that this too, in its own way, counts as a friendship.

(Other part-of-a-couple friends are the friends that came with the marriage, and some of these are friends we could live without. But sometimes, alas, she married our husband's best friend; and sometimes, alas, she *is* our husband's best friend. And so we find ourself dealing with her, somewhat against our will, in a spirit of what I'll call *reluctant* friendship.)

7. Men who are friends. I wanted   25 to write just of women friends, but the women I've talked to won't let me—they say I must mention man-woman friendships too. For these friendships can be just as close and as dear as those that we form with women. Listen to Lucy's description of one such friendship:

"We've found we have things to talk about that are different from what he talks about with my husband and

Continued >

different from what I talk about with his wife. So sometimes we call on the phone or meet for lunch. There are similar intellectual interests—we always pass on to each other the books that we love—but there's also something tender and caring too."

In a couple of crises, Lucy says, "he offered himself for talking and for helping. And when someone died in his family he wanted me there. The sexual, flirty part of our friendship is very small, but *some*—just enough to make it fun and different." She thinks—and I agree—that the sexual part, though small, is always *some*, is always there when a man and a woman are friends.

It's only in the past few years that I've made friends with men, in the sense of a friendship that's *mine*, not just part of two couples. And achieving with them the ease and the trust I've found with women friends has value indeed. Under the dryer at home last week, putting on mascara and rouge, I comfortably sat and talked with a fellow named Peter. Peter, I finally decided, could handle the shock of me minus mascara under the dryer. Because we care for each other. Because we're friends.

8. There are medium friends, and pretty good friends, and very good friends indeed, and these friendships are defined by their level of intimacy. And what we'll reveal at each of these levels of intimacy is calibrated with care. We might tell a medium friend, for example, that yesterday we had a fight with our husband. And we might tell a pretty good friend that this fight with our husband made us so mad that we slept on the couch. And we might tell a very good friend that the reason we got so mad in that fight that we slept on the couch had something to do with that girl that works in his office. But it's only to our very best friends that we're willing to tell all, to tell what's going on with that girl in his office.

The best of friends, I still believe,   30
totally love and support and trust each other, and bare to each other the secrets of their souls, and run—no questions asked—to help each other, and tell harsh truths to each other when they must be told.

But we needn't agree about everything (only twelve-year-old girlfriends agree about *everything*) to tolerate each other's point of view. To accept without judgment. To give and to take without ever keeping score. And to *be* there, as I am for them and as they are for me, to comfort our sorrows, to celebrate our joys.

Understanding the Reading

1. **Thesis**   What is Viorst's thesis? Where does she state it most directly?

2. **Principle of classification**   What is Viorst's main principle of classification in the essay?

3. **Introduction**   How do Viorst's opening paragraphs lead up to her thesis? What contrast is she making?

4. **Conclusion**   How does Viorst's concluding category relate specifically to her opening paragraphs?

5. **Vocabulary** Using context clues (p. 34), write a brief definition of each of the following words as it is used in the reading, consulting a dictionary if necessary: *harsh* (para. 1), *ardor* (2), *sibling rivalry* (16), *dormant* (19), and *reluctant* (24).

6. **Structure** To visualize the structure of the essay, complete the graphic organizer below.

Analyzing the Reading

1. **Audience** How would you define Viorst's intended audience? What makes you think as you do? What does she hope to communicate to this audience?

2. **Use of detail** Choose one of Viorst's categories and analyze how she develops it. What kinds of details does she provide?

Title	"Friends, Good Friends—Such Good Friends"
Introduction	**Topic:** Friends
	Background: Explains Viorst's former view that "a friend is a friend all the way."
	Thesis:
Body paragraphs: types of friendship	**Category 1:**
	Characteristic:
	Category 2:
	Characteristic:
	Category 3:
	Characteristic:
	Category 4:
	Characteristic:
	Category 5:
	Characteristic:
	Category 6:
	Characteristic:
	Category 7:
	Characteristic:
	Category 8:
	Characteristic:
Conclusion	Best friends offer total love, support, and trust but don't need to agree on everything.

3. **Technique** Does Viorst present her categories in any particular order? Explain.

4. **Sentences** Reread the long sentence that makes up paragraph 14. How does Viorst make it possible to follow this sentence?

5. **Language** Viorst uses the phrase "I once would have said" three times in her opening paragraphs. What is the effect of this repetition?

6. **Language** Notice Viorst's use of the pronouns *we* and *our* in paragraphs 14–15. What is unusual about the use of the plural first person, rather than *I* and *my*, here?

Evaluating the Reading

1. **Appeal to audience** Do you think Viorst's essay appeals to men as well as to women? Why, or why not?

2. **Categories** Do you identify more closely with some rather than with other of Viorst's categories? How do the categories relate to your experience?

3. **Technique** For her final category, beginning in paragraph 29, Viorst doesn't provide a label as she does for her other categories. Do you think she should have? Why, or why not? What would be a good label for the last category?

4. **Presentation** This essay was originally published in 1977, thirty-six years ago. Does it seem dated to you? Why, or why not?

Discussing the Reading

1. Based on your own experience, do you agree that friendships serve a variety of different functions in your life? Do you define friendship essentially as Viorst does?

2. Viorst writes a lot about intimacy in the essay. How do you define *intimacy*? What would you reveal only to an intimate friend?

3. Can you add to Viorst's categories? That is, are there people you consider friends who don't fit into one of the categories she classifies? If so, what name would you give to that category?

Writing about the Reading

1. **Paragraph** In a paragraph, use your own experience to develop a classification of the different types of friends you have. You may include categories that Viorst describes if they are relevant. (Hint: Like Viorst, present specific examples from your life to develop each category.)

2. **Essay** Viorst classifies friendships, in part, according to their "many levels of intensity" (para. 3). Write an essay classifying relationships more generally in terms of their levels of intensity. Include types of friendships, but also think about family relationships, romantic relationships, and any others that occur

to you. (Hint: Start by brainstorming a list of meaningful relationships in your life, then sort these according to their level of intensity. Finally, narrow your potential categories down to a manageable number to deal with in an essay.) As you draft, develop each category with representative examples.

3. **Essay** Viorst refers to different stages of relationships throughout one's life. Write a classification or division essay about some of the stages in people's lives. You might focus on stages according to age, education, and job opportunities, interpersonal relationships, or something else. Or you might choose one stage and analyze its parts or characteristics. Whatever you choose, be sure to state clearly in your thesis what you intend to analyze. Use relevant supporting details.

A Brush with Reality: Surprises in the Tube

David Bodanis is a journalist and an academic trained in mathematics, physics, and economics. He has taught social science courses at Oxford University, consulted with businesses on energy policy and sustainable development, and written several books. The following essay is from *The Secret House* (1986), his examination of the foods eaten and products consumed by a family over the course of a day.

Reading Tip

In this piece, Bodanis examines the substances that are put together to make toothpaste. Notice the deadpan tone he uses to describe the ingredients and the words he chooses in order to leave a particular impression on readers.

Preview the Reading

Preview the reading (see pp. 23–24 for guidelines), and then decide what the author's purpose is in writing this division.

A Brush with Reality: Surprises in the Tube

══ DAVID BODANIS ══

Into the bathroom goes our male resident, and after the most pressing need is satisfied it's time to brush the teeth. The tube of toothpaste is squeezed, its pinched metal seams are splayed, pressure waves are generated inside, and the paste begins to flow. But what's in this toothpaste, so carefully being extruded out?

Water mostly, 30 to 45% in most brands: ordinary, everyday simple tap water. It's there because people like to have a big gob of toothpaste to spread on the brush, and water is the cheapest stuff there is when it comes to making big gobs. Dripping a bit from the tap onto your brush would cost virtually nothing; whipped in with the rest of the toothpaste the manufacturers can sell it at a neat and accountant-pleasing $2 per pound equivalent. Toothpaste manufacture is a very lucrative occupation.

Second to water in quantity is chalk: exactly the same material that schoolteachers use to write on blackboards. It is collected from the crushed remains of long-dead ocean creatures. In the Cretaceous[1] seas chalk particles served as part of the wickedly sharp outer skeleton that these creatures had to wrap around

[1] **Cretaceous** The last part of the age of dinosaurs, 144 to 65 million years ago.

themselves to keep from getting chomped by all the slightly larger other ocean creatures they met. Their massed graves are our present chalk deposits.

The individual chalk particles—the size of the smallest mud particles in your garden—have kept their toughness over the aeons,[2] and now on the toothbrush they'll need it. The enamel outer coating of the tooth they'll have to face is the hardest substance in the body—tougher than skull, or bone, or nail. Only the chalk particles in toothpaste can successfully grind into the teeth during brushing, ripping off the surface layers like an abrading wheel[3] grinding down a boulder in a quarry.

The craters, slashes, and channels that the chalk tears into the teeth will also remove a certain amount of build-up yellow in the carnage, and it is for that polishing function that it's there. A certain amount of unduly enlarged extra-abrasive chalk fragments tear such cavernous pits into the teeth that future decay bacteria will be able to bunker down there and thrive; the quality control people find it almost impossible to screen out these errant super-chalk pieces, and government regulations allow them to stay in. 5

In case even the gouging doesn't get all the yellow off, another substance is worked into the toothpaste cream. This is titanium dioxide. It comes in tiny spheres, and it's the stuff bobbing around in white wall paint to make it come out white. Splashed around onto your teeth during the brushing it coats much of the yellow that remains. Being water soluble it leaks off in the next few hours and is swallowed, but at least for the quick glance up in the mirror after finishing it will make the user think his teeth are truly white. Some manufacturers add optical whitening dye—the stuff more commonly found in washing machine bleach—to make extra sure that that glance in the mirror shows reassuring white.

These ingredients alone would not make a very attractive concoction. They would stick in the tube like a sloppy white plastic lump, hard to squeeze out as well as revolting to the touch. Few consumers would savor rubbing in a mixture of water, ground-up blackboard chalk, and the whitener from latex paint first thing in the morning. To get around that finicky distaste the manufacturers have mixed in a host of other goodies.

To keep the glop from drying out, a mixture including glycerine glycol—related to the most common car antifreeze ingredient—is whipped in with the chalk and water, and to give that concoction a bit of substance (all we really have so far is wet colored chalk) a large helping is added of gummy molecules from the seaweed Chondrus Crispus. This seaweed ooze spreads in among the chalk, paint, and antifreeze, then stretches itself in all directions to hold the whole mass together. A bit of paraffin oil (the fuel that flickers in camping lamps) is pumped in with it to help the moss ooze keep the whole substance smooth.

---

[2] **aeons** *Eons*—an eternity.
[3] **abrading wheel** Tool that wears down material by applying friction and pressure from a rotating disk.

Continued >

With the glycol, ooze, and paraffin we're almost there. Only two major chemicals are left to make the refreshing, cleansing substance we know as toothpaste. The ingredients so far are fine for cleaning, but they wouldn't make much of the satisfying foam we have come to expect in the morning brushing.

To remedy that, every toothpaste on the market has a big dollop of deter- 10 gent added too. You've seen the suds detergent will make in a washing machine. The same substance added here will duplicate that inside the mouth. It's not particularly necessary, but it sells. The only problem is that by itself this ingredient tastes, well, too like detergent. It's horribly bitter and harsh. The chalk put in toothpaste is pretty foul-tasting too for that matter. It's to get around that gustatory discomfort that the manufacturers put in the ingredient they tout perhaps the most of all. This is the flavoring, and it has to be strong. Double rectified peppermint oil is used—a flavorer so powerful that chemists know better than to sniff it in the raw state in the laboratory. Menthol crystals and saccharin or other sugar simulators are added to complete the camouflage operation.

Is that it? Chalk, water, paint, seaweed, antifreeze, paraffin oil, detergent, and peppermint? Not quite. A mix like that would be irresistible to the hundreds of thousands of individual bacteria lying on the surface of even an immaculately cleaned bathroom sink. They would get in, float in the water bubbles, ingest the ooze and paraffin, maybe even spray out enzymes to break down the chalk. The result would be an uninviting mess. The way manufacturers avoid that final obstacle is by putting something in to kill the bacteria. Something good and strong is needed, something that will zap any accidentally intrudant bacteria into oblivion. And that something is formaldehyde—the disinfectant used in anatomy labs.

So it's chalk, water, paint, seaweed, antifreeze, paraffin oil, detergent, peppermint, formaldehyde, and fluoride (which can go some way towards preserving children's teeth)—that's the usual mixture raised to the mouth on the toothbrush for a fresh morning's clean. If it sounds too unfortunate, take heart. Studies show that thorough brushing with just plain water will often do as good a job.

Understanding the Reading

1. **Division** What are the ingredients in toothpaste?
2. **Background information** Why did the author include information about the origins of chalk?
3. **Division** What is put in toothpaste to inhibit the growth of bacteria?
4. **Conclusion** What does the author present as a final thought on the subject?

Analyzing the Reading

1. **Thesis** Analyze the effectiveness of using an implied thesis. Is the author's purpose in writing clear? Why, or why not?

2. **Parts** How successful is Bodanis in presenting his parts? Is the division of the ingredients in toothpaste complete? Do any parts overlap?

3. **Details** Name some especially effective details that are included for each category. Are some parts better explained than others? Explain your answer.

4. **Conclusion** What does Bodanis's conclusion imply about his feelings about toothpaste?

5. **Language** What does the author mean by the phrase "reassuring white" in paragraph 6?

Evaluating the Reading

1. **Drawing conclusions** When drawing conclusions, one makes reasoned decisions or opinions on the basis of available facts. What conclusion does Bodanis draw about the fact that water is the most plentiful ingredient in toothpaste?

2. **Drawing conclusions** Throughout the essay, Bodanis refers repeatedly to the consumers of toothpaste. Reread paragraphs 6, 7, and 10. What conclusion is he drawing about consumers?

3. **Implied conclusion** Just as the thesis is implied, the main conclusion is not stated directly. Based on his use of details, what conclusion do you think Bodanis is drawing about the use of toothpaste?

4. **Conclusion** Did you find the conclusion satisfying? Is there additional information that you would find helpful?

5. **Language** Evaluate the expressions "finicky distaste" and "host of other goodies" (para. 7). What is the author trying to express? How effective is he at making his point?

6. **Organization** To better understand the structure Bodanis uses in this essay, create a graphic organizer or outline that shows all the major divisions, plus the thesis and conclusion. Then, evaluate how effective this organization is. How might you have organized it differently?

Discussing the Reading

1. Discuss the role of dental hygiene in our society. Why do we place such great importance on our teeth?

2. Discuss the strategies that manufacturers use to make their products appealing to consumers.

3. In class or in your journal, explore the various reasons some people choose to buy "natural" personal-care products.

Writing about the Reading

1. **Essay** Conduct a study of one advertising medium: TV, radio, the Internet, newspapers, or magazines. Take notes on what you see, hear, and read. Then write a classification essay describing the different types of ads according to aspects such as content, intended audience, or placement. Be sure to indicate what effect the ads had on you.

2. **Essay** How much do people know about what they consume and use? Choose a common processed food or household product, and ask three to five friends to tell you what they think it contains; take notes on their comments. Then compare their answers to the actual ingredients. Write a classification or division essay describing the degrees of knowledge people have about this food or product. Make recommendations about how consumers can learn more about what they eat and use.

3. **Internet research** Choose a product that you use daily, such as shampoo or deodorant. Using the label of ingredients as a starting point, use the Internet to research what the product really contains. Then write a division essay that identifies the product's components and explains each, as Bodanis does for toothpaste in his essay.

COMBINING THE PATTERNS

The Dog Ate My Flash Drive

Carolyn Foster Segal retired in 2011 from teaching English at Cedar Crest College, where she specialized in American literature, poetry, creative writing, and women's film. She has published many essays in the *Chronicle of Higher Education*, a weekly newspaper for college faculty and administrators. The following piece appeared in the *Chronicle* in 2000. With the author's permission, it has been revised slightly to update some technological references.

Reading Tip

As you read, notice how Segal's classification essay also uses description and illustration to fully explain each category she identifies.

Previewing the Reading

Preview the reading (see pp. 23–24 for guidelines), and determine whether it uses classification or division.

CAROLYN FOSTER SEGAL

The Dog Ate My Flash Drive

Taped to the door of my office is a cartoon that features a cat explaining to his feline teacher, "The dog ate my homework." It is intended as a gently humorous reminder to my students that I will not accept excuses for late work, and it, like the lengthy warning on my syllabus, has had absolutely no effect. With a show of energy and creativity that would be admirable if applied to the (missing) assignments in question, my students persist, week after week, semester after semester, year after year, in offering excuses about why their work is not ready. Those reasons fall into several broad categories: the family, the best friend, the evils of dorm life, the evils of technology, and the totally bizarre.

The Family. The death of the grandfather/grandmother is, of course, the grandmother of all excuses. What heartless teacher would dare to question a student's grief or veracity? What heartless student would lie, wishing death on a revered family member, just to avoid a deadline? Creative students may win extra extensions (and days off) with a little careful planning and fuller plot development, as in the sequence of "My grandfather/grandmother is sick"; "Now my grandfather/grandmother is in the hospital"; and finally, "We could all see it coming—my grandfather/grandmother is dead."

Another favorite excuse is "the family emergency," which (always) goes like this: "There was an emergency at home, and I had to help my family." It's a lovely sentiment, one that conjures up images of Louisa May Alcott's little women rushing off with baskets of food and copies of *Pilgrim's Progress*, but I do not understand why anyone would turn to my most irresponsible students in times of trouble.

The Best Friend. This heartwarming concern for others extends beyond

Continued >

HOMEWORK DONE only $1.00

HOMEWORK EATEN only 50¢

the family to friends, as in, "My best friend was up all night and I had to (a) stay up with her in the dorm, (b) drive her to the hospital, or (c) drive to her college because (1) her boyfriend broke up with her, (2) she was throwing up blood [no one catches a cold anymore; everyone throws up blood], or (3) her grandfather/grandmother died."

5   At one private university where I worked as an adjunct,[1] I heard an interesting spin that incorporated the motifs of both best friend and dead relative: "My best friend's mother killed herself." One has to admire the cleverness here: A mysterious woman in the prime of her life has allegedly committed suicide, and no professor can prove otherwise! And I admit I was moved, until finally I had to point out to my students that it was amazing how the simple act of my assigning a topic for a paper seemed to drive large numbers of otherwise happy and healthy middle-aged women to their deaths. I was careful to make that

[1] **adjunct** A part-time instructor.

point during an off week, during which no deaths were reported.

The Evils of Dorm Life. These stories are usually fairly predictable; almost always feature the evil roommate or hall-mate, with my student in the role of the innocent victim; and can be summed up as follows: My roommate, who is a horrible person, likes to party, and I, who am a good person, cannot concentrate on my work when he or she is partying. Variations include stories about the two people next door who were running around and crying loudly last night because (a) one of them had boyfriend/girlfriend problems; (b) one of them was throwing up blood; or (c) someone, somewhere, died. A friend of mine in graduate school had a student who claimed that his roommate attacked him with a hammer. That, in fact, was a true story; it came out in court when the bad roommate was tried for killing his grandfather.

The Evils of Technology. The computer age has revolutionized the student story, inspiring almost as many new excuses as it has Internet businesses. Here are just a few electronically enhanced explanations:

- The computer wouldn't let me save my work.
- The printer wouldn't print.
- The printer wouldn't print this file.
- The printer wouldn't give me time to proofread.
- The printer made a black line run through all my words, and I know you can't read this, but do you still want it, or wait, here, take my flash drive. File name? I don't know what you mean.
- I swear I attached it.
- It's my roommate's computer, and she usually helps me, but she had to go to the hospital because she was throwing up blood.
- I did write to the Listserv, but all my messages came back to me.
- I just found out that all my other Listserv messages came up under a diferent name. I just want you to know that its really me who wrote all those messages, you can tel which ones our mine because I didnt use the spelcheck! But it was yours truely :) Anyway, just in case you missed those messages or don't belief its my writting, I'll repeat what I sad: I thought the last movie we watched in clas was borring.

The Totally Bizarre. I call the first story "The Pennsylvania Chain Saw Episode." A commuter student called to explain why she had missed my morning class. She had gotten up early so that she would be wide awake for class. Having a bit of extra time, she walked outside to see her neighbor, who was cutting some wood. She called out to him, and he waved back to her with the saw. Wouldn't you know it, the safety catch wasn't on or was broken, and the blade flew right out of the saw and across his lawn and over her fence and across her yard and severed a tendon in her right hand. So she was calling me from the hospital, where she was waiting for surgery. Luckily, she reassured me, she had remembered to bring her paper and a stamped envelope (in a plastic bag, to avoid bloodstains) along with her in the ambulance, and a nurse was mailing everything to me even as we spoke.

That wasn't her first absence. In fact, this student had missed most of the class meetings, and I had already recommended that she withdraw from the course. Now I suggested again that it might be best if she dropped the class. I didn't harp on the absences (what if even some of this story were true?). I did mention that she would need time to recuperate and that making up so much missed work might be difficult. "Oh, no," she said, "I can't drop this course. I had been planning to go on to medical school and become a surgeon, but since I won't be able to operate because of my accident, I'll have to major in English, and this course is more important than ever to me." She did come to the next class, wearing—as evidence of her recent trauma—a bedraggled Ace bandage on her left hand.

You may be thinking that nothing 10 could top that excuse, but in fact I have one more story, provided by the same student, who sent me a letter to explain why her final assignment would be late. While recuperating from her surgery, she had begun corresponding on the Internet with a man who lived in Germany. After a one-week, whirlwind Web romance, they had agreed to meet in Rome, to *rendezvous* (her phrase) at the papal Easter Mass. Regrettably, the time of her flight made it impossible for her to attend class, but she trusted that I—just this once—would accept late work if the pope wrote a note.

Continued >

Understanding the Reading

1. **Categories** Identify the categories of student excuses that Segal identifies.
2. **Examples** Do some student excuses turn out to be legitimate? Give an example from the reading.
3. **Examples** What obvious mistake was made by the student who offered the chain-saw excuse?
4. **Vocabulary** Explain the meaning of each of the following words as it is used in the reading: *bizarre* (para. 1), *veracity* (2), *conjures* (3), *motifs* (5), and *harp* (9). Refer to your dictionary as needed.

Analyzing the Reading

1. **Thesis** Is it helpful or unnecessary for Segal to list her five categories in her thesis?
2. **Title** What is the function of the essay's title?
3. **Audience** Who is Segal's audience? How can you tell?
4. **Combining patterns** What other patterns of development does Segal use in the essay?
5. **Supporting evidence** What types of supporting information does Segal supply to make her categories seem real and believable? Review the reading and complete the chart below by filling in at least one type of support for each category. The first entry has been done for you.

Category	Types of Support
1. The Family	Examples (death of grandmother/ grandfather), quotations
2. The Best Friend	
3. The Evils of Dorm Life	
4. The Evils of Technology	
5. The Totally Bizarre	

Evaluating the Reading

1. **Categories** What other categories could be included in this essay?
2. **Language** What is the connotation of "an interesting spin" (para. 5)?

3. **Sources** Other than students, what sources does Segal use? Explain why the essay would or would not benefit from more sources.

4. **Detail** Does Segal provide sufficient detail in each category? What other kinds of details might she have included?

5. **Classification** Is the classification appropriate for Segal's purpose? Why or why not?

6. **Tone** Describe the tone of the essay. What does it reveal about Segal's attitude toward students?

7. **Visuals** What does the inclusion of the cartoon add to the essay? Why is the boy selling "Homework Done" frowning and the boy selling "Homework Eaten" smiling? What is the implied message? What other visual differences do you notice between the two boys?

Discussing the Reading

1. As a student, how do you react to the essay? Have you observed these excuses being made (or perhaps even made them yourself)? Do you agree that they are overused? Or did you find the essay inaccurate, unfair, or even upsetting?

2. How do you think instructors should handle students who make false excuses? Should circumstances matter?

3. In your opinion, are excuses more common in school situations than in other areas of life? What are some other situations in which making excuses might be common?

Writing about the Reading

1. **Essay** Not only students make excuses. Write an essay classifying other kinds of excuses—for example, those that coworkers or supervisors make to justify their poor performance, tardiness, or irresponsibility, or those children make to their parents to account for perceived bad behavior. You may come up with other excuse makers to write about.

2. **Essay** Write an essay classifying teachers according to their performance in the classroom. Brainstorm first to determine various bases of classification—presentation skills, perhaps, or grading policies. Then choose one of these as the focus for your essay. Try to come up with interesting identifying names for each category, and be sure to include descriptive examples.

3. **Combined patterns** Write an essay in which you use classification and/or division to support an argument about college education or the college experience. You might focus on the relative value of different types of graduation requirements, the importance of what you learn in various campus settings, how you think tuition revenue should be divided among services offered by the institution, or some other issue worth making a case about.

📖 **TEXTBOOK**

Types of Message Appeals

Michael R. Solomon is a professor of marketing at Saint Joseph's University who studies consumer behavior and the psychology of fashion. His textbook *Consumer Behavior: Buying, Having, and Being* analyzes why people buy things and how their purchases shape them. This selection is excerpted from a chapter on attitudes and persuasion from that book.

Reading Tip

Consider the effect of the examples the author uses in this selection. What do they contribute to your understanding of the text?

Previewing the Reading

Preview the reading (pp. 23–24), and list as many types of appeals as you can recall.

Types of Message Appeals
Michael R. Solomon

A persuasive message can tug at the heartstrings or scare you, make you laugh, make you cry, or leave you yearning to learn more. In this section, we'll review the major alternatives available to communicators.

Emotional Versus Rational Appeals

Colgate-Palmolive's Total brand was the first toothpaste to claim that it fights gingivitis, a benefit that let Colgate inch ahead of Procter & Gamble's Crest for the first time in decades. Colgate initially made a scientific pitch for its new entry as it emphasized Total's germ-fighting abilities. In newer ads, however, former model Brooke Shields cavorts with two children (not hers) as soft music plays in the background. She states, "Having a healthy smile is important to me. Not just as an actress but as a mom."

So, which is better: to appeal to the head or to the heart? The answer often depends on the nature of the product and the type of relationship consumers have with it. It's hard to gauge the precise effects of rational versus emotional appeals. Although recall of ad content tends to be better for "thinking" ads than for "feeling" ads, conventional measures of advertising effectiveness (e.g., day-after recall) may not be adequate to assess cumulative effects of emotional ads. These open-ended measures assess cognitive responses, and they may penalize feeling ads because the reactions are not as easy to articulate.

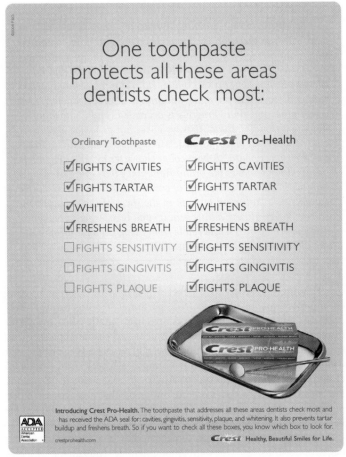

The Crest Pro-Health campaign emphasizes information over emotion as it focuses on the toothpaste's health benefits. *Source:* © Procter & Gamble Company, 2007. Used with permission.

Sex Appeals

Mars recently introduced Fling, a low-calorie chocolate bar targeted to women it describes as "Naughty, but not that naughty." In the candy's first commercial spot, a woman enters a dressing room that already has a man inside and the two get undressed and do uncandy-like things. But as the camera pans over the top it turns out they're actually in two separate rooms and in reality she's nibbling on a Fling. The campaign uses taglines like "Your boyfriend doesn't need to know," and "Pleasure yourself."

Continued >

ECONsumer Behavior

In a departure for mainstream advertising, several ad campaigns deal with the recession as they evoke strong negative emotions that acknowledge the fear and uncertainty many consumers experience. Eastman Kodak's ads for a line of printers and inkjet cartridges rant about a "$5 billion stain" on the economy when companies overpay for other ink brands. Post Shredded Wheat cereal proclaims that "Progress is overrated" and "Innovation is not your friend." JetBlue Airways pokes fun at senior executives who no longer fly on corporate jets as it greets them with a sarcastic "Welcome aboard." A blue-collar character in Miller High Life ads gleefully removes the brand from fancy bars and restaurants that he thinks take advantage of customers. An agency executive commented, "You need to walk in the shoes of the average consumers today. They're a little beat up and their wallets are lighter, and the people they trusted stole from them." At least for now, it's not all hearts and flowers in the ad biz.

Echoing the widely held belief that "sex sells," many marketing 5
communications for products from perfumes to autos feature heavy doses of erotic suggestions that range from subtle hints to blatant displays of skin. Of course, the prevalence of sexual appeals varies from country to country. Even American firms run ads elsewhere that would not go over at home. For example, a "cheeky" ad campaign designed to boost the appeal of American-made Lee jeans among Europeans features a series of bare buttocks. The messages are based on the concept that if bottoms could choose jeans, they would opt for Lee: "Bottoms feel better in Lee Jeans."

Perhaps not surprisingly, female nudity in print ads generates negative feelings and tension among female consumers, whereas men's reactions are more positive—although women with more liberal attitudes toward sex are more likely to be receptive. In a case of turnabout being fair play, another study found that males dislike nude males in ads, whereas females responded well to undressed males— but not totally nude ones. Women also respond more positively to sexual themes when they occur in the context of a committed relationship rather than just gratuitous lust.

So, does sex work? Although erotic content does appear to draw attention to an ad, its use may actually be counterproductive. In one survey, an overwhelming 61% of the respondents said that sexual imagery in a product's ad makes them less likely to buy it. Ironically, a provocative picture can be *too* effective; it can attract so much attention as to hinder processing and recall of the ad's contents. Sexual appeals appear to be ineffective when marketers use them merely as a "trick" to grab attention. They do, however, appear to work when the product is *itself* related to sex (e.g., lingerie or Viagra).

MARKETING PITFALL

The campaign for a Commercial-Free Childhood (CCFC) protested when Nickelodeon and Burger King showed what it called a "highly sexualized" commercial for Burger King's SpongeBob Kids Meal. In the spot BK's weird spokescharacter The King sings a remix of Sir Mix-A-Lot's 1990s hit song "Baby Got Back," with the new lyrics: "I like square butts and I cannot lie." The CCFC objected to the inclusion of women who shake their rear ends as SpongeBob dances and to Sir Mix-A-Lot's statement (in reference to the offer): "Booty is booty." Burger King responded that the commercial's intent is to speak to adults who take their kids to BK, and it requires the purchase of an adult Value Meal.

A research firm recently explored how men and women look at sexually themed ads and what effect, if any, what they choose to look at might have on the ads' effectiveness. One part of the study used special software to follow the visual behavior of respondents as they looked at ten print ads. The ad sample consisted of two U.S. print ads, one sexual and one nonsexual, from each of five product categories. When the participants looked at a sexual ad, men tended to ignore the text as they focused instead on the woman in it, whereas the women participants tended first to explore the ad's text elements. Men said they liked the sexual ads more, liked the products advertised in them more, and would be more likely to buy those products. Women scored the sexual ads lower than nonsexual ones on all three of those criteria.

MARKETING PITFALL

A series of funny ads a German agency created didn't make everyone laugh. Grey Germany did three condom ads for a pharmacy chain. They implied that if more people used condoms the world would have been spared such figures as Mao Tse-Tung, Adolf Hitler, and Osama bin Laden. Each execution depicted a swimming sperm with a likeness of one of the despised characters. Critics complained the ads were racist, offensive, and inappropriate; the campaign apparently didn't exactly enhance the retailer's image.

Continued >

Humorous appeals can be effective when marketeers use them properly.

Humorous Appeals

A TV commercial for Metamucil showed a National Park Service ranger who pours a glass of the laxative down Old Faithful and announces that the product keeps the famous geyser "regular." Yellowstone National Park started getting letters from offended viewers such as this one who wrote, "I suppose that in an era when people sell naming rights to sports arenas . . . that some in the National Park Service would see nothing wrong with selling the image of a National Park ranger for the marketing of a product promoting bowel regularity." Park officials also had their own concerns—they didn't want people to think that the geyser needed "help" or that it's OK to throw things down into it!

Does humor work? Overall, humorous advertisements do get 10 attention. One study found that recognition scores for humorous liquor ads were better than average. However, the verdict is mixed as to whether humor affects recall or product attitudes in a significant way. One reason silly ads may shift opinions is that they provide a source of *distraction*. A funny ad inhibits *counterarguing* (in which a consumer thinks of reasons why he doesn't agree with the message), so this increases the likelihood of message acceptance because he doesn't come up with arguments against the product.

Humor is more likely to be effective when the ad clearly identifies the brand and the funny material does not "swamp" the message. This danger is similar to one we've already discussed about beautiful models who divert attention from copy points. Subtle humor is usually better, as is humor that does not make fun of the potential consumer. Finally, humor should be appropriate to the product's image. Hint: An undertaker or a bank might want to avoid humor, as well as a company that accepted U.S. government bailout money.

Fear Appeals

Volkswagen's advertising campaign to promote the safety of its Jetta model really got people's attention. The spots depict graphic car crashes from the perspective of the passengers who chatter away as they drive down the street. Without warning, other vehicles come out of nowhere and brutally smash into their cars. In one spot, viewers see a passenger's head striking an airbag. The spots end with shots of stunned passengers, the damaged Jetta, and the slogan: "Safe happens." The ads look so realistic that consumers called the company to ask if any of the actors were hurt.

Fear appeals emphasize the negative consequences that can occur unless the consumer changes a behavior or an attitude. Fear appeals are fairly common in advertising, although they are more common in social marketing contexts in which organizations encourage people to convert to healthier lifestyles by quitting smoking, using contraception, relying on a designated driver, or perhaps driving a Jetta. In a typical recent campaign for Brink's Home Security, sales jumped 10% after ads depicted families' peaceful lives that get disrupted by a home invasion. In one spot, a Brink's siren saves a woman who is home alone after a creepy-looking guy tries to kick in her door.

This tactic worked for Brink's—but does a fear appeal work more generally for marketers that don't happen to be in the security business? Most research on this topic indicates that these negative messages are most effective when the advertiser uses only a moderate threat and when the ad presents a solution to the problem. Otherwise, consumers will tune out the ad because they can do nothing to solve the threat.

When a weak threat is ineffective, there may be insufficient elaboration of the harmful consequences of engaging in the behavior. When a strong threat doesn't work, there may be too much elaboration that interferes with the processing of the recommended change in behavior—the receiver is too busy thinking of reasons the message doesn't apply to her to pay attention to the offered solution. A study that manipulated subjects' degree of anxiety about AIDS, for example, found that they evaluated condom ads most positively when they

15

Continued >

used a moderate threat. Copy that promoted the use of the condom because "Sex is a risky business" (moderate threat) resulted in more attitude change than either a weaker threat that emphasized the product's sensitivity or a strong threat that discussed the certainty of death from AIDS.

Similarly, scare tactics have not generally been an effective way to convince teenagers to curb their use of alcohol or drugs. Teens simply tune out the message or deny its relevance to them. However, a study of adolescent responses to social versus physical threat appeals in drug prevention messages found that social threat (such as being ostracized by one's peer) is a more effective strategy.

Understanding the Reading

1. **Thesis** What is the central thesis of this selection? What main ideas do you learn from reading it?

2. **Predicting exam questions** If an instructor were to give a pop quiz on this selection, what three questions might be included? How would you answer each?

3. **Language** In his discussion of humorous appeals, the author italicizes the terms *distraction* and *counterarguing* to emphasize them. What do these words mean in context?

4. **Meaning** What point does the author seem to be making about the effectiveness of the various appeals he categorizes?

Analyzing the Reading

1. **Technique** Reread the selection, and highlight the questions the author poses. What is the purpose of the questions, and how do they affect you as a reader?

2. **Visuals** The text includes a print ad for Crest Pro-Health toothpaste and for Old Spice body spray. What do these advertisements illustrate about message appeals?

3. **Boxed material** The text includes two types of boxes, "ECONsumer Behavior" and "Marketing Pitfall." What is the purpose of each? How important is it to learn the content of each?

4. **Audience** Do you think the author is writing primarily to students studying for a career in marketing and advertising? Or is a broader audience intended? What makes you think so?

5. **Other patterns** Where in the selection does the author use comparison and contrast extensively? Why is this method important to the point being made?

⬛ Evaluating the Reading

1. **Examples** How well do the examples of advertising the author cites help you understand the points being made? Are the examples presented in sufficient detail?

2. **Visual** Do you agree that the Old Spice ad exemplifies the effective use of humorous appeal? Why, or why not?

3. **Presentation** The author doesn't seem to recommend one of the types of appeals he discusses as being more effective than any others. Do you think he should have done more to evaluate the appeals in terms of their effectiveness relative to one another?

Discussing the Reading

1. Of the advertising message appeals the author describes here, which do you personally find most effective? What kinds of ads are you most likely to remember and to respond positively to?

2. In one of the "Marketing Pitfall" boxes, the author describes a Burger King ad for its SpongeBob Kids Meal that was criticized as being "highly sexualized" in an inappropriate manner. Given Burger King's defense of the ad, do you agree that it was inappropriate? Why, or why not?

3. Would you boycott a product because you found the company's advertising offensive? What kinds of appeals do you find offensive?

Writing about the Reading

1. **Essay** Using the types of message appeals presented in the selection, write a classification essay about advertising. Provide your own examples for each category from print, television, and online advertising. Assume that your audience has not read much about message appeals in advertising.

2. **Essay** Choose a print ad that you think effectively conveys a message about the product being advertised. Then write an essay analyzing the ad by dividing it into its primary parts—picture, text, use of print and type size, and so forth. Be sure to develop a thesis about why you find the ad effective.

3. **Essay** This selection classifies types of message appeals in advertising geared to various consumers. Write an essay in which you classify types of consumers—that is, types of shoppers—according to a basis of classification you develop yourself. Begin by brainstorming a list of consumer types. Then develop a thesis that suggests the categories they fall into. As you draft your essay, provide clear examples for each category.

Writing Your Own Classification or Division Essay

Now that you have learned about the major characteristics, structure, and purposes of classification and division essays, you know everything necessary to write your own. In this section you will read a student's classification essay and get advice on finding ideas, drafting your essay, and revising and editing it. You may want to use the essay prompts in "Readings for Practice, Ideas for Writing" (p. 449) or choose your own topic.

A Student Model Classification Essay

For her introductory sociology course, Maris Vasquez was asked to write an essay about people's use of technology. She chose to discuss Facebook users. As you read the essay, notice how Vasquez uses classification as her primary method of organization.

Title: identifies subject

A Profile of Facebook Users

Maris Vasquez

Introduction: Vasquez establishes expertise on topic

As a college student, I have spent a good amount of my life on Facebook. I use it to procrastinate, discover what friends are doing at other colleges, or determine who a person is. Facebook is a great Web site from which to observe human activity. In my travels across all kinds of profiles, I have drawn one conclusion. Based on posts, photos, profile pictures, likes, comments, and other Facebook activities, users can generally be grouped into five categories that characterize their purpose in using Facebook: creepers, socialites, politicians, philosophers, and amateur photographers.

Thesis: lists categories and includes basis of classification

Category 1: creepers

The first category is what I like to call the creepers. When one hears the word *creeper*, one might think of bugs and other sorts of creepy, crawly creatures. That is just what this kind of Facebook user does. She (this user often happens to be female) makes her way across Facebook profiles, discovering bits and pieces about the users she observes, much like a bug crawling across the earth. The creeper rarely comments on the things she observes or leaves clues that she was reading along. She simply takes in the information and adds it to her repertoire of gossip. Her own Facebook page is often creeper proof. She spends a great deal of time perfecting her privacy settings so that no one can peek in

Characteristic 1: rarely comments

Characteristic 2: prevents others from finding out her information on her. What she does post is perfectly edited, be it a picture or a status, so that no one can make any false judgments. Her status is often about how dumb other people are. This status is usually posted after a thorough thirty-minute creeping session. The word *stalking* is often synonymous with *creeping*.

Characteristic 3: Her messages are a judgment on others.

Category 2: socialites

Characteristic 1: posts party photos frequently

The socialites are, in many ways, the opposite of the creepers. The socialite (also known as the partier) posts every picture from every party she goes to. She is not discrete in her postings and makes it quite clear that she doesn't particularly care what other people did on their weekend. She tags herself in pictures that the nightclubs post and is known for a certain type of status, which often includes at least three other users, who are tagged, and lists their location. Themed parties are her favorite. Before, during, and after photos are a must, even if the evidence turns undignified. An intoxicated word-salad status is quite common, but finding them later can be difficult as they're often deleted the next morning. Morning-after statuses often say something like "Last night was crazy! Love my girls." Profile pictures are never "selfies" but always show her with at least two other people, preferably at a nightclub. The socialite does not particularly care if potential employers see photos of her drinking because she assumes that, as former college kids, they'll excuse her actions.

Characteristic 2: posts status updates while intoxicated but deletes them later

Characteristic 3: not concerned with the impression her profile makes

Category 3: politicians

Characteristic 1: posts news articles and partisan political information

The politician uses Facebook for a completely different type of self-promotion. He posts provocative articles on recent news developments, campaign videos from his favorite professional politicians, and his own witty responses to the day's events. His status is often controversial; it attracts many "likes" from his political followers and angry comments from his detractors. It isn't really a successful month on Facebook unless he's started at least one Facebook fight in which he must defend his position against users of the opposite political persuasion. The politician's profile frequently features a campaign logo or a photograph of himself posing with an actual politician.

Characteristic 2: purposefully starts debates online

Characteristic 3: photos relate to his politics

Category 4: philosophers

Characteristic 1: posts romantic quotes

Characteristic 2: black-and-white photos

Similar to the politician, but deserving of her own category, is the philosopher. She posts sappy quotes about life or song lyrics, which are usually thinly disguised comments on her love interests. Her profile pictures are often in black and white and never feature her smiling. The caption usually includes one of her sappy quotes, occasionally with a heart or other symbol featured prominently.

5

Category 5: amateur photographers

Characteristic 1: photos of objects

Characteristic 2: posts answers to questions about camera equipment

Characteristic 3: uses pictures rather than words

Conclusion

Categories may overlap but each type exists.

Finally, the photographer uses Facebook like his second Tumblr account. He posts albums of completely random objects like his cat, his shoe laces, and his pens. He favors black and white, and his profile picture is often of him taking a picture of something, sometimes of the person taking the picture of him. He uses Facebook to convince others how artsy he is. He posts statuses about whether or not he should get a fisheye lens and answers any questions anyone posts about cameras, whether he knows the person or not. His statuses are few and far between because he prefers to speak through pictures. When he does post a status, his words often resemble those of the philosopher.

Most people on Facebook are probably a combination of all these categories, but when you see one of these stereotypical Facebook users, you know it. Statuses, photos, profile pictures, comments, and the like can tell a lot about a person. In combination, these things can inform you as to a user's ultimate intention in using Facebook.

Responding to Vasquez's Essay

1. How well does the writer's opening paragraph create interest in her classification essay? Does her thesis make you want to read on?

2. Are Vasquez's categories equally well developed? How clearly do you understand each?

3. How well do Vasquez's topic sentences make transitions from one category to the next?

4. Do you think her mentioning in the conclusion that the categories she has established can often be combined helps or hurts Vasquez's essay?

Finding Ideas for Your Classification or Division Essay

One way to find ideas to write about is to look for topics *as you read* material from this book, for other classes, or in your spare time. As you read classification or division pieces, think of other ways of classifying or dividing the topic. For example, consider an essay that classifies exercise programs according to their health benefits. Alternatively, exercise programs could be classified according to cost, degree of strenuousness, types of exercise, and so forth. A classification or division essay provides the reader with one particular viewpoint on the subject. Be sure to keep in mind that it is *only* one viewpoint. Once you identify alternative viewpoints, choose one to write about.

Planning Your Classification or Division Essay

Your first step is to choose a subject to classify or divide. Once you've done so, you need to come up with details about the subject and its categories or parts. Often it works best to generate details first and then use the details to identify categories or parts. Begin with one or more of the following strategies for generating details about your topic.

1. **Visit a place where you can observe the topic or the people associated with it.** For example, to generate details about sports fans, attend a sporting event or watch one on television. Take notes on what you see and hear. Be specific; record conversations, physical characteristics, behaviors, and so forth.

2. **Discuss the topic with a classmate or friend.** Focus on the qualities and characteristics of the topic. Allow the perspective of your classmate or friend to open your mind to new details on your topic.

3. **Brainstorm a list of all the features or characteristics of the topic.** Jot down everything that comes to mind; one feature will serve as a springboard for further characteristics.

4. **Draw a map or diagram that illustrates the topic's features and characteristics.** This map or diagram will help you discover relationships and connections among the characteristics.

5. **Conduct library or Internet research to discover facts, examples, and other details about the topic.** Research will suggest new possibilities and help you expand upon your own ideas.

Choosing a Principle of Classification or Division

Your next task is to decide the principle or basis on which to classify or divide the subject. Read through your details, thinking about the kinds of categories that might be relevant to discussing your subject or the parts into which you could usefully divide it. If the topic is highway drivers, for instance, you could classify them by gender, age, type of car driven, or driving habits. If the topic is a sports team, you could divide it into coaches, assistants, primary players, back-up players, and so forth. Experiment with several principles of classification or division until you find one that fits your purpose and audience.

Choosing Categories or Parts

With your principle of classification or division in mind, use the following suggestions to determine categories or parts.

1. **Make sure that your categories or parts are comprehensive—that your categories could include all items or that you haven't left out any parts.** For example, in a division essay about parts of a baseball stadium, you would not exclude the infield or the bleachers.

2. **Be sure the categories or parts are exclusive; each item being categorized should fit into one category only and parts should not overlap.** For example, in a classification essay about annoying driving habits, the categories "reckless drivers" and "aggressive drivers" are not exclusive, as many drivers would fit into both.

3. **Create categories or parts that will engage your readers.** For example, a division essay on players' facilities in a baseball stadium—dugout, locker room, and bullpen—would be more interesting to sports fans than an essay describing different seating sections of the stadium.

4. **Once you establish categories or parts, you may need to do additional brainstorming or some other type of prewriting to generate enough details to explain each category or part adequately.**

5. **Choose names that effectively describe the categories or parts.** For example, in the essay classifying highway drivers with annoying habits, you might assign names like "I-own-the-road" drivers and "I'm-daydreaming" drivers.

Identifying the Key Features of Each Category or Part

Once you have a workable list of categories or parts, go back to the details and identify key features. These are the features that you will use to explain and differentiate each category or part. Recall how Judith Viorst, in "Friends, Good Friends—Such Good Friends," clearly describes the major characteristics of each type of friendship she has experienced or observed.

Consider again the categories of annoying highway drivers. You might distinguish each type of driver by the key characteristics listed here.

"I-OWN-THE-ROAD" DRIVERS	Inconsiderate of other drivers; weave in and out of traffic; honk horns or flash lights to intimidate others into letting them pass
"I'M-DAYDREAMING" DRIVERS	Fail to observe other drivers; fail to signal when changing lanes; wander over the dividing line or onto the shoulder

As you identify characteristics for each category or part, you may find that two categories or parts overlap or that a category or part is too broad. Do not hesitate to create, combine, or eliminate categories or parts as you work.

For some classification or division essays, it may be easier to start with categories or parts and then fill in the details. In other words, you may want to reverse—to some extent—the process just described. If you do so, be sure not to skip any steps.

Drafting Your Classification or Division Essay

After evaluating categories or parts and reviewing your thesis, you are ready to organize your ideas and draft the essay. Choose the method of organization that best suits your purpose. One method that works well in classification essays is the least-to-most arrangement whereby categories are addressed in increasing order of importance or from least to most common, difficult, or frequent. Spatial order often works well in division essays, as does order of importance. In describing the parts of a baseball stadium, you might move from stands to playing field (spatial order). In writing about the parts of a hospital, you might describe the most important areas first (operating rooms and emergency room) and then move to less important facilities (waiting rooms and cafeteria).

Once you decide how to organize your categories or parts, the next step is to write a first draft. Use the following guidelines.

1. **Write an effective introduction.** See "How Is a Classification or Division Essay Structured?" (p. 438) for advice on introductions.

2. **Explain each category or part.** Begin by defining each category or part, taking into account the complexity of the topic and the background knowledge of the audience. For example, in a division essay about a baseball stadium, you might need to define *infield* and *outfield* if the audience includes a large number of people who are not sports fans.

3. **Provide details that describe each category or part.** Be sure to show how each category or part is distinct from the others. Include a wide range of details—sensory details, personal experiences, examples, and comparisons and contrasts.

4. **Generally, allow one or more paragraphs for each category or part.**

5. **Use transitions.** Your readers need transitions to keep on track as you move from one category or part to another. Transitions such as "the *third* category of . . . ," "an *additional* characteristic of . . . ," and "it *also* contains . . ." will help distinguish key features between and within categories or parts.

6. **Provide roughly the same amount and kind of detail and description for each category or part.** For instance, if you give an example of one type of mental disorder, then you should give an example for every other type discussed in the essay.

7. **Consider adding headings or lists to make the categories or parts clear and distinct.** Headings or lists can be especially useful if there is a large number of categories or parts.

8. **Consider adding a visual such as a diagram or flowchart to make your system of classification or division clearer for readers.**

9. **Write a satisfying conclusion.** If you have trouble finding an appropriate way to conclude, return to your statement about why the classification or division is significant and try to elaborate on it.

Figure 15.3 Revising a Classification or Division Essay

QUESTIONS		REVISION STRATEGIES

1. Thesis and introduction Do they explain your principle of classification or division and suggest its importance?

No →
- Revise your thesis to make your justification stronger or more apparent.
- Add explanatory information to your introduction.

Yes ↓

2. Principle of classification Do you use it consistently throughout the essay? Does it fit your audience and purpose and clearly relate to your thesis?

No →
- Brainstorm other possible principles of classification of your topic that better fit your audience and purpose.
- Revise your categories and parts to fit either your existing principle or a new one.
- Rewrite your thesis to reflect your principle of classification.

Yes ↓

3. Categories or parts Do they cover all or most members of the group or all major parts of the topic? Are your categories or parts exclusive (not overlapping)?

No →
- Brainstorm or do research to add categories or parts.
- Revise your categories or parts so that each item fits into one group only.

Yes ↓

4. Details of each category Does your essay use details to fully explain each category? (If it reads like a list, answer "No.")

No →
- Brainstorm or do research to discover more details.
- Add examples, definitions, facts, and expert testimony to improve your explanations.

Yes ↓

5. Organization Is the organization clear? Does the method you use suit your audience and purpose? Have you followed it consistently?

No →
- Refer to Chapter 6 to discover a more appropriate organizing plan.
- Revise the order of your categories or parts.
- Add transitions to make your organization clear.

Yes ↓

6. Topic sentences Is each paragraph focused on a separate category or part?

No →
- Consider combining paragraphs that cover a single category or part and splitting paragraphs that cover more than one.

Yes ↓

7. Conclusion Does it offer a new insight or perspective on the topic?

No →
- Build the importance of the classification or division into the conclusion.

Revising Your Classification or Division Essay

If possible, set your draft aside for a day or two before rereading and revising it. As you review the draft, focus on content and ideas, not on grammar, punctuation, or mechanics. Use the flowchart in Figure 15.3 to guide your analysis of the strengths and weaknesses in your draft essay.

Editing and Proofreading Your Essay

The last step is to check your revised essay for errors in grammar, spelling, punctuation, and mechanics. In addition, watch out for the types of errors you tend to make in writing assignments, whether for this class or another situation. When editing a classification or division essay, pay attention to two particular kinds of grammatical error: choppy sentences and omitted commas following introductory elements.

1. **Avoid a series of short, choppy sentences.** These can make a classification or division sound dull and mechanical. Instead, combine short sentences and vary sentence patterns and lengths.

   ▶ Working dogs are another one of the American Kennel Club's breed
   , such as German shepherds and sheepherding dogs,
   categories. ~~These include German shepherds and sheepherding dogs.~~

   ▶ The fountain pen, one
   One standard type of writing instrument ~~is the fountain pen.~~ , It is sometimes messy and inconvenient to use. It often leaks.

2. **Use a comma to separate introductory words, phrases, and clauses from the rest of the sentence.**

   ▶ When describing types of college students , be sure to consider variations in age.

   ▶ Although there are many types of cameras , most are easy to operate.

Chapter 16

Definition:
Explaining What You Mean

Quick Start: This photograph shows someone painting a picture on the side of a building. Do public images like this count as art? Does art need to appear in a museum? Does art include graffiti? Who creates art? In a small group, brainstorm the characteristics of art. Then use your list to create a definition of the term *art*. Use examples and sensory details to help define exactly what you think constitutes art.

What Is Definition?

A **definition** explains what a term means or which meaning is intended when a word has several different meanings. For instance, you might need to define *slicing* to someone unfamiliar with golf or the term *koi* to someone unfamiliar with tropical fish. If you call a friend a *nonconformist*, she might ask you for your definition of that word. You and a friend might disagree over what constitutes *feminism* even though you share similar politics. Clearly, definitions are an important part of daily communication.

When members of a group share a set of terms with commonly understood meanings, communication is simplified. For example, many sports and hobby enthusiasts have their own special vocabulary: Hockey fans know terms such as *high-sticking, icing, puck*, and *blueline*; cooking enthusiasts know terms such as *sauté, parboil*, and *fillet*. Members of professions and academic fields also have specialized terminology: A surgeon, for example, asks for the *scalpel*, not for "the small, straight knife with the thin, sharp blade." As you can see, terms and meanings make communication precise, helping avoid misunderstandings and confusion.

Many academic and work situations require that you write or learn definitions, as the following examples illustrate. On an exam for a health and fitness course, you might find the short-answer question, Define the term *wellness*. As a chemical engineer responsible for your department's compliance with company standards, you might be asked to write a brief memo to your staff defining the terms *safety* and *work efficiency*.

There will be many occasions to use definition in your writing. For example, when you suspect your reader may not understand a key term, offer a brief definition. Often, however, a standard definition will not be sufficient to explain a complex idea. At times you may need a paragraph or an entire essay to define a single term. For instance, if you had to define *happiness*, you would probably have trouble coming up with a brief definition because the emotion is experienced in a variety of situations and in somewhat different ways. In an essay-length piece of writing, however, you could explore the term and explain all that it means to you. Such a lengthy, detailed definition is an **extended definition**.

Definition does the following things.

1. Definition often includes a brief explanation of the term.
2. Definition is specific and focused.
3. Definition makes a point.
4. Definition uses other patterns of development.
5. Definition may use negation and address misconceptions.

1. Definition Often Includes a Brief Explanation of the Term

Almost any kind of essay will include a brief definition of an important **term**. Even in an extended-definition essay, it is useful to include a brief definition to help readers begin to grasp the concept. A brief or standard definition (the kind found in a dictionary) consists of three parts:

- the *term* itself,
- the *class* to which the term belongs, and
- the *characteristics or details* that distinguish the term from all others in its class.

For example, a *wedding band* is a piece of jewelry. "Jewelry" is the **class**, or group, of objects that includes wedding bands. To show how a wedding band differs from other members of that class, you would need to identify its **distinguishing characteristics**—the features that make it different from other types of jewelry.

In the following excerpt from a magazine article, the author successfully provides a brief definition of the term *bully* while providing the class (a behavior) and distinguishing characteristics.

Term	The term bully does not have a standard definition, but Dan Olweus, professor of psychology at the University of Bergen, has honed the definition to three core elements —
Three characteristics	bullying involves a pattern of *repeated aggressive behavior* with *negative intent* directed from one child to another where there is a *power difference*. Either a larger child or several children pick on one child, or one child is clearly
Distinguishes this term from similar terms	more dominant than the others. Bullying is not the same as garden-variety aggression; although aggression may involve similar acts, it happens between two people of
Explanation of power difference	equal status. By definition, the bully's target has difficulty defending him- or herself, and the bully's aggressive behavior is intended to cause distress.

—Hara Estroff Marano, "Big. Bad. Bully."

2. Definition Is Specific and Focused

An extended definition focuses on a specific term and discusses it in detail. For instance, an essay that explores *freeganism*, an environmental movement whose members live primarily on things that other people throw away, would go beyond a simple definition (like the one in this sentence). In order to help readers better understand the lifestyle, the author would present the term and could then go on to describe the philosophy behind the movement, how and where freegans find food, and the safety measures they take.

3. Definition Makes a Point

The thesis of an extended-definition essay tells why the term is worth reading about. The following thesis statements include a brief definition and make a point about the term.

Produced by the body, hormones are chemicals that are important to physical as well as emotional development.

Euthanasia, the act of ending the life of someone suffering from a terminal illness, should not be legislated; rather, it should be a matter of personal choice.

Note that writers sometimes choose to separate the brief definition from their thesis, so it is important to look for both parts as you read and to be sure to include both as you write.

4. *Definition Uses Other Patterns of Development*

To explain the meaning of a term, writers usually integrate one or more patterns of development. Here are some examples of how other patterns might be used in an extended definition.

Pattern of Development	Defining the Term *Lurking*
Narration (Chapter 10)	Relate a story about learning something important by lurking.
Description (Chapter 11)	Describe the experience of lurking.
Illustration (Chapter 12)	Give examples of typical situations involving lurking.
Process analysis (Chapter 13)	Explain how to lurk in an Internet chat room.
Comparison and contrast (Chapter 14)	Compare and contrast lurking to other forms of observation.
Classification and division (Chapter 15)	Classify the reasons people lurk— for information, entertainment, and so on.
Cause and effect (Chapter 17)	Explain what might lead to lurking and what its benefits or outcomes might be.
Argument (Chapter 18)	Argue that lurking is an ethical (or unethical) practice.

For a brief overview of the patterns, see Chapter 9, "Patterns: An Introduction."

5. *Definition May Use Negation and Address Misconceptions*

When the term being defined is so similar to other terms in the same class that it can be confused with them, a writer may use **negation** to explain how the term is different from the others. This strategy involves explaining what a term *is not* as well as what it *is*. For example, in the following excerpt from a mass-communication textbook, the authors define public relations by explaining how it is different from advertising.

Similarity: Persuasion **Characteristics of ads** **Negation:** Characteristics of PR that differ from advertising	While public relations may sound very similar to advertising, which also seeks to persuade audiences, it differs in important respects. Advertising uses simple and fixed messages ("Our appliance is the most efficient and affordable") transmitted directly to the public through the purchase of ads for specific products or services. Whereas advertising focuses mainly on sales, public relations develops a marketable image for a person, an organization, a product, a service, or an issue. In doing so, public relations creates more complex messages that may evolve over time (for example a political campaign, or a long-term strategy to dispel unfavorable reports about "fatty processed foods"). PR may be transmitted to the public indirectly, often through articles and reports in the news media.

—*Media Essentials: A Brief Introduction*, Richard Campbell, Christopher R. Martin, and Bettina Fabos

In addition, an extended definition may need to address popular misconceptions about the term. In an essay defining *plagiarism*, for instance, you might correct the mistaken idea that plagiarism involves only passing off another writer's entire paper as your own, since it also includes using other writers' quotes or general phrases without giving them credit.

Reading and Writing Definition Essays

In this section you will learn about the structure of a definition essay, read a sample essay, and practice using the guidelines for understanding, analyzing, and evaluating definition essays. This will help you skillfully read and write essays that use definition.

How Is a Definition Essay Structured?

1. The **introduction** presents the term, provides background information, and includes the **thesis statement**.

2. **Body paragraphs** use one or more patterns of development to describe the distinguishing characteristics of the term and the supporting details.

3. The **conclusion** refers back to the thesis and brings the essay to a satisfying close.

Figure 16.1 represents these major components visually.

Figure 16.1   Graphic Organizer for a Definition Essay

Title	
Introduction	Introduces the term
	Provides background information
	Thesis statement: Gives standard definition and reveals the importance or significance of the term
	⬇
Body paragraphs: organized using one or more patterns of development	Distinguishing characteristic(s)
	Supporting details
	Distinguishing characteristic(s)
	Supporting details
	Distinguishing characteristic(s)
	Supporting details
	⬇
Conclusion	Refers back to thesis
	Draws essay to a satisfying close

1.   THE INTRODUCTION AND THESIS STATEMENT IDENTIFY THE TERM BEING DEFINED

The introduction should identify the term being defined and provide necessary background information. It may also suggest the importance or value of understanding the term. When introducing the term, it may be helpful to use negation, explaining what the term *is* and *is not*. (See p. 492 for more on negation.) Your thesis should include a brief standard definition of the term as well as a perspective or point of view about the term.

Notice how the following weak thesis statement can be revised to reveal the writer's main point.

WEAK   Wireless cable is a means of transmitting television signals through the air by microwave.

REVISED   The future of wireless cable, a method of transmitting television signals through the air using microwaves, is uncertain.

Notice that the preceding revised thesis includes a standard definition as well as an assertion about the term.

Avoid "is when . . ." and "is where . . ." statements such as "Friendship is when . . ." or "Crime is where . . ." Instead, name the class to which the term belongs (see p. 490).

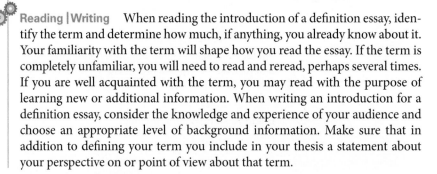

Reading | Writing   When reading the introduction of a definition essay, identify the term and determine how much, if anything, you already know about it. Your familiarity with the term will shape how you read the essay. If the term is completely unfamiliar, you will need to read and reread, perhaps several times. If you are well acquainted with the term, you may read with the purpose of learning new or additional information. When writing an introduction for a definition essay, consider the knowledge and experience of your audience and choose an appropriate level of background information. Make sure that in addition to defining your term you include in your thesis a statement about your perspective on or point of view about that term.

2.   THE BODY OFFERS DETAILS TO MAKE THE TERM UNDERSTANDABLE

The body of a definition essay explains the term's class and presents characteristics that distinguish the term from others in the class. For example, an essay that defines *identity theft* would explain the term as belonging to the class "criminal behaviors." The body paragraphs would present characteristics that distinguish identity theft from other types of crime, such as burglary or white-collar crime.

The body may also present facts, examples, descriptions, and so forth to make the term understandable. It should be organized using one or more patterns of development depending on the type of supporting information used, as well as on the intended audience and purpose. (See "Definition Uses Other Patterns of Development," p. 491.) The body also includes sufficient information to enable readers to understand each characteristic.

Reading | Writing   When reading the body of a definition essay, be sure to identify and highlight each distinguishing characteristic. Make sure you understand how each characteristic is unique and how it relates to the term. When writing the body of the essay, be sure to make your definition easy for your reader to follow. Consider devoting one paragraph to each characteristic and using transitions to move from one distinguishing characteristic to another.

3. THE CONCLUSION BRINGS THE ESSAY TO A SATISFYING CLOSE

The conclusion should pull together information presented in the essay and leave the reader with a final impression of the term.

 Reading | Writing   When reading the conclusion of a definition essay, be sure to test yourself. If you can define the term in your own words, without looking back at the essay, then you understand it. If you cannot, continue to work with the essay until you are able to do so, consulting with classmates or doing further research if necessary. When writing the conclusion of a definition essay, it may be helpful to first read through your essay. Look for points or ideas that need repetition or review.

A Model Definition Essay

Title

The Hoarding Syndrome: When Clutter Goes Out of Control

Deborah Branscum

Deborah Branscum has been a contributing editor to *Newsweek*, a columnist for Fortune.com, and research chief at *Mother Jones*. In 2002, Branscum moved from the San Francisco Bay area to Sweden, a process that sparked her interest in "possessions, clutter, and organization." This penchant is apparent in the following article, which was published by *Reader's Digest* in 2007.

Introduction

As the caseworker from Child Protective Services approached Sue Howard's home last year, she knew something was wrong. Outside the one-story brick house on a quiet, leafy street in Nacogdoches, Texas, a blue dresser stood against one wall. The front porch was crowded with papers, books, an open bag of cat food, toys, a bunch of shoes, and several pairs of roller skates. The white steel front door, which had fallen off its hinges, was propped up in the door frame.

Background information: extended example introduces idea of hoarding

Inside the house it was much worse. The entry hall was crammed with a love seat, boxes, and so much clothing, the caseworker had to step on it to get to the dark, wood-paneled living room and then the dining area, where piles of papers, books, and other objects (including boxes and boxes of past-their-prime Girl Scout Cookies) were stacked on nearly every surface.

ILLUSTRATED BY MATT MUHURIN

This clinical obsessive-compulsive disorder transforms the everyday act of throwing away an object into a deeply wrenching, personal violation.

About nine years ago, Howard, now forty-two, began to feel trapped by poverty. "I thought, What can I do? I'll do what my grandma did." From that moment, Howard refused to discard anything she considered potentially useful.

In 2001, when her husband went to graduate school, Howard began selling books online. She took pride in snapping up bargains for her four children and her business at thrift stores, garage sales, and Wal-Mart. But those bargains gradually took over the household, adding to the tension of an already troubled marriage. The scuffed kitchen floor was sometimes sticky, and appliances, including the dishwasher and refrigerator, were often on the fritz. Howard was too embarrassed to allow a stranger in to do repairs and too overwhelmed to clean up a home filled with clutter. Every time the doorbell rang, her stomach knotted in fear.

Between 2002 and 2005, caseworkers visited Howard's home at least five times in response to anonymous calls. They gave Howard and her husband time to clean up the property, which they always did. But the visit in May 2006 was different. By then, Howard had separated from her husband and was rasing Kelsie, sixteen, Zachary, fifteen, Clay, ten, and Ben, eight, on her own for almost a year and a half. The clutter was getting worse — and potentially dangerous. The caseworker told Howard to move the children to their father's apartment.

Dangerous Compulsion

Thesis: When saving things becomes a compulsion, it can become dangerous.
Body paragraphs
(Distinguishing characteristics of hoarding)

Saving stuff, in moderation, is usually considered normal. But this otherwise healthy impulse can go too far and develop into what some experts consider a clinical obsessive-compulsive disorder. Compulsive hoarding can't be chalked up to eccentricity or a character flaw. It's more serious and harder to control than that. "This is not laziness, criminal negligence, or failure to attend to the responsibilities of life," explains Sanjaya Saxena, MD, director of the Obsessive-Compulsive Disorders Program at the University of California, San Diego. "It is, in fact,

Defining characteristic 1: a compulsive disorder

a neuropsychiatric disorder that will not get better unless the person is treated."

Defining characteristic 2: may result in tragic consequences

Specific detail

And it can lead to tragic consequences. One of the most famous cases involved the wealthy and reclusive Collyer brothers. In 1947, their bodies were discovered in a crumbling New York City mansion packed with more than 100 tons of junk. Last year, a resident of Shelton, Washington, was smothered when a massive pile of clothes toppled on her. And a few fatal fires have even made headlines. Hoarders tend to fill their homes with flammable material and often block hallways and exits in the process, which can make escaping a fire impossible.

Defining characteristic 3: may require treatment

Hoarding can affect people of all ages and backgrounds. As many as three million to six million Americans may be afflicted at some level, and Saxena warns that hoarding often requires extensive treatment. But many deny that they have too much stuff or that the clutter is a problem. And even those who seek treatment can't always find or afford the currently recommended approach: cognitive-behavioral therapy (sometimes paired with medication) from a specialist.

Specific details

Defining characteristic 4: Compared to others, they see more things as being beautiful, useful, or important things, not just junk.

And it's a myth that hoarders keep only junk. Like the rest of us, they may save things that are beautiful, useful, or have sentimental value, say national experts Gail Steketee, PhD, professor and acting dean at the School of Social Work at Boston University, and Randy O. Frost, PhD, a psychologist at Smith College. The difference is that hoarders often find beauty, utility, and meaning where others don't.

Specific detail

Most people, for example, can recycle an old newspaper without a second thought. But a hoarder who saves old newspapers may see an archive of valuable, potentially life-changing information. From that perspective, discarding a newspaper is wasteful, foolish, perhaps even a personal failure. And so this clinical disorder transforms the everyday act of throwing away an object into a deeply wrenching, personal violation.

10

Defining characteristic 5: Hoarders can't organize their things.

Specific detail

Organization is also a nightmare. Steketee and Frost say that compulsive hoarders usually have trouble categorizing items, find it difficult to make decisions, and worry that objects not in sight will be forgotten. They might leave clothes on top of a bureau, for example, instead of putting them in drawers. Over time, a few items piled here and there grow into mountains of dangerous clutter.

Defining characteristic 6: associated with the wide range of dangers

Specific details

How dangerous? The dust, mildew, mold, and rodent droppings commonly found in extreme clutter can irritate allergies or lead to headaches or respiratory problems like asthma for hoarders and their families. In some cases, home maintenance suffers, so individuals may endure freezing winters without heat and sweltering summers with no air conditioning. Clutter also places hoarders and their families, especially the elderly, at high risk of injuring themselves in a fall.

Conclusion

Hoarding affects whole communities, too.

Extreme hoarding endangers not only the residents but also neighbors and firefighters, who face greater risk of injury and death when battling clutter-fed flames. It can become a financial threat to communities as well. Making a hoarder's home safe and habitable can be staggeringly expensive, and hoarders can't always pick up that tab. One year, the health department of a small town spent approximately 75% of the community's entire budget on cleaning out a hoarder's home, according to Frost. A mere eighteen months later, "the home was back the way it was before."

Understanding, Analyzing, and Evaluating Definition Essays

In reading definition essays, you want to be able to do more than merely understand the content of the essays you're reading.

 Reading | Writing   Truly skillful reading and writing require the abilities to understand, analyze, *and* evaluate material. These abilities are important to you as a reader because they give you a systematic, thorough method of examining a reading. They're important to you as a writer because they help you decide what to revise, rewrite, drop, and replace, allowing you to produce a well-written, engaging essay.

Understanding a Definition Essay

Preview the essay before reading to identify the subject being defined and its general definition. Then read it slowly, using the skills you learned in Chapter 2, and look for answers to the following questions.

- **What term is being defined and in what context?** An essay may define the term *green computing*, but as the reader, it is up to you to determine

Figure 16.2   Graphic Organizer for "The Hoarding Syndrome: When Clutter Goes Out of Control"

Title	"The Hoarding Syndrome: When Clutter Goes Out of Control"
Introduction	Extended example of a hoarder (paras. 1–5)
	Thesis (note this occurs in body): When savings things becomes a compulsion, it can become dangerous.
Body paragraphs: distinguishing characteristics of hoarding	**Defining characteristic 1:** A compulsive disorder
	Defining characteristic 2: May result in tragic consequences
	Defining characteristic 3: May require treatment
	Defining characteristic 4: Hoarders see many things as beautiful, useful, or important
	Defining characteristic 5: Unable to organize their things
	Defining characteristic 6: Associated with wide range of dangers
Conclusion	Hoarding affects whole communities, too.

whether it is being defined from an industrial/manufacturing viewpoint, an environmental viewpoint, or a business sales perspective.

- **Why is the term useful or important to know?** Understanding this will give you a purpose for reading and will help you maintain your interest.

- **To what class does the term belong?** Knowing the class will help you place the term within a framework of your knowledge and experience. If an essay defines the practice of *paying forward*, the idea of helping others because someone helped you, knowing that the practice belongs to the general class of Good Samaritan activities may help you set it in your mind.

- **What are the distinguishing characteristics?** These will help you understand how the term is unique and distinct from other members of the same class. Creating a graphic organizer can help you identify the distinguishing characteristics. Figure 16.2 shows a graphic organizer for "The Hoarding Syndrome: When Clutter Goes Out of Control."

- **What examples or other practical explanations are provided?** These supporting details are useful for making the term real and understandable.

- **How does the term differ from similar terms?** This is especially important if similar terms are presented. If a textbook or an article does not explain sufficiently how two or more terms differ, check the terms in a standard dictionary. If the difference is still unclear, check the terms in a specialized subject dictionary.

Understanding in Action

Following is one student's summary of the opening example of the definition of hoarding (paras. 1–6) from "The Hoarding Syndrome: When Clutter Goes Out of Control." Write your own summary of the rest of the essay.

> The essay opens with an example of hoarding. Sue Howard lives in Texas, and her house is filled with clutter. There is everything from piles of stuff on the front porch and the crammed entry hall to the stacked surfaces everywhere in the dining and living rooms. Because of her fear of poverty, years ago Howard began to save anything she thought might someday be useful. She also started buying anything that seemed like a bargain. Now all these things have taken over her house. Appliances often don't work because Howard is ashamed to let repair people in who'll see the mess. Social workers have warned her to clean up the place for the safety of her children. But once her husband moved out, it all just got worse. Now she's about to lose her four children.

Analyzing a Definition Essay

Analyzing a definition essay involves examining how clearly, thoroughly, and effectively the term is defined. Use the following questions to guide your analysis.

- **Is the term's class described clearly and specifically?** The class should be broad enough to be recognizable and meaningful but not so broad that you are not able to place it in a context.
- **Do the characteristics make the term distinguishable from other similar terms or other members of the same class?** Together, the characteristics should define the term uniquely, so it doesn't overlap with any other term.
- **Is each characteristic named or titled?** The author should make it easy for you to identify each and to follow along as he or she moves from one characteristic to another.

- **Is each characteristic distinct?** The author should make it clear how each characteristic differs from others, using details, descriptions, examples, comparisons or contrasts, or personal experiences to make those distinctions throughout the essay.
- **Is each characteristic understandable?** Each characteristic should be clearly explained and should not require background knowledge the reader does not have.

Analysis in Action

The student who wrote the summary for Understanding in Action also annotated paragraph 7 of "The Hoarding Syndrome." Use this annotation as a model to annotate paragraphs 9–13 of that essay.

Characteristic: *Can be tragic*	And it can lead to tragic consequences. One of the most famous cases involved the wealthy and reclusive Collyer brothers. In 1947, their bodies were discovered in a
Clear examples of the dangers of hoarding	crumbling New York City mansion packed with more than 100 tons of junk. Last year, a resident of Shelton, Washington, was smothered when a massive pile of clothes toppled on her. And a few fatal fires have even
Extreme! Makes it clear why treatment is important	made headlines. Hoarders tend to fill their homes with flammable material and often block hallways and exits in the process, which can make escaping fire impossible.

📊 Evaluating a Definition Essay

Evaluating a definition essay involves judging how accurately and effectively the author has explained the term. Use the following questions to guide your evaluation of definition essays.

- **Is the definition comprehensive and complete?** Determine whether the author covers all the important characteristics.
- **Does each characteristic have fair and equal coverage?** Each characteristic should be given roughly the same amount of coverage and use the same level of detail.
- **Are the writer's definitions objective or subjective?** In some essays, the purpose may be to persuade the reader to take a particular action or accept a specific viewpoint. In such essays, subjective or emotional language may be used to influence the reader. For example, a writer who defines the term

liberal as "someone who wants to allow criminals to run free on the streets while sacrificing the rights of innocent victims" reveals a negative bias toward liberals and probably intends to make the reader dislike them.

- **Do you agree with the writer's definition of the term?** Determine whether it is accurate, correct, and consistent with what you already know about the term.

- **Do you think the characteristics the author identified apply to all members of the group that the term covers?** Evaluate whether the characteristics commonly apply in a wide variety of situations. For example, if a writer defining *college students* states that a characteristic of college students is that they are "attending school primarily to please their parents," you might rightly question whether such a characteristic accurately applies to most college students.

Evaluation in Action

Below is an evaluation of "The Hoarding Syndrome" opening paragraph written by the same student who summarized it in Understanding in Action. After reading it, write your own evaluation of this definition essay.

The opening example helps make clear what hoarding is and some of the causes of the condition. It also suggests the dangers of hoarding that the rest of the essay covers in more detail. I just wish the author had given the story of Sue Howard a more definite conclusion. I got involved in her problems and would like to know what happened to her and her children. I also wonder if her story is similar to many other hoarders' stories or if her case is more extreme.

Readings for Practice, Ideas for Writing

On Dumpster Diving

Lars Eighner began writing essays and fiction after graduating from the University of Texas at Austin. The following selection is an abridged version of a nonfiction piece originally published in the *Threepenny Review*. His works include *Travels with Lizbeth* (1993), a book about the homelessness he experienced after losing his job at a mental hospital.

Reading Tip

Eighner's essay is written in the first person. Notice how this point of view gives added depth and intimacy to the topic. Also, pay attention to the author's tone and his attitude toward Dumpster diving.

Previewing the Reading

Preview the reading using the guidelines on pages 23–24, and then answer the following questions.

1. What is Dumpster diving?
2. Give some examples of items the author collects from Dumpsters.

On Dumpster Diving

Lars Eighner

I began Dumpster diving about a year before I became homeless.

I prefer the word *scavenging* and use the word *scrounging* when I mean to be obscure. I have heard people, evidently meaning to be polite, use the word *foraging*, but I prefer to reserve that word for gathering nuts and berries and such, which I do also according to the season and the opportunity. *Dumpster diving* seems to me to be a little too cute and, in my case, inaccurate because I lack the athletic ability to lower myself into the Dumpsters as the true divers do, much to their increased profit.

I like the frankness of the word *scavenging*, which I can hardly think of without picturing a big black snail on an aquarium wall. I live from the refuse of others. I am a scavenger. I think it a sound and honorable niche, although if I could I would naturally prefer to live the comfortable consumer life, perhaps—and only perhaps—as a slightly less wasteful consumer, owing to what I have learned as a scavenger.

While Lizbeth and I were still living in the shack on Avenue B as my savings ran out, I put almost all of my sporadic income into rent. The necessities of daily life I began to extract from Dumpsters. Yes, we ate from them. Except for jeans, all my clothes came from Dumpsters. Boom boxes, candles,

Continued >

bedding, toilet paper, a virgin male love doll, medicine, books, a typewriter, dishes, furnishings, and change, sometimes amounting to many dollars—I acquired many things from the Dumpsters.

5   After all, the finding of objects is becoming something of an urban art. Even respectable employed people will sometimes find something tempting sticking out of a Dumpster or standing beside one. Quite a number of people, not all of them of the bohemian type, are willing to brag that they found this or that piece in the trash. But eating from Dumpsters is what separates the dilettanti from the professionals. Eating safely from the Dumpsters involves three principles: using the senses and common sense to evaluate the condition of the found materials, knowing the Dumpsters of a given area and checking them regularly, and seeking always to answer the question "Why was this discarded?"

Perhaps everyone who has a kitchen and a regular supply of groceries has, at one time or another, made a sandwich and eaten half of it before discovering mold on the bread or got a mouthful of milk before realizing the milk had turned. Nothing of the sort is likely to happen to a Dumpster diver because he is constantly reminded that most food is discarded for a reason. Yet a lot of perfectly good food can be found in Dumpsters.

Canned goods, for example, turn up fairly often in the Dumpsters I frequent. All except the most phobic people would be willing to eat from a can, even if it came from a Dumpster. Canned goods are among the safest of foods to be found in Dumpsters but are not utterly foolproof.

For myself I have few qualms about dry foods such as crackers, cookies, cereal, chips, and pasta if they are free of visible contaminates and still dry and crisp. Most often such things are found in the original packaging, which is not so much a positive sign as it is the absence of a negative one.

Raw fruits and vegetables with intact skins seem perfectly safe to me, excluding of course the obviously rotten. Many are discarded for minor imperfections that can be pared away. Leafy vegetables, grapes, cauliflower, broccoli, and similar things may be contaminated by liquids and may be impractical to wash.

10   Students throw food away around breaks because they do not know whether it has spoiled or will spoil before they return. A typical discard is a half jar of peanut butter. In fact, nonorganic peanut butter does not require refrigeration and is unlikely to spoil in any reasonable time. The student does not know that, and since it is Daddy's money, the student decides not to take a chance. Opened containers require caution and some attention to the question. "Why was this discarded?" But in the case of discards from student apartments, the answer may be that the item was thrown out through carelessness, ignorance, or wastefulness. This can sometimes be deduced when the item is found with many others, including some that are obviously perfectly good.

Yogurt, cheese, and sour cream are items that are often thrown out while they are still good. Occasionally I find a cheese with a spot of mold, which of course I just pare off, and because it is obvious why such a cheese was discarded, I treat it with less suspicion than an apparently perfect cheese found in similar circumstances. Yogurt is often discarded, still sealed, only because the expiration date on the carton had passed. This is one of my favorite finds because yogurt will keep for several days, even in warm weather.

No matter how careful I am I still get dysentery[1] at least once a month, oftener in warm weather. I do not want to paint too romantic a picture. Dumpster diving has serious drawbacks as a way of life.

I learned to scavenge gradually, on my own. Since then I have initiated several companions into the trade. I have learned that there is a predictable series of stages a person goes through in learning to scavenge.

At first the new scavenger is filled with disgust and self-loathing. He is ashamed of being seen and may lurk around, trying to duck behind things, or he may try to dive at night. (In fact, most people instinctively look away from a scavenger. By skulking around, the novice calls attention to himself and arouses suspicion. Diving at night is ineffective and needlessly messy.)

15   Every grain of rice seems to be a maggot. Everything seems to stink. He can wipe the egg yolk off the found can, but he cannot erase from his mind the stigma of eating garbage.

That stage passes with experience. The scavenger finds a pair of running shoes that fit and look and smell brand-new. He finds a pocket calculator in perfect working order. He finds pristine ice cream, still frozen, more than he can eat or keep. He begins to understand: People throw away perfectly good stuff, a lot of perfectly good stuff.

At this stage, Dumpster shyness begins to dissipate. The diver, after all, has the last laugh. He is finding all manner of good things that are his for the taking. Those who disparage his profession are the fools, not he.

He may begin to hang on to some perfectly good things for which he has neither a use nor a market. Then he begins to take note of the things that are not perfectly good but are nearly so. He mates a Walkman with broken earphones and one that is missing a battery cover. He picks up things that he can repair.

At this stage he may become lost and never recover. Dumpsters are full of things of some potential value to someone and also of things that never have much intrinsic value but are interesting. All the Dumpster divers I have known come to the point of trying to acquire everything they touch. Why not take it, they reason, since it is all free? This is, of course, hopeless. Most divers come to realize that they must restrict themselves to items of relatively immediate utility. But in some cases the diver simply cannot control himself. I have met several of these pack-rat types. Their ideas of the values of various pieces of junk verge on the psychotic. Every bit of glass may be a diamond, they think, and all that glistens, gold.

I find from the experience of   20 scavenging two rather deep lessons. The first is to take what you can use and let the rest go by. I have come to think that there is no value in the abstract. A thing I cannot use or make useful, perhaps by trading, has no value however rare or fine it may be. I mean useful in a broad sense — some art I would find useful and some otherwise.

I was shocked to realize that some things are not worth acquiring, but now I think it is so. Some material things are white elephants that eat up the possessor's substance. The second lesson is the transience[2] of material being. This has not quite converted me

---

[1] **dysentery** An intestinal infection marked by abdominal pain, fever, and diarrhea.

[2] **transience** Temporary quality, short-lived.

Continued >

to a dualist,[3] but it has made some headway in that direction. I do not suppose that ideas are immortal, but certainly mental things are longer lived than other material things.

Once I was the sort of person who invests objects with sentimental value. Now I no longer have those objects, but I have the sentiments yet.

Many times in our travels I have lost everything but the clothes I was wearing and Lizbeth. The things I find in Dumpsters, the love letters and rag dolls of so many lives, remind me of

[3] **dualist** One who believes that substances are either material or mental.

this lesson. Now I hardly pick up a thing without envisioning the time I will cast it aside. This I think is a healthy state of mind. Almost everything I have now has already been cast out at least once, proving that what I own is valueless to someone.

Anyway, I find my desire to grab for the gaudy bauble has been largely sated. I think this is an attitude I share with the very wealthy—we both know there is plenty more where what we have came from. Between us are the rat-race millions who nightly scavenge the cable channels looking for they know not what.

I am sorry for them.   25

Understanding the Reading

1. **Background information** According to Eighner, what stages do people go through before becoming "professional" Dumpster divers?

2. **Detail** What risks associated with Dumpster diving does the author mention?

3. **Purpose** What lessons does Eighner share about his experiences Dumpster diving?

4. **Viewpoint** What attitude does Eighner say he shares with the wealthy?

5. **Language** According to Eighner, what is the difference between *scavenging* and *foraging* (paras. 2–3)?

6. **Language** Explain the phrase "gaudy bauble" as used in paragraph 24.

7. **Vocabulary** Using context clues, define each of the following words as it is used in the essay, consulting a dictionary if necessary: *niche* (para. 3), *bohemian* (5), *dilettanti* (5), *phobic* (7), *pristine* (16), *dissipate* (17), and *disparage* (17).

8. **Organization** To analyze Eighner's organization, complete the graphic organizer that follows. Keep in mind that he doesn't only use definition as a pattern.

Analyzing the Reading

1. **Technique** The primary pattern of development in Eighner's essay is definition. To make Dumpster diving clear to his readers, Eighner uses other patterns as well. What other patterns does he use? (See Chapter 9, "Patterns: An Introduction," for a brief overview.)

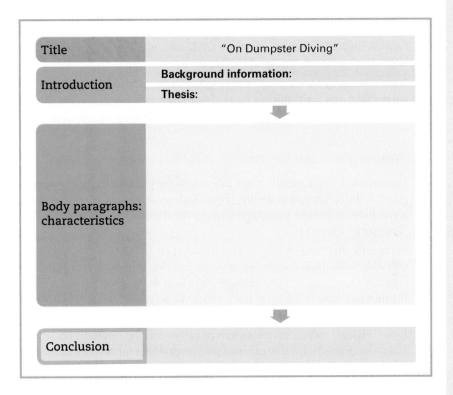

2. **Details** What kinds of sensory details does Eighner include? Highlight several particularly effective examples. What do these details contribute to the essay?

3. **Thesis** What is the author's main point? What examples support this assertion?

4. **Conclusion** Eighner begins his conclusion in paragraph 20. How does he signal the transition to his conclusion?

Evaluating the Reading

1. **Purpose** Did this essay alter your opinion of the homeless? Did any of your preconceptions about the homeless affect your response? Why, or why not?

2. **Presentation** How did you react to learning that Eighner eats out of Dumpsters? Does this reaction affect your response to the writer?

3. **Technique** Eighner's essay both opens and closes with a single-sentence paragraph. Do you find these effective? Explain.

4. **Definition** Does the essay give you a good sense of what Dumpster diving is and what it involves? How would you evaluate the level of detail here?

Discussing the Reading

1. Discuss Eighner's attitude toward materialism, wealth, and personal possessions. How do these correspond to your own?

2. Does *scavenging* have a positive or negative connotation? Is shopping at garage sales and thrift stores a form of scavenging?

3. In class or in your journal, discuss the possible reasons for homelessness.

Writing about the Reading

1. **Paragraph** Using Eighner's essay as a source for information, write a paragraph defining Dumpster diving. (Hint: Eighner writes in the first person about himself. In your paragraph write in the third person using the subject "Dumpster divers.")

2. **Paragraph** Brainstorm a list of activities that are important to you on an everyday basis. Then choose one that you can define in detail in a paragraph entitled "On _____" (for example, "On Text-Messaging"). (Hint: Like Eighner has done in his essay, use a variety of personal examples to develop your definition.)

3. **Essay** Eighner comments on American values and the emphasis on acquiring and owning goods. He also explains how he provides for his own daily needs. Write an essay in which you explain your view on consumerism, defining that term as you see it. How important is consumption as an American value?

Gullible Travels

Bethe Dufresne is a freelance journalist based in Connecticut. In 2009 she traveled to Kenya to report on the launch of the first free school for girls in East Africa's largest slum. The following article, first published in the Catholic magazine *Commonweal*, grew out of her experience there.

Reading Tip

The author of this definition essay offers different names for her topic. What are they, and how does her including them relate to her purpose?

Previewing the Reading

Preview the reading using the guidelines on pages 23–24. Then answer the following questions.

1. What, specifically, is the author defining in this essay?
2. List one fact you learned about this topic.

Gullible Travels[1]

Bethe Dufresne

In the lobby of Nairobi's Boulevard Hotel you'll see signs promoting all manner of tourist sites, from a Maasai crafts market to animal parks. For now, at least, you're unlikely to see any signs promoting tours of Nairobi's infamous Kibera slum, the largest in East Africa. Yet such tours aren't difficult to find.

As a reporter covering the debut of Kibera's first free school for girls in 2009, I made multiple visits to the massive slum, where an estimated 1.5 million people eke out an existence mostly without basic services such as electricity, running water, sanitation, and police protection. I was shocked to learn that this was a popular tourist destination.

Kibera is one of the leading attractions of "poverty tourism"—a trend that has been given many names, including "slum safaris" and "poverty porn." From Soweto to São Paulo, Jakarta to Chicago, urban "slumming" has become a global phenomenon, even as a lively debate rages about the ethics of what promoters call "reality tourism."

The fuss over slum tours may be just a footnote to the great international-aid debate, but the same hot-button issues arise: Who really reaps the economic benefits? What are the long-term effects? And where—for the poor who are the prime attraction—is the protection and oversight?

Of course, no one who promotes slum tours actually says, "Come with us to gawk at desperately poor people."

[1] **Gullible Travels** The title is a reference to *Gulliver's Travels*, the classic novel by Jonathan Swift. It is a traveler's narrative but also pokes fun at human nature.

5

Continued >

Tourists flock to the Dharavi slum in Mumbai, which was featured in the movie *Slumdog Millionaire.*

The typical pitch targets travelers' desire for authentic experiences, as if authenticity can only be found in suffering. But the broader appeal is to travelers' charitable impulses: Take this tour and help slum dwellers in the process, because — it is claimed — part of the profits go to schools, orphanages, and other worthy projects.

Prices vary. A short tour of Mumbai's Dharavi slum can be had for $11, while a private tour that includes interaction with residents costs $71. Alex Ndambo, who books all types of tours for Real Adventures Africa from Nairobi's Boulevard Hotel, told me a day tour of Kibera costs $50 to $80. He said he'd "heard" that 35 to 45% goes to the community, where most people live on less than a dollar a day.

Slum tours have existed in some form for a long time. Nineteenth-century New Yorkers toured the Bowery

to satisfy their curiosity, and perhaps to stimulate their charitable instincts. Today, however, the Internet has helped popularize the concept as never before: Travelers in almost any major city can find or arrange a tour of the urban underbelly. A 2009 article in *National Geographic Traveler* called reality tourism "the latest frontier in travel" and credited its growth to tourists' eschewing "indulgent vacations in favor of more meaningful travel experiences." The same article gave tips for "the right way to slum it," like inquiring about how much of the cost goes to the slum community, but it neglected to mention how difficult that information is to verify.

All tour promoters claim the best intentions. Most tours have rules for patrons: No photos without permission from the subject, no peering into windows, and no handing out treats or money to the children who chant "How are you?" while reaching out to brush white skin. After tours end, guides typically solicit donations of cash or goods on behalf of residents, pledging to pass along the loot.

10   The biggest markets for slum tours are Kibera, Rio de Janeiro's favelas (shantytowns), and the Dharavi district of Mumbai. The obvious reasons are their scale, both in square footage and degree of human misery, and the fact that all three have been featured prominently in major films. For Kibera, it was *The Constant Gardener* (2005); for Rio, *City of God* (2002); and for Mumbai, *Slumdog Millionaire* (2008). Those films didn't create slum tourism, but they have certainly bolstered it.

Kennedy Odede, a cofounder of Kibera's first free girls' school, wrote an opinion piece for the *New York Times* . . . describing how, as a teenager outside his Kibera shack, he spied a white woman taking his picture and "felt like a tiger in a cage." He recalled another occasion when a tour guide — someone he knew — led a group into a private home to photograph a woman giving birth.

For my part, I had a job to do in Kibera and an invitation to be there. Yet I have to wonder what made me so different from slum tourists, driven as I was by curiosity, seeking the satisfaction of doing good, and attracted, like many journalists, to danger and despair.

My husband and I traveled around Kibera under the guidance of a resident named Bangkok, a nickname he acquired after a trip to Thailand as part of a youth boxing team. With a scar on one cheek and long, muscular limbs, Bangkok moved with leonine grace and assurance. Kibera is said to have "a thousand corners," and every time we

rounded another it was plain from the deference we were accorded that no one messed with Bangkok. "You get into any trouble," he said, "just say Bangkok."

Each time we returned to Kibera, the residents seemed less beaten down and foreign, and we appreciated their resourcefulness and vitality more. Once we got over the initial shock of the place, we could begin to see Kibera as a community, not just a slum. But this takes time, and a tour is by definition a glimpse, a chance to skim the surface.

Bangkok also led commercial slum   15 tours, and in the midst of such extreme poverty I questioned my right to criticize how he made a living. He told me he made sure Kibera residents got a cut of the profits. Perhaps they did. But to date there appears to be no real accounting, there or anywhere else, of how much tourism money actually makes its way into slums.

Robert Frank, blogging for the *Wall Street Journal*'s *Wealth Report* in February 2010, wrote that the slum tourism debate has so far been "fueled by emotion and politics, with little research." That may change, he added, with a study by British researcher Fabian Frenzel, who is attempting to quantify the economic impact of tourism in Rio's favelas.

When I asked Ndambo in Nairobi what Kenyan lawmakers thought about Kibera tours, he said they encourage them because it inspires charitable giving. You could also say it helps let the leaders off the hook when it comes to addressing the poverty in their midst.

Brazil is trying a different approach with "Rio Top Tour: Rio de Janeiro in a Different Perspective," through which the government partners with slum residents to promote tours celebrating local arts and culture, and marketing

Continued >

something other than poverty to tourists. A bit of shrewd politics in advance of hosting the 2016 Summer Olympics, perhaps, but it also shows how slum tours could evolve into something genuinely beneficial to residents.

Curious about the demographics of slum tourists, I asked Ndambo who is most apt to book a Kibera tour. "Americans," he answered without hesitation. Asked why he thought that was the case, he replied, "I suppose it's because Americans are so kind."

20   "Thoughtless" is more like it, if you ask Wayne and Emely Silver, cofounders of American Friends of Kenya (AFK). Since 2004 their Connecticut-based nonprofit has provided partnership on projects driven by Kenyans. No one associated with AFK is paid. Twice I've joined the Silvers in an ethics class at Three Rivers Community College in

Norwich, Connecticut, to discuss working in developing nations. Slum tours were a hot topic, and I found the "reality television" generation primed to give them a chance. Most tourists probably want to help, students theorized, and as long as they are respectful, where is the harm?

Wayne Silver insisted that the tours are "inherently disrespectful" because there can be "no real zone of privacy" where homes are shacks and all neighborhood life is on the streets. Students listened respectfully, but not all were convinced. "Eyes are being opened," one said. "It all depends on what you do with what you see," said another.

To this Emely Silver offered a challenge. The plane ticket alone makes any trip to Africa an expensive proposition, she said, "so if you can afford to go to Africa to take a slum tour, you can afford to go and work with us."

Understanding the Reading

1. **Thesis** Where in the essay does Dufresne state the thesis that introduces her definition?

2. **Viewpoint** What is Dufresne's personal connection to her subject? How does she compare herself to others who tour slum areas?

3. **Characteristics** What term does Dufresne define? What are the primary characteristics of the term?

4. **Meaning** What is the "broader appeal" of slum tours (para. 6)? What is Dufresne's response to this stated goal?

5. **Meaning** How has the Brazilian government modified the idea of slum tours?

6. **Vocabulary** Using context clues (p. 34), define each of the following words as it is used in the reading, consulting a dictionary if necessary: *infamous* (para. 1), *debut* (2), *massive* (2), *gawk* (5), *urban underbelly* (8), *eschewing* (8), *leonine* (13), *quantify* (16), *shrewd* (18), *demographics* (19), and *inherently* (21).

Analyzing the Reading

1. **Combining patterns** In her extended-definition essay, what patterns of development in addition to definition does Dufresne use? Annotate the reading to identify the various patterns of development. (See Chapter 9, "Patterns: An Introduction," for a brief overview.)

2. **Technique** Does Dufresne put her term in a larger class? What is that class? Does she state it implicitly or explictly?

3. **Technique** Dufresene uses quotation throughout the essay. Why, in particular, does she use quotation in paragraphs 5, 8, 11, 21, and 22?

4. **Voice** How does Dufresne characterize herself in terms of slum tourists in paragraphs 2, 12, 14, and 15? Why does she make it a point to do so in these parts of the essay?

Evaluating the Reading

1. **Definition** Do you think Dufresne succeeds in fully defining her subject? Does she provide sufficient detail?

2. **Presentation** Is Dufresne's definition objective? Do you think her personal feelings color the presentation? Explain your answer with specific examples from the essay.

3. **Visuals** Why was the photograph of an Indian slum included in the essay? What message does it convey?

4. **Language** In paragraph 9, Dufresne writes that slum-tour operators solicit donations from tourists and promise "to pass along the loot." Is this a fair use of language?

Discussing the Reading

1. Would you have any interest in participating in a slum tour? Why, or why not?

2. What do you think of the claim that slum tours open people's eyes in a way that ultimately benefits slum dwellers? Is the attraction to such tours primarily "charitable" in your view?

3. How do you respond to Emely Silver's challenge quoted in the final paragraph? How does what she suggests relate to slum-tour operators' offer of "reality tourism"?

Writing about the Reading

1. **Paragraph** Write a paragraph in which you define Dufresne's subject in your own words. (Hint: You'll first need to choose the term that you wish to define. Defresne primarily uses the term *slum tourism*, but she also offers alternatives such as *poverty porn* and *reality tourism*. Your choice of term will influence the basis of your definition.)

2. **Essay** Dufresne quotes Wayne Silver as criticizing slum tourism as "disrespectful" because there is "no real zone of privacy" in slums. Do you think our society values respect and privacy? Is there a trend toward the acceptance of disrespectful behavior and/or the loss of privacy? Write an essay in which you define respectful (or disrespectful) behavior or in which you define privacy or its loss. Think about how your definition of the concept you choose is or is not reflected in examples you see around you.

3. **Essay** Dufresne writes in paragraph 14 about being able to see Kibera "as a community, not just a slum." Write an essay in which you define a particular "community" that you are familiar with. Begin by brainstorming examples of different kinds of communities, and then choose one and brainstorm its characteristics.

Can You See Me Now? Deaf America

Stefany Anne Golberg is a multimedia artist, musician, and writer, and teaches at the Maryland Institute College of Art. She is also a cofounder of the Flux Factory, a nonprofit that fosters art innovation. The following piece is excerpted from *The Smart Set*, a Web magazine that covers culture, ideas, and everything in between. In this essay Golberg defines the deaf culture.

Reading Tip

As you read, consider why the author, who is not deaf, holds the "Deaf-World," as she terms it, in such high regard.

Previewing the Reading

Preview the reading (see pp. 23–24 for guidelines), and then list two things you already learned about the deaf culture.

---

thesmartset.com

Can You See Me Now? Deaf America

By Stefany Anne Golberg

For most deaf Americans, being deaf is not the inability to hear but rather the ability to perceive life in a different way from hearing people. For many, it's a blessing.

I first decided to take up American Sign Language as a teenager. Sadly, I had no deaf friends or family members with whom to practice ASL. I didn't know any deaf people at all, in fact. I was driven mostly by fascination with the silent language itself, which is powered by a clarity and expressiveness absent from everyday spoken English.

There is an illustrated diagram in my ASL textbook explaining that to properly ask a

Continued >

question in ASL you first make a statement and then shrug your shoulders, cock your head to one side, and open your eyes wide, perhaps adding an inquisitive expression to your face. To a hearing person, this feels like overkill—like donning a Greek theater mask every time you need to find the bathroom. But communicating with your whole body is a fundamental part of ASL. It's a visual idiom, a language of the eye.

Modern deaf poetry is filled with intense imagery, as in J. Schuyler Long's "The Poetry of Motion":

> In the poetry of motion there is music if one sees,
> In the soaring birds above us there are moving symphonies.
> There is music in the movement of a ship upon the wave
> And the sunbeams dancing o'er it, that the minstrels never gave.
>
> . . . in harmony of motion there are songs that Nature sings.
> And there is music all around us if we have the eyes to see.

What deaf people have realized about themselves in the past century is that being deaf opens up a new mode of experience. ASL is the language of that experience. They are creating their own world. But it's a world they have to defend.   5

Deaf activists have argued for decades that deafness is not a defect but a character trait, even a benefit. In their 2011 book *The People of the Eye*, authors Harlan Lane, Richard C. Pillard, and Ulf Hedberg go one step further. They assert that deafness is an ethnicity that, like all officially classed ethnicities, must be given its due politically and culturally [and grammatically, which is why the classification is capitalized throughout the rest of this piece].

Deaf identity is based not on religion, race, or class, say the authors, but "there is no more authentic expression of an ethnic group than its language." And language is the core of American Deaf life. With the emergence of Deaf schools, literacy allowed Deaf people to better communicate in the hearing world. As ASL developed, Deaf Americans could better communicate with each other, and with this came the creation of a Deaf culture, even a new way of being.

ASL signers say that they spend much more time thinking about and dealing with language than most Americans, resulting in a rich and independent tradition of Deaf literature, theater, and journalism. Deaf people have their own clubs, their own rituals, their own places of worship, their own newspapers, and their own sense of humor. In *The People of the Eye*, readers learn how the fully embodied language of ASL and Deaf pride created a culture of storytelling in the Deaf-World, and how this storytelling developed a unique narrative structure based on the particularities of ASL.

American signers also share a common history and even ancestry. Indeed, *The People of the Eye* is chock-full of ancestral accounts and pedigree diagrams that would make a Mormon genealogist proud.

Americans have been searching for ways to eliminate deafness for a long time. These 10 remedies have ranged from the abusive to the absurd, from so-called oralism (forcing Deaf people to speak and lip-read instead of sign); to sticking twigs, urine, or electricity in the ears; to divine intervention. Charles Lindbergh reportedly would charge $50 to take Deaf people up in a little plane and perform acrobatic stunts to "rouse the slumbering hearing apparatus."

Today, thanks to the cochlear implant, deafness can, in effect, be "cured." An estimated 71,000 adults and children have had the treatment, and daytime television is rife with heartwarming stories about people whose lives have been dramatically changed by the device.

The cochlear implant resembles a sea parasite escaped from Radio Shack and looks like it is feasting on the side of the human head. But unlike a hearing aid, which rests outside the ear and amplifies sound, the implants are surgically attached to the cochlea.[1] On its Web site, the National Institute on Deafness and Other Communication Disorders explains that cochlear implants "bypass damaged portions of the ear and directly stimulate the auditory nerve. Signals generated by the implant are sent by way of the auditory nerve to the brain, which recognizes the signals as sound."

Recognizing signals as sound is not a restoration of complete hearing capacity, but cochlear implants do seem to help those who want to better perceive sound, as well as increase their ability to communicate orally. And the technology is improving all the time.

It seems as if all of this progress is good progress. For adults who have grown up in the Deaf-World and live in it as happy citizens, though, the suggestion that they should get a cochlear implant can sound downright insulting, prejudiced even. After all, the authors of *The People of the Eye* posit, if one accepts the argument that Deaf is an ethnicity, aren't plans to eradicate it to be seen as an act of genocide?[2] And even if deafness is a choice, does this make it any lass valid than, say, Judaism? Many of the qualities we hold inviolable,[3] as true to our identities, to our "ethnicities," are mutable,[4] after all. (As the Inquisition[5] demonstrated, even

[1] **cochlea** Part of the inner ear that converts sound vibrations into nerve impulses.
[2] **genocide** The deliberate extermination of a group of people.
[3] **inviolable** Cannot be changed, broken, or destroyed.
[4] **mutable** Able to be changed.
[5] **Inquisition** Group of institutions within the Roman Catholic Church justice system who fought against heretics (disbelievers).

Continued >

white Protestants can be cured.) But because they can be changed does not mean they must be.

These are tough, uncomfortable questions. Are cures an acceptable way to address   15
human diversity? Are deviations from the norm to be embraced, with education and social sensitivity, or eliminated? What of Deaf children, who are too young to understand the implications of the potential loss of their Deaf identity? Or who may not want to grow up in the Deaf-World but are unable to make the choice? And what of the hearing parents of a Deaf child? How could they encourage their child to be Deaf, especially given the option of a cochlear implant? Even the most permissive, who might accept their Deaf child's different ethnicity as one would for an adopted child, would have to come to terms with leaving their child to the unfamiliar Deaf-World. In doing so, would they lose their own connection to the world of their child?

What authors Lane, Pillard, and Hedberg want hearing people to understand is that most Deaf Americans would not assimilate[6] even if they could. Deaf people tend to marry other Deaf people, go to Deaf schools, have Deaf friends and even surrogate[7] Deaf parents when hearing parents are insufficient to bolster a Deaf identity (or who threaten that identity by attempting to cure them). The Deaf-World, born of necessity, has now become a fortress against the invading hordes of the hearing. There are ASL signers who dream of a Deaf homeland, where visual communication is the norm. Deaf people who gain too much success in the hearing world or marry into it can be looked on with suspicion.

In *Understanding Deaf Culture: In Search of Deafhood*, author Paddy Ladd draws a distinction between deafness and what he calls Deafhood. Deafness, says Ladd, is a term given by the hearing. It presents being Deaf as a finite state. "Deafhood is not, however, a 'static' medical condition life 'deafness,'" Ladd writes. "Instead, it represents a process—the struggle by each Deaf child, Deaf family, and Deaf adult to explain to themselves and each other their own existence in the world. In sharing their lives with each other as a community, and enacting those explanations rather than writing books about them, Deaf people are engaged in a daily praxis,[8] a continuing internal and external dialogue."

When we look at it this way, maybe considering Deaf as an ethnicity is itself a process of reconsidering what a Deaf person is or can be. Maybe it's not an end but a beginning, for hearing and Deaf alike.

---

[6] **assimilate** To be or become absorbed.
[7] **surrogate** Person acting for another, substitute.
[8] **praxis** Regular activity involving a skill.

Understanding the Reading

1. **Thesis** What is the thesis of this definition essay, and where does Golberg state it directly?

2. **Audience** Who are Golberg's intended readers? What effect does she apparently hope her essay will have on these readers?

3. **Meaning** What does Golberg suggest defines deaf culture and qualifies it as an "ethnicity"?

4. **Language** What distinction is made between "deafness" and "Deafhood" in paragraph 17?

Analyzing the Reading

1. **Introduction** How does Golberg's opening paragraph serve to summarize the main point of her definition? Highlight specific words in the paragraph that do this.

2. **Technique** Why does Golberg write in such detail about American Sign Language in paragraph 3?

3. **Technique** Paragraph 15 consists almost completely of a series of questions. What is the function of this paragraph in terms of the audience to whom Golberg is appealing?

4. **Technique** How do the final three paragraphs of the essay deal with the questions raised in paragraph 15?

5. **Language** Consider Golberg's use of vocabulary in describing cochlear implants in paragraphs 12–14: "cured" (in quotation marks), "heartwarming stories," "sea parasite . . . feasting on the side of the human head," and "recognizes the signals as sound." What do these words and phrases contribute to the impression she hopes to create?

6. **Meaning** Why does Golberg write about deafness being a "choice" (para. 14)? What larger point is she making?

7. **Visual** What do you think the visual that accompanies the reading means?

Evaluating the Reading

1. **Method** How effective do you find Golberg's essay as a definition? Do you think she makes her point fully and clearly? Does she convince you of her thesis?

2. **Development** Golberg writes in paragraph 2 that ASL "is powered by a clarity and expressiveness absent from everyday spoken English." Do you think she offers sufficient evidence to support this point?

3. **Visuals** Consider the drawing that accompanies this piece. How does it contribute to the definition Golberg presents? From whose perspective does it seem to be drawn? How does it contribute to the tone of the essay?

4. **Language** Paraphrasing defenders of deaf culture, Golberg writes in paragraph 14 that attempts to cure deafness medically and technologically can be seen "as an act of genocide." Do you think this language is apt?

5. **Language** Golberg writes of the "Deaf-World" as a "fortress against the invading hordes of the hearing" (para. 16). Does her essay make you sympathize with this characterization?

Discussing the Reading

1. Golberg asserts in paragraph 16 that most deaf people don't want to "assimilate." Do you think that assimilation into mainstream culture is generally a good thing or a bad thing? Why?

2. In paragraph 14, Golberg writes that just because innate personal qualities "can be changed does not mean they must be." How broadly do you think this statement can be applied?

3. How do you answer the questions Golberg poses in paragraph 15?

Writing about the Reading

1. **Essay** Write an essay in which you define the primary culture, subculture (group of people who share a common interest or characteristic), or ethnicity you see yourself belonging to. You may belong to several cultures or subcultures. You belong to the subculture of college students, for example. Other subcultures include members of a particular community service organization or players of a particular sport. (Hint: As you plan your essay, think about stereotypes of your culture versus the reality you see.) You may take a humorous approach to this assignment if you wish.

2. **Essay** Golberg uses the term *ethnicity* throughout her essay. Write an essay of extended definition in which you consider the concept of ethnicity, using Golberg's definition of the term as a starting point.

3. **Essay** Write an essay about the various aspects of assimilation. Choose a subculture (group of people who share a common interest or characteristic) that you are familiar with or part of. You might choose a work, school, or sport subculture. Briefly define what the subculture is and explain its characteristics. Then discuss what is involved in assimilating to the group—that is, in becoming part of that group.

COMBINING THE PATTERNS

Latino Heritage Month

Luis J. Rodriguez is a poet, journalist, fiction writer, children's book writer, critic, and social activist. In an effort to curb gang violence, Rodriguez cofounded Tia Chucha's Centro Cultural, a multiarts, multimedia cultural center in the northeast San Fernando Valley. The son of Mexican immigrants, he considers the notion of Latino heritage in this 2011 article from the *Huffington Post.*

Reading Tip

As you read, annotate the essay to highlight the diversity of Latino culture as the author defines it.

Previewing the Reading

Preview the reading (see pp. 23–24 for guidelines), and then think about the author's purpose. What does he want to communicate about Latino heritage?

---

huffingtonpost.com

Latino Heritage Month

By Luis J. Rodriguez

I recently visited Orlando, Florida, home to more Puerto Ricans on the mainland other than New York City. I was there to spend time with my grandson Ricardo, who earlier this year graduated from high school with honors and is now into his first year of college. Ricardo is part of the Puerto Rican side of my family, wonderful law-abiding Christians, who worked hard and provided a loving home for my grandson when the world around him seemed bleak.

For fifteen years, I lived in a mostly Puerto Rican community of Chicago, where Ricardo's mother grew up. Although I am Chicano, born on the Mexico-U.S. border, I've also lived among Mexican migrants, Central Americans, African Americans, Asians, Cuban Americans, and European Americans in Los Angeles, the San Francisco Bay Area, Miami, San Bernardino, and San Fernando. For years, I've spoken at and participated in ceremonies in Native American reservations (a Navajo medicine man and his wife around ten years ago adopted my present wife). My other grandchildren are half German, half Scottish-Irish, and half Hungarian.

My former wives and live-in girlfriends include a barrio-raised Chicana, an undocumented Mexican, a Mexican/Colombian, a poor white mother of two, and an African American.

Continued >

My own roots are with the indigenous Tarahumara (who call themselves Raramuri) of Chihuahua on my mother's side. My father—and you could see this on his face and in his hair—was native, Spanish, and African from the Mexican state of Guerrero.

In fact, Ricardo's girlfriend is from Guyana, whose family was originally from India.

To say the least, my extended family is complex and vibrant, made up of all skin   5
colors, ethnicities, and languages . . . and as "American" as apple pie (or burritos, for that matter, since these were created on the U.S. side of that border).

Purportedly I'm a Latino, although I rarely call myself this. I mean the original Latinos are Italians, right? Yet Italian Americans are not considered Latinos in this country. And so-called Latinos have origins in Native America, Africa, Europe, Asia, and a vast array of mixtures thereof. We are known as the largest "minority" group in the United States, yet we do not constitute one ethnic group or culture.

Let me put it this way: Despite the umbrella of "Latino" above our heads, Puerto Ricans are not the same as Dominicans. And many Salvadorans I know don't want to be confused with being Mexican.

Still, today we officially launch Latino Heritage Month, configured to run from September 15 to October 15, largely to coincide with the Independence Days of countries like Mexico, El Salvador, and others. Unofficially, of course, people who claim roots in Latino countries celebrate every day—they're also into the Fourth of July, Christmas, Martin Luther King Jr. Day, Hanukah, and Native American Sun Dance ceremonies. Regardless of their country of origin, these people are central to the American soul and deeply intertwined with the social fabric.

Despite this Latinos seem to be a rumor in the country, a "middle people," neither black nor white, hardly in the popular culture, mostly shadows and shouts in the distance.

Maybe what we celebrate is the complexities, the richness, the expansiveness of   10
who we are. Maybe we celebrate that Latinos have bled and sweated for this country. Hundreds from the Dominican Republic, Colombia, Mexico, Ecuador, Argentina, and other Latin American countries died during the 9/11 attacks. People with Spanish or Portuguese surnames garnered more medals of honor during World War II and had a disproportionate number of casualties during the Vietnam War. The first known U.S. death from the Iraq War was a young man originally from Guatemala.

Perhaps we celebrate that Latinos have worked in the auto plants of Detroit, steel mills of Chicago, cotton fields of Texas, textile centers of Massachusetts, and crop fields of California. That they are among the best in professional sports, and I'm not limiting this to soccer—they have been some of the world's best boxers, baseball players, football players, golfers, and tennis players.

Let's celebrate that Latinos have been in the forefront of the organized labor movement and fought alongside African Americans against slavery and for Civil Rights. That they are among the oldest residents of the continent, as indigenous peoples from places like Mexico, Central America, or Peru. And they are the majority of this country's most recent arrivals.

Let's recognize that U.S. Latinos can be found among scientists, professors, doctors, politicians, and judges. That renowned actors, musicians, and writers include Carlos Santana, Ricky Martin, Jennifer Lopez, George Lopez, Danny Trejo, Celia Cruz, Oscar Hijuelos, Sandra Cisneros, Junot Diaz, Salma Hayek, Antonio Banderas, Los Lobos, Cheech Marin, Shakira, Javier Bardem, Penelope Cruz, Eva Mendes, and Bruno Mars.

Our ancestors were former slaves and former slaveholders, peons and nobles, poets and conquistadors, African miners and native rebels. They include practitioners of the Flamenco and canto hondo with ties to the Roma people (so-called Gypsies) and the Arab/Muslim world, which once ruled Spain for close to 800 years. And so-called Latinos still use words, herbs, dance, and clothing from the wondrous civilizations of the Olmeca, Mexica (so-called Aztec), Maya, and Inca.

The fact is Latino heritage is U.S. heritage. You wouldn't have such "American"   15
phenomena as cowboys, guitars, rubber balls, gold mining, horses, corn, and even Jazz, Rock-and-Roll, and Hip Hop, without the contribution of Latinos. And besides the hundreds of Spanish words that now grace the English language (lariat, rodeo, buckaroo, adios, cafeteria, hasta la vista, baby), there are also indigenous words that English can't do without . . . chocolate, ocelot, coyote, tomato, avocado, maize, and barbecue, among others.

Unfortunately, as we contemplate what Latino Heritage means, we have to be reminded that Latinos have been among the most scapegoated[1] during the current financial crisis. States have established more laws against brown-skinned undocumented migrants while Arizona is trying to outlaw teachings on Mexican/Ethnic history and culture. They are also among the poorest, least healthy, and most neglected Americans. Spanish-surnamed people are now the majority in the federal prison system and the largest single group in state penitentiaries of California, New Mexico, and Texas. And they are concentrated among this country's homeless and drug-addicted populations.

[1] **scapegoated** Made to accept the blame for others.

Continued >

huffingtonpost.com

So while all Americans have much to celebrate in Latino heritage, like most Americans we also have a long way to go.

Whatever one thinks of Latinos, one thing is for sure: They have given much to this country, and have much more to give. I'm convinced any revolutionary changes in the economy, politics, technology, cultural life, social equity, and justice must have Latinos (regardless of race, background, religion, social class, or political strain) at the heart of them. They are integral to the past, present, and future of this country.

And this is a beautiful thing, baby.

Understanding the Reading

1. **Thesis** In a sentence or two, summarize Rodriguez's central point about what he feels should be celebrated during Latino Heritage Month.

2. **Author's presentation** In the first five paragraphs, Rodriguez focuses on his own life. What do you learn about him and his relation to Latino culture?

3. **Meaning** What point is Rodriguez making in paragraphs 8–9?

4. **Meaning** Paragraphs 10–15 stand in contrast to paragraph 16. What is the contrast?

5. **Language** Explain what Rodriguez means when he writes in paragraph 6 that "the original Latinos are Italians, right?"

Analyzing the Reading

1. **Audience** Who would you say is Rodriguez's intended audience here— Latinos, non-Latinos, or both? Explain your answer.

2. **Technique** Rodriguez uses illustration in paragraphs 10–13. What do these examples contribute to his overall purpose?

3. **Technique** Why do you think Rodriguez waits until paragraph 16 to suggest some of the ills facing Latinos in the United States? And why do you think he mentions these at all in an essay about celebrating Latino Heritage Month?

4. **Combining patterns** What patterns other than definition and illustration does Rodriguez use to develop his essay?

5. **Language** Why does Rodriguez preface the word *Latinos* with *so-called* in paragraphs 6 and 14? How does this contribute to his definition?

6. **Language** Rodriguez opens his next-to-last paragraph with "Whatever one thinks of Latinos," implying that readers might have various responses, some of which may even be negative. Why do you think he does this?

Evaluating the Reading

1. **Author's voice** How do you respond to what Rodriguez reveals about himself in his opening paragraphs? Do you think he comes across as a sympathetic representative of Latino culture?

2. **Argument** In paragraph 9, Rodriguez writes that Latinos exist in the "shadows" of the United States, "hardly in the popular culture." Do you think he adequately supports this argument? Do you agree with his assertion?

3. **Argument** Does Rodriguez convincingly make the case that "Latino heritage is U.S. heritage" (para. 15)? Explain your answer.

4. **Conclusion** How do you respond to Rodriguez's single-sentence concluding paragraph?

Discussing the Reading

1. Cultural groups in the United States celebrate a variety of ethnically oriented occasions—from Italian American festivals to St. Patrick's Day parades to Black History Month. Do you think these generally contribute to friendship and understanding among groups? Or do they reinforce cultural differences?

2. In paragraph 13, Rodriguez singles out primarily entertainers to make his point about the contributions of Latinos in the United States. Why do you suppose he focuses on entertainers rather than Latinos who have made achievements in other fields?

3. In paragraph 16, Rodriguez touches on the current debate about undocumented aliens in the United States and official and unofficial hostility toward Latinos. Why do you think Latinos are being seen as a threat by some non-Latinos?

Writing about the Reading

1. **Essay** Rodriguez states that "Latino heritage is U.S. heritage." Choose another cultural or ethnic group and define it in terms of the contributions it makes to U.S. heritage.

2. **Essay** We talk a lot about differences among the people who make up the U.S. population—political differences, ethnic differences, religious differences, differences in sexual orientation, and so forth. Are there things in the American character that go beyond these differences? Write an essay in which you define what it means to be an American in the broadest sense and thereby create a definition that unites this diverse population.

3. **Combined patterns** In paragraph 8, Rodriguez lists a number of holidays in which people may participate. Choose a particular holiday that has special meaning to you, and write an essay explaining its significance in detail, using narration, description, examples, process analysis, and any other patterns that seem appropriate. (Hint: Find a way to personalize the opening of your essay to attract readers' interest, as Rodriguez does in his essay.)

📖 **TEXTBOOK**

Cybergroups

William E. Thompson is a professor of sociology and criminal justice at Texas A&M University–Commerce. With **Joseph V. Hickey**, a former professor of anthropology at Emporia State University, he coauthored *Society in Focus: An Introduction to Sociology*. That textbook is the source of the following selection.

Reading Tip

As you read, highlight some of the differences the authors suggest between cybergroup interaction and face-to-face interaction.

Previewing the Reading

Preview the reading, keeping in mind that it is from a chapter in a sociology textbook focusing more generally on dynamics within groups. What are some of the main traits that define the subset of "cybergroups"?

Cybergroups
William E. Thompson and Joseph V. Hickey

A colleague returned home recently to find his fourteen-year-old son alone at the computer, playing a game. When he asked his son how his day had been, the boy responded, "Just a minute, Dad, I'm with two other guys." The father was confused. As it turned out, the son was playing a computer game with two other people, but this play group was a cybergroup that consisted of a fourteen-year-old boy in the United States and two adult men—a U.S. serviceman in England and a sixty-year-old mechanic in Poland.

In 2001, the Kyodo News Service in Japan reported, "Police arrested five teenage members of 'Mad Wing Angels,' a virtual motorcycle gang that met via media texting, including members who didn't own motorcycles, and had never gathered in one place at the same time. The leader had never met the four Tokyo girls she ordered to beat and torture a fifth gang member who asked permission to leave the group to study abroad" (Rheingold 2002a:4). Sociologists are conducting research in this important new area. Several exploratory studies have examined how a limited social presence (compared to face-to-face interaction) affects group dynamics and decision making. In cybergroups, most of the social cues that help to guide everyday interactions are either absent or unclear. For example, in cybergroups there are neither verbal cues nor body language to help with the interaction. Likewise, observable information about social contexts and social characteristics (e.g., race, class, gender, age) of group members may also be lacking, ambiguous, or potentially false. These ambiguities and the anonymity afforded by Internet and computer-mediated interaction force sociologists to substantially adapt their methods of research and analysis (Garcia et al., 2009).

This is not to say that there are no detectable status differences in cyberspace. People can provide status cues like titles (senior vice president) and can demonstrate status and competence through computer language, prestigious email addresses, and names that protect anonymity, but are well-known online. A new computer **lexicon** that is developing includes icons for all sorts of emotions, from smiling faces to express happiness or agreement to flames to express anger or contempt. But most of the trappings and seeming certainties of real-life power and authority become less certain in computer-mediated interactions, where people are both socially and physically distant. Perhaps the most noteworthy difference between cybergroups and face-to-face groups is "the emphasis on shared interests rather than social characteristics" (Wellman et al., 1996:225).

lexicon: dictionary, list of words or symbols and their meanings

Another major difference between cybergroups and face-to-face interaction relates to group size. In real life, most people regularly interact with fewer than twenty-five kin, friends, and coworkers, whereas they are acquainted with perhaps as many as one thousand people. Computers have expanded these numbers dramatically, making it possible to interact with an unlimited number of people and groups, all across the globe, and to create new groups and terminate others instantaneously. Research in the 1990s suggested that participation in online groups might reduce offline social interaction—especially interaction with kin, friends, neighbors. Research in the twenty-first century, however, suggests the opposite is the case. Studies have found that numerous "virtual" social connections actually "reinforce pre-existing social, political, and cultural patterns." That is, for people who are already active members of numerous "offline groups" the Internet adds a new layer of communication opportunities (Matei and Ball-Rokeach, 2002:405). Interestingly, one study of ethnically diverse neighborhoods in Los Angeles found that most new online social connections tended to be made within one's ethnic group. Asian Americans in particular seemed more cautious in venturing outside their groups and social networks, with some believing that online relationships outside one's in-groups were shallow, unsavory, or even dangerous. As one Korean woman put it, "Online friends are just for fun, not for serious relationships" (Matei and Ball-Rokeach, 2002:420).

Studies have found cybergroups to resemble both primary and secondary groups—but not to fit either ideal type very well. One sociologist defined cybergroup ties as "moderately strong intimate

Continued >

Do you think these people are taking part in small-group behavior? Should our definition of face-to-face interaction change now that cybergroups exist?

secondary relationships" (Wireman, cited in Wellman et al., 1996:222). They can be simultaneously detached and intensively emotional, enduring or brief. Most cybergroup interactions are relatively superficial, yet they can also produce powerful emotional bonds and lasting ties—even marriages, as in the case of an American woman who quit her job and flew to England to marry a fellow Net user whom she had never met (Wellman et al., 1996).

TAKING A CLOSER LOOK

How might the proliferation of cybergroups affect people's understandings of groups in the future? Use your own experiences online and offline to chart future directions.

---

primary group: people who regularly interact and have close and long-lasting relationships

secondary group: people who interact on a formal and impersonal basis to accomplish a specific goal

egalitarian: belief in the equality of all people

This strange comingling of **primary** and **secondary group** traits is explained in part by the special nature of computer-mediated interactions. They tend to be more open, **egalitarian**, and creative than groups in everyday life. People communicate more freely and easily in cybergroups, and relative anonymity makes it easier to express inner thoughts and feelings. This gives cybergroups the potential of becoming very effective support groups. Likewise, because individuals are less constrained by group pressures and opinions online, cybergroups tend to be very creative. People seem to be more willing to take risks online than they would in real life. Such freedoms, of course, have a downside. Without clear patterns of authority and leadership, group consensus is often difficult to reach online. And cybergroups seem to have difficulty reaching decisions that would be considered simple and routine in face-to-face interactions. Moreover, the social solidarity that is associated with traditional work groups is often lacking in cybergroups, where "each person is at the center of a unique personal community and work group" (Wellman et al., 1996:232). Sociologists also want to know what new dilemmas will emerge as more people shift back and forth between cybergroups and groups in real life.

Sources: Nancy K. Baym. "The Emergence of Online Community." *CyberSociety 2.0: Revisiting Computer-Mediated Communication and Community.* Thousand Oaks, CA: Sage, 1998:35–68. Angela C. Garcia, Alecea I. Standlee, Jennifer Bechkoff, and Yan Cul. "Ethnographic Approaches to the Internet and Computer-Mediated Communication." *Journal of Contemporary Ethnography* 38(1), 2009:52–84. Barry Wellman, Janet Salaff, Dimitrina Dimitrova, Laura Garton, Milena Gulia, and Caroline Haythornthwaite. "Computer Networks as Social Networks: Collaborative Work, Telework, and Virtual Community." *Annual Review of Sociology* 22, 1996:213–238.

Understanding the Reading

1. **Textbook reading** This relatively brief textbook excerpt defines cybergroups in relation to face-to-face groups. List what you think are five of the most important defining differences between these groups.

2. **Thesis** Do you think this excerpt has a thesis? Can you summarize one overall point about cybergroups the authors make?

3. **Language** In paragraph 5, the authors make a distinction between "primary" and "secondary" groups. Explain why cybergroups don't "fit either ideal type very well."

4. **Vocabulary** Define the following words as they are used in the reading: *ambiguous* (para. 2), *anonymity* (2), *status* (3), *trappings* (3), *instantaneously* (4), *comingling* (6), and *dilemmas* (6). Consult a dictionary if needed.

Analyzing the Reading

1. **Introduction** The authors open by describing two examples of people participating in cybergroups (paras. 1–2). How do the specifics of these examples help stress the importance of understanding cybergroups?

2. **Presentation** The authors give considerable attention to the concept of status in paragraph 3. Why might the authors present this as an important issue in terms of how groups interact?

3. **Language** Consider how cybergroups are described in the final paragraph. Do you think the authors consider them positively, negatively, or neutrally? What makes you think so?

📊 Evaluating the Reading

1. **Reading** The paragraphs in the selection are, for the most part, quite long. How does this affect your reading?

2. **Complexity** Which parts of this excerpt do you find most accessible and which parts difficult to follow? Which reading techniques did you use to ensure that you understood the complex parts of the piece?

3. **Visuals** Do the photo of Japanese teens texting and the accompanying caption represent the message of the excerpt well?

4. **Central idea** Based on this excerpt, how well do you understand the idea of cybergroups? What past knowledge of and experience with cybergroups, if any, did you bring to your reading?

Discussing the Reading

1. Answer the question the authors pose in the "Taking a Closer Look" box. How do you think cybergroups will affect how people will think about face-to-face groups?

2. The authors write in paragraph 2 about girls in a cybergroup who beat and tortured another member at the direction of a leader they'd never met. Do you think this sort of behavior is more likely in cybergroups than in face-to-face groups?

3. How closely does the authors' description of cybergroup participation reflect what you know about people's participation in cybergroups? Do you think the various research studies cited correspond to the reality of such groups?

Writing about the Reading

1. **Essay** Using the information presented here and your own experience if appropriate, write an essay defining and explaining cybergroups for readers of a general-interest magazine, such as *Time* or *Newsweek*. (Hint: Make sure that your language and level of presentation are more suitable for this audience than the textbook excerpt's are.)

2. **Essay** Think about a group you belong to—a close circle of friends who spend a lot of time together, a team or musical group that meets regularly, the people you work closely with, or perhaps even a cybergroup. Write an

essay in which you define the relationships within this group using some of the concepts the authors write about here—status and authority, intimacy and detachment, expressivity, creativity, decision making, and so forth. (Hint: Start by brainstorming to characterize the group's dynamic in four or five specific words. Then use those words to develop your thesis.)

3. **Essay** The caption below the photograph in this selection asks whether technology is altering "our definition of face-to-face interaction." How would you answer this question? In an essay, define what you think face-to-face interaction means in the modern world.

Writing Your Own Definition Essay

Now that you have learned about the major characteristics, structure, and purposes of a definition essay, you know everything necessary to write your own. In this section you will read a student's definition essay and get advice on finding ideas, drafting your essay, and revising and editing it. You may want to use the essay prompts in "Readings for Practice, Ideas for Writing" (p. 503) or choose your own topic.

A Student Model Definition Essay

In the following essay, Brent Schwartz explores planking, an Internet phenomenon that has become popular in the past few years. As you read, notice the ways in which Schwartz extends the definition beyond a simple explanation to discuss its importance. Also take note of the sources he uses and his citations of those sources.

Title: Cleverly introduces term

Planking: A Flat Phenomenon

Brent Schwartz

Introduction
The class of the subject is *trend*.

Trends come and go all the time, everything from things we buy to words we say. Sometimes it's something subtle like using the word *rad* or more drastic like extreme body piercings. Somewhere in the middle of this spectrum of fads is planking.

Thesis: Brief definition provided and purpose expressed

Planking occurs when one person lies face down and straight, like a "plank" board, in some unusual area while another person takes a photo. While it may seem absurd, planking has reached mainstream status in the past couple of years.

Defining characteristic 1: mysterious, unclear origins

Specific detail

The origins of planking are just as mysterious and unclear as the appeal of the action itself. Several people claim to have inspired the practice. Comedian Tom Green claims to have first participated in planking during a skit on his 1994 Canadian public access television show where he laid face down on a street while a hidden camera captured the reactions of those passing by (Bershad). More recently, two men in England, Gary Clarkson and Christian Langdon, have cited themselves as the fad's creators with the inception of "The Lying Down Game" in 2000 ("Who, What, Why").

Sources: Schwartz uses sources throughout the paper.

Defining characteristic 2: spread by mainstream news and celebrities

Specific detail

In 2011, planking became so popular that it was picked up by mainstream news sources such as MSNBC and CBS. Celebrities also started taking an interest in planking in the same year. Photos of Public Enemy hype man Flava Flav, *Juno* star Ellen Page, Justin Bieber, and many other celebrities planking began to appear on the Internet. This helped raise the visibility of the obscure cultural sensation.

Defining characteristic 3: done in an unusual place

Popular places to plank include benches, desks, cars, and playgrounds. However, the real key is to find the most creative and unusual place. The quest for more extreme planking spots has led to some backlash from law enforcement and parts of the public. In 2009, a group of seven doctors in Swindon, England, were put on suspension after they planked while on duty (Savill).

Specific detail:

Even more extreme, in May 2011 a man in Brisbane, Australia, plummeted to his death when trying to plank on a seventy-fourth story balcony ("Australia Man"). These safety violations, among other reports, have made many people weary and skeptical of this fad.

Defining characteristic 4: has inspired similar activities

The influence of planking has inspired others to create their own odd, compelling poses for photos. While not quite as popular as their inspiration, they keep with the same concept of performing the act in an unusual place. "Batmanning" involves hanging upside down by your feet. "Horsemanning," inspired by the Headless Horseman from "The Legend of Sleepy Hollow," occurs when two people pose to give the perception of a head detached from its body. Another variation called "owling" simply has a person perch on a surface like an owl.

Conclusion

Suggests that act of planking is ongoing

Whether planking is going to be a fading fad or if it will continue to be a prominent fixture in popular culture is unclear. While there are some safety concerns, when done with caution planking can provide weird and simple entertainment. It is possible that planking may always be around but take place in a different form. With influence from the media and high-profile figures, it seems likely that people will continue to put their creative energy into this offbeat hobby.

Sources: Schwartz properly cites sources in MLA format

Works Cited

"Australia Man Plunges to 'Planking' Death." *MSNBC.msn.com*. MSN, 15 May 2011. Web. 23 Apr. 2012.

Bershad, Jon. "You Know That Internet Phenomenon 'Planking'? Seems That Tom Green Invented It in 1994." *Mediaite.com*. Mediaite, 13 July 2011. Web. 20 Apr. 2012.

Savill, Richard. "Hospital Staff Suspended over Facebook 'Lying Down Game' Pictures." *Telegraph.org*. Telegraph Media Group Limited, 9 Sept. 2009. Web. 22 Apr. 2012.

"Who, What, Why: What Is Planking?" *BBC.co.uk*. BBC, 16 May 2011. Web. 22 Apr. 2012.

Responding to Schwartz's Essay

1. Is Schwartz's brief description of planking in his introduction sufficient for you to understand the phenomenon?
2. How well does Schwartz establish the popularity of planking?
3. What is the appeal of planking? Do you agree that this "offbeat hobby" will continue to interest people?
4. In his fifth paragraph, Schwartz describes some similar activities that planking has inspired. Can you think of any others?

Finding Ideas for Your Definition Essay

As you read an extended definition or an article containing brief definitions, jot down any additional characteristics or examples that come to mind. When responding to the article, you might indicate how the definition could be expanded to include these additional characteristics or examples. You might also try the following strategies.

- Think of other terms in the same class.
- Try to relate the definitions to your own experience. Where or when have you observed the characteristics described? Your personal experiences might be useful in an essay in which you agree with or challenge the writer's definitions.
- If the writer has not already done so, you might use negation to expand the meaning of the term, or you might explore its etymology.

Planning Your Definition Essay

The first step is to select a topic and narrow it to a more specific term. For example, the term *celebrity* is probably too broad a topic for a brief essay, but it can be narrowed to a particular type of celebrity, such as *sports celebrity*, *Hollywood celebrity*, *local celebrity*, or *political celebrity*. Consider your readers as well. When the audience is unfamiliar with the term, you will need to explain it in greater detail than when the audience already is familiar with it.

The following suggestions will help you identify distinguishing characteristics and supporting details for the term you intend to define.

1. **Define the term out loud for a classmate.** Then discuss the term with your classmate, making notes about anything that was unclear.
2. **Brainstorm a list of (a) words that describe your term, (b) people and actions that might serve as examples of it, and (c) everything a person would need to know to fully understand it.**

3. **Observe a person who is associated with the term or who performs some aspect of it.** Take notes on your observations, including the qualities and characteristics of what you see.

4. **Look up the term's etymology, or origin, in the *Oxford English Dictionary*, *A Dictionary of American English*, or *A Dictionary of Americanisms*, all of which are available in the reference section of your library.** Take notes; the word's etymology may indicate some of its characteristics and details, which might give you ideas on how to organize the essay.

5. **Think of incidents or situations that reveal the meaning of the term.**

6. **Think of similar and different terms with which your readers are likely to be more familiar.**

7. **Do a search for the term on the Internet.** Visit three or four Web sites, and take notes on what you discover.

Drafting Your Definition Essay

Once you have evaluated your term's distinguishing characteristics, supporting details, and the thesis, it is time to organize your ideas and draft your essay.

To a considerable extent, the organization of a definition essay depends on the other pattern(s) of development you decide to use (see the examples on p. 491). With your pattern(s) firmly in mind, think about how to organize your term's characteristics and details. For example, consider an essay defining *marathon runner*. An essay that focuses on *classifying* different types of marathon runners would probably follow a least-to-most or most-to-least organization, whereas an essay *narrating* a story about marathon runners might be most effectively related in chronological order.

Once you have decided on a method of organization, use the following guidelines to draft the essay.

1. **Describe the class as specifically as possible.** Narrowing the class will make it easier for readers to understand the term. For example, in an essay defining *Dalmatian*, the class should not be the broad category "animal" or "mammal" but rather the more specific "breed of dog."

2. **Do not use the term (or forms of the term) as part of your definition.** Synonyms may be helpful as substitutes for a term. For example, do not write, "*Mastery* means that one has *mastered* a skill." In place of *mastered*, you could use *truly learned*.

3. **Include enough distinguishing characteristics so that readers will not mistake the term for something similar within the class.** If you define *answering machine* as "a machine that records messages," your definition would be incomplete because other machines (such as computers) also record messages.

Figure 16.3 Revising a Definition Essay

QUESTIONS	REVISION STRATEGIES
1. Thesis Does it include a brief definition of the term? Does it indicate why your definition is useful, interesting, or important?	• Incorporate the distinguishing characteristics of your term and a standard definition into your thesis. • In your thesis answer the question, Why is this definition worth reading about?

QUESTIONS	REVISION STRATEGIES
2. Distinguishing character-istics Do they make your term distinct from similar terms? Is each characteristic true in all cases?	• Do additional research or prewriting to discover more characteristics and details to add. • Eliminate characteristics and details that limit the definition too much.

QUESTIONS	REVISION STRATEGIES
3. Patterns of development Identify the patterns you use in your definition. Does each clearly connect your details and help explain the distinguishing characteristics of your term?	• Review the patterns (Chapter 9) and consider substituting or adding one or more of them to enhance your definition.

QUESTIONS	REVISION STRATEGIES
4. Negotiation and misconcep-tions Does each section eliminate possible misunderstandings? Are there other places where you need to do so?	• Revise your explanation of what your term is not. • Add facts or expert opinion to correct readers' mistaken notions about the term.

QUESTIONS	REVISION STRATEGIES
5. Topic sentences Does each paragraph have a clear topic sentence and focus on a particular characteristic? Is each paragraph well developed?	• Consider combining paragraphs that cover the same characteristic or splitting paragraphs that cover more than one. • Add or revise topic sentences and supporting details.

QUESTIONS	REVISION STRATEGIES
6. Introduction and conclusion Does the introduction provide necessary background information? Does your conclusion bring the essay to a satisfying close?	• Add background information that sets a context for the term you are defining. • Revise your introduction and conclusion so that they meet the guidelines presented in Chapter 6.

(Arrows between each question are labeled "Yes" flowing down; "No" arrows point from each question to its revision strategies.)

4. **Do not limit the definition so much that it becomes inaccurate.** Defining *bacon* as "a smoked, salted meat from a pig that is served at breakfast" would be too limited because bacon is also served at other mealtimes (at lunch, for instance, as part of a bacon, lettuce, and tomato sandwich) and other salted, smoked pork products are sometimes served at breakfast (ham, for instance).

5. **Use transitions.** When moving from characteristic to characteristic, be sure to use transitional words or phrases to signal each change. The transitions *another*, *also*, and *in addition* are especially useful in extended definitions.

6. **Consider including the etymology of the term.** The etymology, or origin, of a term may be of interest to readers. Alternatively, you might include a brief history of the term in your introduction or elsewhere in your essay.

Revising Your Definition Essay

If possible, set your draft aside for a day or two before rereading and revising it. As you review it, concentrate on your ideas and organization, not on grammar or mechanics. Use the flowchart in Figure 16.3 to discover the strengths and weaknesses of your definition essay.

Editing and Proofreading Your Essay

The final step is to check your revised essay for errors in grammar, spelling, punctuation, and mechanics. In addition, look for the types of errors you commonly make in any writing, whether for this class or another situation. As you edit and proofread your definition essay, watch out for the following types of errors commonly found in this pattern of writing.

1. **Make sure to avoid awkward expressions such as *is when* or *is where* in defining the term.** Name the class to which the term belongs.

   ▶ Early bird specials ~~is when~~ restaurants *are reduced-price dinners served in* ~~offer reduced priced dinners~~ late in the afternoon and early in the evening.

   ▶ A rollover is ~~where an employee transfers money from one retirement~~ *a transaction in which funds from one investment are transferred* to another, often without the holder of the funds taking possession of them. ~~account to another.~~

2. **Make sure subjects and verbs agree in number.** When two subjects are joined by *and*, the verb should be plural.

   ▶ The upbeat rhythm and intense lyrics of hip-hop music ~~excites~~ *excite* the crowd, making people want to get up and dance.

When two nouns are joined by *or*, the verb should agree with the noun closest to it.

▶   For the birds, the markings or wingspan ~~are~~ *is* easily observed with a pair of good binoculars.

When the subject and verb are separated by a prepositional phrase, the verb should agree with the subject, not with the noun in the phrase.

▶   The features of a hot-air balloon ~~is~~ *are* best learned by studying the attached diagram.

Chapter 17

Cause and Effect: Using Reasons and Results to Explain

Quick Start: Assume you are a journalist for your local newspaper reporting on a natural disaster that occurred in a nearby town. Your immediate task is to write a brief article to accompany the photograph shown on this page. Write a paragraph telling readers why the disaster occurred and what happened as a result of it. For the purpose of this activity, make up a plausible account of the event that led up to the scene depicted in the photograph.

What Is Cause and Effect?

A **cause-and-effect** essay, also called a *causal-analysis* essay, analyzes (1) **causes**—why an event or phenomenon happens, (2) **effects**—what happens because of the event or phenomenon, or (3) both causes and effects. The essay generally shows how one event or phenomenon brings about another—for example, how losing your car keys (the cause) leads you to be late for class (the effect).

Many everyday occasions require the use of causal analysis. If your child is injured in an accident, the doctor may ask what effects the accident had on him or her. In a note to a manufacturer, you may need to explain what problems with a product have led to you to request a refund. You will have many occasions to use causal analysis in college and on the job, as suggested by the following examples: For an essay exam in your twentieth-century history course, you might be required to discuss the causes of U.S. involvement in the Korean conflict; should you become an investment analyst, you might need to explain to a client why a certain company was profitable this year.

Causal analysis does the following:

1. It explains causes, effects, or both causes and effects.
2. It has a clear purpose.
3. It explains each cause or effect fully.
4. It may recognize or dispel readers' assumptions about the topic.

1. Causal Analysis Explains Causes, Effects, or Both

In deciding whether to consider causes, effects, or both, it is important to distinguish the causes from the effects. To do this, think of causes as the *reasons that something happened* and effects as the *results of the thing that happened*.

CAUSE   **EFFECT**

Event X happened because . . .   ← EVENT X →   The result of Event X was . . .

Sometimes causes and effects are relatively easy to identify. In complex situations, however, the causes and effects are often less clear. For example, the causes for a weight problem are complex, and causes may not always be clearly separable from effects. Some people have an obsession with dieting (*effect*) because they have a poor body image (*cause*). Yet an obsession with dieting (*cause*) can lead to a poor body image (*effect*).

One cause and effect   In some cases, there is a single cause, which has one effect.

      CAUSE   **EFFECT**

You get a flat tire. ⎯⎯⎯⎯⎯⎯⎯⎯⎯→ You are late for work.

Multiple causes and/or effects   Causal analysis can be complex when it deals with an event or a phenomenon that has multiple causes, multiple effects, or both. Several causes may produce a single effect. For example, you probably chose the college you attend now (*one effect*) for a number of reasons, including the availability of courses in your major, the cost of tuition, the reputation of the school, and its distance from your home (*multiple causes*).

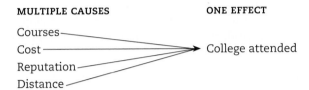

Alternatively, one cause may have several effects. For instance, your decision to quit your part-time job (*one cause*) will result in more study time, less pressure, and less spending money (*multiple effects*).

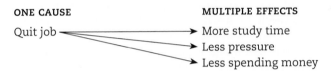

Related events or phenomena may have both multiple causes and multiple effects. For instance, an increase in the number of police officers patrolling the street in urban areas along with the formation of citizen watch groups (*multiple causes*) will result in less street crime and the growth of small businesses (*multiple effects*).

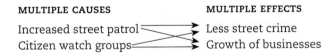

Chain of events   In some cases a series of events forms a chain in which each event is both the effect of what happened before it and the cause of the next event. In other words, a simple event can produce a chain of consequences.

CAUSE	EFFECT/CAUSE	EFFECT/CAUSE	EFFECT
You cannot find your car keys.	→ You are late for class.	→ You miss a surprise quiz.	→ Your A quiz average is lowered to a B.

Once you clearly separate causes and effects, you can decide whether to focus on causes, effects, or both.

2. Causal Analysis Has a Clear Purpose

A cause-and-effect essay may be expressive, but more often it is informative, persuasive, or both. In an essay about the effects of the death of a close relative, for example, you would express your feelings about the person by showing how the loss has affected you. However, an essay describing the sources (*causes*) of the pollution of a local river could be primarily informative, or it could be informative and persuasive if it also stresses the positive results (*effects*) of enforcing antipollution laws.

Some cause-and-effect essays have more than one purpose. For example, an essay may examine the causes of academic cheating (*informative*) and propose policies that would alleviate the problem (*persuasive*).

3. Causal Analysis Explains Each Cause or Effect Fully

A causal analysis presents each cause or effect in a detailed and understandable way, using examples, facts, descriptions, comparisons, statistics, and/or anecdotes.

For most cause-and-effect essays, you will need to research the topic to locate evidence that will support the thesis. In an essay about the effects on children of viewing violence on television, for instance, you might need to locate research or statistics that document changes in children's behavior after watching violent programs. In addition to statistical data, expert opinion is often used as evidence. For example, to support a thesis that reading aloud to preschool children helps them develop prereading skills, you might cite the opinions of reading specialists or psychologists who specialize in child development.

4. Causal Analysis May Recognize or Dispel Readers' Assumptions

Some cause-and-effect essays recognize or dispel popular ideas that readers assume to be true. For example, an essay on the effects of capital punishment might attempt to dispel the notion that it is a deterrent to crime. Recognizing in your essay the causes or effects that readers assume to be most important, regardless of whether you support or refute them, lends credibility to your writing. In an informative essay, this recognition conveys the impression that nothing has been overlooked. In a persuasive essay, it reassures readers that other viewpoints have been acknowledged.

Reading and Writing Cause-and-Effect Essays

In this section you will learn about the structure of a cause-and-effect essay, read a sample essay, and practice using the guidelines for understanding, analyzing, and evaluating cause-and-effect essays. This will help you skillfully read and write essays that use this pattern.

How Is a Cause-and-Effect Essay Structured?

The structure of a cause-and-effect essay can take many different forms depending on your purpose for writing it. No matter what your purpose, a cause-and-effect essay should always have an introduction and conclusion.

1. The **introduction** identifies the event, provides background information, and states a **thesis**.
2. **Body paragraphs** connect the causes and effects of the event and support the thesis.
3. The **conclusion** reminds readers of the thesis and presents a final statement about the event.

There are three types of cause-and-effect essays, as shown in the graphic organizers in Figures 17.1, 17.2, and 17.3. Figure 17.1 shows the organization of an essay with multiple causes *or* multiple effects. Figure 17.2 shows how an essay with both multiple causes and multiple effects is organized. Figure 17.3 presents the organization of an essay concerned with a chain of causes and effects. Notice that causes are presented before effects. Although this is the typical arrangement, writers sometimes reverse it, discussing effects first and then causes to create a sense of drama or surprise. When you incorporate causes, effects, or both into an essay that is not primarily a causal analysis, you can adapt one of these organizational plans to suit your purpose.

Figure 17.1   Graphic Organizer for an Essay on Multiple Causes or Multiple Effects

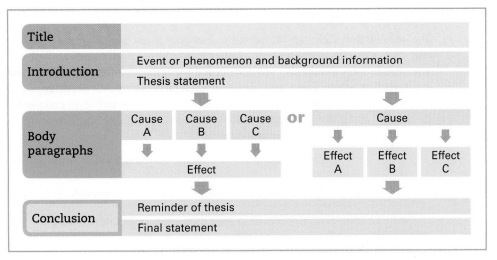

Figure 17.2   Graphic Organizer for an Essay on Multiple Causes and Multiple Effects

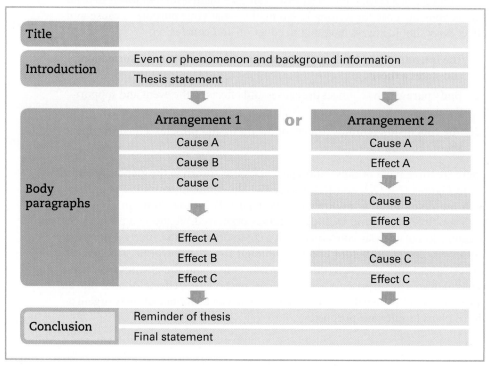

1. THE INTRODUCTION IDENTIFIES THE EVENT, PROVIDES BACKGROUND INFORMATION, AND STATES THE THESIS

The introduction identifies the event the essay will focus on. Essays may address only causes or effects of an event, or they may address both causes and effects. The introduction should also provide needed background information about the event, such as where, when, why, or under what circumstances it occurred.

The thesis statement should identify the topic—the event or phenomenon discussed—and make an assertion about its causes, effects, or both. This example shows the parts of a strong thesis statement.

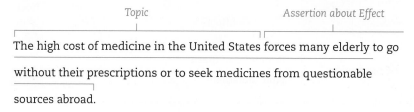

The high cost of medicine in the United States forces many elderly to go

without their prescriptions or to seek medicines from questionable

sources abroad.

Figure 17.3   Graphic Organizer for an Essay on a Chain of Causes and Effects

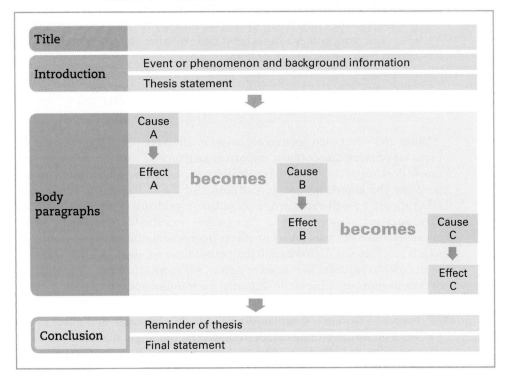

The thesis statement should make clear the cause-and-effect relationship. Here is an example of weak and revised thesis statements.

WEAK   Breathing paint fumes in a closed environment can be dangerous for people suffering from asthma and other lung disorders.

REVISED   Breathing paint fumes in a closed environment can be dangerous for people suffering from asthma and other lung disorders because their lungs are especially sensitive to irritants.

The revised thesis statement makes the cause-and-effect connection explicit by using the word *because* and by including necessary information about the problem.

When you write cause-and-effect essays for college classes, try to express your thesis in a single sentence. Professional writers, however, sometimes express their theses in a less direct way, using two or more sentences.

Reading | Writing   When reading the introduction of a cause-and-effect essay, be sure to identify the topic and assess your familiarity with it. Your knowledge and experience, or lack of such, will determine how closely you need to read the essay. When writing the introduction of a cause-and-effect essay, help your reader by making it clear whether your essay will be concerned with causes, effects, or both.

2.   BODY PARAGRAPHS CONNECT THE CAUSES AND EFFECTS OF THE
     EVENT AND SUPPORT THE THESIS USING A LOGICAL ORGANIZATION

A cause-and-effect essay focuses on causes or effects or both. The essay should focus on *primary causes* (more important causes) and may discuss *secondary causes* (less important or related causes) as well, depending on the author's purpose and the knowledge and sophistication of the audience. Each cause and effect should be well explained, with sufficient evidence provided to indicate that the casual relationship exists. The essay is organized logically and systematically. It often presents causes or effects in chronological order—the order in which they happened. However, it may instead use a most-to-least or least-to-most order to sequence the causes or effects. For more information on methods of organization, see Chapter 9, "Patterns: An Introduction" (p. 175).

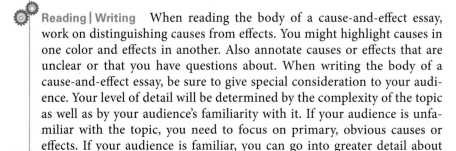 **Reading | Writing**   When reading the body of a cause-and-effect essay, work on distinguishing causes from effects. You might highlight causes in one color and effects in another. Also annotate causes or effects that are unclear or that you have questions about. When writing the body of a cause-and-effect essay, be sure to give special consideration to your audience. Your level of detail will be determined by the complexity of the topic as well as by your audience's familiarity with it. If your audience is unfamiliar with the topic, you need to focus on primary, obvious causes or effects. If your audience is familiar, you can go into greater detail about secondary causes or effects.

3.   THE CONCLUSION REMINDS READERS OF THE THESIS
     AND SUMMARIZES THE ESSAY

The conclusion should reaffirm or solidify the cause-and-effect relationship and leave the reader with a strong final impression.

 Reading | Writing   When reading the conclusion of a cause-and-effect essay, check that you understand the relationship discussed by writing a two-column list of causes and of effects or by drawing a graphic organizer. If you cannot clearly express or draw the cause-and-effect relationship, reread the essay and discuss it with a classmate if necessary. Testing your recall will also help you remember what you read for later analysis or class discussion. When writing the conclusion of a casual-analysis essay, concentrate on leaving your readers with a concise review or summary of the cause-and-effect relationship.

A Model Cause-and-Effect Essay

Title

E. coli on the Rocks

Amy Tan

Amy Tan has written two children's books and several novels, including *The Joy Luck Club.* She has also contributed articles to such magazines as the *New Yorker* and *National Geographic.* Her work has been translated into French, Finnish, and thirty-three other languages.

Introduction

Background information: presents a common misconception about "germ-free" ice

Thesis: New information suggests that the water you think is clean is not.

Body paragraphs (multiple causes and effects)

Cause 1: E.coli can live on ice (primary cause).

Cause 2: People do not wash their hands, transferring bacteria to ice (secondary cause).

Background information: details from experts on the primary cause

If you're like me, you've assumed that anything frozen is naturally germ free. The cold would kill the nasties. Furthermore, the only bad ice cubes are those made with dirty water. Tap water in China, for example. Clean water from U.S. taps makes for worry-free clean ice cubes. Wrong.

Just when you thought Purell solved all your public hygiene needs, now there's news that the lovely crystalline form of water you get in a restaurant may be dirtier than water from your toilet. The specific culprit is E. coli. The chilling reason your drink may be afloat with this bacteria stems purely from people's lack of toilet hygiene. Simply put, a lot of people in a lot of restaurants who handle ice don't wash their hands.

This is very mysterious to me—this dirty-hand syndrome. Whenever I have been in a public restroom, I have never seen anyone exit a toilet stall and not wash their hands. This leads me to think that some people wash their hands only when someone is watching.

One of the news reports mentioned how many colonies were found on a single ice cube. Colonies! I thought it would be only a few rogue E. coli microbes. But colonies made me imagine an ice floe with a thousand swaying porta-potties and no sinks.

I started recalling friends who had come over to our house and said, "I can help myself," and they helped themselves to ice by grabbing the cubes with their bare hands rather than using the ice scoop. I have no doubt that they wash their hands.

5

Effect 1: People may unknowingly transfer bacteria.

But what if they were just in a store to pick up a bottle of wine to bring to our house? What if that bottle had been handled by someone who washed their hands only when someone was watching? That is why I'm emptying out my freezer and starting over. Fresh ice. Ice scoops firmly planted in full view. No more packages of Boca Burgers and edamame near the ice tray.

Effect 2: The author changes her habits based on new information.

The next time you order a drink, do what my mainland Chinese relatives and friends do. Hold up your hand, palm out, and say: "No ice." Two simple words. They can save your life.

Conclusion

Advice to readers to solve problem

Understanding, Analyzing, and Evaluating Cause-and-Effect Essays

In reading and writing cause-and-effect essays, your goal is to get beyond mere competence: That is, you want to be able to do more than merely understand the content of the essays you're reading or convey just your basic ideas to the audience you're writing for.

 Reading | Writing   Truly skillful reading and writing require the abilities to **understand, analyze,** *and* **evaluate** material. These abilities are important to you as a reader because they give you a systematic, thorough method of examining a reading. They're important to you as a writer because they help you decide what to revise, rewrite, drop, and replace, allowing you to produce a well-written, persuasive essay.

📊 Understanding a Cause-and-Effect Essay

Preview the essay before reading it to identify the event or situation being explained and, if possible, to determine whether the essay will focus on causes, effects, or both. Then read it slowly, to identify specific causes and effects. As you read and reread, use the skills you learned in Chapter 2 and look for answers to the following questions.

- **What is the author's thesis?** Determine what point or assertion the thesis makes about the topic.

- **What is the event or situation being explained?** Think about what you already know about the event or situation and use that information to maintain your interest and to formulate questions.

Figure 17.4   Graphic Organizer for "E. coli on the Rocks"

Title	"E. coli on the Rocks"
Introduction	Background information on water: Common conception that ice made with clean water is free of germs. Wrong.
Body paragraphs	**Cause A:** Restaurant servers handle ice but don't wash their hands after going to the bathroom.
	Effect A: Ice they handle may be afloat with the bacteria E. coli.
	Cause B: People wash their hands in bathrooms if other people are there to see.
	Effect B: If the bathroom is empty, people are more likely not to wash their hands.
	Cause C: Tan recalls friends at her home insisting on picking up ice with their hands.
	Effect C: Tan will be much more careful about ice use and how she stores frozen food.
Conclusion	**Advice:** Always say you want no ice when ordering a drink.

- **What are the primary causes and primary effects?** **Primary** causes are those that are most directly related to the effect and are considered most important. Identify each and begin to think about how and why they are connected. Drawing a graphic organizer can help you determine the primary causes and effects (as well as secondary causes and effects) when reading or writing. Figure 17.4 shows a graphic organizer for Amy Tan's "E. coli on the Rocks."

Understanding in Action

Below is one student's summary of the first two paragraphs of Tan's essay. Use it as a model to write your own summary of the rest of the essay.

Tan has always assumed that ice cubes made with clean water are germ free because the cold would kill any possible germs. But it turns out that ice handled by servers in restaurants may be covered in the bacteria E. coli because those servers haven't washed their hands after going to the bathroom.

- **What are the secondary causes and/or effects?** Secondary effects are less important effects and are often less obviously related to the cause. Determine how the author distinguishes them from primary causes and look for evidence showing their relationship to the primary causes.

Analyzing a Cause-and-Effect Essay

Analyzing a cause-and-effect essay involves examining how the events or situations presented are related and how the selection is organized. Use the following questions to guide your analysis.

- **Is the assertion in the thesis statement fully explained and supported?** The assertion should be focused and limited so that it is fully and completely covered in the remainder of the essay.
- **Is the causal relationship clearly explained?** Determine if the author provided sufficient evidence that the causal relationship exists and examine the types of evidence provided.
- **Is the sequence of events clear?** Not all essays are organized chronologically. Some authors may discuss the effect(s) before presenting the cause(s). Other authors may not mention key events in the order in which they occurred. Understanding a causal relationship sometimes requires putting events in order.
- **Does the author use a clear method of organization to help you follow the essay?** The author may devote a separate paragraph to each cause or effect and may arrange the paragraphs using one of the organizations shown in Figures 17.1 (p. 543), 17.2 (p. 544), and 17.3 (p. 545).
- **Does the author use transitions to help you move from one cause or effect to another?** Transitional words, phrases, or sentences work as guideposts, helping you anticipate what the author will discuss next.

Evaluating a Cause-and-Effect Essay

Evaluating a cause-and-effect essay involves judging how accurately and effectively the author has established and demonstrated the causal relationship. Use the following questions to guide your evaluation of cause-and-effect essays.

- **Does the writer cover all major causes or effects?** Consider whether the author presents a fair description of the causal relationship. For instance, a writer arguing in favor of using animals for medical

Analysis in Action

Below is Tan's first paragraph annotated by the same student who wrote the summary for Understanding in Action. Use annotations of your own to analyze the rest of the essay.

Appeals directly to readers	If you're like me, you've assumed that anything frozen is naturally germ free. The cold would
Casual tone emphasizes "ick" factor	kill the nasties. Furthermore, the only bad ice cubes are those made with dirty water. Tap water in China, for example. Clean water from
Interesting way to introduce thesis	U.S. taps makes for worry-free clean ice cubes. Wrong.

Evaluation in Action

This evaluation of the two opening paragraphs of Tan's "E. coli on the Rocks" was written by the same student who summarized and annotated the essay in the Understanding in Action and Analysis in Action boxes. Use it as a model for writing your own evaluation of the essay.

I like that Tan pulls me in as a reader with her first sentence. I also think that it's effective in the first paragraph that she sounds like she's speaking directly to her readers, almost as if they were friends. The final "Wrong" really makes me want to read on. Then saying that ice in restaurants may be "dirtier than water from your toilet" is also effective in making clear how disgusting it is that people don't wash their hands after going to the bathroom.

research might fail to mention the painful effects of the testing on the animals.

- **Does the writer provide sufficient evidence for the causal relationship?** Look closely at the supporting evidence and determine whether it is sufficient to make sure the relationship exists. Suppose, for example, a writer asserts that medical doctors often order unnecessary medical tests to prevent possible lawsuits and only supports the assertion using personal experiences; a few anecdotes are not sufficient evidence.

- **What is the writer's purpose?** Does the writer describe certain causes or effects to urge you to accept a particular viewpoint or position? For example, a graphic description of the physical effects of an experimental drug on laboratory animals may strengthen a writer's argument against the use of animals in medical research.

- **Does the author make assumptions?** If so, are they supported by the reasons given and the evidence? A writer, for example, may assume that cosmetics should be tested on animals to assure their safety for humans. But unless the author explains and documents this assumption, you are not obliged to accept or agree with it.

Readings for Practice, Ideas for Writing

Why Do People Watch Sports on TV?

John Clifton is a Texas-based freelancer who has written about dating, music, finance, and more. He contributes to AskDeb.com, an online resource for everyday questions. This selection is an answer to one of them.

Reading Tip

As you read, highlight and annotate the essay to identify the specific evidence the author provides to explain each of the causes he offers in answering the question in his title.

Previewing the Reading

Preview the reading using the guidelines on pages 23–24, and then answer the following questions.

1. What do you predict the author's attitude toward sports to be?
2. What are several reasons the author offers to explain why people watch sports on television?

AskDeb.com

Why Do People Watch Sports on TV?

By John Clifton

People who don't enjoy watching sports on TV often don't get why the rest of us enjoy sports viewing so much. For instance, why does someone get so passionate about a vicarious competition, since we have no particular effect on the outcome? When we're watching sports on television, we're pulling for or against people we've likely never met and likely never will meet.

The thing is, there are countless reasons people watch sports on TV. For those who think we sports fans are crazy, let me try to explain a few of the major reasons people view sports on television.

A Sense of Community

Supporting the local team allows for a sense of community. Sports allows for a sense of common identity with people in your local city, state, or community. The local fandom has something in common. If you hate sports but love some kind of music,

Continued >

think about meeting some other fan of your favorite band. The two of you have something to talk about, something in common. That's the way it is with sports.

I always come back to that scene from the movie *City Slickers* where Daniel Stern's girlfriend asks why guys love sports so much. Billy Crystal's character mentions that when he was eighteen and he and his dad had nothing in common, the two of them could still talk about the Mets. That's what I'm talking about when I mention a sense of community. Sports brings together people when they have nothing else in common. You get two strangers who love the L.A. Lakers talking about the team, and the next thing you know, these people are like old friends.

It's Unscripted[1]

A lot of people enjoy watching sports on TV because it's unscripted. They don't know who's going to win. With a movie or TV show, you generally have a pretty good idea what the ending is going to look like. With sports, you never know the outcome. Every game has a favorite, but sayings like "That's why they play the game" or "Games are won on the field" exist for a reason. Upsets happen, surprise twists occur, and it's all unscripted and unrehearsed. Sports is organic.[2] People might consider something like boxing barbaric, but there's nothing like watching a big championship match when you never know what might happen with the next fist thrown. It's just an entirely different dynamic than watching *Rocky* for the tenth time and knowing the ending.

That's why the idea of sports athletes betting on games is such a big deal. The drama of sports is not knowing what's coming next. Once you realize that players or referees are fixing games, then you are watching professional wrestling, not a competition. This hardly ever happens, and sports leagues are quick to stamp out any sign that a game is fixed.

Of course, you might reply that a good movie doesn't tip its hand, either. Or you might say that most sports events don't go down to the wire and therefore the ending isn't dramatic all that often. This misses the experience of being a rabid[3] sports fan. Whether you rejoice in a close victory or suffer the indignity of a blowout defeat, sports is about picking a team and following their story—no matter the outcome.

Sports Fanatics

If sports on TV looks boring or mind-numbing, you need to know something about sports. Watching a sport is only interesting if you have something on the line. If you could care less about either team or competitor in a sporting event, you're probably

---

[1] **unscripted** Not planned.
[2] **organic** Living, alive.
[3] **rabid** Extreme, fanatical.

going to find even a close game fairly boring. Sports and passion go hand in hand. It lends itself to fanaticism.

Let's equate it to a fictional story. Whether you like books, plays, or movies, think what makes an entertaining story. You need to care about the characters. You want a protagonist[4] you care about and empathize with. You want an antagonist or villain who you really want to see go down. To a sports fan watching TV, that's what the game is like. They pick sides and the game really "matters" to them. That's when it becomes interesting.

Think about it: *Fan* is short for *fanatic*. Sports watching needs someone to care about the outcome of the game. The fan is on the edge of his or her seat. Emotions well up as a tightly contested game sits in the balance. Win or lose, the sports watcher goes through an emotional journey. Sports becomes an outlet for unspent emotions. Sports allows for a certain amount of catharsis[5] in people's lives.   10

Of course, not everybody falls naturally into the role of the sports fan. To some people, caring about the outcome of a game seems pointless. Even then, though, certain people find new ways to personalize a sports competition for themselves.

Money on the Line

Some people bet on the outcome of sporting events so they have something on the line. This is the only way they can care about the outcome of a game, or it "spices things up" and makes the average game really mean something to them. I'm not advocating that someone who doesn't enjoy sports start betting on games to get interested; I'm only suggesting that's one of the reasons people watch sports on TV.

The next time you see someone sweating over every play of a sports broadcast, ask them if they have any money on the line. A lot of the time, you'll find they do. It's amazing how much more interesting a ball game becomes when there's a little bit of money riding on the outcome of the sport.

The same goes for fantasy sports. Fantasy football and fantasy baseball are another way people personalize the sports they watch. These people select teams of individual players and track the statistical success of the players themselves—not the teams involved. Often, fantasy sports owners have money on the line for the winner of the competition. Just as often, bragging rights mean as much as the side bet. There's a lot to be said for "outsmarting" all your friends, even if it's over something as random and meaningless as fantasy sports.

[4] **protagonist** Leading character or figure.
[5] **catharsis** Release of emotions or tensions.

Continued >

Free Family Entertainment

I'm overlooking one major reason people watch sports on television: Watching sports   15
on TV is free. There's also the fact that you're never watching a rerun.

A third factor is that people started watching sports as a kid. Maybe they watch
major league baseball because they play Little League baseball. Maybe they
check out the Premiership, because they play select soccer in their local
community. Whatever the case, kids often watch sports, because it's something
they can relate to.

Also, parents look at sports as better entertainment than other parts of the pop
culture. If your child is watching a movie, there's no telling what kinds of nudity,
violence, or bad language they're exposed to. A parent doesn't have to worry about
that when their kid is watching sports. The worst they have to concern themselves
with are displays of bad sportsmanship or out-of-control athletes, but those are
almost universally condemned in the setting of a game on TV and are often shunted
to the side during TV broadcasts in favor of "the game on the field." The family and
child aspect of sports is one reason that sports commissioners are so quick to punish
"morals" transgressions in their sports.

I know of a couple of people who love sports who grew up in strict, religious families.
There wasn't much of anything on television their parents didn't disapprove of, so they
started watching sports. They became sports encyclopedias, because that was the
only "wholesome" TV watching they enjoyed. So when you ask yourself why people
seem so obsessed with watching sports on TV, you need to remind yourself that most
of them got in the habit at a really early age—and that sports is comparatively
harmless TV viewing.

So sports is free to watch; it's always something new; it's unscripted; parents
don't have to freak out about what their kids are watching; sports gives people an
outlet to vent; and being a fan of a sports team or competitor allows people to
identify with something relatively harmless and build a sense of community with
like-minded fans around them. So the next time you watch a bunch of mindless
sports fans watching TV at the local restaurant or sports bar and behaving like
morons after every play, remember that sports is entertainment, that it's a whole
lot more entertaining when you blow off steam by acting like a moron, and that
sports is harmless fun.

📊 Understanding the Reading

1. **Thesis** Where does the author state his opening thesis?

2. **Causes** Summarize the causes the author offers for why people watch sports on television.

3. **Development** Briefly summarize how the author's major points explain each cause.

4. **Audience** How does the author envision his intended audience, and what does he hope to achieve with this audience? How can you tell?

5. **Vocabulary** Using context clues (p. 34), define each of the following words as it is used in the essay, consulting a dictionary if necessary: *vicarious* (para. 1), *barbaric* (5), *empathize* (9), *antagonist* (9), *shunted* (17), and *transgressions* (17).

6. **Organization** Complete the following graphic organizer to help you see the organization of the essay.

Title	"Why Do People Watch Sports on TV?"
Introduction	People who aren't sports fans may wonder why the rest of us enjoy watching sports on TV. There are many reasons for this.
Body paragraphs	Cause 1:
	Support:
	Cause 2:
	Support:
	Cause 3:
	Support:
	Cause 4:
	Support:
	Cause 5:
	Support:
Conclusion	Summarizes the causes explained in the essay

Analyzing the Reading

1. **Introduction and conclusion** How do the first two paragraphs relate to the final paragraph?

2. **Examples** What are some of the specific examples Clifton includes here? How do they help develop his explanations of causes?

3. **Audience** Where in the essay does Clifton anticipate readers' possible objections to the case he is making? How does he deal with these?

4. **Purpose** Clifton suggests comparisons between what sports fans enjoy and what nonsports fans might enjoy (paras. 3 and 9). What is the purpose of these comparisons?

5. **Language** Overall, how would you characterize the level of language Clifton uses in the essay? How does his language in general contribute to the impression you get of him? Point to some specific examples to explain your answer.

Evaluating the Reading

1. **Presentation** How well does Clifton explain the reasons people enjoy watching sports on TV? If you're not a sports fan, do his points make sense? If you are a sports fan, do you think he covers all the reasons you and other fans you know have for enjoying televised sports?

2. **Organization** Does Clifton present his list of causes in a meaningful order? Can you determine a clear method to his organization?

3. **Conclusion** Clifton's conclusion is a bit repetitive. Should he have revised it to be more concise? How would you revise it?

4. **Language** In his conclusion, Clifton refers to sports fans as sometimes "behaving like morons." Do you find this language appropriate?

5. **Presentation** In paragraph 14, Clifton switches his topic to fantasy sports. Do you think this subject fits in with the rest of the essay?

Discussing the Reading

1. Why do some people really enjoy sports while others have no interest in it at all? What might separate the two types in terms of personality?

2. In your view, what is the most important reason Clifton offers in his essay? Which reason do you think is most common among sports fans? Which might be least common?

3. Clifton argues that watching sports on TV is wholesome for children, that parents don't have to worry about them being exposed to negative influences. Do you agree?

Writing about the Reading

1. **Paragraph** In a paragraph, describe your personal attitude toward watching sports on television. (Hint: First, draft a topic sentence that summarizes your attitude. Then develop your paragraph by explaining the reasons for your attitude.)

2. **Paragraph** What are you a fanatic about? Whether you are passionate about a particular team or band, as Clifton suggests, or some activity that occupies much of your time, write a paragraph in which you explain what causes your enthusiasm for this particular subject. (Hint: Make sure to clearly introduce the object of your fanaticism in your opening sentences.)

3. **Essay** Write an essay titled "Why Do People _____ ?" (Fill in the blank with your subject, of course.) Start by brainstorming a number of different subjects, focusing on interests of your own that you could explain to readers. Then choose one for which you can come up with four or five reasons people pursue and enjoy the activity. Alternatively, you might have as your topic an activity, such as smoking, that people choose to do even though it has negative outcomes. (Hint: Like Clifton, create topic headings that summarize each reason you explain in that section.)

The Clan of One-Breasted Women

Terry Tempest Williams is a naturalist, environmental activist, and award-winning writer. In 1991 she published *Refuge: An Unnatural History of Family and Place*, a memoir about the rise of the Great Salt Lake, the flooding of the Bear River Migratory Bird Refuge, and her mother's diagnosis with ovarian cancer. This essay about the cancer that has ravaged her family was originally published as the epilogue to *Refuge*.

Reading Tip

Williams starts with a very personal description of the effect that cancer has had in her family. Notice how this sets the tone for her intimate, honest essay. Also, pay attention to the primary and secondary causes she identifies and how she uses vivid and interesting language to explain them.

Previewing the Reading

1. What do the members of the clan of one-breasted women have in common?
2. Predict how this essay is organized.

The Clan of One-Breasted Women

===== TERRY TEMPEST WILLIAMS =====

I belong to a Clan of One-Breasted Women. My mother, my grandmothers, and six aunts have all had mastectomies. Seven are dead. The two who survive have just completed rounds of chemotherapy and radiation.

I've had my own problems: two biopsies for breast cancer and a small tumor between my ribs diagnosed as a "borderline malignancy."

This is my family history.

Most statistics tell us breast cancer is genetic, hereditary, with rising percentages attached to fatty diets, childlessness, or becoming pregnant after thirty. What they don't say is living in Utah may be the greatest hazard of all.

We are a Mormon family with roots in Utah since 1847. The "word of wisdom" in my family aligned us with good foods—no coffee, no tea, tobacco, or alcohol. For the most part, our women were finished having their babies by the time they were thirty. And only one faced breast cancer prior to 1960. Traditionally, as a group of people, Mormons have a low rate of cancer. 5

Is our family a cultural anomaly?[1] The truth is, we didn't think about it. Those who did, usually the men, simply said, "bad genes." The women's attitude

---

[1] **anomaly** Abnormality, oddity.

was stoic. Cancer was part of life. On February 16, 1971, the eve of my mother's surgery, I accidentally picked up the telephone and overheard her ask my grandmother what she could expect.

"Diane, it is one of the most spiritual experiences you will ever encounter."

I quietly put down the receiver.

Two days later, my father took my brothers and me to the hospital to visit her. She met us in the lobby in a wheelchair. No bandages were visible. I'll never forget her radiance, the way she held herself in a purple velvet robe, and how she gathered us around her.

"Children, I am fine. I want you to know I felt the arms of God around me."   10

We believed her. My father cried. Our mother, his wife, was thirty-eight years old.

A little over a year after Mother's death, Dad and I were having dinner together. He had just returned from St. George, where the Tempest Company was completing the gas lines that would service southern Utah. He spoke of his love for the country, the sandstoned landscape, bare-boned and beautiful. He had just finished hiking the Kolob trail in Zion National Park. We got caught up in reminiscing, recalling with fondness our walk up Angel's Landing on his fiftieth birthday and the years our family had vacationed there.

Over dessert, I shared a recurring dream of mine. I told my father that for years, as long as I could remember, I saw this flash of light in the night in the desert—that this image had so permeated my being that I could not venture south without seeing it again, on the horizon, illuminating buttes and mesas.[2]

"You did see it," he said.

"Saw what?"   15

"The bomb. The cloud. We were driving home from Riverside, California. You were sitting on Diane's lap. She was pregnant. In fact, I remember the day, September 7, 1957. We had just gotten out of the Service. We were driving north, past Las Vegas. It was an hour or so before dawn, when this explosion went off. We not only heard it, but felt it. I thought the oil tanker in front of us had blown up. We pulled over and suddenly, rising from the desert floor, we saw it, clearly, this golden-stemmed cloud, the mushroom. The sky seemed to vibrate with an eerie pink glow. Within a few minutes, a light ash was raining on the car."

I stared at my father.

"I thought you knew that," he said. "It was a common occurrence in the fifties."

It was at this moment that I realized the deceit I had been living under. Children growing up in the American Southwest, drinking contaminated milk from contaminated cows, even from the contaminated breasts of their mothers, my mother—members, years later, of the Clan of One-Breasted Women.

It is a well-known story in the Desert West, "The Day We Bombed Utah," or   20
more accurately, the years we bombed Utah: Above ground atomic testing in

[2] **buttes and mesas** Steep-sided flat-topped hills.

Continued >

Nevada took place from January 27, 1951, through July 11, 1962. Not only were the winds blowing north covering "low-use segments of the population" with fallout and leaving sheep dead in their tracks, but the climate was right. The United States of the 1950s was red, white, and blue. The Korean War was raging. McCarthyism[3] was rampant. Ike[4] was it, and the cold war was hot. If you were against nuclear testing, you were for a communist regime.

Much has been written about this "American nuclear tragedy." Public health was secondary to national security. The Atomic Energy Commissioner, Thomas Murray, said, "Gentlemen, we must not let anything interfere with this series of tests, nothing."

Again and again, the American public was told by its government, in spite of burns, blisters, and nausea, "It has been found that the tests may be conducted with adequate assurance of safety under conditions prevailing at the bombing reservations." Assuaging public fears was simply a matter of public relations. "Your best action," an Atomic Energy Commission booklet read, "is not to be worried about fallout." A news release typical of the times stated, "We find no basis for concluding that harm to any individual has resulted from radioactive fallout."

On August 30, 1979, during Jimmy Carter's presidency, a suit was filed, *Irene Allen v. The United States of America*. Mrs. Allen's case was the first on an alphabetical list of twenty-four test cases, representative of nearly twelve hundred plaintiffs seeking compensation from the United States government for cancers caused by nuclear testing in Nevada.

Irene Allen lived in Hurricane, Utah. She was the mother of five children and had been widowed twice. Her first husband, with their two oldest boys, had watched the tests from the roof of the local high school. He died of leukemia in 1956. Her second husband died of pancreatic cancer in 1978.

In a town meeting conducted by Utah senator Orrin Hatch, shortly before   25
the suit was filed, Mrs. Allen said, "I am not blaming the government, I want you to know that, Senator Hatch. But I thought if my testimony could help in any way so this wouldn't happen again to any of the generations coming up after us . . . I am happy to be here this day to bear testimony of this."

God-fearing people. This is just one story in an anthology of thousands.

On May 10, 1984, Judge Bruce S. Jenkins handed down his opinion. Ten of the plaintiffs were awarded damages. It was the first time a federal court had determined that nuclear tests had been the cause of cancers. For the remaining fourteen test cases, the proof of causation was not sufficient. In spite of the split decision, it was considered a landmark ruling. It was not to remain so for long.

In April 1987, the Tenth Circuit Court of Appeals overturned Judge Jenkins's ruling on the ground that the United States was protected from suit by the legal

[3] **McCarthyism** Period of anticommunism in the late 1940s and 1950s named for Senator Joseph McCarthy.
[4] **Ike** Dwight D. Eisenhower, the thirty-fourth U.S. president (1953–1961).

doctrine of sovereign immunity, a centuries-old idea from England in the days of absolute monarchs.

In January 1988, the Supreme Court refused to review the Appeals Court decision. To our court system it does not matter whether the United States government was irresponsible, whether it lied to its citizens, or even that citizens died from the fallout of nuclear testing. What matters is that our government is immune: "The King can do no wrong."

In Mormon culture, authority is respected, obedience is revered, and inde- 30 pendent thinking is not. I was taught as a young girl not to "make waves" or "rock the boat."

"Just let it go," Mother would say. "You know how you feel, that's what counts."

For many years, I have done just that—listened, observed, and quietly formed my own opinions, in a culture that rarely asks questions because it has all the answers. But one by one, I have watched the women in my family die common, heroic deaths. We sat in waiting rooms hoping for good news, but always receiving the bad. I cared for them, bathed their scarred bodies, and kept their secrets. I watched beautiful women become bald as Cytoxan, cisplatin, and Adriamycin were injected into their veins. I held their foreheads as they vomited green-black bile, and I shot them with morphine when the pain became inhuman. In the end, I witnessed their last peaceful breaths, becoming a midwife to the rebirth of their souls.

The price of obedience has become too high.

The fear and inability to question authority that ultimately killed rural communities in Utah during atmospheric testing of atomic weapons is the same fear I saw in my mother's body. Sheep. Dead sheep. The evidence is buried.

I cannot prove that my mother, Diane Dixon Tempest, or my grandmothers, 35 Lettie Romney Dixon and Kathryn Blackett Tempest, along with my aunts developed cancer from nuclear fallout in Utah. But I can't prove they didn't.

My father's memory was correct. The September blast we drove through in 1957 was part of Operation Plumbbob, one of the most intensive series of bomb tests to be initiated. The flash of light in the night in the desert, which I had always thought was a dream, developed into a family nightmare. It took fourteen years, from 1957 to 1971, for cancer to manifest in my mother—the same time, Howard L. Andrews, an authority in radioactive fallout at the National Institutes of Health, says radiation cancer requires to become evident. The more I learn about what it means to be a "downwinder," the more questions I drown in.

What I do know, however, is that as a Mormon woman of the fifth generation of Latter-day Saints, I must question everything, even if it means losing my faith, even if it means becoming a member of a border tribe among my own people. Tolerating blind obedience in the name of patriotism or religion ultimately takes our lives.

When the Atomic Energy Commission described the country north of the Nevada Test Site as "virtually uninhabited desert terrain," my family and the birds at Great Salt Lake were some of the "virtual uninhabitants."

Continued >

One night, I dreamed women from all over the world circled a blazing fire in the desert. They spoke of change, how they hold the moon in their bellies and wax and wane with its phases. They mocked the presumption of even-tempered beings and made promises that they would never fear the witch inside themselves. The women danced wildly as sparks broke away from the flames and entered the night sky as stars.

And they sang a song given to them by Shoshone grandmothers: 40

Ah ne nah, nah	Consider the rabbits
nin nah nah—	How gently they walk on the earth—
ah ne nah, nah	Consider the rabbits
nin nah nah—	How gently they walk on the earth —
Nyaga mutzi	We remember them
oh ne nay—	We can walk gently also—
Nyaga mutzi	We remember them
oh ne nay—	We can walk gently also—

The women danced and drummed and sang for weeks, preparing themselves for what was to come. They would reclaim the desert for the sake of their children, for the sake of the land.

A few miles downwind from the fire circle, bombs were being tested. Rabbits felt the tremors. Their soft leather pads on paws and feet recognized the shaking sands, while the roots of mesquite and sage were smoldering. Rocks were hot from the inside out and dust devils hummed unnaturally. And each time there was another nuclear test, ravens watched the desert heave. Stretch marks appeared. The land was losing its muscle.

The women couldn't bear it any longer. They were mothers. They had suffered labor pains but always under the promise of birth. The red hot pains beneath the desert promised death only, as each bomb became a stillborn. A contract had been made and broken between human beings and the land. A new contract was being drawn by the women, who understood the fate of the earth as their own.

Under the cover of darkness, ten women slipped under a barbed-wire fence and entered the contaminated country. They were trespassing. They walked toward the town of Mercury, in moonlight, taking their cues from coyote, kit fox, antelope squirrel, and quail. They moved quietly and deliberately through the maze of Joshua trees. When a hint of daylight appeared they rested, drinking tea and sharing their rations of food. The women closed their eyes. The time had come to protest with the heart, that to deny one's genealogy[5] with the earth was to commit treason against one's soul.

At dawn, the women draped themselves in mylar, wrapping long streamers of silver plastic around their arms to blow in the breeze. They wore clear masks, that became the faces of humanity. And when they arrived at the edge of Mercury,

---

[5] **genealogy** Record or account of ancestry or family history.

they carried all the butterflies of a summer day in their wombs. They paused to allow their courage to settle.

The town that forbids pregnant women and children to enter because of radi- 45 ation risks was asleep. The women moved through the streets as winged messengers, twirling around each other in slow motion, peeking inside homes and watching the easy sleep of men and women. They were astonished by such stillness and periodically would utter a shrill note or low cry just to verify life.

The residents finally awoke to these strange apparitions.[6] Some simply stared. Others called authorities, and in time, the women were apprehended by wary soldiers dressed in desert fatigues. They were taken to a white, square building on the other edge of Mercury. When asked who they were and why they were there, the women replied, "We are mothers and we have come to reclaim the desert for our children."

The soldiers arrested them. As the ten women were blindfolded and handcuffed, they began singing:

> *You can't forbid us everything*
> *You can't forbid us to think—*
> *You can't forbid our tears to flow*
> *And you can't stop the songs that we sing.*

The women continued to sing louder and louder, until they heard the voices of their sisters moving across the mesa:

> *Ah ne nah, nah*
> *nin nah nah—*
> *Ah ne nah, nah*
> *nin nah nah—*
> *Nyaga mutzi*
> *oh ne nay—*
> *Nyaga mutzi*
> *oh ne nay—*

"Call for reinforcements," one soldier said.

"We have," interrupted one woman, "we have—and you have no idea of our numbers."

I crossed the line at the Nevada Test Site and was arrested with nine other Utahans for trespassing on military lands. They are still conducting nuclear tests in the desert. Ours was an act of civil disobedience. But as I walked toward the town of Mercury, it was more than a gesture of peace. It was a gesture on behalf of the Clan of One-Breasted Women.

As one officer cinched the handcuffs around my wrists, another frisked my 50 body. She found a pen and a pad of paper tucked inside my left boot.

---

[6] **apparitions** Supernatural appearance of a person or thing, strange or startling.

Continued >

"And these?" she asked sternly.

"Weapons," I replied.

Our eyes met. I smiled. She pulled the leg of my trousers back over my boot.

"Step forward, please," she said as she took my arm.

We were booked under an afternoon sun and bused to Tonopah, Nevada. It   55
was a two-hour ride. This was familiar country. The Joshua trees standing their
ground had been named by my ancestors, who believed they looked like prophets
pointing west to the Promised Land. These were the same trees that bloomed
each spring, flowers appearing like white flames in the Mojave. And I recalled a
full moon in May, when Mother and I had walked among them, flushing out
mourning doves and owls.

The bus stopped short of town. We were released.

The officials thought it was a cruel joke to leave us stranded in the desert with
no way to get home. What they didn't realize was that we were home, soul-
centered and strong, women who recognized the sweet smell of sage as fuel for
our spirits.

Understanding the Reading

1. **Detail** What is the recurring dream cited by Williams at the start of the essay? What does she learn from her father about this vision?

2. **Cause** According to Williams, what caused the cancer in her family?

3. **Background information** What factors made it easy for the government to conduct nuclear tests in Utah in the 1950s and 1960s? How did the government respond to the rise in cancer rates years later?

4. **Detail** What dream does the author describe toward the end of the essay? How does this story relate to the action that she and other protesters take?

Analyzing the Reading

1. **Purpose** What main point does the author make, and how does that relate to her purpose in writing?

2. **Cause and effect** Identify the causes and effects discussed in Williams's essay. Is each cause and effect explained in a detailed and understandable way? Does she provide sufficient supporting evidence to prove the existence of a causal relationship between events? Explain.

3. **Language** What is the meaning of the metaphor "becoming a midwife to the rebirth of their souls" (para. 32)?

4. **Language** Explain the doublespeak that Williams quotes, such as "low-use segments of the population" (para. 20) and "virtually uninhabited desert terrain" (38).

Evaluating the Reading

1. **Language** Evaluate the author's use of descriptive language. Highlight several examples in which she expresses her thoughts through sensory details.

2. **Patterns** What other patterns of development does the author use? How do these patterns enhance the causal analysis?

3. **Conclusion** Consider Williams's conclusion. In what ways does it reinforce her main assertion about the topic? Do you find this ending satisfying? Why, or why not?

4. **Visualizing fact and opinion** Because authors often include both facts and opinions in their writing, it is up to the reader to distinguish between what are true and verifiable facts and what are opinions or statements of belief. Use your knowledge of fact and opinion to identify whether the following statements from the article are facts or opinions. For each, include a brief explanation of why you think it is one or the other.

Statement	Fact or Opinion?
"Most statistics tell us breast cancer is genetic . . ." (para. 4)	
". . . living in Utah may be the greatest hazard of all." (para. 4)	
"Within a few minutes, a light ash was raining on the car." (para. 16)	
"Irene Allen lived in Hurricane, Utah." (para. 24)	
"Tolerating blind obedience in the name of patriotism or religion ultimately takes our lives." (para. 37)	
"Ours was an act of civil disobedience." (para. 49)	

Discussing the Reading

1. Discuss the development and testing of nuclear weapons. Should any country be allowed to continue to possess and develop such weapons? What restrictions and safeguards should apply?

2. Discuss the notion of blind obedience. Do you agree or disagree with Williams's statement that "[t]olerating blind obedience in the name of patriotism or religion ultimately takes our lives" (para. 37)? Defend your position.

Writing about the Reading

1. **Paragraph** Williams held the memory of the bomb's flash from when she was a very young child. Using cause and effect, write a paragraph about one of your earliest memories. Why do you think it remains so vivid for you?

2. **Essay** Brainstorm a list of ways that government affects your life. Choose one, and write a cause-and-effect essay for your classmates describing the policy, law, or agency and how it influences you. Be sure to fully explain the multiple causes and effects, and recognize or dispel any assumptions your readers might have about this role of government.

3. **Internet research** Since the time of the atomic bomb tests described in the essay, new and equally dangerous threats to public safety have evolved. Using cause and effect, write an essay that explores the threats civilian populations face today from nuclear weapons and other weapons of mass destruction. To keep your topic manageable, narrow it to a single issue, such as the threats posed by biological weapons. Consider examining the Department of Homeland Security's Web site and the Web site for the Federation of American Scientists, an organization dedicated to ending the arms race, at www.fas.org.

Sins of the Grandfathers

Sharon Begley is a science writer and editor who currently serves as the senior health and science correspondent at Reuters. She has authored and coauthored multiple books, most recently *The Emotional Life of Your Brain* (2012) with Richard J. Davidson. The following article was published in 2010 on the news Web site the *Daily Beast*.

Reading Tip

Because of the scientific nature of the subject, the technical vocabulary in this reading is relatively complex. As you read, highlight any words or phrases that you have trouble understanding. Then read on to see whether the context that follows helps you understand the terms. Consult a dictionary if necessary.

Previewing the Reading

Preview the reading (see pp. 23–24), and then see if you can form a tentative idea of what the "sins-of-the-grandfathers effect" mentioned in the final paragraph is.

Sins of the Grandfathers

Sharon Begley

What happens in Vegas could affect your offspring. How early life experiences could cause permanent changes in sperm and eggs.

Michael Skinner has just uttered an astounding sentence, but by now he is so used to slaying scientific dogma[1] that his listener has to interrupt and ask if he realizes what he just said. Which was this: "We just published a paper last month confirming epigenetic changes in sperm which are carried forward transgenerationally. This confirms that these changes can become permanently programed."

OK, so it's not bumper-sticker ready. But if Skinner, a molecular biologist at Washington State University, were as proficient with soundbites as he is with mass spectrometry, he might have explained it this way: The life experiences of grandparents and even great-grandparents alter their eggs and

ILLUSTRATION BY BRIAN REA

[1] **dogma** Established beliefs or principles.

Continued >

sperm so indelibly that the change is passed on to their children, grandchildren, and beyond. It's called transgenerational epigenetic inheritance: the phenomenon in which something in the environment alters the health not only of the individual exposed to it, but also of that individual's descendants.

The astounding part of Skinner's statement is that this altered inheritance does not occur the way generations of biologists have been taught. Instead of changing the DNA sequences that make up the genes that ancestors pass down to descendants—the As, Ts, Cs, and Gs, that spell out the genetic code— something more subtle occurs in epigenetic inheritance. A life experience—in Skinner's study, exposing rats to a fungicide called vinclozolin—alters the on-off switches that control DNA in sperm or eggs. Biologists have long known about the switches, which are clusters of atoms called methyl groups. The cluster can silence a gene it attaches to; when the cluster is removed, the gene is active again. (This silencing is why the DNA for, say, insulin is turned off in brain cells but active in pancreas cells.) But biologists believed that when sperm and eggs grew up, as it were, and created an embryo, the tags were reset, nature's way of scrubbing the sins of the fathers and mothers before they could afflict the next generation.

Skinner's discovery that not all those marks are erased, but are instead permanently modified (at least as far out as he bred his rats: four generations), has challenged a decades-old tenet[2] of reproductive biology . . . which, when it's brought to his attention, he acknowledges with an *Oh, right*: "The 'permanently' does astonish me," he concedes.

"I guess it's why we got such pushback from the medical community."

Skinner's findings are far from anomalous. For one thing, they're not confined to rats or to the fungicide he fed them. Other labs, too, are finding that experiences—everything from a lab animal being exposed to a toxic chemical to a person smoking, being malnourished in childhood, or overeating—leaves an imprint[3] on eggs or sperm, an imprint so tenacious that it affects not only those individuals' children but their grandchildren as well.

Skinner and his team have gone the furthest in showing how this works. By analyzing the on-off settings of switches on every bit of sperm DNA, they found that sixteen had been altered, turned on when the normal position was off, or off when the normal position was on. Those alterations appeared in the sons of mothers exposed to the fungicide when they were pregnant, in the sons of the sons, and in the sons of the sons' sons. The tags on the sperm DNA did not vanish, as textbooks say. As a result, because some genes that were supposed to be dormant were instead active, and some genes that were supposed to be active were squelched, the sons and grandsons developed abnormalities in their testes, prostates, and kidneys. The point is not that this fungicide causes these problems in people—humans are exposed to much lower doses—but a proof of principle: By altering sperm in an enduring way, an environmental exposure can leave its mark on at least four subsequent generations.

The environmental exposure doesn't have to be as extreme as chowing down on a fungicide. Scientists at Australia's University of New South Wales fed

---

[2] **tenet** Principle.

[3] **imprint** Character or distinguishing feature.

healthy, svelte, male rats a high-fat diet (43% of calories from fat — a typical American diet). Not surprisingly, the rats put on weight and fat, and developed insulin resistance and glucose intolerance — basically, type 2 diabetes, the scientists reported . . . in *Nature*. None of that was surprising. What made the scientists take notice was the daughters these rats sired: Although their mothers were of normal weight and ate a healthy diet while pregnant, daughters of the high-fat-diet dads developed insulin resistance and glucose resistance as adults — even though they never ate a high-fat diet themselves.

Mothers' diet while pregnant affects their children's health as adults because of how nutrients and toxic compounds pass through the placenta.[4] But fathers have no contact with their daughters except through the sperm that created them. These rat fathers were not genetically diabetic. The conclusion is therefore inescapable: The fathers' high-fat diet altered their sperm in a way that induced adult-onset disease in their daughters. (The next step is to see whether grandchildren develop it, too.) Emma Whitelaw of Queensland Institute of Medical Research, who has found similar transgenerational effects, has called it "a molecular memory of the parent's experience — in this case, diet." Reminiscent of Skinner's finding that sons and grandsons of his fungicide-exposed rats had abnormal on-off switches in their sperm DNA, the Australian team found that 642 genes in the pancreas (which makes insulin) of the daughters of the high-fat-diet fathers had on-off switches in the wrong position. The result raises the intriguing possibility that the childhood-obesity epidemic is at least in part due to alterations in sperm caused by fathers-to-be eating a high-fat diet. After all, while it's fine to blame kids' couch-potato ways and fattening diets, that does not explain why obesity in babies has risen 73% since 1980.

Transgenerational effects do not have to be harmful. When fifteen-day-old female mice frolicked for two weeks in an enriched environment, one filled with exercise wheels, novel objects, and lots of other mice for social stimulation, it strengthened the brain mechanism that underlies memory. That much had been shown many times before: Animals raised in an enriched environment remember mazes better. But . . . , scientists led by Larry Feig of Tufts University reported in the *Journal of Neuroscience* that the neuronal effect shows up in the mice's offspring — even when those offspring never lived in an enriched environment, and even though those offspring were not so much as a gleam in their mothers' eyes when they lived in the enriched environment. "The idea that qualities acquired from experience can be transmitted to future offspring has long been considered [heresy[5]]," Feig's team wrote. If something similar occurs in humans, how good your memory is during adolescence "can be influenced by environmental stimulation experienced by one's mother during her youth."

One reason that is not so far-fetched: Transgenerational effects are showing up not only in lab rats but also in people, as if the ghosts of our ancestors haunt our very genes. In 2006 scientists announced the findings of a study in a town in Sweden called Överkalix

10

---

[4] **placenta** An organ that provides nourishment to a fetus.

[5] **heresy** Opinion at odds with accepted beliefs.

Continued >

(chosen because it keeps excellent birth and death records). If a father began smoking before the age of eleven, found Marcus Pembrey of the Institute of Child Health in London, his sons had a greater body-mass index, on average, than did sons of men who took up smoking as adults. In this same population, if a man suffered food shortages as an eight- to twelve-year-old child, his sons' sons were more likely to die young; if a woman suffered food shortages as a child, her son's daughters were. Another study in Överkalix found that if a man overate in childhood, his sons' children were four times more likely to develop diabetes and cardiovascular disease.

At the time these studies were done, it cost about $10,000 per sample to scan DNA for changes in the on-off switches that show this sins-of-the-grandfathers effect. But the cost is dropping fast, says Skinner, making it feasible to see whether life experiences leave indelible marks on the sperm or eggs that give rise to children and grandchildren. Since the answer so far is yes, consider it a warning to hold off on your unhealthy behavior until after you have kids.

Understanding the Reading

1. **Thesis** What is Begley's thesis, and where does she state it directly?

2. **Cause-and-effect relationship** In your own words, explain the causal relationship Begley details. What implications does she suggest for this fairly recent scientific discovery?

3. **Meaning** What is Begley's point in the final sentence of paragraph 6?

4. **Meaning** What specific comparison does Begley make in paragraphs 7–8, and what tentative conclusion does she draw?

5. **Development** In terms of how she has previously developed her subject, what contrast does Begley make in paragraph 9?

6. **Visuals** What does the drawing that accompanies the piece represent?

Analyzing the Reading

1. **Audience** How do you think Begley defined her audience for the piece, and what makes you think so? Is her purpose basically to inform, or do you think she is making a larger argument here?

2. **Technical language** Reread paragraph 3. Why do you think Begley's presentation of the topic gets so much more technical in this paragraph than in most of the rest of the essay?

3. **Thesis** Where in the essay does Begley rephrase and repeat her thesis? Why might she have done so?

4. **Visuals** How does the drawing that accompanies the piece contribute to the overall tone of the piece? Is it more in keeping with the technical language in paragraph 3 or with the rest of the piece?

5. **Conclusion** How does Begley try to connect directly to readers in her final paragraph?

Evaluating the Reading

1. **Language** In her opening, Begley quotes the phrase "epigenetic changes in sperm which are carried forward transgenerationally." Does she go on to define this phrase adequately for you? Could you translate it so that it is "bumper-sticker ready"?

2. **Cause-and-effect relationship** How clearly do you think Begley explains the causal relationship that is the subject of her essay? After reading it, do you still have any unanswered questions?

3. **Presentation** Most of Begley's examples used to prove genetic environmental effects crossing generations involve lab rats. Do you find the studies involving humans she cites in her final paragraph convincing?

4. **Personal response** Are you likely to change any of your behaviors based on the possibility of passing on effects to future generations, as Begley advises in her final paragraph?

Discussing the Reading

1. As Begley describes, lab researchers often deliberately compromise the health of animal subjects to benefit humans. Do you think this is ethical?

2. In paragraph 9, Begley repeats the well-established point that raising rats in a stimulating environment makes them more intelligent later in life. What implications does this have for human beings?

3. Do you think the term *sins*, as Begley uses it in her title and final paragraph, is appropriate for the point she is making?

Writing about the Reading

1. **Essay** Based on your response to question 1 of Discussing the Reading, write an essay in which you present what you feel is the proper relationship between medical research that causes suffering to animals and the ultimate outcomes that benefit human beings. In your view, what results for humans, if any, can justify increasing levels of suffering for animals, if any?

2. **Essay** Write a cause-and-effect essay in which you explore how you developed into the person you are today. Think about traits likely passed down to you genetically, as well as the kinds of experiences that you believe shaped your

core identity. To begin, brainstorm words you would use to describe yourself. Then choose three or four of these specific personality traits and explain their possible causes in your essay.

3. **Internet research** Write an essay focusing on the causes, the effects, or both of the childhood-obesity epidemic Begley refers to in paragraph 8. You'll want to begin by researching this phenomenon. Be sure to clearly identify the sources you come up with so you can cite them correctly in your essay (see Chapter 19, "Finding and Using Sources.")

COMBINING THE PATTERNS

How Science Can Help You Fall in Love

Robert Epstein is a contributing editor at *Scientific American Mind,* where the following article appeared in 2010. He holds a Ph.D. in psychology from Harvard University and seeks to educate the public about mental health and behavioral science. To that end, he has written fifteen books and hosted several radio programs.

Reading Tip

As you read, annotate the selection to highlight the specific advice the author offers to help readers enhance their romantic relationships.

Previewing the Reading

Preview the reading (see pp. 23–24 for guidelines), and then briefly summarize the central cause-and-effect relationship the essay analyzes.

How Science Can Help You Fall in Love

Robert Epstein

The best way to get students interested in scientific studies is to give them hands-on experiences that get them excited about the subject matter. In chemistry courses, teachers accomplish that with test tubes and mysterious liquids. In a course I taught recently at the University of California, San Diego, on relationship science, I piqued my students' interest with exercises on, well, *love.*

To begin, I invited eight students who did not know each other to come to the front of the auditorium, where I paired them up randomly. I then asked each individual to rate, on a scale of 1 to 10, how much he or she liked, loved, or felt close to his or her partner. Then I asked the couples to look deeply into each other's eyes in an exercise I call Soul Gazing.

There was some giggling at first and then some very intense gazing. After two minutes, I again asked for the numbers. The result? A modest 7% increase in loving (meaning 1 point added for one person in the couple), an 11% increase in liking, and a whopping 45% increase in closeness. There were gasps and cheers in the audience. When I asked everyone in the class to pair up for two minutes of gazing, 89% of the students said the exercise increased feelings of intimacy.

And that was just the beginning . . . .

Continued >

Eye Contact

5 About 50% of first marriages fail in the United States, as do two-thirds of second marriages and three-quarters of third marriages. So much for practice! We fail in large part because we enter into relationships with poor skills for maintaining them and highly unrealistic expectations. We also tend to pick unsuitable partners, mistakenly believing that we're in love simply because we feel physical attraction.

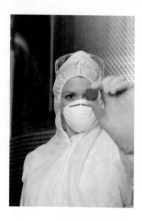

Love-Building Exercises

Here are some fun exercises, all inspired by scientific studies, that you can use to deliberately create emotional intimacy with a partner—even someone you barely know:

1. **Two as One.** Embracing each other gently, begin to sense your partner's breathing and gradually try to synchronize your breathing with his or hers. After a few minutes, you might feel that the two of you have merged.
2. **Soul Gazing.** Standing or sitting about two feet away from each other, look deeply into each other's eyes, trying to look into the very core of your beings. Do this for about two minutes and then talk about what you saw.
3. **Monkey Love.** Standing or sitting fairly near each other, start moving your hands, arms and legs any way you like—but in a fashion that perfectly imitates your partner. This is fun but also challenging. You will both feel as if you are moving voluntarily, but your actions are also linked to those of your partner.
4. **Falling in Love.** This is a trust exercise, one of many that increase mutual feelings of vulnerability.

From a standing position, simply let yourself fall backward into the arms of your partner. Then trade places. Repeat several times and then talk about your feelings. Strangers who do this exercise sometimes feel connected to each other for years.

5. **Secret Swap.** Write down a deep secret and have your partner do the same. Then trade papers and talk about what you read. You can continue this process until you have run out of secrets. Better yet, save some of your secrets for another day.
6. **Mind-Reading Game.** Write down a thought that you want to convey to your partner. Then spend a few minutes wordlessly trying to broadcast that thought to him or her, as he or she tries to guess what it is. If he or she cannot guess, reveal what you were thinking. Then switch roles.
7. **Let Me Inside.** Stand about four feet away from each other and focus on each other. Every 10 seconds or so move a bit closer until, after several shifts, you are well inside each other's personal space (the boundary is about 18 inches). Get as close as you can without touching.

(My students tell me this exercise often ends with kissing.)

8. **Love Aura.** Place the palm of your hand as close as possible to your partner's palm without actually touching. Do this for several minutes, during which you will feel not only heat but also, sometimes, eerie kinds of sparks.

—*R.E.*

That combination of factors sets us up for failure: Eventually—often within a mere eighteen months—the fog of passion dissipates, and we begin to see our partner with new clarity. All too often we react by saying, "Who are *you*?" or "You've *changed*." We might try hard for years after that to keep things going, especially if children are in the picture. But if we start out with the wrong person and lack basic tools for resolving conflicts and communicating, the chances that we will succeed are slim to none.

Over the years, having looked carefully at the fast-growing scientific literature on relationship science and having conducted some new research of my own, I have come to believe that there is a definite fix for our poor performance in romantic relationships. The fix is to extract a practical technology from the research and then to teach people how to use it.

At least eighty scientific studies help to reveal how people learn to love each other. A 1989 study by psychologist James D. Laird of Clark University and his colleagues inspired my Soul Gazing exercise. The researchers showed that mutual eye gazing (but not gazing at hands) produced rapid increases in feelings of both liking and loving in total strangers. Mutual gazing is like staring, but with an important difference: For many mammalian species, staring is both intended and received as a threat. Try it on a New York subway if you have any doubts about its efficacy. In mutual gazing, however, people are giving each other *permission* to stare; that is, they are being vulnerable[1] to each other, and that is the key element in emotional bonding. The vulnerability created when people are in war zones can create powerful emotional bonds in seconds, and even hostages sometimes develop strong attachments to their captors, a phenomenon called the Stockholm syndrome.

Signs of vulnerability in an animal or another person bring out tendencies in many people to provide care and protection—to be drawn to that being and to like or even love him or her. And as research in social psychology has shown for decades, when a person is feeling vulnerable and thus agitated or otherwise aroused, he or she often looks around for clues about how to interpret and label those feelings. The body is saying, "I'm aroused, but I'm not sure why," and the environment is suggesting an answer, namely, that you're in love.

A Technology of Affection

Soul Gazing is one of dozens of exercises I have distilled from scientific studies that make people feel vulnerable and increase intimacy. Love Aura, Let Me Inside, and Secret Swap are other examples of fun, bond-building activities that any couple can learn and practice.

Students could earn extra credit in my course by trying out such techniques with friends, romantic interests, or even total strangers. More than 90% of the students in the course reported using

[1] **vulnerable** Open to attack or danger.

Continued >

these methods successfully to improve their relationships, and more than 50 of the 213 students submitted detailed reports about their experiences. Nearly all the reports documented increases in liking, loving, closeness, or attraction of between 3 and 30% over about a month. In a few cases, ratings tripled. (Students did not need to enhance their relationships to receive extra credit; all they had to do was document their use of the techniques.)

The few exceptions I saw made sense. One heterosexual male saw no positive effects when he tried the exercises with another male; moreover, the experience made him "uncomfortable." When he tried them with a female, however, his intimacy ratings increased by 25% — and *hers* increased by 144%!

A student named Olivia attempted the exercises with her brother, mother, a good friend, and a relative stranger. Soul Gazing failed with her brother because he could not stop giggling. When she and her mom tried the Secret Swap — an activity that creates vulnerability when people disclose secrets to each other — intimacy ratings increased by 31%. Exercises she tried with her friend boosted ratings between 10 and 19%, but most impressive was the outcome of gazing with someone she barely knew: a 70% increase in intimacy.

One student did the assignment with her husband of five years. The couple, Asa and Gill, tried out eight different exercises, and even though their "before" scores were usually very high (9s and 10s), every exercise they tried increased their scores by at least 3%. Overall, Asa wrote, "I noticed a drastic change in our bond for one another. My husband seems more affectionate now

than he was, for which I am really grateful." She also reported a bonus: a substantial drop in the frequency with which she and her spouse called attention to their past mistakes. This change probably came about because the couple was now, as a result of my course, broadly interested in enhancing their relationship.

Taking Control

The students in my course were doing something new — taking *control* over their love lives. We grow up on fairy tales and movies in which magical forces help people find their soul mates, with whom they effortlessly live happily ever after. The fairy tales leave us powerless, putting our love lives into the hands of the Fates.

But here is a surprise: Most of the world has never heard of those fairy tales. Instead more than half of marriages on our globe are brokered by parents or professional matchmakers, whose main concerns are long-term suitability and family harmony. In India an estimated 95% of the marriages are arranged, and although divorce is legal, India has one of the lowest divorce rates in the world. (This is starting to change, of course, as Western ways encroach on traditional society.)

Young couples in India generally have a choice about whether to proceed, and the combination of choice and sound guidance probably accounts for the fact that studies of arranged marriages in India indicate that they measure up well — in, for example, longevity, satisfaction, and love — against Western marriages. Indeed, the love experienced by Indian couples in arranged marriages appears to be even more robust than the love people experience in "love marriages." In a 1982 study psychologists Usha Gupta and Pushpa Singh of the University of Rajasthan in Jaipur, India, used the Rubin Love Scale, which gauges intense, romantic, Western-style love, to determine that love in love marriages in India does exactly what it does in love marriages here: It starts high and declines fairly rapidly. But love in the arranged marriages they examined started out low and gradually *increased*, surpassing the love in the love marriage about five years out. Ten years into the marriage the love was nearly twice as strong.

Kaiser and Shelly Haque of Minneapolis met only once before their marriage was arranged in Bangladesh more than eleven years ago. Since then, the couple's love for each other has grown, an emotional trajectory that is not uncommon in arranged marriages.

How do they do it? How do people in some arranged marriages build love deliberately over time—and can we do it, too?

Over the past few years I have been interviewing people in arranged marriages in which love has grown over time. One of these couples is Kaiser and Shelly Haque of Minneapolis, who have been happily married for eleven years and have two bright, well-adjusted children. Once he had a secure life in the United States, Kaiser, an immigrant from Bangladesh, returned to his native country to let his family know he was ready for matrimony. The family did the rest. After just one meeting with Shelly—where, Kaiser said, there was "like at first sight"—the arrangements were made. "We've grown to love each other and to get to know each other over time," Kaiser says. "The sparks are getting bigger, and I think we can do even better in the future."

20   Kaiser and Shelly are not atypical. A study that Mansi Thakar, a student at the University of Southern California, and I presented at the November 2009 meeting of the National Council on Family Relations included thirty individuals from nine countries of origin and five different religions. Their love had grown, on average, from 3.9 to 8.5 on a 10-point scale in marriages lasting an average of 19.4 years.

These individuals identified eleven factors that contributed to the growth of their love, ten of which dovetailed beautifully with the scientific research I reviewed in my course. The most important factor was commitment, followed by good communication skills. The couples also identified sharing secrets with a spouse, as well as accommodation— that is, the voluntary altering of a partner's behavior to meet the other person's needs. Seeing a spouse in a vulnerable state (caused by injury or illness) was also singled out. There are many possible lessons here for Westerners, among them: Do things deliberately that make you vulnerable to each other. Try experiencing

Continued >

danger, or thrilling simulations[2] of it, as a couple.

The results conflicted with those of American studies in only one respect: Several of the subjects said their love grew when they had children with their spouse. Studies in the United States routinely find parenting to be a threat to feelings of spousal love, but perhaps that tendency results from the strong feelings and unrealistic expectations that launch our relationships. The stress of raising children tends to disrupt those expectations and ultimately our positive feelings for each other.

[2] **simulations** Imitations, pretend situations.

Creating Love

A careful look at arranged marriage, combined with the knowledge accumulating in relationship science, has the potential to give us real control over our love lives — without practicing arranged marriage. Americans want it all — the freedom to choose a partner and the deep, lasting love of fantasies and fairy tales. We can achieve that kind of love by learning about and practicing techniques that build love over time. And when our love is fading, we can use such techniques to rebuild that love. The alternative — leaving it to chance — makes little sense.

📊 Understanding the Reading

1. **Thesis** Epstein waits until his final paragraph to state his thesis. Based on the entire reading, restate this thesis in your own words.

2. **Audience** Epstein is a professor of psychology. How do you think he defined the readers for this essay: as other psychology professionals, as psychology students, as general readers, or as another audience? What makes you think so?

3. **Purpose** What is Epstein's point in paragraphs 5–6? How does this help you understand his underlying purpose?

4. **Meaning** The heading that introduces paragraph 10 refers to the "technology of affection." How would you define this term?

5. **Other methods** The section that begins with paragraph 15 is developed through comparison and contrast. What are the subjects being compared, and how are they similar and different?

6. **Visuals** How does the photograph of the uniformed researcher on page 576 help summarize the main point of the essay?

📊 Analyzing the Reading

1. **Introduction** Why does Epstein open his essay by describing a course he teaches and one of the methods he uses with students in that course (paras. 1–3)? What does this have to do with his central point?

2. **Language** Epstein italicizes one word in the sixth sentence of paragraph 8. Why?

3. **Presentation** Why does Epstein write about fairy tales in paragraph 15? What transition is he setting up?

4. **Visuals** What does the photograph of the Haques on their wedding day (p. 579) contribute to Epstein's discussion of the couple's eleven-year marriage (para. 19)?

Evaluating the Reading

1. **Personal response** What are the most important ideas you take away after reading this essay? Would you apply any of the lessons Epstein presents to your own life? Why, or why not?

2. **Statistical evidence** Paragraphs 3, 11–14, and 20 present statistical comparisons to demonstrate a causal effect about relationship development. Do you find this numerical evidence convincing?

3. **Presentation and visual** In his discussion of arranged marriages, Epstein cites the Haques as an example of a couple whose love has grown since their wedding (para. 19). But he only provides a quotation from the husband to support this claim. Do you find this evidence sufficient? Is the photograph of the couple useful or helpful?

4. **Thesis** Do you think that Epstein successfully establishes the basis for his concluding thesis? Are you convinced that people can practice "techniques that build love over time" and that can "rebuild" love that is "fading" (para. 23)?

Discussing the Reading

1. Epstein writes in paragraph 15 that our concept of love is based on fairy tales and movies in which "magical forces" help couples "effortlessly live happily ever after." How accurate do you find this characterization?

2. According to studies Epstein cites in paragraph 22, U.S. couples' relationships are threatened by the "stress of raising children." Do you agree that having children can "disrupt" the positive feeling couples share? Can the presence of children bring couples closer together?

3. Epstein seemingly allows no exception to his final point that "leaving [love] to chance . . . makes little sense." Is maintaining love the calculated act he suggests it is?

4. Examine the visuals that accompany the essay. Compare and contrast the subjects. What does the use of these two photos imply about the relationship between science and life? How do they contribute to the tone of the essay and its subject matter?

Writing about the Reading

1. **Essay** Based on the "Love-Building Exercises" box and Epstein's discussion of the love-building exercises, write an essay in which you explain to readers each exercise in terms of its intended effect, as well as the intended cumulative effect of all the exercises. (Hint: As you think about your audience, decide whether you're writing primarily to people not currently in a relationship, couples at the beginning of a relationship, or couples who have been together for some time.)

2. **Essay** Epstein suggests the causal effect of sheer physical attraction and of the model provided in fairy tales and movies, but how do you think people determine what it means to fall in love? Based on your own experience and what you've observed in others, write an essay analyzing how people fall in love. Moreover, how do couples maintain loving relationships?

3. **Combined patterns/Internet research** Epstein writes that arranged marriages throughout the world and in various cultures are ultimately fulfilling for both husband and wife over the course of their years together. Research arranged marriages, focusing initially on those cultures in which they are most common, and why certain cultures value them. Then write an essay in which you first define arranged marriage and explain the process through which such couples are brought together. Go on to develop your topic by considering the extent to which you believe such marriages succeed and what, in your opinion, accounts for this relative level of success.

📖 TEXTBOOK

Warming Planet, Decreasing Biodiversity

Michèle Shuster and **Janet Vigna** teach biology at New Mexico State University and Grand Valley State University, respectively. **Gunjan Sinha** is a science journalist, and **Matthew Tontonoz** has edited textbooks on biology, evolution, and environmental science. All four collaborated on *Biology for a Changing World*, an introductory textbook to the discipline. This selection is excerpted from a chapter on ecosystem ecology.

Reading Tip

As you read, make notes about how the two "infographics" accompanying the excerpt contribute to explaining the ideas the authors present.

Previewing the Reading

Preview the reading (see pp. 23–24 for guidelines), and briefly define the cause being explained and what, in general, is being affected in this causal relationship.

Warming Planet, Decreasing Biodiversity
Michèle Shuster, Janet Vigna, Gunjan Sinha, and Matthew Tontonoz

Although temperature swings and shifts in the ranges of organisms are natural phenomena, the amount of warming in recent years is unprecedented, and evidence suggests that the change is not merely part of a natural cycle. From 1880 until 2010, the earth's surface has warmed, on average, by about 0.8°C (1.4°F), according to a 2010 study by NASA's Goddard Institute for Space Studies. That may not sound like a lot. But consider this: The difference in global average temperatures between today and the last ice age—when much of North America was buried under ice—is only about 5°C (9°F). Where global temperatures are concerned, even a one-degree change is significant.

The rate of warming has increased as well. Eighteen of the warmest years on record occurred in just the past twenty years. The last decade, from 2000 to 2010, was the hottest decade so far, with 2010 tying 2005 for the title of hottest year on record. Much of this warming is attributable to the **greenhouse effect**, the trapping of heat in the earth's atmosphere. As sunlight shines on our planet, it warms the earth's surface. This heat radiates back to the atmosphere, where it is absorbed by **greenhouse gases** such as carbon dioxide. The heat trapped by greenhouse gases raises the temperature of the atmosphere, and in turn, the surface of the earth (see Infographic 1).

Continued >

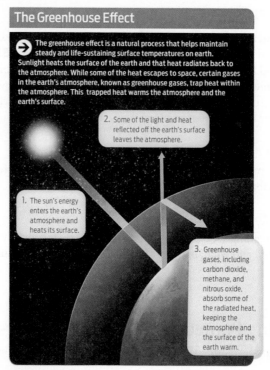

The Greenhouse Effect

The greenhouse effect is a natural process that helps maintain steady and life-sustaining surface temperatures on earth. Sunlight heats the surface of the earth and that heat radiates back to the atmosphere. While some of the heat escapes to space, certain gases in the earth's atmosphere, known as greenhouse gases, trap heat within the atmosphere. This trapped heat warms the atmosphere and the earth's surface.

2. Some of the light and heat reflected off the earth's surface leaves the atmosphere.

1. The sun's energy enters the earth's atmosphere and heats its surface.

3. Greenhouse gases, including carbon dioxide, methane, and nitrous oxide, absorb some of the radiated heat, keeping the atmosphere and the surface of the earth warm.

Infographic 1

Cause and Effect

The greenhouse effect is a natural process that helps maintain life-supporting temperatures on earth. Without this greenhouse effect, the average surface temperature of the planet would be a frigid –18°C (0°F). In recent years, however, rising levels of greenhouse gases have increased the strength of the greenhouse effect, a phenomenon known as the enhanced greenhouse effect. As the amount of greenhouse gases in the atmosphere has increased, so have temperatures. The result is **global warming**, an overall increase in the earth's average temperature (see Infographic 2).

For ecologist Hector Galbraith, director of the Climate Change Initiative at the Manomet Center for Conservation Sciences, in Massachusetts, one of the most worrying things about climate change is how quickly it is happening, and how sensitive species are to the changes. "Most people think of climate change as something that's thirty years out," says Galbraith. But that's simply not true, he notes. "We began seeing responses in **ecosystems** twenty years ago. The ecosystems knew about it before we did."

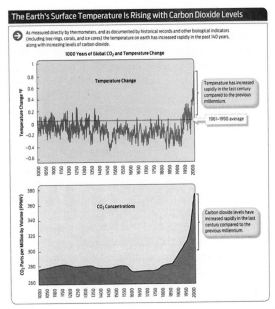

Infographic 2

Plants, of course, are slower to adapt than animals; they cannot 5
simply get up and move (although they may change their range over
time by dispersing seeds into more favorable climes). But some animals can change their ranges quite quickly. "A bird can simply open
its wings, and within two hours it's fifty miles farther north," says
Galbraith.

What will be the outcome of all these changes? The answer, says
Galbraith, is that we don't really know. "We're seeing changes to systems that have been relatively stable for thousands of years. . . . The
really scary thing about climate change is it's very difficult to predict
the ecosystem effects of these changes."

Nevertheless, there are disturbing scenarios. Take the relationship between birds and insects. Many forests are susceptible to insect
attacks. Given their insect-rich diet, flycatchers are a natural form of
pest control. If the birds move north, as evidence suggests they are
doing, they leave behind a forest susceptible to predation by insects
that might be less vulnerable to the changed climate or more adaptable. The maple-tree-loving pear thrip and the forest tent caterpillar
are just two examples of insects that might be happy to see the flycatchers go. More insects means more dead trees, which in turn
means more fuel for forest fires.

Not all species will be negatively affected by climate change—
some may actually benefit. But one species' success in coping with

Continued >

climate change may contribute to another's demise. For example, the adaptable red fox (*Vulpes vulpes*), found throughout the Northern Hemisphere, is venturing into the range of the endangered Arctic fox (*Vulpes lagopus*), whose habitat—the Arctic tundra—has gotten warmer. When the two species share a range, the Arctic fox inevitably suffers because the red fox out-competes it for food and also preys on Arctic fox pups.

While some species can adapt to a changing climate by shifting range, future global warming will likely exceed the ability of many species to adapt, as hospitable habitats can no longer be found or accessed. According to a 2004 study published in the journal *Nature*, as many as a million species could be driven to extinction by 2050 because of climate change. Using computer models, a group of fifteen investigators from around the world estimated that between 15% and 37% of a sample of 1,103 species of plants, mammals, birds, reptiles, amphibians, and invertebrates would be "committed to extinction" because of warming temperatures.

The study's authors found that for many of these species, rising 10 temperatures will make suitable habitat impossible to find or reach. The natural residents of mountaintops are especially vulnerable: As temperatures rise, species may move up to higher, colder elevations, but eventually they have nowhere left to go.

Understanding the Reading

1. **Textbook reading** What is the "greenhouse effect" (para. 2)? What do the authors mean by the "enhanced greenhouse effect" (para. 3)? How does the difference between the two relate to the subject of the selection?

2. **Examples** The selection presents several examples of species responding to potential climate change (paras. 5, 7, 8, and 10). How do these examples help answer the question posed at the beginning of paragraph 6?

3. **Causal chain** What causal chain is presented in paragraph 6? Explain it in your own words.

4. **Graphics** What visual point is being made in the second infographic, which presents changes in the earth's temperature and in carbon dioxide levels over the same period of time?

Analyzing the Reading

1. **Development** Why in the opening paragraph does the author compare the warming of the earth's surface between 1880 and 2010 with differences in temperatures today and during the last ice age?

2. **Graphics** How does the infographic about the greenhouse effect relate to paragraph 2, in which it is cross-referenced?

3. **Causal explanation** Where do the authors begin to develop the relationship between the two topics mentioned in the title? What is the purpose of the preceding paragraphs?

Evaluating the Reading

1. **Quotation** How do you respond to the quotation in paragraph 6 that the "really scary thing about climate change" is that its effects are difficult to predict? Do the authors seem to agree about this unpredictability?

2. **Evidence** Paragraph 9 cites a study conducted in 2004 that argues that "as many as a million species could be driven to extinction by 2050." As presented here, do you find this to be convincing evidence?

3. **Graphics** How helpful do you find infographic 1? How could you use it to study/learn the content it illustrates?

4. **Language and audience** Given the level of language and presentation in this selection, how do you think the authors envisioned the textbook's readers? You might compare the level of this selection to that of the textbook selections in previous chapters.

Discussing the Reading

1. There is some controversy surrounding the idea of global warming and climate change. A number of experts insist that, despite what these authors write, it is all part of a natural cycle. Discuss whether textbook authors should present "both sides," so to speak.

2. The enhanced greenhouse effect described here is ultimately the result of technological advances over the last century, which some people see as beneficial to humans. Do you think that what benefits humans should have priority over the biodiversity of the earth's plant and animal life?

3. The authors write in paragraph 7 about "disturbing scenarios" related to global warming. How seriously do you take these scenarios? Are you concerned that changes will affect your lifestyle?

Writing about the Reading

1. **Essay** The relationship between greenhouse gases and climate change is arguably a topic of concern for governmental policy worldwide. But how might individuals in the United States change their behavior in ways that could diminish greenhouse gas emission? After researching this topic, brainstorm a list of ways consumers contribute to global warming. Then in an essay offer specific advice about lifestyle changes that could make a difference.

2. **Internet research** This selection focuses on how global warming affects plant and animal life. But how might humans be affected by continued rapid global warming? Again, research the topic in order to write an essay about the potential effects of climate change on the earth's human population.

3. **Internet research** The authors write in paragraph 3 about how rising levels of greenhouse gases have led to temperature increases worldwide. Do some research about what has caused the global increase in these gases, and write an essay in which you explore this cause-and-effect relationship over the last century or so.

Writing Your Own Cause-and-Effect Essay

Now that you have learned about the major characteristics, structure, and purposes of a cause-and-effect essay, you know everything necessary to write your own causal analysis. In this section you will read a student's cause-and-effect essay and get advice on finding ideas, drafting your essay, and revising and editing it. You may want to use the essay prompts in "Readings for Practice, Ideas for Writing" (p. 553) or choose your own topic.

A Student Model Cause-and-Effect Essay

Nathan Nguyen was a first-year liberal arts major when he wrote this essay in response to an assignment for his writing class. He was asked to explain the causes and effects of a current social problem. As you read, notice how Nguyen presents a chain of causes and effects, in which an initial cause has an effect, which in turn becomes a cause of another effect, and so on.

Title: suggests importance of topic

Gambling on Our Future

Nathan Nguyen

Introduction: opening example catches readers' interest

Marge Simpson is a junkie. Are you surprised? Marge has always been the moral anchor that kept *The Simpsons* squarely in the mainstream. She was the stay-at-home mom who tempered Lisa's progressive politics, the sober wife who supported Homer during his drunken misadventures, and the upstanding citizen who taught Bart how to live in society. If Marge had an intravenous drug habit, Americans everywhere would be up in arms. But it's just gambling, and in this day and age, few things are more mainstream. In fact, inspired by the huge revenues generated by Las Vegas, states are turning to gambling to boost their post-recession economies and their ailing educational

Thesis: suggests essay will focus on chain of events

systems and urban centers. As states open up their laws to all kinds of gambling, it has become more widespread and convenient, leading to an increase in addiction and problem gambling.

Cause A: Nevada legalizes gambling

The passage of the 1931 bill allowing gambling in Nevada was originally designed to generate revenue for the state and its ailing educational system. The result was little less than a phenomenon, establishing Las Vegas as a tourist playground and a symbol of American decadence but also changing forever the way politicians

Effect A/Cause B: Las Vegas becomes popular; economic boon
Source

tax the people. Recently, the Las Vegas tourism and hospitality industry, which includes gambling, has accounted for 46% of the state's income and yielded $16 billion-a-year (Nevada Resort Assoc.; Las Vegas Convention and Visitors Auth. 1). The economic boon to the state was watched enviously by lawmakers around the country; over time, what was once viewed as sinful has captured the dreams and imaginations of politicians and constituents alike.

Effect B/Cause C: seeing the boom, other states legalize gambling

Use of quote from source

Even before the nation's most recent economic struggles, cities and states had entered the business of gambling, desperate to re-create the rags-to-riches story of Las Vegas. According to the journal *American Family Physician*, "in 1978 only two states had legalized gambling; in 1998, however, only two states had not legalized gambling" (Unwin, Davis, and De Leeuw 741). The business of legalized gambling takes many forms. For example, a landmark Supreme Court decision in 1987 opened up the door to Native American gaming on tribal lands. The ensuing increase to economic development on some of these lands has caught the imagination of other impoverished areas. Struggling urban centers, such as Detroit and St. Louis, have opened large luxury casinos in the hopes of bringing money in from the wealthy suburbs to revitalize decaying downtown districts.

Effect C/Cause D: once legal, access to gambling becomes widespread

But gambling is not confined to casinos alone. Forty-three states now have casinos of a sort in every grocery, convenience store, and gas station, in the form of the lottery. Moreover, because hopeful lawmakers eased limitations on Internet gambling to boost state revenues, there are opportunities for "casinos" to be reached legally from every household and office in the country (Berzon). The problem now is not how to find legal gambling, but how to escape it.

Effect D/Cause E: Lotteries and the Internet have increased the acceptance of gambling.

The dramatic acceptance of state lotteries and Internet gaming across the nation has had the largest impact on how Americans view gambling. The lottery, like its big brother Las Vegas, was originally set up to subsidize state educational systems. Since 1964 when New Hampshire began its lottery, states have turned to lotteries as a way of increasing revenues without raising taxes and now they expect Internet gaming to do the same. While the revenues of state-run lotteries are often lauded, according to the *Final Report* by the National Gambling Impact Study Commission, the "actual contributions are exceedingly modest" (2-4). Furthermore, the American Gaming Association predicted that Internet gaming, such as poker,

Sources: cites statistic and expert opinion

5

"would generate . . . a fraction of what states get from their lotteries" (Cooper). Despite this, Americans continue to support the lottery, making it one of the top forms of gambling in the country. Even before the economic downturn, 86% of Americans had admitted to gambling at least once in their lives (Natl. Gambling Impact Study Commission 1). But as "states have become active agents for the expansion of gambling," public welfare has taken a backseat to revenue raising (3-4).

Effect E/Cause F: with acceptance of gambling, addiction is common

The abundance of opportunities to gamble has created more compulsive gamblers by exposing people to an "illness" they might not otherwise have developed and by giving reformed gamblers more chances to fall off the wagon. While most gamblers are able to do it healthily, a majority of the benefit derived from gambling is at the expense of the ill. A study by Duke University professors Charles Clotfelter and Philip Cook found that "5% of lottery players account for 51% of total lottery sales." Their research indicates that those who make under $10,000 spend "more than any other income group" and that lotteries rely on players who are

Sources: Research study documents appeal of gambling to the poor.

"disproportionately poor, black, and have failed to complete a high school education" (Natl. Gambling Impact Study Commission 7-10). People joke that it is a tax on the stupid, but in fact it is a tax on hope, especially with the rise of online gambling.

Effect F: increase in social problems associated with gambling addiction

Regarding the effects of Internet gaming, Keith Whyte, executive director of the National Council on Problem Gambling, argues that pathological gambling "definitely can be heightened" in this "immersive environment where you can lose track of time and money" (Berzon). College students are particularly vulnerable, precisely because they are more prone to taking risks than other groups and because people who begin gambling at a young age are at a much higher risk for developing a gambling problem later in life (Natl. Gambling Impact Study Commission 4-12). The rising rates in problem gambling correspond to the growth of legalized gambling across the country.

Conclusion: restates chain of events and emphasizes thesis

The promise of a Las Vegas miracle has lured states into expanding gambling and putting a mini Vegas in every 7-11 store and Internet device. As states increasingly turn to gambling, more people are exposed to it, a cycle that leads to ever-rising rates of problem gambling and addiction. The hope of a Vegas miracle lures people, often poor and occasionally very sick, to a casino, to the lottery, or to online betting. The trickle-down effect from this is the often unseen side to the promise of the big jackpot: Bankruptcy, job loss, divorce, alcoholism, drug addiction, and welfare are just some

Use of gambling jargon suggests author's opinion of the trend

of the costs associated with gambling addiction. The question then is, are states willing to gamble with our future? For now, the trend continues, but the odds of winning are a million to one.

Sources: Nyugen documents sources

Works Cited

Berzon, Alexandra. "States Cleared for Online Bets." *Wall Street Journal.* Dow Jones & Company, Inc., 27 Dec. 2011. Web. 29 Feb. 2012.

Cooper, Michael. "As States Weigh Online Gambling, Profit May Be Small." *New York Times.* New York Times, 17 Jan. 2012. Web. 1 Mar. 2012.

Las Vegas Convention and Visitors Authority. "2011 Las Vegas Year-to-Date Executive Summary." *Only Vegas.* Las Vegas Convention and Visitors Auth., 2012. Web. 28 Feb. 2012.

National Gambling Impact Study Commission. *Final Report.* National Gambling Impact Study Commission, 3 Aug. 1999. Web. 1 Mar. 2012.

Nevada Resort Association. "How Gaming Benefits Nevada." *Nevada Resort Association.* Nevada Resort Assoc., 2011. Web. 28 Feb. 2012.

Unwin, Brian K., Mark K. Davis, and Jason B. De Leeuw. "Pathologic Gambling." *American Family Physician* 3 (2000): 741–49. Print.

Responding to Nguyen's Essay

1. Suggest an alternative title that more directly reflects the essay's thesis.
2. Evaluate Nguyen's introduction. Is the opening reference to Marge Simpson an effective strategy? How would it appeal to those who are unfamiliar with *The Simpsons?* Discuss alternative ways to introduce the topic.
3. Nguyen does not include examples of real people and their gambling addictions. Would such examples strengthen the essay? Why, or why not?
4. Nguyen concludes by reiterating his thesis. What alternative ways might he have chosen to end the essay?

Finding Ideas for Your Cause-and-Effect Essay

Look for ideas for cause-and-effect essays as you do your reading for this and other classes. By thinking critically—understanding, analyzing, and evaluating—about the texts you read, you can find inspiration for your own writing. Here are a few approaches to take.

- When reading an essay that discusses the causes of an event or a phenomenon, consider writing about the effects; when reading about the effects of an event or a phenomenon, consider writing about the causes.

- Think of other possible causes or effects than those given in an essay you have read.
- For a chain-of-events essay, imagine what might have happened if the chain had been broken at some point.
- Consider the secondary causes or effects the writer does not mention.
- Write about a cause-and-effect relationship from your own life that is similar to one in the essay.

Selecting an Event to Write About

The first step is to select an event or a phenomenon to write about. Be sure to choose one with which you are familiar or about which you can find information in the library or on the Internet. Then decide on your purpose and whether to focus on causes, effects, or both. Keep the length of your essay in mind as you think about these issues. It would be unrealistic, for example, to try to discuss both the causes and the effects of child abuse in a five-page paper.

Discovering Causes and Effects

The next step is to discover causes, effects, or both. You can approach this task in a number of ways.

1. **Brainstorm** Write your topic in the middle of a blank page, turning the page sideways to allow for extra writing space. Brainstorm all possible causes and effects, writing causes on the left and effects on the right.
2. **Visualize** Replay the event in your mind. Focus on one or both of the following questions: Why did the event happen? What happened as a result of it? Make notes on your answers.
3. **Ask questions** Try asking questions and writing assertions about the problem or phenomenon. Did a chain of events cause the phenomenon? What effects are not so obvious?
4. **Discuss** Talk about your topic with a classmate or friend. Ask his or her opinion on the topic's causes, effects, or both.
5. **Research** Look up your topic at the library or on the Internet. Make notes on possible causes and effects, or print out or photocopy relevant information you discover.

Identifying Primary Causes and Effects

Once you have a list of causes or effects (or both), the next task is to sort through them and decide which ones are *primary*, or most important. For example, if your topic is the possible effects of television violence on young viewers, two primary effects might be an increase in aggressive behavior and a willingness to accept violence as normal. Less important, or *secondary*, effects might include learning inappropriate or offensive words and spending less time viewing family-oriented shows. In essays about controversial issues, which causes or effects are primary and which are secondary may depend on the writer's interests.

Use the following questions to help you decide which causes and effects are most important.

Causes

- What are the most obvious and immediate causes?
- What cause(s), if eliminated, would drastically change the event, problem, or phenomenon?

Effects

- What are the obvious effects of the event, problem, or phenomenon?
- Which effects have the most serious consequences? For whom?

After you identify primary and secondary causes and effects, examine them to be sure you have not overlooked any *hidden* causes or effects. For example, if a child often reports to the nurse's office complaining of a stomachache, a parent may assume that the child has digestive problems. However, a closer study of the behavior may reveal that the child is worried about attending a physical-education class and that the stomachaches are the result of stress and anxiety. The physical-education class is the hidden cause. As you analyze causes and effects, do not assume that the most obvious or simplest explanation is the only one.

You should also be on the lookout for assumptions that involve errors in reasoning. For example, the fact that Event A precedes Event B does not necessarily mean that Event A is the cause of Event B. Suppose you decide against having a cup of coffee one morning and later that day you score higher than ever before on a political science exam. Although one event followed the other in time, you cannot assume that reducing your coffee intake caused the high grade. To avoid such errors, look for evidence that one event did indeed cause the other.

Once you feel confident about your list of causes and effects, you need to provide a complete explanation of each primary cause or effect that will be included in the essay. To do so, you'll probably use one or more other patterns of development. For example, you may need to narrate events, present descriptive details, define important terms, explain unfamiliar processes, include examples, or make comparisons to explain unfamiliar concepts. At this point, it is a good idea to do some additional prewriting or research to gather evidence to support the causes, effects, or both. Try to discover several types of evidence, including facts, expert opinion, personal observation, quotations, and statistics.

Developing Your Thesis

Once you are satisfied with the causes and effects and the evidence you have generated to support them, the next step is to develop a working thesis. As noted earlier, the thesis for a causal analysis identifies the topic, makes an assertion about the topic, and tells whether the essay will focus on causes, effects, or both. Use the following tips to develop your thesis.

1. Avoid overly broad or absolute assertions. Such statements are difficult or impossible to support.

2. Use qualifying words. Unless a cause-and-effect relationship is well established and accepted, qualify your thesis statement.

3. Avoid an overly assertive or dogmatic tone. The tone of your essay, including the thesis, should be confident but not overbearing. You want readers to accept your premise based on its merits; an essay with a hostile or dismissive tone will alienate an audience before they have a chance to evaluate its position.

Drafting Your Cause-and-Effect Essay

Once you have evaluated the cause-and-effect relationship and thesis, it is time to organize your ideas and draft your essay. Review Figures 17.1, 17.2, and 17.3 (pp. 543–45) to see which is closest to your essay's basic structure. Then choose a method of organization that will present your ideas effectively (see pp. 117–20).

After you decide how to organize the essay, the next step is to write a first draft. Use the following guidelines to draft your essay.

1. **Write an effective introduction.** Your introduction should identify the topic and causal relationship as well as draw readers into the essay.

2. **Provide well-developed explanations.** Be sure to provide sufficient evidence that the causal relationship exists. Offer a number of reasons and choose a variety of types of evidence (examples, statistics, expert opinion, etc.). Try to develop each cause or effect into a detailed paragraph with a clear topic sentence.

3. **Use strong transitions.** Use a transition each time you move from an explanation of one cause or effect to an explanation of another. Transitional words and phrases that are useful in cause-and-effect essays include *because*, *since*, *as a result*, and *therefore*.

4. **Avoid overstating causal relationships.** When writing about causes and effects, avoid words and phrases that overstate the causal relationship, such as *it is obvious*, *without doubt*, *always*, and *never*. These words and phrases wrongly suggest that a causal relationship is absolute and without exception. Instead, use words and phrases that qualify, such as *it is possible*, *it is likely*, and *most likely*.

5. **Write a satisfying conclusion.** Your conclusion may remind readers of the thesis and draw the essay to a satisfying close. You might also summon the readers to action, as Sharon Begley does at the end of "Sins of the Grandfathers" when she recommends that people wait until they finish having children before engaging in unhealthy behaviors.

Figure 17.5 Revising a Cause-and-Effect Essay

QUESTIONS		REVISION STRATEGIES
1. Thesis Does it express a qualified, manageable assertion? (Can you prove your thesis?)	No	• Use a branching diagram to narrow your topic (see Chapter 4). • Revise to focus only on primary causes or effects. • Add qualifying words or phrases to your thesis.
Yes		
2. Using causes and effects Does your essay clearly focus on causes, effects, or both?	No	• Reconsider whether you want to explain causes, effects, or both. Will the essay be skimpy if you focus on only one or too long or complicated if you use both?
Yes		
3. Explanations of causes and effects Is each explained fully?	No	• Add anecdotes or observations from personal experience or other details and examples. • Do research to locate facts, research studies, statistics, and expert opinions.
Yes		
4. Organization Did you use chronological, least-to-most, or most-to-least organization? Is it clear and effective? Do your ideas progress logically?	No	• Choose a different order if necessary. • Rearrange your causes, effects, or both.
Yes		
5. Readers' assumptions Have you identified all likely preconceptions and challenged or addressed them?	No	• Brainstorm popular ideas readers might assume about your topic and either support or challenge them.
Yes		
6. Topic sentence Is each paragraph focused on a separate cause or effect?	No	• Be sure each paragraph has a topic sentence and supporting details (see Chapter 7). • Consider combining closely related paragraphs. • Split paragraphs that cover more than one cause or effect.
Yes		
7. Introduction and conclusion Are they effective?	No	• Revise your introduction and conclusion so that they meet the guidelines presented in Chapter 6.

Revising Your Cause-and-Effect Essay

If possible, set your draft aside for a day or two before rereading and revising it. As you review the draft, concentrate on how you organize and present your ideas, not on grammar, punctuation, or mechanics. Use the flowchart in Figure 17.5 to guide your analysis of the strengths and weaknesses of your draft.

Editing and Proofreading Your Essay

The final step is to check your revised essay for errors in grammar, spelling, punctuation, and mechanics. In addition, check for the types of errors you commonly make in any writing assignments, whether for this class or another situation. As you edit and proofread your causal-analysis essay, watch out for two types of errors commonly found in this type of writing: wordy sentences and mixed constructions.

1. **Look for and revise wordy sentences.** When explaining causal relationships, writers often use complex and compound-complex sentences (sentences with multiple dependent and independent clauses). Because such sentences can become wordy and confusing, you should look for ways to eliminate empty phrases and simplify your wording.

   ▶   *Certain types of computer*
   ~~As you are already well aware,~~ viruses ~~of certain types in a computer file~~
   often create errors that you cannot explain ~~in documents~~ and may
   eventually result in lost data.

2. **Revise to eliminate mixed constructions.** A mixed construction occurs when a writer connects phrases, clauses, or both that do not work together logically, leading to confusion in meaning.

   ▶   *Although*   *Samantha*
   ~~Samantha, although~~ she was late for work, ~~but~~ was not reprimanded by
   her boss.

Using both *although* and *but* makes this a mixed construction. To avoid mixed constructions, check words that join phrases and clauses. Pay attention to prepositions and conjunctions. Also, check to be sure that the subjects of every sentence can perform the action described by the verb. If not, revise the sentence by supplying the appropriate verb.

Chapter 18

Argumentation: Supporting a Claim

THE U.S. DISTRIBUTION OF WEALTH

OCCUPYGEORGE.COM

Quick Start: Study this image of a dollar bill stamped by supporters of the Occupy Wall Street movement, which arose in 2011 to protest inequality. What does the modified dollar bill represent? Identify the issue addressed and the position taken on this issue. How effective is the modified bill in conveying this message? In what ways is it convincing? Write a paragraph that could be used in place of the bill. Make a statement about the issue, and give several reasons to support the position on the issue.

What Is Argument?

The paragraph you wrote in response to the Quick Start prompt makes an argument. It makes a claim about wealth in the United States and supports it with reasons. In everyday conversation, an argument can be a heated exchange of ideas between two people: For example, college roommates might argue over who should clean the sink or who left the door unlocked last night. An effective **argument** is a logical, well-thought-out presentation of ideas that makes a claim about an issue and supports that claim with reasons and evidence. An ineffective argument may be an irrational, emotional release of feelings and frustrations. Many sound arguments, however, combine emotion with logic. A casual conversation can also take the form of a reasoned argument.

An argument has three basic parts: an **issue**, a **claim**, and **support**. In most arguments it is also important to argue against opposing viewpoints, which is known as **refutation**. The ability to construct and write sound arguments is an important skill in many aspects of life. Political, social, and economic issues, for instance, are often resolved through public and private debate. Knowing how to construct an effective argument is also essential to success in college and on the job, as the following examples show. For a health science course, you may be asked to write an essay claiming that the results of genetic testing, which can predict a person's likelihood of contracting serious diseases, should be kept confidential. As a lawyer representing a client whose hand was seriously injured on the job, you might have to argue to a jury that your client deserves compensation for the work-related injury.

Argument does the following:

1. It focuses on a narrowed issue.
2. It states a specific claim in a thesis.
3. It depends on careful audience analysis.
4. It presents reasons supported by convincing evidence.
5. It avoids errors in reasoning.
6. It appeals to readers' needs and values.
7. It recognizes opposing views.

1. Argument Focuses on a Narrowed Issue

An **issue** is a controversy—a problem or an idea about which people disagree. In choosing an issue, therefore, be sure it is arguable—that is, an issue that people have differing opinions on. For example, arguing that education is important in today's job market is pointless because people generally agree on that issue. It is worthwhile, however, to argue the merits of a liberal arts education versus technical training as preparation for after-graduation employment.

Depending on the issue you choose and the intended audience, your readers may need background information. In an argument to your classmates about organ donation, for example, you would give information about how there are not enough organs to meet the needs of people awaiting transplants.

In addition, the issue you choose should be narrow enough to address adequately in an essay-length argument. When you narrow the issue, your thesis will be more precise and your evidence more specific. You will also be able to provide more effective arguments against an opposing viewpoint. A detailed and specific argument is a strong argument, leaving no "holes" or gaps for opponents to uncover.

2. Argument States a Specific Claim

To build a convincing argument, you need a clear and specific **claim**—a statement that tells readers your position on the issue. An argument may claim that stronger laws are needed to control cyberbullying or that recycling should be mandatory, for example.

While all arguments make and support a claim, some also call for action. An essay opposing human cloning, for example, might argue for a ban on that practice and urge readers to take action against it, such as by voicing their opinions in letters to congressional representatives. Regardless of the argument, be careful about the way you state your claim.

3. Argument Depends on Careful Audience Analysis

Because an argument is intended to influence readers' thinking, it is important to determine not only how familiar readers are with the issue but also their likely position: Will they be likely to agree with your claim, be neutral about or waver on it, or disagree with it?

Agreeing audiences   When writing for an audience that will likely agree with your claim, the focus is usually on urging readers to take action. Instead of presenting large amounts of evidence, concentrate on reinforcing your shared viewpoint and building emotional ties with the audience. By doing so, you encourage readers to act on their beliefs.

Neutral or wavering audiences   Neutral readers may be somewhat familiar with the issue, but they usually do not have strong feelings about it. Instead, they may have questions or misunderstandings about it, or may simply be uninterested. In writing for this type of audience, be straightforward. Emphasize the importance of the issue, and offer explanations that clear up possible misunderstandings. Your goals are to establish your credibility, engender readers' trust, and present solid evidence in support of your claim.

Disagreeing audiences   The most challenging type of audience is the disagreeing audience because they believe their position is correct and are not eager to accept your views. They may also distrust you because you don't share their views on something they care deeply about.

In writing for a disagreeing audience, the goal is to persuade readers to consider your views on the issue. Be sure to follow a logical line of reasoning. Rather than stating your claim early in the essay, for this type of audience it may be more effective to build slowly to your thesis. First establish **common ground**—a basis of trust and goodwill—with readers by mentioning interests, concerns, and experiences that you share. Then, when you state your claim, the audience may be more open to considering your argument.

4. Argument Presents Reasons Supported by Convincing Evidence

In developing an argument, you need to have reasons for making a claim. A **reason** is a general statement that backs up a claim; it answers the question, Why do I have this opinion about the issue? You also need to support each reason with evidence. Suppose, for example, you argue that high-school uniforms should be mandatory for three reasons: The uniforms (1) reduce clothing costs for parents, (2) eliminate distractions in the classroom, thus improving academic performance, and (3) reduce peer pressure. Each reason would need to be supported by **evidence**—facts, statistics, examples, personal experience, or expert testimony. Carefully linking evidence to reasons helps readers see how the evidence supports the claim.

Be sure to choose reasons and evidence that will appeal to your audience. In an argument about mandatory school uniforms, high-school students would probably not be impressed by the first reason listed above—reduced clothing costs for parents—but they might consider the second and third reasons if you cite evidence that appeals to them, such as personal anecdotes from students. For an audience of parents, however, facts and statistics about reduced clothing costs and improved academic performance would be appealing types of evidence.

5. Argument Avoids Errors in Reasoning

In an argument essay, it is important to avoid introducing **fallacies**, or errors in reasoning or thinking. Fallacies are of various types and can weaken an argument and call into question the believability of supporting evidence. Following is a brief review of the most common types of faulty reasoning.

- **Circular reasoning**, also called **begging the question**, occurs when a writer simply repeats the claim in different words and uses the rewording as evidence. The statement "*Cruel* and unusual experimentation on helpless animals is *inhumane*" is an example.
- A **hasty generalization** occurs when the writer draws a conclusion based on insufficient evidence. If you were to taste three pieces of chocolate cake and then conclude that all chocolate cakes are overly sweet, you would be making a hasty generalization.

- A **sweeping generalization** is a claim that something applies to all situations without exception. To claim that all cameras are easy to use is a sweeping generalization.

- A **false analogy** results when a writer compares two situations that are not sufficiently similar. Just because two items or events are alike in *some* ways does not mean they are alike in *all* ways. If you wrote, "Just as a human body needs rest after strenuous work, a car needs rest after a long trip," you would be falsely comparing the human body with an automobile.

- A **non sequitur** (which means "it does not follow") occurs when no logical relationship exists between two or more connected ideas. "Because my sister is rich, she will make a good parent" is a non sequitur because no logical relationship exists between wealth and good parenting.

- A **red herring** distracts readers from the main issue by raising an irrelevant point. For example, suppose you are arguing that television commercials for alcoholic beverages should be banned. To mention that some parents actually give sips of alcohol to their children creates a red herring, distracting readers from the issue of television commercials for alcohol.

- A **post hoc fallacy** occurs when a writer assumes that Event A caused Event B simply because B followed A. The claim "Student enrollment fell dramatically this semester because of the appointment of the new college president" is a post hoc fallacy because other factors might have contributed to the decline in enrollment (such as changes in the economy or in the availability of financial aid).

- An **either-or fallacy** occurs when a writer argues as if there were only two sides to an issue, with one side being correct. For instance, on the issue of legalizing drugs, a writer may argue that all drugs must be *either* legalized *or* banned, ignoring other positions (such as legalizing marijuana use for cancer patients undergoing chemotherapy).

6. Argument Appeals to Readers' Needs and Values

Although an effective argument relies mainly on credible evidence and logical reasoning, emotional appeals can support and enhance a sound argument. **Emotional appeals** are directed toward readers' needs and values. **Needs** may be biological—such as the need to eat food and to drink—or psychological—such as the need to belong and to have self-esteem. **Values** are principles or qualities that readers consider important, worthwhile, or desirable (honesty, loyalty, privacy, and patriotism, for example).

7. Argument Recognizes Opposing Views

Recognizing opposing arguments forces you to think hard about your own claims—and perhaps to adjust them. In addition, readers will be more willing to consider your claim if you take their point of view into account. There are three methods of recognizing opposing views in an argument essay: acknowledgment, accommodation, and refutation.

When you **acknowledge** an opposing viewpoint, you admit that it exists and indicate that you have given it serious consideration. When you **accommodate** an opposing viewpoint, you acknowledge readers' concerns, accept some of them, and incorporate them into your own argument. When you **refute** an opposing viewpoint, you demonstrate its weaknesses. Consider how the author refutes an opposing viewpoint in the following paragraph.

Acknowledges argument that good speech will trump bad speech	At the core of the argument that we should resist all government regulation of speech is the ideal that the best cure for bad speech is good, that ideas that affirm equality and the worth of all individuals will ultimately prevail. This is an empty ideal unless
Refutation of that argument strengthens his.	those of us who would fight racism are vigilant and unequivocal in that fight. We must look for ways to offer assistance and support to students whose speech and political participation are chilled in a climate of racial harassment.

—Charles R. Lawrence III, "On Racist Speech"

Here the author refutes a common view of free speech. By acknowledging and refuting this view, the author strengthens his own argument that recognizes the downside of unchecked freedom of speech.

Reading and Writing Argument Essays

In this section, you will learn about the structure of an argument essay, read a sample essay, and practice using the guidelines for understanding, analyzing, and evaluating argument essays. This will help you skillfully read and write essays that use argument.

How Is an Argument Essay Structured?

In an argument essay that is effectively structured, each part of the essay plays a role in helping to make the argument clear and compelling to readers.

1. The **introduction** identifies the issue and often presents the thesis statement, or claim.

2. The **body paragraphs** present the reasons and evidence to support the thesis and may include emotional appeals and address opposing viewpoints.

3. The **conclusion** reinforces the thesis, makes a final appeal, and may urge readers to action.

Figure 18.1 (p. 604) represents these major components visually.

Figure 18.1   Graphic Organizer for an Argument Essay

Title	

	Issue
Introduction	Background information
	Definition of terms
	Thesis statement* (the claim)

Body paragraphs	**Reasons and evidence**	Reason 1
		Various types of evidence
		Reason 2
		Various types of evidence
		Reason 3
		Various types of evidence
	Emotional appeals	Need or value 1
		Need or value 2
		Need or value 3
	Opposing viewpoints	Opposing view 1
		Acknowledgment, accommodation, or refutation
		Opposing view 2
		Acknowledgment, accommodation, or refutation

	Restatement of claim
Conclusion	Final appeal to needs or values
	Request that readers take action

*The thesis statement may appear elsewhere within the argument.

1. THE INTRODUCTION AND THESIS STATEMENT IDENTIFY THE ISSUE AND THE CLAIM

The introduction, which usually includes the thesis statement, may provide background information about the issue. It might also suggest why the issue is important and define terms to be used in the argument. The thesis statement in an argument essay makes a claim about the issue. The claim should be narrow and as specific as possible. Here is an example of how a general claim can be narrowed to become a clear and specific thesis statement.

GENERAL   The use of animals in testing should be prohibited.

SPECIFIC   The testing of cosmetics and skin-care products on animals should be prohibited.

The introduction should also engage readers and create a sense of goodwill and trust toward the writer.

Reading | Writing   When reading the introduction to an argument essay, identify the issue and the claim. Then determine what you already know about the issue. This will help you decide how to read and what strategies to use to build comprehension and recall. If you already have a position on the issue, determine whether the essay agrees or disagrees with your position. When writing argument essays, especially if the practice is new to you, it is usually best to state your claim in a strong thesis early in the piece. Doing so will help keep your argument on track. As you gain experience writing arguments, you can experiment with placing the thesis later in the essay.

2. THE BODY PARAGRAPHS PRESENT THE REASONS AND EVIDENCE TO SUPPORT THE THESIS

The body paragraphs should provide detailed reasons, supported by evidence, to back up the claim. Each reason should be stated clearly and supported by evidence. Often one paragraph is devoted to each reason. The reason may be stated in the topic sentence, with the remainder of the paragraph consisting of evidence supporting it. Research and statistics are often cited as evidence. The body may make emotional appeals, tied to the needs and values of the audience. It may also recognize or refute opposing viewpoints.

Reading | Writing   When reading the body of an argument essay, consider whether you are in agreement or disagreement with the claim. Be aware that if you disagree with it, you may be inclined to quickly discount or ignore reasons or evidence, or if you agree with it, you may tend to accept the author's reasoning and evidence without analyzing it carefully. When writing the body of an argument essay, be sure to use a tone appropriate for your audience. The tone you choose will depend on the issue, the claim, and whether your audience agrees, disagrees, or is neutral. For a weighty issue, such as use of the death penalty, a serious, even somber, tone would be appropriate. For a claim that calls for action, an energetic or enthusiastic tone would help motivate readers. For a disagreeing audience, you might use a friendly, nonthreatening tone.

3. THE CONCLUSION REINFORCES THE THESIS, MAKES A FINAL APPEAL, AND MAY URGE READERS TO ACTION

An argument may end in a number of ways, such as by restating the thesis, making a final appeal to values, projecting into the future, urging a specific action, or calling for further research.

Reading | Writing   When reading the conclusion of an argument essay, ask yourself, Am I convinced? Why, or why not? When writing the conclusion of an argument essay, reread your essay and ask yourself: Have I provided convincing evidence? What final statement will make my claim stick in my reader's mind or push neutral or disagreeing audiences toward agreement? Revise your conclusion as necessary.

A Model Argument Essay

Title

Eating Meat for the Environment
Lisa M. Hamilton

Lisa M. Hamilton is a writer and photographer who focuses on agricultural issues. She is the author of *Deeply Rooted: Unconventional Farmers in the Age of Agribusiness* (2009) and *Farming to Create Heaven on Earth* (2007). Her works have been published in *The Nation, Harper's, National Geographic Traveler, Orion,* and *Audubon,* where this essay originally appeared.

Introduction
Background
information: A
proposal — to fight
global warming, eat
less meat.
Background
information:
Statistics show
livestock contribution
to greenhouse gases.

In fall 2008 Rajendra Pachauri, head of the United Nations Intergovernmental Panel on Climate Change, offered a simple directive for combating global warming: Eat less meat.
    Critics pointed out that the economist and environmental scientist is a vegetarian, but the numbers back up his idea. A 2006 U.N. report found that 18 percent of the world's greenhouse gas emissions come from raising livestock for food. While Pachauri's advice is good overall, I would propose a corollary: At the same time that we begin eating less meat, we should be eating more of it.

Thesis: We should eat more meat — but pasture-raised meat.

More of a different kind, that is. Animals reared on organic pasture have a different climate equation from those raised in confinement on imported feed. Much of the emissions associated with livestock production come as the result of dismantling the natural farm system and replacing it with an artificial environment. For instance, in large-scale confinement systems, or CAFOs (concentrated animal feeding operations), manure has nowhere to go. Managed in human-made lagoons, it produces millions of tons of methane and nitrous oxide every year through anaerobic decomposition. On pasture, that same manure is simply assimilated back into the soil with a carbon cost close to zero.

Reason 1: Manure of pasture-raised animals goes back to the soil, with no carbon cost.

Opposing view: just the lesser of two evils

Some would argue that pasture-raised animals are just the lesser of two evils. Given that livestock make for some emissions no matter where they're raised—cows, for instance, like any other ruminant, produce methane as a by-product of their digestion— wouldn't it be better to have no livestock at all? Not according to farmer Jason Mann, who grows produce and raises chickens, hogs, and cattle on pasture outside Athens, Georgia. In the age of CAFOs, many people have come to regard livestock as a problem to be solved. But on a sustainable farm system like his, animals are an essential part of the equation.

Refutation: According to Jason Mann, a farmer, animals are an essential part of the equation.

Mann likens his farm to a bank account: Every time he harvests an ear of corn or a head of lettuce, he withdraws from the soil's fertility. If he doesn't redeposit that fertility, his account will hit zero. He could certainly truck in compost from 250 miles away or apply chemical fertilizers to make his vegetables grow. But by his own carbon calculation the best option is to return that fertility to the soil by using livestock, particularly cows. They do more than keep his soil rich. When cattle are managed properly, they can boost soil's ability to sequester carbon. Their manure adds organic matter to the soil, their grazing symbiotically encourages plant growth, and their heavy hooves help break down dead plant residue. Some proponents argue that highly managed, intensive grazing can shift cattle's carbon count so dramatically that the animals actually help reduce greenhouse gases. . . .

5

Reason 2: Manure from pasture-raised animals returns fertility to the soil.

Reason 3: Managed properly, these animals can reduce greenhouse gases.

In addition to completing the farm's ecology, Mann's livestock also complement the farm's economy with critical revenue for the real bank account—which keeps the operation afloat in a way that lettuce alone cannot. But that happens only when animals become meat. With the exception of laying hens, if animals stand around eating all day but never produce more than manure, they are a

Reason 4: Selling animals for meat helps farmers like Mann to keep their farms going.

net loss. In order for livestock to be worthwhile in a whole farm system, they must be eaten. For Mann's farm to be sustainable, his neighbors must buy and eat his meat.

Reason 5: By buying pasture-raised meat we can help this kind of farming to expand.

The same applies on a larger scale: In order for pasture-based livestock to become a significant part of the meat industry, we need to eat more of its meat, not less. As it is, grass-fed beef accounts for less than 1 percent of U.S. beef consumption, and the numbers for chicken and pork hardly register. Even where the industry is growing, it is stunted by inadequate infrastructure. The greatest challenge is a lack of small-scale slaughterhouses, but it also suffers from a dearth of research, outreach for new producers, and investment in breeding for pasture-based systems. And those things will change only as the market grows.

Evidence: statistic that now less than 1% of meat in US is pasture raised

Conclusion: refers back to opening, with a call to action

So by all means follow Rajendra Pachauri's suggestion and enjoy a meatless Monday. But on Tuesday, have a grass-fed burger—and feel good about it.

Emotional appeal: By eating this meat, you'll help the environment.

Understanding, Analyzing, and Evaluating Argument Essays

In reading and writing argument essays, your goal is to get beyond mere competence: That is, you want to be able to do more than merely understand the content of the essays you're reading or convey just your basic ideas to the audience you're writing for.

 Reading | Writing   Truly skillful reading and writing require the abilities to **understand, analyze,** *and* **evaluate** material. These abilities are important to you as a reader because they give you a systematic, thorough method of examining a reading. They're important to you as a writer because they help you decide what to revise, rewrite, drop, and replace, allowing you to produce a well-written, persuasive essay.

Understanding an Argument Essay

Reading arguments requires careful attention and analysis, so you should plan on reading an argument several times. Preview it to identify the issue and assess the overall level of difficulty. Read it once to get an overview. Then read it several times more to analyze and critique it. As you read and reread, use the skills you learned in Chapter 2 and look for answers to the following questions.

- **What does the title suggest about the focus and purpose of the essay?** A title such as "Voting: Why Not Make It Mandatory?" clearly suggests the writer will advocate mandatory voting, while a title such as "Confusion in the Streets: A Call for Caring Treatment of Street People" will urge action on behalf of the homeless.

- **Who is the author, what are his or her credentials, and where was the essay published?** Some authors and publications are known for a particular point of view, so be sure to read all headnotes, footnotes, and citations for information related to point of view, as well as to determine when the essay was first published and what qualifies the author to write on the subject. If the publication or author has a particular viewpoint or audience—such as liberal or conservative—you can sometimes predict the stand an essay will take on a particular issue.

- **What is the issue?** Highlight the issue, and notice how the writer introduces it and any background information. Highlight definitions of key terms.

- **What do you already know about the issue?** Before reading, create two columns for pros and cons about the issue, and list as many ideas as you can in each column. By thinking this through before reading, you will be less influenced by the writer's appeals and more likely to maintain an objective, critical viewpoint.

- **What is the claim?** Highlight the writer's claim. Notice any qualifying or limiting words.

- **What reasons and evidence does the author offer?** Study and highlight the types of evidence used to support the claim—facts, statistics, expert opinion, examples, and personal experience. Add annotations indicating

Understanding in Action

Following is one student's summary of the introduction of "Eating Meat for the Environment," including its thesis. Use it as a model to write your own summary of the whole essay.

Based on evidence that almost one-fifth of greenhouse gases are from livestock being raised for meat, the United Nations recommended that people eat less meat. The author agrees with this recommendation but says we should also eat more meat that comes from animals that are pasture raised.

your initial reactions to or questions about the reasons or evidence. Make marginal notes summarizing reasons and key supporting evidence.

- **Which terms are unfamiliar or undefined?** Because an argument can depend on terms used in specific ways with specific meanings, highlight key terms and make sure to note exactly how they are defined.

- **Does the writer acknowledge, accommodate, or refute opposing views?** Highlight each instance. It may help to create a graphic organizer to keep track of the author's view as well as his or her treatment of opposing positions. Figure 18.2 is a graphic organizer for "Eating Meat for the Environment."

Analyzing an Argument Essay

Analyzing an argument essay involves examining the reasons and evidence provided to support the claim. Use the following questions to guide your analysis.

- **Is the claim narrow and specific?** The claim should be narrow enough to be fully addressed and supported in the essay.

- **What is the author's purpose?** Ask yourself, Why does the writer want to convince me of this? What, if anything, does he or she stand to gain? If a writer stands to profit personally from the acceptance of an argument, be particularly cautious and critical.

Analysis in Action

Here the student who wrote the summary for Understanding in Action annotated the first two paragraphs of the essay. Annotate the rest of "Eating Meat for the Environment" on your own.

Can the U.N. tell people to do this? And what's the connection? Meaning Pachauri? 18% is a lot!	In fall 2008 Rajendra Pachauri, head of the United Nations Intergovernmental Panel on Climate Change, offered a simple directive for combating global warming: Eat less meat.
What is a corollary? This doesn't seem possible!	Critics pointed out that the economist and environmental scientist is a vegetarian, but the numbers back up his idea. A 2006 U.N. report found that 18 percent of the world's greenhouse gas emissions come from raising livestock for food. While Pachauri's advice is good overall, I would propose a corollary: At the same time that we begin eating less meat, we should be eating more of it.

Figure 18.2 Graphic Organizer for "Eating Meat for the Environment"

Title	"Eating Meat for the Environment"
Introduction	**Issue:** Eating meat and its effect on global warming
	Background: U.N. report showing 18% of greenhouse gases are from raising livestock for food, and call to eat less meat
	Claim (thesis): We should eat more meat from pasture-raised animals.
Body paragraphs	**Reason 1:** Unlike CAFO animals, pasture-raised animals are not bad for the environment.
	Evidence: Manure of animals raised on CAFOs produces greenhouse gases; manure from pasture-raised animals goes back in the soil.
	Opposing view: Pasture-raised animals are just the lesser of two evils.
	Refutation/Reason 2: Pasture-raised animals are actually good for the environment, perhaps even reducing greenhouse gases.
	Evidence: From Jason Mann, who raises crops and livestock sustainably: Pasture-raised animals return fertility to the soil; their grazing and hooves result in better plant growth.
	Reason 3: Sale of meat from pasture-raised animals helps make environmentally sustainable farms economically profitable.
	Evidence: Vegetables and animal manure alone wouldn't support these farms.
	Reason 4: To encourage pasture-based livestock, and get its benefits, we need to support the farmers by eating more of their meat.
	Evidence: Today less than 1% of U.S. beef, pork, and chicken comes from pasture-raised animals.
	Evidence: The pasture-raised livestock industry has many infrastructure needs that require more of a market.
Conclusion	**Emotional appeal:** Eating (the right) meat can lead to feelings of doing the environmentally right thing, rather than of guilt.
	Returns to idea in introduction of eating less meat (a viewpoint that's been accommodated) and to opening claim, urging readers to eat pasture-raised meat

- **Is each reason supported with convincing, detailed evidence?** The evidence should be presented in a clear, understandable way.

- **Are key terms defined clearly and used consistently?** Each term should have one specific meaning that is used throughout the essay.

- **Is the argument presented in a logical and organized way?** Expect authors to use paragraphing, headings, and transitional words and phrases to help readers follow the presentation of ideas.

- **Does the author provide source citations where needed?** Sources, when used, should be properly and correctly documented. Both paraphrases and quotations should be cited.

- **Are opposing viewpoints addressed?** The author should recognize, accommodate, or refute opposing ideas.

▐ *Evaluating an Argument Essay*

Evaluating an argument essay involves judging how accurately and effectively the author presents and supports his or her claim. Use the following questions to guide your evaluation of argument essays.

- **Is the claim reasonable and logical?** The claim should be realistic, reasonable, and practical.

- **Is the evidence relevant, accurate, current, and typical?** Facts offered as evidence should be accurate, current, complete, and taken from reliable sources.

- **Is there sufficient evidence?** The author should provide a sufficient number of facts, statistics, examples, and so forth to fully support each reason. A variety of types of evidence should be offered.

Evaluation in Action

The same student who wrote the summary and the annotation also wrote the following response to the essay's argument. Use it as a springboard to write your own response to "Eating Meat for the Environment."

> Since I'm a vegetarian, this isn't an easy argument for me to agree with! I am impressed by the way Hamilton shows that if farmers raise animals for meat the right way, this can even reduce greenhouse gases. But if 99% of people are buying regular meat that isn't raised this way (maybe partly because they can't afford pasture-raised meat), it might be that there's no way to change things enough to make eating meat be good for the environment.

- **Does the writer rely on emotional appeals?** Appeals are a legitimate part of an argument, but the writer should not attempt to manipulate your emotions to distract you from the issue and the evidence.

- **Are opposing viewpoints dealt with fairly?** The writer should not denegrate or ridicule opposing ideas. Instead, he or she should present reasoned responses to the ideas of others. When refuting opposing viewpoints, the writer should clearly show why they are wrong or inappropriate.

- **Does the author avoid errors in reasoning?** If a writer makes errors in reasoning, you have the right to question his or her credibility.

Readings for Practice, Ideas for Writing

Globe High School Censors Its Student Newspaper

Sarah Fenske is editor of *LA Weekly*, a paper that covers local news, music, movies, restaurants, and events in Los Angeles. She previously served as managing editor at the *Riverfront Times* in St. Louis and as a columnist in Phoenix. This article, published in 2008 by the *Phoenix New Times*, comes from her days as a columnist.

Reading Tip

As you read, identify the writer's attitude toward Globe High School's student newspaper as compared to her attitude toward the Channel One news broadcasts students watch daily.

Previewing the Reading

Preview the reading using the guidelines on pages 23–24, and then answer the following questions.

1. What is the issue this reading explores?
2. Why is the writer concerned about what happened at Globe High School?

SARAH FENSKE

Globe High School Censors Its Student Newspaper

Every morning, students at Globe High School are forced to watch TV.

Sounds weird, I know, but it's not unusual. An estimated six million kids—one-third of all American teens—start their day with a twelve-minute news program broadcast by a company called Channel One.

The deal is a bit tawdry[1]: Channel One donates TVs to school districts and, in return, the districts promise to

force their students to watch the insipid[2] broadcast—and, of course, commercial after commercial. Buy Skittles. Drink Coke. Lately, Channel One has also been broadcasting ads for the TRUTH, the ten-year-old but still oh-so-edgy ad campaign warning teens about Big Tobacco's skullduggery. The latest TRUTH ads are called "Whudafxup," and the word appears prominently in most of the spots.

Controversial, right? With that f-bomb tucked into the slang you'd think the puritans would be raising hell. But at Globe High School, the controversy came only because a student dared to—gasp!—write about the campaign in the school newspaper.

After the December 7 issue of the   5 Globe High School *Papoose* was

[1] **tawdry** Gaudy, showy, cheap.

[2] **insipid** Lacking taste, interest, or stimulation.

propaganda[3] featuring the word *Whudafxup*, but if a student dares to repeat the word while critiquing the propaganda in question, seven hundred newspapers need to be destroyed? And high school administrators wonder why students are so sullen these days. Pretty hard to smile when your education is being managed by idiots.

High school students don't enjoy all the rights that adults do. They can't drink and can't vote. Most of them can't even buy a pack of those demon cigarettes. But they do have the freedom of speech. The First Amendment applies even to high school newspapers—and when I consulted a lawyer who specialized in the issue, I was surprised to learn just how many rights high school journalists have.

Frank LoMonte is the executive director of the Student Press Law Center in Arlington, Virginia. He says that high schools have greater latitude[4] to censor publications than, say, colleges, "but that is not unlimited. . . . Even in a situation where a school sets itself up as the absolute arbiter[5] of what goes into a student newspaper, they can't just censor willy-nilly," LoMonte tells me. For twenty-five years, U.S. Supreme Court precedent has held that schools censoring student publications must have a "valid educational purpose," LoMonte says. If the students have done a terrible job and the paper is littered with grammatical errors, for example, the school can intervene. Or if, say, the students wanted to publish a graphic sexual description, the school could argue that

printed, but before the student journalists could begin distribution, the principal announced that he was confiscating all seven hundred copies and destroying them. Future issues of the paper, the principal warned, would be subject to strict review. The paper's coeditors, seniors Nathan O'Neal and Shelby McLoughlin, say that they were given two reasons for the school's censorship. One was an editorial written by O'Neal, who described a "sullen and gloomy atmosphere" in the hallways and a lack of motivation among both students and teachers. The nerve of that kid!

The other problem, O'Neal and McLoughlin say, was a headline: "Whudafxup with that?" Staff writer Taylor Rainwater had written an essay criticizing the TRUTH campaign—and dared to put the ad's title in the story's headline. That was inappropriate, the students were told. So, it's appropriate for Globe students to be subjected to

[3] **propaganda** The organized spread of information intended to promote or damage its subject.
[4] **latitude** Freedom.
[5] **arbiter** Person in control.

Continued >

it needs to protect its students and remove the offensive story.

But destroying the entire print run because a student used a word frequently shown on classroom TVs? That's a hard sell. For that matter, so is banning an editorial just because it has a negative take on the school. If administrators allow a student newspaper to write positive editorials about school functions, LoMonte says, it needs to allow negative ones, too. "If a student wrote an editorial saying that school spirit is at an all-time high, I have a feeling that editorial would be published," he says. "From the facts as you describe them, the school engaged in the most noxious form of censorship."

10   Suffice it to say, Sherrill Stephens, the principal at Globe High School, doesn't quite see things this way. Globe is a small town, with just about eight thousand residents, and it seems even smaller by virtue of its isolation. Tucked into the Pinal Mountains, at the edge of the Tonto National Forest, it feels a world away from the bustling Valley—never mind that it takes only an hour and a half to drive there. Principal Stephens agreed to take my call, after an admirably short period on hold. But when he got on the phone, and I again explained my purpose, Stephens's befuddlement was clear.

Why, he asked, would anyone in Phoenix care about the *Papoose*? "It's really not much of a story," Stephens drawled, good-old-boy style. Then he refused to tell me why he ordered the issue's destruction. "If you saw it, you'd know why," he said. I told him I had seen it. And I simply couldn't fathom what the problem was. "The superintendent and I decided it was not appropriate," he said, again refusing to give particulars. "There were inappropriate things. We are in a small

town. That is why. And we're doing a lot of good things here." Maybe that's true. Maybe the football team notched some wins and the cheerleaders are pretty. But Globe High School is certainly not teaching its students much about good journalism—much less critical thinking.

The *Papoose* used to come out five or six times a year. I looked at a few years of back issues, and I was impressed. It's an attractive tabloid, with design good enough for a small college newspaper. It wins awards—including, last year, second place in "overall excellence" from the Arizona Newspaper Association's high school division. The two coeditors are serious enough about their work that both attended journalism workshops during last year's summer break. This year, though, the *Papoose* has struggled. The longtime adviser retired, and last semester, the paper was stuck with a new teacher just arrived from the Philippines, a guy who made it clear he had little interest in newspapers. It didn't help that the school district auctioned off the newspaper's Macs and replaced them with a new computer system incapable of printing the newspaper's layouts, coeditors O'Neal and McLoughlin tell me.

It wasn't until December that the students managed to complete their first issue. Just getting it to the presses was something of a triumph. It's a shame that the rest of the school never got to see it. What's even worse: O'Neal and McLoughlin tell me their next attempt at an issue didn't even get that far. After the December 7 issue was junked, they say, they were told that the next issues would have to be vetted by no fewer than four teachers and administrators—and one school office worker. Not surprisingly, the late December issue didn't even get through half that roster before someone objected to an editorial about the Plan B "morning after" pill. That issue has yet to be printed. (Principal Stephens denied knowing anything about its existence, much less the controversy over the Plan B editorial.) McLoughlin and O'Neal say it's no longer timely; they've given up on getting it out.

And here's the kicker. Now, the students say, the school is suggesting that its journalism class ought to help the district to publish a newsletter instead of putting out a real newspaper. "They tried to assign us to do articles about the school and articles that could go out to the parents," McLoughlin says, rolling her eyes. "They wanted a public relations tool," O'Neal says.

15   LoMonte, of the Student Press Law Center, says the students could have a decent lawsuit over the censored issues—and that there are plenty of lawyers around the country who take cases like this pro bono.[6] God Bless America, eh?

[6] **pro bono** Services performed without charge.

But neither editor wants to pursue it. They're getting ready to graduate, and they can't wait to get out of Globe to study journalism at Arizona State or, in O'Neal's case, perhaps, the University of Southern California. McLoughlin says, "I want to see justice done, but . . ." "But we only have four months left," O'Neal finishes. I don't blame them for moving on. Still, it's unsettling that the students at Globe High School got to see plenty of commercials this year but, so far, haven't seen a single issue of their supposedly student-run newspaper.

"We are constantly being preached 'professionalism' and responsibility, but how can we be expected to perform to these standards if the boundaries are constantly being altered?" That's the last line of Nathan O'Neal's editorial from December 7, the editorial Globe High School wasn't allowed to read. Principal Stephens may not agree, but I think it's a really good question—and it's safe to say the students aren't going to find the answer on Channel One.

Understanding the Reading

1. **Thesis** Summarize Fenske's claim, or thesis. Where does she state it most directly?

2. **Reasons** On what primary basis does Fenske object to the school's action in censoring the student newspaper?

3. **Evidence** What evidence does Fenske offer to support her argument against censorship of high-school newspapers?

4. **Opposing views** Where does Fenske present the opposition to her argument? How detailed is the presentation of this opposing view?

5. **Meaning** Why was it difficult for the staff to put out a subsequent issue of the school newspaper? What did school administrators want them to work on instead?

6. **Vocabulary** Using context clues (p. 34), define each of the following words as it is used in the essay, consulting a dictionary if necessary: *skullduggery* (3),

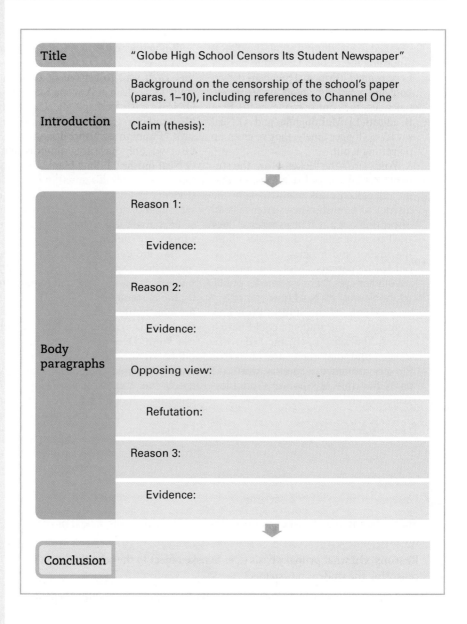

Title	"Globe High School Censors Its Student Newspaper"
Introduction	Background on the censorship of the school's paper (paras. 1–10), including references to Channel One
	Claim (thesis):
Body paragraphs	Reason 1:
	Evidence:
	Reason 2:
	Evidence:
	Opposing view:
	Refutation:
	Reason 3:
	Evidence:
Conclusion	

confiscating (5), *sullen* (5), *subjected* (6), *critiquing* (6), *noxious* (9), *befuddlement* (10), *fathom* (11), and *vetted* (13).

7. **Organization** To help understand the essay's organization, complete the graphic organizer above.

8. **Visuals** Describe the cartoon that accompanies this piece. What does it depict? What claim does it make?

Analyzing the Reading

1. **Introduction** Why does Fenske open with a detailed presentation of how Channel One is used in high-school classrooms? Why is this point important?

2. **Evidence** How does Fenske produce her primary evidence that the school acted inappropriately in censoring the student newspaper?

3. **Presentation** Why does Fenske take the time she does in paragraph 10 to describe the town of Globe?

4. **Audience** How sympathetic do you think Fenske expects her readers to be toward her argument? What makes you think so?

5. **Language** In paragraph 11, Fenske writes that while responding to a question from her, Principal Stephens "drawled, good-old-boy style." What is she suggesting about his response?

Evaluating the Reading

1. **Issue** Fenske obviously thinks that censorship of student newspapers is a significant issue. Do you agree?

2. **Evidence** Do you think that Fenske effectively makes a case against censorship of student newspapers? Does she rely too much on quoting Frank LoMonte, or does she present enough other evidence to convince you?

3. **Emotional appeals** What does Fenske's characterization of the paper's co-editors and the school's principal contribute to the point of her argument? What does she make you feel about each?

Discussing the Reading

1. What is your opinion about companies like Channel One that broadcast into schools—including commercials and editorial content—in exchange for providing TVs for so-called educational use?

2. Do you think that school administrators have an absolute right to control publication of student speech? What boundaries, if any, would you set?

3. In your opinion should coeditors O'Neal and McLoughlin have pursued their school's censorship issue further? Or were they right in just "moving on"?

Writing about the Reading

1. **Paragraph** Write a paragraph summarizing the argument made here against censorship of school newspapers. Use quotations from the essay that help make your point. (Hint: State your claim clearly. You might open with it as a topic sentence or close with it.)

2. **Paragraph** What do you think students should do when they feel school administrators are treating them unfairly? Write a paragraph arguing for a specific course of action in such situations.

3. **Essay** What rights do you think high-school students should be granted in their academic life? Should administrators have total control? Or should there be a give-and-take between administrators and students? Write an essay arguing about the degree to which students should have rights in high school.

Why Would Anyone Miss War?

Sebastian Junger is the best-selling author of *The Perfect Storm*, *A Death in Belmont*, *Fire*, and *WAR*. He also codirected the documentary *Restrepo*, which won a Grand Jury Prize at the 2010 Sundance Film Festival. This opinion piece appeared in the *New York Times* in 2011.

Reading Tip

As you read, highlight those sentences in the text that best summarize the writer's main argument.

Previewing the Reading

Preview the reading using the guidelines on pages 23–24, and then answer the following questions.

1. What war is this essay primarily concerned with?
2. What is the writer's attitude toward war?

SEBASTIAN JUNGER

Why Would Anyone Miss War?

Several years ago I spent time with a platoon of army infantry at a remote outpost in eastern Afghanistan, and after the deployment I was surprised that only one of the soldiers chose to leave the military at the end of his contract; many others re-upped and eventually went on to fight for another year in the same area. The soldier who got out, Brendan O'Byrne, remained a good friend of mine as he struggled to fit in to civilian life back home.

About a year later I invited Brendan to a dinner party, and a woman asked him if he missed anything at all about life at the outpost. It was a good question: The platoon had endured a year without Internet, running water, or hot food and had been in more combat than almost any platoon in the United States

military. By any measure it was hell, but Brendan didn't hesitate: "Ma'am," he said, "I miss almost all of it."

Civilians are often confused, if not appalled,[1] by that answer. The idea that a psychologically healthy person could miss war seems an affront to the idea that war is evil. Combat is supposed to feel bad because undeniably bad things happen in it, but a fully human reaction is far more complex than that. If we civilians don't understand that complexity, we won't do a very good job of bringing these people home and making a place for them in our society.

My understanding of that truth came partly from my own time in Afghanistan and partly from my conversations with a Vietnam veteran named Karl Marlantes, who wrote about his experiences in a devastating novel called *Matterhorn*. Some time after I met Karl, a woman asked me why soldiers "compartmentalize"[2] the experience of war, and I

[1] **appalled** Overcome with shock or horror.
[2] **compartmentalize** Separate or set aside from other experiences.

Continued >

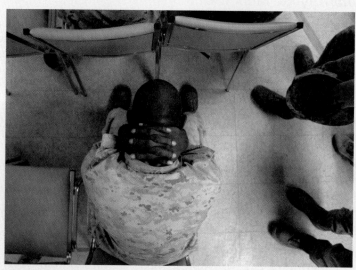

Marine waits to take psychological tests at the Marine Corps Air Ground Combat Center in Twentynine Palms, CA.

answered as I imagined Karl might have: because society does. We avoid any direct look at the reality of war. And both sides of the political spectrum indulge in this; liberals tend to be scandalized that war can be tremendously alluring to young men, and conservatives rarely acknowledge that war kills far more innocent people than guilty ones. Soldiers understand both of these things but don't know how to talk about them when met with blank stares from friends and family back home.

5   "For a while I started thinking that God hated me because I had sinned," Brendan told me after he got back from Afghanistan. "Everyone tells you that you did what you had to do, and I just hate that comment because I didn't have to do any of it. I didn't have to join the army; I didn't have to become airborne infantry. But I did. And that comment—'You did what you had to do'—just drives me insane. Because is that what God's going to say—'You

did what you had to do? Welcome to heaven?' I don't think so."

If society were willing to acknowledge the very real horrors of war—even a just war, as I believe some are—then men like Brendan would not have to struggle with the gap between their worldview and ours. Every year on the anniversary of D-Day, for example, we acknowledge the heroism and sacrifice of those who stormed the beaches of Normandy. But for a full and honest understanding of that war, we must also remember the firebombing of Dresden, Frankfurt, and Hamburg that killed as many as 100,000 Germans, as well as both conventional and nuclear strikes against Japan that killed hundreds of thousands more.

Photographs taken after Allied air raids in Germany show piles of bodies 10 or 15 feet high being soaked in gasoline for burning. At first you think you're looking at images from Nazi concentration camps, but you're not—you're looking at people we killed.

I am in no way questioning the strategic necessity of those actions; frankly, few of us are qualified to do so after so much time. I am simply pointing out that if we as a nation avoid coming to terms with events like these, the airmen who drop the bombs have a much harder time coming to terms with them as individuals. And they bear almost all the psychic harm.

Change history a bit, however, and imagine those men coming back after World War II to a country that has collectively taken responsibility for the decision to firebomb German cities. (Firebombing inflicted mass civilian casualties and nearly wiped out cities.) This would be no admission of wrongdoing—many wars, like Afghanistan and World War II, were triggered by attacks against us. It would simply be a way to commemorate the loss of life, as one might after a terrible earthquake or a flood. Imagine how much better the bomber crews of World War II might have handled their confusion and grief if the entire country had been struggling with those same feelings. Imagine how much better they might have fared if there had been a monument for them to visit that commemorated all the people they were ordered to kill.

10   At first, such a monument might be controversial—but so was the Vietnam memorial on the Mall in Washington. Eventually, however, that memorial proved to be extremely therapeutic for veterans struggling with feelings of guilt and loss after the war.

Every war kills civilians, and thankfully our military now goes to great lengths to keep those deaths to a minimum. Personally, I believe that our involvement in Afghanistan has saved far more civilian lives than it has cost. I was there in the 1990s; I know how horrific that civil war was. But that knowledge is of faint comfort to the American soldiers I know who mistakenly emptied their rifles into a truck full of civilians because they thought they were about to be blown up. A monument to the civilian dead of Iraq and Afghanistan would not only provide comfort to these young men but also signal to the world that our nation understands the cost of war.

It doesn't matter that most civilian deaths in Iraq and Afghanistan were caused by insurgent[3] attacks; if our soldiers died for freedom there—as presidents are fond of saying—then those people did as well. They, too, are among the casualties of 9/11. Nearly a decade after that terrible day, what a powerful message we would send to the world by honoring those deaths with our grief.

[3] **insurgent** A person who fights against lawful authority.

Understanding the Reading

1. **Thesis** What is the thesis of Junger's argument, and where does he state it most directly and completely?

2. **Reasons** What reasons for his argument does Junger offer in paragraph 3?

3. **Evidence** What is the point of Junger's inclusion of two quotations from Brendan O'Byrne in paragraphs 2 and 5? How do they support his claim in paragraph 3?

4. **Viewpoint** Why does Junger feel as he does about honoring those killed by U.S. forces? Where do his sympathies lie?

5. **Conclusion** What is Junger's underlying point in his final sentence about "what a powerful message we would send to the world"?

Analyzing the Reading

1. **Introduction** How does the opening paragraph establish Junger's relationship to the subject?

2. **Presentation** What contrast does Junger describe in paragraph 4, and how does it relate to his topic?

3. **Evidence** Why does Junger devote so much time to World War II in paragraphs 6–9?

4. **Visuals** How does the photograph that accompanies this piece relate to the author's argument? How does it help Junger present his argument and contribute to the tone of the piece?

5. **Conclusion** Why does Junger make the point in his final paragraph that "most civilian deaths in Iraq and Afghanistan were caused by insurgent attacks"?

Evaluating the Reading

1. **Title** How well do you think the title of the essay predicts and summarizes its argument?

2. **Language** In paragraph 3, Junger presents the idea that most people see war as "evil," and in paragraph 5 returning soldier O'Byrne is quoted as wondering whether he had "sinned" in combat. How appropriate is such language to the point Junger is making?

3. **Main point** Do you think Junger's thesis about creating a memorial for those killed by American soldiers in wartime has merit? Do you think erecting such a memorial would help achieve his stated goals?

Discussing the Reading

1. Why do you think Brendan O'Byrne says he misses "almost all" of his time in combat (para. 2)? Are you "appalled" by this?

2. Do you, as Junger suggests in paragraph 4, "avoid any direct look at the reality of war"? Why, or why not?

3. Junger is essentially supportive of the actions of the military, even if those actions result in civilian casualties. What's your response to this?

Writing about the Reading

1. **Paragraph** In a paragraph, respond to what Brendan O'Byrne has to say about his wartime experiences in paragraphs 2 and 5. Do you think he did "what he had to do"?

2. **Internet research** Junger makes the point in his opening paragraph that returning veterans face numerous difficulties when they come home. Research this issue, and then write an essay arguing for specific policies that would ease their transition.

3. **Essay** Is there such a thing as a "just war," or do you believe that war is inherently "evil"? In an essay, argue for your own beliefs about the necessity or the futility of war.

I Have a Dream

Martin Luther King Jr. was one of the planners and organizers of the 1963 March on Washington for Jobs and Freedom to promote civil rights for African Americans. That year, King was heavily involved in the nonviolent protests against segregation in Birmingham, Alabama, where peaceful marchers had faced police dogs and fire hoses turned on them by order of the city's police chief. On August 28, 1963, King was the final speaker at the march. He roused the crowd with a stirring speech, "I Have a Dream," on the steps of the Lincoln Memorial. This speech in whole or in part has been widely published in newspapers, including the *New York Times* and *Washington Post*. As you read the speech, which reportedly was improvised, note King's masterful use of repetition. In addition, pay attention to the imagery he uses to include all Americans in his vision.

Reading Tip

This is a famous speech that many people have heard many times. As you read, carefully track the types of appeals King uses.

Previewing the Reading

Preview the reading using the guidelines on pages 23–24 to discover what the dream referred to in the title is.

MARTIN LUTHER KING JR.

I Have a Dream[1]

Five score years ago, a great American, in whose symbolic shadow we stand, signed the Emancipation Proclamation.[2] This momentous decree came as a great beacon light of hope to millions of Negro slaves who had been seared in the flames of withering injustice. It came as a joyous daybreak to end the long night of captivity.

But one hundred years later, we must face the tragic fact that the Negro is still not free. One hundred years later, the life of the Negro is still sadly crippled by the manacles of segregation and the chains of discrimination. One hundred years later, the Negro lives on a lonely island of poverty in the midst of a vast ocean of material prosperity. One hundred years later, the Negro is still languishing in the corners of American society and finds himself an exile in his own land. So we have come here today to dramatize an appalling condition.

In a sense we have come to our nation's Capitol to cash a check. When the architects of our republic wrote the magnificent words of the Constitution and the Declaration of Independence, they were signing a promissory note to which every American was to fall heir. This note was a promise that all men would be guaranteed the unalienable

[1] You can watch a video of the speech on YouTube and listen to the audio version at http://www.americanrhetoric.com/speeches /mlkihaveadream.htm.
[2] **Emancipation Proclamation** 1862 act issued by Abraham Lincoln during the Civil War to free the slaves in states that had seceded from the Union.

rights of life, liberty, and the pursuit of happiness.

It is obvious today that America has defaulted on this promissory note insofar as her citizens of color are concerned. Instead of honoring this sacred obligation, America has given the Negro people a bad check; a check which has come back marked "insufficient funds." But we refuse to believe that the bank of justice is bankrupt. We refuse to believe that there are insufficient funds in the great vaults of opportunity of this nation. So we have come to cash this check—a check that will give us upon demand the riches of freedom and the security of justice. We have also come to this hallowed spot to remind America of the fierce urgency of *now*. This is no time to engage in the luxury of cooling off or to take the tranquilizing drug of gradualism. *Now* is the time to make real the promises of Democracy. *Now* is the time to rise from the dark and desolate valley of segregation to the sunlit path of racial justice. *Now* is the time to open the doors of opportunity to all of God's children. *Now* is the time to lift our nation from the quicksands of racial injustice to the solid rock of brotherhood.

5   It would be fatal for the nation to overlook the urgency of the moment and to underestimate the determination of the Negro. This sweltering summer of the Negro's legitimate discontent will not pass until there is an invigorating autumn of freedom and equality. 1963 is not an end, but a beginning. Those who hope that the Negro needed to blow off steam and will now be content will have a rude awakening if the nation returns to business as usual. There will be neither rest nor tranquility in America until the Negro is granted his citizenship rights. The whirlwinds of revolt will continue to shake the foundations of our nation until the bright day of justice emerges.

But there is something I must say to my people who stand on the warm threshold which leads into the palace of justice. In the process of gaining our rightful place we must not be guilty of wrongful deeds. Let us not seek to satisfy our thirst for freedom by drinking from the cup of bitterness and hatred. We must forever conduct our struggle on the high plane of dignity and discipline. We must not allow our creative protest to degenerate into physical violence. Again and again we must rise to the majestic heights of meeting physical force with soul force. The marvelous new militancy which has engulfed the Negro community must not lead us to a distrust of all white people, for many of our white brothers, as evidenced by their presence here today, have come to realize that their destiny is tied up with our destiny and their freedom is inextricably bound to our freedom. We cannot walk alone.

And as we walk, we must make the pledge that we shall march ahead. We cannot turn back. There are those who are asking the devotees of civil rights, "When will you be satisfied?" We can never be satisfied as long as the Negro is the victim of the unspeakable horrors of police brutality. We can never be satisfied as long as our bodies, heavy with the fatigue of travel, cannot gain lodging in the motels of the highways and the hotels of the cities. We cannot be satisfied as long as the Negro's basic mobility is from a smaller ghetto to a larger one. We can never be satisfied as long as a Negro in Mississippi cannot vote and a Negro in New York believes he has nothing for which to vote. No, no, we are not satisfied, and we will not be satisfied until justice rolls down like waters and righteousness like a mighty stream.

Continued >

I am not unmindful that some of you have come here out of great trials and tribulations. Some of you have come fresh from narrow jail cells. Some of you have come from areas where your quest for freedom left you battered by the storms of persecution and staggered by the winds of police brutality. You have been the veterans of creative suffering. Continue to work with the faith that unearned suffering is redemptive.

Go back to Mississippi, go back to Alabama, go back to South Carolina, go back to Georgia, go back to Louisiana, go back to the slums and ghettoes of our northern cities, knowing that somehow this situation can and will be changed. Let us not wallow in the valley of despair.

10   I say to you today, my friends, that in spite of the difficulties and frustrations of the moment I still have a dream. It is a dream deeply rooted in the American dream.

I have a dream that one day this nation will rise up and live out the true meaning of its creed: "We hold these truths to be self-evident; that all men are created equal."[3]

I have a dream that one day on the red hills of Georgia the sons of former slaves and the sons of former slaveowners will be able to sit down together at the table of brotherhood.

I have a dream that the state of Mississippi, a desert state sweltering with the heat of injustice and oppression, will be transformed into an oasis of freedom and justice.

I have a dream that my four little children will one day live in a nation where they will not be judged by the color of their skin but by the content of their character.

I have a dream today.   15

I have a dream that the state of Alabama, whose governor's lips are presently dripping with the words of interposition[4] and nullification, will be transformed into a situation where little black boys and black girls will be able to join hands with little white boys and white girls and walk together as sisters and brothers.

I have a dream today.

I have a dream that one day every valley shall be exalted, every hill and mountain shall be made low, the rough places will be made plain, and the crooked places will be made straight, and the glory of the Lord shall be revealed, and all flesh shall see it together.

This is our hope. This is the faith with which I return to the South. With this faith we will be able to hew out of the mountain of despair a stone of hope. With this faith we will be able to transform the jangling discords of our nation into a beautiful symphony of brotherhood. With this faith we will be able to work together, to pray together, to struggle together, to go to jail together, to stand up for freedom together, knowing that we will be free one day.

This will be the day when all of   20 God's children will be able to sing with new meaning.

My country, 'tis of thee
Sweet land of liberty,
  Of thee I sing:
Land where my fathers died,
Land of the pilgrims' pride,
From every mountainside
  Let freedom ring.

---

[3] **"We hold these truths to be self-evident; that all men are created equal"** Famous line from the Declaration of Independence.

[4] **interposition** Controversial view that states have the right to decide if the federal government has exceeded its power.

And if America is to be a great nation this must become true. So let freedom ring from the prodigious hilltops of New Hampshire. Let freedom ring from the mighty mountains of New York. Let freedom ring from the heightening Alleghenies of Pennsylvania!

Let freedom ring from the snow-capped Rockies of Colorado!

Let freedom ring from the curva-ceous peaks of California!

But not only that; let freedom ring from Stone Mountain of Georgia!

25   Let freedom ring from Lookout Mountain of Tennessee!

Let freedom ring from every hill and molehill of Mississippi. From every mountainside, let freedom ring.

When we let freedom ring, when we let it ring from every village and every hamlet, from every state and every city, we will be able to speed up that day when all of God's children, black men and white men, Jews and Gentiles, Protestants and Catholics, will be able to join hands and sing in the words of the old Negro spiritual, "Free at last! free at last! thank God almighty, we are free at last!"

Understanding the Reading

1. **Detail** According to King, what problems did African Americans still face one hundred years after the signing of the Emancipation Proclamation?

2. **Analogy** Explain the analogy King makes between America's promise and a bad check. What does he say America owes African Americans?

3. **Purpose** For what purpose does King urge his followers to return to Missis-sippi, Alabama, and other states and communities?

4. **Conclusion** According to King, what must still happen in order for America "to be a great nation" (para. 21)? In a sentence or two, summarize King's dream.

Analyzing the Reading

1. **Audience** King delivered "I Have a Dream" to a crowd assembled for a civil rights march. What kind of audience was King addressing — agreeing, neu-tral or wavering, or disagreeing — and how did that affect his argument?

2. **Claim** What claim does King make? How does he present it?

3. **Evidence** What kinds of reasons and evidence does King use to support his claim? Are his details convincing and persuasive? Why, or why not?

4. **Emotional appeals** Identify the needs and values that King appeals to. How effectively do these emotional appeals strengthen his argument? Explain.

5. **Opposing views** What opposing viewpoints does King address? Explain how he recognizes and counters them.

Evaluating the Reading

1. **Structure of a speech** A well-written speech captures the audience's attention and keeps them interested. How does King accomplish this in "I Have a Dream"?

2. **Word choice** What repeated words and catchphrases does King use? Do they help build his argument, or are they merely devices to engage the listener? Explain.

3. **Conclusion** Evaluate the conclusion of the speech. What final impression does it make? Explain how it appeals to values, projects into the future, or urges listeners to take action — or a combination of all three.

4. **Figurative language** Evaluate King's use of figurative language by completing the following chart. For each figurative expression listed, explain what it means and how it strengthens King's argument. The first one has been done for you.

Figurative Expression	Meaning
"…we have come to our nation's Capitol to cash a check." (para. 3)	Implies an obligation established by the words of the Constitution and the Declaration of Independence regarding the rights of African Americans. Use of this analogy gives the cause a sense of importance and legitimacy.
"*Now* is the time to lift our nation from the quicksands of racial injustice to the solid rock of brotherhood." (para. 4)	
"The whirlwinds of revolt will continue to shake the foundations of our nation until the bright day of justice emerges." (para. 5)	
"Let us not seek to satisfy our thirst for freedom by drinking from the cup of bitterness and hatred." (para. 6)	
"You have been the veterans of creative suffering." (para. 8)	
"With this faith we will be able to transform the jangling discords of our nation into a beautiful symphony of brotherhood." (para. 19)	

5. **Language** Evaluate the light and dark imagery in the first paragraph.

Discussing the Reading

1. Discuss what you know about the civil rights movement in America. What has been accomplished since the 1960s, and what remains to be done?

2. Martin Luther King Jr. was a charismatic leader who encouraged people to take action. Are there any similar figures today to whom people look for leadership? Choose one figure and compare him or her to King.

Writing about the Reading

1. **Essay** How far have Americans come in avoiding judging people by the color of their skin? Has skin color been replaced by other factors (for example, income, age, sex, health, housing, education)? Choose a factor indicating that inequality still exists in this nation, and write an argument essay that demonstrates its existence and suggests a remedy.

2. **Essay** As a pivotal figure in the civil rights movement, King rallied hundreds of thousands of people to action. As citizens, it is our obligation to become involved if we want to effect change. One of the most basic levels of involvement is voting, yet voting rates have been declining since the 1960s. In an essay, argue for the importance of voting. Your audience is young voters in their late teens and early twenties.

3. **Internet research** Listen to some speeches from the History Channel's archive (www.history.com/speeches) or another Web site that archives historical speeches. Browse the collection, and choose a speech that uses argument to call people to action. Evaluate its effectiveness, and then write an essay that argues whether the speech does or does not have relevance today. To better understand the context of the speech, it may be necessary to conduct further online research about the historical circumstances surrounding it.

COMBINING THE PATTERNS

Why I Dumped My iPhone — And Why I'm Not Going Back

Sam Graham-Felsen speaks and writes about technology, politics, and social movements. He has lectured at the United Nations World Urban Forum and contributed articles to the *Nation, New York* magazine, and the *Washington Post*. In 2008 he served as the chief blogger for Barack Obama's presidential campaign. His interest in technology is on display in the following article, first published by the media organization *GOOD* in 2011.

Reading Tip

As you read, note when the writer made his decision to "dump" his iPhone. What led to this decision?

Previewing the Reading

Preview the reading (see pp. 23–24 for guidelines), and then predict reasons why the author dumped his iPhone.

Why I Dumped My iPhone— And Why I'm Not Going Back

Sam Graham-Felsen

On Black Friday in 2009, I said goodbye to my iPhone. And when Steve Jobs's successor announces the newest version today, I'm going to ignore the whole spectacle. Or try to, anyway.

In 2007 I was one of those people who obsessively monitored MacRumors.com for iPhone scuttlebutt, then waited in line for hours and bought one the first day it came out. At the time, I was working on Barack Obama's digital campaign team in Chicago, and I was wide-eyed about the iPhone's potential to empower the grass roots. A volunteer, I imagined, could pull up a map and find five doors of likely voters to knock on; or share streaming videos of Obama speeches at local diners and farmers markets—or even collect credit card donations at rallies. It would be easier than ever to change the world.

Indeed, the iPhone changed my life. Before I got my iPhone, rushing to the airport was a harrowing experience; after, it was actually kind of fun. I could check in en route to my flight and instantly get my boarding pass, use the extra half hour to find a cheap but critically lauded Mexican place in my destination city. I was never bored. Whenever I came to a red light or a long line, I reflexively reached for my iPhone. The Terminal 3 waiting area became the most interesting place in the world.

I could easily spend three straight hours on my phone without even noticing. If I'd spent three straight hours watching TV, I would be disgusted with myself. But I was convinced that the Internet was more edifying than television—even though most of my online diet consisted of gossipy garbage—because it was "interactive." I couldn't possibly be a zombie, because everyone knows zombies don't comment and share.

5   Yet it was nearly impossible for me to sit through dinner without reaching for my iPhone. Even when my wife was in the middle of telling me something important, I couldn't resist peeking at that tiny screen under the table to find out whether a high school acquaintance liked my latest status update. "What is so important?" she demanded, and I knew I had no good answer.

Soon after another iPhone-related argument, I traveled to Turkey to give a presentation about my experiences on the Obama campaign and about how tools like the iPhone could be used to build a movement. But for all my talk about the liberating power of technology, I was beginning to see how imprisoned I was by it. On the long flight home, my iPhone on airplane mode, I began reading Henry David Thoreau's *Walden*. It was one of several dozen classics that I'd downloaded for free in a fit of literary quixotism, then ignored.

I was almost embarrassed by the degree to which *Walden* felt directed toward me. I was particularly stung by his withering take on news junkies: "Hardly a man takes a half-hour's nap after dinner, but when he wakes he holds up his head and asks, 'What's the news?' as if the rest of mankind had stood his sentinels. . . . Pray tell me anything new that has happened to a man anywhere on this globe," he wrote in 1854.

And when I came across his famous verdict—"Men have become tools of their tools"—I felt like an enormous tool.

The next morning, I was in Boston with my family for Thanksgiving. Jet-lagged and jarred by Thoreau, I woke up at 5 A.M. I got a bike out of my parent's basement, took out my iPhone, and looked up directions to Walden Pond.

When I arrived, I read *Walden*'s most   10 celebrated lines: "I went to the woods because I wished to live deliberately, to front only the essential facts of life." I thought about how it's become fashionable to pooh-pooh Thoreau as a weak-willed hypocrite who lived a short walk away from civilization and had his mother deliver food to his doorstep. Many of these Thoreau skeptics dismiss critics of technology as curmudgeonly alarmists. Of course, I was one of those people.

I read on: "I wanted to live deep and suck out all the marrow of life, to live so sturdily and Spartan-like as to put to rout all that was not life. . . ."

No matter how impure Thoreau's experiment in simple living may have been, there was something undeniable in his suggestion that we often have to strip convenience from our lives to feel alive. The iPhone had certainly made my life easier, but had it made my life better?

First thing the next morning, I went to the AT&T store. I had to explain several times that I didn't want to trade my iPhone in for a new model, or a Droid, or anything with the Internet. I just wanted something that would allow me to make calls. The salesclerk looked at me with an expression that read: "Who gets something *worse* on Black Friday?" I walked out with a ridiculously unsleek '90s-era Nokia that my friends still tease me about.

Continued >

Since then, I haven't become a Renaissance man or a soulful motorcycle mechanic, but my daily life has improved. Commutes are no longer opportunities to catch up on email or Twitter, so I'm reading books again. It feels a little like getting a new contact lens prescription: Things that were blurred together feel sharper and more distinctly colored. And of course, I'm no longer engaged in half conversations with the people in front of me and half conversations with the Internet.

15   There are, of course, inconveniences. I had to buy a printer for my boarding passes. I handwrite driving directions or text them to myself. If I'm in an unfamiliar neighborhood or a new city, I actually have to do some planning before I bolt out the door. And when I get lost and am too embarrassed to ask a stranger, I have to call my wife, who has an iPhone, for directions.

One of the hardest things to get used to was being unable to instantly share my awesome and horrible experiences with my friends online. Now, I write down my impressions in a notebook, and by the time I get back to a computer, they rarely feel like must-tweets. I'm forced to slog through the tedium of waiting, to wrestle with dull passages and slow scenes, to grapple with confusing and sometimes scary situations on my own. I'm able to savor an idea and allow it to gestate.

When I had an iPhone, the Internet was no longer a destination; it was on me every day, like a piece of clothing I put on first thing in the morning. When I get tempted to return to that life, I ask myself: Do I really want the Internet to be something I feel naked without?

I still covet the thinner, faster, lighter iPhone 5. But I'm sticking with my boring little Nokia.

Understanding the Reading

1. **Thesis** What is Graham-Felsen's central point? Where does he state it most directly?

2. **Reasons** What main reason does Graham-Felsen give for trading in his iPhone?

3. **Evidence** How, according to Graham-Felsen, has getting rid of his iPhone improved his life?

4. **Opposing arguments** How does Graham-Felsen say getting rid of his iPhone has inconvenienced him?

Analyzing the Reading

1. **Organization and other patterns** How does Graham-Felsen structure his argument? What patterns does he use to support his argument? Highlight the transitional phrases that indicate this structure. (You might create a graphic organizer as well.)

2. **Evidence** What comparison does Graham-Felsen make to demonstrate that he had begun to spend far too much time on his iPhone for his own liking?

3. **Introduction** Why does Graham-Felsen open by noting that he gave up his iPhone on Black Friday? How does he return to this point later?

4. **Language** How is the word *tool* used in three different senses in paragraph 8?

5. **Language** In paragraph 17, the writer uses the image of a "piece of clothing" to describe how he felt about the Internet. How does he develop this image, and what does it contribute to his argument?

Evaluating the Reading

1. **Introduction** How do you respond to Graham-Felsen's claim in paragraph 2 that he acquired his iPhone idealistically, purely as a working tool to "change the world"?

2. **Evidence** How well do you think Graham-Felsen makes the case that he was "imprisoned" (para. 6) by his iPhone?

3. **Quotation and evidence** Graham-Felsen quotes extensively from Thoreau's *Walden* in paragraphs 7–11. How convincing do you find these quotations as evidence to argue against regular and extensive iPhone use?

4. **Voice** Graham-Felsen's argument is quite personal, based very much on his own experience. Are you sympathetic to his experience and feelings? Or do you have a different response? Why?

Discussing the Reading

1. The writer says he would be "disgusted" with himself if he spent "three straight hours watching TV." What's the difference between spending time watching television and spending the same time logged on to an "interactive" electronic communication device?

2. How do you feel when someone you're talking to face-to-face constantly checks phone messages? Is this something you do, too?

3. Discuss the meaning of the following quotation cited from *Walden* regarding keeping up with current events: "Pray tell me anything new that has happened to a man anywhere on this globe" (para. 7).

Writing about the Reading

1. **Essay** Using Graham-Felsen's essay as a starting point, write an essay making an argument about electronic communication (email, texting, social-network sites, and so forth) versus direct human interaction. (Hint: Start by brainstorming evidence from your own experience about how such communication experiences differ. Then develop a thesis that values one over the other.)

2. **Essay** Smartphones, tablets, social-media sites — all are popularized by various forms of marketing, as Graham-Felsen suggests in his second paragraph

regarding MacRumors.com. Do you think Americans are overly manipulated by advertising? Write an essay presenting your opinion about the positive or negative effects of advertising, using examples to defend your position.

3. **Combining patterns** Like Graham-Felsen, write an argument in favor of a lifestyle change that arose specifically from a decision you made for yourself or your family. Tell the story of your decision as a narrative, but also offer convincing evidence of the benefits of this change. (Hint: Note that Graham-Felsen also acknowledges some drawbacks of his decision.)

📖 **TEXTBOOK**

The Age of Music Piracy Is Officially Over

Paul Boutin is a technology writer who contributes to such publications as the *New York Times*, the *Wall Street Journal*, and *Wired*. Before turning to journalism, Boutin worked in information technology at MIT. The following article was originally published by *Wired* in 2010. This article was also included in an information technology college textbook titled *Digital Planet: Tomorrow's Technology* (2011). It was featured in a boxed insert, "Crosscurrents," that spotlights short essays that illustrate society's relationship with technology.

Reading Tip

As you read, annotate and highlight the changes record labels and online retailers have made in response to the complaints of music downloaders.

Previewing the Reading

Preview the reading (see pp. 23–24 for guidelines), and predict the author's position on the issue of music piracy.

The Age of Music Piracy Is Officially Over
Paul Boutin

The music industry hasn't adjusted easily to the digital revolution. Steadily declining revenues have devastated publishing companies, record companies, record stores, and musicians. Most observers place the blame on music piracy — illegal duplication and downloading of "free" music. This article, first published in the December 2010 issue of Wired*, addresses the most common reasons for music piracy and argues that most of those reasons are no longer valid. (Ironically, the Beatles' music library was released on iTunes between the time the column was written and the time the magazine was released.)*

Mark down the date: The age of stealing music via the Internet is officially over. It's time for everybody to go legit. The reason: We won. And all of you audiophiles and copyfighters, you know who fixed our problems? The record labels and online stores we loved to hate.

Granted, when Apple launched the iTunes Music Store in 2003 there was a lot to complain about. Tracks you bought on computer A often refused to play on gadget B, thanks to that old netizen bogeyman, digital rights management. (It's crippleware!) My local Apple store was actually picketed by nerds in hazmat suits attempting to educate passerby on the evils of DRM.

Continued >

Well played, protesters: In January 2009, Apple announced that it would remove the copyright protection wrapper from every song in its store. Today, Amazon and Walmart both sell music encoded as MP3s, which don't even have hooks for copyright-protection locks. The battle is over, comrades.

A few years ago, audiophiles dismissed iTunes' 128-Kbps resolution as anemic, even though it supposedly passed rigid blind testing against full-bandwidth CD tracks of the same song. The sound is compressed, connoisseurs said. The high end is mangled. Good work, audiophiles: Online stores have cranked up the audio quality to a fat 256 Kbps. To most ears, it's indistinguishable from a CD. (Actually, most ears are listening through crummy earbuds anyway, but whatever.) It's certainly better than most of the stuff out on BitTorrent. If you still hate the sound of digital music, you probably need to go back to vinyl. You can get a pretty good turntable for around $500. Which, I'll just point out, is not free. And when you steal vinyl records, it's called shoplifting.

Haters might get a bit more traction with the gripe that official 5 stores still don't carry every track ever recorded. You won't find, say, AC/DC or the Beatles in iTunes. For other artists, contract restrictions mean some songs can't be downloaded in every country, which indeed seems dumb for a store on the border-free Internet. Americans, for example, can't buy Daniel Zueras's 2007 Spanish hit "No Quiero Enamorarme" from the iTunes store for Spain. Still, the available inventory keeps growing, including artists' back catalogs. I recently discovered that Salt City Orchestra's limited-edition, vinyl-only 1997 nightclub fave "The Book" has been kicking around iTunes since 2008. Way back in the day, I had to trade favors with a pro DJ to get that record. It's getting harder and harder to find the few holdouts to hang a reasonable complaint on.

That leaves one last war cry: Music should be free! It's art! Friends, a song costs a *dollar*. Walmart has pushed some of its MP3s down to 64 cents. At Grooveshark, you can sample any song you want before you buy. Rdio charges $5 a month for all the music you can eat, served up via the cloud.

So there's really no reason not to buy — and surely you understand by now that there are reasons why you should. When you buy instead of bootlegging, you're paying the band. Most download retailers send about 70 percent of each sale to the record companies that own the music. Artists with 15 percent royalty deals get 15 percent of that 70 percent, or about 10.5 cents per dollar of sales. Those who write their own music and own their own music publishing companies — an increasingly common arrangement — get another 9.1 cents in "mechanical royalties." Every download sends almost 20 cents straight to the band.

A recent court ruling against Universal Records — and in favor of the rapper Eminem — might even lead to downloads of older music being treated not as sales but as licensed music. (Newly written contracts tend to address digital music sales directly.) That would bump the artist's split with the label from around 15 percent to an average of 50 percent. If that happens and you can still rationalize not throwing four dimes Eminem's way, then maybe there's another reason you're still pirating music: You're cheap.

Understanding the Reading

1. **Textbook reading** Why was this essay included in an information technology textbook? What does it illustrate about society and technology?

2. **Reasons and evidence** What are the main reasons presented in the selection for purchasing music online legitimately rather than pirating it? What evidence is offered for each reason?

3. **Introduction** The opening paragraph is a separate introduction to the selection, which the textbook writer reprints from *Wired* magazine. What main point does it make about the "digital revolution"?

Analyzing the Reading

1. **Questioning** Draft three questions that an instructor might pose on a quiz about this reading. Then briefly answer your questions.

2. **Audience** How does the writer try to reach out to and connect with his audience in paragraphs 2–4? What does this strategy contribute to his argument?

3. **Meaning** What is the point of the parenthetical sentence about earbuds in paragraph 4? And why does the writer end this paragraph by saying that to "steal vinyl records" is called "shoplifting"?

4. **Conclusion** How do the writer's final three paragraphs lead up to his concluding sentence? What is the basic argument here?

Evaluating the Reading

1. **Introduction** In the opening paragraph, the writer uses first-person plural pronouns three times (*we, our, we*). Do you think that aligning himself with the "haters" (para. 5) in this way helps establish him as a credible advocate for his position?

2. **Evidence** In his final three paragraphs, the writer cites evidence regarding what buyers pay for and what artists receive from downloaded music sales. Do these numbers convince you to reject the idea leading off the discussion that "[m]usic should be free"?

3. **Language** How do you respond to the writer's final characterization of music piraters as "cheap"? Is this a reasonable use of vocabulary?

4. **Opposing arguments** Do you think the writer fairly presents the opposing arguments he wants to refute?

Discussing the Reading

1. How do you define *music piracy*? In your view is it comparable to shoplifting?

2. What's your response to the claim, "Music should be free! It's art!"?

3. Do you believe that revenue declines in the music industry are primarily the result of piracy? What else might contribute to this trend?

Writing about the Reading

1. **Essay** In an essay, present your own viewpoint on the practice of downloading music without paying artists and record companies. What is your feeling about the sites that encourage such illegal duplication of music files? (Hint: In your argument consider the trade-offs between those who gain from such downloads and those who suffer.)

2. **Essay** How might artists, record companies, and record retailers remedy the downturn in music-industry profits? Brainstorm some possible solutions and then develop a thesis based on what you see as the best of those solutions before you begin to draft.

3. **Essay** Music fans can access and purchase recordings by their favorite artists in a number of ways. But why do you think fans are willing to spend considerably more money to see those performers live in concert? Write an essay presenting reasons and evidence for the popularity of live concerts.

ARGUMENT PAIR: DEBATING THE DREAM ACT

What's Wrong with the DREAM Act[1]

Margaret "Peggy" Sands is the credentialed congressional correspondent for the *Hispanic Outlook in Higher Education*, a magazine covering Hispanic education at the post-secondary level. She has also written a book, *Immigration and the American Dream: Battling the Political Hype and Hysteria*. The following article, first published by *AOL News* in 2010, is characteristic of her work in its attention to immigration policy and the U.S. Hispanic community.

Reading Tip

As you read, highlight the main reasons the writer opposes the DREAM Act.

Previewing the Reading

Preview the reading (see pp. 23–24 for guidelines), and then write a brief definition of the DREAM Act and explain why the writer thinks it won't become a law.

---

[1] In 2012 President Obama announced that his administration would stop deporting young illegal immigrants who fulfilled certain criteria specified by the DREAM Act.

aolnews.com

What's Wrong with the DREAM Act

By Peggy Sands

As soon as today, the Senate may vote on the DREAM Act. This law would, according to backers, offer people brought into the United States illegally as children and who graduated from high school a better chance of making a life here. It's a noble goal, but passage is a long shot. It isn't just a problem with timing. While the legislation addresses the compelling plight of the illegal immigrant high-school graduate, it suffers major flaws that make it patently unfair. Here are several big flaws.

It discriminates against children of legal immigrants. Under the law, for example, high-school graduates under age thirty who were brought to the country illegally before age sixteen would have access to in-state tuition, publicly funded student loans, and a green card. But foreign-born high-school graduates in those same age groups who were brought into the country legally wouldn't qualify for these invaluable benefits. The DREAM Act benefits illegal immigrants only.

Continued >

Likewise, these illegal immigrants would only need to serve in the military for two years to expedite citizenship. Legal immigrants have to put their life on the line for three years before getting that benefit. That's a difference that's not just unfair, but potentially deadly.

By favoring millions of illegal immigrants over legal ones, the DREAM Act surely will encourage more young foreign nationals to enter and/or stay in the United States illegally. While the bill is limited only to those currently in the country, it's highly likely that once granted, the "dream" will be extended to future young illegal immigrants who graduate from an American high school "or its equivalent." With such benefits, why come in legally?

The age range is too broad. Because of the generous qualifying age range of before   5
sixteen and up to thirty years old, an estimated two million adult illegal immigrants would qualify immediately for green cards under the DREAM Act, according to the nonpartisan[1] Migration Policy Institute — twice as many as normally are given out in a single year. Opponents call this unacceptable "sneak amnesty."

Some proponents also recognize this to be extreme and, last week, the upper age limit was reduced to thirty from thirty-five years old. But some argue that the upper range should be reduced to twenty-four, while the lower age limit should be set at ten or even eight years old. That would better reflect the goal of the act to benefit students who've only known the United States as home.

It's being falsely marketed. Backers say the DREAM Act is the only way for illegal immigrant high-school graduates to go to college. The fact is, they already can attend many highly tolerant colleges throughout the country. "We don't ask students about their immigration status. If they've graduated from high school and qualify academically, they're admitted," Charles B. Reed, chancellor of the California State University system, told me in June. The California Supreme Court ruled in favor of his position in November.

To be sure, the DREAM Act does fulfill one dream — the dream of colleges and universities for more Hispanic students. Last winter the powerful Hispanic Association of College and Universities urged passage of the act, saying that it not only would send a positive message to Latinos, but would also help colleges qualify for a new $1 billion U.S. Department of Education fund aimed exclusively at Hispanic-serving institutions. To apply, colleges need to document that 25% of their students are Hispanic. The DREAM Act would be a rich source of such students.

There are many compelling reason's why any immigrant who was brought into the country as a very young child and goes on to complete high school, college, or serve

[1] **nonpartisan** Not supported or controlled by a political party.

aolnews.com

in the armed forces with a clean record should be allowed to apply for permanent legal status.

The DREAM Act can be fixed to benefit this more limited population. But that would   10
require lawmakers to be brutally honest about the law's real purpose. It's about obtaining a permanent legal residency work permit (a green card). After all, what is the use of attending an expensive U.S. college if you don't have the right to stay and work, if you can be deported at any time?

Of course, looking at the DREAM Act as a work-permit bill makes it much more difficult to pass during a recession with at least 10% of American workers unemployed or underemployed. It's much easier to pitch it as fulfilling the dreams of wonderful young immigrants who are in the country illegally to go to college.

This spin is the DREAM Act's biggest problem and why it probably won't become law.

Understanding the Reading

1. **Thesis** What is Sands's basic opposition to the DREAM Act? Where does she summarize this position most clearly?

2. **Reasons** What main reasons does Sands offer to oppose the DREAM Act? How does she highlight these reasons?

3. **Evidence** What specific evidence does Sands offer to support her reasoning? Consider paragraphs 2, 5, and 9–10 in particular.

4. **Organization** Complete the graphic organizer on page 644 for help in understanding the organization of the argument.

Analyzing the Reading

1. **Methods of development** Where does Sands focus on comparison and contrast in her argument? What is her purpose in this section?

2. **Methods of development** Why does Sands point to a cause-and-effect relationship in paragraph 4, and how does this relate to her point in paragraph 11?

3. **Appeal to readers** Why does Sands offer some support for the goals of the DREAM Act in paragraph 9? How does she differentiate her beliefs from those of the act's backers?

4. **Definition** How does Sands redefine the DREAM Act in her next-to-last paragraph? What does this redefinition contribute to her argument?

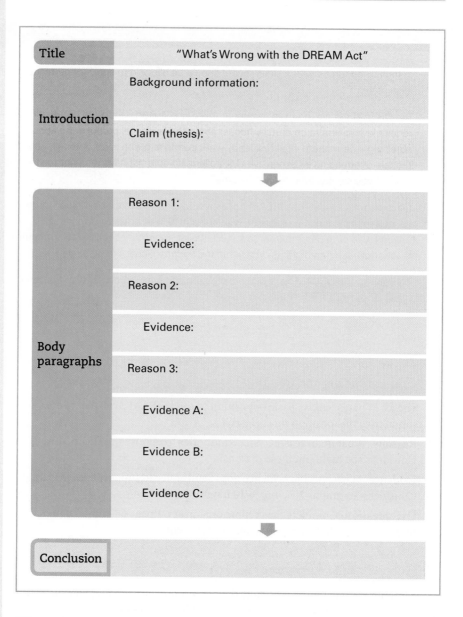

Title	"What's Wrong with the DREAM Act"
Introduction	Background information:
	Claim (thesis):
Body paragraphs	Reason 1:
	Evidence:
	Reason 2:
	Evidence:
	Reason 3:
	Evidence A:
	Evidence B:
	Evidence C:
Conclusion	

Evaluating the Reading

1. **Reasons** Which do you think is Sands's most convincing reason for opposing the DREAM Act? In general do you think she makes a strong argument, or do some of her reasons fail to convince you?

2. **Evidence** Sands suggests in paragraph 8 that colleges and universities stand to benefit from passage of the DREAM Act. Does she make a clear connection between this supposed benefit and support for the act?

3. **Language** Why do you think Sands refers specifically to an "expensive" college in paragraph 10? What is she suggesting about DREAM Act beneficiaries? Do you think this is a fair characterization?

4. **Purpose and audience** In both her opening and conclusion, Sands suggests pretty directly that passage of the DREAM Act is unlikely. What, then, seems to be the purpose of her argument, and who might her intended audience be? How effective do you find the strategy she uses in appealing to this audience?

Discussing the Reading

1. Does Sands convince you that the DREAM Act is "patently unfair" to legal immigrants? Why, or why not?

2. How well do you understand the age range Sands writes about in paragraphs 5–6? Do you find her explanation clear?

3. The DREAM Act is officially titled the "Development, Relief, and Education for Alien Minors" Act. Propose a different title with which you think the author would agree.

Writing about the Reading

1. **Essay** In difficult economic times, many cuts are made to education budgets, and many costs are passed on to students. Based on your own perspective and experience, brainstorm a list of how your education is affected by the current economic climate. Then write an essay directed to school administrators expressing your viewpoint about what has happened to your educational prospects. Suggest solutions of your own for making education better for students.

2. **Essay** Sands concedes that young children who are brought into the United States as illegal immigrants but who graduate high school or college or serve in the military should be allowed to apply for legal status. Do you agree? Write an essay arguing for or against this claim.

3. **Essay** As has often been noted, the United States is a nation of people with mostly immigrant forebears, legal or not. Why, then, are recent immigrants so often regarded negatively by people whose own families may have been here for only a few generations? Write an argument expressing your views on the status of recent immigrants—legal and illegal—in the United States. (You might, for example, consider legislation in Arizona allowing people only suspected of being in the country illegally to be stopped by police and required to prove legal residency.) Research the topic, as needed, to locate supporting information.

Pass the DREAM Act

The **Chicago Tribune** is a daily newspaper with over a million readers. Founded in 1847, it is now an industry leader in American journalism. The *Tribune* published the following editorial on September 20, 2010.

Reading Tip

As you read, highlight and comment on the benefits of the DREAM Act that the editorial writer presents.

Previewing the Reading

Preview the reading (see pp. 23–24 for guidelines), and then predict the author's position on the issue.

CHICAGO TRIBUNE

Pass the DREAM Act

They're members of what sociologists call "the 1.5 generation"—children brought to the United States at a young age, raised as Americans with little connection to the country where they were born. They speak English, attend school, join the Girl Scouts and Little League. And they're here illegally.

In recent months, they've been standing publicly to reveal their names and immigration status, risking arrest and deportation to push for a federal law that would help them gain legal status by attending college or serving in the military. They've staged sit-ins in the office of Senator John McCain, R-Arizona, a one-time champion whose support for their cause has faded, in the halls of Congress and in rallies across the country, including in Chicago. Now the Development, Relief and Education

for Alien Minors Act—DREAM Act for short—could be up for a vote in the U.S. Senate this week. It's a good deal for them, and for the country.

Every year, 65,000 youngsters who are here illegally graduate from high school to an uncertain future. They don't qualify for most scholarships, student loans or resident tuition rates; they also can't work here legally. Those who can afford tuition hesitate to apply for fear of being deported. With no ties to any other country, most end up staying and working underground. U.S. taxpayers, meanwhile, are deprived of the talent and legal labor of hundreds of thousands of young men and women they paid to school.

The DREAM Act would give those youngsters six years of conditional legal residency in which to attend college or enlist in the armed forces. They would be eligible for federal loans and work study programs, but not for government education grants. After two years of college or military service, they could get a green card, which allows them to live and work here legally and apply for citizenship.

5   Only high-school graduates (or GED holders) who qualify for college or military service would be eligible.

The DREAM Act, sponsored by Senator Dick Durbin, is supported by business, religious, and educational groups that recognize it as a net plus for the country. It would help young people get significantly better jobs, which translates into greater earning power, more tax revenue, more consumer spending—and less public money spent on health and social services. The U.S. Defense Department is eager to tap this pool of top-quality recruits.

So what's the holdup? The harshest immigration hawks have labeled the DREAM Act "youth amnesty."[1] They don't want to make concessions to parents who brought their children here illegally. For others, it's a more calculated political move. Some feel the DREAM Act should be part of a comprehensive immigration overhaul because its broader bipartisan[2] support could offset more controversial parts of the bill, such as a path to citizenship for longtime illegal workers. Others believe it should be a stand-alone bill, not freighted with so many unpopular measures.

Senate President Harry Reid, D-Nevada, now wants to attach it to the defense authorization bill, which includes critical spending for operations in Iraq and Afghanistan and pay increases for U.S. troops. With midterm elections looming, Democrats—especially Reid—could use a boost from grateful Latino voters. The DREAM Act could be just the ticket.

But things are getting complicated. The House version of the defense spending bill includes $485 million—a mere down payment—to develop a fighter jet engine the Pentagon says it doesn't need or want. Supporters are trying to add it to the Senate version, too. Both bills also include a repeal of the "don't ask, don't tell" policy that keeps gays from serving openly in the U.S. military.

10   President Barack Obama supports both the "don't ask, don't tell" repeal and the DREAM Act—as do we—but he's promised to veto the bill if it includes funding for the wasteful engine project. And he should.

Reid can't count on the DREAM Act to carry him on Election Day. But there are better reasons to pass it. Congress should find a way to do it, and soon.

[1] **amnesty** Pardon or forgiveness.
[2] **bipartisan** Including members from two political parties.

Understanding the Reading

1. **Thesis** What is the thesis of the editorial? Where is it summarized most clearly?

2. **Topic** How does the editorial characterize those who would benefit from the DREAM Act? Why is their future currently "uncertain"?

3. **Evidence** According to the editorial, who supports the DREAM Act, and what is the basis of this support?

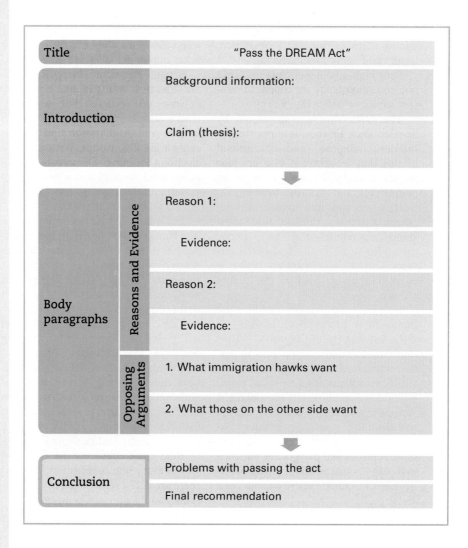

Title	"Pass the DREAM Act"		
Introduction	Background information:		
	Claim (thesis):		

Body paragraphs	**Reasons and Evidence**	Reason 1:
		Evidence:
		Reason 2:
		Evidence:
	Opposing Arguments	1. What immigration hawks want
		2. What those on the other side want

| **Conclusion** | Problems with passing the act |
| | Final recommendation |

4. **Opposing arguments** Why do "immigrant hawks" oppose the DREAM Act?

5. **Organization** Complete the graphic organizer above to help you understand the organization of the argument.

Analyzing the Reading

1. **Introduction** Why does the writer open by quoting how "sociologists" define children illegally brought into the United States at a young age? What kind of appeal is being made?

2. **Emotional appeal** Paragraph 2 describes the actions of young people who support the DREAM Act. How does the writer expect readers to respond here?

3. **Method of presentation** What is the purpose of paragraph 5, which makes its point in only a single sentence? What is being highlighted?

4. **Conclusion** Why does the writer focus on a congressional defense authorization bill in paragraphs 8–10? What does this have to do with the DREAM Act?

Evaluating the Reading

1. **Appeal to readers** Do you think that the argument establishes sympathy for the potential beneficiaries of the DREAM Act? Why, or why not?

2. **Opposing arguments** In your view, does the reading present and refute opposing arguments as fully as it should? In formulating your response, you might consider the arguments made in the preceding essay by Peggy Sands.

3. **Language** In paragraph 6, the writer states that the effect of passing the DREAM Act would be a "net plus." How do you interpret this phrase, and do you find the point convincing?

4. **Conclusion** Evaluate the argument's conclusion, which begins in paragraph 8. Does it provide a strong enough restatement of the thesis? What does it suggest to you about the intended audience?

Discussing the Reading

1. Have you ever thought about "the 1.5 generation"? How does this label affect your feelings about these illegal residents who were brought to the United States at a very young age?

2. How would you recommend that your representatives in Washington vote on the DREAM Act? Why do you think as you do?

3. Do you think it makes sense that provisions of the DREAM Act would be attached to a bill being voted on to authorize defense spending? What does this suggest to you about how Congress works?

Writing about the Reading

1. **Essay** The editorial suggests that young people are right to risk arrest when protesting for causes they believe in. What causes would you be willing to go to jail for? Or do you believe that such protest is simply wrong? Write an essay arguing for or against the ethics and the ultimate effectiveness of public protest. (Hint: Be sure to present and refute opposing arguments in developing your thesis.)

2. **Essay** The DREAM Act seems to equate going to college with serving in the military in terms of how young people would benefit. Do you think this is fair? Should people who risk their lives for their country be accorded only the

same status by the government as those who simply pursue a college degree? Write an essay arguing for or against special governmental help for veterans. Be specific about what such help might entail.

3. **Research** Conduct research to determine the current status of the DREAM Act. Write an essay summarizing your findings and commenting on the action or inaction.

Comparing the Arguments

1. Compare how Sands and the editorial writer introduce the issue. In what context does each writer frame the issue?

2. Evaluate the evidence the authors offer in support of their claims. Which author presents more substantial evidence? Explain.

3. Which writer's argument do you find to be more convincing? Why?

4. How do you think Sands might respond to the *Chicago Tribune*'s claim?

5. What did you learn about this topic from the essays? Can you reach a conclusion about the DREAM Act on the basis of these two sources? Explain.

ARGUMENT PAIR: DEBATING MULTITASKING

How (and Why) to Stop Multitasking

Peter Bregman is a leadership consultant and CEO of Bregman Partners, Inc., a global management consulting firm. He is the author of *Point B: A Short Guide to Leading a Big Change* (2007) and *18 Minutes: Find Your Focus, Master Distraction, and Get the Right Things Done* (2011). He also blogs for *Harvard Business Review*, where this essay appeared in 2010.

Reading Tip

Bregman focuses primarily on personal experience in this argument. Pay close attention to how he uses data in his argument and consider how he balances personal experience and outside information.

Previewing the Reading

Preview the reading (see pp. 23–24 for guidelines), and list at least one reason why the author opposes multitasking.

---

blogs.hbr.org

How (and Why) to Stop Multitasking

By Peter Bregman

During a conference call with the executive committee of a nonprofit board on which I sit, I decided to send an email to a client. I know, I know. You'd think I'd have learned. Last week I wrote about the dangers of using a cell phone while driving. Multitasking is dangerous. And so I proposed a way to stop. But when I sent that email, I wasn't in a car. I was safe at my desk. What could go wrong?

Well, I sent the client the message. Then I had to send him another one, this time with the attachment I had forgotten to append. Finally, my third email to him explained why that attachment wasn't what he was expecting. When I eventually refocused on the call, I realized I hadn't heard a question the chair of the board had asked me.

I swear I wasn't smoking anything. But I might as well have been. A study showed that people distracted by incoming email and phone calls saw a 10-point fall in their IQs. What's the impact of a 10-point drop? The same as losing a night of sleep. More than twice the effect of smoking marijuana.

Continued >

Doing several things at once is a trick we play on ourselves, thinking we're getting more done. In reality, our productivity goes down by as much as 40%. We don't actually multitask. We switch-task, rapidly shifing from one thing to another, interrupting ourselves unproductively, and losing time in the process.

You might think you're different, that you've done it so much you've become good at   5
it. Practice makes perfect and all that. But you'd be wrong. Research shows that heavy multitaskers are *less competent* at doing several things at once than light multitaskers. In other words, in contrast to almost everything else in your life, the more you multitask, the worse you are at it. Practice, in this case, works against you.

I decided to do an experiment. For one week I would do no multiasking and see what happened. What techniques would help? Could I sustain a focus on one thing at a time for that long? For the most part, I succeeded. If I was on the phone, all I did was talk or listen on the phone. In a meeting I did nothing but focus on the meeting. Any interruptions—email, a knock on the door—I held off until I finished what I was working on.

During the week I discovered six things:

- **First, it was delightful.** I noticed this most dramatically when I was with my children. I shut my cell phone off and found myself much more deeply engaged and present with them. I never realized how significantly a short moment of checking my email disengaged me from the people and things right there in front of me. Don't laugh, but I actually—for the first time in a while—noticed the beauty of leaves blowing in the wind.
- **Second, I made significant progress on challenging projects,** the kind that—like writing or strategizing—require thought and persistence. The kind I usually try to distract myself from. I stayed with each project when it got hard, and experienced a number of breakthroughs.
- **Third, my stress dropped dramatically.** Research shows that multitasking isn't just inefficient, it's stressful. And I found that to be true. It was a relief to do only one thing at a time. I felt liberated from the strain of keeping so many balls in the air at each moment. It felt reassuring to finish one thing before going to the next.
- **Fourth, I lost all patience for things I felt were not a good use of my time.** An hour-long meeting seemed interminably long. A meandering pointless conversation was excruciating. I became laser-focused on getting things done. Since I wasn't doing anything else, I got bored much more quickly. I had no tolerance for wasted time.
- **Fifth, I had tremendous patience for things I felt were useful and enjoyable.** When I listened to my wife Eleanor, I was in no rush. When I was brainstorming about a difficult problem, I stuck with it. Nothing else was competing for my attention so I was able to settle into the one thing I was doing.

- **Sixth, there was no downside.** I lost nothing by not multitasking. No projects were left unfinished. No one became frustrated with me for not answering a call or failing to return an email the second I received it.

That's why it's so surprising that multitasking is so hard to resist. If there's no downside to stopping, why don't we all just stop? I think it's because our minds move considerably faster than the outside world. You can hear far more words a minute than someone else can speak. We have so much to do, why waste any time? So, while you're on the phone listening to someone, why not use that *extra* brain power to book a trip to Florence? What we neglect to realize is that we're already using that brain power to pick up nuance, think about what we're hearing, access our creativity, and stay connected to what's happening around us. It's not really extra brain power, and diverting it has negative consequences.

So how do we resist the temptation? First, the obvious: The best way to avoid interruptions is to turn them off. Often I write at 6 A.M. when there's nothing to distract me, I disconnect my computer from its wireless connection and turn my phone off. In my car, I leave my phone in the trunk. Drastic? Maybe. But most of us shouldn't trust ourselves. Second, the less obvious: Use your loss of patience to your advantage. Create unrealistically short deadlines. Cut all meetings in half. Give yourself a third of the time you think you need to accomplish something. There's nothing like a deadline to keep things moving. And when things are moving fast, we can't help but focus on them. How many people run a race while texting? If you really only have thirty minutes to finish a presentation you thought would take an hour, are you really going to answer an interrupting call? Interestingly, because multitasking is so stressful, single-tasking to meet a tight deadline will actually reduce your stress. In other words, giving yourself less time to do things could make you more productive and relaxed.

Finally, it's good to remember that we're not perfect. Every once in a while it might be 10 OK to allow for a little multitasking. As I was writing this, Daniel, my two-year-old son, walked into my office, climbed on my lap, and said "*Monsters, Inc.* movie please." So, here we are, I'm finishing this piece on the left side of my computer screen while Daniel is on my lap watching a movie on the right side of my computer screen. Sometimes, it is simply impossible to resist a little multitasking.

Understanding the Reading

1. **Claim** Why does Bregman believe we should stop most of our multitasking?

2. **Opposing view** Summarize the opposing views favoring multitasking that Bregman refutes.

3. **Evidence** What did Bregman discover after he stopped multitasking?

4. **Vocabulary** Explain the meaning of each of the following words as it is used in the reading, consulting a dictionary as necessary: *refocused* (para. 2), *competent* (5), *disengaged* (7), *persistence* (7), and *meandering* (7).

5. **Organization** Create a graphic organizer for the argument in this essay.

Analyzing the Reading

1. **Claim** What is Bregman's claim? What is the author's purpose in making the claim?

2. **Emotional appeals** What types of emotional appeals does Bregman make? Identify the needs and values to which he appeals.

3. **Evidence** What types of evidence does Bregman use to support his claim?

4. **Reasoning** Are there any errors in Bregman's reasoning? If so, what are they and where in the selection do they occur?

Evaluating the Reading

1. **Tone** Describe Bregman's tone. Highlight several words or phrases that reveal this tone.

2. **Sources** Bregman mentions research but fails to cite his sources. How does that influence the effectiveness of his argument?

3. **Language** What is the connotation of *delightful* (para. 7)?

4. **Language** What is "smoking anything" (para. 3) a euphemism for?

Discussing the Reading

1. Evaluate Bregman's description of his discoveries when he stopped multitasking. Are they persuasive? Could he have added anything that would make them more persuasive?

2. What do you think of Bregman's tips on how to stop multitasking? Are these things you could apply to your life? Why, or why not?

Writing about the Reading

1. **Essay** Keep a journal for a day, and record all the times you multitask and how doing so affects you. Then, write an essay describing your experiences with multitasking. Offer examples of why it has or has not been useful for you.

2. **Essay** Pick another habit or activity that you often do that, like multitasking, has benefits and disadvantages, and try to give it up for a week. Then write an essay like Bregman's that either argues for or against the habit based on your experience. Consider including in your essay a list of discoveries like Bregman's.

3. **Internet research** Bregman provides statistics about multitasking but does not cite his sources. Do some library and Internet research on recent studies on multitasking. Based on the information you find, write an essay that either supports or argues against Bregman's claims. Remember to consider opposing viewpoints in your argument.

In Defense of Multitasking

David Silverman has worked in business and taught business writing. He is the author of *Typo: The Last American Typesetter or How I Made and Lost 4 Million Dollars* (2007). He blogs for *Harvard Business Review*, where this essay appeared in 2010, three weeks after "How (and Why) to Stop Multitasking."

Reading Tip

Silverman's piece is a direct response to Peter Bregman's "How (and Why) to Stop Multitasking" (p. 651). As you read, pay careful attention to the ways he uses Bregman's structure to make his own argument.

Previewing the Reading

Preview the reading (see pp. 23–24 for guidelines), and list several reasons why the author defends multitasking.

---

blogs.hbr.org

In Defense of Multitasking

By David Silverman

HBR.org blogger Peter Bregman recently made some excellent points about the downside of multitasking. I will not deny that single-minded devotion often produces high quality. Nor will I attempt to join the misguided (and scientifically discredited) many who say, "Yeah, other people can't do it, but I'm super awesome at doing ten things at once."

But let's remember, unitasking has a downside too—namely, what works for one person slows down others. Multitasking isn't just an addiction for the short-attention-spanned among us; it's crucial to survival in today's workplace. To see why, take a look at computing, where the concept of multitasking came from.

Long ago, in the days of vacuum tubes and relays, computers worked in "batch" mode. Jobs were loaded from punched cards, and each job waited until the one before it was completed. This created serious problems. You didn't know if your job had an error until it ran, which could be hours after you submitted it. You didn't know if it would cause an infinite loop and block all the other jobs from starting. And any changes in external information that occurred during processing couldn't be accounted for.

The invention of time-sharing resolved these issues: Multiple tasks can now be done concurrently, and you can interrupt a task in an emergency. Incoming missile? Stop the backup tape and send an alert to HQ. So, how does all that apply to the way people work? In several ways:

1. **Multitasking helps us get and give critical information faster.** You can get responses to questions quickly, even if the person you're asking is on another task. For example: I was at an all-day off-site (no BlackBerrys allowed) when one of my direct reports received a request from an internal customer to make a slide. Since I was unreachable by phone when he started on it, my employee worked the entire afternoon on something that, after I finally read my email and called him, took us only thirty minutes to do together because I had information he didn't have.

2. **It keeps others from being held up.** If I don't allow for distractions in an attempt to be more efficient, other people may be held up waiting for me. This is the classic batch job problem. Going back to my slide example: The next day, the person who had requested the slide said he only needed a couple of bullet points. Had he been reachable earlier, and not devoted to a single task and blocking all interruptions, we wouldn't have wasted what ended up being nearly six hours of work time (my employee's and mine).

3. **It gives you something to turn to when you're stuck.** Sometimes it's good to butt your head against a task that is challenging. And sometimes it's good to walk away, do something else, and let your subconscious ponder the ponderable. When you return twenty-five minutes later, maybe you'll reach a better solution than you would have if you'd just stuck it out. And in the meantime, you've finished some other task, such as writing a blog post. (By the way, my 10.6 minute attempt to uncover how many minutes it takes to get back to a task after an interruption yielded a variety of answers—11, 25, 30—and links to a lot of dubious research, such as a University of California study of thirty-six workers and a study that tracked "eleven experienced Microsoft Windows users [three female].")

4. **The higher up you are in the organization, the more important multitasking is.** The fewer things you have to do, the more you should concentrate on them. If I'm painting my house, and I'm on a ladder, I've got to keep on that one task. But if I'm the general contractor, I need to stay on top of the house painter, the carpenter, the electrician, and the guy swinging that big ball on the end of a giant chain, lest the wrong wall or an unsuspecting worker get demolished. To take this to the logical extreme: Does Barack Obama get to unitask? Can he say, "I'm not available for the rest of the day, because I'll be working on that spreadsheet I've been trying to get done on the number of my Facebook friends who aren't updating their pages with posts about their pet cats?" Or does he have to keep doing his job while handling whatever spilled milk (or, say, zillions of gallons of oil) comes his way?

Continued >

blogs.hbr.org

What do you think? Are we comfortable pretending we really can live our lives not   5
multitasking? Or are we like my father and others who say smoking is bad but can be
found on the front porch in the dead of night, a small red glow at their lips, puffing
away while texting their BFFs and playing Words with Friends?

Before you answer, think about the eight *Washington Post* reporters who tried to go a
week without the Internet and failed miserably. The truth is, we need multitasking as
much as we need air.

Understanding the Reading

1. **Claim** What claim does Silverman make?
2. **Reasons** Summarize Silverman's reasons for defending multitasking.
3. **Message** What message does Silverman convey by discussing his father in the next-to-last paragraph?
4. **Vocabulary** Explain the meaning of each of the following words as it is used in the reading: *discredited* (para. 1), *unitasking* (2), *concurrently* (4), *ponderable* (4), and *lest* (4).
5. **Organization** Create a graphic organizer for the argument in this essay.

Analyzing the Reading

1. **Analogy** Explain Silverman's analogy about computers. What is he trying to show with it?
2. **Effectiveness** Is Silverman's analogy about computers effective? Why, or why not?
3. **Evidence** What additional information, evidence, or explanation would make this essay more convincing?
4. **Evidence** The end of the essay talks about multitasking and the presidency. Is this an effective example? How useful is it in applying the issues in this essay to regular people?
5. **Audience** Who is Silverman's intended audience?

Evaluating the Reading

1. **Appeals** To what needs and values does Silverman appeal?
2. **Fallacies** What fallacies, if any, can you find in Silverman's essay?

3. **Sources** Evaluate Silverman's use of sources in this essay. What kinds of sources could he have added?

4. **Opposing viewpoints** How does Silverman present opposing viewpoints? Does he refute them? If so, how?

5. **Fact versus opinion** Discuss whether Silverman's essay is made up primarily of fact or of opinion. How does this balance affect the success of his argument?

6. **Language** What are the connotations of *addiction* in paragraph 2 and *missile* in paragraph 4?

Discussing the Reading

1. Do you agree or disagree with Silverman's assertion that multitasking is essential for survival at work? Why?

2. Imagine you are having surgery under local anesthetic and discover your surgeon multitasking while performing the procedure. Discuss your response.

Writing about the Reading

1. **Essay** Write an essay describing how and why multitasking might have developed as a human behavior. When would it have been a valuable skill? How would it have helped early humans?

2. **Essay** Try working on *only* one task at a time for one day, and in an essay, report what you accomplished, your level of productivity, and/or what you missed.

3. **Essay** Find a professional essay that presents an argument you disagree with. (You may use one of the essays in this book or, perhaps, an opinion piece in a school, local, or national newspaper or on a Web site.) Write an essay arguing against the piece.

Comparing the Arguments

1. Which writer's argument did you find more convincing? Why?

2. Compare how each writer introduces the issue. In what context does each writer frame it?

3. In their discussions of what people try to do when they multitask, Silverman and Bregman do not seem to be talking about exactly the same kinds of activities. How do you think this difference affects their opinions of multitasking?

4. What is the primary difference in the ways that Bregman and Silverman view multitasking? Do they define it differently? If so, describe how each might define it.

5. How do you think Bregman might respond to Silverman's claims?

Writing Your Own Argument Essay

Now that you have learned about the major characteristics, structure, and purposes of an argument essay, you know everything necessary to write your own argument. In this section you will read a student's argument essay and get advice on finding ideas, drafting your essay, and revising and editing it. You may want to use the essay prompts in "Readings for Practice, Ideas for Writing" (p. 614) or choose your own topic.

A Student Model Argument Essay

James Sturm wrote this essay when he was a student at Kalamazoo College, where he graduated with a degree in international and area studies. As you read, notice how Sturm uses comparison and contrast as well as illustration to strengthen his argument.

Title: indicates position

Introduction: establishes common ground

Thesis statement: clearly states claim

Background information: government regulation and record labeling

Source citation

Transition

Reason 1: Music influences listeners' attitudes.

Pull the Plug on Explicit Lyrics

James Sturm

Many kids pass through a rebellious phase in middle school. If the teacher asks them to stop throwing pencils, they toss one more. If the sign reads "No Trespassing," they cross the line. If they hear their father listening to classical music, they tune in to rap and punk rock. This is exactly what I did, although I now look back with regret on my actions. Having matured significantly since my middle-school days, I understand the negative effect that explicit lyrics have on youth, and I believe such music should be off-limits until the age of sixteen.

Currently, the government takes a rather laissez-faire attitude with regard to the music industry. Thousands of albums are readily available to young people regardless of explicit content. In fact, the main control mechanism for protecting youthful consumers from harmful content comes from the recording companies themselves. Under the Parental Advisory campaign of the Recording Industry Association of America (RIAA), it is the responsibility of artists and record labels themselves to decide if their albums should receive the infamous "Parental Advisory: Explicit Content" label. Children are allowed to purchase the albums regardless ("Parental Advisory").

This lack of regulation would not be a problem if the music did not produce negative effects on its listeners. Although it is difficult to prove statistically that music full of hateful content fuels similar attitudes in its listeners, it requires only common sense to understand why. That is, people are influenced by what they think about. If a child thinks, for example, that he is unimportant or unloved, then he will act out in various ways to gain attention from his peers. Problem thinking is a result of a variety of influences, including friends, parents, and the media. Negative music, if listened to frequently enough, naturally implants negative thoughts in the minds of its listeners.

Furthermore, consider the unique influence of music as opposed to other forms of media. Unlike movies, video games, and magazines, music has a way of saturating one's mind. Everyone knows the feeling of having a song "stuck" in their head, repeating itself throughout the day. Unlike a movie, which is seen once, discussed among friends, and then forgotten, a song can remain lodged in one's mind for weeks on end. And if the songs are steeped in content such as violence against women, happiness found in harmful drugs, and hatred of the police, these themes will continue reverberating in the minds of the listeners, slowly desensitizing them to otherwise repulsive ideas. Becoming numb to such ideas is the first step toward passively agreeing with them or even personally acting upon them.

Whereas adults can usually listen to such music with no behavioral ramifications, children are far more susceptible to its subtle influence. With less experience of life, a lower level of maturity, and a lack of long-term thinking, young people are prone to make impulsive decisions. Providing them with access to music that fuels negative and harmful thoughts is a dangerous decision. We live in an age where violent tragedies such as school shootings are increasingly commonplace. Although various factors contribute to such acts of violence, hatred-themed music is likely a part of the equation. Therefore, given the influential power of music and the heightened effect it can have on those still in the developmental stage of their lives, young people should have limited access to music with explicit lyrics.

I propose sixteen years of age as a reasonable cutoff. Until children reach that age, they should not be allowed to purchase music with a Parental Advisory label. At sixteen, they are becoming young adults and making more and more of their own decisions. Before sixteen, they are weathering the turbulent transition from middle school to high school. This transition should not be accompanied by music that promotes rebellion as a means of coping with stress and difficulty. After reaching age sixteen,

---

Reason 2: Music is more influential than other entertainment.

Evidence: We all know what getting a song stuck in our heads feels like.

Reason 3: Children are strongly influenced by music.

Evidence: accommodates opposing view while connecting music and violence

Offers an explanation for choosing sixteen as age cutoff

5

however, most young people will have obtained a driver's license, and the freedom that it allows eliminates the possibility of protecting youth from certain music. That is, those with a driver's license can seek out their own venues to hear explicit content, whether concerts or elsewhere.

Opposing view: Three views are expressed.

The main critique of my position is not new. Many say that it's pointless to censor music's explicit content because, as the RIAA's Web site contends, "music is a reflection, not a cause; it doesn't create the problems our society faces, it forces us to confront them" ("Freedom of Speech"). It is true that music reflects our culture. But it is also true that music fuels the perpetuation of that culture, for better or for worse. Guarding youth from explicit music does not equate to ignoring the issues raised in the music. It merely delegates that task to adults rather than to children.

Another critique says that limiting youth access to explicit music would take a financial toll on the music industry. This is true, but it would also force the music industry to adapt. We can either allow the youth of our nation to adapt to the music industry, or we can force the industry to adapt to an impressionable generation of kids.

A third critique is that even if explicit music were restricted to those of a certain age, younger kids would find access to it anyway. This is a legitimate concern, especially given the explosion of music-downloading software. But if not only music outlet stores but also online companies such as Amazon.com and iTunes were included in the regulations, progress would surely come.

Conclusion: quotes hip-hop artist to offer final support for claim

Hip-hop artist Ja Rule has spoken in favor of the current Parental Advisory system, saying, "That's what we can do as musicians to try to deter the kids from getting that lyrical content." But he added, "I don't think it deters the kids—it's just another sticker on the tape right now" (Bowes). Even hip-hop artists agree that protecting the minds of our youth is a necessity. But until laws are passed to restrict access to this music, the "Parental Advisory" label will just be another logo on the CD cover.

10

Sources: documents sources used

Works Cited

Bowes, Peter. "Spotlight on Explicit Lyrics Warning." *BBC News World Edition*. BBC, 27 May 2002. Web. 18 Sept. 2012.

"Freedom of Speech." *RIAA*. Recording Industry Association of America, n.d. Web. 17 Sept. 2012.

"Parental Advisory." *RIAA*. Recording Industry Association of America, n.d. Web. 18 Sept. 2012.

Responding to Sturm's Essay

1. Discuss Sturm's proposal to ban the sale of "explicit music" to children. How are other media — such as books, movies, magazines, and TV shows — treated similarly or differently when it comes to children?

2. What is the benefit, if any, of having explicit lyrics in music? Why are they needed, or why should they be allowed at all?

3. Write an essay discussing the following dilemma: A middle-school student wants to listen to explicit music, but it is not legally available to her age group. Her parents do not want her to have access to such music. Is there a compromise position? What advice would you offer to each side?

Finding Ideas for Your Argument Essay

Reading assignments for this class and your other college courses are good sources of ideas for argument essays. Class discussions and college lectures are other good sources. You can also discover issues by reading or listening to the national news, reading print or online magazines, reading blogs, checking social media, and so forth. If you keep a writing journal, you may find good ideas there, as well. Here are a few guidelines to use in choosing an issue.

- Think about issues on which you've heard different positions. These can be school or community issues or national or international ones—or they can simply be issues related to people's everyday lives.

- Think about a topic on which you *haven't* heard different positions. Are there nevertheless different positions that could be taken?

- Brainstorm about *various*—not just two—different sides of an issue. Think of reasons and evidence that support these different viewpoints.

- Look online to see what people are saying about a topic that is of interest to you. Or go to an online newspaper and read people's comments on articles.

Selecting an Issue to Write About

The first step is to choose an issue that interests you and that you want to learn more about. Also consider how much you already know about the topic; if you choose an unfamiliar issue, you will need to conduct extensive research. To discover a workable issue, try some of the prewriting strategies discussed in Chapter 4. Regardless of the issue you choose, make sure that it is arguable and that it is narrow enough for an essay-length argument.

Considering Your Audience

Once you choose an issue, be sure to consider the audience. The reasons and the types of evidence you offer, the needs and values to which you appeal, and the common ground you establish all depend on the audience. Use the following questions to analyze your intended readers.

- What do my readers already know about the issue? What do they still need to know?
- Do my readers care about the issue? Why, or why not?
- Is my audience an agreeing, a neutral or wavering, or a disagreeing audience? What opinions do they have on the issue?
- What do I have in common with my readers? What shared views or concerns can I use to establish common ground?

Developing a Claim in Your Thesis

Research is often an essential part of developing an argument. Reading what others have written on the issue helps you gather crucial background information, reliable evidence, and alternative viewpoints. For many arguments, you will need to consult both library and Internet sources.

After doing research about the issue, your views on it may soften, harden, or change in some other way. For instance, research on the mandatory use of seat belts may turn up statistics, expert testimony, and firsthand accounts of lives saved by seat belts in automobile accidents, leading you to reconsider your earlier view opposing mandatory use. Therefore, before developing a thesis and making a claim, reconsider your views in light of your research.

As noted earlier, the thesis for an argument essay makes a claim about the issue. As you draft your thesis, be careful to avoid general statements that are not arguable. Instead, make your claim arguable and specific, and state it clearly. Note the difference between a vague statement and a specific claim in the following examples.

VAGUE   In recent years, U.S. citizens have experienced an increase in credit-card fraud.

SPECIFIC   Although the carelessness of merchants and electronic tampering contribute to the problem, U.S. consumers are largely to blame for the recent increase in credit-card fraud.

The first example merely states a fact and is not a valid thesis for an argument. The second example makes a specific claim about an issue that is arguable.

Considering Opposing Viewpoints

Once you are satisfied with your claim and reasons and evidence, you are ready to consider opposing viewpoints; it is time to decide how to acknowledge, accommodate, and/or refute them. If you fail to at least acknowledge opposing viewpoints, readers may assume you did not think the issue through or that you dismissed alternative views without seriously considering them. In some situations, you may choose merely to acknowledge opposing ideas. At other times, you may need to accommodate opposing views, refute them, or both.

Create a list of all the pros and cons on your issue, if you haven't already done so. Then make another list of all possible objections to your argument. Try to group the objections to form two or more points of opposition.

To acknowledge an opposing viewpoint without refuting it, you can mention the opposition in your claim, as shown in this claim about sexual harassment.

▶ **Although mere insensitivity may occasionally be confused with sexual harassment, most instances of sexual harassment are clear-cut.**

The opposing viewpoint mentioned here is that insensitivity may be confused wih sexual harassment. By including it as part of the claim, the writer shows that he or she takes it seriously.

To accommodate an opposing viewpoint, find a portion of the opposing argument that you can build into your own argument. One common way to accommodate readers' objections is to suggest alternative causes for a particular situation. For example, suppose your argument defends the competency of most high-school teachers. You suspect, however, that some readers think the quality of most high-school instruction is poor and attribute it to teachers' laziness or lack of skill. You can accommodate this opposing view by recognizing that there are some high schools in which poor instruction is widespread. You could then suggest that the problem is often owing to a lack of instructional supplies and the disruptive behavior of students rather than to teachers' incompetence.

If you choose to argue that an opposing view is not sound, you must refute it by pointing out problems or flaws in your opponent's reasoning or evidence. Check to see if your opponent uses faulty reasoning or fallacies. To refute an opponent's evidence, use one or more of the following guidelines.

1. **Give a counterexample, or exception, to the opposing view.** For instance, if an opponent argues that dogs are protective, give an example of a situation in which a dog did not protect its owner.

2. **Question the opponent's facts.** If an opponent claims that few professors give essay exams, present statistics demonstrating that a significant percentage of professors do give essay exams.

3. **Demonstrate that an example is not representative.** If an opponent argues that professional athletes are overpaid and cites the salaries of two famous quarterbacks, cite statistics showing that these salaries are not representative of all professional athletes.

4. **Demonstrate that the examples are insufficient.** If an opponent argues that horseback riding is a dangerous sport and offers two examples of

riders who were seriously injured, point out that two examples are not sufficient proof.

5. **Question the credibility of an authority.** If an opponent quotes a television personality regarding welfare reform, point out that she is not a sociologist or a public-policy expert and therefore is not an authority on welfare reform.

6. **Question outdated examples, facts, or statistics.** If an opponent presents evidence that is not recent on the need for more campus parking, you can argue that the situation has changed (for example, enrollment has declined or bus service has increased).

7. **Present the full context of a quotation or statistical evidence.** If an opponent quotes an authority selectively or cites incomplete statistics from a research study linking sunburn and skin cancer, the full context may show that your opponent has "edited" the evidence to suit his or her claim.

Drafting Your Argument Essay

You are now ready to organize your ideas and draft your essay. Organizing and drafting an argument involve deciding on a line of reasoning, choosing a method of organization, and developing the essay accordingly.

Here are four common ways to organize an argument.

Method I	Method II	Method III	Method IV
Claim/thesis	Claim/thesis	Support	Opposing viewpoints
Support	Opposing viewpoints	Opposing viewpoints	Support
Opposing viewpoints	Support	Claim/thesis	Claim/thesis

The method you choose depends on your particular audience, purpose, and issue. Often, it is best to state your claim at the outset. In some cases, however, stating the claim at the end of the argument is more effective. You also need to decide whether to present reasons and supporting evidence before or after you discuss opposing viewpoints. Finally, decide the order in which you will discuss your reasons and supporting evidence: Will you arrange them from strongest to weakest? From most to least obvious? From familiar to unfamiliar?

Once you have chosen a method of organization, it is time to write the first draft. Use the following guidelines.

1. **Write an effective introduction.** The introduction should identify the issue and offer background information based on the audience's knowledge and experience. Many argument essays also include a thesis in the introduction, where the writers make their *claim*. To engage your readers, you might relate a personal experience, make an attention-getting remark, or recognize a counterargument.

2. **Clearly state the reasons for your claim, and provide supporting evidence.** Each reason can be used to anchor the evidence that follows it. One approach is to use each reason as a topic sentence. The rest of the paragraph and perhaps those that follow would then consist of evidence supporting that particular reason.

3. **Cite the sources of your research.** As you present the evidence, you must include a citation for each quotation, summary, or paraphrase of ideas or information you borrowed from sources.

4. **Use transitions to help readers follow your argument.** Make sure you use transitions to move clearly from reason to reason, as in "*Also relevant* to the issue . . ." and "*Furthermore*, it is important to consider. . . ." Also, be certain to distinguish your reasons and evidence from those of the opposition. Use a transitional sentence — such as "Those opposed to the death penalty claim . . ." — to indicate that you are about to introduce an opposing viewpoint. A transition can also be used to signal a refutation, such as "Contrary to what those in favor of the death penalty maintain . . . ."

Revising Your Argument Essay

If possible, set your draft aside for a day or two before rereading and revising it. Then, as you review your draft, focus on discovering weak areas and strengthening the overall argument, not on grammar or mechanics. Use the flowchart in Figure 18.3 to guide your analysis.

Editing and Proofreading Your Essay

The last step is to check your revised essay for errors in grammar, spelling, punctuation, and mechanics. In addition, be sure to look for the types of errors you tend to make in any writing, whether for this class or another situation. As you edit and proofread, look out for the following two grammatical errors in particular.

1. **Make sure to use the subjunctive mood correctly.** Because argument essays often address what would or might happen in the future, you will often use the subjunctive mood, which expresses a wish, suggestion, or condition contrary to fact. When using the verb *be* to speculate about conditions in the future, remember to say *were* in place of *was* to indicate a hypothetical situation.

Figure 18.3 Revising an Argument Essay

QUESTIONS	REVISION STRATEGIES
1. Introducing the issue Is the issue clearly defined? Is enough information provided? Is the issue sufficiently narrow? **No**	• Ask a friend unfamiliar with the issue to read this section and identify missing information. • Use a branching diagram or questions to limit your issue (see Chapter 4).
Yes	
2. Thesis Is your claim stated clearly in your thesis? Is it arguable? Is it sufficiently specific and limited? **No**	• Write a one-sentence summary of what the essay intends to prove. • Try limiting the claim. • Add a qualifying word or phrase (*may, possibly*) to your thesis.
Yes	
3. Intended audience Is your essay targeted to your readers—to their knowledge and attitudes? Do you appeal to their needs and values? **No**	• Add more background information. • Add reasons and evidence based on the needs, values, and experiences you share with your readers.
Yes	
4. Reasons and evidence Do you have enough reasons and evidence? Will they be convincing and appealing to your audience? **No**	• Brainstorm or conduct research to discover more reasons, stronger evidence, or more appealing reasons and evidence.
Yes	
5. Argument progression Does each step follow a logical progression? Is your reasoning free of errors? **No**	• Check progression by creating an outline or a graphic organizer. • Omit faulty reasoning and fallacies.
Yes	
6. Organization Is your method of organization clear? Is it effective? **No**	• Experiment with one or more other methods of organization (see Chapter 6).
Yes	
7. Opposing viewpoints Do you acknowledge, accommodate, or refute opposing viewpoints? **No**	• Acknowledge an opposing viewpoint. • Build an opposing viewpoint into your argument. • Refute an opponent's evidence.
Yes	
8. Introduction and conclusion Are they effective? **No**	• Revise your introduction and conclusion so that they meet the guidelines in Chapter 6.

> ►   If all animal research ~~was~~ *were* outlawed, progress in the control of human

> diseases would be slowed dramatically.

2. **Look for and correct pronouns that don't refer back to a clear antecedent.**
    A pronoun must refer to another noun or pronoun, called its *antecedent*.
    The pronoun's antecedent should be clearly named, not just implied.

> ►   Children of divorced parents often are shuttled between two homes,
>
>   and ~~that~~ *this lack of stability* can be confusing and disturbing to them.

Student Resource Guide

Chapter 19

Finding and Using Sources

Quick Start: Suppose that for an American history course you have been assigned to write a five-to-seven page research paper on the history of an American monument and what it represents. You decided to write about the World Trade Center Memorial, shown above. Write a brief statement summarizing what you already know about the memorial and indicating what further information you would need to write about it in detail.

When you responded to the Quick Start prompt, you began the research process: You evaluated what you knew and what you needed to find out. In this chapter you will learn where to look for such information, how to ascertain its value, and how to cite and document it properly.

Sources of information come in many forms. They include materials that come in both print and electronic form (such as books, newspapers, magazines, brochures, and scholarly journals), media sources (DVDs, television, radio), and electronic sources (blogs and podcasts, email). Interviews, personal observations, and surveys are also sources of information.

You can use sources in a variety of ways. For instance, you may plan a paper that is based on your own experiences but discover that you need additional support from outside sources for aspects of the topic. At other times you may start a paper by checking several sources to narrow your topic or become more familiar with it. Finally, you may be asked to write a research paper, which requires the most extensive use of sources.

When Should You Use Sources?

You should use sources whenever the topic requires more factual information than you can provide from your own personal knowledge and experience. Here are some warning signs that may suggest the need for sources.

- You feel as though you do not have enough to say.
- You do not feel comfortable with your topic.
- You have avoided certain aspects of your topic because you do not know enough about them.
- You have unanswered questions about your topic.
- Your essay is too short, but you do not know what to add.

When you plan and develop an essay using sources, you will follow the same process described in Chapters 4, 5, and 6. Use the following guidelines to make your paper with sources successful.

1. **Start with your own ideas.** Your essay should be based on your own ideas. Starting with the sources themselves would result in a summary, not an essay.

2. **Use sources to support your ideas.** Once you have identified the main points of your paper, decide what information is needed to support them. Incorporate sources that will make your ideas believable and acceptable to the reader.

3. **Focus on ideas, not facts.** To maintain a focus on ideas, ask yourself, "What do all these facts add up to?" For example, when writing about campaign-finance reform, instead of concentrating on the amount of money corporations give to politicians, consider what impact the money has on the politicians' agendas.

4. **Avoid strings of facts and quotations.** Writing that strings together fact after fact or quotation after quotation is dull and does not convey ideas effectively. Try to refer to no more than one or two sources per paragraph.

Primary and Secondary Sources

Sources are classified as *primary* or *secondary.* **Primary sources** include historical documents (letters, diaries, speeches); literary works; autobiographies; original research reports; eyewitness accounts; and your own interviews, observations, or correspondence. For example, a report on a study of heart disease written by the researcher who conducted the study is a primary source, as is a novel by William Faulkner. **Secondary sources** report or comment on primary sources. A journal article that reviews several previously published research reports on heart disease is a secondary source. A book written about Faulkner by a literary critic or biographer is a secondary source.

How to Locate Sources

Sources of information range from books and videos to interviews and Web sites. To locate and then evaluate and use sources, you'll find a systematic process helpful (see Figure 19.1).

Figure 19.1 Locating and Using Sources: An Overview

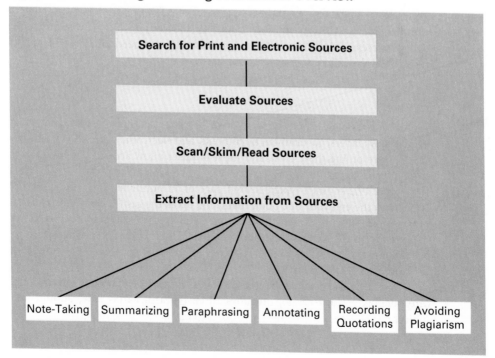

Figure 19.2   Library Catalog Search Page

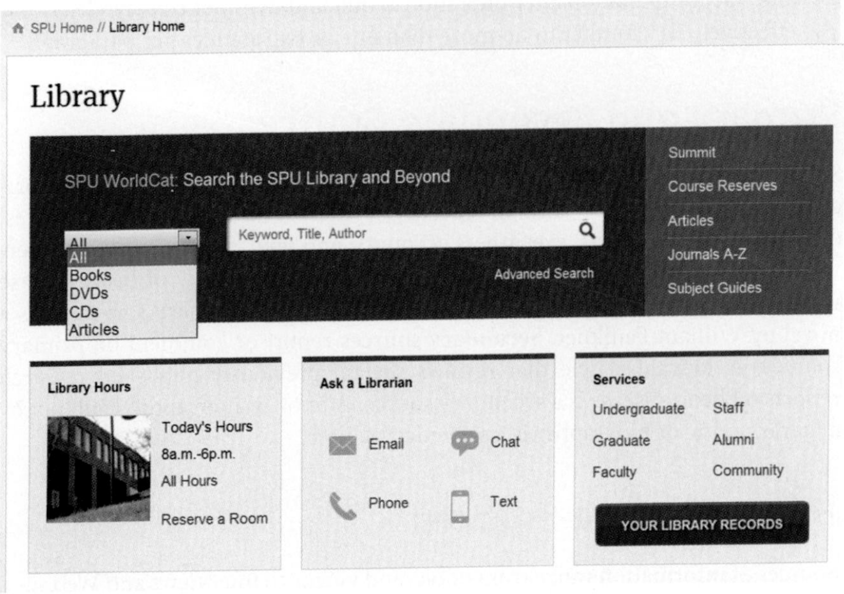

Locating Useful Library Sources

Your college library is one of the best sources of reference materials. Learning to use the library will help you locate sources effectively, which is imperative for college success. To get the most out of your library, you need to know which of its research tools are best for your purposes.

THE LIBRARY CATALOG

A library's catalog lists books owned by the library. It may also list available magazines, newspapers, government documents, and electronic sources. Most library catalogs are online these days, and most libraries allow access to their catalogs from outside computers, at home or in a computer lab on campus.

Figure 19.2 shows a typical search page of an online library catalog. Figure 19.3 shows the entry for one book that came up as the result of an online search of the subject *human-animal relationships*. Catalog entries often indicate whether the book is on the shelves, whether it has been checked out, and when it is due back. Some systems allow you to reserve the book by entering your request on the computer.

For older or special collections, some libraries still maintain a traditional card catalog. A card catalog includes three types of cards: title, author, and subject.

Figure 19.3   Library Catalog Search Results

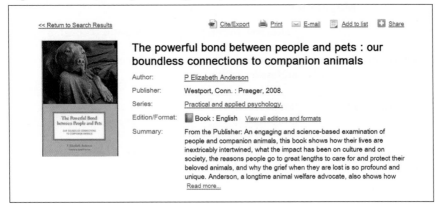

All catalogs provide call numbers that tell you where to locate books on the library's shelves. Once you have a specific call number, use your library's floor plan and the call-number guides posted on shelves to locate the appropriate section of the library and the book you need. Be sure to scan the surrounding books, which are usually on related topics. You may discover other useful sources that you overlooked in the catalog.

LOCATING ARTICLES USING PERIODICAL DATABASES

Periodicals include newspapers, popular magazines, and scholarly journals. Because periodicals are published daily, weekly, or monthly, they often contain up-to-date information about a subject. Table 19.1 on page 678 summarizes the differences between popular magazines (such as *People*) and scholarly journals (such as the *American Journal of Psychology*). For academic essays, it is best not to rely solely on information from popular magazines.

A library's catalog does not list specific articles from magazines or journals. To find such articles, you must consult a periodical database. Most electronic library catalogs provide access to a number of such databases, and more and more of these periodical databases give users access to full-text articles.

When you are searching for articles in a periodical database, look for options that allow you to refine your search. Many databases allow users to limit results by date and publication type. Look for a place to choose "peer reviewed" or "newspapers and magazines" if you need to locate an article from a particular kind of source. Once you locate a relevant article, if full text is available online, find out what your options are for emailing, printing, and saving it. If the full text is not available online, check your library catalog to see whether the library subscribes to the periodical. If not, check with the librarian for interlibrary loan options.

Table 19.1   A Comparison of Scholarly Journals and Popular Magazines

	Scholarly Journal	Popular Magazine
Who reads it?	Researchers, professionals, students	General public
Who writes it?	Researchers, professionals	Reporters, journalists, freelance writers
Who decides what to publish in it?	Other researchers (peer review)	Editors, publishers
What does It look like?	Mostly text, some charts and graphs, little or no advertising	Many photos, many advertisements, eye-catching layout
What kind of information does it contain?	Results of research studies and experiments, statistics and analysis, in-depth evaluations of specialized topics, overviews of all the research on a subject (literature review), bibliographies and references	Articles of general interest, easy-to-understand language, news items, interviews, opinion pieces, no bibliographies (sources cited informally within the article)
Where is it available?	Sometimes by subscription only, large bookstores, large public library branches, college/university libraries, online	Newsstands, most bookstores, most public library branches, online
How often is it published?	Monthly to quarterly	Weekly to monthly
What are some examples?	*Journal of Bioethics, American Journal of Family Law, Film Quarterly*	*Popular Science, Psychology Today, Time*

Some databases list articles on a wide range of subjects. Others are specialized and have articles from scholarly journals in particular fields. Figure 19.4 shows a sample result from a search on the topic of *human-animal relationships* in *Academic Search Premier*, a database that indexes both scholarly *and* popular periodicals.

Figure 19.4   **Result from Search in *Academic Search Premier***

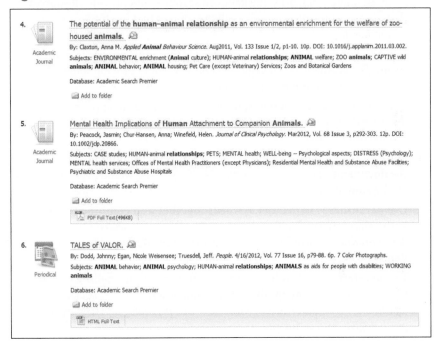

Doing Research on the World Wide Web

The Web contains millions of Web sites, so you will have to use a search engine to locate the information you need. A **search engine** is an application that locates information on a particular topic when a keyword, phrase, or question is entered into a search box. Six commonly used search engines and their URLs follow.

Useful Search Engines

Search Engine	URL
Ask	www.ask.com
Bing	www.bing.com
Go.com	www.go.com
Google	www.google.com
Google Scholar	http://scholar.google.com
Yahoo!	www.yahoo.com

If a keyword or phrase is too general, a search could turn up hundreds or perhaps thousands of sites, most of which will not be helpful to you. Your searches will be more productive if you use the following guidelines for keyword searches.

1. **Place quotation marks around a phrase to limit your search.** For example, "single motherhood" will give you topics related to single motherhood. Without quotation marks, the keyword search would provide all sources that use the word *single* as well as all the sources that use the word *motherhood.*

2. **Use AND or a plus sign (+) to join words that must appear in a document.** For example, *psychology* AND *history* would provide sources that mention both psychology and history.

3. **Use OR to indicate synonyms, when only one needs to appear in the document.** For example, *job* OR *career* would provide more options than just *job* or just *career.*

4. **Place NOT or a minus sign (−) before words that should not appear in the document.** For example, *camels* NOT *cigarettes* would provide sources on the animal only.

5. **Use parentheses to group keywords together and combine them with other keywords.** For example, (*timepiece* OR *watch* OR *clock*) AND *production* would provide sources on production of any of these items.

6. **Use an asterisk (*) to indicate letters that may vary in spelling or words that may have variant endings.** For example, a search for "social psycholog*" will find sources with the words *psychology, psychologist, psychologists,* and so forth.

Evaluating Sources for Relevance and Reliability

Many students make the mistake of photocopying many articles, printing out dozens of Web pages, and lugging home numerous books only to find that the sources are not useful or that several contain identical information. Save yourself time by thinking about which sources will be most relevant and reliable.

Questions for Evaluating Sources for Relevance

A *relevant source* contains information that helps you answer one or more of your research questions. Answering the following questions will help you determine whether a source is relevant.

1. **Is the source appropriate—not too general or too specialized—for your intended audience?** Some sources may not contain the detailed information your audience requires; others may be too technical and require background knowledge that your audience does not have. For example, suppose you are writing about the environmental effects of recycling cans and bottles for an audience of science majors. An article in *Reader's Digest* might be too general. An article in *Environmental Science and Technology*, written for scientists, may be a bit too technical.

2. **Is the source recent enough for your purposes?** In rapidly changing fields of study, outdated sources are not useful unless you need to give a historical perspective. For example, a ten-year-old article on using air bags to improve car safety will not include information on recent discoveries about the dangers that air bags pose to children riding in the front passenger seat.

Questions for Evaluating Sources for Reliability

A *reliable source is* honest, accurate, and credible. Answering the questions below will help you determine whether a source is reliable. (To check the reliability of an Internet source, consult pp. 682–83 as well.)

1. **Is the source scholarly?** Although scholars often disagree with one another, they make a serious attempt to present accurate information. In addition, an article that appears in a scholarly journal or textbook has been reviewed by a panel of professionals in the field prior to publication. Therefore, scholarly sources tend to be trustworthy. For more on the differences between scholarly and popular sources, refer to Table 19.1 on page 678.

2. **Does the source have a solid reputation?** Some popular magazines, such as *Time* and *Newsweek*, are known for responsible reporting, whereas others have a reputation for sensationalism and should be avoided or approached skeptically. Web sites, too, may or may not be reputable.

3. **Is the author an expert in the field?** Check the author's credentials. Information about authors may be given in a headnote; at the end of an article; on a home page in a link; or in the preface, on the dust jacket, or at the beginning or end of a book.

4. **Does the author approach the topic fairly and objectively?** A writer who states a strong opinion is not necessarily biased. However, a writer who ignores opposing views, distorts facts, or ignores information that does not fit his or her opinion is presenting a biased and incomplete view of a topic. Although you can use a biased source to understand a particular viewpoint, you must also seek out other sources that present alternative views.

Table 19.2   Evaluating Internet Sources

Purpose	• Who sponsors or publishes the site — an organization, a corporation, a government agency, or an individual? • What are the sponsor's goals — to present information or news, to voice opinions, to sell products, or to promote fun?
Author	• Who wrote the information on the site? • Is the information clearly presented and well written?
Accuracy	• Are ideas supported by credible evidence? Is there a works-cited list or bibliography? • Is the information presented verifiable? • Are opinions clearly identified as such?
Timeliness	• When was the site first created? What is the date of the last revision? • Does the specific document you are using have a date? • Are the links up-to-date?

Evaluating Internet Sources

The Internet offers many excellent and reputable sources. However, misinformation often appears on the Web, so it is especially important to evaluate Web sources carefully. Use the following questions to evaluate the reliability of Internet sources. (Table 19.2 summarizes these questions.)

WHAT IS THE SITE'S PURPOSE?

Web sites have many different purposes. They may provide information or news, advocate a particular point of view, or try to sell a product. Many sites have more than one purpose. A pharmaceutical company's site, for instance, may offer health advice in addition to advertising its own drugs. Understanding the purposes of an Internet source will help you deal with its potential biases.

To determine the purpose of any site, start by identifying the sponsor of the site—the organization or person who paid to place it on the Web. The copyright usually reveals the owner of a site, and often a link labeled "About Us," "About Me," or "Mission Statement" will take you to a description of the sponsor.

WHAT ARE THE AUTHOR'S CREDENTIALS?

It helps to know who wrote the Web page you are looking at. The sponsors of many Web sites have professionals write their content. When this is the case, the writer's name and credentials are usually listed, and his or her email address may be provided. If information about an author is not available on the site or is sketchy, you might conduct a search for the author's name on the Web.

Regardless of who the author of the site is, the information should be well written and organized. If the sponsor did not spend time presenting information correctly and clearly, the information itself may not be very accurate.

IS THE SITE'S INFORMATION ACCURATE?

In addition to paying attention to how a site's material is written and organized, ask yourself the following questions.

- **Is a bibliography or a list of works cited provided?** If sources are not included, you should question the accuracy of the site.
- **Can the accuracy of the information be checked elsewhere?** In most instances you should be able to verify Internet information by checking another source, often simply by clicking on links in the original source.
- **Is the document in complete form?** If you're looking at a summary, use the site to try to find the original source. Original information generally has fewer errors and is often preferred in academic papers.

IS THE SITE UP-TO-DATE?

You can check the timeliness of a site by asking yourself the following questions about dates.

- **If the site has been revised, what is the date of the last revision?** Updating a site regularly is essential for sites that feature current events or report time-sensitive data.
- **When was the document you are looking at posted to the site?** Has it been updated?

This kind of information generally appears at the bottom of a site's home page or at the end of a particular document. If no dates are given, check some of the links. If the links are outdated and nonfunctioning, the information at the site is probably outdated as well.

Working with Text: Reading Sources

Reading sources involves some special skills. Unlike textbook reading, in which your purpose is to learn and recall the material, you usually read sources to extract the information you need about a topic. Therefore, you can often read sources selectively, reading only the relevant parts and skipping over the rest. Use the following strategies for reading sources: scan, skim, and then read closely.

Scanning a Source

Scanning means "looking for" the information you seek without actually reading a source from beginning to end. Just as you scan a phone directory to locate a phone number, you scan a source to extract needed information.

Use the following guidelines to scan sources effectively.

1. **Determine how the source is organized.** For example, is it organized chronologically or by topic?
2. **For journal articles, check the abstract or summary; for books, scan the index and table of contents.** You can quickly determine whether the source contains the information you need and, if so, approximately where to find it.
3. **Keep key words or phrases in mind as you scan.** For example, if you are searching for information on welfare reform, key phrases might include *welfare system, entitlement programs, benefits,* and *welfare spending.*
4. **Scan systematically.** Follow a pattern as you sweep your eyes across the material. For charts, tables, and indexes, use a downward sweep. For prose material, use a zigzag or Z-pattern, sweeping across several lines of print at a time.

Skimming a Source

Skimming (also called *previewing*) is a quick way to find out whether a source suits your purposes and, if so, whether any sections deserve close reading. As you skim a source, mark or jot down sections that might be worth returning to later.

Use the guidelines on pages 23–24 to skim a source effectively; adapt them to fit each particular source.

Reading a Source Closely

Once you identify the sections within a source that contain the information you need—by scanning, skimming, or both—*read* those sections closely and carefully. To be sure you do not take information out of context, also read the paragraphs before and after the material you have chosen. (For more on strategies for close reading, see Chapters 2 and 3.)

Improving Your Reading of Electronic Sources

When you read material on the Internet, you often need some different reading strategies. The following advice should help you read Web sites more productively.

- **When you reach a new site, explore it quickly to discover how it is organized and what information is available.** Find out if there is a search option or a guide to the site (a site map). Doing an initial exploration is especially important on large and complex sites.

- **Keep in mind that text on Web sites does not usually follow the traditional text pattern.** Instead of containing paragraphs, a Web page may show a list of topic sentences that you have to click on to get details. In addition, electronic pages are often designed to stand alone: They are brief and do not depend on other pages for meaning. In many instances, background information is not supplied.

- **Follow your own learning style in making decisions about what paths to follow.** Because Web sites have menus and links, readers create their own texts by following or ignoring different paths. Some readers may prefer to begin with "the big picture" and then move to the details; others may prefer to do the opposite. All readers should make sure that they don't skip over important content.

- **Focus on your purpose.** Keep in mind the information you are looking for. If you don't focus on your purpose, you may wander aimlessly through the site and waste valuable research time.

Extracting Information from Sources

As you read sources, you will need to take notes to use later. Different note-taking systems can help you with summaries, paraphrases, and quotations. Careful note-taking can help you avoid plagiarism.

Gathering Necessary Citation Information

As you work with print sources, be sure to record information for each source. Figure 19.5 on page 686 provides an example of a form showing the information you'll need. Recording this information will help you locate the source again—in case you need to verify something or find additional information. It will also give you the information you need for citing the source.

When using electronic sources, be sure to print out all the information you might need to cite the source. For Web sources, this includes the author and title

Figure 19.5   Bibliographic Information Worksheet for Print Sources

Author(s) _____

Title _____

Beginning Page _____   Ending Page _____

Title of Periodical _____

Volume Number _____   Issue Number _____

Date of Issue _____

Call Number _____

Publisher _____

Place of Publication _____

Copyright Date _____

of the document; the title of the site; the sponsoring organization; the date of publication or of the last update; the number of pages, paragraphs, sections, or screens, if they are numbered in the document; the access date; and the URL. For an online periodical article, be sure your printouts also include the periodical name, any volume and issue numbers, and the print publication information (periodical name, publisher, date, and so on) if the article was originally published in print.

Systems of Note-Taking

When you take research notes, you'll probably need to copy quotes, write paraphrases, and make summary notes. There are three ways to record your research—on note cards, on your computer, or on copies of source material.

Regardless of the system you use, be sure to designate a place to record your own ideas, such as different-colored index cards, a notepad, or a computer folder. Be careful as well not to simply record (or highlight) quotations. Writing summary notes or paraphrases helps you think about the ideas in your source, how they fit with other ideas, and how they might work in your research paper.

NOTE CARDS

Some researchers use 4- by 6-inch or 5- by 8-inch index cards for note-taking. If you use this system, put information from only one source or about only one subtopic on each card. At the top of the card, indicate the author of

Figure 19.6   Sample Note Card

Schmoke & Roques, 17-25

Medicalization

Medicalization is a system in which the government would control the release of narcotics to drug addicts.
 —would work like a prescription does now — only gov't official would write prescription
  — addicts would be required to get counseling and health services
  — would take drug control out of hands of drug traffickers (paraphrase, 18)

the source and the subtopic that the note covers. Be sure to include page numbers in case you need to go back and reread the article or passage. If you copy an author's exact words, place the information in quotation marks and include the term *direct quotation* and the page number in parentheses. If you write a summary note (see p. 688) or paraphrase (see pp. 689–90), write *paraphrase* or *summary* on the card and the page number of the source. When you use this system, you can rearrange your cards and experiment with different ways of organizing as you plan your paper. Figure 19.6 shows a sample note card.

COMPUTERIZED NOTE-TAKING

Another option is to type your notes into computer files and organize your files by subtopic. To do so, use a computer notebook to create small "note cards," or use a hypertext card program. As with note cards, keep track of sources by including the author's name and the page numbers for each source, and make a back-up copy of your notes. If you have access to a computer in the library, you can type in summaries, paraphrases, and direct quotations while you are doing the research.

ANNOTATED COPIES OF SOURCES

This approach is most appropriate for very short papers that do not involve numerous sources or extensive research. To use this system, photocopy or print the source material; underline or highlight useful information; and write your reactions, paraphrases, and summary notes in the margins or on attachments to the appropriate page. Annotating source material often saves time because you don't need to copy quotations or write lengthy notes. The disadvantage, in addition to the expense of photocopying, is that this system does not allow you to sort and rearrange notes by subtopic. For advice on highlighting and annotating, see Chapters 2 and 3, pages 33–34 and pages 78–79.

Writing Summary Notes

Much of your note-taking will be in the form of summary notes, which condense information from sources. Take summary notes when you want to record the gist of an author's ideas but do not need the exact wording or a paraphrase. Use the guidelines below to write effective summary notes. Remember that everything you put in summary notes must be in your own words.

1. **Record only information that relates to your topic and purpose.** Do not include irrelevant information.

2. **Write notes that condense the author's ideas into your own words.** Include key terms and concepts. Do not include specific examples, quotations, or anything that is not essential to the main point. (You can include any comments in a separate note, as suggested earlier.)

3. **Record the ideas in the order in which they appear in the original source.** Reordering ideas might affect the meaning.

4. **Reread your summary to determine whether it contains sufficient information.** Would it be understandable to someone who has not read the original source? If not, revise the summary to include additional information.

5. **Jot down the publication information for the sources you summarize.** Unless you summarize an entire book or poem, you will need page references to cite your sources.

A sample summary is shown below. It summarizes the first three paragraphs of the essay "The Lady in Red," which appears in Chapter 10 (pp. 202–204). Read the paragraphs, and then study the summary.

Sample Summary

In Poubsbo, on Thanksgiving Day, 2002, Richard LeMieux spent his last money on a hamburger for his dog, Willow. Because he was low on gas, hungry, and out of money, he turned to begging. Prior to this day, he held successful jobs, including sportswriting and sales. Working within a corporate environment required him to work with people and dress appropriately. In sales he had to convince people to invest in his product. He found begging to be more challenging.

Writing Paraphrases

When you **paraphrase**, you restate the author's ideas in your own words. You do not condense ideas or eliminate details as you do in a summary. Instead, you use different sentence patterns and vocabulary but keep the author's meaning. In most cases, a paraphrase is approximately the same length as the original material. Compose a paraphrase when you want to record the author's ideas and details but do not want to use a direct quotation. When paraphrasing, be especially careful not to use the author's sentence patterns or vocabulary, as doing so would result in *plagiarism* (see pp. 690–92). Read the excerpt from a source below; then compare it to the paraphrase that follows.

Excerpt from Original

Learning some items may interfere with retrieving others, especially when the items are similar. If someone gives you a phone number to remember, you may be able to recall it later. But if two more people give you their numbers, each successive number will be more difficult to recall. Such proactive interference occurs when something you learned earlier disrupts recall of something you experienced later. As you collect more and more information, your mental attic never fills, but it certainly gets cluttered.

—David G. Myers, *Psychology*

Paraphrase

When proactive interference happens, things you have already learned prevent you from remembering things you learn later. In other words, details you learn first may make it harder to recall closely related details you learn subsequently. You can think of your memory as an attic. As you add more junk to it, it will become messy and disorganized. For example, you can remember one new phone number, but if you have two or more new numbers to remember, the task becomes harder.

Writing paraphrases can be tricky, both because there are so many ways to paraphrase a particular passage and because an author's language can easily "creep in." The following guidelines should help you write effective paraphrases.

1. **Read first; then write.** You may find it helpful to read material more than once before you try paraphrasing.

2. **If you must use any of the author's wording, enclose it in quotation marks.** If you do not use quotation marks, you may inadvertently use the same wording in your paper, which would result in plagiarism.

3. **Work sentence by sentence, restating each in your own words.** To avoid copying an author's words, read a sentence, cover it up, and then write. Be sure your version is accurate but not too similar to the original. As a rule of

thumb, no more than two or three consecutive words should be the same as in the original.

4. **Choose synonyms that do not change the author's meaning or intent.** Consult a dictionary if necessary.

5. **Use your own sentence structure.** Using an author's sentence structure can be considered plagiarism. If the original uses lengthy sentences, for example, your paraphrase of it should use shorter sentences.

6. **Record the publication information.** You will need this information to document the sources in your paper.

Recording Quotations

Sometimes it is advisable, and even necessary, to use a direct quotation—a writer's words exactly as they appear in the original source. Use quotations to record wording that is unusual or striking or to report the exact words of an expert on your topic. Such quotations, when used sparingly, can be effective in a paper. When using a direct quotation, be sure to record it precisely as it appears in the source. The author's spelling, punctuation, and capitalization must be recorded exactly. Also write down the page number on which the material being quoted appears in the source. Be sure to indicate that you are copying a direct quotation by writing *direct quotation* in parentheses.

You may delete a word, phrase, or sentence from a quotation as long as you do not change the meaning of the quotation. Use an ellipsis mark (three spaced periods)— . . . —to indicate that you have made a deletion.

Avoiding Plagiarism

In writing a paper with sources, you must avoid **plagiarism**—using someone else's ideas, wording, organization, or sentence structure as if they were your own. Plagiarizing is intellectually dishonest and considered a form of cheating because it involves submitting someone else's work as your own. Harsh academic penalties are applied to students found guilty of plagiarism; these often include receiving a failing grade on the paper, failing the entire course, or even being dismissed from the institution.

What Counts as Plagiarism

There are two types of plagiarism—intentional (deliberate) and unintentional (accidental). They are equally serious and carry the same academic penalties. The following count as plagiarism:

- **using information copied word for word but without appropriate quotation marks,** even if you acknowledge the source;

- **paraphrasing, summarizing, or otherwise using information without acknowledging** the source;
- **using someone else's visual material** (graphs, tables, charts, maps, diagrams) **without acknowledging** the source;
- **using another student's work or purchasing a paper online** and submitting it as your own.

Cyberplagiarism, or plagiarism involving Internet sources, may also be intentional or unintentional and is as serious as any other plagiarism. Cyberplagiarism takes several common forms:

- **borrowing information from the Internet without giving credit** to the source posting the information,
- **"cut-and-paste plagiarism"**—copying text directly from an Internet source and pasting it into your own essay without giving credit,
- **purchasing a student paper on the Internet** and submitting it as your own work.

How to Avoid Plagiarism

To avoid plagiarism, you need to be very careful both when taking notes and when composing your paper. Here are some guidelines to follow when note-taking.

- **Place anything you copy in quotation marks and record the source.**
- **Record the source for any information** you paraphrase, summarize, or otherwise include in your notes.
- **Be sure to separate your own ideas from ideas expressed in your sources.** Try using two different colors of ink or two different print sizes for your ideas and your sources' ideas. Alternatively, use two different sections of a notebook or two different computer files.

When you are working with Internet sources, follow these suggestions.

- **Always cut and paste information you want to save into a file for notes,** rather than directly into your paper.
- **When you make notes on ideas, opinions, or other information you encounter on the Internet, be sure to include source information for each item.**
- **Be sure to record all information for each source—the name of the site, the date of access, and so on.**

When you compose your paper, having followed these guidelines should help you avoid plagiarism. In addition, keep these tips in mind.

- **Acknowledge all information from your sources unless it is common knowledge. Common knowledge** includes well-known facts (everyday information, scientific facts, historical events, and so on).

- **Place in quotation marks everything you copy directly from a source.**

- **Make sure that a paraphrase does not mix the author's wording and your own.**

- **Always acknowledge the ideas or opinions of others, even if you do not quote them directly and regardless of whether they are in print or another medium.** For example, movies, videos, documentaries, interviews, and computerized sources all require acknowledgment.

Documenting Your Sources: MLA Style

To avoid plagiarism, you need to acknowledge your sources by **documenting** them. Documentation also helps interested readers find those sources.

There are various systems of documentation that have become the standards for specific disciplines. The system described in this section is recommended by the Modern Language Association (MLA). MLA style is commonly used in English and the humanities. If you are unsure as to whether or not to use the MLA system, check with your instructor.

In the MLA system, documentation has two parts that work together.

1. In-text citations identify sources within the text of the paper.

2. A list of works cited, at the end of the paper, gives full information on each of the sources.

This chapter provides models for documenting some common types of sources. For more information, consult:

   MLA Handbook for Writers of Research Papers, 7th ed. New York: MLA, 2009. Print.

The student paper that appears later in this chapter uses MLA style (see pp. 709–16), as do student papers in Chapters 14 and 16–18.

In-Text Citations

When you paraphrase, summarize, or quote from a source, you must credit the source by providing an in-text citation at that point in your paper. The in-text citation includes a brief reference to the source, for which there is more complete information in the list of works cited, and tells the reader where in your source the material came from. There are two basic ways to write an in-text citation: (1) an attribution with parenthetical source information or (2) an entirely parenthetical citation.

USE AN ATTRIBUTION

When you use an attribution, you mention the author's name before presenting the borrowed material. Use the author's full name for the first mention; subsequent mentions generally include only the last name. (Upon first mention, you might also provide background context that establishes the source as relevant.) The parenthetical content, with the page number(s) and sometimes a shortened title of the source, immediately follows the borrowed material.

> Jo-Ellan Dimitius, a jury-selection consultant whose book *Reading People* discusses methods of predicting behavior, observes that big spenders often suffer from low self-esteem (35).

USE A PARENTHETICAL CITATION

When citing a source parenthetically, include both the author's last name and the page number(s) in parentheses at the end of the sentence. Do not separate the name and page number with a comma.

> Big spenders often suffer from low self-esteem (Dimitius 35).

RULES FOR IN-TEXT CITATIONS

Many instructors prefer that you use attributions rather than parenthetical citations. For either type of citation, the following rules apply.

- Do not use the word *page* or the abbreviations *p.* or *pp.*
- Place the sentence period after the closing parenthesis, unless the citation follows a block quotation (see below).
- Insert closing quotation marks before the parentheses.

> "Countercultures reject the conventional wisdom and standards of the dominant culture and provide alternatives to mainstream culture" (Thompson and Hickey 76).

In MLA style, lengthy quotations (more than three lines of poetry or more than four typed lines of prose) are indented in *block form*, one inch from the left margin. Double-space a block quotation and do not put it in quotation marks. Introduce a block quotation in the sentence that precedes it; a colon is often used at the end of the introduction. The parenthetical citation appears at the end of the block quotation, *after* the final sentence's period.

Block Quotation, MLA Style

Although a business is a profit-making organization, it is also a social organization. As Hicks and Gwynne note:

> In Western society, businesses are essentially economic organizations, with both the organizations themselves and the individuals in them dedicated to making as much money as possible in the most efficient way. But businesses are also social organizations, each of which has its unique culture. Like all social groups, businesses are made up of people of both sexes and a wide range of ages, who play different

roles, occupy different positions in the group, and behave in different ways while at work. (174)

SOME MLA IN-TEXT CITATION MODELS

The following are some examples for in-text citations for some common types of sources.

One Author

> According to Vance Packard . . . (58).
>
> . . . (Packard 58).

Two or Three Authors   Include all authors' names, in either an attribution or a parenthetical citation.

> Marquez and Allison assert . . . (74).
>
> . . . (Marquez and Allison 74).

Four or More Authors   You may use all of the authors' last names or the first author's last name followed by either a phrase referring to the other authors (in an attribution) or *et al.*, Latin for "and others" (in a parenthetical citation). Whichever option you choose, apply it consistently within your paper.

> Hong and colleagues maintain . . . (198).
>
> . . . (Hong et al. 198).

Two or More Works by the Same Author   When citing two or more sources by the same author, include the full or abbreviated title to indicate the proper work.

First Work

In *For God, Country, and Coca-Cola*, Pendergrast describes . . . (96).

Pendergrast describes . . . (*For God* 96).

. . . (Pendergrast, *For God* 96).

Second Work

In *Uncommon Grounds*, Pendergrast maintains . . . (42).

Pendergrast maintains . . . (*Uncommon* 42).

. . . (Pendergrast, *Uncommon* 42).

Corporate or Organizational Author   When the author is given as a corporation, an organization, or a government office, reference the organization's name as the author name. Use abbreviations such as *Natl.* and *Cong.* in parenthetical references.

According to the National Institute of Mental Health . . . (2).

. . . (Natl. Institute of Mental Health 2).

Unknown Author   Use the full title in an attribution or a shortened form in parentheses.

According to the article "Medical Mysteries and Surgical Surprises," . . . (79).

. . . ("Medical Mysteries" 79).

Entire Work   To refer to an entire work, such as a Web site, a film, or a book, use the author's name, preferably within the text; do not include page numbers. The title is optional.

In *For God, Country, and Coca-Cola,* Pendergrast presents an unauthorized

history of Coca-Cola, the soft drink and the company that produces it.

Chapter in an Edited Book or Work in an Anthology   An **anthology** is a collection of writings by different authors. In the in-text citation, name the author who wrote the work (not the editor of the anthology), and include the page number(s) from the anthology.

According to Ina Ferris . . . (239).

. . . (Ferris 239).

Indirect Source   When quoting an indirect source (someone whose ideas came to you through another source, such as a magazine article or book), make this clear by adding, in parentheses, the last name and page number of the source in which the quote or information appeared, preceded by the abbreviation *qtd. in.*

According to Ephron (qtd. in Thomas 33), . . .

Personal Interview, Letter, Email, Conversation   Give the name of the person in your text.

In an interview with Professor Lopez, . . .

Literature and Poetry   Include information that will help readers locate the material in any edition of the literary work. Include page numbers from the edition you use.

- *For novels:* Cite page and chapter numbers.

  (109; ch. 5)

- *For poems:* Cite line numbers instead of page numbers; use the word *line* or *lines* in the first reference only.

  First reference   (lines 12–15)

  Later references   (16–18)

- *For plays:* Give the act, scene, and line numbers in arabic numerals, separated by periods.

(*Macbeth* 2.1.32–37)

Include complete publication information for the edition you use in the list of works cited.

Internet Sources   In general, Internet sources are cited like their printed counterparts. Give enough information in the citation so that readers can locate the source in your list of works cited. If the electronic source provides page numbers, you should provide them, too. If the source uses another ordering system, such as paragraphs (*par.* or *pars.*), sections (*sec.*), or screens (*screen*), provide the abbreviation with the appropriate number.

Brian Beckman argues that "centrifugal force is a fiction" (par. 6).

. . . (Beckman, par. 6).

If the source does not have paragraphs or page numbers, which is often the case, then cite the work by author, title of the document or site, or sponsor of the site, whichever begins your entry in the list of works cited.

Author

Teresa Schmidt discusses . . .

. . . (Schmidt).

Title

The "Band of Brothers" section of the History Channel site . . .

. . . ("Band").

Sponsor

According to a Web page posted by the Council for Indigenous Arts and Culture, . . .

. . . (Council).

The List of Works Cited

Follow these general guidelines for preparing the list.

1. **List only the sources you cite in your paper.** If you consulted a source but did not cite it in your paper, do not include it in the list of works cited.

2. **Put the list on a separate page at the end of your paper.** The heading *Works Cited* should be centered an inch below the top of the page. Do not use quotation marks, underlining, or bold type for the heading.

3. **Alphabetize the list by authors' last names.** For works with multiple authors, invert only the first author's name. If no author is listed, begin the entry with the title.

> Trask, R. L., and Robert M. C. Millar. *Why Do Languages Change?* Cambridge: Cambridge UP, 2010. Print.

4. **Capitalize the first word and all other words in a title except *a, an, the, to,* coordinating conjunctions, and prepositions.**

5. **Italicize or underline titles of books and names of periodicals.**

6. **Give inclusive page numbers of articles in periodicals.** Do not use the word *page* or the abbreviation *p.* or *pp.*

7. **Indent the second and all subsequent lines half an inch or five spaces.** This is known as the *hanging indent* style.

8. **Double-space the entire list.**

The following sections describe how to format works-cited entries for books, periodicals, Internet sources, and other sources.

BOOKS

General guidelines and sample entries for books follow. Include the elements listed below, which you will find on the book's title page and copyright page (see Figure 19.7).

1 *Author.* Begin with the author's last name, followed by the first name.

2 *Title.* Provide the full title of the book, including the subtitle. It should be capitalized and italicized.

3 *Place of publication.* Include only the city.

4 *Publisher.* Use a shortened form of the publisher's name; usually one word is sufficient (*Houghton Mifflin* is listed as *Houghton*). Abbreviate *University Press* as *UP*.

5 *Date.* Use the most recent publication date listed on the book's copyright page.

6 *Medium.* For printed books, the medium of publication is *Print*.

MLA Format for Citing a Book

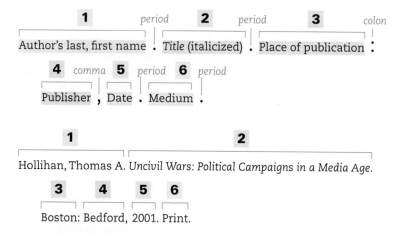

Hollihan, Thomas A. *Uncivil Wars: Political Campaigns in a Media Age.*

Boston: Bedford, 2001. Print.

Book with One Author

> Rybczynski, Witold. *Makeshift Metropolis: Ideas about Cities.* New York: Scribner, 2010. Print.

Book with Two or More Authors   List the names in the order they appear on the title page of the book, and separate the names with commas. The second and subsequent authors' names are *not* reversed. For books with four or more authors, you can either list all names or list only the first author's name followed by *et al.*

Figure 19.7 Where to Find Documentation Information for a Book

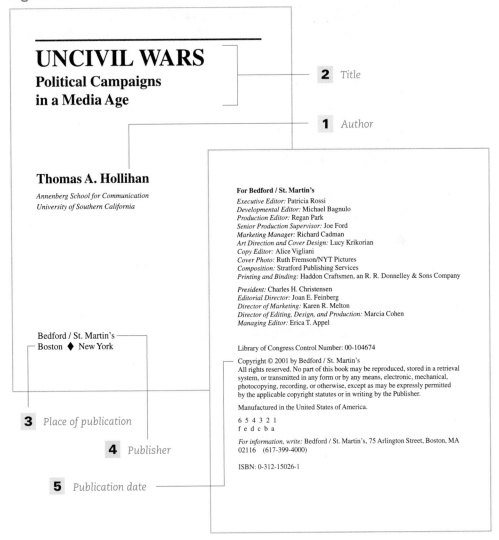

Two or Three Authors

Postel, Sandra, and Brian Richter. *Rivers for Life: Managing Water for People and Nature.* Washington: Island, 2003. Print.

Four or More Authors

Lewin, Benjamin, Jocelyn E. Krebs, Stephen T. Kilpatrick, and Elliott S. Goldstein. *Lewin's Genes X.* Sudbury: Jones, 2011. Print.

Lewin, Benjamin, et al. *Lewin's Genes X.* Sudbury: Jones, 2011. Print.

Book with No Named Author   Put the title first and alphabetize the entry by title. (Do not consider the words *A, An,* and *The* when alphabetizing.)

> *The New Interpreter's Dictionary of the Bible.* Nashville: Abingdon, 2006. Print.

Book by a Corporation or an Organization   List the organization or corporation as the author, omitting any initial article (*A, An, The*).

> American Red Cross. *First Aid and Safety for Babies and Children.* Yardley: StayWell, 2009. Print.

Government Publication   If there is no author, list the government followed by the department and agency of the government. Use abbreviations such as *Dept.* and *Natl.* if the meaning is clear.

> United States. Office of Management and Budget. *A New Era of Responsibility: Renewing America's Promise.* Washington: GPO, 2009. Print.

Edited Book or Anthology   List the editor's name followed by a comma and the abbreviation *ed.* or *eds.*

> Szeman, Imre, and Timothy Kaposy, eds. *Cultural Theory: An Anthology.* Chichester: Wiley-Blackwell, 2011. Print.

Chapter in an Edited Book or Work in an Anthology   List the author and title of the work, followed by the title and editor of the anthology (*Ed.* is the abbreviation for "Edited by"); city, publisher, and date; and the pages where the work appears.

> Tillman, Barrett. "Pearl Harbor." *Today's Best Military Writing: The Finest Articles on the Past, Present, and Future of the U.S. Military.* Ed. Walter J. Boyne. New York: Forge, 2004. 311–20. Print.

Introduction, Preface, Foreword, or Afterword

> Aaron, Hank. Foreword. *We Are the Ship: The Story of Negro League Baseball.* By Kadir Nelson. New York: Jump at the Sun, 2008. Print.

Two or More Works by the Same Author(s)   Use the author's name for only the first entry. For subsequent entries, use three hyphens followed by a period. List the entries in alphabetical order by title. List works for which the person is the only author before those for which he or she is the first coauthor.

> Adams, Ryan. *Hellosunshine.* New York: Akashic, 2009. Print.
>
> ---. *Infinity Blues.* New York: Akashic, 2009. Print.
>
> Myers, Walter D. *Lockdown.* New York: Amistad, 2010. Print.

Myers, Walter D., and Christopher Myers. *Jazz*. New York: Holiday, 2006.

Print.

Edition Other than the First   Indicate the number of the edition following the title.

Barker, Ellen M. *Neuroscience Nursing*. 3rd ed. St. Louis: Mosby-Elsevier, 2008.

Print.

Encyclopedia or Dictionary Entry   Note that when citing well-known reference books, you do not need to give the full publication information, just the edition and year.

Teixeira, Robert. "Suffrage Movement." *Encyclopedia of Gender and Society*. Ed.

Jodi O'Brien. Los Angeles: Sage, 2009. Print.

Note: If more than one of these rules applies to a source, cite the necessary information in the order given in the preceding examples.

ARTICLES IN PERIODICALS

A periodical is a publication that appears at regular intervals: newspapers generally appear daily, magazines weekly or monthly, and scholarly journals quarterly. General guidelines and sample entries for various types of periodical articles follow. Include the elements listed below, most of which you should find on the first page of the article (see Figure 19.8 on page 703).

1 *Author*. Use the same format for listing authors' names as for books (see p. 698). If no author is listed, begin the entry with the article title and alphabetize the entry by its title (ignore *The*, *An*, or *A*).

2 *Article title*. The title should appear in double quotation marks; a period falls inside the ending quotation mark.

3 *Periodical title*. Italicize or underline the title of the periodical. Do *not* include the word *A*, *An*, or *The* at the beginning: *Journal of the American Medical Association*, *New York Times*.

4 *Date or volume/issue (year)*. For magazines and newspapers, list the date in the following order: day, month, year; abbreviate the names of months except for *May*, *June*, and *July*. For scholarly journals, give the volume and issue numbers and year in parentheses: 72.2 (2005).

5 *Page(s)*. If an article begins in one place, such as on pages 19 to 21, and is continued elsewhere, such as on pages 79 to 80, write *19+* for the page numbers (*not* 19-80). Otherwise, include the first and last page number separated by a hyphen (39-43).

6 *Medium*. For printed periodicals, the medium of publication is *Print*.

The basic format for citing a periodical article is as follows.

MLA Format for Citing an Article in a Periodical

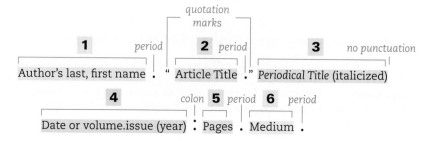

Article in a Magazine

Article in a Newspaper

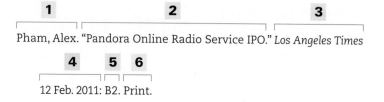

Article in a Scholarly Journal

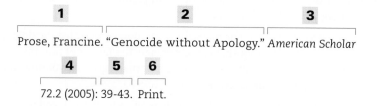

Article in a Monthly Magazine

Killingsworth, Jason. "The Unbearable Lightness of Being Jonsi." *Paste Magazine* May 2010: 49-53. Print.

Figure 19.8   Where to Find Documentation Information for an Article

Article in an Edition of a Newspaper   If an edition name (*natl. ed.*) appears on the newspaper's first page, include it after the date.

> Urbina, Ian. "Gas Wells Recycle Water, but Toxic Risks Persist." *New York Times* 2 Mar. 2011, late ed., A1+. Print.

Editorial or Letter to the Editor   Begin with the author's name (if provided), and add the word *Editorial* or *Letter* followed by a period after the title. Often, editorials are unsigned and letters to the editor omit titles.

"The Search for Livable Worlds." Editorial. *New York Times* 8 Sept. 2004: A22. Print.

Wolansky, Taras. Letter. *Wired* May 2004: 25. Print.

Book or Film Review   List the reviewer's name and title of the review. After the title, add *Rev. of* and give the title and author of the book. For a film review, replace *by* with *dir.* Include publication information for the review itself, not for the material reviewed.

Gabler, Neal. "Ephemera: The Rise and Rise of Celebrity Journalism." Rev. of *The Untold Story: My Twenty Years Running the* National Enquirer, by Iain Calder, and *The Importance of Being Famous: Behind the Scenes of the Celebrity Industrial Complex,* by Maureen Orth. *Columbia Journalism Review* 42.3 (2004): 48-51. Print.

INTERNET SOURCES

Citations for Internet sources should include enough information to enable readers to locate the sources. Since URLs are long and subject to change, the MLA suggests including them only when the information listed below is unlikely to be enough to enable readers to find the source.

Citing Internet sources may not be as straightforward as citing print sources because Web sites differ in how much information they provide and where and how they provide it. As a general rule, give as many of the following elements as possible, and list them in the order shown.

1   *Author.* Include the name of the person or organization if it is available.

2   *Title of the work.* Enclose titles of Web pages in quotation marks; italicize the titles of Web sites and other longer works.

3   *Print publication information.* If the material was originally published in print, tell where and when it was originally published. Include volume and issue numbers, names of periodicals, names of publishers, dates, and so forth.

4   *Electronic publication information.* The information here will differ depending on the type of source.
    a. To cite an entire Web site or a document on a Web site, provide as many of the following as are available: title of site (italicized), the sponsoring organization, and date of publication or last update.
    b. To cite an article in an online periodical, give the periodical title (italicized), the sponsoring organization or publisher, and the volume/issue or date. Also include the name of any database (italicized) through which you accessed the article.

    c. To cite an e-book, give all the information you would give for a print book.

5 *Medium.* For Internet sources, the medium of publication is *Web.* For e-books, include the file format (PDF file, Kindle e-book file) as the medium.

6 *Access date.* Include the date you accessed the document (day, month, year).

Some sample citations for different kinds of Internet sources are given below.

MLA Format for Citing Internet Sources

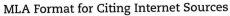

1	period **2** period	**3**
Author's last name, first name	. Title of work .	Print publication

               period   **4**   period **5** period

information . Electronic publication information . Medium .

      6   period

Access date .

Entire Web Site

            1   **2**

LaMoreaux, Andrew M., ed. *The Huntington Archive of Buddhist*

                                 4a

and Related Art. College of the Arts, Ohio State U, 15 Oct. 1995.

  5   **6**

Web. 8 Sept. 2011.

Document on a Web Site

    1   **2**   **4b**

Hogan, Marc. "Live Transmission." *Pitchfork.* Pitchfork Media Inc.,

              5   **6**

7 Feb. 2001. Web. 3 Mar. 2012.

E-book

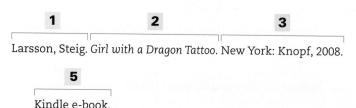

Larsson, Steig. *Girl with a Dragon Tattoo.* New York: Knopf, 2008.

Kindle e-book.

Article in an Online Newspaper or Magazine

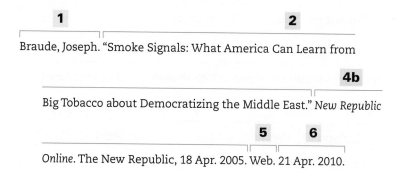

Braude, Joseph. "Smoke Signals: What America Can Learn from

Big Tobacco about Democratizing the Middle East." *New Republic*

Online. The New Republic, 18 Apr. 2005. Web. 21 Apr. 2010.

Article from an Online Journal

Edmonson, Cole. "Moral Courage and the Nurse Leader." *Online Journal of Issues in Nursing* 15.3 (2010): n. pag. Web. 14 Feb. 2011.

Article from an Online Periodical Database

Williams, D. M., A. Fraser, and D. A. Lawlor. "Associations of Vitamin D, Parathyroid Hormone and Calcium with Cardiovascular Risk Factors in US Adolescents." *Heart* 97.4 (2011): 315-20. *CINAHL Plus.* Web. 15 Feb. 2011.

Online Government Document

United States. Office of the Dir. of Natl. Intelligence. Natl. Intelligence Council. *The Terrorist Threat to the U.S. Homeland. National Intelligence Council.* Office of the Dir. of Natl. Intelligence, July 2007. Web. 3 Mar. 2011.

Posting to an Online Discussion List or Newsgroup For a discussion group, include the author's name, the title or subject line enclosed in quotation marks, the name of the Web site on which the group is found, the sponsor of the site, the date of posting, the medium, and the date of access. If possible, cite an archived version. If the posting has no title, label it *Online posting.*

Jones, John. "The End of Species." *ILovePhilosophy.com*. I Love Philosophy

Forum, 12 Feb. 2011. Web. 15 Feb. 2011.

Online Book   Include the author's name; title (italicized); the name of any editor, translator, or compiler; original publication information (if available); the name of the Web site on which the online book appears; the medium; and date of access.

Dickens, Charles. *Great Expectations*. Boston: Estes, 1881. *Google Books*. Web.

14 Feb. 2011.

OTHER SOURCES

DVD-ROM or CD-ROM   Include the title, the version (if specified), the publication information, and the medium.

Poulter, Patricia A., and Anne Griffin Perry. *Mosby's Nursing Skills 2.0. Student

Version*. St Louis: Mosby, 2006. CD-ROM.

Personal Communication (Interview, Letter, Email)   Indicate the name of the person, followed by the type of communication and the date. For interviews you conducted, indicate the type of interview (telephone, personal, email, and so forth). For a letter, include the designation *MS* for a manuscript (a letter written by hand) or *TS* for a typescript (a letter composed on a machine). For emails, include the subject line (if available) in quotation marks.

Burrow, Alby. Telephone interview. 28 Jan. 2011.

Gomez, Pedro. Letter to the author. 19 May 2010. TS.

Adams, Alex. "Pet Care Advice." Message to Rudy Simmons. 19 Feb. 2011. Email.

Published Interview   List the person interviewed, and then list the title of the interview in quotation marks. If the interview has no title, label it *Interview*. Give the publication details for the source in which the interview was found.

Richards, Eric. "Observation and Memory: An Interview with Eric Richards."

American Music 27.2 (2009): 180-203.

Film, Video, or DVD   Begin with the title, followed by the director and key performer(s), unless you are focusing on the work of the director or another contributor. Include the name of the distributor, the release date, and the medium (*Film*). For a film on DVD, add the original release date (if relevant) before the distributor, and change the medium to DVD.

The Lady Eve. Dir. Preston Sturges. Perf. Barbara Stanwyck and Henry Fonda.

1941. Criterion, 2001. DVD.

Television or Radio Program   Unless you are focusing on the work of a contributor, list the title of the episode, if any (in quotation marks), and the title of
the program (italicized) first. Then give key names (narrator, producer, director,
actors) as necessary. Identify the network, local station and city of broadcast (if
available), and broadcast date before the medium.

> "Mugged." *Flight of the Conchords*. Perf. Jermain Clement. HBO. 1 July 2008.
> Television.

Music Recording   Begin with a contributor or title of the work, depending on
your focus. Include the composer (*Comp.*) or performer (*Perf.*), and the title of
the recording or composition as well as the production company, the date, and
the medium (CD, audiocassette, LP, audiotape). Titles of recordings should be
italicized, but titles of compositions identified by form (for example, Symphony
No. 5) should not.

> Wilco. *Yankee Hotel Foxtrot*. Perf. Jeff Tweedy, John Stirratt, and Nels Cline.
> Nonesuch Records, 2002. CD.

A Student Model MLA-Style Paper

The following research paper was written by Nicholas Destino for his first-year
writing course at Niagara County Community College. Destino used MLA style
for formatting his paper and documenting his sources. Notice how he uses in-
text citations and quotations to provide evidence that supports his thesis.

Destino 1

Nicholas Destino

Professor Thomas

English 101

11 Mar. 2011

Double-spaced
identification:
writer's name,
instructor's name,
course title, and
date

Do Animals Have Emotions?

Double-spaced
throughout

Title centered

Somewhere in the savannas of Africa a mother elephant

is dying in the company of many other pachyderms. Some

of them are part of her family; some are fellow members

of her herd. The dying elephant tips from side to side and

seems to be balancing on a thin thread in order to sustain

her life. Many of the other elephants surround her as she

struggles to regain her balance. They also try to help by

feeding and caressing her. After many attempts by the herd

to save her life, they seem to realize that there is simply

nothing more that can be done. She finally collapses to the

ground in the presence of her companions. Most of the other

elephants move away from the scene. There are, however,

two elephants who remain behind with the dead elephant--

another mother and her calf. The mother turns her back to

the body and taps it with one foot. Soon the other elephants

call for them to follow and eventually they do (Masson

and McCarthy, *When Elephants Weep* 95). These movements,

which are slow and ritualistic, suggest that elephants may

be capable of interpreting and responding to the notion of

death.

In-text citation of
a work with two
authors; short title
included because
another work by
these authors is
cited later in the
essay

The topic of animal emotions is one that, until recently,

has rarely been discussed or studied by scientists. However,

since the now-famous comprehensive field studies of

chimpanzees by the internationally renowned primatologist

Jane Goodall, those who study animal behavior have begun to

look more closely at the notion that animals feel emotions. As

Header: student's
name and page
number

a result of their observations of various species of animals, a
number of these researchers have come to the conclusion that
animals do exhibit a wide range of emotions, such as grief,
sympathy, and joy.

One of the major reasons that research into animal
emotions was traditionally avoided is that scientists fear
being accused of *anthropomorphism*--the act of attributing
human qualities to animals. To do so is perceived as
unscientific (Masson and McCarthy, "Hope and Joy" xviii).
Frans de Waal, of the Yerkes Regional Primate Research
Center in Atlanta, believes that if people are not open to
the possibility of animals having emotions, they may be
overlooking important information about both animals and
humans. He explains his position in his article "Are We in

Attribution of
summaries and
quotations within
text

Anthropodenial?" The term *anthropodenial*, which he coined,
refers to "a blindness to the humanlike characteristics
of other animals, or the animal-like characteristics of

Page numbers
follow quotations

ourselves" (52). De Waal proposes that because humans
and animals are so closely related, it would be impossible
for one not to have some characteristics of the other. He

Attributions of
paraphrase and
quotation

contends, "If two closely related species act in the same
manner, their underlying mental processes are probably
the same, too" (53). If de Waal is correct, then humans can
presume that animals do have emotions because of the
many similarities between human and animal behavior.

Grief has been observed in many different species. In
many instances, their behaviors (and presumably, therefore,
their emotions) are uncannily similar to the behaviors of
humans. Birds, which mate for life, have been observed
showing obvious signs of grief when their mates die. In *The
Human Nature of Birds*, Theodore Barber includes a report from

one Dr. Franklin, who witnessed a male parrot caring for his mate by feeding her and trying to help her raise herself when she was dying. Franklin observed the following scene:

> Her unhappy spouse moved around her incessantly,
> his attention and tender cares redoubled. He
> even tried to open her beak to give her some
> nourishment.... At intervals, he uttered the most
> plaintive cries, then with his eyes fixed on her, kept a
> mournful silence. At length his companion breathed
> her last; from that moment he pined away, and died
> in the course of a few weeks. (qtd. in Barber 116)

Veterinarian Susan Wynn, discussing the physiological symptoms brought on by emotional trauma in animals, notes that "[a]nimals definitely exhibit grief when they lose an owner or another companion animal.... Signs of grief vary widely, including lethargy, loss of appetite, hiding ..." (5). This observation reinforces de Waal's position that animals experience some of the same emotions as humans.

Perhaps the most extreme case of grief experienced by an animal is exemplified by the true story of Flint, a chimp, when Flo, his mother, died. In her book *Through a Window*, which elaborates on her thirty years of experience studying and living among the chimps in Gombe, Tanzania, Jane Goodall gives the following account of Flint's experience with grief.

> Flint became increasingly lethargic, refused most
> food and, with his immune system thus weakened,
> fell sick. The last time I saw him alive, he was hollow-
> eyed, gaunt and utterly depressed, huddled in the
> vegetation close to where Flo had died.... The last
> short journey he made, pausing to rest every few feet,
> was to the very place where Flo's body had lain. There

Quotation longer than four lines indented one inch and not enclosed in quotation marks; period precedes citation

Citation for an indirect source

First letter of a quotation changed to lowercase to fit into sentence; ellipsis marks used to indicate omitted material

Source's credentials included within the text

Destino 4

he stayed for several hours, sometimes staring and staring into the water. He struggled on a little further, then curled up--and never moved again. (196-97)

Of course, animal emotions are not limited to despair, sadness, and grief. Indeed, substantial evidence indicates that animals experience other, more uplifting emotions, such as sympathy, altruism, and joy.

Many scientists who study animal behavior have found that several species demonstrate sympathy for one another. In other words, they act as if they care about one another in much the same way as humans do. It is probably safe to assume that no animal is more sympathetic, or at least displays more behaviors associated with the emotion of sympathy, than chimpanzees. Those who have studied apes in the wild, including de Waal, have observed that animals who had been fighting make up with one another by kissing and hugging. Although other primates also engage in similar behaviors, chimps even go so far as to embrace and attempt to console the defeated animal ("Going Ape"). Another striking example of one animal showing sympathy for another is the account cited by Barber of a parrot comforting its sick mate. It is not, however, the only example of this type of behavior, especially among birds. Barber cites several other instances as well. According to Barber, documented records show that responsible observers have seen robins trying to keep each other alive. Also, terns have been known to lift a handicapped tern by its wing and transport it to safety. Likewise, a jay has been known to successfully seek human help when a newborn bird of a different species falls out of its nest. What makes this latter example particularly noteworthy is that the newborn wasn't a jay but an altogether different type of bird.

Information from a source paraphrased

Title used in citation since source does not indicate author; page number not given since the article is on only one page in the journal

Information from a source summarized

Destino 5

Had the jay been helping another jay, it would be easy to assume that the act of caring was the result of what scientists call *genetic altruism*--the sociobiological theory that animals help each other to keep their own genes alive so that they can reproduce and not become extinct. Simply put, scientists who believe in genetic altruism assume that when animals of the same species help each other out, they do so because there is something in it for them--namely, the assurance that their species will continue. This theory certainly provides an adequate, unbiased scientific explanation for why animals such as birds might behave in a caring manner. However, if animals really help each other out only when doing so will perpetuate their species, then the jay would have had no genetic reason to help the newborn bird.

There is another popular explanation for why a bird of one species might help a bird of another species, however. Scientists who favor a related scientific theory called *mutual altruism* believe that animals will help each other because some day they themselves may need help, and then they will be able to count on reciprocal help (Hemelrijk 479-81). This theory is a plausible, nonanthropomorphic explanation for why animals show sympathy, regardless of whether they actually feel sympathy. This point is crucial because, after all, humans can't actually observe how an animal feels; we can only observe how it behaves. It is then up to the observer to draw some logical conclusion about why animals behave in the ways they do. The mutual altruism theory, however, also can be disputed. In many cases, animals have helped others even when the receiver of the help would probably never be in a position to return the favor. For example, there are many accounts of dolphins helping drowning or otherwise

Information in this paragraph can be found in many sources so does not need to be documented

Destino 6

endangered swimmers. Phil Mercer, on the BBC Web site,
reported that dolphins stopped a shark from attacking
swimmers off the coast of New Zealand. The animals
surrounded the swimmers for about forty minutes while the
great white shark circled. When the swimmers reached the
shore, they remarked that they were sure that the dolphins
acted deliberately to save them. Marathon swimmer Martin
Strel also believes that he was deliberately helped by pink
dolphins during his 2007 swim of the entire Amazon River,
even believing that he heard them communicating (Butler).

Not only do animals show sympathy, but they are also
clearly able to express joy. For example, on many occasions
primate experts have heard apes laugh while in the presence
of other apes. These experts are sure that the noise they heard
was laughter because of the clarity and tone of the sound. In
their book, *Visions of Caliban*, Dale Peterson and Jane Goodall
describe this laughter in detail:

> I'm not referring to a sort of pinched vocalization that
> might be roughly compared with human laughter,
> as in the "laughter" of a hyena. I'm referring to real
> laughter, fully recognizable laughter, the kind where
> you lie down on the ground and shake in a paroxysm
> of clear amusement and simple pleasure. (181)

Although Peterson and Goodall felt that only four species
(chimpanzees, gorillas, bonobos, and orangutans), in addition
to humans, have the capacity to be amused and to show
their amusement by laughing, Elizabeth Walter reports that
researchers have found that dogs and rats are also capable of
laughter.

Even the actions of animals who are not able to laugh
uproariously indicate that they feel joy. Many animals engage

Destino 7

in playful behavior that can emanate only from a sense of joy. In "Hope and Joy among the Animals," Masson and McCarthy tell an amusing, yet true, story about an elephant named Norma.

> A traveling circus once pitched its tents next to a schoolyard with a set of swings. The older elephants were chained, but Norma, a young elephant, was left loose. When Norma saw children swinging, she was greatly intrigued. Before long, she went over, waved the children away with her trunk, backed up to a swing, and attempted to sit on it. She was notably unsuccessful, even using her tail to hold the swing in place. (45)

Geese, according to experts, have an "emotional body language which can be read: goose posture, gestures, and sounds can indicate feelings such as uncertain, tense, glad, victorious, sad, alert, relaxed or threatening." Additionally, birds can sometimes be seen moving their wings back and forth while listening to sounds they find pleasant (McHugh).

In short, animals exhibit a large number of behaviors that indicate that they possess not only the capacity to feel but the capacity to express those feelings in some overt way, often through body language. If these are not proof enough that animals have emotions, people need look no further than their own beloved cat or dog. Pets are so frequently the cause of joy, humor, love, sympathy, empathy, and even grief that it is difficult to imagine that animals could elicit such emotions in humans without actually having these emotions themselves. The question, then, is not, Do animals have emotions? but, Which emotions do animals have, and to what degree do they feel them?

Entire title of article included in attribution because two works by Masson and McCarthy are cited

Destino presents his own conclusion about animal emotions.

The works-cited list appears on a new page; the heading is centered.

Double-spaced throughout

Entries are alphabetized by authors' last names.

First line of each entry is flush with the left margin; subsequent lines are indented half an inch.

Works Cited

Barber, Theodore Xenophone. *The Human Nature of Birds: A Scientific Discovery with Startling Implications.* New York: St. Martin's, 1993. Print.

Butler, Rhett A. "Marathon Swimmer: An Interview with the First Man to Swim the Length of the Amazon." *Mongabay .com.* Mongabay.com, 23 Jan. 2011. Web. 14 Feb. 2012.

de Waal, Frans. "Are We in Anthropodenial?" *Discover* July 1997: 50-53. Print.

"Going Ape." *Economist* 17 Feb. 1997: 78. Print.

Goodall, Jane. *Through a Window.* Boston: Houghton, 1990. Print.

Hemelrijk, Charlotte K. "Support for Being Groomed in Long-Tailed Macaques, Macaca Fascicularis." *Animal Behaviour* 48 (1994): 479-81. Print.

Masson, Jeffrey Moussaieff, and Susan McCarthy. "Hope and Joy among the Animals." *Utne Reader* July-Aug. 1995: 44-46. Print.

---. *When Elephants Weep: The Emotional Lives of Animals.* New York: Delacorte, 1995. Print.

McHugh, Mary. "The Emotional Lives of Animals." *Global:Ideas:Bank.* Global Ideas Bank, 1998. Web. 5 Mar. 2012.

Mercer, Phil. "Dolphins Prevent NZ Shark Attack." *BBC News.* BBC, 23 Nov. 2004. Web. 6 Mar. 2012.

Peterson, Dale, and Jane Goodall. *Visions of Caliban: On Chimpanzees and People.* New York: Houghton, 1993. Print.

Walter, Elizabeth. "Tickled Pink: Why Scientists Want to Make Rats Laugh." *Greater Good.* Greater Good Science Center, Summer 2008. Web. 14 Feb. 2012.

Wynn, Susan G. "The Treatment of Trauma in Pet Animals: What Constitutes Trauma?" *Homeopathy Online* 5 (1998): n. pag. Web. 9 Mar. 2012.

Glossary

Academic image The way a student is perceived by instructors and classmates.

Accommodate In an **argument**, a method in which the writer recognizes opposing views, by not only acknowledging readers' concerns but also accepting some of them and incorporating these into the argument.

Acknowledge In an **argument**, a method in which the writer recognizes opposing views, by admitting that these views exist and indicating that he or she has considered them.

Active reading A process of reading for better understanding. It includes **previewing** the text before reading, annotating and highlighting while reading, and reviewing after reading.

Active voice The form of the verb in sentences where the subject of the sentence performs the action of the verb. *See also* **passive voice**. For example, *She hit the ball.*

Analogy An extended comparison in which one subject is used to explain another. Analogies can make complicated ideas easier to understand, make unfamiliar objects easier to imagine, or show something in a new light. *The world's largest rodent, the capybara, is as roly-poly and water loving as a hippopotamus, though not nearly as big* makes the unfamiliar capybara easier to imagine.

Analyzing Examining a piece of writing to answer such questions as how and why the writer wrote the material.

Annotations Notes that a reader makes in the margins while reading, recording his or her ideas, impressions, reactions, and questions.

Anthology A collection of writings by different authors.

Argument A **pattern of development** used by writers to make a logical, well-considered case for or against an issue. An effective argument supports a position, or **claim**, on an **issue**, with **reasons** and **evidence**.

Assertion A statement that takes a position or expresses a viewpoint. In an **essay**, an effective **thesis statement** makes a clear assertion about the topic of the essay, rather than just presenting a **fact**. For example, *Global warming will disrupt millions of lives by triggering heat waves, droughts, and floods.*

Assumption An idea that an author believes to be true but does not try to prove. Often, writers' assumptions are not directly stated.

Audience The readers of a particular piece of writing. A writer should always keep the audience in mind when planning and writing an essay. *See also* **intended audience**.

Basis of comparison The shared characteristic(s) that an author chooses to focus on in order to make a comparison between two things. An author might choose to compare Italian and Chinese cuisines on the basis of their healthfulness or their popularity, for example. *See also* **points of comparison**.

Begging the question *See* **circular reasoning.**

Bias A writer's prejudice in favor of or against what he or she is writing about. Writers show bias when they present only one side of an argument without considering other views.

Body paragraph All the **paragraphs** of an **essay** except those in the **introduction** and **conclusion**. The body paragraphs of an essay each support the thesis of the essay, in different ways depending on the **patterns of development** used.

Brainstorming A **prewriting** technique for generating ideas about a topic that involves jotting down a list of everything that comes to mind relating to the topic within a time limit.

Cause and effect Also known as *causal analysis*, a **pattern of development** that analyzes why something happened (**causes**) and/or what happened because of something (**effects**).

Causes The reasons why an event or phenomenon happens, often a focus of cause-and-effect essays. *See also* **cause and effect, effects,** and **primary** and **secondary.**

Central thought *See* **thesis statement.**

Chronological order The sequence in which events occur; a method of organization in which details are in the order in which they occurred. Writers often use chronological order in **narrative** or **process analysis** essays.

Circular reasoning Also called *begging the question*, a **fallacy** that occurs when a writer simply repeats a **claim** in different words and uses the rewording as evidence. For example, *Physical punishment of children is wrong because children should never be spanked or otherwise hit.*

Claim A basic part of an **argument** — a statement that reveals the writer's position on an **issue.** The writer's claim usually appears as part of the **thesis statement.**

Class A part of a **definition** — the group to which the thing that is being defined belongs. For example, *necklace* belongs to the class *jewelry.*

Classification A kind of **classification and division,** in which people, things, or ideas are sorted into categories.

Classification and division A **pattern of development** used to sort people, things, or ideas into categories (**classification**) or to break one thing down into parts (**division**).

Climax The point in a **narrative** at which **tension** is at its highest, just before the **resolution** of the **conflict.**

Clustering *See* **mapping.**

Coherence The situation when the ideas in a **paragraph** or other piece of writing flow smoothly, so that readers can follow easily. Coherence comes through organization, **transitions,** and **repetition.**

Common ground A basis of trust and goodwill between an author and his or her **audience.** Establishing common ground — by mentioning mutual interests, concerns, or experiences — may make readers more open to considering an **argument** and is especially useful when writing for a disagreeing audience.

Comparison and contrast A **pattern of development** used to show the similarities (comparison) and differences (contrast) between two things.

Conclusion The final **paragraph** or paragraphs that draw an **essay** to a close. While conclusions vary, depending partly on the **patterns of development** used, they often reinforce the **thesis.**

Conflict A struggle, question, or problem that the characters in a **narrative** confront. The conflict can be between participants or between a participant and an outside force, such as the law, a moral or value, or an act of nature.

Connotation The set of feelings or associations that a word evokes in a reader; the meanings a word has taken on in addition to its **denotation.** Words with similar denotations can have different connotations; for example, *fat* has a more negative connotation than *overweight.*

Critical thinking A process of thinking that uses skills that go beyond basic understanding and are related to analysis and evaluation. Like critical reading, to which it is related, critical thinking is important in college.

Cyberplagiarism **Plagiarism** that involves Internet sources — and, like any other use of others' ideas or language without giving them credit, a serious academic offence. Cyberplagiarism may be **intentional plagiarism** or **unintentional plagiarism.**

Definition An explanation of the meaning of a term; a **pattern of development** that writers use to explain what something means. *See also* **extended definition.**

Denotation A word's literal meaning, or dictionary definition, as opposed to its **connotation.**

Description A **pattern of development** in which information is presented in a way that appeals to some or all of the five senses — sight, hearing, smell, taste, touch — usually with the aim of evoking a specific feeling or impression.

Details *See* **supporting details.**

Dialogue Conversation among characters in a **narrative.** Dialogue can be used to dramatize the action, emphasize the **conflict,** and give readers an impression of the characters.

Distinguishing characteristics In a definition, the features of the thing being defined that make it different from other members of its **class.** For example, having a single horn is a distinguishing characteristic of a rhinoceros.

Division A kind of **classification and division,** in which one item is broken down into its parts.

Documenting For a paper with sources, the process of acknowledging sources, and thereby avoiding **plagiarism,** usually by following a system of documentation, for example, that of the Modern Language Association (MLA style).

Dominant impression The overall attitude, mood, or feeling about a subject that a piece of writing conveys to a reader. In a **description,** the dominant impression is the **implied thesis.**

Doublespeak Unclear or evasive language used intentionally (for example, by politicians, governments, or corporations) to hide or soften unpleasant realities. For example, in the military, *collateral damage* is doublespeak for unintentional deaths. Doublespeak is a type of **euphemism.**

Drafting Creating a tentative or preliminary version of a paragraph or essay.

Editing Reviewing and revising an **essay** for such local issues as **style,** mechanical and grammatical correctness, and word choice.

Effects The things that happen as the result of an event or phenomenon, often a focus of cause-and-effect essays. *See also* **cause and effect, causes,** and **primary** and **secondary.**

Either-or fallacy A **fallacy** that occurs when a writer says there are only two sides to an issue and only one side is correct. For example, a politician might argue that either government programs must be cut or the state won't have enough money, ignoring other possibilities such as raising taxes.

Emotional appeals Parts of an **argument** that are directed at readers' feelings and beliefs, rather than being based on reason and evidence. Emotional appeals, which can enhance a sound argument, are directed toward readers' **needs** and **values.**

Essay Generally, a reading that presents information on a specific topic from the writer's **point of view.**

Euphemism A polite or neutral word or phrase used to avoid an unpleasant, embarrassing, or otherwise objectionable word. For example, *passed away* is a commonly used euphemism for *died.*

Evaluating Examining the quality, relevance, and adequacy of the ideas presented.

Evidence Any type of information — including examples, statistics, quotations, and research findings — used as support to convince the reader that the **thesis** is reasonable or correct.

Extended definition A lengthy, detailed **definition** that explores a term and all that it means; such a definition might require a long paragraph, a full essay, or an entire book.

Facts Objective statements of information that can be confirmed to be true. Examples of facts are statistics, research findings, and personal experiences.

Fallacies Errors in reasoning and thinking. Fallacies can weaken an **argument** and call into question the believability of its supporting **evidence**. *See also* **circular reasoning, hasty generalization, sweeping generalization, false analogy, non sequitur, red herring, post hoc fallacy,** and **either-or fallacy.**

False analogy A **fallacy** that occurs when a writer compares two situations that are not sufficiently similar (just because two items are alike in *some* ways does not mean they are alike in *all* ways). For example, *Giving workers higher pay is an incentive for them to work more, so to get students to study more, they should be given higher grades.*

Figure of speech Language used in nonliteral, imaginative ways to create a striking impression. For example, *The traffic moved along like a herd of cows heading home.* **Metaphor, personification,** and **simile** are specific kinds of figures of speech. See Table 2.4 on pages 36–37 for these and other figures of speech.

Flashback A step backward in **narrative** time. Authors often explain a scene or event by using a flashback to return to past events.

Foreshadowing In a **narrative,** a hinting at events that will happen later.

Formal outline A type of outline that uses a standard format with Roman numerals (I, II), Arabic numbers (1, 2), and capital and lowercase letters to show levels of importance in an **essay**. A formal outline may be either a **topic outline** or a **sentence outline**. *See also* **informal outline.**

Freewriting A **prewriting** technique for exploring a topic that involves writing non-stop whatever comes to mind about the topic for a specific period of time.

Generalization A broad statement about a topic. The **thesis statement** of an **illustration** essay frequently contains a generalization.

Glossary In some books, including most textbooks, a list (usually at the end of the book) of key terms, in alphabetical order, along with their definitions.

Graphics A type of visual aid that generally presents or summarizes information. Common types of graphics include pie charts, bar graphs, line graphs, and diagrams and flowcharts (see Figure 2.4, on page 49).

Graphic organizer A diagram of the structure and main points of an **essay** or other reading, useful for understanding the reading. A graphic organizer for a reading includes all its key elements (title, **introduction, main idea** and key **supporting details** of **body paragraphs,** and **conclusion**).

Hasty generalization A **fallacy** that occurs when a writer draws a conclusion based on insufficient evidence. For example, someone who goes to a new neighborhood and sees a violent incident and concludes that the neighborhood is dangerous would be making a hasty generalization.

How-it-works essay A **process analysis** that explains how something works or is done for readers who want to understand the process but not actually perform it.

How-to essay A **process analysis** that explains how something works or is done for readers who want to perform the process.

Illustration A **pattern of development** that uses examples to support a point and to make ideas concrete and easier to understand.

Images A type of visual aid based on a picture of some kind. Image-based visual aids include photos, cartoons, advertisements, and illustrations.

Implied thesis The main point or position in an **essay** when it is suggested rather than directly stated. Professional authors sometimes use an implied thesis, but students and other academic writers should usually state their thesis directly in a **thesis statement.**

Index In many books, including most textbooks, an alphabetical listing, at the end of the book, of all key topics, terms, places, and names in the book. Each item in an index has one or more page numbers, so readers can find all relevant discussions.

Inference An educated, reasonable guess about what is not known based on what is known. Inferences are based on available **facts** and information, experience, and content in the reading. They are logical connections between what the writer states directly and what the writer implies.

Informal outline A type of outline, also known as a *scratch outline*, that uses key words and phrases to list the main points and subpoints of an essay. *See also* **formal outline**.

Intended audience The group of people a writer expects to read his or her work. The intended audience influences a writer's **style**.

Intentional plagiarism Deliberately using an author's ideas or language as if they were one's own, a serious academic offense. *See also* **plagiarism** and **unintentional plagiarism**.

Introduction The opening **paragraph** or paragraphs of an **essay**. Effective introductions generally identify the topic, provide background information about it, and, often, include the **thesis statement**.

Issue A basic part of an **argument** — the controversy that the argument will address. *See also* **claim** and **support**.

Journal A notebook or computer file for recording and exploring ideas and observations, including responses to reading assignments. Journals can also be a source of ideas for papers.

Key details The most important **supporting details** writers use to develop their **main ideas**.

Least-to-most order A method of organization in which **supporting details** are organized from least to most important, familiar, interesting, or persuasive.

Main idea Of a **paragraph**, the most important point the paragraph is trying to make. The main idea expresses the writer's viewpoint and is often found in a **topic sentence**.

Mapping A **prewriting** strategy also known as *clustering* in which a writer creates a visual depiction of the relationships among ideas to respond to assignments and readings. Mapping offers a visual way to discover ideas and relationships about a topic.

Metaphor A **figure of speech** that makes an indirect comparison between two things, describing one thing as if it were another, without using *like* or *as*. For example, *The air-conditioned office was an oasis on the scorching July day.*

Mixed metaphor An unintentional combining of **figures of speech**. Mixed metaphors can be puzzling to readers. For example, *Her eyes shot daggers at me, melting my resistance.*

Most-to-least order A method of organization in which **supporting details** are organized from most to least important, familiar, interesting, or persuasive.

Narration *See* **narrative**.

Narrative A relation of a series of events, real or imaginary, in an organized sequence; a story that makes a point. Narration is one of the **patterns of development**.

Needs One of two main targets of **emotional appeals** in **argument**; readers' needs that the writer appeals to may be biological (for example, the need for food and drink) or psychological (for example, the need to belong and to have self-esteem).

Negation The method of defining a **term** by explaining what it is not. A writer may use negation to explain how a term is different from other terms in its **class**. For example, *A volunteer is not a paid worker.*

Non sequitur From the Latin for "it does not follow," a **fallacy** that occurs when a writer connects up ideas that have no logical relationship. For example, *Because my sister is rich, she'll make a good parent.*

Objective Written to inform — to present information or communicate ideas without **bias** or emotion. A **description** that is objective describes only what the writer observes or experiences.

Opinions Statements that are **subjective**, expressing attitudes, beliefs, or feelings, and that cannot be established as true or false. It is important to distinguish opinions from **facts**.

Outlining. *See* **formal outline** and **informal outline.**

Paragraph A group of sentences that explains or develops one idea. A paragraph can be a single sentence or go on for pages. A paragraph includes a **topic**, a **main idea** and **topic sentence, supporting details,** and **transitions.**

Paraphrase Rewriting material from a reading in one's own words. Paraphrasing can help readers to think about and understand what they read.

Passive voice The form of the verb in sentences in which the subject of the sentence is acted upon. *See also* **active voice.** For example, *She was hit by the ball.*

Patterns of development Nine methods used to develop and organize an **essay** or other information: **narration, description, illustration, process analysis, comparison and contrast, classification and division, definition, cause and effect,** and **argument.** These patterns can be used alone or combined to develop an **essay** or used when **prewriting** to generate ideas about a topic. They help writers organize their ideas and help readers follow writers' key points. For a summary, see Table 9.1 (pp. 177–79).

Peer review A process in which two or more students read and comment on one other's **essays.**

Periodicals Publications such as newspapers, magazines, and scholarly journals.

Personification A **figure of speech** in which an object is given human qualities or characteristics. For example, *The tender, reassuring rays of the rising sun caressed her cheeks.*

Plagiarize Use an author's ideas or language (wording, organization, or sentence structure) as if they were one's own, neglecting to give the author credit. Plagiarism is considered cheating and a highly serious academic offense. *See also* **intentional plagiarism, unintentional plagiarism,** and **cyberplagiarism.**

Point of view The perspective from which an author writes, or the "person" the author becomes as he or she writes. The point of view used most commonly in essays is first person (*I, we, mine, ours*) or, especially for academic essays, third person (*he, she, they*). Less frequently, writers use second person (*you, your*). In choosing a point of view, consider your **topic, purpose,** and **audience.**

Point-by-point organization A method of organization used in an **essay** of **comparison and contrast** in which the author alternates things being compared, focusing on one characteristic at a time. *See also* **subject-by-subject organization.**

Points of comparison The points or **evidence** related to the **basis of comparison** that a writer develops in comparing two subjects. In a comparison between two breeds of dog, the basis of comparison might be *attractiveness*, and the points of comparison might be *fur texture, expressiveness of eyes,* and *shape of face.*

Post hoc fallacy A **fallacy** that occurs when a writer assumes that Event A caused Event B simply because B followed A. For example, *Every morning after the sun comes up, the highways fill with cars* is a post hoc fallacy if the sunrise is assumed to cause the traffic.

Previewing An **active reading** strategy that provides a quick way to become familiar with an essay's content and organization.

When previewing, read the title and author information, the **introduction**, any headings and the first sentence following them, **topic sentences**, the **conclusion**, and any prereading or end-of-assignment questions. Review also any photographs, tables, charts, or drawings that accompany the text.

Prewriting The stage in the writing process when the writer chooses a topic, narrows it down to a manageable scope, and develops a **thesis**. To discover ideas, the following prewriting strategies can be used: **brainstorming**, **freewriting**, **questioning**, and **mapping**.

Primary In a cause-and-effect **essay**, the most important **cause** or **effect**. *See also* **cause and effect** and **secondary**.

Primary sources Any material, as for a research paper, that is someone's firsthand evidence — for example, historical documents (letters, diaries, speeches); literary works; autobiographies; eyewitness accounts; and the writer's own interviews, observations, or correspondence. *See also* **secondary sources**.

Process analysis A **pattern of development** used to explain in step-by-step fashion how something works, or is done, or is made. *See also* **how-it-works essay** and **how-to essay**.

Procrastination Putting off tasks that need to be done.

Proofreading Reading through an essay to catch and correct surface errors — errors in grammar, punctuation, spelling, and mechanics — as well as keyboarding and typographical mistakes.

Purpose The reason an author writes a particular piece. Common purposes for writing are to entertain, to express feelings and elicit feelings from readers, to inform or educate, and to persuade or to advocate for a cause. The author's purpose in writing a piece influences its words, details, and **style**.

Questioning A **prewriting** strategy used to discover ideas about a topic. Questioning involves writing down all the questions that come to mind about a topic.

Reason A general statement that backs up a **claim** in **argument**.

Red herring A **fallacy** in which a writer introduces an irrelevant point, generally to distract readers. For example, a politician is using a red herring if he argues against his opponent's proposals on public education by pointing out that the opponent sends her children to private school.

Refutation In **argument** essays, making an argument against opposing viewpoints, demonstrating their weaknesses.

Refute To make a **refutation**.

Repetition A way of achieving **coherence** in **paragraphs** and other pieces of writing, in which key terms (or pronouns that stand for key terms) are repeated.

Resolution The solution for the **conflict** in a **narrative** and the point at which this occurs, following the **climax**.

Responding Reacting and recording reactions to a reading, in order to understand it better. The responses can be recorded through **annotations**, **journal** entries, or a **response paper**.

Response paper An assignment that involves writing about some aspect of an **essay** after reading and analyzing it.

Revision The process of making changes to improve both what is said and how it is said.

Scratch outline *See* **informal outline**.

Search engine An application for locating information online through keyword or other searches.

Secondary In a cause-and-effect **essay**, the less important **causes** or **effects**. *See also* **cause and effect** and **primary**.

Secondary sources Any material, as for a research paper, that reports or comments on **primary sources**.

Sensory details Details that appeal to one or more of the five senses: sight, hearing, smell, taste, and touch. Writers use sensory details to help the reader experience the object, sensation, event, or person being described.

Sentence outline A **formal outline** that uses complete sentences.

Simile A **figure of speech** that makes a direct comparison using *like* or *as*. For example, *The dog was as black as coal.*

Sketching *See* **visualizing.**

Spatial order A method of organization that presents details about a subject according to their position in space. An author using spatial order might describe a place or object from top to bottom, from inside to outside, or from near to far away.

Style The characteristics of the language a writer uses in a piece of writing; for example, short sentences and common words or longer, flowery sentences and more complicated words. **Purpose** and **intended audience** influence style.

Subject-by-subject organization A method of organization in an **essay** of **comparison and contrast** in which the author addresses all of the points about the first subject before addressing the same points about the second subject. *See also* **point-by-point organization.**

Subjective Written, often in the first person (*I, me, mine*), to create an emotional response. A **description** that is subjective includes not only observations and experiences but also the writer's feelings about them.

Summary The major points of an **essay** or other reading stated in the reader's own words. Because summaries do not include any details, they are brief.

Summary notes Marginal **annotations** of a reading that briefly state the key points in each **paragraph**. Readers can use their summary notes to write a **summary.**

Support A basic part of an **argument** — the **evidence** and **reasons** presented to persuade readers of the **claim** about an **issue.**

Supporting details The **facts**, examples, and ideas that writers include to fully explain the **main ideas** of **paragraphs.** Supporting details are needed to make paragraphs developed and convincing.

Sweeping generalization A **fallacy** that results from claiming that something applies to *all* situations. Trains may often be late, but someone who says they are always late is making a sweeping generalization.

Synonyms Words that have similar meanings — for example, *courageous* and *brave.*

Tension The suspense created as the story in a **narrative** unfolds and the reader wonders how the **conflict** will be resolved.

Term In a **definition**, the thing that is being defined.

Thesis statement (or **thesis**) Also known as *central thought*, the single main idea of an **essay** or other reading. It explains what the reading is about and expresses the writer's position. The thesis statement often appears in an essay's **introduction**, and it often is expressed in a single sentence.

Tone The way a reading sounds to its **audience**, influenced by an author's approach to the topic and the **audience**. A reading's tone comes from the writer's word choice and sentence patterns and other aspects of **style.** For example, the tone might be bitter, surprised, admiring, amused, or grateful.

Topic Of a **paragraph**, the general subject — what the entire paragraph is about.

Topic outline A **formal outline** that uses key words and phrases, rather than sentences.

Topic sentence The sentence that states the **main point** of a **paragraph.** The topic sentence is often the first sentence of the paragraph.

Transitions (or **transitional expressions**) Words, phrases, or even clauses or sentences that lead the reader from one idea to another in **paragraphs** and **essays**, signaling what comes next. By connecting ideas, transitions keep writing from seeming choppy and clarifying relationships among ideas. Some common transitions are *nevertheless, finally,* and *for example.* For other commonly used transitions, see Table 7.1, on page 147.

Understanding Grasping the ideas an author presents and being able to explain them in one's own words.

Unintentional plagiarism Accidentally using an author's ideas or language as though they were one's own, for example, by using language too similar to that of the original source or forgetting to put quotation marks around a direct quotation. Although accidental, unintentional plagiarism is a serious academic offense. *See also* **plagiarism, cyberplagiarism,** and **intentional plagiarism.**

Unity The quality and arrangement of parts of an essay so they work together to achieve a single purpose and support the thesis.

Values One of two main targets of **emotional appeals** in **argument** — principles or qualities that readers consider important or desirable (for example, honesty, loyalty, privacy, or patriotism).

Vantage point The position from which a **description** is written. With a *fixed vantage point,* a writer describes what he or she sees from a single position. With a *moving vantage point,* a writer describes the subject from various positions.

Visualizing A **prewriting** technique, also known as **sketching,** that involves closing the eyes, thinking about the topic, and then making notes about or drawing a sketch of what's visualized.

Working outline *See* **informal outline.**

Working thesis *See* **thesis statement.**

Writing assertions A **prewriting** technique for looking at a topic from different perspectives. This technique involves writing **assertions** (statements that take a position) on the topic and then choosing an assertion and **brainstorming, freewriting,** or **mapping** to generate ideas about it.

Writing patterns *See* **patterns of development.**

Acknowledgments

Dr. Judith Allen. "The End of a Relationship: How to Recover from a Broken Heart" from *NetCounselors.com*. Copyright © Dr. Judith L. Allen. Reprinted by permission of the author.

Sherry Amatenstein. "Talking a Stranger through the Night," from *Newsweek*, Nov. 2, 2002. Copyright © 2002 by The Newsweek/Daily Beast Company LLC. All rights reserved. Used by permission and protected by the Copyright Laws of the United States. The printing, copying, redistribution, or retransmission of the Material without express written permission is prohibited.

Dave Barry. "We've Got the Dirt on Guy Brains." From *The Miami Herald*, Nov. 23, 2003. Copyright © 2003 by Dave Barry. Reprinted by permission of the author.

Andrew Bast. "The Warrior's Brain" from *Newsweek*, Nov. 22, 2010. Copyright © 2010 The Newsweek/Daily Beast Company LLC. All rights reserved. Used by permission and protected by the Copyright Laws of the United States. The printing, copying, redistribution, or retransmission of the Material without express written permission is prohibited.

George Beekman and Ben Beekman. "History of the Future," from DIGITAL PLANET: TOMORROW'S TECHNOLOGY AND YOU, 10th Edition. Copyright © 2012. Reprinted by permission of Pearson Education, Inc., Upper Saddle River, NJ.

Sharon Begley. "Sins of the Grandfathers" from *Newsweek*, Oct. 7, 2010. Copyright © 2010 by The Newsweek/Daily Beast Company, LLC. All rights reserved. Used by permission and protected by the Copyright Laws of the United States. The printing, copying, redistribution, or retransmission of the Material without express written permission is prohibited.

David Bodanis. "A Brush with Reality: Surprises in the Tube" from THE SECRET HOUSE. Copyright © 1986 by David Bodanis. Reprinted by permission of the Carol Mann Agency.

Paul Boutin. "The Age of Music Piracy Is Officially Over" from *Wired* magazine, Nov. 29, 2010. Copyright © 2010 by Conde Nast. All rights reserved. Reprinted by permission.

Deborah Branscum. "The Hoarding Syndrome: When Clutter Goes Out of Control," from *Reader's Digest*, March 2007. Copyright © 2007 by The Reader's Digest Association, Inc. Reprinted by permission of Reader's Digest.

Peter Bregman. "How (and Why) to Stop Multitasking," Harvard Business Review Blog, May 20, 2010. Copyright © 2010 by Harvard Business Publishing. All rights reserved. Reprinted by permission.

Bill Bryson. "Snoopers at Work" from I'M A STRANGER HERE MYSELF, copyright © 1999 by Bill Bryson. Used by permission of Broadway Books, a division of Random House, Inc. and Random House Canada.

Veronica Chambers. "The Secret Latina" from *Essence*, July 2000. Reprinted by permission of the author.

Chicago Tribune. "Pass the Dream Act," Sept. 10, 2010, copyright © 2010 by *Chicago Tribune*. All rights reserved. Used by permission and protected by the Copyright Laws of the United States. The printing, copying, redistribution, or retransmission of this Content without express written permission is prohibited.

Amy Chua. "Why Chinese Mothers Are Superior" from *The Wall Street Journal*, Jan. 8, 2011. Copyright © 2011 by Dow Jones & Co., Inc. All rights reserved worldwide. Reprinted by permission of the publisher.

Cindy Chupack. "Dater's Remorse," from BETWEEN BOYFRIENDS. Copyright © 2003 by Cindy Chupack. Reprinted by permission of St. Martin's Press. All rights reserved.

Saundra K. Ciccarelli and J. Noland White. "Secrets for Surviving College," from PSYCHOLOGY: AN EXPLORATION, 1st Edition. Copyright © 2010. Reprinted by permission of Pearson Education, Inc., Upper Saddle River, NJ.

John Clifton. "Why Do People Watch Sports on TV?" is reprinted by permission of askdeb.com, http://www.askdeb.com/.

Brian Doyle. "The Hawk," from *The Sun*, Feb. 2011. Reprinted by permission of the author.

Bethe Dufresne. "Gullible Travels" from *Utne Reader*, excerpted from *Commonweal* magazine, Dec. 17, 2010. Copyright © 2010 by Commonweal Foundation. Reprinted with permission of Commonweal Foundation, www.commonwealmagazine.org.

The *Economist*. "A Step in the Right Direction." Copyright © 2010 by The Economist Newspaper Ltd., London. Reprinted from the March 4, 2010 issue by permission of the publisher.

Lars Eighner. "On Dumpster Diving," from TRAVELS WITH LIZBETH. Copyright ©1993 by Lars Eighner. Reprinted by permission of St. Martin's Press. All rights reserved.

Robert Epstein. "How Science Can Help You Fall in Love," from *Scientific American*, January/February 2010. Copyright © 2010 by Scientific American, a division of Nature America, Inc. Reprinted by permission. All rights reserved.

Sarah Fenske. "Globe High School Censors Its Student Newspaper" from *Phoenix New Times*, Feb. 7, 2008. Reprinted by permission of Phoenix New Times, a Village Voice Media publication.

Patrick Frank, Duane Preble, and Sarah Preble. "Issue-Oriented Art and Street Art," from PREBLES' ARTFORMS, 9th Edition. Copyright © 2009. Used by permission of Pearson Education, Inc., Upper Saddle River, NJ.

Joshua Fruhlinger. "Five Things to Avoid When Dating Online," from www.switched.com, August 7, 2008. Original publication copyright © 2007 by Joshua Fruhlinger. Reprinted by permission of the author.

Louis Giannetti. "Costumes," from UNDERSTANDING MOVIES 12th EDITION. Copyright © 2011. Used by permission of Pearson Education, Inc., Upper Saddle River, NJ.

Stefany Anne Golberg. "Can You See Me Now? Deaf America" from *Utne Reader*, September/October 2011. Excerpted from *The Smart Set*, May 23, 2011, www.thesmartset.com. Reprinted by permission of the author.

Sam Graham-Felsen. "Why I Dumped My iPhone," by GOOD and Sam Graham-Felsen. Originally appeared on www.GOOD.com, Oct. 4, 2011. Reprinted with permission from GOOD.

Janel Healy. "Singing for the Cameras: Reality TV = Community Exposure?" from *Communities* magazine, Summer 2011, Issue # 151. Copyright © 2011 by Janel Healy and *Communities* magazine. Reprinted with permission of the publisher, commmunities.ic.org.

Leslie Jamison. "It's a Mad, Mad, Marathon" was originally published in *The Believer*. Copyright © 2011 by Leslie Jamison. Used by permission of The Wylie Agency LLC.

Sebastian Junger. "Why Would Anyone Miss War?" from *The New York Times*, July 16, 2011. Copyright © 2011 by Sebastian Junger. Reprinted by permission of the Stuart Krichevsky Literary Agency, Inc.

Mindy Kaling. "Types of Women in Romantic Comedies Who Are Not Real," from IS EVERYONE HANGING OUT WITHOUT ME? (AND OTHER CONCERNS). Copyright © 2011 by Mindy Kaling. Used by permission of Crown Archetype, a division of Random House, Inc.

Richard LeMieux. "The Lady in Red" from BREAKFAST AT SALLY'S (2008). Reprinted by special arrangement with Skyhorse Publishing, Inc.

Martin Luther King Jr., "I Have a Dream" speech, copyright ©1963 Dr. Martin Luther King, Jr., copyright © renewed 1991 Coretta Scott King. Reprinted by arrangement with The Heirs to the Estate of Martin Luther King Jr., c/o Writers House as agent for the proprietor, New York, NY.

Morgan Lowrie. "Comparing Online and Traditional Education" from helium.com, February 11, 2009. Reprinted by permission of the author.

Jeremy MacClancy, excerpt from "Eating Chili Peppers." From CONSUMING CULTURE: WHY YOU EAT WHAT YOU EAT by Jeremy MacClancy. Copyright © 1992 by Jeremy MacClancy. Reprinted by permission of Henry Holt and Company, LLC.

Tom and Ray Magliozzi. "Inside the Engine" from CAR TALK by Tom and Ray Magliozzi. Copyright © 1991 by Tom and Ray Magliozzi. Used by permission of Dell Publishing, a division of Random House, Inc. E-rights by arrangement with International Creative Management, Inc.

Zach Miners. "Twitter Goes to College," originally published as "Twitter Takes a Trip to College" from *U.S. News & World Report*, Sept. 1, 2009. Reprinted by permission of the publisher.

Celestina Phillips. "Thinking Purple and Living Green" from the *Fort Worth Business Press*, vol. 20, issue 42, Oct. 27, 2008. Reprinted by permission of the publisher.

Luis J. Rodriguez. "Latino Heritage Month: Who We Are — And Why We Celebrate." First published in *The Huffington Post*, Sept. 15, 2011. Used by permission of Susan Bergholz Literary Services, New York, NY and Lamy, NM. All rights reserved.

Cris Rouvalis. "Hey, Mom, Dad, May I Have My Room Back?" from the *Pittsburgh Post-Gazette*, Aug, 31, 2008. Copyright © 2008 by Pittsburgh Post-Gazette. All rights reserved. Reprinted with permission of the publisher.

William Saletan. "Gabby Giffords: Portrait of a Brain Being Rebuilt," from *Slate*, Nov. 15, 2011, copyright © 2011 by The Slate Group. All rights reserved. Used by permission and protected by the Copyright Laws of the United States. The printing, copying, redistribution, or retransmission of the Material without express written permission is prohibited.

Peggy Sands. "What's Wrong with the DREAM Act." From AOL Opinion, December 8, 2010. Reprinted by permission of the author, Margaret Orchowski (Peggy Sands).

John Scalzi. "Unstoppable Double-Fudge Chocolate Mudslide Explosion." Previously published as "Chocolate" in *The Culinarian*, February 2005. Reprinted by permission of the author.

Carolyn Foster Segal. "The Dog Ate My Flash Drive," originally appeared as "The Dog Ate My Disk and Other Tales of Woe" in *The Chronicle of Higher Education*, Aug. 11, 2000. Reprinted by permission of the author.

Richard Selzer. "The Discus Thrower," from CONFESSIONS OF A KNIFE. Copyright © 1989, 2001 by Richard Selzer. Reprinted by permission of Georges Borchardt, Inc. on behalf of the author.

Michèle Shuster, Janet Vigna, Gunjan Sinha, and Matthew Tontonoz. "Warming Planet, Decreasing Biodiversity," from BIOLOGY FOR A CHANGING WORLD. Copyright © 2011 by W.H. Freeman and Company. Used with permission of W.H. Freeman and Company.

David Silverman. "In Defense of Multitasking." Harvard Business Review, May 9, 2010, www.hbr .org. Copyright © 2010 by Harvard Business Publishing. All rights reserved. Reprinted by permission.

Michael R. Solomon, "Types of Message Appeals" from CONSUMER BEHAVIOR 9th Edition. Copyright © 2011. Used by permission of Pearson Education, Inc., Upper Saddle River, NJ.

Sarah Spigelman. "New York vs. Chicago Pizza" from Bites.Today.com, Oct. 20, 2011. Used by permission of MSNBC Interactive News LLC via Copyright Clearance Center.

Brent Staples. "Just Walk On By: A Black Man Ponders His Power to Alter Public Space" is reprinted by permission of the author. Originally published as "Black Men and Public Space" in the December 1986 issue of *Harper's Magazine*.

Amy Tan. "E. coli on the Rocks" first appeared on AmyTan.net. Copyright © 2009 by Amy Tan. Reprinted by permission of the author and the Sandra Dijkstra Literary Agency.

Deborah Tannen. "Sex, Lies, and Conversation." From *The Washington Post*, June 24, 1990. Copyright © 1990 by Deborah Tannen. Adapted from YOU JUST DON'T UNDERSTAND: WOMEN AND MEN IN CONVERSATION (HarperCollins). Reprinted with permission of the author.

William E. Thompson and Joseph V. Hickey. "Cybergroups," from SOCIETY IN FOCUS: AN INTRODUCTION TO SOCIOLOGY, 7th Edition. Copyright © 2011. Used by permission of Pearson Education, Inc., Upper Saddle River, NJ.

Judith Viorst. " "Friends, Good Friends — Such Good Friends," from *Redbook*, October 1977. Copyright © 1977 by Judith Viorst. Reprinted by permission of The Choate Agency, LLC.

Carole Wade and Carol Tavris. "Taking Psychology with You: Dealing with Cultural Differences" from INVITATION TO PSYCHOLOGY 5th Edition. Copyright © 2012. Used by permission of Pearson Education, Inc., Upper Saddle River, NJ.

Alton Fitzgerald White. "Right Place, Wrong Face." Adapted from "Ragtime, My Time" from the Oct. 11, 1999 issue of *The Nation*. Reprinted by permission of The Nation. For subscription information, call 1-800-333-8536. Portions of each week's magazine can be accessed at http://www.thenation.com.

Terry Tempest Williams. "The Clan of One-Breasted Women" from REFUGE: AN UNNATURAL HISTORY OF FAMILY AND PLACE, copyright © 1991 by Terry Tempest Williams. Used by permission of Pantheon Books, a division of Random House, Inc.

PHOTO CREDITS

3, Michael Doolittle/Alamy; **20,** © Juice Images/Alamy; **26,** Digital Vision/Getty Images; **26,** Hybrid Images/Getty Images; **51,** From The Human Mosaic: A Cultural Approach to Human Geography, 12/e by Domosh et al. ©2013 by W.H. Freeman and Company. Used with permission.; **53,** Richard Levine/Alamy; **84,** Geri Lavrov/Getty Images; **104,** © John Caldwell/The New Yorker Collection/www.

Index

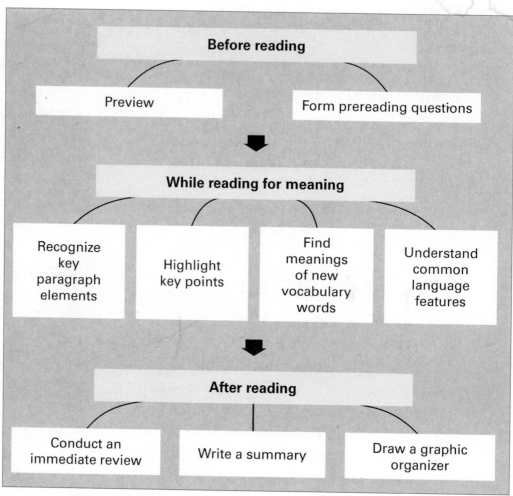

Before reading

Preview

Form prereading questions

While reading for meaning

Recognize key paragraph elements

Highlight key points

Find meanings of new vocabulary words

Understand common language features

After reading

Conduct an immediate review

Write a summary

Draw a graphic organizer

Strategies for Active Reading
(see Chapter 2, p. 23)